ROYALS AND THE REICH

Also by Jonathan Petropoulos
The Faustian Bargain: The Art World in Nazi Germany
Art as Politics in the Third Reich

ROYALS
AND THE
REICH

THE PRINCES von HESSEN
IN NAZI GERMANY

Jonathan Petropoulos

OXFORD
UNIVERSITY PRESS

OXFORD

UNIVERSITY PRESS

Oxford University Press, Inc., publishes works that further
Oxford University's objective of excellence
in research, scholarship, and education.

Oxford New York
Auckland Cape Town Dar es Salaam Hong Kong Karachi
Kuala Lumpur Madrid Melbourne Mexico City Nairobi
New Delhi Shanghai Taipei Toronto

With offices in
Argentina Austria Brazil Chile Czech Republic France Greece
Guatemala Hungary Italy Japan Poland Portugal Singapore
South Korea Switzerland Thailand Turkey Ukraine Vietnam

Copyright © 2006 by Jonathan Petropoulos

Published by Oxford University Press, Inc.
198 Madison Avenue, New York, NY 10016
www.oup.com

First issued as on Oxford University Press paperback, 2008

Oxford is a registered trademark of Oxford University Press

Library of Congress Cataloging-in-Publication Data
Petropoulos, Jonathan.
Royals and the Reich : the princes von Hessen in Nazi Germany / by Jonathan
Petropoulos.
p. cm. Includes bibliographical references.
ISBN 978-0-19-533927-7 (pbk.)
1. Hessen, Philipp von, b. 1896.
2. Hessen, Christoph von, 1901–1943.
3. Princes—Germany—History—20th century—Biography.
4. Germany—History—1933–1945.
5. National socialism—Social aspects.
I. Title.
DD247.H373P48 2005
943.086′086′21—dc22
2005018109

1 3 5 7 9 8 6 4 2
Printed in the United States of America
on acid-free paper

To Jack and Kingsley Croul,
with respect and friendship.

Contents

List of Illustrations

Acknowledgments

This book would have been very different without the cooperation of the Hessen family. In particular, I thank Prince Moritz, Landgrave von Hessen, and his cousin, Rainer von Hessen—sons of the two main figures in this history. They put many important documents at my disposal, shared vivid and often difficult memories, and exhibited great patience as I struggled with a challenging and complex topic. Rainer von Hessen, in particular, guided me through many treacherous passages. I bear sole responsibility for the mistakes in this book, but without him there would be many more. I also thank Her Majesty, Queen Elizabeth II, for permission to conduct research in the Royal Archives at Windsor Castle, and Prince Philip, Duke of Edinburgh, for his willingness to discuss the history of his German relations. I am also grateful to Prince Hermann von Hessen, of the Philippsthal-Barchfeld branch of the family, who was also most gracious in answering my queries.

There have been many other individuals and institutions that have supported my research. I express my deep gratitude to John and Kingsley Croul, who have honored me by endowing the chair that I hold at Claremont McKenna College in Southern California, and who provided the support that permitted me to make frequent trips to archives in both Europe and the United States. The Crouls' interest in my work and their friendship have encouraged me throughout this project. Many other friends and colleagues at Claremont McKenna College have also been supportive of my research: in particular President Pamela Gann, Dean

William Ascher, and Vice-President for Development Dennis Mulhaupt, who made it possible for me to combine scholarship and teaching in a productive and personally satisfying way. I owe a special debt to Professor John Roth, the director of the college's Center for the Study of the Holocaust, Genocide, and Human Rights; his dedication to scholarship and students has been nothing short of inspirational. In addition to my splendid colleagues in Claremont, I extend thanks to the Alexander von Humboldt Foundation and my host in Germany, Professor Andreas Wirsching, who enabled me to carry out the research that provided the foundation for this project. I express my appreciation to the President and Fellows of Clare Hall at Cambridge University in the United Kingdom, who granted me a Visiting Fellowship that permitted the completion of this book.

A number of scholars read drafts or portions of this manuscript and offered constructive suggestions. I thank Professor Eckhart Franz, Christian Goeschel, Dr. Lothar Machtan, Hugo Vickers, and Professor Gerhard Weinberg for their helpful comments. Others who helped me in significant ways and answered queries include Dr. Gerard Aalders, Martin Allen, Professor Günter Bischof, Miranda Carter, Professor Stephen Dorril, Lord Max Egremont, Professor Christian Gerlach, Dr. Patricia Heberer, Charles Higham, Professor Michael Kater, Dr. Isabel Kobus, Dr. Stephan Malinowski, Professor John C. G. Röhl, Dr. Timothy Ryback, and Nancy Yeide. I reiterate that I alone bear responsibility for the short-comings of this study.

Among the archivists who assisted me, I recognize Christine Klössel at the Archiv der Hessischen Hausstiftung at Schloss Fasanerie; Pamela Clark at the Royal Archives at Windsor Castle; and Dr. Diether Degreif of the Hessisches Hauptstaatsarchiv in Wiesbaden. Matthias Koch and Monica Bernhardt at the Hessisches Staatsarchiv in Darmstadt were also extremely helpful. I express my gratitude to Babette Heusterberg at the Bundesarchiv Berlin-Lichterfelde, Berit Pistora at the Bundesarchiv Koblenz, Martin Luchterhandt at the Landesarchiv Berlin, and Herbert Karbach at the Political Archives of the Foreign Office in Berlin. In Kassel, I thank Dr. Bernhard Schnackenburg at the Staatliche Museen Kassel, and Frank-Roland Klaube, the head of the Kassel Stadtarchiv. In Kronberg, thanks to Frau Imke for the tour of the Burg and family cemetery. Dr. Jameson at the Library of Congress in Washington, DC, as well Michael Kurtz, Greg Bradsher, Michael Hussey, and Holly Reed at the National Archives and Records Administration in College Park, MD, were unfailingly supportive. I also thank Tanya Middelbro at the National Archives of Canada, who sent me useful documents, as well as Lord Romsey for providing me with papers from the archives at Broadlands. I thank Karen Robson in the Department of Special Collections in the Hartley

Library at the University of Southampton for her assistance with the Mountbatten papers. Stephanie Wachalec at Kent State University assisted me with the papers of Queen Marie of Romania. Tanya Chebotarev at the Bakhmeteff Archive at Columbia University permitted me to work with the papers of Prince Paul of Yugoslavia and Cheryl Gunselman at Washington State University, assisted with the papers of Prince Alexander Friedrich von Hessen. Dr. Cordula Grewe, then at the German Historical Institute in Washington, DC, provided me with the documents concerning the Kronberg thefts. Dr. Anja Heuss and Ian Locke sent me important materials concerning the fate of artworks during and after the Third Reich.

I was fortunate to have a wonderful cohort of research assistants: notably, Nicole Gallagher, Clayton Schroers, Julie Jacoby, Meredith Perry, Nate Hansen, Stefanie Altman, Cynthia Scott, Garrett Hodge, Amy Walter, Sarah Jagels, and Richard Helke. I express special thanks to my colleagues in Claremont: Richard Drake, the assistant director of the Gould Center for Humanistic Studies, and Tracy Vienna in the History Department, both of whom helped in numerous ways in the preparation of the manuscript.

I thank literary agents Agnes Krup and Michael Carlisle for their confidence in this project and their wise counsel. I am also exceptionally fortunate to be able to work with Peter Ginna at Oxford University Press: his combination of enthusiasm and "tough love" helped make for a better book. His colleague at OUP, Laura Stickney, also provided a thoughtful close reading, for which I am grateful. I also express my appreciation for the efforts of Mary Sutherland and Helen Mules for copyediting the manuscript.

I owe my family more than words can express. I thank my parents, George and Maureen Petropoulos, for their unflagging support over the years. My wife, Kimberly, has encouraged me throughout the project and given me not only sensible advice on myriad issues, but has also been instrumental in creating a supportive environment. I also thank Astrid and Isabel Petropoulos for their patience with their father, who too often seems to be working.

Cambridge, U.K.   JP
April 2005

A Note about Nomenclature

M ost noble titles in this book have been translated into English. It is important to note that titles, per se, ceased to exist in Germany after 1918; members of the nobility usually circumvented this prohibition by incorporating the title into their names. They themselves (and many in society) continued to recognize the various noble designations, and it is consistent with the atmosphere of the times to retain them. Similarly, most of the Christian and family names have not been Anglicized. In order to capture a sense of the subjects' time and place, it was deemed useful to keep aristocratic prefixes in German (usually "von" and "zu") as well as the German versions of names (for example, Moritz rather than Maurice, or von Preussen rather than "of Prussia"). In certain instances, Hessen-Kassel is rendered as Hesse-Kassel, and this too relates to German grammatical practices. Because of the tendency among aristocrats to use traditional family Christian names, many individuals had very similar names. In order to provide some clarity, birth and death dates for most figures have been listed the first time they are mentioned in the text, as well as in the index. The family tree of the Hesse-Kassel family in appendix 2 may also help guide the reader.

Abbreviations

AHH	Archiv der Hessischen Hausstiftung (Archive of the Hessen House Foundation, Eichenzell)
APA	Archiv des Auswärtigen Amt (Archive of the German Foreign Ministry)
ASHCAN	Allied Supreme Headquarters for Axis Nationals
BAB	Bundesarchiv Berlin-Lichterfelde (German Federal Archives, Berlin)
BAK	Bundesarchiv Koblenz (German Federal Archives, Koblenz)
BDC	Berlin Document Center
BHSA	Bayerisches Hauptstaatsarchiv (Bavarian Main State Archives, Munich)
BSB	Bayerische Staatsbibliothek (Munich)
CIC	Counter Intelligence Corps
CIR	Consolidated Interrogation Report (of the Art Looting Investigation Unit)
CULBA	Columbia University Libraries, Bakhmeteff Archive
DAG	Deutsche Adelsgenossenschaft (German Noble Society)
DNVP	Deutschnationale Volkspartei (German National People's Party)
ERR	Einsatzstab Reichsleiter Rosenberg (Special Task Force of Reich Leader Rosenberg)
FA	Forschungsamt (Research Office in the Reich Air Ministry)
FOIA	Freedom of Information Act

GDR	German Democratic Republic
GF	Grossherzogliche Familienarchiv (Grand Ducal Archive, Darmstadt)
GStAPK	Geheimes Staatsarchiv Preussischer Kulturbesitz (Secret State Archive of the Prussian Cultural Foundation, Berlin)
HHStAW	Hessisches Hauptstaatsarchiv (Hessian Main State Archives, Wiesbaden)
HMS	His (Her) Majesty's Ship
HStAD	Hessisches Staatsarchiv Darmstadt (Hessian State Archives, Darmstadt)
HStAM	Hessisches Staatsarchiv Marburg
IfZG	Institut für Zeitgeschichte (Institute for Contemporary History, Munich)
IMT	International Military Tribunal at Nuremberg
LC	Library of Congress, Washington DC
NARA	National Archives and Records Administration, College Park
NL	Nachlass (papers)
NSDAP	Nationalsozialistische Deutsche Arbeiterpartei (Nazi Party)
NSKK	Nationalsozialistisches Kraftfahrer Korps (National Socialist Drivers' Corps)
OMGUS	Office of the Military Government of Germany, United States
OSS	Office of Strategic Services
PA	Personalakte (personal file)
PRO	Public Records Office (British National Archives, Kew Gardens)
RA	Royal Archives, Windsor Castle
RAF	Royal Air Force
RSHA	Reichssicherheits Hauptamt (Reich Security Head Office)
RuSHA	Rasse und Siedlungs-Hauptamt (Race and Settlement Head Office)
RvH	Private Papers of Rainer von Hessen
SA	Sturmabteilung (Storm Troop, brownshirts)
SAK	Stadtarchiv Kassel (City Archives, Kassel)
SD	Sicherheitsdienst (Security Service)
SHAEF	Supreme Headquarters Allied Expeditionary Forces
SOE	British Special Operations Executive
SS	Schutz-Staffel (blackshirts)
ULC	University Library, Cambridge

Category I	major offender
Category II	opportunist offender
Category III	lesser offender/opportunist
Category IV	fellow traveler
Category V	exonerated

To be sure, he was not a "typical" aristocrat: but in the course of his own lifetime, the aristocracy changed, adapted, dispersed, and declined so much that it would be difficult to suggest anyone who was.

David Cannadine (on Winston Churchill)

There was a lot of interchange. The princely families of Europe knew each other. They met each other a lot and it was all the way across. France being Roman Catholic, there were very few matrimonial connections. There were some with Belgium, but that was fairly distant. Of course, there was Scandinavia. But the nearest other Protestant country that produced wives or husbands was Germany, so there was much more familial contact that way.

HRH Prince Philip, Duke of Edinburgh

Introduction

Two vignettes reflect many of the themes treated in this book. The first is set on 15 December 1930. Prince Christoph von Hessen, from the illustrious dynasty that ruled the area surrounding Kassel in central Germany until 1866, is to wed Princess Sophia of Greece and Denmark. Their families have gathered north of Frankfurt at Kronberg—and more specifically, at Schloss Friedrichshof. This castle, which was one of many belonging to the Hessens, had been built in the 1890s by Christoph's grandmother (the eldest daughter of Queen Victoria) as a monument to her recently deceased husband, German emperor Friedrich III. Friedrichshof has been closed for most of the previous decade, its sumptuous furniture and precious artworks covered with white sheets and the world-renowned porcelain collection locked away, as the family suffered the tribulations of the crisis-ridden Weimar Republic. But this is a glorious day for the Hessens and their relatives—or at least those who are able to attend (Christoph's uncle, ex-Kaiser Wilhelm II, for example, is stranded in exile in Holland, unable to return to Germany). Christoph's older brother, Prince Philipp, who recently married Princess Mafalda, a daughter of the king of Italy, has traveled up from Rome. Most of Princess Sophia's family members have also made the trip, including her father, Prince Andrea, and her nine-year-old brother, Philip (the future Duke of Edinburgh), who will carry the train of her wedding dress. Prince Andrea and his family have also had a difficult decade—he, barely escaping with his life after being charged with treason by the Greek revolutionary government in 1922. But this day

Prince Christoph, Princess Sophia, and guests at the 1930 wedding. Prince Philip of Greece and Denmark, the future Duke of Edinburgh, sits at the feet of the bride and groom. Prince Philipp von Hessen is top center.

is different. The servants are in livery uniforms, and the Hessens even lend Sophia a diamond tiara from the family jewels.

But amid the splendor and high spirits, there is a substratum of tension and complexity. Princess Sophia is but sixteen years of age (b. 1914)—young, even within the peculiar world of European royalty. She is, however, mature for her age and possesses great poise and beauty. There is also the quiet acknowledgment that she has been a virtual orphan for the past few years, her mother in a sanitarium in Switzerland struggling with her mental health, and her father leading the existence of a bon vivant in Paris and Monte Carlo. Christoph has also been struggling in his life, failing to complete his university degree or to hold down jobs on rural estates or in an automobile factory. Yet the two so clearly adore one another, and such issues are put aside. Even the religious differences are resolved in a creative manner. There are two ceremonies: a protestant service in the Kronberg town chapel and second one officiated by a Greek Orthodox priest, brought in specifically for the purpose by Prince Andrea. Politics also lie beneath the surface. Christoph's brother Prince Philipp has just joined the Nazi Party. He had met Hitler earlier that autumn and took the leap in October —signing the papers in the Berlin apartment of Hermann Göring, as the latter's Swedish (and noble) wife Carin spurred him on, querying, "Are you to belong to this great movement?" Christoph has also been meeting with the Görings to discuss politics: within a year of his wedding, Prince Christoph will also join the Nazi Party (and by February 1932 become a member of the SS).

Fast forward sixteen years to November 1946: Prince Philipp is in an American internment facility in Darmstadt—the twenty-second camp that he has been in as a prisoner of both the Nazis and the Allies. It is a sprawling, grim complex. Twenty thousand inmates, most of them former Nazis, sit in desolate barracks and tents awaiting trial before one of the camp's ten denazification tribunals. Philipp is a broken man—gaunt, laconic, and somewhat bewildered. He cannot understand what happened. He had risen to the pinnacle of the Third Reich: the Oberpräsident (governor) of his home province of Hessen-Nassau, the Führer's personal emissary to Mussolini, and a glittering member of Nazi high society. One moment, in September 1943, he was sitting in the Führer Headquarters, staying up until past 2:00 a.m. listening to Hitler (delivering a rant that passed for conversation);

Prince Philipp as a prisoner of the Americans at ASHCAN, 1945.

the next moment he was arrested by SS guards and sent on his way to the Flossenbürg concentration camp. Philipp tries to make sense of it all. He can call on other inmates who had witnessed much of this mercurial history: his cousin and close friend Prince August Wilhelm ("Auwi"), the fourth son of the ex-Kaiser, who had played an instrumental role in inducing him to join the Nazi Party; his twin brother Wolfgang (1896–1989), who had also been part of Göring's menagerie and who had held the post as Landrat (county commissioner) of Bad Homburg, the affluent community north of Frankfurt; and even Otto Skorzeny (1908–75), the famed SS commando who had led the mission to spring Mussolini from his imprisonment on the Gran Sasso in September 1943. But they cannot explain how one of Hitler's favorites became an enemy of the Reich; how this privileged prince, who had once been an interior designer specializing in the decoration of noble homes, was now accused of complicity in the killing of more than ten thousand people at Hadamar as part of the T-4 (or so-called euthanasia) program—although these charges were eventually dropped.

This book aims to explain how an entire generation of the princes von Hessen-Kassel became Nazis and how they reacted to the regime's criminal policies. Their experiences are placed in the broader context of aristocrats' involvement with the Nazi regime. More specifically, this is a study of two brothers, Princes Philipp and Christoph, and their extraordinary lives during the Third Reich. Prince Christoph became the head of the *Forschungsamt* (research office) in the Reich Air Ministry, the most important signals intelligence agency in Nazi Germany. Akin to the National Security Agency in the United States, the Forschungsamt tapped telephones and intercepted thirty-four thousand telegrams per day on average, passing along the "intelligence" to Göring and other Nazi leaders (to the latter on a need-to-know basis). This clandestine agency spied on not only diplomats and businessmen but also a range of other declared enemies: trade union officials, socialists, and clergy. In short, Prince Christoph was a member of the SS and one of the top intelligence officials during the Third Reich.

Perhaps the most remarkable aspect concerning Prince Philipp was his closeness to Hitler. Historian Lothar Machtan, who has studied Hitler's personal life in detail, maintains that from 1938 until 1942, Philipp, next to Speer, was "Hitler's closest friend in terms of a foremost unpolitical relationship."[1] Albert Speer himself wrote of Prince Philipp:

> He was one of the few followers whom Hitler had always treated with deference and respect. Philipp had often been useful to him, and especially in the early years of the Third Reich had arranged contacts with the head of Italian Fascism. In addition he had helped Hitler purchase valuable art works. The prince had been able to arrange their export from Italy through his connections with the Italian royal house, to which he was related. . . . [Hitler] continued to treat him with the greatest outward courtesy and invited him to his meals. But the members of Hitler's entourage, who until then had been so fond of talking with a "real prince," avoided him as if he had a contagious disease.[2]

While Philipp did indeed experience a fall from Hitler's grace, he stood at the core of the Third Reich. It is striking that he has been so overlooked by historians. Even though there are magisterial biographies of Hitler— two volumes by Ian Kershaw and an eight-hundred-page-plus effort by Joachim Fest, for example—Prince Philipp is scarcely mentioned.[3] Philipp was important not just because of his intense relationship with Hitler but also because of his role as Hitler's special envoy in foreign relations with Italy, as well as his position as Oberpräsident, the highest-ranking state official in the province of Hesse-Nassau. It is also notable that the *Almanach de Gotha*, the "bible" for nobility, put Prince Philipp's picture on the frontispiece in the 1941 edition—an extraordinary honor that speaks to his visibility at the time not only in Germany, but in Europe more generally.[4] Like his brother Christoph, he was an important second rank leader—the echelon in the National Socialist state that rightly deserves to command the attention of the current generation of historians.[5] Although Christoph was

ALMANACH DE GOTHA

ANNUAIRE GÉNÉALOGIQUE
DIPLOMATIQUE ET
STATISTIQUE
1 9 4 1

178e ANNÉE

GOTHA: JUSTUS PERTHES

PHILIPPE PRINCE DE HESSE

Prince Philipp on the frontispiece of the 1941 Almanach de Gotha, *wearing his Iron Cross and the Nazi Party pin, among other decorations. Note that he wears a German military uniform with a swastika armband.*

not a public figure like his brother Philipp, he too was well acquainted with many top Nazi leaders.

Beyond the individual lives of Philipp and Christoph, this book explores the experiences of a cohort of German princes who supported Hitler and the Nazi regime. Because Germany unified so late (1871), there were nearly two dozen houses that retained their designation as princely (*Fürstenhäuser*)—even after the end of the Imperial era in 1918.[6] One document in the German Federal Archives (see appendix 1) contains a list of 270 members of princely families who joined the Nazi Party.[7] While it is difficult to provide an exact percentage of princes who joined the party (it depends on which families one counts as princely), it appears that between a third and a half of the princes eligible to do so joined the National Socialist German Workers' Party (NSDAP). If princes had constituted a profession (which one might quip they did in a certain way), they would have rivaled physicians as the most Nazified in the Third Reich (doctors' membership peaked in 1937 at 43 percent).[8] Although each family, and each individual member, possesses a distinctive history, certain traits emerge: great wealth and privilege, especially prior to 1914; an awareness of ancestry and a loyalty to family (nearly all members of the high nobility could recite genealogical tables from memory); a romanticized conception of military service; self-sacrifice and loss during World War I; a disaffection from the fledgling Weimar Republic, which most viewed as threatening their families and the cause of wider problems (economic dislocation and social unrest); a susceptibility to the entreaties of Hitler, Göring, Himmler, and other Nazi leaders; a sense of duty that sometimes led to complicity in the crimes of the regime; a gradual but escalating alienation from the Nazis; hardship and suffering during the last stages of the war and in the postwar period; a reluctance to engage the National Socialist past in the postwar period; and the survival (and in many cases, revival) of their illustrious families. These points, of course, fit a general outline—a kind of "ideal type"—and not every member of the high aristocracy would correspond in all respects. The challenge for the historian is to preserve what is distinctive and understand what it is that has greater significance.

At a broader level, this history concerns class relations and the relative power of those in different strata. Princeton historian Arno Mayer, among others, has argued that the nobility retained its dominant position in European society up to the Great War.[9] Germany is now a democratic, postfeudal country, which raises the question, when did the nobility lose its predominance? The answer is that the epochal shift in influence, which started with the fall of the monarchy at the end of World War I and continued throughout the Weimar Republic, played out during the Third Reich and the years immediately following World War II. The broader narrative described here centers on how the Nazis successfully courted many members of the nobility. It is a sign of the continuing influence of the traditional elite that the Nazis worked so hard to win their support. For the older generation, Hitler frequently appealed to them by expressing sympathy for a restoration of the monarchy; for the younger, there was the hope of careers and influence in the Third Reich. For both, the Nazis offered financial incentives: measures to help secure their property (or in the case of the Hohenzollern, outright payments). The alliance, or whatever one would call it, did not last. Hitler could brook no challenge to his power. He could not help but view the old rulers as rivals. When a Hohenzollern prince fell in battle in May 1940 (Prince Wilhelm—the son of the crown prince), and a reported fifty thousand people turned out for his funeral in Potsdam, Hitler felt threatened.[10] He still sought to use the princes for his own purposes, but he felt frustration in this regard. When the ex-Kaiser died in June 1941, Hitler wanted a state funeral in Berlin in which he himself would star; but Wilhelm II had issued instructions before his death and wanted to be buried in Doorn. Hitler restricted attendance and blocked out news coverage.

Hitler's paranoia grew in proportion to Germany's military defeats: could these princes with their cosmopolitan families be trusted in the intensifying war? He began to have doubts, and in May 1943 issued a "secret order" (*Geheim-Erlass*), "The Decree Concerning Internationally Connected Men in the State, Party, and Armed Forces."[11] This order, which went to certain members of the Nazi bureaucracy but not the public at large, entailed compiling a list of all the members of the high nobility in these three spheres and then conducting a review. Some were permitted to stay on—such as Prince Josias zu Waldeck und Pyrmont (1896–1967). Most of the princes were forced out of the Wehrmacht (something that angered nearly every one of them). In the wake of the failed July 20 plot to kill Hitler, many aristocrats and their families were imprisoned by the Nazis. This applied not just to the Stauffenbergs and Moltkes (families of the conspirators) but to the Wittelsbach and many others. The Nazis invoked and perverted the ancient Germanic custom of *Sippenhaft*—or a kith-and-kin reprisal. Leaders such as Propaganda Minister Joseph Goebbels and German Work Front chief Robert Ley delivered vitriolic harangues against the nobility (cursing the "blue-blooded swine").[12] Himmler articulated one fantasy to his doctor that entailed lining up the nobles, making them walk through the streets of Berlin where the masses would spit on them, and then hanging them in a public square.[13] In the 1950s, there were reports that as many as five thousand nobles had died as a result of kith-and-kin reprisals.[14] This was not the case. There were thousands in camps, but most were "privileged" prisoners and survived the war (although the end, which involved being taken into the Alps as potential hostages, was indeed harrowing). Sociologist Ralf Dahrendorf suggested in his sweeping study of German society written in the 1960s that the Nazi regime carried out "the functional equivalent" of what elsewhere was called a bourgeois revolution.[15]

The decline of the nobility continued in various ways after 1945. While the German Democratic Republic was far less murderous than the Nazi regime, nobles in the East suffered as their estates were nationalized and communist leaders harassed them. Many, like the East Prussian author and publisher of the influential weekly *Die Zeit*, Countess Marion von Dönhoff, fled to the West. The Allies in the West also pursued a program of "defeudalization," believing that Prussian *Junkers* lay at the root of "the German catastrophe" of the twentieth century. The German nobility was never quite the same. Aristocrats in general, and princes more specifically, had lost their predominant position. While one found individuals like Princes Philipp, Wolfgang, and Christoph von Hessen in high-ranking government positions before the war, one would be hard-pressed to find princes in similar positions after 1945. As a symbol of this broader transformation, monarchical rule came to an end during or shortly after World War II in Italy, Yugoslavia, Romania, Bulgaria, and Albania. A transformation that had been so noticeable after World War I—with the collapse of the German,

Russian, and Austro-Hungarian empires—took several more decades to play out. The process, however, did not simply entail collapse and a consignment to oblivion. Princely families, or at least those in Germany, proved resilient. As we will see in the final chapter of this book, the Hessens, like many of their counterparts, adapted to the democratic and capitalist system of the Federal Republic and reemerged as a wealthy and highly visible family.

There are many other challenges confronting the historian writing about princely families. One concerns archival access. Because most families possess private archives that are not subject to German archival laws, they are permitted to keep their files closed. This is what historian Anke Schmeling confronted when she set out to write the history of Hereditary Prince zu Waldeck und Pyrmont, the Higher SS and Police Leader (*Höhere SS und Polizei Führer*) of Weimar with jurisdictional authority over the Buchenwald concentration camp. Even though Prince zu Waldeck died in 1967, Schmeling was unable to examine his papers in the early 1990s. She made repeated requests to family members and was always turned away.[16] The Habsburg family archive, to take another example, is also closed.[17] As Prince Michael of Greece recently observed, in a comment about royals in general, "The royal clan has its customs, its tastes, its crazes, its hobbies (jewels and genealogy), its codes, and its secrets, and it keeps a whole crowd of skeletons closely guarded in its closets."[18]

Among the most secretive of the royals—and of considerable relevance for this book—is the House of Windsor. Of Germanic origin and cousins of the Hohenzollern and the Hessens (among others), the British royals were viewed during the first half of the twentieth century as a source of hope by many who sought a rapprochement between Germany and Britain. The archives of the British royal family could indeed shed considerable light on the history of German princes during the Third Reich. Most of these records are housed in Windsor Castle in the so-called Round Tower. While certain documents in the Royal Archives are accessible to researchers, it appears that many others have been held back. For example, despite visiting the Royal Archives on two research trips, I was unable to see a single document relating to the Duke of Kent's activities in the 1930s (and there were other documents cited in official biographies that were withheld). The royal family's connection to German princes is a subject that raises uncomfortable questions, and the queen's staff has internalized this protective outlook: one experienced researcher who has received considerable support from the Windsors acknowledged that the subject of the royal family and the Nazis made the archivists "really nervous."

The history of the Hessens also intersects with that of Pius XII (Eugenio Pacelli) (1876–1958)—the pope from 1939 to 1958 who led the church through the war and the Holocaust. Prince Philipp von Hessen and Pius

XII met on many occasions, and, as Philipp testified in 1947, there was one particularly sensitive mission in 1940 that had important political implications. In his denazification trial, Prince Philipp declined to give specifics about the initiative, and the Vatican also refused to divulge information, saying that it was a private matter between the pope and the prince. The denazification board accepted this explanation and did not pursue the matter. The Vatican archives for this period, of course, are closed to scholars. Admirers of Pius XII continue to press for beatification and canonization, but because of the culture of secrecy that permeates the Holy See, the pontiff's relationship with this Nazi prince remains enigmatic. One is therefore left with tantalizing clues, such as the diary entry of 8 January 1940 from Italian Foreign Minister Count Ciano (1903–44): "I receive the Prince of Hesse. For the *n*th time he announces that the conclusion of a *modus vivendi* between the pope and the Reich is close at hand."[19]

Among the most valuable but problematic sources are the denazification files. The *Spruchkammer* file of Prince Philipp provided many of the most important documents for this study. His file, housed in the Hessian Central State Archives in Wiesbaden, contains nearly a thousand pages. It includes numerous accounts of his life and career—a mixture of prosecutorial briefs detailing complicity in the history of the Third Reich, but also of exculpatory statements, written by Philipp himself and many others who knew him. Documents generated by the defense predominate in the files of the denazification boards, and therein lies a danger. It is easy to adopt Philipp's view of events—to rationalize and minimize the consequences of very problematic actions. Scholars have recently debated the usefulness of denazification records: some believe that the circumstances in which they were created (with the defendant trying to save his neck) compromise them as sources.[20] I proceed knowing that many of the denazification records reflect a concerted attempt at exoneration.

The Hessens have collected many of their family members' private papers and placed them in a private archive in Schloss Fasanerie near Fulda. My initial requests for access to papers from the twentieth century were denied. I was informed, given the nature of these letters (many of them not yet sorted through and catalogued), that they were not accessible to scholars. But the family ultimately decided to be helpful and permitted me to see many, if not all, of the family papers. Prince Christoph's son, Rainer von Hessen, a historian living in France, played a crucial role in this generous cooperation. He made available copies of many of the documents from the family archive in his possession. In the course of researching this book, certain documents believed to be missing were located (the disappearance of many valuable records, especially records of nobles from east of the Elbe River lost amidst total war on the Eastern Front and the subsequent depredations of the Soviet Red Army, remains a challenge). In the case of Prince Christoph, his wartime letters to his wife, Princess Sophia, were found in her home in the Bavarian Alps. They had been stored in the cellar and were found by one of her daughters as she helped to clear the house after her mother's death. These letters astonished her family.[21] While this discovery represents a valuable, if partial, recovery of Prince Christoph's papers, the bigger picture regarding princely records is one of displacement, destruction, and the denial of access to archival records. These obstacles have created lacunae in the history of the Third Reich, not to mention twentieth-century Europe. The former ruling elite, who have for so long fascinated observers (and continue to do so—one need only look at the many glossy magazines of Europe where page after page is devoted to the scions of nobility), have avoided scrutiny where Nazi Germany is concerned. In a recent bibliography concerning the history of the Third Reich, which lists more than thirty-seven thousand items, only a fraction concern the nobility (and even fewer focus on princely families).[22]

Another challenge posed by this history stems from the pervasiveness of myths and legends. For example, among the founding myths of the Federal Republic of Germany is that aristocrats opposed the Nazi regime, and that their martyrs, the July 20 conspirators, sacrificed themselves in a manner that absolved the others of guilt. Germany is still a class-conscious country, and the nobility still commands considerable respect. This translates into difficulties when it comes to writing about unpleasantly "brown" pasts of the traditional elite. German historian Christian Gerlach, for example, wrote an article that appeared in a scholarly volume accompanying the controversial *Wehrmacht Exhibition*. Gerlach studied military documents —mostly from Army Group Center—and showed how certain July 20 conspirators were complicitous in the genocide: more bureaucrats than shooters but still cogs in the machine. Individuals who eventually joined the resistance, such as Baron Rudolf-Christoph von Gersdorff (1905–80), Henning von Tresckow (1901–44), and Count Peter Yorck von Wartenburg (1904–44), were officers who had a detailed knowledge of the murders, and still performed tasks that were part of the genocidal war in the East (Gersdorff, for example, was a counterintelligence officer, and Yorck von Wartenburg helped pillage in his post within the Haupttreuhandstelle Ost).[23] Gerlach's piece elicited a response in the German weekly *Die Zeit* from former German president Richard von Weizsäcker (whose unit was implicated) and Countess Marion von Dönhoff, among others. *Die Zeit*, according to Gerlach, then refused to publish his response.[24] The cumulative effect of this combination of secrecy, intimidation, and counter-propaganda has been a fuzzy, legend-ridden understanding of the nobility in twentieth-century Germany.

A second, more specific, legend that pertains to this book is best related by author Martin Allen (although he himself treats the story as fact). He

Prince Christoph von Hessen in Luftwaffe uniform ca. 1941.

asserts that Prince Christoph von Hessen was the pilot on a Messerschmidt 110 fighter-bomber plane that attacked Buckingham Palace on 13 September 1940. Allen describes in vivid detail how the plane passed "low over Admiralty Arch . . . [and] thundered along the Mall at nearly 250 miles per hour brushing tree tops" before delivering its payload—six bombs that very nearly killed King George VI.[25] His portrait is so deftly drawn— he even renders the scene through the eyes of the king, who "apparently saw the Messerschmidt as it rushed toward [him]"—that his rendition appears credible. This is a legend with remarkable counterfactual implications: a royal trying to kill his cousin and commit regicide, bringing a pro-appeasement figure to the throne. A successfully executed mission could have decisively altered the course of the war. Two questions arise: the first is whether Martin Allen's account is true, and why would such a legend take hold? Indeed, others have rendered the story besides Martin Allen, but none has furnished conclusive evidence or disclosed their sources of information.[26] A careful examination of the extant documentation shows that Prince Christoph was not aboard any plane that bombed Buckingham Palace. But the existence of this legend is in itself significant and telling.

Legends help make overwhelmingly complex phenomena more coherent and comprehensible. Often rendered in dramatic and even poetic terms, legends frequently take hold because there is a core of historical truth to them.[27] The first legend mentioned above, about aristocrats as anti-Nazi members of the resistance, is grounded in an element of historical fact (there were aristocrats in the July 20 plot); yet it also speaks to the need for "a useable past"—to employ Charles Maier's phrase.[28] Not just aristocrats but many segments in the West German public felt a need to identify figures that embodied positive attributes and traditions. This would help with the creation of a democratic system in the years after World War II. Despite the plebiscitary support for the Nazi regime, there had been "good Germans," to be found first and foremost within the aristocracy.[29] These were usually portrayed as self-sacrificing and cultured (a photo of the von Stauffenberg brothers with poet Stefan George proved very effective in this regard).[30] Granted, the patriotism of the resisters was sometimes questioned, and the legend was far from a straightforward hagiography.[31] But many West Germans nurtured key components of this myth as they implemented the "economic miracle" and simultaneously proclaimed, "*Wir sind wieder wer*" (we are again somebody). The second legend, about Christoph as the alleged pilot on a plane that bombed Buckingham Palace, is also based on certain facts: he had joined the Luftwaffe and was stationed at a base in France that served as a launching site for raids against London during the Battle of Britain. But the legend speaks more to a mistrust of royalty that was pervasive in the 1990s, to a frustration about the inaccessibility of archival sources, and to our tabloid culture that encourages sensational revelations. The origins and propagation of legends are subjects treated in this book: this includes the allegation that Prince Philipp von Hessen met with the Duke of Windsor during the early stages of the war in an effort to secure a negotiated peace. Another unproved assertion maintains that British intelligence agent (and Soviet spy) Anthony Blunt found sensitive correspondence between the two men when he traveled with Royal Archivist Owen Morshead to Schloss Friedrichshof in August 1945.

As the generation of the Third Reich and World War II passes, it is now time to render a more sober and nuanced version of this history—one that challenges not only myths but also taboos. This would entail, for example, acknowledging the sacrifices of aristocrats who resisted the Nazis but also would study those who supported the regime. Historian Stephan Malinowski has found that among 312 families from the "old aristocracy" there were 3,592 who joined the Nazi Party—962 (26.9 percent) before Hitler came to power in 1933.[32] This accounting is not exhaustive, but rather a highly suggestive sampling. There were other aristocrats who joined the Nazi

Party, although no scholar has yet offered a precise figure (or calculated a percentage based on the sixty thousand to eighty thousand aristocrats in Germany at the time).[33] But with regard to Nazi Party membership, it appears that aristocrats exceeded the general 10 percent average for the Third Reich.[34] Malinowski's survey has permitted him to discern various trends among the interwar nobility: for example, that the less wealthy "small aristocrats" (*Kleinadeligen*) in Prussia were more seriously affected by the loss of World War I and the collapse of the monarchy; that nearly every East Elbian noble family had at least one member in the Nazi Party; that the old Catholic aristocracy in Bavaria less often joined the party; that the younger generation were more likely to be activists; and that aristocratic women became party members at a higher rate than their nonnoble counterparts.[35] It is also notable that a cohort of historians is now working together to study aristocrats during the Third Reich in a more systematic way (the German Research Foundation has funded one important initiative).[36] While there are multiple approaches to the topic, including the use of Weberian ideal types and a more social-scientific synthesis of data, quite a few scholars are endeavoring to understand the experiences of specific aristocrats.[37] Indeed, many see biography and prosopography as an important way to move forward in understanding nobility during the Third Reich.[38]

This book will not focus on scandal or represent what the Germans call "*Enthüllungsgeschichte*"—that is, "the unmasking, for its own sake, of the 'brown parts' of numerous [individuals]."[39] It will also refrain from explicit moral judgments. As Ian Kershaw has noted, "for an outsider, a non-German who has never experienced Nazism, it is perhaps too easy to criticise, to expect standards of behavior which it was well-nigh impossible to attain in the circumstances."[40] This is especially the case when one examines members of the high nobility: people from not only a different social stratum but also, in a certain sense, from a different world. Ethical considerations factor into this history, but it will be up to the reader to judge. My project here will be to render the members of princely families in human terms and offer an understanding of their complicated thought processes.

The goal is to provide comprehensive portraits—and this would include the recognition of positive attributes. Philipp, who spoke three foreign languages (English, Italian, and French), was described by the head of the State Theater in Kassel as "an educated, good European." He added that "one gained the impression that he was a very correct man raised according to the English style."[41] Prince Christoph, like Philipp, possessed considerable charm. Indeed, the younger brother was more extroverted and had a more lively sense of humor (even some of the photographs of him in his SS uniform show him with a hint of a smile). His brother-in-law, Prince Philip, the current Duke of Edinburgh, described him as "a solid fellow. He was a very gentle person, interestingly enough, and very balanced actually. He

Prince Philipp in Berlin on Unter den Linden in 1925.

was kind and had a good sense of humor. So he actually was the complete opposite of what you'd expect, I suppose."[42] Christoph also spoke fluent English and was proficient in French. Almost the exact same height as Philipp (5′10″), he too had lost most of his blond hair by the mid-1930s. With a trim physique and sharp, almost angular features, most regarded him as striking and attractive. Christoph suffered from an array of relatively minor physical ailments: the most serious was a sensitive stomach that was occasionally ulcerous. This did not prevent him from being very athletic; indeed, he had a passion for a wide array of sports. He raced cars and motorcycles and developed into a world-class equestrian, participating in competitions across Europe. These two men possessed considerable ability and combined a commitment to their illustrious family with a love of country. Indeed, their gravitation to National Socialism was motivated by a certain idealism. They believed that Hitler and his cohorts were the best answer to Germany's considerable problems, including economic instability, the onerous Treaty of Versailles, and Bolshevism. Princes Philipp and Christoph embodied contradictory qualities and cannot be portrayed in an entirely negative or, conversely, entirely positive light. Like so many others, especially in the era in which they lived, they fell somewhere in between in a gray area.[43]

The interwar years featured the complex and in certain ways contradictory phenomenon of the "fascist gentleman." In many ways, Philipp and Christoph conformed to the archetype—an image that has gradually gained greater currency in novels and films: for example, Kazuo Ishiguro's *The Remains of the Day*, Michael Ondaatje's *The English Patient*—to name but two novels that were highly successful as films (with regard to the latter, one could add Luchino Visconti's film *The Damned* (1969) about a Krupp-like family of German industrialists and Franco Zeffirelli's 1999 *Tea with Mussolini*, among others). Whether it was the pro-appeasement Lord Londonderry and certain of his British friends, Colonel de la Rocque and the elitist French fascists of the Croix de Feu and Jeunesse Patriotes, or the haughty and anti-Semitic Central European nobility (see Gregor von Rezzori's *Memoirs of an Anti-Semite*); this "ideal type" was an international phenomenon.[44]

Philipp and Christoph embodied this outlook and lifestyle as they criss-crossed Europe visiting family and like-minded friends. The two princes retained a sense of class-awareness; like most royals, they were almost invariably conscious of being part of a larger world. They made decisions to support Hitler with an eye to the fortunes of their social stratum. Class was at the root of so much of their thinking, contributing to a pronounced anti-Bolshevism, a fear of social unrest, and a belief in leadership skills (*Führertum*).[45] While they were prepared to assert their individuality and even to be the "black sheep" of their family—which they were at times, such as when they first joined the Nazi Party—they remained part of a tight-knit family.[46] Indeed, their parents and siblings also joined the Nazi Party. Princes Philipp and Christoph were remarkable individuals, but in many ways, they were more than that.

1

The Interconnectedness
of the Nobility:
Strategies to Preserve Privilege
Through the Great War

In order to understand the Hessens' view of the world, one must have some knowledge of the context in which they lived in late-nineteenth- and early twentieth-century Europe. This includes the class structure that prevailed in Germany, the interrelatedness of the most illustrious families, the material wealth that they possessed, and the aristocratic customs that prevailed. Indeed, these considerations shaped both the Hessens' relations with the outside world and their intrafamily interactions. The Hessens, one could say, occupied a stratum that one might describe as "the bottom of the top." This top was comprised of the ruling houses of Europe—the Windsors (Sachsen-Coburgs or the Saxe-Coburgs), Romanovs, Habsburgs, and with ever increasing importance, the Hohenzollern. Within the German Reich the Hohenzollern held a unique place, but they were followed closely by other royal houses, such as those of Hannover, Saxony (Wettin), Württemberg, and Bavaria (Wittelsbach). Indeed, even prior to the dissolution of the Holy Roman Empire in 1806, the German Reich was characterized by relatively weak imperial authority and strong princely houses.[1] There had once been many princely houses, but as the German lands gradually unified in the nineteenth century—going from more than three hundred independent states prior to the Congress of Vienna to 38 in the 1815 settlement to just one in 1871, the number of princely houses decreased. It remained difficult to sort out all the families—in part because of widespread intermarriage but also because of the existence of subsidiary lines. The *Almanach de Gotha* offers one organizational schema, dividing the nobility into three parts: first, the sovereign houses of Europe; second, the seigniorial houses; and third, the princely nonsovereign families.[2] The sovereign houses that in most cases ruled over independent states up until the unification of Germany in 1871 included the Hohenzollern of Prussia, the House of Wittelsbach in Bavaria, the Hannover (the city is spelled Hanover in English), the House of Württemberg in the southwest, and the Hessen.[3] Many of the families in the second part, the *Maisons seigneuriales* (the *Almanach de Gotha* is written in French), are also illustrious. These would include the following: Hohenlohe, Thurn und Taxis, Fürstenberg, Arenberg, Fugger, and Waldenburg-Schillingsfürst. Oftentimes, members of families in part three, the nonsovereign houses, would also have the title of prince or princess. Among the better known of these families in Germany are the Bismarcks, the Hardenbergs, and the Donha-Schlobitten.

The Hessens were a part of this rarified world of princely houses, a strata so elevated that it was even set apart from the general aristocracy, let alone the nonnoble part of society. The German language denotes this special status: the princely families warranted not just the word *Adel* (nobility/aristocracy) but *Hochadel* (high nobility)—and it is significant that the Germans would have a specific word (*hoch*) to designate this niveau. The Hochadel was so powerful that between 1815 and the first German unification in 1871 that these thirty-six princes in the German Bund had the right to ennoble individuals within their territories—a right that eventually fell exclusively to the emperor.[4] Within the Hochadel, of course, there were a number of terms conveying different kinds of status. At the top, one would find *kaiserlich* (imperial) or *königlich* (a ruling royal house). Not quite so exalted was *fürstlich* (princely). But even here—with the title of *Fürst*—there would be further distinctions: most notably between the traditional feudal nobility and the monarchical service nobility. The Kaiser had the ability to elevate noble men to the status of *Fürst*, as Kaiser Wilhelm I did with Otto von Bismarck. The lineage of a family—with the older the better (and with designation *Ur-Adel* or "foundational nobility" dating back to the early Middle Ages as an especially prized quality) factored significantly into considerations of rank. Indeed, a baron (*Freiherr*) from an old family would usually be more highly regarded than a count (*Graf*) from a more recently elevated line, even though the ranking of titles in and of themselves would normally be reversed.[5] Most aristocrats would have been sensitive to these various gradations: they were raised with an acute awareness of hierarchy, lineage, and protocol, and a trained bureaucracy emerged to assist them in maintaining this order. There was a remarkable degree of precision in maintaining genealogies and family histories: this included a host of professionals who compiled and maintained volumes such as the *Genealogisches Handbuch des Adels, Fürstliche Häuser,* and the *Gotha'ische Almanach.*[6] The Institute for German Aristocratic Research in

Marburg to this day continues to publish a journal titled *Aus dem Deutsches Adelsarchiv* that focuses on the 1945–59 period, and above all, on the fate of aristocrats in the eastern regions of the former Reich. It has an Internet site advertised as "Your Internet Platform to German Aristocracy."[7] This attention to hierarchy is crucial in gaining a sense of their own social understanding. While the formal meetings of the princes—the *Fürstentag*—no longer take place, representatives of the royal houses still convene on a regular basis to discuss issues of concern, the most notable involving genealogy. Landgrave Moritz reported how the heads of the houses would discuss thorny subjects, which included not only tax laws but also how one regards adopted children.

Members of the Hessen family therefore retain a clear picture of where they stand in the noble hierarchy. This is somewhat remarkable because aristocratic titles were abolished during the Weimar Republic after the fall of the monarchy. As of 1919 aristocratic titles were merged into the individual's name. Therefore, the Prince of Bavaria or the Prince of Baden actually was not a title but a name. Rainer von Hessen (son of Prince Christoph), noted, "Strictly speaking 'Landgrave' is no longer a title, but the law permitted titles to be changed into names. So, to enable the head to be called landgrave, every member of the family carries in his passport the name Prinz und Landgraf (or Prinzessin und Landgräfin) von Hessen." Rainer von Hessen continued, "actually, most people today confuse the name with a title. They also use expressions like 'Royal Highness,' 'Highness,' and 'Serene Highness's (*Durchlaucht*), as forms of address and forget that we live in a republic."[8] Despite the absence of a legal foundation, many members of the nobility continue to monitor the use of titles. The head of the House of Hesse-Kassel and his heir, the eldest son, are nonetheless referred to as His Royal Highness.[9]

The Hessens were comprised of three branches, divided between two main branches: the older northern Kassel branch (the main focus of this book), the southern Grand Ducal house in Darmstadt, as well as the side line of Hessen-Philippsthal-Barchfeld.[10] The Hessens had begun splitting into multiple branches in the late sixteenth century when Landgrave Philipp divided his territory (*Landgrafschaft*) among his four sons. Because two of the sons were childless, there was partial consolidation into the Landgrafschaft Hesse-Darmstadt (which became a Grand Duchy or *Grossherzogtum* in 1806) and into the *Landgrafschaft* of the Hessen-Kassels (whose heads of the family became electors or *Kurfürsten* beginning in 1803). While there was occasional intermarriage between the branches, the houses remained separated until recently: in the 1960s, the head of the Hesse-Darmstadt family, Prince Ludwig (1908–68), adopted his nephew, the heir to the Hesse-Kassels, Landgrave Moritz (son of Prince Philipp) (b. 1926). Upon the death of Ludwig's wife—Margaret ("Peg") von Hessen-Darmstadt (1913–97)—Moritz became the chief of both houses. Still, it is easy to confuse the families; it is no surprise that when the Hessen jewels were stolen after World War II by American officers, authorities at first were not sure which branch was the proper owner.[11]

The Hesse-Kassels were related to a remarkable array of monarchs. As noted earlier, the most important links were with the Hohenzollern and the British royal house: the mother of Philipp and Christoph, Princess Margarethe von Preussen (1872–1954), was the sister of Kaiser Wilhelm II as well as the daughter of Queen Victoria's eldest daughter, Princess Victoria (1840–1901). Princess Victoria had married the Prussian heir, later Kaiser Friedrich III (1831–88)—who ruled for three months before his death from cancer in 1888. This meant that Princess Margarethe was the niece of British King Edward VII (1841–1910). (There were also other ancestral ties linking the Hessens and the Windsors.)[12] The Windsors, as is well known, stemmed from the houses of Hannover and Sachsen-Coburg, and retained a decidedly German cast well into the twentieth century. In fact, they used the family name of Saxony-Coburg until 1917. In light of the fiercely anti-German sentiment running throughout the British population (one writer quipped with some hyperbole, "people refused to

Royals meet at Schloss Friedrichshof, Kronberg, 1906. From left: Princess Margarethe von Hessen, Grand Duchess Marie of Russia, King Edward VII of Great Britain, and Kaiser Wilhelm II.

drink German wines and kicked dachshunds in the street"), King George V (1865–1936), decided, "with an inspired flamboyance worthy of any medieval monarch, to renounce his German ancestry and proclaim the House of Windsor."[13] The Mountbattens also changed their name from Battenberg in 1917, as did Queen Mary's family, the Tecks, who took the name Cambridge. Queen Victoria had "been brought up by one Coburg [her mother—her father was descended from the House of Hannover] and married another: Prince Albert of Sachsen-Coburg (1819–61)."[14] She spoke German without an accent and saw most of her children marry German princes: besides her eldest daughter marrying a Hohenzollern, Alice (1843–78) married Ludwig IV, Grand Duke of Hessen of the Darmstadt line (1837–92); Helen (1843–1923) married Prince Christian von Schleswig-Holstein; Arthur (1850–1942) married Princess Louise Margaret von Preussen (1860–1917); Leopold (1853–84) wed Princess Helene zu Waldeck und Pyrmont (1861–1922); and Beatrice (1857–1944) married Prince Heinrich von Battenberg (1858–96).[15] The Windsors, Battenbergs, and the two branches of the Hessens intermarried to an extent that their family trees are virtually inseparable. The Hohenzollern were not far out of the picture, and Queen Victoria's German-ness is perhaps most vividly conveyed by the fact that when she fell gravely ill on the Isle of Wight in January 1901, her grandson, Kaiser Wilhelm II, rushed from Weimar, where he was attending the opera, and braved stormy seas to be by her side. The Queen of Great Britain and Ireland and Empress of India, "died at age eighty-one, literally in the Kaiser's arms, on 22 January 1901."[16]

This is but the tip of the iceberg in terms of royal relations. As noted earlier, Prince Philipp married Princess Mafalda (1902–44), daughter of the king of Italy, Vittorio Emmanuele III (1869–1947) and Queen Elena (1873–1952); and Prince Christoph married Princess Sophia of Greece (1914–2001), the sister of Prince Philip (now Duke of Edinburgh). Mafalda's and Philipp's brother-in-law was Tsar Boris of Bulgaria (1894–1943), a member of the Sachsen-Coburg und Gotha family. If one factors in the connections of their cousins, the Hessen-Darmstadt, the interrelatedness of the Hessens to European royal families is all the more impressive. Princess Alix von Hessen married her cousin, Tsar Nicholas II and was, of course, the last Tsarina. Also telling, if more general, is a document from after World War II, where Philipp listed the trips he made abroad after 1918: whether it was Italy (on numerous occasions), Holland (1931), Egypt and Greece (1933), Bulgaria (1935), Yugoslavia (1935), or Greece (1938), the reason given for the trip was always the same: "to visit relatives."[17] The royals actively cultivated close family ties through a variety of means, including travel, from an early age. This is still the case today, as Prince Alexander zu Schaumburg-Lippe (b. 1958) noted, "The fact is, we are all part of a living tradition."[18]

European royal families generally practiced endogamy, or marriage within a group, caste, or class. The panoply of royals throughout Europe deemed suitable for matchmaking provided them with enough variety to sustain lines, although the interconnectedness was such that it is easy to understand the genetic problems of inbreeding, such as hemophilia, an illness that is especially notable among the descendents of Queen Victoria in the families of Hesse-Darmstadt, Prussia, Russia, and Spain.[19] Historians sometimes talk about the "Grandparents of Europe"—Queen Victoria and Christian IX of Denmark (1818–1906) (the latter was from the House of Schleswig-Holstein-Sonderburg-Glücksburg and became Danish king in 1863 when his brother-in-law, the then Landgrave von Hessen, waived his rights to the throne).[20] One would be justified to suggest that before there was the European Union, there were the descendents of Victoria and Christian. Royals and their observers sometimes talk about a "north–south split" that grew out of religious differences. As Prince Michael of Greece noted, "since the papacy discouraged Catholics from marrying members of other Christian denominations, the Catholic monarchies of Southern Europe —France, Spain, Portugal, Italy, and Austria—married with one another. Their common language, to this day, is French. As the more tolerant Protestant and Orthodox churches accepted mixed marriages, the northern monarchies made up another bloc, in which Orthodox Russia, later joined by the Orthodox Balkans, married with Protestant Scandinavia, Germany, and England. Among them, the common language remains English."[21]

These generalizations can be seen in the case of the wife of Prince Christoph, Sophia, who held the title Princess of Greece and Denmark (the name of the House was Schleswig-Holstein-Sonderburg-Glücksburg). Although one might not normally associate these two countries with one another, the linkage had come about in 1863 when Prince William of Denmark became King George I of Greece after an insurrection forced out the previous Wittelsbach ruler. Her parents were Prince Andrea of Greece (1882–1944) and Princess Alice von Battenberg (1885–1969). Prince Andrea's "paternal origins were two parts Danish (including his grandfather, King Christian IX of Denmark), one part Dutch and five parts German. . . ."[22] He was also related to the Romanovs on his mother's side. Princess Alice was born a Battenberg and stemmed from a morganatic marriage in the Hesse-Darmstadt grand-ducal family (as compared to the Hesse-Kassel branch of her husband Christoph). Therefore, Sophia, like her husband and distant cousin Christoph, was directly related to Queen Victoria (1819–1901). Alice and Prince Andrea had five children, including not only Sophia but also Prince Philip (b. 1921). In order to marry Elizabeth in 1947, Philip was adopted by his uncle Louis Mountbatten (1900–79), became a naturalized British subject, and renounced his Greek title.[23] One sign of the complexity of royal intermarriage is that despite stemming from the Greek royal family and having Greek citizenship for many years, neither Sophia nor Philip possesses any Greek ancestry.[24] This situation is similar to that in Romania (House Hohenzollern) and Bulgaria (House of Sachsen-Coburg), where the ruling families are not indigenous but German.[25] These modest but nevertheless highly complex examples permit one to understand why Lord Louis Mountbatten devised a code to map royal genealogy. Conceived in 1939 when he was at home at Broadlands in Hampshire, Lord Louis's code used letters and numbers to document the Mountbattens' connections to fifteen ruling families across Europe.[26] The *Tables*, as they were known after they were published in India in 1947, were so complicated that they might have challenged some of the wartime code-breakers at Bletchley Park.

Despite the interrelatedness of the European royals, there was none-theless some infusion of new blood, often with attractive women marrying the male heirs. The great example was the Battenbergs, when the Prince Alexander von Hessen-Darmstadt (1823–88) defied the order of his brother-in-law, Tsar Alexander II, and married Julie von Hauke (1825–95) in 1851.[27] Her situation is in certain respects reminiscent of Diana, Princess of Wales: the Spencers were a distinguished old family, but nonroyal (for the British royal house the concept of equal birth—an *Ebenbürtigkeitsprinzip*—does not apply in the same way as on the Continent).[28] Still, in the early twentieth century, it was more often the case that women, rather than men, would ascend the hierarchy into princely or royal stations.

Decisions about marriage, especially of the morganatic kind (where royals married nonroyals) were made with great care. Although it was increasingly common to marry for love, the decision about whom to wed was not a personal one for those involved. As the deposed Kaiser Wilhelm II told his son, also named Wilhelm, who wished to marry a member of the minor nobility, "Remember, there is every possible form of horse. We are thoroughbreds, however, and when we conclude a marriage such as with Fräulein Salviati, it produces mongrels, and that may not happen."[29] If individuals defied parents and other relations and chose the mate they preferred, they risked being ostracized (and even cut off from family funds). When Grand Duke Ludwig IV von Hessen-Darmstadt, who was widowed in 1878, married a divorcée, Countess Alexandrine Kolémine in 1884, Queen Victoria "ordered that this union be dissolved."[30] Unlike the Prince of Wales (later the Duke of Windsor), who some fifty years later chose Wallis Simpson over the throne, Ludwig IV complied and separated from the countess, leaving her with a pension until her death in 1941.[31] The definition of the word "morganatic" suggests the problems often associ-ated with "unequal" matches: "a form of legitimate marriage between a member of certain royal families of Europe and a person of inferior rank, in which the titles and estates are not shared by the inferior partner or their children."[32] Even the verb associated with such marriages is suggestive: in royal circles, one "commits" a morganatic marriage. The royals of Europe would, of course, usually provide for the offspring of such marriages, while taking care to preserve the family patrimony. Royals, in fact, pioneered the practice of prenuptial agreements in order to preserve the family property and protect it from those perceived as outsiders.

Royal matches typically contained a paradoxical combination of homogeneity and heterogeneity. Prince Michael of Greece captured these contradictory qualities when he observed, "Almost all the royals of my generation, who are now in their sixties, can boast of a similar family tree. Indeed, back then, royals could marry only among themselves. And since there was only one royal family per country [with the exception of Germany], they had no choice but to seek partners abroad."[33] Considering the international nature of royal matches, as well as the religious divisions that existed, the German aristocracy was never monolithic. Geographic considerations also came into play, including a certain "East-West opposition." Most notably, the *Junkers* who resided east of the Elbe River and were known for certain predilections (conservatism, piety, service to the state, and military prowess), stood out from other groups. German historian Heinz Reif has argued for "relatively autonomous aristocratic groups," distinguished by wealth, origin, the quality of nobility (feudal aristocracy vs. monarchic service aristocracy), and their favored areas of activity.[34] Compared to the nobility in general, the princely families exhibited more similarities: they were a smaller group and had more contact with one another. But while there were tendencies and ideas that applied to princes as a whole, there were also areas of divergence. The Hessens, then, provide insight into this world, but no one family can capture all the qualities present among the German princes.

The House of Hesse: a Princely Dynasty

The Hessen were affected by tradition in profound ways well into the twentieth century. Like most princely houses, they were an old family, with the dynasty dating back to the Middle Ages. The Hohenzollern were relative upstarts; their ancestors began ruling Brandenburg in the fifteenth century. More common would be the Princes zu Waldeck und Pyrmont, who were a rich and powerful family in the twelfth century and who acquired their family seat, the Burg Waldeck, in 1150. The Hessens date the advent of their dynastic line back to the thirteenth century when, as a result of the Thuringian-Hessen War of Succession (1247–64), Heinrich I, Landgrave von Hessen, made Marburg his capital.[35] Heinrich established the family's coat of arms—the red and white striped banner on a blue background with lions—which he took from his Thuringian relatives. It is still used by the family today (and versions are symbols for both provinces, Hesse and Thuringia). Philipp the Magnanimous moved the family seat to Kassel in the sixteenth century. When the city was badly damaged in the Seven Years' War (1756–63), the princes rebuilt in grand style so as to include the Museum Fridercianum, the building most often cited as the first separate museum in a German state. At this time the museum held the collection of Landgrave Frederick II, "best known to American historians for allegedly having supplied Hessian mercenaries to the British during the Revolutionary War."[36]

After the Austro-Prussian War of 1866 and the creation of the North German Confederation, the Hesse-Kassels lost their status as a ruling family, and this meant losing further control over much of their property (but the head of the House kept the title of *Landgraf* or Landgrave, a hereditary title without territorial authority). However, the Grand Dukes of Hesse-Darmstadt continued to exist as a ruling family until 1918. In the Austro-Prussian War of 1866, the head of the Hesse-Kassel house—Elector (*Kurfürst*) Friedrich Wilhelm I (1787–1867)—had sided with the Austrians in an attempt to defend the federal constitution that governed relations between the thirty-eight German states. While Bismarck gave the cousin of the Elector and presumptive heir the opportunity to join with the Prussians, and promised to reward him with the regency of Hessen, the cousin, Landgrave Friedrich Wilhelm, declined, viewing this as an illegitimate act.[37] The 1866 war progressed rapidly: even before the battle at Königgrätz, the land of Hessen was occupied by Prussian troops without firing a shot. Bismarck annexed Hesse-Kassel, as well as Hanover, Nassau, and Frankfurt, and turned these states into Prussian provinces. Bismarck also ordered the confiscation of much of the Hessen family property. The Elector went into exile and died shortly thereafter. It was left to his successor, his cousin Landgrave Friedrich Wilhelm von Hessen (1820–84), to repair the situation. It helped that he had married Princess Anna von Preussen (1836–1918), a niece of the Hohenzollern king. However, Bismarck kept most of the *kurfürstliche* fortune for his own notorious slush fund—the *Reptilienfonds*.[38]

Indeed, it was only in 1873, two years subsequent to German unification, that the Hessens and the Prussian Crown concluded a treaty that restored some of the property. Landgrave Friedrich Wilhelm agreed to forego his claims to the Hessian throne and in return received three castles, an income from the Prussian state (*Staatsrente*), and most of the Hesse-Kassel family's inventory of art and household goods. In the contract, this property was declared *gebundenen Besitz*—or entailed property—which meant that it could not be divided, nor sold, or even given on loan. Indeed, this was a key point in the legal process that subsequently culminated in the creation of the Hessen House Foundation (*Hausstiftung*) in the twentieth century. The Hessens lost a great deal in the German wars of unification—including the *Residenz* in Kassel and a number of other castles in the region. In 1866, the magnificent Schloss Wilhelmshöhe in Kassel, for example, became the property of the Prussian ruling family: after being used to imprison Napoleon III in the wake of his capture in 1870, the imposing Schloss later became the favorite summer residence of Kaiser Wilhelm II. For the Hessens, the Kaiser's presence there served as a painful reminder of the earlier defeat.[39] While the Hesse-Kassels were hardly left penniless, German unification brought diminished independence, and they experienced something akin to a hostile takeover on the part of the Prussians.

Despite the considerable losses as well as the profound humiliation, the Hessens gradually rebounded. The properties of the Hesse-Kassels were similarly immense, even if they did not approach the holdings of the Hohenzollern, the Hohenlohe, the Solms, and the Ratibor (the largest landowners in Germany).[40] They had retained Schloss Panker in Holstein near the North Sea—a property that had previously escaped confiscation by the Prussians because it was not *kurfürstliche* (it dated back to the Hessens' ties to the Swedish royal family). They also had Schloss Adolphseck near Fulda, which today houses the most important part of the family's art collection. Once the summer residence of the Prince Bishop (*Fürstbischof*) of Fulda, it was expanded in the eighteenth century, when, following the vogue of the Enlightenment, it took on a French name, Schloss Fasanerie (the name was changed back to Adolphseck in 1877 after the Hessens recovered it from the Prussian crown). Featuring ochre-colored walls and sweeping elegant lines, the baroque castle sits amid an expansive park (it was known as a hunting retreat or *Jagdschloss*). When Napoleon invaded the German lands in 1806, he presented the Schloss to Marshal Duroc as a gift. The Hessens recovered the property after the Congress of Vienna and remodeled it.[41] It still houses a regal *kurfürstlicher* throne room, decorated with a massive crystal chandelier, an expansive baroque carpet, gilt furniture, and, of course, a red velvet throne adorned with the family coat of arms.

Several other properties belonging to the Hessens warrant mention. Schloss Philippsruhe near Hanau was a majestic eighteenth-century baroque castle and the primary residence of Landgrave Alexander Friedrich von Hessen (1863–1945), the head of the House until 1925 when he renounced the position in favor of his younger brother Friedrich Karl (1868–1940)—the father of Philipp and Christoph. Blind and devoted to music, Alexander Friedrich counted among his friends Clara Schumann, Edvard Grieg, Richard Strauss, and Siegfried Wagner, and would host them at Philippsruhe.[42] Schloss Philippsruhe also became the headquarters for the family foundation in the 1920s. Schloss Rumpenheim near

Offenbach, just east of Frankfurt, was the first home of Prince Friedrich Karl and Princess Margarethe (before they became the Landgrave and Landgravine respectively, in 1925) and was where the first four children were raised. Wolfgang recalled, "when we were at Rumpenheim, there was always a singular feeling among us brothers. The Schloss had a certain smell that old castles have and that never exists in a new house."[43] With a view of the Main River, a "splendid park" in which the boys played, and the proximity to Frankfurt, the castle was one of the favorites of most family members.[44] There was also Palais Bellevue in Kassel, which Philipp took over when he became Oberpräsident of Hesse-Nassau. This urban residence was part of a complex of buildings located on the rim of the city, with a view down to the Fulda river and across to the rolling hills of the Hessian countryside (hence the name Bellevue). Most of the complex had been lost to the Prussians during the wars of German unification, but the Palais Bellevue, which was recovered by the family, would prove ideal for Philipp—more than large enough for his family and a short five-minute walk to his office on the Adolf Hitler Platz.

In the twentieth century, the property that served as the center for the Hesse-Kassels was Schloss Friedrichshof in Kronberg. Designed by Ernst Eberhard Ihne (1848–1917), the castle, which was commissioned in 1892 by his widow, Empress Friedrich, was a monument to the emperor (above the portal to the main entrance carved in stone is the inscription *Frederici Memoriae*).[45] An ambitious exercise in historicist architecture, Friedrichshof incorporated various strands in the history of German, Italian, Dutch, Renaissance, and English Tudor-style architecture, and then combined them with the British landscape and interior design. Portions of the exterior were half-timbered, giving it the style of the region. The interior design featured traditional wood paneling, open fireplaces, and an important art collection. Many of the portraits were of British ancestors, and the library was stocked with books by British authors.[46] A number of illustrious guests, including Queen Victoria, Czar Nicholas II, and Kaiser Wilhelm II, also planted trees, including massive sequoias.[47] The effect, then, was a mixture of German Schloss and English country house. One should note that there were also modern features: from the start it was lit by electricity, making it one of the first residences with this amenity (initially it had its own generator), and it had an elevator, as well as bathrooms with hot and cold water. Despite being a curious structure, Friedrichshof "worked" as a building. Prince Philipp commented about his grandmother's project, "many of the castles and castlelike houses that later arose, especially in America, drew their inspiration here. Perhaps it doesn't conform any longer to our contemporary taste, but for the turn-of-the-century, it was a sensation."[48] One indication of the successful historicist architecture was that Wilhelm II, after seeing the Schloss, commissioned the architect Ernst Ihne to design

Schloss Friedrichshof at Kronberg, the castle constructed by Empress Friedrich in the 1890s as a monument to her deceased husband.

the Kaiser Friedrich Museum because he "could be confident that Ihne was uncontaminated by modernist fads."[49] The Kaiser's decision was also apparently motivated by his disappointment at not inheriting the castle. Despite the fact that he had well over one hundred grand residences, it bothered him that his mother had bequeathed it and the medieval castle in the town (as well as her jewels and art collection) to his younger sister Margarethe—even though the latter had been the devoted companion and caretaker of Empress Friedrich.[50]

For centuries, aristocrats, who were prohibited by feudal custom from engaging in retail trade, invested their wealth in land, precious metals, and art. Princely wealth was often material and, thus, impressive in a palpable way. When compared with modern-day financial assets, which are often in the form of stocks, bonds, savings, and such—the wealth of the nobility was outwardly more imposing. The Hessens were typical in this regard. Even their vast agricultural holdings would stir the imagination. This was partly due to the geographic diversity: they owned huge estates not just in Hesse but also in the north of Germany, above all in Holstein, near the Danish border. In addition to their castles, they had more than a half-dozen estates (signified in German by the word *Gut*).[51] Like many princes, most of the Hessens were brought up to consider money and finances as something "dirty" or beneath them and hired professional estate managers. This was the case with Landgrave Friedrich Karl, who was induced after World War I by his son Wolfgang to engage Heinrich Lange (Wolfgang's superior in the army) to restructure the family's finances. Lange transferred many of the assets to the family foundation, the Hessische Hausstiftung, diversified the foundation's holdings, and arranged for it to acquire numerous properties in Munich and Berlin.[52] This included thirty-one listings in Munich alone—many with the best addresses on the Leopoldstrasse and the Nymphenburgstrasse—but also some tenement houses in working-class districts. The Hessens also had holdings in Wiesbaden, Frankfurt, and Hanau, among other cities.[53] After World War II, the American occupation forces placed the total value of the real estate at over RM 9 million ($3.6 million —although one must multiply this 1945 figure by at least a factor of thirty to approach current value).[54] These numbers reveal in a microcosm the vastness of princely real estate holdings—even after the division and loss of property during the Weimar Republic. Of course, the scope of princely property during the Imperial era was even more stunning: in 1917 within Prussia (which had absorbed the provinces of Hessen in the nineteenth century), noble foundations possessed 7.3 percent of the property versus a national average of 6.8 percent (Silesia had the highest rate of noble ownership at about 15 percent).[55]

In light of these vast and diverse holdings, it was never easy to arrive at a valuation of the Hessens' wealth. They also owned a considerable amount of stock, usually in blue-chip German companies like I. G. Farben, AEG, and the Löwenbräu brewery in Munich. The Hessens also put money into many local industrial concerns, such as the Gelsenkirchener mine and the Mitteldeutsche steel works. (This perhaps helps explain why Prince Philipp would profess such an avid interest in workers.) The American occupation authorities were also able to locate approximately two dozen accounts in various financial institutions totaling RM 968,630 ($388,000).[56] The Hessens' diverse portfolio was typical of princely families, who often restructured their finances on a more rational basis beginning during the closing years of the nineteenth century. Even if they did not opt for hands-on control of financial matters, they would fashion themselves as what David Cannadine called, "that curious hybrid, part businessman and part landowner: the aristocratic millionaire."[57] Despite these considerable and varied resources, the Hessens were a tradition-bound family, and accordingly, most of their assets were in real estate and cultural property. The art collection, mentioned above, was by all accounts the most significant in the Land of Hesse (with the exception of the formerly *kurfürstliche* and now state collections in Kassel, including the famous works by Rembrandt and

Rubens). The family jewelry was also stunning: after American soldiers stole much of it from Schloss Friedrichshof at war's end, the estimates ranged up to RM 15 million ($6 million), although the insurance value of RM 5 million ($2.5 million) was ultimately used.[58] The contents of their castles was also appraised at RM 5 million by, a "special expert," who inventoried the furniture, carpets, fixtures, and porcelain, among other objects.

When the head of the family Landgrave Friedrich Karl died in 1940, Prince Philipp became the "legal successor," and among other things, the chairman of the Kurhessische Hausstiftung.[59] This meant that he was charged with making many of the decisions concerning the disposition of the property: what would be kept and how it would be utilized; what artwork would be placed where; and sometimes, which family member lived in which property. Although the Weimar constitution tried to abolish the custom of primogeniture—Article 155 ordered the dissolving the trusts (*Fideikommisse*) and entailed property (*gebundene Vermögen*)—in an effort to provide for the equal division of inherited property among family members, the princes usually circumvented these measures. In the case of the Hessens, they did this by structuring the family foundation in such a way that the head of the house would receive half the income, while the other family members would divide the other half. However, payments from the foundation occurred only when the annual balance showed a clear profit; with maintenance costs and other expenditures often quite significant, the foundation did not represent a steady source of revenue for family members. One finds incomes that were considerable, but not off the charts. To give some perspective, Philipp reported the following annual earnings:

1939: RM 30,779
1940: RM 35,295
1941: RM 183,331
1942: RM 40,407
1943: RM 42,007
1944: RM 24,026.[60]

With the exception of the year 1941 (the year after his father died and Philipp became head of the House of Hessen), Philipp appeared prosperous, but he did not have an extraordinarily high income. Although the average annual salary of an industrial worker in Nazi Germany was only about RM 1,800 per year, Philipp's income did not match those for great industrialists, who would have earned hundreds of thousands of marks per year.[61] The Hessens were conservative with their wealth and, as noted above, kept most assets in the traditional aristocratic forms of real estate, jewelry, and art. Still, Philipp's assets in 1940 amounted to RM 416,000, and by 1944, he was worth RM 686,000.[62]

The properties of the Hessens—even if legally owned by the Kurhessische Hausstiftung after 1928—had many qualities that gave them a feudal atmosphere. For example, in the denazification trial of Prince Philipp, the chief administrator (*Schlossverwalter*) at Schloss Fasanerie testified that "his grandfather was in the princely service for many years, as was the case of his father until his death."[63] It was not uncommon to have three generations simultaneously working for a princely family, and both the employees and the Hessens appeared to take comfort in this generational continuity. The Kurhessische Hausstiftung employed quite a number of people and then cared for those who made it to old age: in 1946, thirty-one people employed by the Hessens had pensions (the oldest was Adam Schreiber at age ninety-six—born in 1850).[64] Of course, one must avoid an overly nostalgic or sentimental view of the lives of staffers. Author Anne de Courcy captures the two-edged sword of disregard and commitment when she notes, "Servants were frequently regarded almost as another piece of personal property and anyone attempting to 'poach' a good cook, butler or maid, as the moral equivalent of the cat burglar. It was not quite so bad if the current and prospective employers did not know each other, but to lure away the cook or nanny of a friend was considered an act of the basest treachery."[65] Among the Hessens it was often the case that staff moved from the employ of one family member to another, but most stayed on in some capacity: Adelheid Fliege, who was engaged as Mafalda's secretary in 1934 after Philipp had become Oberpräsident, continued to work for Philipp after the war—"in purely personal matters."[66] Heinrich Lange, who as mentioned earlier fought with Prince Wolfgang during World War I, became the chief administrator not only for Friedrich Karl but later also for Philipp—a tenure of more than twenty-five years in 1946.[67] There were certain reciprocal bonds between the Hessens and their employees, whereby the princes would look out for the welfare of their employees. As one journalist noted recently, "The code of old-time servitude meant that the more marginal classes were sort of adopted by the rich, provided for some security in terms of medical care and old age."[68] The Hessens appeared to believe in this code—even if there was no conscious avowal by family members. The economic crises of the 1920s were all the more traumatic for them because they were forced to release some employees.

Of course, there was the flip side to these feudal traditions, most notably the overwhelming influence of the ruling family. Throughout the German lands, it had long been the law (since the Peace of Augsburg in 1555) that inhabitants of a region had to adhere to the religion of the princely family. In Hesse, as in Waldeck, the denomination was Evangelical Lutheran.[69] Politically, one would talk of the locals and their ties (*Verbundenheit*) with the *Fürstenhaus*.[70] This raises the question of political influence of royals, which traditionally, was very strong in German lands. It is interesting that in statements made for the denazification board, the servants and staff all testified that they did not know of any cases where Philipp "tried to influence the managers, clerks, and workers of the princely administration in a National Socialist sense."[71] But he did not really need to pressure subordinates. The example he set was powerful in itself. Prince Philipp was also capable of tolerating a few individuals who were not supporters of the regime. Chief administrator Heinrich Lange stated that he was an "opponent of the [Nazi] movement . . . therefore I avoided political conversations with the prince, since I had an opposing viewpoint."[72] Clearly, there was the expectation that dissenters would suppress their views. Although there was significant regional variation, there remained undercurrents of tradition whereby locals paid heed to the politics of the princes. This is one of the reasons that the Nazis would later court them.

Philipp's Early Years (1896–1920)

Prince Phillip von Hessen was born along with his twin brother Wolfgang on 6 November 1896 in Schloss Rumpenheim on the Main River. Quite remarkably, another set of twins would arrive five years later when Christoph and Richard were born (twins did not run in the family). According to a *New York Times* article from 1924, "These two batches of royal Hessian twins constitute the only known and authenticated cases in the history of dual births of Princes of the blood."[73] Philipp and Wolfgang were the third and fourth sons of Prince Friedrich Karl von Hessen (1868–1940) and Princess Margarethe Beatrice Feodora von Preussen (1872–1954). Because the two older brothers would die in World War I, birth order became significant. Philipp was born minutes ahead of Wolfgang and therefore later became the Landgrave and head of the house.

The parents, as often is the case with aristocrats, had disarmingly playful nicknames (even Queen Elizabeth II since childhood has had the name "Lilibet"): Friedrich Karl was known as "Fischy" and Margarethe as "Mossy." Within the family, their sons had similarly amusing, not to mention mostly rhyming, monikers: Philipp was known as "Phli" (pronounced "flea"), Christoph was known as "Chri" (pronounced "kree"), Richard was "Ri", and Wolfgang was called "Bogie." It was not just that they had nicknames —this is common in many social milieu, often growing out of children's difficulties with pronunciation—but that they continued to use these names throughout their lives. From time to time, new nicknames would arise within the family: "Chri" was called, for a time, "Doggie," by his brothers. Additionally, they would resort to private codes when writing about political figures in letters to one another: for instance, "big B" for the Kaiser. Throughout the 1930s, the Hessens referred to Hitler as "Ini," an

The Hessens at Friedrichshof, ca. 1904: from left, Friedrich Wilhelm, Richard, Philipp, Princess Margarethe, Christoph, Maximilian, Prince Friedrich Karl, and Wolfgang.

appellation that remains a mystery. They would also sometimes adopt quirky little habits. Whenever Friedrich Karl met his brother-in-law Andrea, the two men would greet one another by turning their backs and bowing in the opposite direction—a peculiar play on royal etiquette.[74] But such silliness hardly disguised their serious and often imposing demeanor.

Landgrave Friedrich Karl was a formidable but complex man. While he was in many ways a type from an earlier era, and believed in an aristocracy committed to military service, he twice resigned his commission—the first time in 1893 at age twenty-five when he retired to Rumpenheim to "devote himself to his scholarly and artistic streak." The Kaiser, however, would not grant him his leave and wrote to his mother Empress Friedrich that with Prince Friedrich Karl's "'philosophizing, melancholy' character, he needed 'contact with soldiers and military service' to provide 'the necessary counterbalance."[75] Later, he temporarily resigned his post in 1911 in order to spend more time with his family.[76] Friedrich Karl was studious and had a passion for archeology, art, and literature, which he passed on to Philipp. During the second tenure in the Prussian Army, he assumed the command of a regiment in the local garrison in Frankfurt and established his family in a home in Frankfurt so that he could be closer to the barracks. While not nearly as committed to a martial ethos as his Prussian relations, he permitted his sons to pursue careers in the military. Three of the six boys attended the Lichterfelde Cadet Academy in Berlin where they endured a Spartan and even brutal education ("Thrice daily every cadet had to polish his boots and the metal buttons on his tunic").[77] Friedrich Karl, not surprisingly, had a romanticized conception of war. Like many others in 1914, he expected something similar to the nineteenth-century variant. But he also thought himself modern in certain respects: for example, he told his sons that unlike their cousins, the Hohenzollern princes, they would enjoy no special privileges at the Cadet Academy and must succeed on their own merits.

With the outbreak of war in 1914, Friedrich Karl himself abjured a posting to the General Staff and instead insisted on remaining with his regiment. Observers were shocked that he would not take advantage of the royal perk, the post at headquarters that would keep him from the line of fire. Indeed, according to his grandson, Rainer von Hessen, some royals considered him "insane" for staying with his regiment as they advanced to the front.[78] But in addition to an anachronistic conception of fighting, Friedrich Karl was an idealist, and he believed in loyalty to his troops. Additionally, he suffered from something of an inferiority complex. The prince had married "up" by landing the Kaiser's sister, and he was sensitive about not measuring up in the eyes of his in-laws. At the time of his wedding he was not head of the House of Hessen: the position was held by his older and virtually blind brother, Landgrave Alexander Friedrich, who relinquished it in the mid-1920s in order to enter into an "unequal" marriage to Baroness Stockhorner von Starein (1884–1965). Prince Friedrich Karl, as was his title when he married, elicited the address "Highness" (*Hoheit*), while his wife warranted "Royal Highness" (*Königliche Hoheit*). This disparity came to an end in 1925 when Friedrich Karl became the head of the house, but that was decades later (the precise nomenclature and its history was duly noted at the time by aides to the British king George V).[79] In order to marry the Princess of Prussia, Friedrich Karl had needed to secure the permission of her brother, Kaiser Wilhelm II—which he did in 1892 via a written request and a face-to-face meeting: the latter occurred on the occasion of a visit by the king and queen of Italy, just prior to the parade of princes from the ruling houses who processed before the Kaiser and his royal guests.[80] The Kaiser attended the January 1893 wedding at the Hohenzollern *Stadtschloss* in Berlin; perhaps more remarkable was that the heir to the Russian throne, Tsarevich Nicholas (who succeeded his father the following year), also accepted an invitation to attend. While Wilhelm attempted to forge closer relations between the two empires—with limited success—the wedding had other "momentous consequences": the Tsarevich significantly advanced his courtship of the Kaiser's cousin, Princess Alix von Hessen-Darmstadt, his future wife.[81]

Prince Friedrich Karl possessed a complex personality, with certain countervailing views and interests. For starters, he resented the Hohenzollern in many ways—a sentiment that had its origins in the Prussian annexation of Hesse in 1866. Part of the reason the prince chose to command a regiment in Frankfurt was that he wanted no part of the military headquarters in Potsdam, despite the power and respect associated with the Prussian General Staff. Indeed, he frequently criticized the lifestyle of Prussian officers of elite regiments where there was widespread drinking, gambling, and dueling. It is telling that one of his best friends from his youth was the relatively liberal Prince Max von Baden (1867–1929), the last chancellor of Imperial Germany who played a key role in the Kaiser's abdication. Prince Max, who studied with Friedrich Karl at the university in Freiburg, would later help found the progressive school in Salem. The two men combined a high regard for tradition with heterodox and sometimes progressive ideas.

Landgravine Margarethe was also quite prepossessing. She was born in the Hohenzollern's imposing *Neues Palais* in Potsdam and had grown up amid great privilege and formality (Prince Louis Ferdinand von Preussen described Potsdam as "a mixture between a convent and a barracks lacking that simple cheerfulness which makes even the most difficult conditions in life endurable").[82] Margarethe was widely regarded as the most popular of Kaiser Wilhelm II's sisters, and she maintained good relations with a wide array of family members.[83] Some of her early letters to her cousins in Darmstadt from the first decade of the twentieth century were written on the stationery of Buckingham Palace, while others detailed her plans to travel to Holland to meet up with her cousin, Czar Nicholas II.[84] These letters are indeed very revealing: first, because they exhibit how correspondence served to keep family members connected; second, how women excelled with regard to epistolary communication; and third, because they suggest some of the places where these semi-nomadic members of the high aristocracy would meet (to palaces and great country houses one would add certain fashionable spas and resorts). Women like Princess Margarethe played key roles in helping establish important social networks.

In 1901 Margarethe inherited her mother's Schloss Friedrichshof, which was so impressive that even Prince Friedrich Karl was prepared to eschew the other Hessen properties and make it the primary seat of the family. This was not an easy decision for Friedrich Karl—he was attached to Panker in Holstein, the seventeenth-century Schloss where he was born, and also to Schloss Rumpenheim, the couple's initial home, which he found especially agreeable. In tradition-bound high aristocracy, it was highly unconventional for a husband to reside in his wife's home. But because there were good reasons—notably Margarethe's commitment to maintaining the house of her mother's and the great expense that this entailed—and

Princess Margarethe riding sidesaddle at Friedrichshof before World War I.

in light of her strong personality, the family moved to Friedrichshof. As a young woman, Princess Margarethe had fallen for Prince Max von Baden. Prince Max did not reciprocate affections and Princess Margarethe therefore moved on to her second choice, Max's close friend, Friedrich Karl. Margarethe would always seem more secure and grounded than her husband, and this found expression in her personality. Very much the matriarch, she was at the center of the large and dynamic family. Later, during and after World War II, she would take care of many of her grandchildren and try to preserve a center at Friedrichshof as their parents faced various tribulations.

Friedrich Karl and Margarethe raised their children in an environment that was simultaneously traditional and cosmopolitan. The boys, for example, were clothed in old-fashioned dresses until about the age of three.[85] They were raised by a series of English governesses, who also helped with their education. This was often the case with European princes: American-born socialite and British MP Sir Henry "Chips" Channon noted in his diary in 1936, "I spent the morning with Philipp of Hesse and we talked of how most of the royalties of Europe have a cockney accent acquired from English nannies. At one moment English nannies played a great role and indeed directed the politics of Europe—and what a hash they made of it."[86] Princess Margaret ("Peg") von Hessen-Darmstadt (née Geddes and born in Dublin) noted: "a great deal of English was spoken in the house as a result of the English nannies, who supervised all six brothers when they were children."[87] Philipp also later recalled, "Before World War I, I was in England every year."[88] The English connections of the family were consciously emphasized. Peg von Hessen added, "Prince Philipp, just like his brothers, was raised democratically. They went to school in England and so in their own experiences got to know about 'fair play.' There was no trace of a Prussian officer's spirit in his house."[89] This statement must be viewed from the perspective of the time (she was trying to impress the denazification board) and in relation to the Prussian pomp and ostentation (which the Hessens deplored). While the Hessens may have been "modern" and democratically inclined relative to the households of the Hohenzollern or the Wittelsbach, where private tutors oversaw the education of the children to a more advanced age, the environment in the Hessen home would strike us today as remarkably tradition bound.[90] It is nonetheless striking that Prince Christoph wrote the majority of his letters to his mother in English (especially from 1924 to 1932) and that Philipp and Mafalda mostly spoke English to one another.[91]

As was common practice for not only aristocratic families but also those of higher civil servants and clergy, most of the children went away to boarding school. Many towns, such as Kronberg, did not have schools that granted the *Abitur* (the diploma needed for university). All but the two youngest sons, Christoph and Richard, went away to school. Yet they did so largely on their own accord. In the case of Wolfgang, who attended the Lichterfelde Cadet Academy, it was his wish because, as he disclosed later (and not at the time to his parents), a male tutor in the household was making sexual advances that left him feeling very uncomfortable. That Wolfgang was unable to tell his parents about this situation and that he chose the demanding regimen of a military academy speaks to the constraints that persisted in the Hessen family, as well as more broadly in Imperial Germany. Still, relations between parents and children were strikingly close. Christoph, for example, would write his mother about his romantic life, even confiding episodes of infatuation and heartbreak.

Prince Philipp left the family home in 1910 at the age of fourteen to go to school in southern England. He was apparently unhappy there, despite the fact that the school was located in Bexhill-on-Sea, which, as one local history notes, "became the playground for the aristocracy" during the Edwardian period (it was the first resort to permit "mixed" bathing and the site of the first motor race in Britain in 1902).[92] The reasons for Philipp's unhappiness remain unspecified. His twin-brother, Wolfgang, recalled that a great deal of sport was played there and that Philipp returned home

Cadets at the Berlin Lichterfelde Academy performing martial exercises. Prince Max von Hessen holds the standard.

looking much healthier than when he had left two years earlier. Philipp also had some fond memories of his time in England. He recalled how he, along with other family members, attended the birthday party of Princess Victoria, the second daughter of King Edward VII, held at Buckingham Palace (he was there on several occasions). The party included fireworks that would release parachutes holding charming toys, such as Japanese ivory carvings, which the children would collect. During one party, Philipp pursued the toys with such zeal that he did not notice that his family had departed. Struck with panic, he approached the only person whom he recognized—King Edward VII. Grabbing the king's pant legs, he said, "I am lost." The king asked, "But who is your mother?" Philipp replied, "Mossy." The king then began to laugh raucously and called to a page, who arranged to return him to his family.[93] While the episode drips with nostalgia, harkening back to what scholar George Steiner labeled "the imagined garden" of pre-World War I Europe, it also speaks to the lavish lifestyle of the British royal family, a monarchy (as distinct from the Hessens and other nonruling German princely families) that paid no taxes.[94]

After his return from England, Philipp's parents granted him a short period living at home, where he attended a *Musterschule* in Frankfurt. This was a kind of progressive school where modern languages were taught (as compared to only Greek and Latin). Philipp was a sensitive child and gravitated to art and music—dominant interests in later years. This extended to dabbling with art. Princess "Peg" von Hessen-Darmstadt once observed, "he is not a painter in a literal sense, but he is gifted at drawing."[95] It is therefore understandable that Philipp subsequently went off to a *Realgymnasium* in Potsdam. His parents did not send this gentle and artistically inclined boy to the Cadet Academy; instead, he attended a more traditional school nearby. This was the recommendation of General von Gontard, the tutor of the Kaiser's sons. Philipp was under the supervision of Colonel von Steuben, the director of the military orphanage there. Even though the Realgymnasium was relatively less harsh than the academy, it was difficult for Philipp to be away from home and to live at the orphanage with boys, mostly sons of lower-ranking officers who had died. Philipp recalled that the orphanage and school was the idea of his father, who wanted that "he should imbibe some of the German spirit," and he added "I never could feel really at home there. It was all too foreign."[96] The privileged existence that Philipp enjoyed had costs. His was a youth that began with governesses and ended with boarding school, and this evidently contributed to a lack of self-confidence and to longings for acceptance. That Philipp was the only one in his family at the Realgymnasium and that most of his brothers attended the more prestigious Cadet Academy made him feel all the more marginalized. It is possible to interpret later behavior—including posturing with Nazi leaders—as an outgrowth of this adolescent experience where he longed for recognition.

Despite a certain melancholia and sense of loneliness, Philipp fared surprisingly well in Potsdam. His brothers were nearby, and they met quite frequently. They were often invited on weekends to the *Neues Palais* to be with the Kaiser and his family, and Philipp became close to his Prussian cousins, especially Prince August Wilhelm (1887–1949), who was to play an important role in Philipp's gravitation to the Nazis. Prince "Auwi" later recalled that Philipp became something of "an adopted son" of the Hohenzollern in Potsdam and that Philipp helped nurture his passion for art and antiques.[97] Philipp often found time to escape into the city to go to the theater. Yet he was a relatively assiduous student, earning honors (*Primareife*) when he took the exit exam, or Abitur in 1915. He spoke English, Italian, and French, and had done well enough in math and science to qualify for a university course in architecture. Philipp was clearly quite exceptional: he was the only one of the four older brothers not to pursue a military education (that option was closed off for the younger twins). He swam against the stream for a male member of the high aristocracy: in Germany, even more so than in Britain, there was the expectation that one would pursue a career as an officer. Wolfgang, for example, recalled in his memoirs, "From my youth on, I had never known another goal other than becoming an officer." Yet in the case of Philipp, a fitting image is provided by his son, Landgrave Moritz, who chuckled as he told how Philipp preferred to sit in the stands and watch his brothers in the military parades rather than participate in them.[98]

In 1914, however, even Philipp became caught up in the events that led to World War I. In July 1914, just prior to the outbreak of war but in the wake of the assassination of Crown Prince Franz Ferdinand von Habsburg, Philipp and Wolfgang had accompanied their mother and her sister Sophie, queen of Greece, on a trip to England. On 14 July, they were invited to Marlborough House to lunch with Queen Alexandra (the widow of King Edward VII), as well as King George V and Queen Mary.[99] Queen Alexandra became panicky and predicted that war stood just outside the door. This upset Margarethe and Sophia to such an extent that they immediately contacted the German Ambassador in London, Prince Felix Lichnowsky. He reassured the two ladies that there was no danger of war— not with England in any case. Nonetheless, the Hessens embarked for Germany in late July on one of the last ships to leave Britain. Wolfgang later recalled that none of them could believe that the two countries would go to war but that there were unnerving signs on their trip back home: soldiers at all train stations, pyramids of luggage, and an atmosphere of almost palpable tension.[100]

Despite his artistic temperament and nonmilitary demeanor, Phillip registered for the Grand Ducal Hessian Prince Dragoon (Leibdragoner) Regiment on 6 August 1914, just days after all the Great Powers of Europe had declared war on one another (4 August had been the crucial day when German troops invaded Belgium and the scope of the war expanded). One senses, however, a hint of reluctance on Philipp's part (but he was not alone in this regard).[101] Philipp was certainly outdone by his brothers. Wolfgang, for example, raced back to the Cadet Academy after his return from England. Like most of the cadets he was immediately sent off to an active regiment. While the members of the Hessen family evinced enthusiasm for the war, they and the other German princes do not bear direct or inordinate responsibility for the conflagration. Historian Golo Mann has noted "the princes didn't precipitate the war, no less lead it. . . . The dynasties and individual state governments more or less had to go along, as they had been forced to do earlier in 1870 or even in 1813; they were, in the end, also German."[102]

In accordance with the philosophy of his father, Philipp did not avail himself of the privileges normally accorded the high nobility to take up a commission as an officer. In a statement before the denazification board, his attorney wrote, "the concerned party did not make use of the then existing right of high nobility to serve in the officer corps, but entered the Dragoon-Regiment Nr. 24 in Darmstadt as a volunteer, where he served as a soldier of the pike. In the course of the war, he was promoted to lieutenant."[103] Just as Friedrich Karl declined a post on the General Staff, and just as the Hessen princes at the Lichterfelde Academy had to live as a regular cadets, it was expected that they would earn their rank as soldiers.[104] Philipp later presented the decision not to avail himself of an appointment as an officer as evidence of his modern thinking—as a sign of his solidarity with the German people. In any case, Philipp did not expect his low-ranking position to endure very long. In 1914, prior to entering active service, he trained as a *Fahnenjunker*: that is, as an ensign who aspired to become an officer. With his education, not to mention his status, the prince was hardly a typical "officer of the pike." Later, he was granted a leave in order to finish his Abitur. He did this in autumn 1915, through a mechanism invented for soldiers called the *Notabitur* (emergency degree) that enabled students to take the exam verbally—in other words, in an expeditious manner—so that they could return to their units.

Philipp began active service as a cadet in February 1915 and was initially sent to Belgium. Just as Wolfgang and his eldest brother Friedrich Wilhelm fought together in the same Ulan cavalry regiment (the Sixth), Philipp and his brother Max both joined the Twenty-fourth Dragoon infantry regiment. By April 1915, Philipp had been redeployed to the East on the staff of the Twenty-fifth cavalry brigade, where he contributed to the Kurland offensive. Philipp worked mostly in staff jobs involving the procurement of munitions and did not see action for much of the war. Yet he was a member of a unit that was frequently posted to front-line areas, and this included battles in Kovno in April 1915 and near Brody in Galicia (today in Ukraine) from August 1915 to November 1916, as well as on the Siegfried Front in Belgium in March and April 1917.[105] Philipp sent postcards and letters home to family and to other relations. Some of his missives to his uncle Grand Duke Ernst Ludwig von Hessen-Darmstadt (1868–1937) and his wife, Grand Duchess Eleonore (1871–1937), have been preserved in the Darmstadt archives: they range from a postcard in 1914, when he was completing his officer's training as a *Fahnenjunker*—this card featured a photograph of the Queen Louise Bridge over the Memel in Tilsit—to a letter dated 10 June 1917, when he was stationed in Belgium.[106] The latter included the observation, "from here there is nothing interesting to report" (except that he liked the new division commander). This situation soon changed. Ironically, he experienced the most dramatic and dangerous moments of his military career after the death of two of his brothers, which prompted the Kaiser to issue orders keeping him and Wolfgang out of harm's way. The Kaiser's order led to Wolfgang's transfer to the staff of Field Marshal August von Mackensen (1849–1945), where the famous general (often associated with his striking death's-head Hussar's uniform) watched over "his little Hessen prince."[107] Wolfgang, however, who had served in the north of France, Serbia, Macedonia, and Romania, had seen a great deal of fighting and truly earned his Iron Cross before being moved away from the front.

Philipp appears to have participated in combat only during the last year of the war, although in the absence of his memoirs, it is difficult to know precisely what he experienced. He was awarded a series of medals, including the Iron Cross First and Second Class, the Hessian Cross of Bravery, and the Austrian Service Cross, among other medals.[108] It is not certain that he actually earned these medals: they may have been more a result of his social status and seem remarkable in light of the desk job he held for most of the war (he also emerged from the war holding the relatively low rank of lieutenant). Yet Philipp reported in questionnaires filed during the Third Reich that he participated in actual combat when he and his unit returned to the Ukraine in 1918. His son, Landgrave Moritz, recalls hearing of his father being shot in the leg, although it was not sufficiently serious for him to mention in subsequent accounts of his military service.[109] Philipp also reported involvement in a battle near Chilkowa in Ukraine on 21 March 1918.[110] Later, in September 1918, he wrote to his mother from Sienkowo that he was with a machine-gun squadron and had been in charge for a few days because the commanding officer was absent. One of his squadron's assignments was to help keep the Ukrainian troops in line (he told his mother of their "disquiet").[111] The fledgling Soviet regime had precipitated a civil war, which complicated the conflict. Philipp's activities during the last phase of the war remain murky: if he was indeed seeing active combat, it is not clear against whom he was fighting. Although one would expect an aristocrat to fight along with the "Whites" against Lenin's regime, it was the Germans who had transported the communist leader from Switzerland to St. Petersburg in a sealed army train and supported the Bolsheviks in their initial quest for power. Philipp's movements become somewhat clearer only in the autumn of 1918, when Friedrich Karl called his sons back to Friedrichshof for consultations about the family's future. Philipp returned immediately and arranged for his aide-de-camp to send along his dog—Philipp's pet having accompanied him during most of his wartime service.

Prince Philipp's largely administrative experience during the Great War was rather exceptional for the Hessens. Indeed, they, like many German nobles, were not simply about pomp, circumstance, and orders from far behind the front lines. They wanted to fight and were often prepared to die—an outlook, as historian Marcus Funck has noted, that was common among many noble groups (especially the Junkers in Prussia).[112] Clan sacrifice was transformed into national sacrifice, an idea that gained support from national patriotic associations during the Wilhelmine era. Thus, the Hohenzollern princes, for example, all assumed positions in army regiments, and several of them participated in active fighting: Prince Eitel Friedrich (1883–1942) saw service in Russia (winning the Pour le Mérite) and at the Somme; while his younger brother, Prince Oskar (1888–1958), a lieutenant colonel commanding the Liegnitz King's Grenadier Regiment, led front-line charges against the French.[113] One Junker family studied by Marcus Funck, the Wedels, lost twenty-four members during World War I. While notions of self- and family sacrifice became the stuff of myth, there was also a harsh reality underlying the often romanticized conceptions. Prince Wolfgang noted, "from my class, which consisted of approximately twenty-eight cadets, I am the only one that survived World War I. Nearly all of my classmates perished in 1914."[114] While there are no precise figures for noble losses, the war took the lives of approximately 7.5 percent of German aristocrats as a whole, and 22 percent of adult males.[115] The percentages for royals appear similarly high: sixty-eight members of princely houses fell.[116] This was a devastating toll, especially for this male-dominated caste.

As noted earlier, Friedrich Karl turned down an offer for a staff position and led the Eighty-first Infantry Regiment into battle in the Belgian part of the Ardennes mountains. The regimental history tells of their "baptism of fire" on 22 August 1914, just two days after the regiment had crossed the Belgian border near Bertix—a middle position among the armies that moved westward as part of the Schlieffen Plan. Encountering French

Prince Friedrich Karl von Hessen during World War I.

troops equipped with tremendous fire-power, the Eighty-first suffered heavy losses. When a battalion flag bearer was shot by the enemy, Friedrich Karl, a lieutenant general, proceeded to grab the flag and continue the advance, exhorting his troops to continue the fight.[117] For him, as his grandson Rainer noted, war was a kind of martial exercise (*Geländespiel*) that bore little relationship to reality.[118] This reckless enthusiasm for war displayed by the prince was to become increasingly uncommon after the trenches were dug and the armies settled in to slaughter one another in the years that followed. Yet during the Great War, the social elite on both sides suffered very high casualty rates: the junior officers, who were often recruited from this segment of society, fell victim in particularly large numbers.[119] On 7 September 1914, in combat near the village of Etrépy, Friedrich Karl was injured by grenade fragments that covered the left side of his body—the shrapnel, along with pieces of his uniform, gave him blood poisoning. He was operated on in a Frankfurt hospital, but the doctors could not remove all the fragments on the first try and he was subjected to repeated procedures. While he soon overcame the threat to his life, Friedrich Karl was left debilitated (suffering from a heart condition as well) and was no longer fit for combat.

Friedrich Karl's two eldest sons were killed in battle. Prince Maximilian (b. 1894), the second oldest, was the first to die, as he fell at St. Jean-Chappel near Bailleul in Flanders on 12 October 1914. A member of the Grand Ducal Hessen Dragoon regiment, the twenty-year-old prince was badly wounded by machine-gun fire in an engagement with British cavalry. He was evacuated by his comrades to a Trappist monastery at Mont des Cats, where the monks cared for him. The British advanced quickly and took control of the cloister, thereby capturing the severely wounded lieutenant. According to one account, while being treated at a British field hospital, "he told an army doctor that he was the great-grandson of Queen Victoria, and gave him a locket to send to his mother in Germany. The British doctor promised to do so. Prince Maximilian died within a few hours and three days later the doctor was killed when a German shell hit the field hospital. The locket with a note by [the doctor] was sent to [the doctor's] widow in England, who forwarded it to Queen Mary; it eventually reached Princess Margarethe of Hesse" through the Grand Duchess of Baden and the Crown Princess of Sweden—both relations of Margarethe who, like many other noble women, worked for the Red Cross.[120] One sees evidence of the special treatment afforded princes: the mayor of the town where Max died ordered a craftsman to construct a coffin, which he did out of an elm tree; he was then buried in a nearby cemetery and the grave was marked with a cross. One observer reported, "this was not done for any other officer."[121] Locals learned of his grave, and because they had suffered greatly in the fighting, they protested, whereupon the coffin was exhumed and moved to a secret location. Later on, in 1926, British king George V, assisted the family in recovering the body and arranging its transport to Kronberg. The death of Prince Max quickly became the stuff of legend. An inaccurate and romanticized version of events was even propagated by the *New York Times* in a 1924 article.[122] If nothing else, the press reports offered an indication of the standing of the Hessen family and of the political culture of the times, which remained attuned to the high aristocracy.

The eldest son, Friedrich Wilhelm died at Curu Orman in Romania on 12 September 1916. Always regarded by Friedrich Karl as the ideal son, Friedrich Wilhelm is remembered in the family for valor and even chivalry.[123] Friedrich Wilhelm ("Fri") was killed in what his younger brother Wolfgang called "close fighting." Wolfgang, who was in the same Ulan regiment, noted later that he did not see very much of his brother during the war (partly because Fri had been wounded in an early engagement and took time to recover). But Wolfgang was close enough that he was brought to view the corpse and discern that Friedrich had had his throat slit by an enemy bayonet—the blood-flecked dagger was found resting on the chest of the dead prince.[124] While it is hard to assess the consequences of losing these two brothers during the Great War, their deaths certainly shook family members profoundly. Prince Wolfgang noted that Max had been his mother's favorite, while Friedrich Wilhelm was viewed in a similar manner by their father. Upon receiving word of Fri's death, most of the family, including many members of the Hessen-Darmstadt branch, convened at Kronberg, where they held a vigil throughout the entire night. Wolfgang recalled, "for years my mother went almost every day by foot from Friedrichshof to the Burg in order to see the coffin of her son, later her two sons."[125] So profound was the loss that historian E. H. Cookridge has even suggested that Prince Christoph "may never have forgiven the British for killing his brother in battle," and that this helped pushed him toward National Socialism.[126] While this interpretation is highly dubious—Prince Christoph, for example, had English friends after 1918—the deaths of the cherished older brothers added significantly to the trauma felt by nearly all members of the Hessen family.

For the Hessen family, there was a curious denouement at the end of World War I. In the early autumn of 1918, Friedrich Karl was approached by a Finnish delegation with the idea of making him king of Finland. It is striking that in the twentieth century, royals from houses that no longer governed often sustained hopes of finding a country that would call on them. For example, Friedrich Christian zu Schaumburg Lippe (1906–83), who worked for Goebbels, earnestly believed that he was on the verge of being made king of Iceland during the Third Reich.[127] At times, politicians or other royals would entertain plans to place individuals on thrones. Sir Eric Phipps (1875–1945), British ambassador to Berlin, reported back to the Foreign Office in 1934 about various restoration schemes in Germany and Austria: "the Austrians had no objection to Philipp of Hesse or some other South German candidate."[128] Another unlikely proposal involving Prince Philipp pointed to him becoming the sovereign of Romania: a British diplomat noted in July 1941 that "The Germans wish[ed] to depose King Michael [of Romania] and place instead Friedrich of Hohenzollern-Sigmaringen, but the Italians would prefer Phillippe (*sic*) of Hesse."[129]

The scenarios involving Prince Philipp and Prince zu Schaumburg-Lippe were farces in comparison with the serious deliberations undertaken by Friedrich Karl and the Finns. In the wake of the Russian Revolution, the Finns had gained their independence and, after a workers' revolt against the first government was put down with the violent intervention of German troops in the spring of 1918, plans for a constitutional monarchy proceeded afoot. At this point, the Finnish leaders still believed that the Germans would win the war, and furthermore, they trusted that the Kaiser's troops would protect them from another Bolshevik uprising. They thus set upon the idea of turning to a German prince and consulted Kaiser Wilhelm II, who apparently recommended his brother-in-law.[130] An initial approach was made to Friedrich Karl on 5 September 1918, and after receiving a positive response, the Finnish parliament elected him monarch (as King Väinö) on 9 October 1918—that is, approximately a month before the end of the war. Friedrich Karl decided to go forward and receive the parliamentary delegation at Kronberg, and the Finns presented him with gold buttons featuring the country's coat of arms for him to wear on his blazer. In October 1918, Friedrich Karl called back his sons from their military postings in order to discuss the matter. While Philipp would have remained in Germany and succeeded his father as Landgrave (head of the house), Wolfgang was envisioned as the crown prince of Finland.[131] The two eldest surviving sons took part in the deliberations surrounding the accession: Philipp even met with an architect to discuss the design of the future royal palace and then traveled with Wolfgang to Munich to shop for furniture.[132]

Friedrich Karl was still unsure whether it was best for him to ascend to the throne but nonetheless made preparations to do so. He worked with Finnish tutors to learn the language and studied so as to become more familiar with the country and its people. A problem arose when a representative of the German Foreign Office wrote him and said that his assumption of the Finnish crown might suggest that the Germans had an imperialistic program to dominate Eastern Europe and therefore undermine peace negotiations with President Woodrow Wilson. The British were also exerting pressure on the Finnish government: Sir Alexander Hardinge in the Foreign Office in London wrote that while the British had nothing against the Finns choosing a monarchical form of government, they would not recognize the brother-in-law of the Kaiser as king (the French sent a

similar message).[133] With the sudden German capitulation and the abdication of his brother-in-law the Kaiser in November 1918, the decision was
effectively made for him. Friedrich Karl waited while the Finnish representative, Baron Carl Gustav von Mannerheim (1867–1951), made one last-
ditch effort to discuss the matter with the British and French. But it made
little sense from a geopolitical perspective to take a ruler from a vanquished
nation. With the French troops having already occupied the bridgehead
Mainz, including Kronberg, Prince Friedrich Karl withdrew his candidacy
on 20 December 1918. Finland became a republic in July 1919.

Exertions of a Younger Sibling: Christoph Prince von Hessen

Prince Christoph and his elder twin Prince Richard (1901–69) were born
in Frankfurt on 14 May 1901. Because Friedrich Karl had taken over the
command of Regiment Eighty-one of the local garrison, the family lived
in the city. They rented a house on the Main river, at Untermainkai 12, just
up the way from the Rothschild palace. The house next door was occupied
by another general at the garrison, and it featured two guards before the
entrance. Prince Wolfgang recalled, "My mother, who as a member of the
royal family was also entitled to guards, did not avail herself of this prerog-
ative."[134] Indeed, the Hessens did not avail themselves of all the privileges
that they were due, and the guards offer a fitting symbol. Granted,
Christoph and his family would spend much of the summer at Schloss
Friedrichshof in nearby Kronberg, where their surroundings were anything but modest. But even at the Schloss, the focus would be on horses and
dogs, rather than pomp and circumstance. There was also an emphasis on
family—the immediate clan, of course, but also relations who came to visit.
Margarethe's sister Sophie (1870–1932) had married King Constantine I of
Greece (1868–1923), and despite the latter's relocation to Athens, she
would visit her sister at Friedrichshof most summers. Christoph was particularly close to his Greek cousin Paul (1901–64), a future king of Greece;
indeed, Wolfgang described his Greek cousins as veritable siblings.[135]
Often they would be in Kronberg, but Christoph also traveled to visit his
relations in Athens. Christoph and his brothers, like most other princes,
were raised with a profound regard for family, and the parents made a concerted effort to nurture relations between cousins. Other relations with
whom he was particularly close were Prince Donatus and Prince Ludwig
von Hessen-Darmstadt, sons of Grand Duke Ernst Louis, as well as Prince
Berthold von Baden (son of Prince Max).[136]

Christoph attended the Musterschule in Frankfurt, but unlike his older
brother Philipp, he remained there for the remainder of his secondary
school education. Like Philipp, he learned to speak English fluently and

had some French. Extroverted, witty, and full of energy, "Chri" replaced Max as the favorite of his mother. The Landgravine undoubtedly played a role in the decision that enabled him to remain at home and, with his twin, Richard, attend the local Reform Realgymnasium. Christoph, however, beneath the easy-going charm, was a highly strung and nervous individual who suffered throughout his life from stomach problems. Indeed, he never completed his Abitur because he was too nervous to take the exam. As Rainer, the younger of his two sons, noted with regard to this crucial test, "he backed out like a race horse from a starting gate."[137] Because Christoph was too young to fight in World War I, he did not have recourse to the "Emergency Abitur" as did Wolfgang and Philipp. Instead, Christoph dodged the exam and remained at home with his parents at war's end.

The years 1918 and 1919 subjected Christoph to a bewildering array of contradictory forces. Despite the losses suffered by the Hessens during the war and the undeniable obsolescence of their romanticized conception of war, he still dreamed of a military career. After 1918, he was forced to abandon this fantasy: the drastically reduced German armed forces in the Weimar Republic had no place for an inexperienced prince; and what's more, he was hardly motivated to defend the Republic. It was also very difficult for the young man to remain at home in Kronberg with a family that was grieving and bitter. While many aristocrats, including the Hessens, were raised to appreciate the importance of self-control (*Selbstbeherrschung*) and never to show one's feelings, this was not in his nature. With a mother mourning her lost sons and, as of November 1918, the forced abdication of her brother, and with a father enduring the tribulations of the Finnish adventure, Kronberg was a gloomy place. French troops occupied the region by year's end, adding further to a stressful environment. It is no wonder that the sensitive and passionate young man felt unable to take his school exams. In that princes were raised with a keen sense of duty—one might think back to Frederick the Great and his notion of "the king as first servant of the state"—Christoph's decision not to sit for his Abitur reflects considerable psychological turmoil.

The Scars of War

While the carnage of the war was itself terrible, it was made worse by the circumstances. This was a war fought for no good reason. It also had flown in the face of the long-held belief that the interrelatedness of European royalty would prevent the outbreak of a European-wide conflagration. This was the view captured so vividly by Barbara Tuchman in her classic *The Guns of August*, where she opens the book by describing the funeral cortege of Edward VII in May 1910: the various sovereigns and their relations "represented seventy nations in the greatest assemblage of royalty and rank ever gathered in one place, and of its kind, the last" (the Hessens joining the Kaiser, his brother Prince Heinrich von Preussen, and Prince Rupprecht of Bavaria, among others).[138] As the war turned into a protracted slaughter, many nobles had the sense that they were precipitating the demise of their class, and they often emerged disoriented and depressed. As historian Robert Weldon Whalen remarked in his study of the war's legacy (and more specifically, in a chapter titled "The Return of the Red Baron"), "disillusionment is too simple an explanation. . . . Words like 'betrayal' and 'lies' fly through the air. The result is not disillusionment, but a bitterly painful sense of dissonance, of *Zerrissenheit*."[139] This was apparently the case with Kaiser Wilhelm II's youngest son, Prince Joachim von Preussen (1890–1920), a cavalry officer who after the war shot himself at the family's hunting lodge near Potsdam. While the war affected nobles in different ways, bitterness and cynicism were common reactions.

The death of the elder brothers contributed to the Hessens' own version of the "stab-in-the-back-myth": superimposed on the more conventional one—that German soldiers had not been defeated on the field of battle but had been betrayed by the civilian leadership (dominated by Jews and socialists)—the Hessens came to believe that they, as a family, had fought valiantly for Germany but had nonetheless been victimized and suffered an unjust loss of status. The family cemetery in the courtyard of the chapel atop the castle at Kronberg became an evolving monument to the suffering of the Hessens. As they waited to recover the corpse of Maximilian, the deaths of the elder and charismatic princes were very much on the minds of the Hessens. Furthermore, there was the contemporaneous blow of seeing their cousin Czarina Alexandra and her family murdered by the Bolsheviks. In Germany, as discussed in the next chapter, their close relation the Kaiser was sent ignominiously into exile. The surviving four brothers reacted in different ways to these traumatic experiences. While Philipp and Christoph traveled and struggled to find rewarding avocations, their twins, Wolfgang and Richard, were able to focus on their work, and they gradually settled into more conventional careers. Rainer von Hessen observed a pattern among his father and uncles: the twins would be markedly different, such that Wolfgang was quiet and unassuming while Philipp more sociable and dynamic; the same applied to Christoph and Richard.

All four of the Princes von Hessen who survived World War I—Philipp, Wolfgang, Christoph, and Richard—joined the Nazi Party. As of 1938, so did Landgrave Friedrich Karl and Landgravine Margarethe. Additionally, their remote cousin, Prince Wilhelm von Hessen (1905–42), part of the Philippsthal branch of family, who married Princess Marianne von Preussen (1913–83) on 30 January 1933—the day that Hitler was appointed Reich chancellor—was a member of both the Nazi Party and the SS. There is no single reason that compelled these various individuals to embrace National Socialism, but there were important shared experiences. Wolfgang reported in his memoirs that the brothers did not discuss politics with one another very often, but each nonetheless found his own ways to National Socialism.[140] The bitterness and disappointment growing out of World War I was a key factor.

The Great War started a process that ended the predominance of the traditional elite, but this process played out over the subsequent decades. While the end of the war and the demise of the *Kaiserreich* signaled a break with the preceding epoch, there were still many areas of continuity. The princes still conceived of themselves as a caste apart, placed tremendous emphasis on preserving family ties, and believed it important to make an appropriate (*ebenbürtig*) marital match. Despite suffering financial setbacks, especially during the Weimar Republic, they still controlled vast resources. Many princes also continued to wield political power: if not by holding high offices themselves, then through their contacts and influence. Furthermore, during the interwar years most Germans remained deferential to the nobility—and especially to the princes.

2

The Princes von Hessen during the Weimar Republic: Tribulations, the High Life, and Fascist Flirtations

E ven though their influence and prestige would continue for several more decades, no other event in the modern era affected German princes as dramatically as the end of the Hohenzollern monarchy and the advent of the Weimar Republic. The end of the Kaiserreich represented a major blow to the German princely houses, and coming in the wake of the Bolshevik Revolution and the murder of the Russian royal family—to whom most German princes were related—many members of the high aristocracy felt that both the world they had known and their very existence were threatened. After the Kaiser's flight to the Netherlands, the remainder of the Hohenzollern property was "reorganized" by the new government. Most royal and princely houses, including the Wittelsbach in Bavaria and the Hessens, were obliged to cede some of their property to the state and create foundations to administer much of the remainder. The changes ushered in by the Weimar government elicited a sense of unease among the princes. The first years after the war were the most trying—exacerbated by the Weimar government's measures aimed specifically at princely houses, as property was being taken and certain bank accounts were frozen. But they ultimately retained most of their wealth and were rarely displaced as members of the social, political, and economic elite. It helped that they had much of their wealth invested in fungible property, including real estate, precious metals, and jewels, as well as art. It also helped that the leaders of the Weimar Republic, although intent on democratizing society, were half-hearted in their pursuit of reform. Indeed, this was the essence of the Weimar Republic: incomplete reform that enabled enemies and critics to persist in their opposition to the new government. For the princes, the situation was characterized by uncertainty and temporary problems, but not their dissolution as a caste. As Golo Mann noted (and overstated), "the disappearance of the [Hohenzollern] dynasty did not mean that all that of dynastic origin and character disappeared. . . . The Revolution altered the political order, not the society."[1]

Many of the changes that came with the transition from monarchy to republic also created new opportunities for members of the high aristocracy. With certain propensities—including travel, an involvement with the arts, and a passion for adventurous pursuits such as flying, automobile and motorcycle racing, horseback-riding, and rowing—many developed a belief in the concept of a "new man" or a "man of action." One role model was Hohenzollern crown prince Wilhelm von Preussen (1882–1951), who returned to Germany from exile in 1923 and was so highly visible in pursuing athletic interests that some observers dubbed him "the crown prince of sport."[2] Such notions extended well beyond aristocratic society, but these ideal types had perceptible upper-class associations. Sir Oswald Mosley, the leader of the British Union of Fascists, initially called his movement the New Party. Described as "youthful, vigorous [and] aristocratic," Mosley attracted a number of his aristocratic supporters—including Winston Churchill's son, Randolph, and Harold Nicolson—who embraced a strange mélange of ideas that were intended to revivify the declining ruling elite.[3] While the "new man" was an international phenomenon, it is telling that certain French fascists in the interwar period were "concerned that their 'new man' was essentially German rather than European."[4] In short, a number of young German elites of the time embraced and helped define the concept. While few individuals combined all elements of this "ideal type" (Philipp, for example, was hardly what one might call a sportsman), they often embraced the more general notions of a belief in an elite, of melding tradition with modernity, and of the value of undertaking dangerous challenges.

The daring and danger that was part of the "New Man" was particularly evident in the passion for flying. One might also think of Hermann Göring and Rudolf Hess—both pilots during World War I—or the Duke of Kent (younger brother of the future George VI) and the Duke of Hamilton (whom Hess tried to reach on his trip to Scotland in 1941): the former was the first member of the British royal family to fly across the Atlantic, and the Duke of Hamilton, while still Lord Clydesdale, had been a dashing amateur pilot and the first man to fly over Mount Everest. In Italy in the 1920s, Mussolini "persuaded the king it was necessary to create a new aristocratic class based on Fascist values," and one found individuals such as Count Galeazzo Ciano, the future Italian Foreign Minister, who neither drank, smoked, or gambled (although he was dubbed "*Il cervo volante*" (the flying stag)—a reference to his passion for flying and his "immoderate consumption of lovers").[5] Historian David Cannadine has explored the question "why did some interwar aristocrats like to be thought 'air-minded'?"— which he defined as "being well-disposed to modernity and technological progress"—and concluded that such thinking was more common among the Germans (and Japanese) than among other nationalities.[6] One can also raise the question about the linkages between "flying and the world-ranging new right," which included Charles Lindbergh and Fascist politician Giuseppe Bottai.[7] While one must take care to preserve distinctions, certain tendencies and values emerged concerning technology, bravery, and leadership.

With greater freedom, but also a steady stream of economic and political crises, many princes struggled to reconcile themselves with "modernity": that is, to preserve their privileges but also adapt to the times. A generational gap surfaced at this time—this was exacerbated by the wartime losses, which had claimed the lives of so many men in or approaching their prime. One scholar of the German nobility even argued that the class was underrepresented in state and society until 1925 because it took time for the "next young generation (born after 1905) to mature and slowly overcome the losses."[8] The younger nobles appeared more prepared to embrace new opportunities, including sometimes supporting the new government (for example, the so-called red counts such as Count Harry Kessler (1868–1937) who worked within the republican system); others gravitated toward National Socialism.[9] The older cohort fought more of a rear-guard battle. They often placed their political hopes in President Paul von Hindenburg, and after 1932, in Reich chancellors Franz von Papen and Kurt von Schleicher, and their "cabinet of barons." As flawed and ineffectual as these reactionaries were, they appear in hindsight to be preferable to the fascist option pursued by many in the younger generation.

Aristocracy and the Weimar Republic

The Republic began with the forced abdication of Kaiser Wilhelm II on 9 November 1918. Prince Max von Baden, the last imperial chancellor, had announced the measure without consulting the Kaiser, then at Supreme Headquarters in the Belgian resort of Spa in the Ardennes mountains. Believing that he would receive more favorable terms from the Entente powers if Wilhelm II was not the monarch, and that he would remove the primary pretext for revolutionary soldiers and sailors who were increasingly emboldened, Prince Max simply proclaimed the Kaiser's abdication. Although Max did not seek to do away with the monarchy and hoped that the Kaiser's departure would enable one of his sons or grandsons to succeed him—and this had been his hope when he had assumed the chancellorship—events soon spun out of control.[10] Prince Max was unable to communicate with Wilhelm II. The Kaiser had surrounded himself with loyal troops at Spa, and he refused to respond to the chancellor's messages. Therefore, on 31 October 1918, Prince Max called Prince Friedrich Karl von Hessen-Kassel and Grand Duke Ernst Ludwig von Hessen-Darmstadt to Berlin and requested that they go to the Kaiser in Belgium and inform him of the necessity of stepping down. The Grand Duke responded that he, as a reigning prince, was not a suitable emissary and turned to his cousin to make the trip. Prince Friedrich Karl initially accepted the assignment, making preparations for the mission, but doubts quickly overtook him: Would the Kaiser's departure appease the leaders of the Entente or mollify the Socialists, who were planning more demonstrations; would this be an act of personal disloyalty; would Wilhelm simply reject his pleas?[11] Prince Friedrich Karl finally answered that if he could not convince himself of the usefulness of the mission, then he could not convince the Kaiser to abdicate. To complicate matters, Prince Max was suffering from the flu (then a global pandemic), which left him completely exhausted; and indeed, his doctor gave him such a strong dose of medicine that he slept for thirty-six hours straight at a crucial juncture in the crisis.[12] The Reich chancellor and his aides thus fumbled about in Berlin as they searched for a way out of the catastrophic situation—a process that culminated with the transfer of power to the Social Democratic leader Friedrich Ebert.

While Prince Max and Prince Friedrich Karl remained friends in the immediate wake of the crisis—Max's daughter Princess Marie Alexandra married Friedrich Karl's son, Prince Wolfgang, in 1924—the events surrounding the Kaiser's abdication were to remain a sensitive topic. Prince Max was frequently portrayed as the one responsible for the collapse of the monarchy, and he himself struggled to demonstrate that he did what he could to bring about a practical compromise. In the autumn of 1926, representatives of the two families, along with other invited notables, convened at the Baden's Schloss Salem near Lake Constance to hear Kurt Hahn (1886–1974), the editor of Prince Max's memoirs, read the chapter that covered the abdication.[13] The Hessens objected to his interpretation, which assigned blame to Friedrich Karl for not traveling to the Kaiser: this, according to the memoirs rendered by Kurt Hahn (who was devoted to Prince Max), would have permitted various possibilities, including the Kaiser naming Prince Max his deputy—a scenario that might have permitted the continuation of the empire. According to Wolfgang, when Max von Baden's memoirs appeared the following year, they, "destroyed a forty-year-long friendship."[14] There continues to be uncertainty about the intentions and role of the liberal prince: Friedrich Ebert characterized him at war's end as enigmatic, and to date, there has been no scholarly biography of the "complicated and conflicted personality."[15]

Amidst the founding of the Republic, there was little time to think about what was to become of the other princes and their considerable property. The Republic was very much a work in progress in late 1918 and early 1919. While there were clear dispositions on the part of certain key figures—the Sparticist leader Karl Liebknecht argued for the nationalization of all property, including that of the feudal elite—this was a matter for careful consideration and negotiation. At the Constituent Assembly held in the National Theater in Weimar in February 1919, where delegates ratified Hugo Preuss's flawed constitution, Friedrich Ebert, who was to be elected the first president of the Republic, "blamed Germany's miseries on 'Kaiserism'" and made a commitment to "a continuous process of the dwindling away of the privileges of birth."[16] Ebert noted in his address to the National Assembly at Weimar in February 1919 that "in the field of politics, the German people has now completely abolished these privileges," and he urged similar transformations in the social and economic realms.[17]

While the Hohenzollern were the focal point of public antipathy, the other princes quickly came under fire, especially as the left-wing elements throughout Germany were invigorated by the prospects of a socialist revolution. This was the time of the *Räterepublik* (republic of councils) in Munich, which forced King Ludwig von Bayern (1845–1921) to flee, and of major uprisings in Kiel and Stuttgart, among other cities. Even though the Hesse-Kassels were not a ruling family, they attracted the attention of many of the revolutionaries. Prince Wolfgang recalled the first sign of the revolution, when crowds absconded with the Hessens' car as well as their horses and wagons, and drove about Frankfurt and the region waiving red banners. The family never recovered this property. Representatives of the workers' and soldiers' councils arrived at Kronberg and made other demands—including billeting insurgents in the Schloss and the stables. Friedrich Karl noted in his diary, "Sergeant Koch [from the Eighty-first Regiment] just came and found us at the breakfast table where he provided the unsettling news of murder threats against me, Mossy, and also the children; he wants to take us to Camberg-Niederselters to his father-in-law who is a gendarme. . . . We decide not to go." Panic-stricken and often tearful friends and employees reported that revolutionary units were due at any moment. Friedrich Karl contemplated taking the family to another of their properties where they might be safer but ultimately decided to evacuate only precious documents and other valuables. Wolfgang searched out loyal troops in Frankfurt, where he tried to induce them to come to Friedrichshof in order to provide protection. One officer responded, "we're not here to guard castles," to which Wolfgang replied, "this doesn't concern castles, but people's lives."[18] Securing no help in guarding Friedrichshof, Wolfgang went to see the head of one of the revolutionary groups who had set up headquarters in the Frankfurter Hof hotel. He was initially subjected to threats, but the leader, who had been a sailor, warmed when he was informed that Friedrich Karl was well-regarded by the troops of the Eighty-first. There were no physical attacks on the Hessens, and little was taken from them, but the events of November 1918 were terrifying and proved instrumental in shaping their views. In the aftermath of the revolution, the dramatic events often loomed large in the minds of many nobles, who suffered what Stephan Malinowski termed "fantasies of loss" (*Verlustphantasien*).[19]

In light of the threats they perceived from revolutionaries, it is not surprising that the Hessen brothers joined units that tried to protect private property and help stabilize the situation. Even seventeen-year-old students Christoph and Richard became auxiliaries (*Hilfsdienst*) in an undertaking coordinated by their school to guard transport carriages until the arrival of French occupation troops. Philipp enlisted in the Transitional Army (*Übergangsheer*), where he formally held a post in the Twenty-fifth Cavalry Brigade up until 26 March 1920.[20] Because Philipp had begun his university studies at this time, his affiliation with the armed forces may have been mostly symbolic (and a pretext for continuing to receive his pay). But Karl Wolff, later a general (Obergruppenführer) of the SS and adjutant to Heinrich Himmler, recalled in 1947, "I know the Prince of Hesse very well, since I was very often with him at war's end in 1919 and later with him in associations in Darmstadt. We both served in a regiment—him as a Major and I as a lieutenant colonel (Oberleutnant)."[21] Philipp's sympathies certainly lay with those opposing the revolutionaries, as was the case with Wolfgang, who helped put down disturbances in Kassel, and then worked in the Army General Command helping oversee the demobilization.

The Hessens discerned another assault on their position; this, in the form of the political and legal reforms undertaken by the new Republic. During the winter of 1918–19, many of the state parliaments took up the issue of the ruling families. The results initially varied a great deal: while certain of the *Landtag* (provincial legislature) and state governments did not have "the slightest disposition to invade the rights of their deposed rulers," others took more radical steps: in Gotha, for example, a communist-socialist coalition "engaged in confiscation without compensation."[22] The new Weimar Constitution that was ratified in 1919 helped clarify the situation: Article 153 stated that the states could exercise the "rights of eminent domain only when accompanied by proper damages."[23] Article 155, as noted in chapter 1, dissolved "entailed property"—a special category of property that had tax advantages. While the more radical measures were annulled, the financial status of princes remained unresolved in many respects. The thrust of the constitution was that princely property would be dealt with in the future, and this left most princes feeling very uneasy, if not directly threatened.

The issue of the princes' legal status continued to be a high profile and controversial issue during the early years of the Republic, partly due to the debates in the state of Prussia that led to the Prussian *Adelsgesetz* (nobility law) of 23 June 1920.[24] Prussia comprised some three-fifths of the population, and was home to the Hesse-Kassels in the West and the Junkers farther to the East. The Adelsgesetz stripped the Prussian nobility of all former privileges. There were no longer special legal codes for aristocrats that afforded them trials by peers and an array of feudal honors.[25] Up until 1918, to take one specific example, only the Hohenzollern were permitted to pass through the central portal of the Brandenburg gate (and the same applied to the Habsburgs in the Hofburg's triumphal arch in Vienna). The law recognized the existence of a nobility, but accorded it no honors or privileges. This was consistent with the Weimar Constitution: Article 109 stated, "the public-legal privileges of birth or social standing are abolished."[26]

The Prussian Adelsgesetz also resulted in the forfeiture of some entailed property belonging to the nobility, but it provided the opportunity to create another kind of tax haven. Paragraph 18 of the law stated that "forests, collections, archives, and communal facilities . . . in so far as their maintenance in a cohesive way appears consistent with the public interest, can be transformed into a foundation (*Stiftung*)."[27] Of course, these transformations had to be negotiated with state authorities, and this was by no means easy; for starters, "the smaller states especially, like those in Thuringia, were simply not in a position to compensate their former princes to the full measure required by civil law."[28] In 1925 alone there were over one hundred such cases before the courts. In the case of the Hesse-Kassels, the negotiations lasted until 1928, when the Kurhessische Hausstiftung formally came into existence.[29] The process featured sharp contretemps, with the state authorities threatening wholesale seizures (the Hessens sometimes described this with the German verb "*verstaatlichen*," meaning "to fall to the state"). But the two sides eventually came to an understanding in an agreement that was approved by the High Court in Kassel.[30] In cases involving other princely families, neither side offered much in the way of concessions. The Hesse-Darmstadt family negotiated with the state throughout the entirety of the Weimar Republic: Grand Duke Ernst Ludwig refused to sign the document formally renouncing claims to the throne until property issues were settled (this occurred only in January 1934, when the Nazi Gauleiter Jacob Sprenger simply declared the agreement to be in force without the Grand Duke's signature).[31] The larger point remains that throughout much of the 1920s the princes felt persecuted by the state and by leftist political groups. In February 1926, the Weimar Republic passed the Law of Suspension (*Sperrgesetz*) that provided for a moratorium on claims "until the enactment of a relevant national law," and this only extended the exhausting and debilitating negotiations.[32]

The year 1926 also saw a national referendum on whether to confiscate princely property without compensation. Prince Wolfgang's understanding, which was quite typical of his cohort (and not wholly inaccurate), was that the draft legislation was the work of "Social Democrats and Communists."[33] In 1925, the Communists had submitted a petition to the Reichstag concerning the expropriation of princely property; yet this was rejected. The Communists therefore turned to the referendum, as provided for in the Weimar Constitution (Article 73). If it was to pass, they needed signatures from at least one-tenth of the qualified voters and electoral support from one-half (and in that the electorate was approximately 40 million, this meant some 4 million and 20 million people respectively).[34] Because many Communists and Social Democrats backed the measure, they secured 12.5 million signatures. According to the complicated process, this meant that the Reichstag would first vote on the measure—which they did and rejected it by a vote of 236 to 142. The measure was then put to a popular vote on 20 June 1926.

Prior to the vote, there was intense campaigning. Those on the left had a field day battering the princes. Social Democrat Otto Wels, for example, told a Frankfurt audience "that the Hessian princes had grown rich from the sale of mercenaries and . . . that a big share of the princes properties came from . . . monastic estates that the rulers took from the Catholic Church without [giving it] any compensation at the time of the Reformation."[35] Because of the disastrous economic travails of the early Republic, many considered confiscation to be "a just punishment."[36] On the other hand, President Hindenburg (1846–1934), not surprisingly, came out against the expropriation. So did the National Socialists. Prince Wolfgang attended a Nazi rally in Frankfurt where the issue was discussed at length. The speaker, a deputy of the local Gauleiter remarked, "I and my fellow-fighters are certainly not for the princes. . . . But this law is a *Schweinerei* (filthy disgrace)."[37] The referendum was contested with great passion and as 20 June approached, the police in some localities "prepared for possible violence."[38] Ultimately, the ballot initiative garnered approximately 15.5 million votes and fell short. But this was more votes than Hindenburg had won in the 1925 presidential election, and it alarmed the princes. Indeed, their anxiety provided certain politicians, most notably the Nazis, with an opening. Wolfgang, for example, recalled that the Frankfurt meeting was the first time he had heard a Nazi speaker. The ballot initiative also divided certain centrist parties and hence weakened them, thereby helping the Nazis. Historian Erich Eyck noted that Reichsbank president Hjalmar

Schacht had been "expelled from the Democratic Party—which he had helped to found—over the issue of the expropriation of the princes. His increasing gravitation to the Right was to prove of fatal importance to the Republic."[39]

In retrospect, it was the 1920 Prussian Adelsgesetz that was the key law. It diminished the nobility's legal and political privileges, but enabled them to preserve considerable wealth. Some houses managed this transition with greater ease than others. Fürst Adolf von Schaumburg-Lippe, for example, "was the last German prince forced to abdicate. With regard to property [*Landesvermögen*], the prince and the small state divided it half and half. Enough money therefore remained for him to throw full handfuls out the window."[40] And indeed, members of the Schaumburg-Lippe family, who relied on a fortune created in the Middle Ages on land and investments in Eastern Europe, made a more graceful transition and continued to live in the Schloss at Bückeburg. The Wittelsbach of Bavaria also arranged a compromise with regard to their property that permitted them to enjoy a lavish lifestyle during the Weimar Republic. Part of what had once been private property became state property—and remains so to this day (e.g., the royal palace in the heart of Munich). But the Wittelsbach created foundations that took custody of much of the family's art and certain castles, such as Schloss Berg on Lake Starnberg (where King Ludwig II drowned), and Schloss Hohenschwangau near Füssen.[41] The princely families, because they enjoyed higher status and greater wealth than most other nobles, rarely had to scrape bottom in coping with the changes of the republic. While one could write with regard to the nobility in general that "many widows were forced to care for their children by themselves and take the overseeing of their estates in their own hands," this would not have applied to the princely houses.[42] As the princes reached settlements with their individual states in the mid-to-late 1920s, they managed to preserve most of their wealth. Their predominance, while challenged, was by no means at an end.

One should mention that the princes had a long history of financial difficulties, although theirs was usually a problem of liquidity. Because of a general reluctance to sell family property, not to mention legal restrictions that prevented them from doing so, there was a long tradition of loans from bankers. One apocryphal story relating to this history comes from the current Prince Alexander von Schaumburg-Lippe, who noted, "at the meeting of the princes (the Fürstentag), all of the wealthy gentlemen rose from their chairs when the banker Baron Rothschild entered the chamber. Only Schaumburg-Lippe remained seated. He was the only one that had no debts to Rothschild." He added that the house was the "smallest" of the Fürstenhäuser, "but [also] probably the wealthiest."[43] This anecdote, of course, exaggerates the indebtedness of the princes to the Rothschilds.

There was in fact a history of the Rothschilds rendering services to the princes in times of need (during the Napoleonic Wars, the Rothschilds helped the then Elector of Hessen evacuate his property so as to keep it out of the hands of Napoleon and then profited from this service). The early 1920s represented another period of crisis. Many members of the nobility, including the Hessens, felt vulnerable to the hyperinflation.[44] In this light, one can more readily understand the nobles' rising anxiety about ceding property to the state as part of the Adelsgesetz: real estate had not only been their main source of income but had also provided them with a buffer against the turbulent economy. The Weimar Republic therefore can generally be characterized as a time of "growing impoverishment" for the nobility that led to certain nonroyals sinking into the upper middle classes, at least economically.[45] The Hessens also had to make certain cutbacks: most visibly, they shut down three-quarters of Schloss Friedrichshof and lived in one wing—the *Wirtschaftsflügel* (housekeeping wing) that included the kitchen. Yet they had been through difficult times before and had good reason to believe that they would weather the storm of the early Weimar Republic.

While the economic circumstances of the early 1920s in themselves would help explain why so many members of the nobility would oppose the Republic, there were political dimensions as well. In the wake of the murder of Foreign Minister Walter Rathenau by right-wing conspirators in 1922, the government passed a law for the protection of the Republic, which included the so-called Emperor's clause: this clause gave the government "the right to prevent members of the former ruling dynasties from entering Germany."[46] While this provision was not implemented in full— only the former Kaiser was prevented from setting foot in Germany—it had symbolic significance. The antipathy of the nobility to the current German government could not help but promote antidemocratic tendencies. They justified their views, therefore, on many levels: nationally, in terms of Germany's catastrophic situation; socially, as part of the ongoing international decline of the feudal elite; and on a familial and personal level, with regard to their own fortunes. Just as they had once retained their hegemonic position by way of a series interlocking allegiances—to nation, family, and myriad traditions—their antidemocratic views featured these mutually reinforcing ideas. The common thread in this worldview was decline—of their country, of their caste, and of society more generally. During the Weimar Republic, there was an acute sense that they were fast losing or had even finally lost their hegemonic position.

There were different ways to continue the fight, and one of the most visible was by working to restore the monarchy. Aristocrats organized in various ways, three of which were particularly significant: the Deutsche Adelsgenossenschaft (German Aristocrats' Association); the Stahlhelm (Steel

Helmet) paramilitary organization; and the Deutsche National Volkspartei. The Deutsche Adelsgenossenschaft (DAG) had been founded in 1874 in Westphalia, and until 1918 it was primarily an organization for northern Protestant nobility. But after 1918, it was revamped to address the broader needs of German nobles—the DAG was a lobbying organization that organized an annual meeting (the *Adelstag*) and published a periodical, the *Deutsche Adelsblatt*. Membership was initially open to all male nobles and then extended to females in 1921. Although the restriction on gender was lifted, the DAG was far from progressive. An avowedly right-wing organization, membership could be revoked if one supported the Weimar Republic; Jews (about 1.5 percent of the nobility as a whole) were excluded through an "Aryan clause" in the early 1920s. Approximately 28 percent of the nobility belonged to the organization, making the DAG a powerful, but not exclusive, voice of the nobility.[47]

Despite claims that it was not a political party, the DAG openly supported the idea of restoring the Hohenzollern monarchy. (This meant that the DAG was de facto anti-Republican.) Because of the wealth and prestige of its members, the government regarded DAG as a threat. In September 1929, the Reich Minister of War prohibited membership in the DAG because he feared that his officers would come under the influence of the organization. Membership in the DAG would also raise the issue of the oath of loyalty taken by members of the military: they had sworn loyalty to the Republic (even if most officers were not enthusiastic about the new form of government), and the mission of the DAG was in conflict with that oath. During the late 1920s, the DAG experienced a number of other challenges as well, with members particularly divided on the issue of support for the National Socialists. Younger members of the DAG exhibited a strong tendency to favor the Nazis, while the older generation was more tentative and noncommittal.[48] The younger faction eventually won out, and the DAG evolved into a highly nazified organization.

The Stahlhelm also exhibited increasing support for the National Socialists, and it was a larger organization with more high profile and influential noble members than the DAG. The honorary chair of the Stahlhelm was Paul von Hindenburg—a position he held until becoming president of the Republic in 1926. With some 400,000 members in 1925, it was the most successful of the *Frontsoldatenbunde* (Front Soldiers' Associations) and was characterized by strident anti-Bolshevism, a commitment to veterans' affairs, and a pro-restoration tenor to its political program.[49] A number of princes also gravitated to the Stahlhelm, including not only Duke Carl Eduard von Sachsen-Coburg und Gotha but many of the Hohenzollern, notably: the eldest, Crown Prince Wilhelm von Preussen (1882–1951); the second eldest of the Kaiser's son, Prince Eitel Friedrich (1883–1942), the fourth eldest, Prince Auwi (1887–1949), and the youngest, Prince Oskar (1888–1958).[50] The 1929 Stahlhelm rally in Munich featured all five Hohenzollern princes marching side by side, which sent a clear message about the organization's support for a restoration. The Stahlhelm actively opposed the Republic, and for this reason joined together in 1931 with the National Socialists and other right-wing groups—an attempt to exhibit the unity of the "National Opposition."

The German National People's Party (DNVP), which attracted many monarchists, also joined in the Harzburg Front. The head of the DNVP, industrialist and media tycoon Alfred Hugenberg (1865–1951), was among the key leaders of the Harzburg Front. The common goal was "opposition to the Brüning government and the Weimar Republic itself"; beyond that there was little in the way of a common political program.[51] Hugenberg eventually threw in his support for Hitler and joined in the Nazi leader's first cabinet in 1933. Like the DAG and the Stahlhelm, Hugenberg and the DNVP were co-opted by the Nazis. There were many monarchists who supported the Nazis. Franz Ritter von Epp (1868–1946), for example, who was a friend of Bavarian Crown Prince Rupprecht (1869–1955), transformed himself from a monarchist to a Nazi and was given a high-ranking post in Bavaria after 1933.[52] Because pro-monarchism took hold in the other right-wing parties, it did not seem out of the question that the Nazis might also support a restoration. Hitler tried to parlay this ambiguity into additional support—a tactic that paid dividends.[53]

Philipp in the 1920s: *Fascisti* and Nazis

Despite the dispiriting German defeat in World War I and the difficult transition for the Hessens as they adjusted to the new republican form of government, Philipp exhibited a certain optimism as he focused on his career plans. As noted earlier, he studied art history and architecture in Darmstadt at the Technical University from 1920 to 1922. He was drawn to the nearby provincial capital in part by Grand Duke Ernst Ludwig (whom he addressed as "Uncle Ernie"). The latter, who had become head of the Hessen-Darmstadt branch in 1892, had revitalized Darmstadt's artistic life, turning the city into one of the centers of art nouveau architecture and design ("in defiance of Prussian bombast").[54] Grand Duke Ernst Ludwig attracted an important colony of artists and craftsmen whose houses and gallery were built on the Mathildenhöhe, just beyond the old city center.[55] Among those who gravitated to the *Jugendstil* (art nouveau) Mathildenhöhe complex were architects Joseph Maria Olbrich, Peter Behrens, and Patriz Huber. Furthermore, Ernst Ludwig commissioned the progressive architect Alfred Messel to design the Grand Ducal Museum, which opened in 1906 and made "Darmstadt one of the last German capitals to build a museum." Messel's building was not as radical as his more modern works, such as the Wertheim department store in Berlin (1904); indeed the Grand Ducal Museum fit in among the traditional historicist buildings that surrounded it, including the neoclassical theater and the grand ducal palace. As historian James Sheehan has noted, "Messel's real talent was for compromise and conciliation."[56] These qualities, and the general artistic vitality of the city, proved alluring to Prince Philipp, who was not just tradition bound but also interested in new ideas.

One would still hesitate to label Philipp a bohemian or progressive during his university years in Darmstadt. He lived very comfortably, first within his uncle's monumental *Neues Palais* on the Wilhelminenplatz in the center of the city, and then, a year later after his younger brother Richard had followed him there and taken over his rooms, Philipp moved to a modest but comfortable gardener's cottage in the Rosenhöhe park, not far from the Mathildenhöhe. Grand Duke Ernst Ludwig took care of his nephews and put these elegant quarters at their disposal. It was common among princes for a senior member of the family to help relations with accommodations: one sees this frequently as those less advantaged—whether due to youth (and lack of inheritance), exile status, or death of a spouse—would benefit from the generosity of a relation who possessed multiple properties. "Uncle Ernie" was especially gracious to his relations from Kassel and provided a comfortable environment that left Philipp free to attend lectures in art history and architecture, and to make trips to Italy and Greece in both 1921 and 1922. These trips, which included long stays with the Hessens' relations in Athens—Philipp's uncle and aunt, King Constantine I (1868–1923) and Queen Sophie (1870–1932), and their family—enabled him to study Greek sculpture in considerable depth.[57] Another indication of Philipp's privileged existence during this period is that he kept a Greek valet—at least until the autumn of 1922—when the servant returned to Greece.[58]

Philipp left university in 1922 without earning a degree, exhibiting a tendency not to complete projects that was pronounced in his youth. He had ceased his studies in order to work at the Kaiser Friedrich Museum in Berlin, where he remained for a year.[59] The legendary museum director, Professor Wilhelm von Bode (the Kaiser Friedrich Museum was renamed the Bode Museum after World War II), had arranged an internship for him in the graphic arts department.[60] Philipp worked on a catalogue of old French drawings that, he wrote a friend, he thought "probably will be published later on." He added, "it is a lot of work but very interesting because nobody has done it before & I keep on making new discoveries every day—besides it is good training for my brain as I have found that I can hardly write decent German anymore."[61] Philipp possessed an impressive knowledge of art history: his friend, British writer Siegfried Sassoon, even regarded him as his guide to European culture on his "grand tour." Sassoon jotted about Philipp in his diary in the summer of 1922, "And of course he

BERLIN. Museum u. Lustgarten *This is the museum I am working in.*

Postcard of the Altes Museum in Berlin sent by Prince Philipp to Siegfried Sassoon, 1923. In Philipp's hand at the top right, "This is the museum I am working in."

is *cultivated*. He knows about baroque and rococo, and all the rest of it."[62] Later, after a visit to the Uffizi and Pitti Palace in Florence in October 1922, Sassoon remarked, "He is an admirable guide, but a little exhausting with his inexhaustible appreciation."[63] Despite his enthusiasm for art history, Philipp did not complete the catalogue. By late 1923, he had moved on to Rome.

Philipp could justify this move to Italy on several grounds: first, he anticipated a career that focused on classical art and archeology, and it therefore made sense to head south in order to get hands-on experience studying objects in their context.[64] Second, the situation in Germany was deteriorating rapidly in 1923, with the occupation of the Ruhr by the French and Belgians early in the year and hyperinflation approaching its November peak. As Philipp wrote Sassoon in May, "I am afraid you won't like my poor Germany anymore as things have changed so much since last year—thanks to the French."[65] By September, Philipp was writing Sassoon and thanking him for sending money. He added, "life has become imposs-ible in Germany now & it is getting worse & worse every day. . . ."[66] Philipp was accustomed to accepting the generosity of others: in Berlin, he had stayed in the flat of Colonel Stewart Roddie (1876–1961), a member of the English Reparations Commission. Later, according to Sassoon, he had "a flat in the house of his friend the American lady."[67] During trips to Munich, Rome, and Venice in the summer of 1922, he had enjoyed a luxurious lifestyle, including the best restaurants and visits to the opera several times a week; these extravagances came largely thanks to various British gentlemen, including Lord Gerald Berners (1883–1950), who shared an interest in music and art.[68] The strong pound (and dollar) made the Continent inexpensive for British and American travelers, and many flocked to Germany and Italy during this period. In this way, Philipp met artist Wyndham Lewis, writers Osbert and Edith Sitwell, and many other notable literati. While Philipp was not parasitic, he took advantage of opportunities such that the generosity of others influenced his decisions about travel.

The entire Hessen family experienced difficulties during the economic upheavals of the early 1920s. Philipp noted, "during the Inflation we were not doing well. All our money was blocked and my parents really had to cut back. As a result I went to Italy. Really only to look around."[69] His twin, Wolfgang, who had apprenticed at the Hamburg bank of Max Warburg in the early 1920s, responded to the upheaval of 1923–24 by traveling to the United States. The future Nazi never commented on how working for a Jewish bank during such troubled times affected him, but it is worth noting that he used a pseudonym, Wolfgang Wildhof. He later maintained that he considered it inappropriate to use his title as a prince while engaged as an apprentice (it was not uncommon for princes to use pseudonyms because they did not wish to be judged by their social status).[70] None of the other employees at the Warburg bank knew his true identity, even though he worked there for almost two years. Wolfgang had fond memories of Max Warburg, who paid for him to travel to New York in autumn 1923 and offered to help him find a position at one of the Warburg affiliates, the International Acceptance Bank. Wolfgang spent only three months at the New York bank, but the trip caused something of a sensation from the outset: upon arriving on the German ship *America*, a fellow passenger recognized the true identity of "*Herr* Wildhof" and revealed it to reporters, who mobbed him at the Hoboken pier. Stories appeared in the American press ("the Prince was met outside the pier barrier by two attractive young women who wore costly fur robes. They drove him to the Waldorf-Astoria"), and even the *New York Times* reported that the prince had come in search of a wealthy bride.[71]

Philipp relocated to Rome in 1923 in order to advance his education and make a career, but also to escape the economic crisis in Germany. The hyperinflation affected Philipp, and he frequently ran out of money. Sassoon continued to send him periodic subventions—once, in 1924, "just in time as things were looking rather bad."[72] According to his mother, "he lived in a garage in Rome; he didn't want to ask his parents for money in these difficult times and therefore made his way alone."[73] Baroness Aliotti had put "quite small rooms in a garage" at his disposal, and did not charge him rent.[74] Still, he wrote in March 1924 that he had "given the order to sell some of my things so I shall be able to stay through Easter."[75] Of course, the Hessens were not alone among aristocrats (or others of means) who suffered economic setbacks during this period. And indeed, this was often a reason to gravitate toward the NSDAP. Historian Volker Dahm noted a number of aristocrats, like later SS-General Eric von dem Bach-Zelewski (1899–1972), who developed an interest in the Nazis in part because "they had lost their existence during the economic crisis."[76] In the 1920s, Bach-Zelewski had struggled to establish a taxi business in Berlin.

In a quest for financial self-sufficiency, Philipp attempted to establish himself in Rome as an interior designer (*Innenarchitekt*). He specialized in the remodeling of rooms in the grand aristocratic style in which he had been raised. He would proffer advice on all aspects of décor, from the physical dimensions of rooms to the selection of furniture, art, and other accoutrements. Understandably, he relied on family connections for most of his commissions (aristocratic networks operated on many levels). Philipp, for example, remodeled rooms for Queen Victoria of Sweden in Rome.[77] He later noted, "my activities consisted primarily of the remodeling of old houses. I recorded good successes."[78] At times, he would describe himself more modestly as a *Liebhaberarchitekt*, which translates alternatively as an amateur architect and one who does so out of genuine interest.[79] This was partly because he recognized that he did not have formal qualifications to call himself an architect. While he did not generate a significant income, it gave him satisfaction to work in a milieu that he understood and loved: sumptuously appointed old homes and castles.

Just as Philipp capitalized on his name and connections as he pursued this work—he was aware that it was socially prestigious for clients to say they had engaged him—his activities as an interior designer also afforded the eligible young bachelor the opportunity to travel more widely in society. Philipp was close friends with fellow-ex-patriot Count Albrecht ("Eddie") von Bismarck (1903–70)—a grandson of the "Iron chancellor" and younger brother of Prince Otto Christian von Bismarck (1897–1975), who was in the German diplomatic corps between the wars. Between them, Philipp and Eddie had impeccable social credentials. The invitations started at the top. As one observer noted: "[A]s a German prince, he was invited to the Italian court and [therefore] formed closer relations to the Italian royal family."[80] Actually, it was the Yugoslav royals who first introduced him to the Savoys: Philipp was the guest of Prince Paul (1893–1977) and Princess Olga (1903–97) of Yugoslavia in the Villa Demidoff in Rome when he first met Mafalda. Their son Heinrich characterized the meeting as "love at first sight," but whether one believes this romantic interpretation, it is clear that Philipp was immediately welcomed by most of the Italian royal family.[81] His presence at court had special political significance: relations between the Hohenzollern and the House of Savoy had been strained by the Italians' decision to fight against Germany and the Central Powers in World War I. The Kaiser had called King Vittorio Emmanuele "a traitor" (and evidently far worse in private).[82] While Philipp went to Italy in a completely private capacity, his links to the Hohenzollern enabled him to help the German and the Italian royals slowly rebuild the relationship.

Her Royal Highness Mafalda Maria Elisabetta Anna Romana, Princess di Savoia, the second daughter of King Vittorio Emmanuele III and Queen Elena, possessed a distinctive charm. Composer Giacomo Puccini was so taken with her, for example, that he dedicated one of his great operas, *Turandot*, to her in the early 1920s.[83] Mafalda had led a very sheltered youth, with a governess educating her and her three sisters: "[T]he princesses received a solid education, primarily in history, literature, Latin, and the arts." But theirs was a highly protective environment: one historian noted, with slight exaggeration, "politics were never discussed in the presence of the Italian princesses."[84] Many other royal families were actually stricter than the Savoys with their daughters; the children of the Bulgarian king, for example, were not even permitted friends their own age. Historian Stéphane Groueff described the upbringing of the Italian princesses: "[T]hey had parties and dances at home, went to picnics and excursions, and played tennis with young Italians of proper families. But there was no question, of course, of ever going anywhere without a chaperone: some youngish *dame-de-compagnie* had to escort them on all occasions."[85] Another observer of European high society, writing about "1939—the last season," elaborated on the custom of chaperones: "[T]his duenna was a fixture by the well-brought-up young woman's side at almost every social event during her debutante year, after which the girl's own principles were trusted to provide the same moral corset."[86] For royal princesses, the tether of a chaperone remained attached until marriage. It was also out of the question for any of them to marry a commoner, but they were permitted to select their spouses. Mafalda's younger sister Giovanna (1907–2000), for example, married King Boris of Bulgaria; and the eldest, Jolanda (1901–86), whom her parents had hoped to match with Edward, Prince of Wales, disappointed by marrying Count Giorgio Calvi di Bergolo (1887–1977), a member of the *piccola nobilitá* who became a general in the Italian army.[87]

With regard to Philipp and Mafalda, members of the House of Savoy were pleased that a younger daughter would marry into such a well-connected family—with direct ties to the Windsors, Hohenzollern, and other northern European ruling houses. The dowager Queen Margarita (1851–1926)—mother of Vittorio Emmanuele III—evidently played a role in the matchmaking.[88] Another sign of support came in 1925: "when the German Embassy in Rome felt it necessary to warn the Quirinal [about Philipp's sympathy for the Fascists and his checkered romantic past] King

Victor Emmanuel was irritated by the interference."[89] Landgrave Friedrich Karl and Landgravine Margarethe were similarly satisfied by Philipp marrying into a ruling house—and the Savoys were the oldest reigning house in Europe, dating back to the eleventh century.[90] For all intents, the match was *ebenbürtig* (appropriate in terms of the families' relative prestige). It also had promise in terms of international affairs—that this alliance would increase the influence and wealth of both families. Prior to the wedding, Landgrave Friedrich Karl had written (in German) to British King George V personally, "announcing his succession to the headship of the Electoral House, and the betrothal of his son to Princess Mafalda of Italy (the king had communicated his letter of reply through the British Consul General in Frankfurt, who had presented it in person)."[91]

Although Philipp and Mafalda's relationship was not without complications, they always preserved warm feelings for one another. Indeed, they cultivated a genuine friendship. It helped greatly that Mafalda possessed a fine sense of humor and alluring informality. Their son Prince Heinrich told a story he had heard about a visit of the Prince of Wales (future King Edward VIII) to Rome at the end of the 1920s: As the procession of notables climbed the steps of the capitol for the reception, an old nobleman, decked out in his heavy regalia, stumbled and fell into Mafalda. The wispy princess tried to pull him up but was unable to do so, which sent her into fits of laughter and caused a commotion. The king and queen, standing with the honored guest, were taken aback at this breach of decorum. The image of a young princess leaning over and pulling on the heavy coat of the old gentlemen, half-paralyzed by a fit of laughter, captures one side of Mafalda.[92] There was enough that was positive between Philip and Mafalda for their staff to draw after the war an idyllic portrait of the couple. One employee used the phrase "unusually happy marriage," and Philipp's chauffeur recalled Princess Mafalda waiting for him when he came home, running across the garden "beaming with joy."[93] Both before and after the wedding in 1925, they enjoyed trips down to Capri, Anacapri, and the surrounding area, where they lived the high life with yachts, nightclubs, and friends. Later, in the 1930s, Mafalda cashed in bonds that her parents had purchased for her and used the money to acquire the Villa Mura, a home on Capri that remained in the possession of the family well into the 1990s.[94]

Their relationship, however, was apparently not completely straightforward. All evidence suggests that Philipp was bisexual. Because homosexual acts were illegal in Germany (and many other countries—but not in Italy until 1931), it was customary to take steps to be cautious in this regard.[95] This is the case with Prince Philipp—with one exception: his affair with British poet and writer Siegfried Sassoon (1886–1967). Sassoon's own diaries include numerous references to a romantic interest identified only as "P"; interestingly, even in the edition of the diaries published in 1981 and annotated by Rupert Hart-Davis, the identity of "P" is left a mystery.[96] But there is no doubt that "P" is Prince Philipp. A series of letters and post-cards that Prince Philipp sent Siegfried Sassoon from the years 1921 to 1925 comprises part of Sassoon's papers housed in the University Library in Cambridge, England. These missives reveal a close friendship with strong emotional bonds. There is no question that the two had a physical relation-ship, and this has now been recognized by several biographers of Sassoon.[97] Because Sassoon possessed extraordinary critical faculties and cared so much for Philipp, he was able to offer perspicacious observations about the prince and their social milieu.

Philipp and Sassoon had met in Rome in October 1921, when the British writer was on a kind of grand tour of the Continent. They had both had fought in World War I, lost brothers in combat, and possessed artistic temperaments. Sassoon was best known for his war poems—the early ones portrayed fighting as a noble enterprise, while the later ones expressed disillusionment.[98] One can well imagine why Philipp might be attracted to the handsome and charismatic British writer, whose "main interests were hunting and poetry."[99] Interestingly, Sassoon was half-Jewish. But he came from a prominent family and his cousin, Sir Philip Sassoon, was extra-ordinarily wealthy and well connected to the British establishment (he also served as Under Secretary in the Air Ministry under Lord Londonderry in the 1930s).[100] The relationship between Prince Philipp and Sassoon had started in Rome that October in 1921: an excursion to Castel Gandolfo and lunch under grapevines with diplomat Harold Nicolson and his wife, writer Vita Sackville-West, served as the setting for their first momentous meeting. It is in itself telling that Philipp would associate with Nicolson and Sackville-West—according to a recent biography, both convinced snobs and racists who themselves engaged in many same-sex liaisons (Nicolson thought Philipp "a nice Prince").[101] Philipp allegedly moved into Sassoon's hotel room three days after the luncheon.[102] That first autumn included a memorable interlude at the Villa d'Este on Lake Como. Sassoon would associate the opulent villa with the prince and he referenced both in his poems, most notably in "Villa d'Este Gardens":

> . . . Waiting you in my thought's high lonely tower
> That looks on star-lit hushed Elysian gloom,
> I know your advent certain as the flower
> Of daybreak that on breathless vales shall bloom.
>
> Oh never hasten now; for time's all sweet,
> And you are clad in the garment of my dreams:
> Led by my heart's enchanted cry, your feet

Portrait of Siegfried Sassoon by Glyn Philpot, 1917.

Move with the murmur of forest-wandering streams
Through earth's adoring darkness to discover
The Paradise of your imperfect lover.[103]

The two men had returned to their respective countries in the winter of 1921–22, but they corresponded while separated. Philipp had written: "Those days at [*sic*] Rome mean a great change in my life & they have made me so happy—happier than I can say. That happiness shall remain in my heart & go back with me to my home where I shall keep it like a precious jewel that no one can take away from me. . . . Now good night & God bless you. My thoughts are with you all the time. Ph."[104] Eleven days later, Philipp wrote Sassoon from Schloss Friedrichshof: "Home again at last finding your dear letter waiting for me here! It brought back everything more vividly than ever: you, your voice, Rome with all its beauty, the murmuring of fountains, some vague melody of Bach played by small untrained fingers, two small rooms in a hotel, & all that happiness. Yes, Sig—you are right: the gods have been very kind to us & I shall be thankful for that all my life."[105] Interestingly, the great war poet Sassoon requested photographs of Philipp in military uniform, which the prince obliged with a picture from

1918. Philipp in turn received not only photos of Sassoon but also copies of his books of poems (and certain poems copied out by hand before they were published).[106]

Philipp and Sassoon were reunited in Munich the following summer. Sassoon was intent to "put [his] friendship on a firmer basis than mere sensualism. I want him to be my link with Europe."[107] This happened, although the relationship began to founder in the autumn of 1922. It was during this period that the British poet sought to understand the German prince—and this is a key reason for exploring their relationship. Sassoon was an acute, if often harsh, critic. Sassoon nonetheless was impressed with Philipp's general knowledge of art, music, architecture, and antiques. He thought that Philipp's "great assets are his charm, his really beautiful manners (always polite), and his essential amiability and kindness."[108] Yet, he thought Philipp was intellectually limited and constrained by his upbringing. Sassoon wrote repeatedly along the lines of his 13 October 1922 diary entry: ". . . much as I love P., I do not regard him as my equal in intellectual things."[109] While Sassoon viewed himself as an artist, he saw Philipp as "merely a cultured person."[110]

Siegfried Sassoon's most damning, and indeed, impassioned, statement about Philipp came in late October 1922, in the evening after the two had spent the day at the Vatican Museum:

> P's mind is extremely *rigid* for a young man [of twenty-six]. He does not easily readjust his opinions—most of which seem to have been formed early; his artistic tastes and admirations derive mainly from the training he received from his father (he acknowledges the indebtedness). In fact P. is an example of conventional culture. He has had the *right things* imposed on him from his boyhood. If he were English he'd probably have revolted against the Parthenon and the primitives and Goethe's *Faust* and Bach's music, and gone in for a little futurism. Also he is impervious to any arguments. He doesn't even pretend to be interested in the other side of a discussion on politics or art. He merely listens and then produces his own stereotyped phrases without reference to anything that has been advanced by the other side. His culture consists in acquiring information without co-coordinating it. He refuses to see any merit in Renoir, Manet, Cezanne (anti-French feeling comes in, of course) and then admires [English book illustrator Arthur] Rackham. I am afraid that this intellectual rigidity will develop into ossification, unless something extraordinary occurs to wake him up. His chief danger, however lies in his not unnatural bitterness about the downfall of his family prestige, and he deeply regrets the disappearance of the environment in which he was brought up. I don't blame him. . . .[111]

The relationship between Sassoon and Philipp failed for a number of reasons, but in large part it was due to the intellectual rigidity and limitations on the part of the prince.

Ironically, there was additional tension in their relationship because Philipp was more open and prone to libertine behavior. Philipp was very open about his relationship with an older American woman living in Bad Homburg (usually referred to as "Baby"). He would telephone her in the evenings, at times when Sassoon was present in the hotel room. Sassoon complained, "I wish he were a little more flexible and not quite so matter of fact"; later he admitted to having "made a spiteful remark . . . you can't do two things at once."[112] Sassoon's concerns about Philipp's promiscuity increased: at one point, he mused, "Am I only one of P's regular succession of 'affairs' "?[113] Sassoon was also offended by Philipp's carousing, complaining when the Prince "went off to join the Worcester crowd, [sitting] with them in the bar at the Continental Hotel till 4 a.m. telling filthy stories. . . . It doesn't seem to enter his mind that I might be disgusted by such goings on."[114] He noted on another occasion, "I resent his inability to distinguish between decent and indecent people. He is quite content to leave me after a pleasant evening, and spend another three hours listening to filth-stories in a cocktail bar. . . . P's craving for amusement and 'amusing' people is almost a vice."[115] Sassoon commented in other entries about the "din of banjo and jazz orchestra" and "people dancing," giving the impression that he and Philipp were "bright young things," either willingly or unwillingly, living scenes from an Evelyn Waugh novel.[116]

Sassoon's doubts about the relationship proved well founded, despite Philipp's interest in keeping the romance going during the subsequent winter and spring. Philipp wrote Sassoon on 3 May 1923: "When your letter arrived I was just leaving for Munich. My parents sent me there to look at a girl which they thought would do as a wife for me. It was a relation of mine—very nice & sweet—but I told them when I came home that I did not care for her & that I was in love with someone whom I could not marry! [. . . .] I must see you & talk to you. You are the only person I am really fond of & the only person I can trust."[117] In March 1924, with Philipp in Rome and Sassoon in Milan, the prince wrote, "Don't you think you could persuade old F. S. [Frankie Schuster] to motor you down here? I somehow have got the feeling that if I don't see you now I shall not see you for a long time."[118] From their correspondence, it appears that the geographical distance that separated them as well as the expectations facing Philipp in terms of finding a suitable wife doomed the relationship. Sassoon's feelings cooled markedly. Toward the end, he wrote, "I have had some splendid times with P., but I know that I shall see him getting heavier and heavier from year to year. And in ten years he will be a bald, self-indulgent, opinionated man—living off the snobbishness of rich people. That sounds cruel and unjust, but I am afraid it will come true. I hope it won't. . . ."[119] Sassoon's predictions, in respects, did come to pass. Philipp continued to have feelings for the British poet: in a remarkable letter from

29 September 1925, just after his marriage to Mafalda, the prince wrote Sassoon, "I have thought of you more than you know. A friendship is a thing that always remains + makes life worthwhile living [*sic*]—it cannot blow away from one day to another. I hope with all my heart to see you soon again + I want you to know that you will always find me unchanged!" Yet, with a sense of closure both literally and figuratively, he indicated that he had moved on: "I must say I am very happy. Lots of love in haste. Ever your old Philipp."[120] The two men did not sustain their relationship, and there is no subsequent correspondence in Sassoon's papers. For his part, Sassoon went on to have a relationship with British aesthete Stephen Tennant and then married Hester Gatty in 1933.

The historical relevance of their relationship is difficult to assess: what does one make of a British veteran taking up with his former enemy, a German prince falling for someone with Jewish ancestry, and both breaking laws in their country? Like many others with the benefit of privilege, Prince Philipp and Sassoon reveled in what they perceived as newly found freedom. The 1920s, as is well known, represented a marked liberalization in terms of social codes of conduct. These two young men captured certain aspects of the "jazz age." Furthermore, the relationship is important to biographers of Prince Philipp and Sassoon—saying something about the character of both men. One can only speculate about the lasting effects of the episode, and, in particular, how it affected Philipp during the Third Reich. In light of the homophobic and persecutory nature of the Nazi regime, it may have been a point of vulnerability for him. Philipp's sexual history was to play a role in his fate. A dossier compiled by Himmler's SS during the war alleged that Philipp was involved in homosexual activities. One of Himmler's intelligence assets in Italy, SS-Major Dr. Eugen Dollmann, filed reports suggesting that Philipp was gay, without stating so explicitly. This might be expected when Dollmann was writing about someone with Philipp's standing (including his closeness to Hitler at the time). Regardless, Dollmann traveled in circles where he had access to gossip.[121] In one report to Himmler, Dollmann wrote, "Count Albrecht von Bismarck is widely known as a homosexual throughout Roman circles." When contemplating steps against "Bismarck" Dollmann noted, "that surely an intervention by the Prince von Hessen, who is closest friends with Count von Bismarck, can be expected." In another missive, Dollmann wrote "Count Albrecht Bismarck, who unfortunately still resides in Capri and who is in the closest contact with the Prince von Hessen, will call forth once again Caprisian-Tiberian memories [where Emperor Tiberius engaged in notorious debauches]; this chapter is itself delicate enough thanks to the prince's connections to the Italian court."[122] Later in 1943, SS General Prince zu Waldeck and his aide at the time, a Gestapo employee, alleged that Philipp was homosexual.[123] It is significant that the issue of Philipp's sexual orientation came up at all. The SS did not ordinarily raise the issue—not with Stauffenberg or any of the July 20 conspirators, for example. While formal charges of homosexuality were never lodged, the allegations represented a long-standing point of vulnerability for the prince.

Certain stereotypes about the sexual practices and morality that prevailed among the upper reaches of society may have fed into the allegations. While one must stress that there was no unifying outlook or code of conduct, the social elite throughout Europe and America often felt exempt from traditional restrictions and taboos. Some aristocrats believed that morals were for the lower classes—something invented to enhance the social and political control of the ruling elite. Another theory was proposed by Lady Diana Mosley, who agreed that "upper-class Englishmen were constantly hopping into bed with each other's wives"; she observed, "I think it is because people had more leisure. Everybody had servants and people had nothing to think about except their lives and emotions and relationships. Nowadays they simply haven't got time." She added, "In England people didn't divorce; they had affairs and stayed married. Divorce came from America."[124] Within "high society," there appears to have been many cases of behavior that transgressed social norms. One might point to Prince Philipp's friend and relation, the Duke of Kent (1902–42), who was the younger brother of King George VI (1895–1952). The Duke of Kent prompted "rumours of encounters with an Argentinean diplomat, an Italian aristocrat, and Noel Coward."[125] According to *The Sunday Times* of London, "one other male lover who passed through Georgie's bed was a young Cambridge graduate and aesthete called Anthony Blunt" (1907–83), who later became keeper of the royal pictures.[126] The duke also had affairs with many women, and consorted with the "fast set"—where his activities apparently included an affair with an African-American revue artist and a "louche liaison" with American Kiki Whitney Preston, who was part of the "infamous Happy Valley set in Kenya" and nicknamed the "girl with the silver syringe" (it is widely believed that "she introduced him to cocaine and morphine, establishing an addiction").[127] Yet with the help of his eldest brother, Edward, the Duke of Kent overcame his problem with substances and became a hard-working and highly valued member of the British royal family in the 1930s, devoting much of his energy to Continental diplomacy. While Philipp was not as promiscuous as the Duke of Kent and evidently refrained from taking drugs (Sassoon noted only that he was very fond of brandy), he shared certain predilections with his British cousin.[128]

Although Philipp may have lived something of a double life with regard to his romantic activities, he and Mafalda remained committed to a family, even as they spent a considerable time apart in the 1930s, with him in Germany and her in Italy. Of course, it was not uncommon for couples among the wealthy elite of Europe to travel alone and spend time apart, just as it was not uncommon to have separate bedrooms (which was the case for them, at least in their German home in Palais Bellevue in Kassel).[129] In general, their lives appeared as normal as one could expect for a princely couple.

Prior to their marriage, the greatest obstacle to the match came on religious grounds. It was for this reason that the parents of Philipp and Mafalda had ambivalent feelings about the marriage. It is hard to comprehend today the sharpness of the divide between confessions in interwar Europe. In Germany, towns often had not only separate churches, schools, and social organizations but sometimes also bakeries, laundries, or other businesses that served a specific denomination.[130] Political life in the German lands, in the words of Gerhard Ritter, "had always possessed a more pronounced religious character than it did elsewhere," with a prince expected to uphold the faith of his kingdom.[131] The Hesse-Kassels looked back with considerable pride to a founding member of the dynasty, Philipp the Magnanimous (1504–67), an evangelical Protestant prince who had been a staunch supporter of Martin Luther.[132] It was a rule of the House of Hesse that its chief must uphold the Protestant tradition. Philipp, the eldest surviving son, was in line for this position, and so this precluded his conversion. The problem of religion was hardly less acute for Mafalda, whose family had such close ties to the Vatican and who offered such a visible symbol for the Italian people. Additionally, Mafalda was devout. Her secretary, Adelheid Fliege, testified after the war, that "she was a very observant Catholic and went to mass every Sunday. . . ."[133]

The couple therefore settled on a compromise. The boys were baptized as Protestants and the daughter as a Catholic.[134] The pope would later chastise Philipp for not raising his children Catholic or sending them to Catholic school. The House of Savoy and the papacy clearly had a special relationship (protocol was such that in contrast to all others, only women from the royal family were accorded the privilege of wearing white clothes in audiences with His Holiness). Philipp and Mafalda's arrangement therefore was viewed as insulting.[135] The compromise was actually problematic for both sides—at least initially. There was very little coverage of the wedding in the German press, which suited the Kaiser and other family members just fine. The Kaiser was notorious for his opposition to Catholicism, and indeed, ordered the ostracism of his aunt, Princess Anna, when she converted in 1901.[136] Wilhelm also had lingering resentments about the Italian royal family: their "betrayal" in World War I had not been forgotten. His view was shared by General Field Marshal August von Mackensen, who remarked about the betrothal, "Are there so few German princesses that the future Landgrave must seek a wife in the enemy camp?"[137] Philipp did not seek his uncle's permission before marrying Mafalda; there had been a "house statute" before 1918 that all marriages in the

Hohenzollern family required the Kaiser's approval, and this included Friedrich Karl who made a formal request before marrying Wilhelm II's sister, but the statute did not enter into play in Philipp's case in the mid-1920s.[138] Although Wilhelm II did not attempt to intercede, he nonetheless put pressure on Philipp's family—and especially his sister the Landgravine—not to attend the wedding. Neither Philipp's parents nor his siblings traveled to Italy for the ceremony. Perhaps somewhat surprisingly, the purportedly stubborn ex-Kaiser soon made up with Philipp and Mafalda. In October 1927, he became the godfather of their son Heinrich (1927–2000). Subsequently, Philipp and Mafalda visited him in Doorn.[139] Landgrave Friedrich Karl and Landgravine Margarethe finessed the situation by accepting an invitation from the king and queen of Italy and paying a private visit to Rome shortly after the wedding.[140]

The wedding of Philipp and Mafalda was nonetheless a high-profile event in Italy. Because of papal criticism of Philipp's refusal to convert, the ceremony was moved from Rome to Turin, where it was held at the Savoy's Raconiggi Palace on 23 September 1925.[141] It was a resplendent affair with Philipp in the Dragoons uniform of his Hessian regiment, adorned with an ostrich-feather-plumed helmet, and Mafalda in an elegant white gown. The guests included royalty from across the Continent, including King Carol of Romania, King George of Greece, and Prince Paul of Yugoslavia. Italian Prime Minister Benito Mussolini was also in attendance, serving as the representative of the state. Philipp claimed after the war this was the first time he met *Il Duce*. Nonetheless, as shown in wedding pictures, the Fascist leader played a prominent role on the occasion.[142] Mussolini posed for pictures with the king and with the bridal couple, and they all played to thousands in the crowd who stood outside the palace gates. While this was an old-world affair in many respects, with a grand setting, ostentatious uniforms and dresses, and more titles, as the saying goes, than a good bookstore, it was tinged by a strong Fascist presence. Mussolini tried to propagate the notion of a glamorous milieu in Fascist Italy, and this pomp, while somewhat different, conformed to his conception of a useful plebiscitary spectacle. Whether it was the "white telephone" movies (a term used by historians of cinema in reference to the elegant, sleek décor of the sets), or the society pages of the censored magazines, this world of prosperity and leisure was actively promoted by Fascist authorities. Philipp and Mafalda, who kept homes in Rome and on Capri, cavorted about Europe and the Middle East in the late-1920s and in many respects lived this fantasy.

After a honeymoon in Capri, the couple traveled to Germany, where Mafalda was introduced to Philipp's family and where they posed for publicity pictures (the prince showed off his new bride—or his "dear little wife" as he referred to her in one letter).[143] The arrival of the princess prompted some curious rituals: at Schloss Panker in northern Germany, for example,

Princess Mafalda and Prince Philipp in dress uniform on their wedding day in September 1925 at the Palazzo Raconiggi.

Mafalda and Philipp were greeted at the border of the property by a delegation of employees and neighbors, the men dressed in black frock-coats and top hats, who escorted them on horseback to the castle.[144] It sounds more elegant than was the case, chiefly because they had to endure torrential rains. A further difficulty emerged because Mafalda initially spoke very little German. While the entire Hessen family could converse in flawless English, one local dignitary greeted her by asking, "Have you had a good *Reis*?" (literally "rice," mistranslating the German word for "trip," "*Reise*"). Mafalda never felt entirely comfortable in Germany, although the Hessen family warmed to her, and the initial challenges created by the union were quickly overcome.

The couple returned to Italy and moved into the Villa Polissena in Rome. According to Philipp's mother, Landgravine Margarethe, they made their home in "a small villa that the King of Italy had given to them both as a gift; they lived there very happily."[145] Philipp himself had written to his old friend Siegfried Sassoon shortly after the wedding, inviting him to

Rome, adding, "I have had a very hard time this year & there was no end of difficulties—Pope, Mussolini, etc.—but I hope all is over now & must say I am very happy!"[146] The Villa Polissena was part of the Villa Savoia, a complex of buildings owned by the king (and his official residence since 1919 when he moved from the Quirinal Palace), which meant that Philipp was separated from his in-laws by only a garden. With no wall in between, the king was often visible from the Hessens' property.[147] Yet the Villa Polissena, with its art nouveau flourishes and the accompanying two hectares of gardens, was by all accounts stunningly beautiful. (A number of scenes of Vittorio De Sica's Academy Award–winning film from 1971, *The Garden of the Finzi-Continis*, were set there, where it served as the refuge of a wealthy Jewish aristocratic family who believed the walls would protect them from Fascism). As its name suggested, it was a villa and not a palace. While there were several representational rooms, most of the house would best be described as comfortable elegance. Philipp used his considerable leisure time to decorate his home. He would spend hours in his study researching objects he had acquired: antique ceramics, marble busts, pictures, and such—deriving special pleasure from determining authenticity and provenance. Philipp also designed and tended to the gardens, which featured numerous fountains, statues, and an antique sarcophagus (according to his son Heinrich, "giving equal weight to the German Romantic and the Italian classical themes").[148] Scholars of formal gardens have noted how this practice was commonly intended as a way to communicate status: Lord Astor did a great deal to make it vogue with his accomplishment at Cliveden.[149] Still, Philipp and Mafalda's lifestyle was not considered particularly grand by the standards of other high nobility. They tended not to entertain lavishly and did not keep a particularly large staff. Moreover, they relied on financial subventions from the king and queen to make ends meet.[150]

In the late 1920s and early 1930s, Philipp enjoyed a life of relative leisure, although his gradually growing family had its demands. Philipp and Mafalda had four children: Moritz (b. 1926), Heinrich (1927–2000), Otto (1937–98), and Elisabeth (b. 1940).[151] They all received family names dating back to the Hessian princes of the Middle Ages, although Otto had the middle name of "Adolf" after his godfather, the German dictator. When the children were young, they were educated in Rome at the Villa Polissena by a tutor, so they were often about the house. Philipp spoke German to them, while Mafalda conversed in Italian. They enjoyed many extravagant privileges. In his memoirs, Heinrich recalls a pet pony, a "fantastic" miniature Bugatti car given as a gift by the famous pilot Francesco de Pinedo, and excursions to the royal stables at the Quirinal where he would ride with his grandfather the king.[152] Later on, in an attempt to socialize the children in a more conventional and less exalted environment, they went off to boarding schools.[153] When at home in Kassel, as compared to Rome, Moritz, Heinrich,

Princess Mafalda with her three sons in 1938: from left, Moritz, Otto, and Heinrich.

and Otto were permitted to play in the streets with other neighboring children. This led to some odd encounters: Heinrich, recalled, for example, being teased by schoolmates as the "Negro Prince" (*Negerprinz*) because his grandfather, Vittorio Emmanuele, was also the emperor of Ethiopia.[154]

The Hessens' lives were complicated by Mafalda's health problems. Already in the late-1920s, Prince Auwi had described her as "diminutive and neurasthenic."[155] In 1937, she developed a life-threatening lung infection, which compelled her to spend most of her time in the warmer climate of Italy. Landgravine Margarethe noted dramatically, Philipp's "very fragile wife was repeatedly near death and thus it came about that the family was in Rome and he lived in Kassel, a situation that did not afford the most orderly family life."[156] Mafalda, however, was far from an invalid; she took up classical dance and continued to provide a center for the family. Most years, she was able to join the family at Kronberg, where they celebrated Christmas.

Princess Mafalda, like many royals and nobles, devoted considerable time and energy to philanthropic work. Much like the British royals today, Mafalda visited sick children in hospitals, attended charity events, and helped raise funds for the disabled and underprivileged. This kind of social commitment had first been championed by Prince Albert von

Sachsen-Coburg, who fostered the ideal in England and later exported it to Germany and other European lands. Historian Niall Ferguson has written about Prince Albert's influence on his daughter, Victoria—and this included pioneering work in the area of philanthropy, especially as it concerned urban housing, the care of veterans, and women's education.[157] The future Empress Friedrich, who was also inspired by Florence Nightingale, helped support forty-one charities in Germany, including clinics for women and children, as well as at the Victoria Lyceum, which focused on educating women.[158] Victoria alienated some conservatives with her philanthropic work, but she paved the way for women and was an important agent for social change. In the twentieth century, charitable work became an essential part of the identity of royal women. Jean Quataert has argued in a recent book that "philanthropy, far from being a simple tool of social discipline, was in fact at the heart of dynastic ritual. . . . Through the ritual of philanthropy, women participated in highly patterned ways in the construction of a viable dynastic national culture."[159]

Princess Mafalda was raised to believe that philanthropic work was one of her chief responsibilities. An aide recalled after the war, "Princess Mafalda was always very committed with regards to social work; also for those sick with tuberculosis. [During one visit to the sick] she even gave a girl a valuable ring as a present because the girl desired it."[160] Mafalda's secretary added, "the princess was [often] in the more impoverished parts of Kassel and did a lot that was good there."[161] When Mafalda's mother, Queen Elena, visited Kassel, their program always included charitable work; the queen herself made financial contributions to a local hospital (one was renamed the Queen Elena Clinic and still exists today).[162] During the war, Queen Elena spent most afternoons with female relations who hailed from across Europe, knitting gloves and sweaters for soldiers.[163] With Mafalda, as with a number of noble women, social work and religious piety were symbiotically linked.[164] This was certainly the case of the mother of Princess Sophia von Hessen, Princess Alice, who founded her own convent dedicated to good works.[165] While Alice represented an extreme, there were many instances when a pronounced social commitment was to be found among the women related to the Hessens. Prince Wolfgang, for example, described the efforts of his wife, Princess Marie-Alexandra, who during World War II helped the victims of bombing and the war-wounded in Frankfurt—literally putting men on her back who had their legs blown off and carrying them from the train so that they could be attended by doctors.[166] Among the princely families, there was a strong feeling of social obligation. While such sentiments extended to the men—Prince Philipp, for example, was featured in the local Kassel newspaper in October 1936 collecting for the Nazi charity the *Winterhilfswerk*—it was first and foremost a domain where women excelled.[167]

Despite the frequent representational duties of Philipp and Mafalda, they nonetheless conceived themselves as a private, and in many ways ordinary, family. Prince Philipp later emphasized the quotidian nature of his life as part of his defense against charges that he had supported Mussolini and the Fascists. He argued that he "concerned himself very little with the political events in Italy and very seldom touched upon political questions with his father-in-law, the king."[168] His defense attorney added, "an active involvement with political questions did not correspond to his inclinations and capabilities, and therefore lay outside his actual areas of interest."[169] Philipp claimed that "as a foreigner he was denied insight into the internal events of Fascist politics."[170] Of course, foreigners have often been perceptive observers of another nation's politics. The *Spruchkammer* (denazification board) was unconvinced by this "head-in-the-sand" argument. The judges agreed that, yes, he might have been "cautious and reticent, but that "he was in the closest circles of the royal family" and lived "in one of the most important segments of Italian and European history."[171]

The Italian royal house was very supportive of the Fascists in the 1920s and 1930s. Philipp noted, "I had the impression that the attitude of my father and brother-in-law [Crown Prince Umberto] was very positive with regards to Mussolini."[172] Historian Robert Katz recalled the glamour and popularity engendered by Mussolini in the 1920s (that is, before the Abyssinian campaign and the shift to a more aggressive foreign policy):

> In the early days, when Fascism was stylish and in its heyday; when Winston Churchill opined of Mussolini, "If I were Italian, I am sure that I would have been with you entirely from the beginning. . . ."; when Lady Chamberlain exclaimed, "What a Man! I have lost my heart!" And Pope Pius XI called him "the man sent from Providence"; in those days the *Duce* would repair to the royal palace in derby and tails, presenting his heroically jutting chin high on a detachable white collar.[173]

Granted, relations between the Italian royal house and *Il Duce* were sometimes strained. Philipp recalled, "after [Mussolini] made a few tasteless indiscretions and attacks against them, relations deteriorated."[174] Yet, "during his nearly half-century reign, Victor Emmanuel III always swam with the tide," and both he and his heir, Crown Prince Umberto (1904–83), remained publicly supportive of Mussolini.[175] For example, in 1936, as the war in Abyssinia began, people began to donate gold and copper to the cause; the queen, in a very visible gesture, was the first to give up her wedding ring.[176] Historians now know that the Italian royal family was more ambivalent about the Fascists than they indicated at the time: Philipp's attorney after the war reflected on the dichotomy between the private and the official when he noted: "although King Vittorio Emmanuele was no friend of Germany's, and by inclination was disposed against Mussolini and Hitler, he was truly fatherly and good to his son-in-law despite this political position.[177]

Prince Philipp, however, grew increasingly enthusiastic about Mussolini and his regime. The prosecutor in his denazification trial wrote that while Philipp was not overtly political, "he regarded Fascism as good, that in the early period ostensibly reaped a good harvest, in which the leader [he uses the word "*Führer*"] of Fascism, Mussolini, attempted to bring about order and cleanliness in Italy. Streets and canals were built, swamps were drained and unemployment reduced. In his political naiveté [Philipp] saw only this side of Fascism and closed his eyes to the other side, which expressed itself in the oppression and removal of opponents of the regime."[178] He admitted after the war that he was enamored with Fascism because of the changes he perceived following Mussolini's seizure of power in 1922. "Fascism interested me very much because I experienced the rise of the Fascists and their unheard of accomplishments. I was impressed by them. I experienced the entire process in Italy. I came to Italy as a young man in 1922 and had seen how circumstances fundamentally improved in the early period."[179] But he also maintained that he was "exactly like so many other foreign visitors and observers of Italy" in being impressed by this "outward transformation."[180] Philipp later claimed, "I had the impression that there was great interest in this transformation, especially in America."

In short, Philipp developed an overly positive view of Italy. He ignored the oppression and violence: "[O]ne said very little about violent measures." Although he admitted to knowledge of the murder of socialist leader Giacomo Matteotti in 1924, he regarded reports of other murders as unreliable: "But I had also heard that many Fascists were murdered. These things, as in all times, had to be evaluated in terms of propaganda." He also heard that the "Liparian islands were reportedly very good and also very beautiful," referring to the islands housing the prison where Antonio Gramsci and other political prisoners were sent.[181] This was part of his rationalization for having supported Mussolini and Fascism—and it gives insight into his thinking. The denazification board was not very impressed with his comments about Fascist Italy: "[H]is conspicuous portrayal of only the bright side of Fascism from 1923 to 1930, in the wake of very questionable one-sidedness and its very extraordinary incompleteness is objectively [speaking] thoroughly false."[182]

Philipp's sympathy for Mussolini and the Fascists in Italy would be a key factor in his gravitation to National Socialism. On a related matter, an open question remains whether he assisted the Nazis in their efforts to forge ties to the more established Fascisti in the 1920s. On one résumé Philipp submitted to the Nazi Party, he claimed to have been "active in Italy in the years before the seizure of power."[183] In his denazification trial, the prosecutor noted "the concerned party traveled to Germany in October 1930 and made a comparison between conditions in Germany and Italy. He was of the opinion that political circumstances, as well as economic conditions, were better in Italy than in Germany, and this prepared the way of the concerned party to fascism."[184] Prince Philipp reasoned that what had worked in Italy might also occur in Germany and talked about a "transfer" of the Fascist system to Germany.[185]

Prince Christoph During the Weimar Republic

Although Prince Christoph had been too young to see military service during the Great War, he witnessed many of the challenges and frustrations of the postwar period in Germany. In addition to experiencing the November 1918 Revolution, he was confronted with the shock of the French troops that moved into the Rhineland in December 1918. For the Hessens, the only positive aspect of the French occupation was that it brought an end to the revolutionary workers' and soldiers' council in Kronberg. The French established three bridgeheads (*Brückenköpfe*) in Cologne, Koblenz, and farther south, in Mainz. Kronberg belonged to the region controlled by the Mainz military contingent. As Wolfgang recalled, "all contact with the outside world, including post, telephone, and travel, was interrupted."[186] Because one needed a special pass every time one entered or left the Brückenkopf, and these required some efforts to procure, Schloss Friedrichshof was effectively cut off from Frankfurt, forcing the Hessens on many occasions to slip out through a rear garden and take a circuitous route around the blockade if they wanted to travel back and forth between the castle and the new urban residence on the Untermainkai (they had decided for financial reasons to give up the big house at Number 12 and move to a more modest place at Number 8).[187] The insult and dishonor of the foreign troops, some of them French-African soldiers, occupying parts of Western Germany came in the wake of reports of German victories throughout the spring of 1918.[188] Christoph, like his brothers and millions of other Germans, believed in a version of the "stab-in-the-back" myth— that the soldiers had not been defeated on the field of battle but lost because of the betrayal of civilian leaders.

The onerous Treaty of Versailles and the humiliation of French occupation forces in the West intensified these resentments. The French troops stationed in the Brückenköpfe were central to the drama that accompanied the German ratification of the treaty. They were part of the leverage exerted by the victorious powers. On 16 June 1919, one week before the deadline for signing the treaty—and with it, accepting legal responsibility for starting the war—French troops forced their way into Friedrichshof and occupied the Schloss. They inhabited the suite of private rooms once used by Empress Friedrich and banished the family to a nearby cottage. Friedrich Karl noted in his diary, "they repeated over and over that they would show who are the masters (*Herren*)."[189] The French made the Hessens even more uncomfortable by stationing military equipment throughout the park surrounding the Schloss, in what was a unmistakable show of force. Even though the French evacuated Friedrichshof once the Germans ratified the treaty, they kept the bridgehead at Mainz until 1930, and this constituted a kind of festering wound for many Germans—especially those who experienced the occupation firsthand. Christoph wrote his mother in March 1920, "I am enraged by these infamous French . . . and what will only come of the Ruhr region."[190] His brother Philipp accused the French of intercepting his letters and wrote to Siegfried Sassoon, "I daresay your gallant allies (filthy pigs) use them for lighting their fires. . . ."[191]

For the princes, then, there were a constellation of factors that alienated them from the fledgling Weimar Republic. Most importantly, as noted earlier, were the statutes that threatened their property and position. But the economic and political crises that followed the war further stretched resources and limited job opportunities. A fundamental realization of many, especially younger aristocrats, was that with the end of the Great War they had lost the world they had known and the opportunities for advancement in the army; and they were unsuccessful with their new professional initiatives. This turned them against the Weimar Republic politically—and above all, placed them against the Communists and therein drew them early on to right-wing organizations such as the *Freikorps*.[192] Prince Christoph was among those who were disillusioned with the fledgling republic: in late March 1920, as the Kapp Putsch was put down and the Weimar government reestablished its authority, Christoph wrote, "All has remained quiet here. But how horrible it looks in the rest of the Reich."[193] The sudden German defeat in 1918, the November Revolution, the French occupation, the Treaty of Versailles, and the various political and economic crises of the 1920s helped turn the young prince against the Weimar Republic and make him susceptible to the Nazis' blandishments.

Even though there was a certain austerity to Christoph's life in the early 1920s, it was offset by his joie de vivre and a network of privileged relations and friends. The young prince was often without money, but he also lived well at times, enjoying the hospitality of others. Right after the war, the prince began exploring a career in what one might call agrarian management. That is, he underwent agricultural training and later helped oversee rural estates belonging to the family and various friends. Already in 1919, he had written to his mother about his *"landwirtschaftliches Herz"* (agricultural heart).[194] Christoph first moved to Holstein, to Gut Panker, the estate where his father had been born. Although the Hessens had lost part of the

Prince Christoph with horses at Schloss Friedrichshof in the 1920s.

six farms there as part of the settlement with the German state in the early years of the Weimar Republic, there were still several working properties, including a stud farm that was of particular interest to the horse-obsessed prince. The first letters back to his mother reveal an enthusiasm for the work, and he was soon personally overseeing the stables. But there were tensions with the manager of the estate, who was accustomed to considerable autonomy running the operations. One sees time and again with royals how managers assumed considerable power and almost came to dominate their superiors. Prince Christoph, however, was not prepared to wrangle with the overseer at Panker, and consumed by a case of *Wanderlust*, he moved on to other properties. He returned to Hesse and spent a year at Gut Thalitter north of Frankenberg, a farm in one of the most scenic parts of the province, located some sixty kilometers west of Kassel.

In 1921 Christoph headed farther afield and relocated to Pomerania near the Baltic Sea, where he spent another six months at Gut Grabow bei Labes. This farm was actually in what the Germans called *Hinterpommern*, the very northeastern region of Germany. This estate was one that had been chartered by the Prussian crown centuries before as they colonized the east. This was the land of the Junkers, the often dour, imposing, and conservative aristocrats, who remained attached to militaristic traditions. Just like farmers throughout Europe, the Junkers were modernizing in terms of agricultural technologies, and there was increasing knowledge of fertilizers and industrial methods. In this outpost of the German Reich, however, it was not unusual to encounter worldviews that were less than enlightened. Very often, landowners subscribed to a German nationalism that they combined with anti-Slavic racism.[195] With the Treaty of Versailles transferring great sections of East Prussia to Poland, Pomeranians became even more acutely aware of their position on the border. In 1922, a new province was created with the official designation *Grenzmark Posen-Westpreussen* (literally, "borderland Posen-West Prussia"). In his correspondence, Christoph captured scenes reminiscent of those in Theodor Fontane's novels. For example, he wrote of attending a funeral in June 1921: "At the beginning, the men were fearfully stiff—even impolite. But if one talks with them longer, they are really nice. It was a true Junker burial." In the same letter, he talked about the workers who did not have a day's rest, about the Polish laborers who were needed for the potato harvest, and about "going on a hunt [where] I shot a very good buck, about which I am very proud."[196] Eastern Pomerania in the 1920s featured a strong feudal legacy and acute resentments growing out of recent geopolitical developments. It was a dangerous mixture—one whose impact would extend beyond the region.[197]

Yet Christoph's letters from Gut Thalitter and Gut Grabow do not reveal the emergence of a proto-Nazi political consciousness. His missives from the first half of 1920s largely concerned cars and motorcycles, horses and dogs, as well as dances and girlfriends. He could scarcely conceal his enthusiasm about the former: he wrote his mother from Berlin, for example, in May 1921, "that it makes me fearfully envious that Phli has a motorcycle. Tell him that if he travels to Berlin, he shouldn't lock it up!"[198] Christoph often resorted to code and shorthand when talking about his private life. While it is in certain respects remarkable that he would confide so much about his romantic interests, he was, after all, a prince, and it was customary for parents and other family elders to play a role in matchmaking. Although Christoph did not reveal the social standing of the women he courted, he was consorting with Prussian high nobility. His letters back home tell of meeting Field Marshal von Mackensen (with whom Wolfgang had served during World War I), and Field Marshal (and later president) Paul von Beneckendorff und von Hindenburg; as well as members of the Bismarck family. But one also gets the sense that he was a young man trying to gain some life experience, and that some of his romantic interests were not *ebenbürtig*—that is, meriting serious consideration for marriage. His many romantic entanglements suggest he was not lacking for personality or charm. In his letters home Christoph also exhibited a lively mind. He wrote about attending the theater, displayed an interest in music (he was thrilled when his British friend Stuart Roddie gave him a gramophone), and offered thoughtful observations about various social issues.

Christoph, however, did not apply himself fully when it came to his studies. He had realized that more formal training would do him good and returned in 1922 for three semesters at the agricultural university (*Landwirtschaftliche Hochschule*) in Munich. This was the most common subject of study for aristocrats, and when one surveys biographies of those who became Nazis, time and again they had studied agriculture—from Ludolf von Alvensleben and Prince zu Waldeck (both Higher SS and Police Leaders) to Wilhelm von Preussen (1906–40), the eldest son of the crown prince (he had wanted to join the army, but this was not an option for a Hohenzollern).[199] While studying in Munich, Prince Christoph lived the *vie bohème* and relied on support from his family (via the chief administrator Heinrich Lange, who sent the money). This was not always a great sum since the family was also forced to take steps to cut back: they had even closed the main house at Friedrichshof in 1921 and lived in one of the cottages on the property.[200] Christoph wrote his mother one amusing and not-so-veiled plea for sympathy, "I have just bought a tin of *Blutwurst* and am going to live on it. I'm sure there are many cats and dogs in it and believe even a fish. At least it smells of it!"[201] While Christoph may have been short of cash, he was still a prince. One gains a sense of his life from an early letter during his tenure as a student: he wrote his mother 1 November 1922, "I have not been able to hear any lectures yet because there are so many formalities to be done before but I hope to begin on Monday. I payed [*sic*] all the visits Papa told me to and luckily most of them were not at home. I saw Rupert [apparently Bavarian crown prince Rupprecht], and he was most kind and told me to send his messages. I shall be awfully thankful for anything to eat that is sent to me because food is terribly expensive."[202] It was a curious, and in its own way, difficult period for the prince during the hyperinflation. While it is perhaps difficult to muster sympathy when his tennis racket broke and a new one, he reported, cost RM 200,000, or when his social obligations interfered with his studies, Christoph described his challenges with a sense of humor and with a certain indifference to formalities. This period as an impoverished student did not last very long, however, and by the end of 1924 Christoph returned to the life of a peripatetic, but nonetheless remunerated, squire in training. As with his Abitur, he failed to complete his degree in agrarian economics.

One striking element in Christoph's life during the early 1920s was the drastic shifts in his financial situation, as he moved from luxury to penury and back again on numerous occasions. He enjoyed extravagant trips to Berlin thanks to Stuart Roddie, and some of Christoph's letters from this period were written on stationery from the Hotel Adlon. As in Italy, those with pounds or dollars, of course, enjoyed fabulous financial advantages (the devalued Reichsmark was on an irregular slide to virtual worthlessness by November 1923). This helps explain the (relatively) high life of expatriates ranging from W. H. Auden and Christopher Isherwood to Thomas Wolfe and Katherine Anne Porter. Roddie facilitated the lavish nights on the town, where the two young men enjoyed some of the stunning Weimar culture: cabarets, theater, and so much more. The grand houses of the country also provided the setting for the occasional sumptuous affair. On another occasion, in this case a wedding, the guests lit lanterns and paraded through the garden of a grand residence, before enjoying a buffet that Christoph described as "huge."[203] Country high society persisted throughout the Weimar Republic—despite certain cutbacks—with anachronistic grandeur. The photographs of such occasions show scenes out of the preceding century: men donning elaborate uniforms (many in those of the Hussars, with massive quantities of gold braid and the imposing death's-head helmet), others in formal attire.

It was common for aristocrats to pursue their education by sampling certain jobs and experiences. Some did this consciously, some more aimlessly. Christoph appears to have fallen in somewhere in between. He envisioned himself as the head of an estate and pursued experiences he thought useful, but he did not exhibit the ability to remain focused. In 1924 Christoph tried a stint at the Kruckwerke in Frankfurt, a factory that produced engines. Not unexpectedly, this did not last, and he fell back into old patterns where he floated between family residences and the homes of friends. He later noted in his résumé about the period from 1925 to 1927, "I had no profession in the following years, since in the wake of the Inflation and the difficult economic circumstances it was not possible for me to acquire an estate."[204] But again, it was a case of self-indulgence and a lack of self-discipline. Prince Christoph preferred to pursue experiences in areas of interest, such as automobiles. He loved cars and motorcycles, and many of his letters to siblings concern the acquisition of some new vehicle. In one, he wrote his twin, Richard, the bad news about a new Lancia sports car they had purchased together that had suffered a dent during transportation from Turin and was delayed for repairs. In another document, one more suggestive but less precise, the ex-Kaiser's private secretary from Doorn wrote in 1928 to the chief administrator Heinrich Lange at Friedrichshof that he was passing on the charges accrued by Prince Christoph for the repair of a car in Doorn.[205] With destinations such as the villa of the ex-Kaiser, automobile excursions permitted both enjoyment and networking. His obsession with cars also gave vent to his occasionally rambunctious behavior. One document that formed part of his SS file noted that Christoph had an accident involving personal injury in February 1931 in Überlingen on Lake Constance near Friedrichshafen, where he was working at the time. The local authorities gave him the option of a thirty Marks fine or three days in jail.[206]

A primary advantage of working in a rural setting was that it permitted Christoph to improve his equestrian skills. Indeed, the prince grew into a

Prince Christoph (driving) *and his twin, Prince Richard, in a Mercedes at a car rally in 1934.*

talented dressage rider and began competing across Germany and then Europe. Horses have long been important in the lives of royals, and dressage, because of its elegance (the rider subtly controls the horse through complex exercises) and its reliance on expensive, well-trained animals, has long had aristocratic associations. Competing at a high level offered other advantages. One would travel, meet people with the means to maintain fine horses, and have access to some of the more exclusive circles. The young Prince von Hessen, with his birthright and charm, was well appreciated by this horsey set. Christoph, in turn, benefited from the social contacts he made through his riding. He wrote his mother one letter suggestive of this world in August 1928, where he talked of the fabulously wealthy Fugger family that hailed from Augsburg:

> The polo was most interesting and amusing. I went to a dinner at Waldfried. 120 people and after dinner another 50 arrived. I met a rather nice and very rich man called Weininger (from Berlin) who showed a lot of interest in my riding. He gave me one of his horses to ride and asked me to come to Berlin in autumn for the hunting season and ride horses. I told him of my plan to take lessons and it seems he said to Fugger that he wanted to offer me one of his horses for this purpose. Fugger says he has Olympic *Pferde* [horses]. I wonder if it is true? Fugger was very nice to me indeed and gave me one of his horses to ride in the games and asked me to come for dinner.[207]

Social aspirations, however, were not the main reason for Christoph's interest in riding. Indeed, he may have argued that the sport was egalitarian in that a horse only recognizes a good rider. The social connections were mostly an agreeable by-product.

Prince Christoph also evinced a love of flying: he took up gliders in the 1920s and had private lessons as a pilot later on.[208] Flying was an avocation that had many connotations: it had been the most glamorous kind of military service during World War I and, because of the air duels, had knightly associations. One historian writing about European aviation and the popular imagination used the phrase "*chevalier* of the skies," and noted, "in control of his fate, handling his airplane with great courage and skill, the aviator appeared to be a genuine war hero, comparable to cavalrymen in Napoleon's era or chivalrous knights in the Middle ages."[209] A common trope in descriptions of aviators has always been the phrase "knights of the air." In addition to suggesting a love of action and a sense of individualism, flying indicated an optimism about technology and modernity. Some scholars have talked about the *Fliegerblick* (glance of the aviator), which often included a belief that "social renewal" would accompany this technological innovation.[210] One sees some of these messages communicated in the Italian Futurists' paintings, the *aeropittura*, that were then promoted by Mussolini as symbols of Fascist values: action, war, chivalry, and progress.

Aviation had particularly nationalistic associations in Germany, where the Treaty of Versailles had prohibited the development of an air force and placed limits on the kind of planes that were developed. During the Weimar Republic, gliders and the associations that promoted them were therefore "widely regarded as a patriotic declaration of faith."[211] Prince Christoph, like many of his generation, had the opportunity to experience the communal effort that came with pulling a glider-plane up a hill, as well as the sense of accomplishment that came from piloting a plane (an experience that many believed "developed character" and promoted "a sense of purpose and confidence").[212] Christoph's uncle, Prince Heinrich von Preussen was a great enthusiast of flying and evidently had an influence on him. Later, the National Socialists developed a Union of Aviators within the party, which one observer called, "the future Luftwaffe in disguise."[213] Prince Paul Metternich-Winneburg (a descendant of the reactionary Austrian chancellor Clemens von Metternich) belonged to the infamous Condor Legion that carried out bombings in Spain in the mid-1930s; he was also a race-car driver.[214] Of course, a love of flying was not limited to Fascists and nationalists.[215] T. E. Lawrence (1888–1935), for example, enlisted in the Royal Air Force after his adventures in the Middle East and his disillusionment at the Paris Peace Conference. Lawrence also embraced the speed, danger, and romance of both airplanes and motorcycles, and, as shown in the opening scene of Sir David Lean's *Lawrence of Arabia*, he lost his life as a result of the latter in 1935. Before his death, Lawrence told a friend, "The air was the only first-class thing that our generation has to do. So everyone should either take to the air themselves or help it forward."[216] In contemporaneous writings, author Antoine de Saint-Exupery featured aviation in a positive light because it offered the opportunity of "binding more closely cities, countries, and peoples" and seemed "to hold out the ideal of a new, more peaceable community of nations."[217] Because Prince Christoph never actually obtained his pilot's license, his romantic yearnings went largely unfulfilled. But he joined the Luftwaffe as a reserve in 1935, underwent subsequent training during the war, and showed an enthusiasm for aviation that was so common in the 1930s.

There has long been a tendency for members of both the European and North American elite to define themselves as vital, heroic, and physically fit. In his study of modern American elites, David Brooks noted, "Families like the Roosevelts adopted a tough, manly ethos in order to restore vigor and self-confidence to the East Coast elite and so preserve its place atop the power structure."[218] During the interwar years, there were striking similarities between the American and German elite—and it was not just that Charles Lindbergh was a hero in both countries. National Socialism, of course, amplified the militaristic tendencies and added a racist caste to all enterprises. For Christoph, it is significant that he missed out on military service during the Great War. As a result, he compensated in certain ways that found expression in his love of cars, planes, and horses.

The Nazis were successful in attracting many of these adventuresome types and in appropriating concepts-associated sports—especially those martial values such as courage, selflessness, and the love of technology. Hitler adopted an approach along the lines of the Italian Fascists and embraced speed and modernity with regard to automobiles and airplanes. He started with an imposing Selve car (which Ernst Hanfstaengl described as "a rattling monster"), which he replaced with a top-of-the line Mercedes convertible.[219] Hitler's obsession with cars extended to ordering a new Mercedes from his jail cell in Landsberg prison that picked him up on his release at the end of 1924. He felt similarly about airplanes, and pioneered their use during the 1932 presidential campaign, when he flew from rally to rally in a manner that astonished many observers.[220] Victor Klemperer, a trained philologist and an astute observer of the Third Reich (and himself an owner of a car), noted:

> Nazi heroism clothed itself [in] the masked figure of the racing driver, his crash helmet, his goggles, his thick gloves. Nazism nurtured all kinds of sport, and purely linguistically, it was influenced by boxing more than all others put together; but the most memorable and widespread image of

heroism in the mid-thirties is provided by the racing driver. . . . If a young man didn't glean his image of heroism from those sinewy warriors depicted on the latest posters or commemorative coins, naked or sporting SA uniforms, then he doubtless did so from racing drivers.[221]

National Socialism appealed to people on many different levels. This is one of the reasons that it drew adherents from such a broad spectrum of society. For some, like Christoph and his twin, Richard, the association of National Socialism with sports, adventure, and modernity proved important in eliciting their support.[222]

Prince Christoph spent the latter half of the 1920s—the "golden years" of the Weimar Republic—preoccupied with horses, motorcycles, and cars. He returned to more regular work in 1930. This time he was employed at the Maybach Werke, a factory that produced various kinds of engines, in Friedrichshafen, on Lake Constance in southern Germany. Christoph spent time in the different departments: automobiles, trucks, Zeppelins, and diesel motors. The position in the engine works represented a significant step down the social hierarchy for the prince. But it was not unheard of for princes to gain some experience in factories; indeed, it was thought useful for a future leadership position. Prince Louis Ferdinand von Preussen (1907–94), a son of Crown Prince Wilhelm, spent time working on the assembly line of the Ford Motor Company in the United States.[223] The position at the Maybach factory permitted Christoph to indulge in one of his passions—his future wife Sophia recalled how he would become so enthralled with his new cars that he would sometimes sleep in them for the first days after acquiring them. Despite this passion, Christoph lost his job in late-1930 due to the layoffs that came with the Depression. He later reported that there was a 50-percent reduction in the labor force at Maybach. The experience of being sacked made him even less sympathetic to the Weimar Republic. Yet Christoph was not a hapless victim of the Depression without recourse to other options. In the winter of 1930/31, he moved to Berlin where he obtained a position at the Viktoria insurance firm. He described his position there as an "independent agent," as he tried to use his social contacts to sell policies.[224] It was his stated occupation when he filled out a résumé for a post in the Nazi government on 21 February 1933.

While Christoph treaded water with his career, he took one substantial step at this time. He married Princess Sophia of Greece and Denmark on 15 December 1930. The two were distant cousins—her mother was a Battenberg, a morganatic branch of the Hesse-Darmstadt line. Sophia recalled that she first met Christoph's brother, Prince Philipp, in 1927 when she was thirteen years old: they became acquainted "on the polo field at the Walfried stud-farm."[225] She met Christoph shortly thereafter.

Christoph's twin, Richard, also took a fancy to her and wanted to court her, but she quickly fell for Christoph. She became engaged to him when she was sixteen. The Greek-German princess, who was born on the Island of Corfu, raised primarily in France, and given the nickname "Tiny" by her family, was strikingly beautiful. Like her mother Princess Alice, it was expected that she would marry into a ruling family (Her younger brother, Philip, certainly met expectations in this respect). Prince Christoph was perhaps not the ultimate fulfillment of these ambitions, but the Hesse-Kassels were still a suitable family. As younger siblings, both Sophia and Christoph had more latitude in selecting a partner than would an heir to the family seat. Furthermore, Sophia was virtually an orphan from an exiled royal family: her father and mother saw little of one another at this point as the father was living a self-indulgent life in France. Just as marriage enabled Sophia to find a way out of a challenging situation, Christoph also found relief: he had experienced several unhappy relationships since the early 1920s, and on at least one occasion, was the target of a matchmaking scheme. Already in December 1921, the ex-Kaiser's adjutant, Sigurd von Ilsemann, reported that Baroness Lilli von Heemstra (Wilhelm II's mistress, who also had had an affair with his son, Crown Prince Wilhelm), had traveled to Friedrichshof with the express purpose of finding a suitable husband (if only as a cover so that she could continue her affair with the ex-Kaiser). Ilsemann reported, "at the beginning she had her eye on the youngest, Prince Christoph, but he was not interested and she then selected his older brother Wolfgang; she immediately secured the permission of the mother [the Landgravine], although the father had not yet been approached."[226] While nothing came of Heemstra's plans for any of the Hessen brothers, it was clear that young royals were expected to find a suitable spouse. When Christoph found someone for whom he had genuine feelings, he leapt at the opportunity.

Theirs was a marriage based on love, which helps explain how Sophia could marry at the age of sixteen. Sophia and Christoph would remain committed to one another (there is no evidence or even a hint of rumor about extramarital affairs), and they carried on a correspondence over the years that reflected tremendous affection. In a representative letter—penned several months after Christoph had reported to the Luftwaffe on 4 November 1939—he wrote Sophia who was then at Wolfsgarten about his return to their Berlin-Dahlem home:

> [H]ow I miss you here and long for you. It is simply terrible. I am so depressed and so miserable that I shall be pleased to get away from this house in which we have spent those lovely happy years together and enjoyed having our little Poonsies [their pet name for the children]. Oh darling if only you were here! When I enter the house I think how often the door used to open like

with magic and then you angel were there waiting for me smiling or laughing and giving me a thrill of happiness I feel a lump in my throat to think of it. I love you, love you, love you, my angel, and you mean everything to me. . . . Lovingly as your old adoring Peech [Christoph].[227]

All of Sophia's sisters married German princes. The eldest, Margarita (1905–81) married Hereditary Prince Gottfried zu Hohenlohe-Langenburg (1897–1960)—another great-grandson of Queen Victoria. The eighth *Fürst* von Hohenlohe was a kind of *Grand seigneur* who lived in Schloss Langenburg in the Hohenloher Land near Crailsheim in Württemberg. "Friedel" joined the Nazi Party in May 1937 (see appendix 1) and had considerable contact with Nazi leaders. For example, he offered his assistance in approaches to British royals during the 1930s and then later served in the Wehrmacht. Prince zu Hohenlohe-Langenburg was a corps commander during the Anschluss of Austria in 1938.[228] Later, after the war, he was president of the exclusive Automobile Association of Germany. Sophia's sister Theodora (1906–69) wed Margrave Berthold of Baden (1906–63) —son of the last imperial chancellor Prince Max—and owner of the castle near Lake Constance that housed Kurt Hahn's famous boarding school at Salem. Theodora and Berthold were instrumental in inducing her youngest sibling, Prince Philip, to come to Salem in 1933; the future Duke of Edinburgh was able to study at Salem thanks to their financial support. Later, when the liberal and Jewish Dr. Hahn was forced to flee to the United Kingdom (where he founded the Gordonstoun school in Scotland), Prince Berthold succeeded him as headmaster. The school has been described as an effort "to breed modern 'princes' of Machiavelli's kind . . . ; leaders in politics and diplomacy, or in industry and commerce."[229] Others have characterized the programs as militaristic asceticism. These descriptions are rather ungenerous: the school featured a significant number of scholarship students from modest backgrounds, and many of its graduates emerged with liberal and progressive views. One of Kurt Hahn's guiding "seven principles" was "to free sons of the wealthy and powerful from the enervating sense of privilege."[230] The school nonetheless underwent a transformation during the Third Reich as Prince Berthold gave "way to Ministry of Education pressures and introduced a rigid, pro-Nazi regime. Though a liberal, he had little choice; he either accepted the Nazi doctrine or closed down completely."[231] While the young Prince Philip experienced the nazified institution—"there was much heel-clicking, and shouts of '*Heil Hitler*' were compulsory for German nationals"—he soon left Theodora and his siblings in Germany and in autumn 1934 followed Hahn to Gordonstoun.[232]

Sophia's other sister, Cécile (1911–37) married Hereditary Grand Duke Georg Donatus von Hessen (1906–37), the son of Ernst Ludwig. Georg

Donatus was similar to Christoph in many ways: an automobile enthusiast —he was an officer in the National Socialist Drivers' Corps (Nationalsozialistische Kraftfahrer Korps or NSKK), an avid sportsman, and an aviator. He and his wife, Cécile, as well as his brother Prince Ludwig, joined the Nazi Party in May 1937 when the party rolls were reopened for certain individuals.[233] Like Christoph, Georg Donatus became a reserve officer in the Luftwaffe. When his father, Grand Duke Ernst Ludwig, died in October 1937, Georg Donatus succeeded him, taking over the position as head of the house. But catastrophe struck several weeks later when he embarked on a flight to London on a Belgian airline to attend the wedding of his brother, Prince Ludwig, who was marrying the daughter of Sir Auckland (later Baron) Geddes (1879–1954), the former Minister of National Service during World War I and then British ambassador to the United States. On 16 November 1937, Georg Donatus, his widowed mother (Grand Duchess Eleonore), his wife, Cécile, two of their children, and six other passengers perished when their plane hit a chimney near Ostende in Belgium. Lord Louis and Lady Edwina Mountbatten had been among those waiting for the Hessian ducal party at the Croydon airfield when they received the news.[234] After a family conference, the decision was made that the betrothal of "Lu" and "Peg" should go ahead; the wedding took place in London on 17 November 1937, with Marina, the Duchess of Kent, and several members of the Mountbatten family joining Ambassador Joachim von Ribbentrop (1893–1946) among the dignitaries at this somber ceremony ("without traditional postwedding celebrations").[235] The funeral followed shortly thereafter in Darmstadt. It was striking to see this collection of princes processing behind the caskets through the streets of Darmstadt in their varied attire—Lord Louis Mountbatten in his British naval uniform, Prince Christoph von Hessen in his SS garb, Prince Philipp von Hessen in his SA brown-shirt, and the future Duke of Edinburgh in formal civilian clothing. The crowd saluted the procession with the outstretched arm of the *"Heil Hitler"* greeting. The intermarriage between German princes today seems almost incredible—especially Cécile and Sophia, two descendants of the Hesse-Darmstadt line, marrying their relations.[236]

There was also remarkable temporal proximity in the marriages of Sophia and Cécile. They were engaged at the same time and made preparations simultaneously. Cécile wrote to their mother of her efforts to prepare their trousseaus while living in Paris: "Tiny's clothes are nearly ready. I saw her trying them on the other day. They are lovely and her wedding dress is too beautiful for words. Satin and quite simple with lace and tulle veil. They have not started mine yet."[237] As described earlier, Greek Orthodox Sophia and Lutheran-Evangelical Christoph decided on dual wedding ceremonies at Kronberg on 15 December 1930. While Sophia and Christoph's wedding ceremony was fairly low-key—held in the small town in the Taunus

Funeral procession in Darmstadt on 19 November 1937 after the airplane crash that killed seven members of the Hesse-Darmstadt family. Leading the procession is the heir, Prince Ludwig von Hessen-Darmstadt. The second row consists of, from left to right, Prince "Friedel" Hohenlohe, Prince Christoph von Hessen (in an SS uniform), Prince Philipp von Hessen (in an SA uniform), Prince Philip (current Duke of Edinburgh), and Prince Berthold von Baden. Lord Louis Mountbatten follows in a peaked naval cap in the row behind. Note that many members of the crown make the Nazi salute.

mountains outside of Frankfurt—her older sister Cécile and Prince Georg Donatus experienced a very different kind of event when they married in Darmstadt six weeks later on 2 February 1931. As was customary, the heir had a grander wedding than a younger sibling: "Men and women lined the streets of Darmstadt, and the car taking Andrea and Cécile to the Alte Schlosskirche was so surrounded that it could not move. They made their way into the courtyard of the Alte Schloss on foot, with much hand-shaking, while Andrea was greeted with cries of '*Hoch der Herr Papa*.' 'It seemed very funny in a "republic" but was a nice sign of the affection of the people for Uncle Ernie & his family,' wrote Victoria to her son Georgie [Second Marques of Milford Haven (1892–1938)]."[238] The nobility here retained much of its social cachet. Yet in the two ceremonies, one can discern some of the differences between the Hesse-Darmstadt and Hesse-Kassel families at this time. The former was a ruling house that kept its position until 1918 and had great public visibility; the latter, while retaining impressive ties to other royalty in Europe, had fallen on harder times

—beginning with the Prussian invasion in 1866 and extending through the first decades of the twentieth century.

Monarchist sentiment was still quite strong during the Weimar Republic, as many in the middle and upper classes remained uncertain about the viability of the fledgling democracy. Ernst ("Putzi") Hanfstaengl, an early Nazi from an affluent German-American family, later recalled about the right-wing groups of the early 1920s, "Many of the titled officers in the affiliated patriotic organizations professed dual loyalties. [Bavarian] Crown Prince Rupprecht used to be referred to quite frequently as 'His Majesty,' and a proportion of the Kampfbund membership was distinctly monarchist in outlook. So much so that for many years Hitler let it be understood that he intended to restore monarchical forms of government, an attitude which later brought considerable Braunschweig, Hesse, and Hohenzollern support, only for all of them to complain about being betrayed in the end."[239] Later, Hanfstaengl added, "Hitler was shrewd enough to realize that monarchist support could be a very important factor and in fact he played on the German royal families' hopes of a restoration for years. 'I consider a monarchy a very suitable form of state organization, particularly in Germany,' he said to me once, and of course he talked in similar terms to whoever wanted to believe it. 'The problem has to be studied very carefully. I would accept the Hohenzollern again at any time, but in the other states we would probably have to put in a regent until we found a suitable prince."[240] Hitler was also known to quip that the only good part of the Social Democrats' platform was their antimonarchy stance. The Nazi leader was inconsistent in his statements about a restoration and about the nobility in general, but he gradually became convinced that it was necessary to court them—at the same time that his self-confidence grew and he became more comfortable in their company.

3

Nazi High Society:
Making Hitler *"salonfähig"*
and Helping the Nazis to Power

Although certain Nazi leaders struggled to overcome the impulse to view members of the high aristocracy as "degenerate" and at odds with their vision for Germany, such thinking was perceived by Hitler and most others with influence as anachronistic and unsuited to the realities they faced in the late 1920s and 1930s. Even the more populist Joseph Goebbels, who had his roots in the "left wing" of the Nazi Party, warmed to the princes, as his diary entries reveal. On 31 January 1931, he recounted an evening at the home of the von Dirksens, influential aristocrats: "many visitors there: a nice girl, the daughter of the Empress, Prince Louis Ferdinand [von Preussen], Prince Philipp von Hessen, the son-in-law of the king of Italy—a very nice and inspirational man."[1] The nazification of Hessens and other princes, as well as their relationships with Nazi leaders, proved important on several levels. First, by meeting with the Nazi elite, the princes helped make them socially acceptable (*salonfähig* or literally, suitable for a salon). Indeed, the presence of the princes at a Nazi Party function added a distinctive luster to the occasion and would be a draw for other potential supporters—including wealthy industrialists such as the Thyssens, Krupps, and Bechsteins—whose financial contributions were crucial to the perpetually cash-strapped party. Moreover, the support of aristocrats sent a message to the population at large that the traditional ruling caste had faith in the Nazis and subscribed to the idea that Hitler could rescue a foundering Germany. The princes were co-opted by the Nazi leaders and joined in this new "high society": an amalgamation of the traditional elite and the new men. This glamorous scene helped provide the "beautiful face of the Third Reich" (along with athletic young people in uniforms and *Autobahnen*, among other potent images).[2]

The symbolism of the princes' support was tremendously important, and recognized as such at the time. Germany, despite its republican government, was still a class-bound society, and centuries of deference to the elite had not been overcome in the short years of the Weimar Republic. As Alexander Schmorell (1917–43) of the White Rose resistance group in Munich observed during the war, "the man in the street can't comprehend everything or decide everything; he isn't that presumptuous, he trusts his leaders, the educated classes, who understand things better than he does."[3] This is not to say that all Germans were inclined to follow the example of the old elite: many members of the proletariat rejected this culture of deference. But there were also numerous instances in which princely support affected the thinking of the uncommitted. Putzi Hanfstaengl, for example, recalled the influence of Prince Auwi: "It was largely through him that I became reconciled with the movement. I felt that if a member of the former royal family was prepared to identify himself with it there was more hope of keeping it within bounds."[4] In sum, it was of great use to the Nazis to have princes, including the former Kaiser's sons, speaking at rallies and posing for pictures. Although it is impossible to answer with certainty the counterfactual question about the absence of the princes' support and what that would have meant for the Nazis' political fortunes, the members of the former ruling families emerged as another useful item in Hitler's political toolbox.

Hitler therefore wooed the royals, and in an attempt to win their support, made all sorts of promises. He vowed that he would respect their views, tolerate their friendships with Jews, and keep an open mind regarding a Hohenzollern restoration.[5] In January 1931, Prince Friedrich zu Eulenburg-Hertefeldt (1874–1937) had an audience with Hitler where the Nazi leader addressed many of the concerns common among the nobility: Prince Eulenburg induced Hitler to authorize the minutes, and then he circulated them to many members of the nobility. "Men with leadership characteristics" were to join together to vanquish Bolshevism.[6] Appeals of this kind proved effective and took some of the stigma out of becoming a Nazi. Still, the majority of the princes who joined the party did so after the seizure of power in January 1933: of the 270 princes on the 1941 list, only 80 had joined before Hitler became chancellor.[7] Apparently the first prince to join the Nazi Party was Hereditary Prince Ernst zur Lippe (1902–87), who signed on in May 1928: he later became an SS-Major (Sturmbannführer) and held a high-ranking post in the SS Race and Settlement Head Office (RuSHA), working as the chief assistant to Reichsleiter Richard Walther Darré (1895–1953).[8] His relation, Prince Friedrich Christian zu

Schaumburg-Lippe followed him into the party in August 1928; the nephew of Queen Wilhelmina of the Netherlands, he became a speaker for the party in 1929 and later served as Goebbels's adjutant.[9] Other early members of the Nazi Party—individuals who would later receive the highly honorific Nazi Party badge of honor—included Hereditary Prince Josias zu Waldeck und Pyrmont (joining in November 1929); and Prince August Wilhelm (Auwi joined the NSDAP in April 1930). Philipp von Hessen followed in October 1930 (more about that momentarily), but there was a steady if slow stream of princes that flowed into the party.

By 1933, there was far less stigma attached to supporting the Nazis. Duke Ernst August von Braunschweig (of Brunswick and Cumberland) (1887–1953), who was married to Princess Viktoria-Luise von Preussen, was the son-in-law of Wilhelm II; while it appears that he never actually joined the party, he evidently was "a regular donor" and had close relations with several Nazi leaders.[10] Society hostess and journalist Bella Fromm reported that the Duke von Braunschweig appeared at an 18 August 1933 party in a brown SA uniform and added, "His son, the Prince of Hannover [also Ernst August (1914–86)], wore the black and silver SS uniform" (evidently of the cavalry, as he had joined the Berlin Reitersturm).[11] The Duke von Braunschweig had been a British peer (Duke of Cumberland) until World War I, when as part of the Titles Deprivation Act of 1917, he was stripped of this honor "for having adhered to the enemies of His Majesty."[12] The same applied to Duke Carl Eduard von Sachsen-Coburg und Gotha, who had been born Prince of Great Britain and Ireland. "Charlie Coburg," as he was called by close British friends, joined the Nazi Party in 1933 and became a Major General (Gruppenführer) of the SA and a delegate in the Reichstag in 1936.[13] Bella Fromm also recalled one evening on 25 November 1933, "after dinner, the unprepossessing Duke [Carl] Eduard strutted around with his Fascist dagger, an honor bestowed on him by Mussolini."[14] Duke Adolf Friedrich von Mecklenburg-Schwerin (1873–1969) was the brother-in-law of the queen of the Netherlands, and, according to Fromm, "devoted himself to the Nazi cause and used his international connections to travel abroad selling Nazi ideas and doing espionage, especially in economic affairs. He was dubbed *Der Grossherzogliche Nazi-Agent.* . . ." (although he evidently did not join the party)[15] A member of the younger generation in the family, Hereditary Grand Duke Friedrich Franz von Mecklenburg-Schwerin (1910–2001), joined the SS in May 1931 and rose through the ranks to SS-Captain (Hauptsturmführer) in 1936. During the war, Prince Friedrich Franz was posted to the German Embassy in Copenhagen where he became the personal aide to SS-General (Obergruppenführer) Werner Best (1903–89), the Nazi plenipotentiary in Denmark. He also served in a Waffen-SS tank corps during the summer of 1944.[16] Count Gottfried von Bismarck-Schönhausen (brother of "Eddie") was also a friend of Philipp von Hessen's, served as District Governor (Regierungspräsident) of Potsdam and member of the Reichstag; he also held the honorary rank of an SS-Lieutenant Colonel (Standartenführer).[17]

Members of certain princely families joined the Nazi Party en masse. The House of Hesse, including its side branch Philippsthal-Barchfeld, had fourteen; Schaumburg-Lippe had ten; Lippe had eighteen; Sachsen-Coburg und Gotha had nine; and the Hohenlohe had no fewer than twenty members in the Nazi Party.[18] This is suggestive of how tight-knit these families could be: when one or two members joined, others often followed. A list of royals who became members of the Nazi Party (see appendix 1) shows that many early supporters were women, such as Princess Marie Adelheid zur Lippe (1895–1993) (May 1930); Princess Lucy zu Sayn-Wittgenstein (1898–1952) (May 1930); Princess Ingeborg-Alix zu Schaumburg-Lippe (1901–96) (October 1930); and Princess Klara von Sachsen-Meiningen (1895–1992) (May 1931). Indeed, at the end of 1934, approximately 30 percent of the members of the *Fürstenhäuser* who had joined the party were women (47 of the 147 listed), as compared to a national average of between 5 and 7.5 percent.[19] Of particular importance were Prince Viktor (1877–1946) and Princess Gisela zu Wied (1891–1975), the latter a physically prepossessing woman of considerable bulk (and minimal beauty) who became particularly enthusiastic about the National Socialists.[20] The acerbic Putzi Hanfstaengl nonetheless described Princess zu Wied as "charming," and she clearly influenced many other notables to support the fledgling party, especially by organizing a kind of "National Socialist salon."[21] Hitler, Göring, and other Nazi leaders, while deeply misogynistic in most respects, made a concerted effort to try to charm the princesses. And indeed, Hitler fared quite well with wealthy and influential women, even of a nonnoble variety, as he combined solicitous good manners (sometimes attributed to his Austrian upbringing) with his charismatic authority. Hitler developed especially close relationships with Winifred Wagner (1897–1980), Helene Bechstein (1876–1951), and Elsa Bruckmann (1856–1946) (wife of renowned publisher Hugo Bruckmann, she was born Princess Cantacuzène of Romania)—all of whom in their own ways regarded him as their "protégé."[22] They induced Hitler to purchase a dinner jacket, starched shirts, and patent-leather shoes, although this horrified some party associates, and it was only the formal shoes that he wore on a regular basis. Still, these women, along with Harvard-educated Ernst Hanfstaengl, worked in the 1920s to make Hitler more *salonfähig*. Historian Wolfgang Schuster also noted how the women brought around their influential husbands: "The help of Bechstein and Bruckmann was directed at Hitler personally and not the NSDAP—[they] sought to support the protégé of their wives as well as advance a political cause. Their wives supported him with grants, such as Frau Bechstein giving him a loan in the form of jewels or art objects."[23]

Beginning in the mid-1930s, Hitler also became friends with Diana and Unity Mitford (1910–2003 and 1911–1948, respectively), two of the daughters of Lord Redesdale. The English aristocrats learned German and sought out Hitler, with Unity pursuing him by waiting at the Munich restaurant Osteria Bavaria. The Mitfords' tactics worked, and Unity in particular became remarkably close to the German dictator. Because she was enthralled with Hitler, she chronicled each conversation they had in her diary by writing about the meeting in red ink (as distinct from black used for the rest of the journal). All told, she had some 140 discussions with Hitler between 1935 and 1939.[24] They met at the Reich Chancellery in Berlin, at Bayreuth, and in Munich, leaving the Obersalzberg primarily to Eva Braun. While few believe that the relationship was consummated sexually, there were personal feelings and an intensity that set it apart from most of Hitler's other relationships (Unity tried to commit suicide by shooting herself in the head when war broke out in September 1939). A biographer of Unity Mitford, David Pryce-Jones, commented, "She was eccentric in the clockwork of her devotion, but then a more ordinary character would not have held Hitler's imagination in its turn. It will always remain a historical freak that Hitler, whose destruction also brought down the old order of England, should have had an English girlfriend brought up at the heart of that old order."[25]

While the Nazi leaders often presented themselves publicly as frugal populists, Hitler sought to keep all doors open, and accordingly not only consorted with the wealthy elite but also relied upon them for financial support. The subject of support for the Nazis offered by big business and other elite has been fraught with controversy (viz. the David Abraham "affair" where he was charged with fabricating evidence implicating "capitalists").[26] But regardless of one's views about the role of elite backers in bringing Hitler to power, there is no question about the emergence of what one might call "Nazi high society," even before the seizure of power in 1933. It entailed a mixture of not only party leaders but also aristocrats, industrialists, diplomats, movie stars, and artists. They met at, among other places, the opera and press balls, at dinners in the Reich Chancellery, and in the Görings's and Goebbels's homes. This mix, which included unlikely figures like the half-Jewish Princess Stephanie zu Hohenlohe (1891–1972) —she kept her ancestry concealed during the 1930s—can be glimpsed in memoirs as well as in seating charts and invitations in the archives.[27] While Hitler and his cohorts derived satisfaction and enjoyment from consorting with this new elite, they also cultivated friendships and contacts with political goals in mind.

Philipp and Christoph Become Nazis

Prince Philipp joined the NSDAP on 1 October 1930 and was given the number 418,991. While there were later suggestions that this number was "back-dated" (Nazi Party numbers were assigned consecutively in the order that individuals joined the party—Hitler was number 55—and a lower number was more prestigious), and Philipp himself said that Göring helped him in this regard, his number was generally appropriate considering the time he joined the Party.[28] It is also significant that Princess Mafalda was persuaded to become a member of the Nazi women's organization, the NS-Frauenschaft. She paid dues of RM 5 per month and gave the impression that she was a party member: her secretary, when questioned after the war, even believed that she had joined the party.[29] Mafalda would attend party events for women, and although she did not participate very frequently, she nevertheless communicated her support for Hitler and the Nazi movement.[30] Their two eldest sons were in the *Jungvolk* and other party youth organizations, as this was obligatory at their school.[31]

Something seemingly as straightforward as party membership was actually mired in complexity and subject to "spin" by Nazi authorities and, after the war, by the individual members and their defenders. This is evident in the cases of Philipp and Christoph's parents—Landgravine Margarethe and Landgrave Friedrich Karl—who joined the Nazi Party in May 1938. The former remained a member until 1945; the latter died in 1940.[32] Margarethe and Friedrich Karl initially resisted the entreaties of the Nazis, despite hosting "Herr Hitler at Kronberg for tea in 1931 and a second time in 1932."[33] After the war, the Landgravine and her defenders portrayed her as skeptical about the Nazis and, along with her husband, rather aloof. In his denazification trial, Philipp offered an account that made his parents appear to be passive actors as they took the momentous step of joining the party: "It occurred on the occasion of my father's seventieth birthday, without him having submitted an application. Just before then I was in Berlin and spoke with Hitler. He asked me where I was heading, and I told him to my parents for the seventieth birthday of my father. He said to me, 'are your parents party members?' I said no, because I knew that my parents had put this off on more than one occasion. As I arrived [back at Kronberg], a confirmation notice of their party membership was there."[34] Philipp portrayed his parents' entry into the party as Hitler's "birthday present."[35] He suggested that it would have been rude and perhaps even impossible for them to opt out of the NSDAP.

One gains a very different impression of the Landgrave and Landgravine's sentiments regarding Hitler and the Nazis in a handwritten letter that the latter sent the dictator shortly after the death of her husband in June 1940. Philipp delivered it personally and it read:

My Führer. I am compelled by my heart to express my deeply felt thanks to you for the wonderful wreath that now lies at the feet of my beloved husband. This gesture of yours is connected to the ceaseless admiration and loyalty that he felt for you and for your work, as well as for the rise of the Fatherland, for which we are thankful, and [these feelings] remain strong in these hours of bitter suffering. Not a day passed when the deceased did not speak of you. He followed until the very end the over-powering events that he had long sensed were coming. The magnificent roses that you sent to him were his last joy. Time and again, when we came to him, he would use his hand to refer to you. May God protect you henceforth my Führer, and may he crown you with success in all the further great goals; that would be my own and my family's lasting wish, as well as that of my beloved husband. In everlasting thanks.[36]

These were not the words of a passive onlooker, disinterested in politics. Indeed, one of the most stunning images of this history is Landgrave Friedrich Karl lying on his deathbed, extending his arm in the *"Heil Hitler!"* salute upon hearing the news of the German victories that came during the first phase of the war. Yet knowing of his sons' attitudes and their important roles in the Third Reich, one might hardly expect less enthusiasm.

As the Hessens gravitated toward the Nazi Party, the magnet was Hermann Göring. It is not entirely clear when Philipp first met Göring: It is possible that they became acquainted prior to World War I, when Göring attended the Lichterfelde Cadet Academy in Berlin with Philipp and Christoph's brothers. Others reported that they first met in Berlin during the war, brought together by Crown Prince Wilhelm.[37] Philipp's number two at the Oberpräsidium in Kassel testified after the war that Philipp "met Göring in Rome in 1923 after the Hitler Putsch."[38] This was disputed by Philipp's mother, the Landgravine.[39] But it is not unlikely that the two would have met, as Göring was also in Italy at this time seeking financial support from the Fascists. One apocryphal story had it that Philipp helped Hermann Göring during his escape from the failed Beer Hall putsch in late 1923, when the Nazi leader, suffering from a painful wound to the groin, fled first to Austria and then to Italy. Several biographers of Göring have maintained that Philipp arranged for the Nazi leader to have an audience with Mussolini in the spring of 1925 and that this favor served as the basis for further contact in the latter part of the decade, but the evidence for their relationship at this time is thin.[40] The important and indisputable contact occurred in 1930, when Philipp and Christoph's cousin, Prince August Wilhelm, brought them together.

Hermann Göring proved very effective in courting potential supporters from the ranks of the princes. As historian Henry Turner has noted, "As the son of a high colonial official in the old imperial government who had gained national attention as an ace fighter pilot during the war, Göring was the closest approximation in the Nazi leadership ranks to a member of the German upper-class establishment."[41] It helped Göring in this respect that his first wife, Carin, (née Baroness von Fock, 1888–1931), was a Swedish-born aristocrat (she died in her early forties from tuberculosis). The future Reichsmarschall so fancied those with titles that the Mitford sisters developed a tongue-in-cheek nickname for him: *"von und zu"* (a reference to German aristocratic prefixes).[42] While imprisoned at Nuremberg after the war, Göring frequently suggested his own aristocratic qualities, stating, "Understand that I am not a moralist, although I have my chivalric code. . . . I revere women and think it unsportsmanlike to kill children."[43] (Protestations aside, Göring bore considerable responsibility for the Holocaust, including the murder of children).

Carin and Hermann Göring engaged many members of the high aristocracy on behalf of the Party, and this included Kaiser Wilhelm II, who was in exile in the Netherlands. Hermann Göring made two visits to Doorn: in January 1931 and May 1932—with the second lasting an entire week.[44] These extended "country weekend" visits featured long discussions, not to mention lavish entertaining (the menu would include pheasant and goose). The Kaiser and Göring stayed up late in the evenings talking politics, and the exchanges were often heated. As Carin recalled after the first visit, the two men "had flown at one another. . . . Both are excitable and so like each other in many ways. The Kaiser has probably never heard anybody express an opinion other than his own, and it was a bit too much for him sometimes."[45] Göring expressed support for the restoration of the monarchy, while the Kaiser wanted more—"the restoration of the entire princely brotherhood."[46] Despite differences, Göring made progress in wooing the ex-emperor. As the Wilhelm's aide Ilsemann noted, "during the first of Göring's visit the Kaiser kept some distance, but this time he has been completely won over."[47] Wilhelm's second wife, Princess Hermine (known as "Hermo") von Schönaich-Carolath (née von Reuss) (1887–1947) was an enthusiastic supporter of the Nazis, as were several of the Kaiser's sons. During the first visit, Princess Hermo "pressed a wad of banknotes" on Göring (ostensibly to permit the gravely ill Carin to pay for a cure), and later, Wilhelm ended up selling the Nazi leader his hunting lodge at Rominten in East Prussia for 700,000 Reichsmarks.[48] The Kaiser exhibited great inconsistency with regard to the Nazis: at certain moments, such as his meetings with Göring, he appeared positively disposed. The financial advantages gained from offering support were not lost on him (he was plagued by financial problems). Later, the Nazi government provided the Kaiser with an annual subvention. This came about as a result of an agreement signed by Göring in his capacity as Prussian Minister President and a representative of the House of Hohenzollern, Friedrich von Berg,

Prince Philipp and Prince August Wilhelm (Auwi) von Preussen locking arms dressed in Nazi uniforms in early 1933.

which was signed in late summer 1933: from then on, "the Kaiser, the Crown Prince and the remaining Prussian princes received a substantial annual allowance from the Prussian state."[49] There were reports that as a condition to the settlement, the Hohenzollern pledged not to criticize publicly Hitler or the Nazis (with the threat of the payments being halted).[50] The Prussian princes clearly had a financial incentive to back the Nazis, and this included their "porcelain factory in Cadinen . . . doing good business . . . turning out busts of Hitler." Nonetheless, Wilhelm II ultimately "thought Hitler a fool," and he clashed with family members who backed the Nazis. Yet, despite Wilhelm's increasing criticism of Hitler, the Hohenzollern as a family offered considerable support for the Nazis and helped make the party seem less "radical and plebeian."[51]

Prince Auwi, the most enthusiastic Nazi among the Hohenzollern (he was given the extremely low and prestigious party number of 24), played a key role in bringing the Hessens into the party.[52] He and Göring orchestrated the crucial meeting with Hitler that brought Philipp into the Nazi fold. They planned the approach with great care: just after the Nazis' electoral breakthrough of 14 September 1930, when they had increased their representation in the Reichstag from 12 seats to 108, and had ceased to be a fringe movement. Prior to the meeting, Philipp was taken to hear Hitler speak. One might regard this a cliché—or a classic example of how many a person fell prey to the "totalitarian temptation."[53] Yet Hitler's remarkable oratorical abilities made a strong impression on Philipp—in the words of one observer "one decisive for his further fate in life."[54] After the speech, Philipp went with Auwi to the Görings's home on the Badenesche Strasse to meet Hitler personally. The Nazi leader and Göring articulated their program in "passionate presentations." Indeed, Hitler in this and in many other instances exhibited considerable political skill in small groups. He, along with the Görings, asked Philipp to join the party, and the prince replied in the affirmative (*allerdings*), although, Philipp stated after the war, he did not believe at this point that he had made "a final commitment with regards to the NSDAP." In offering his self-exculpatory version of events, Philipp recalled how Hitler "spontaneously" stood up, extended his hand, and greeted the "newest party member" with great "enthusiasm."[55] Hitler then "immediately charged Göring with completing the necessary formalities."[56] From the various accounts of the meeting, one gains the sense that Hitler was jumping at the chance to land another prince—and that he wanted to reel him in quickly.

While Philipp joined the NSDAP in part because of the personal contact he had with Nazi leaders, there were also ideological reasons for becoming a Nazi. He later claimed that he joined the party "in an outpouring of idealistic sentiment according to the so-called National Socialist world view—something along the lines of Hitler's speeches, the program of the NSDAP, Hitler's *Mein Kampf*, or Rosenberg's *Myth of the Twentieth Century*" (the latter being a radical if abstruse ideological tract that articulated a racist and expansionist agenda).[57] Yet, when interrogated after the war, Philipp admitted that he, like many others in the party, never read *Mein Kampf* but just leafed through it (*"überblättert"*). He maintained that he believed in the socialist element in the NSDAP. Even after the war, he continued to think that Hitler "had been a worker and had millions of workers behind him."[58] As mentioned earlier with reference to Italian Fascism, Prince Philipp evinced concern for workers and the less fortunate: while his corporatist outlook was tinged with seigneurialism and motivated by the fear that an impoverished and discontented proletariat would be more susceptible to Bolshevism and revolution, there was nevertheless a populist element to his political outlook. Many of his generation explored "national-social ideas," including those advanced earlier by Friedrich Naumann (1860–1919), who argued for a "social monarchy" based on Christian Socialist principles.[59] Putzi Hanfstaengl, an early Nazi and acquaintance of Prince Philipp, avowedly embraced the concept of "social monarchy," which he viewed as a kind of compassionate conservatism.[60]

Philipp was also motivated to join the Nazis for opportunistic reasons, although it was only the Hohenzollern who received outright payments from the Nazis. From the advent of Philipp's contact with Hitler and Göring in 1930, there was talk of rewarding him with a significant political office. As noted in his denazification trial, "[T]he concerned party was presented for the first time here [in the autumn of 1930] with the notion of becoming governor (Oberpräsident) of the province of Hesse-Nassau, since it was of importance to Hitler to engage a man with the name and the reputation of the concerned party for National Socialism."[61] While this was far from a firm offer or commitment, one can understand how the idea of holding the highest office in his native province was alluring to the then underemployed prince in his early thirties. After the war, when called to summarize his career, Philipp wrote for the years 1931–33, "no occupation."[62] Yet he had been raised to believe it his role to play a representative function—to be visible and a figurehead. Hitler played on such ambitions. He also employed a good deal of flattery—noting how suitable and able the prince was. Siegfried Sassoon and others had noted Philipp's weakness for flattery. Hitler added a dose of "idealism" (serving the *Volk* and country), so that the prince might not feel too self-serving. In short, Philipp recognized that the best way for him to assume a leadership role was for the Nazis to come to power.

One question that arises concerns the degree to which Philipp's class-consciousness entered into his decision to support the Nazis. Hitler courted the nobility by sustaining their hopes of a Hohenzollern restoration. Historian Eric Strasser observed, "I have always been puzzled by the fact that in all the discussions on the adherence to Hitler of both Auwi and Philipp von Hessen barely any mention is made of the fact that there was a groundswell of support for a restoration of the Hohenzollern, especially amongst the right of the military. Hindenburg certainly supported the idea. There seems little doubt that Hitler initially indicated a willingness to consider such a move as a bulwark against communism."[63] In September 1932, Hitler told Fritz Thyssen and a number of other "gentlemen" whom the industrialist had invited to his home and that he was "a pacemaker to the monarchy."[64] A British diplomat reported a conversation with then vice-chancellor Franz von Papen in March 1933: "Herr von Papen could not say when the monarchy would be restored but that it would be restored he declared emphatically to be an absolute certainty. . . ."[65] On 9 May 1933, when Hitler traveled to Königsberg to meet with Hindenburg, the president "was anxious to go to his death with an assurance that there would be a restoration. Hitler let him know that he was in favor, but the time was not yet right. He pointed to possible objections from foreign governments."[66] Speculation at the time also raised the possibility that Crown Prince Wilhelm might become king (or as an intermediary step serve as a successor to

Hindenburg as president), or that a younger brother might step forward (the Crown Prince had signed a document on 28 November 1918 renouncing his claim to the throne).[67] The matter was even taken up as a topic of discussion in the cabinet in the spring of 1933.[68] Rumors were so rife that in September 1933, the U.S. ambassador William Dodd noted in his diary a conversation he had with his French counterpart, André François-Poncet, where the latter reported on President Hindenburg's plans to carry-through with a restoration:

> But it won't be a Hohenzollern. Nobody in that family is fit. The Crown Prince is idle and dissolute and has no will of his own, and the sons are not old or promising enough. Nor would Goebbels allow von Hindenburg's will to prevail. He wishes to put the Duke of Hesse on the throne and make himself the real master.[69]

While the idea of Goebbels backing a Hessen as monarch was fanciful, the passage speaks to the uncertainty about the subject that prevailed at the time.[70] Hitler vacillated and sent mixed messages during his quest for power in Germany. At times, such as the meeting with Hindenburg noted above, he would express interest in the idea, or some version of it: he told General Wilhelm von Dommes, an aide to the ex-Kaiser, in April 1934 that "if Germany were ever again to become a monarchy, then this . . . must have its roots in the nation—it must be born in the party, which is the nation." But he would just as quickly turn about face and note that "he had not made the November revolution [the overthrow of the Kaiser in 1918], but it had done one good thing in ridding Germany of the princes."[71]

After World War II, Prince Philipp maintained that he had never been interested in a restoration of the monarchy. He denied that he supported Hitler out of hope for "the restoration of the power of the princely houses" and claimed he was interested in solving the "formidable social problems."[72] Prince Philipp was always very circumspect about any pro-monarchic views that he had, and this was especially the case after World War II, when he was struggling to gain his release from American custody. His sincere views on the subject therefore remain elusive. It appears that Philipp was sympathetic to the idea of a restoration. He was, by his own admission, deeply tied to tradition, and this included a commitment to his class. Many members of his family also sought a revival of the monarchy: Wilhelm II's adjutant Ilsemann, for example, wrote of the Landgravine in the early 1920s, "[S]he wishes with all her heart for a return of the Kaiser to the throne."[73] In the late 1920s, Philipp made efforts to secure his relationship with his uncle: besides making him godfather of his son Heinrich, he paid more regular visits to Doorn.[74] Philipp then, like most members of the Hessen family, would have welcomed a restoration of his Uncle Wilhelm, but it was not a priority for him. He was more sincerely enthusiastic about National Socialism than monarchism. It seemed to matter little to Philipp in the spring of 1933 when Hitler gave a speech in which he "made a clear indication . . . that he was not going to bring back the Hohenzollerns."[75] Philipp continued to forge closer ties to the new regime.

Clearly, a Hohenzollern restoration was not part of Hitler's long-term plans. He and Göring effectively closed the door to a restoration in 1934; President Hindenburg's death in August made this easier to do. Yet even earlier, on the first anniversary of the seizure of power in January 1934, when the Reichstag passed legislation aimed at the reconstruction of the Reich, Hitler had made remarks disparaging the hereditary princes.[76] British ambassador Sir Eric Phipps reported in February 1934, "On 30 January General Göring, in his capacity as chief of the secret police [of Prussia], proposed to the Minister of the Interior that all monarchical associations should be dissolved, and on 2 February Dr. Frick requested the State governments to dissolve and forbid all such bodies immediately." The Nazis also sacked the head of the pro-monarchy Kyffhäuserbund (General von Horn), as well as certain Stahlhelm leaders, and replaced them with more pliable party members. Shortly thereafter, the Stahlhelm was subsumed by the SA. Sir Eric Phipps observed at the time the clear message sent by the fact that Göring, who had been so attached "to the pomp and circumstance of the past," had become "the principal agent of this destruction of monarchist hopes."[77] The Deputy Gauleiter of Berlin, Arthur Görlitzer, was also one of the subleaders who spoke out against the idea of a restoration in early 1934, noting, "We deprecate the action of the gentleman in Doorn in writing letters telling people to get busy and see to it that Germany again becomes really happy by a return to the monarchy. We will treat people who indulge in these activities exactly as we treat those who think they ought to do propaganda for Moscow. For they are even more dangerous than the latter, because they approach intellectual circles and so deprive us of the men we need to help us."[78] The word was out that those working toward a Hohenzollern restoration needed to be more circumspect.

Despite excluding the prospects of a return to the monarchy, and the persistence of a substratum of antiaristocratic sentiment among Nazi populists, Hitler found other ways to appeal to members of the nobility. Throughout the 1930s, he continued to meet regularly with the head of the DAG, Prince Adolf zu Bentheim-Tecklenburg (1889–1967), and the two developed a modus vivendi that entailed seemingly genuine mutual admiration. Prince zu Bentheim and the DAG had earlier implemented measures that excluded aristocrats with Jewish heritage; now they imposed a requirement that all members needed to provide extensive genealogical information dating back centuries. The DAG became so nazified the Kaiser reportedly told Baron von der Heydt in the Netherlands that "the *Adelsgenossenschaft* in calling for family trees back to some prehistoric date was perfectly monstrous, and naturally aroused intense annoyance."[79]

Hitler also exhibited sympathy for the high nobility's wish to revisit the provisions concerning family property that had been drafted during the Weimar Republic. The German dictator and his ministers rewarded supportive princes with legislation that improved their financial situation. There were too many cases of property disputes to go into detail here—especially because each family tended to have extremely complex circumstances—but the princes had begun to lobby Hitler about their economic situation in 1933. Prince Carl Eduard von Sachsen-Coburg und Gotha, for example, wrote "*Lieber Herr Hitler*" in November 1933 about the "extraordinary decline in German forestry" and other related economic problems.[80] Subsequently, the Reich Interior Ministry took the lead in formulating a response to the princes' demands: Reich Minister Frick ordered a careful study (*Denkschrift*) of the princely houses and their assets and the issue of the "legal disputes involving property between the provinces and the previously ruling princely houses."[81] The *Denkschrift*, which was ninety-seven pages long, covered the history of the disputes and laws passed during the Weimar Republic, provided an overview of the assets of each princely house, and then made a series of recommendations. The level of detail in the report was remarkable. It went castle by castle and also covered the status of archives, art collections, hunting rights, and special rights (the Grand Duke von Mecklenburg-Schwerin and his guests had the right to shoot red deer and black boar on certain ancestral lands). A law was finally enacted on 1 February 1939, but it did not affect the status of princely property in any significant way; it basically confirmed the status quo that enabled the princes to have family foundations and kept open the possibility that these foundations would evolve into hereditary holdings (akin to an *Erbhof* or hereditary farm that currently existed for smaller estates).[82] Amid the discussions that preceded the law, there had been calls from several Nazi leaders to divest the princes of some of their property. Reich Minister for Nutrition and Agriculture Darré penned a letter of protest to Lammers in the Reich Chancellery asking whether "the National Socialist state recognizes the misalliance between Adolf Hitler and the princely houses?"[83] The Gauleiter of Thuringia, Fritz Sauckel, also wrote to Hitler complaining about the proposed legislation; a telling response to Sauckel came from Reich Chancellery chief Hans Lammers, who wrote, "the Führer has made it known that a general replay of the conflict with the formerly ruling princely houses is not desired."[84] In other words, up through 1939, Hitler placated the princes. It was an arrangement comparable to the treatment of industrialists: in exchange for financial rewards, they abdicated power to the Nazis. It was not simply a case of the Nazis buying off the princes; there was a stick to go along with the proverbial carrot. Princes often feared the loss of property if they didn't cooperate. Prince Eitel Friedrich wrote his father, the Kaiser, in 1934 and suggested that the family might have to reckon with the expropriation of property if he and his brother Oskar did not sign the oath of loyalty to Hitler required of all Stahlhelm members.[85]

Despite his polite social relationships with various Nazi leaders, Philipp knew that they were violent and radical, and not just about rejuvenating the economy and bridging gaps between social classes. Among his sources of knowledge were his comrades in the Sturm Abteilung (SA). Philipp joined the Storm Troopers in the early 1930s, although there is considerable confusion about the date and manner in which he joined. He himself claimed that he was told at the end of 1932 that Hitler had awarded him an honorary rank (*Ehrenrang*) in the SA. It may well have been that Hitler was thinking strategically, and there were already high nobility in the SS, which ultimately included Hereditary Prince zu Waldeck und Pyrmont, Prince Wilhelm von Hessen, the Prince von Hannover, Prince Franz Josef von Hohenzollern-Emden, Hereditary Grand Duke Friedrich Franz von Mecklenburg, Prince Raphael von Thurn und Taxis (1906–93), Prince Ernst zur Lippe, Prince Stephen zu Schaumburg-Lippe, and Prince Alexander zu Dohna-Schlobitten.[86] Most likely, this was part of Hitler's divide-and-rule philosophy. Furthermore, the head of the SS Heinrich Himmler and the chief of the SA Ernst Röhm would each have wanted princes to command. Philipp's brother Christoph was to join the SS the following year, so the Hessen brothers would be divided between the two main Nazi paramilitary organizations. But there was also a symbolic reason for this appointment: Hitler wanted princes in the SA (Prince Friedrich Christian zu Schaumburg-Lippe, Prince Auwi, and Prince Wolrad zu Schaumburg-Lippe (1887–1962) were also Storm Troopers) to show how the new *Volksgemeinschaft* (people's community) would bring together individuals from all levels of society.[87]

Philipp, however, was not merely a symbolic passive actor in the SA. Regardless of the precise date and reasons for his joining the Brown Shirts, Philipp participated in SA marches in 1931 (that is, a year before the Ehrenrang was awarded), and he soon established regular contact with other comrades there. For example, he paraded with the Storm Troopers, every year at the Nuremberg Party rallies from 1933 until 1937 (and this information comes from a document written in November 1937, so he likely participated in the last rally in September 1938).[88] It is true that Philipp normally wore the notorious brown shirt only on ceremonial occasions.[89] But while he did not engage in street brawls with Communists, like many of his comrades, he participated in a great number of official functions. During one of them, the prince actually suffered an injury. Christoph's wife Sophia wrote Landgravine Margarethe in January 1934, "Philipp rang Chri up this morning, & is here with all the other Führers [for] the trooping of the Friedrichsrodd [a demonstration by SA units]. The doctor has insisted on keeping him here for a few days, as he has developed a blood poisoning of the hand, subsequent to having cut himself on the honorary dagger that Röhm presented to him."[90] One can imagine the prince carrying out the martial exercise with such vigor that he sliced himself on the sharp blade. While Philipp's position in the SA was an honorary one, it had propagandistic significance, both because the paramilitary organization was a bastion for committed Nazis and because it was associated with the idea of an egalitarian "people's community." These messages were underscored by his regular promotions through the ranks—in 1932, 1933, and 1937—the last time to general (Obergruppenführer), the "highest rank under the chief of staff of the SA."[91] This put him on a par with the likes of Gauleiters Fritz Sauckel, Adolf Wagner, and Joseph Bürckel; Munich mayor Karl Fiehler; and Prince Auwi.[92] This 1937 promotion, of course, came from Hitler personally.[93]

Philipp's brothers, Prince Wolfgang and Richard, also joined the SA. The former did so as a means of becoming a Nazi Party member after the rolls had officially been closed in mid-1933. Wolfgang had not joined the Nazi Party earlier, in the words of the local Gauleiter of Hessen-Nassau, Jakob Sprenger (1927–45), "since his training at the chamber of commerce in Frankfurt, as well as in Wiesbaden, is dominated by so many known Jews and Jewish-comrades."[94] In order to enter the SA, Wolfgang was compelled to undergo ideological training, which entailed attending evening meetings where he listened to speeches about National Socialism. He recalled that each meeting featured a rendition of the *Horst Wessel Song* (a sanguinary anti-Semitic party anthem) and that at the end, a member of the Hitler Youth would address the attendees with the refrain, "The small SA man in the lowest formation is a thousand times better than you."[95] The Brown Shirts, as suggested above, stressed the socialist elements of the Nazi Party program, and this often included strongly antiaristocratic sentiments. Wolfgang was forced to shout denouncements of the old order and to endure verbal attacks himself. He later described the training as deeply humiliating and unpleasant. Later, after the Röhm Purge, it came out there was a large dose of hypocrisy amid the SA leadership: despite their rhetoric, the top leaders lived extravagantly, treating themselves to lavish banquets with delicacies and fine wines.[96] In his memoirs, Wolfgang presented his experiences as a Storm Trooper as tiresome, adding that he never felt entirely comfortable in the paramilitary organization. But he did his duty and participated in "great marches" as well as soldierly training.[97] His recollections of his time as a Brown Shirt consisted of sanitized descriptions, with no mention of anti-Semitism, physical assaults, or the intimidation that was so closely associated with the paramilitary organization.

While Philipp was not rampaging through streets in his brown shirt intimidating people or leading a destructive pogrom, he was consorting with such people. There was no disguising the nature of the SA: the rank-and-file members took great pride in their prowess as street fighters. The SA was a bastion of radicalism. While the "Night of the Long Knives," or the purge of SA leader Ernst Röhm and many close associates, curtailed the power of the Brown Shirts and dispelled ideas of a second, or social revolution, the June 1934 purge obviously did not reduce the anti-Semitism, the Führer-worship, and the rabid nationalism that were so central to the organization. Philipp's SA membership was a complicated affair. At his denazification trial, he said that being made a member of the SA was "a matter that I cannot explain to myself"; but he added with some insight, "I later came to the view that it was Hitler's intention to bind me to the party, because my [commitment] was not completely secure."[98] Regardless, Philipp took his duties as a member of the SA seriously. When he was offered the post of Oberpräsident in late spring 1933, he sent a telegram to chief Ernst Röhm, where he wrote, "I ask most obediently if I might assume this post."[99] Later in the 1930s, when he received his Golden Party Badge (the highest honor in the Nazi Party), it was presented to him by Röhm's successor, SA Staff-Chief Viktor Lutze (1890–1943).[100]

Prince Philipp's membership in the SA raises the question of the degree to which he espoused anti-Semitic views. The most probable answer is that, like his brothers, he fell somewhere in the gray zone in this regard. They were by no means radical or vulgar anti-Semites: their longstanding relations with the Frankfurt-based Rothschild family and their friendships with a limited number of patrician Jews are suggestive in this regard. But anti-Semitism, which Stephan Malinowski describes as a "communicative bridge between the aristocracy and the new right," often lurked in the background in the thinking of the Hessens.[101] When Prince Friedrich Karl ordered his officers not to accept invitations from local patrician Jewish bankers, Arthur and Carl von Weinberg—ostensibly because the brothers gave lavish dinner parties and gifts (e.g., gold cigarette cases) that made it difficult or impossible for most officers to reciprocate—he was in part motivated by anti-Semitism.[102] The Hessens embraced, to use the phrase of historian Claudia Koonz in her recent study of the evolution of Nazi ideology, a kind of "*salonfähig* racism." This variation avoided many of the vulgar formulations of the "old fighters"; but, as Koonz noted, this "racism fed by *Judenforschung* [research into Jews] was both more persuasive to non-Nazis and ultimately more lethal because it mentally prepared desk murderers as well as perpetrators at killing sites to conduct thorough, rational 'cleansing' operations."[103]

While one must keep in mind that neither Philipp nor Christoph were active killers during the Holocaust, they were steeped in an anti-Semitic culture in the public and professional spheres, and, to a lesser extent, in their social and familial circles. Prince Philip, Duke of Edinburgh, acknowledged the existence of "inhibitions about the Jews " and "jealously of their success"—although he took care to stress that he "was never conscious of anybody in the family actually expressing anti-Semitic views."[104] In the case of the Hessens, there were instances when their genteel form of anti-Semitism gave way to more vulgar formulations. Philipp, in his capacity as Oberpräsident, signed reports to the Reich Minister of the Interior in 1934 where he remonstrated against the influence of Jews in cattle trading and committed himself to remedy the situation with "diligent work." This report, with its age-old myth about Jews and cattle-trading, was likely written by a subordinate and simply signed by the prince, but Philipp still associated himself with such anti-Semitic views. In a similar report from 1935, he noted "the general charge about the marked assertiveness of Jews in society"; here, he couched his phrasing in a formulation that attributed the sentiment to others.[105] The most explicitly anti-Semitic statement attributed to Philipp came in 1938: in connection with the Anschluss and a report that twenty-five thousand Viennese Jews had escaped across the border, Philipp reportedly said to Göring, "[W]e could leave the border open. . . . We could get rid of the entire scum like that." Göring, who initially considered it a good idea, "pulled up short with an afterthought, 'But not those with any foreign currency . . . the Jews can go but their money they will have to leave behind. It's stolen anyway. . . .'"[106] The Hessens, then, succumbed to many of the shibboleths propagated by the Nazis. Philipp and Christoph's uncle, Landgrave Alexander Friedrich von Hessen, for example, wrote to the conductor Hans Rosbaud in 1941: "But friend Roosewelt [sic], whom I could never stand (I wouldn't trust the fellow to let him out of my sight), is now of all things truly arrogant, conducting himself with his nose in the air, and with his Free Masons, Jews, and friends of Jews, he will make sure that the war is extended as long as possible."[107] Yet more often than not, the Hessens were guarded in their statements and continued to believe that there were acceptable Jews. They would have understood Göring's formulation, "I decide who is a Jew."

Prince Christoph moved toward the Nazis in much the same way as his older brother, with Hermann Göring playing the decisive role as representative of the movement. Christoph attended a gathering at the Görings's home after the opening of Reichstag on 13 October 1930—that is, about a month after Philipp's initial meeting.[108] Göring was then head of the Nazi Party's delegation in the Reichstag, and was soon to become president of the Reichstag as a result of the Nazis's plurality in the July 1932 elections. Göring would go on to hold a dizzying array of offices, including Minister

President of Prussia, Reich Minister for Aviation, head of the Four-Year Plan office, and Reich Hunting Master. Göring and Prince Christoph quickly took a liking to one another—although it is difficult to call their relationship a true friendship. There was an element of mutual exploitation; yet Göring always remained the patron and retained the upper hand in the relationship. Christoph did not initially join the party but held off for the first year. Finally, in October 1931, he took the step and filled out "the membership for entry into the party in the office of party member Hermann Göring in the Badenschen Strasse."[109]

Christoph joined the party with some trepidation. The reasons for his reluctance are not readily apparent. Perhaps he thought it might affect his business selling insurance. Perhaps he was simply less inclined to announce himself for a political party (there is no record of any previous party affiliation). Yet his caution was evident. Although Christoph lived in the Schöneberg quarter of Berlin, he joined a cell in another district. The head of the Spandauer Berg chapter of the Nazi Party, Julius Stilke, addressed an affidavit to Prince Christoph in 1937 where he stated, "in the winter of 1931 the District Leader of that time [Karl] Hanke communicated to me that you would register with me and that I should treat you as a secret party member."[110] The Nazis so wanted Prince Christoph's support that they were prepared to accept him on his terms as a clandestine member. They clearly would have preferred a public declaration, but they accepted this temporary arrangement and registered him in a district where it was easier to maintain secrecy. Spandauer Berg was a largely working class section of Berlin, a place where Christoph had few social contacts. This deceptive arrangement, however, was short-lived, and within a year, Christoph became a dues-paying member of the Sektion Luitpold in the heart of the city (as well as a member of the SS).[111] His situation was not so very different from that of Prince Friedrich Christian zu Schaumburg-Lippe, who began working for the Nazis a full year before his official entry in August 1929.[112] A reason for this kind of caution was related by Prince zu Waldeck, who recalled after the war that when he joined the SS in November 1929, he realized "that he would actually be regarded as a black sheep."[113] While circumstances changed in the subsequent years, there was still a stigma attached—certainly for members of the high aristocracy—and joining the Nazi Party before 1933 indicated a high degree of commitment.

The operation to bring Prince Christoph into the party was so cloaked in secrecy that his registration materials were lost, and this led to considerable confusion about Christoph's party membership. Karl Hanke, later a state secretary in Goebbels's Propaganda Ministry and then the Gauleiter of Upper Silesia, mistakenly sent the application to another district, and it was lost somewhere between the party offices in the central and western districts of Berlin.[114] Christoph filled out another application in the spring of 1933, and, in a sense, joined the party again. He received the membership card number 1,498,608 on 3 July 1933, but they backdated his entry to 1 March 1933.[115] The issue of his entry into the party surfaced again in 1936 because Christoph wanted the prestige accorded those who joined before the Nazi seizure of power. Göring assisted him by ordering State Secretary Pilli Körner to write Martin Bormann in the party headquarters in the Munich *Braune Haus*, requesting that Christoph "receive a lower party number."[116] Göring then wrote a letter for Christoph in January 1936 wherein he testified that Christoph, "has been actively involved in the party since October 1931" (the statement included a handwritten note— "Witness: the Führer").[117] Christoph's Nazi Party number was revised downward in 1937 by some 800,000 as he was given the number 696,176 (as compared to Philipp's 418,991).[118] This drastic revision in his membership number reflected Christoph's importance within the regime. As was appropriate for a party stalwart, his wife, Princess Sophia, joined the Nazis' women's auxiliary, the NS-Frauenschaft, in 1938.[119]

Christoph's commitment to the Nazis also found clear expression in the fact that he joined the SS prior to Hitler's coming to power. In other words, he was not merely an opportunistic "March violet." Christoph entered the SS in February 1932 (with an SS number 35,903), at a time when Hitler was running for president against the incumbent Paul von Hindenburg. To the surprise of many, the Nazi leader mounted a serious challenge. Christoph was duly enthused. He wrote to his mother on 24 April 1932, "We are all terribly excited about the elections. I do hope that they will bring the beginning of the change which we are all longing for so much."[120] While Hitler lost the election (19.36 million to 13.42 million), the Nazis were nonetheless on the rise and poised for their greatest electoral success prior to Hitler's appointment as chancellor: the July Reichstag elections gave them a plurality with 37.4 percent of the vote. Prince Christoph committed himself fully to the cause: On 30 May, Sophia wrote her mother-in-law, "Chri was away twice this week the whole day, but luckily not over night. He is very cheerful, thank goodness, but needs a thorough & complete rest & change badly."[121] The SS had been banned in Prussia by an emergency decree on 13 April, but that clearly had little effect on Christoph. The following month, on the day when Sophia turned eighteen years old, she again wrote the Landgravine, "I spent a very happy [birth] day on Sunday, although Chri was unexpectedly called away on duty this morning."[122] Upon joining the SS, Prince Christoph demonstrated a discipline and a commitment to a cause that was unprecedented in his life.

After the Nazis' seizure of power on 30 January 1933, Christoph's career began to take off, and he associated more frequently with other committed Nazis. He was promoted on 21 February to SS-Sergeant

(Haupttruppenführer) and then again on 30 March to SS-Lieutenant (Sturmführer). This coincided with the start of his tenure at the Prussian Ministry of State. In the interim, in late February, Prince Josias zu Waldeck had come to lunch and, according to Sophia, "had lots of interesting things to say."[123] Waldeck was already in the SS (he had joined in March 1930) and had risen quickly in the organization, serving as Himmler's chief of staff in 1931 and SS-General Sepp Dietrich's chief aide. Christoph and Sophia were now gaining access to those at the highest rank of the Nazi Party and SS, and this fueled their enthusiasm. In the same letter about Waldeck's visit, Sophia described a rally in the Lustgarten in central Berlin: "It was wonderful to see all the *Beamten* [civil servants] march with their flags; the '*Zoll*' [customs] men, the train men, bus men, etc. The policemen wore *Hakenkreuz* [swastika] bands on their arms and sang the *Horst Wessel Lied* as they marched! O glorious feeling. . . ."[124] Sophia's letters are filled with reports of her husband away all night on "marches" or other forms of duty. A typical report of the early years came on 22 January 1934, when Sophia wrote the Landgravine, "On Saturday I didn't see much of Chri, as he couldn't come back for lunch & only turned up late on account of Göring who had been on a round of inspections. At 8:30 [p.m.] he left again & marched all night returning at 2 o'clock in the morning, poor thing, rather stiff but otherwise very well!"[125] One of the reasons for these martial exercises was that in September 1933 Christoph had been given command of his own company, or *Sturm*, consisting of some 160 men. The prince had been raised with great admiration for the military but had missed the opportunity to serve: for members of the Hessen family, as for many princes, the Republican army was an anathema because they viewed the Weimar government as responsible for the overthrow of the monarchy, the Treaty of Versailles, and a host of other failings. The SS seemed to offer a comparable experience.

Of course, the SS was involved much more than marches in stylish uniforms and security for Hitler; it was, for an abundance of reasons, declared a criminal organization by the International Military Tribunal at Nuremberg. The question arises, could one be a member of the SS and not subscribe to racist, anti-Semitic ideas? The answer is most likely no— and Christoph would almost certainly have subscribed to an ideology focused on racism and conquest. His son, Rainer, finds it difficult to escape this conclusion, but he thinks Christoph's primary motivation, rather than hate and conquest, was a wish for what he understood (or misunderstood) to be law and order. Rainer also suggests that his father was naïve about the SS and viewed it as a kind of paramilitary organization, in the way that all big parties had similar entities (the Communists *Rote Front*, etc.). His father was protecting Nazi Party rallies (*Saalschutz*) in a climate of civil war.

Furthermore, when Christoph joined the SS it had not yet gained what he calls its "terrifying nimbus."[126] When the SS emerged from the shadow of the SA after the Röhm Purge, Christoph scaled back his involvement. He had grown tired of night marches and his position at the Forschungsamt (FA) required more time.

Evidence suggests that Christoph was attracted to the SS in large part for personal reasons and not just because he embraced an external political agenda. For someone who had not completed his Abitur nor finished his university studies, and who had not been given an opportunity to distinguish himself on the battlefield, the respect and responsibility that came with being an SS officer enhanced his feelings of self-worth. Speaking more generally, historian Bernd Wegner has noted the high incidence of SS men who "had proved to be lasting professional failures after 1918"—how many feared and perceived a "considerable loss of social prestige"—and how many "did not feel securely integrated into an appropriate social milieu defined by such things as profession family, religion, or lifestyles."[127] While not all these factors apply in Christoph's case (for example, he remained the favorite of his mother and had considerable support from other family members), Christoph's motivations for joining the SS were not first and foremost grounded in an ideology of hate. His extant letters (those up through 1933), contain no racist or anti-Semitic comments. In attempting to understand his initial gravitation to the SS, the personal rather than the political deserves greater emphasis.

Christoph was not the only one in the extended family to join the SS. His remote cousin, Prince Wilhelm von Hessen from the Philippsthal-Barchfeld branch of the family, joined both the Nazi Party and the SS (number 52,711) in April 1932, and served as a member of the SS-Standarte in Fulda-Werra.[128] Wilhelm and his wife, Marianne, born Princess von Preussen (1913–83), lived in a castle, Schloss Augustenau, in Herleshausen an der Werra.[129] This was the estate on which Wilhelm had been raised, and as the eldest son, he inherited it (the castle remains in the family to this day). Wilhelm described his profession as a "business manager" in forest and agricultural enterprises. He remained close to home, as he and his wife, Princess Marianne, raised their three children (born between 1933 and 1937). Indeed, his son explains that Prince Wilhelm's involvement in the SS was "purely regional"—although it is notable that his commanding officer in the Fulda-SS unit was his distant relation, Prince zu Waldeck.[130] Still, Prince Wilhelm von Hessen was far less committed to the SS than Waldeck. He later refused to join a Waffen-SS unit and instead followed "the old family tradition of service in the [regular] Army," which he joined as a reserve officer.[131] This evidently caused him some difficulty among his SS comrades, but he was able to deflect criticisms by pointing to long-standing Nazi Party membership and the importance of preserving tradition.

Despite their increasingly close ties to the Nazi leaders, the Hessens were not completely indoctrinated or fanatical believers. There was a certain emotional distance, a skepticism, a continuation of tradition, that shaped their thinking. Princess Sophia, for example, noted about her brother-in-law Philipp, "now and again we would make fun of the people in the party and their uniforms."[132] In a sense, there was a tension between their commitment to National Socialism and their traditional ways. Christoph retained his self-confident jocularity—a characteristic one normally does not associate with a Nazi. He was certainly not the dour aristocrat (and to complete the stereotype, the officer with monocle), that has sometimes been associated with the German elite.

Christoph and Sophia nonetheless threw their lot in with the Nazis and benefited in many ways as a result. Like his brother Philipp, Christoph's economic situation stabilized after the Nazi seizure of power. He gave up his work at the Viktoria Insurance firm in order to take a position in the regime. The couple, who had been living in the center of Berlin, moved to a new apartment in 1933, and then, in 1936 settled in Berlin Dahlem, a neighborhood of grand houses, where they constructed a beautiful red brick villa with spacious gardens at Auf dem Grat 8/10.[133] They remained in this home until September 1939, when Christoph went off to fight and Sophia took the children to Kronberg. Their Dahlem villa was sufficiently prepossessing that after the war it served as the residence of the British High Commissioner stationed in Berlin. In fact, it had been financed by the Kurhessische Hausstiftung when Christoph was granted credit on his future paternal inheritance. But it was the kind of dwelling one would expect from a prince with such close ties to the leaders at the apex of the Nazi regime.

Helping the Nazis to Power

As noted above, the princes of Hessen helped the Nazi cause in two general ways: by bolstering public support, and by helping them court other wealthy and influential elite. In both respects, they took their lead from their Hohenzollern cousins, Prince Auwi and his son Prince Alexander Ferdinand (1912–85). Prince Auwi, as noted earlier, was a highly visible figure and campaigned vigorously for the Nazis. He would join Hitler, Göring, Goebbels, and other leaders on stage (he was an official speaker or *Reichsredner*), and thus helped imbue them with certain respectability. It was also significant that Auwi's older brother, the Crown Prince Friedrich Wilhelm (known as Wilhelm), as of 1932 "clearly went all out for the NSDAP" and then, on 21 March 1933, joined his brother during the "Day at Potsdam," when the parliament opened for the first time after

Crown Prince Wilhelm von Preussen campaigning for Hitler in the presidential election of 1932.

the Reichstag fire.[134] The princes represented tradition and suggested a return to imperial greatness: in a deeply symbolic scene, with Auwi in an SA uniform and Wilhelm in Hussar's death's-head regalia, "Hindenburg walked past the crown prince and bowed, then pointed to the emperor's empty chair with his field marshal's baton."[135] In the Day at Potsdam, Hitler sought to link himself to the august Prussian tradition, and the Hohenzollern princes in attendance dutifully played their roles.[136] The Hessens, in turn, did their part, and this included flying the Nazi flag over their castles. As Princess Sophia noted in February 1933, "... when [Prince zu Waldeck] flew with Hitler in one of the election campaigns, they flew over Friedrichshof, and he says he saw the flag on the Burg!"[137] Prince Wolfgang acknowledged later, that the *Hakenkreuz* banner atop the castle "attracted great attention in Kronberg. It was regarded as a signal that our family had publicly embraced National Socialism."[138] Hitler and his cohorts realized the usefulness of Prince Auwi, the Hessens, and other nobles. Prince Philipp also eventually came to this realization, telling his American captors after the war that "he was prepared to believe that he himself was welcomed by the party leaders for a time as something of a façade for the movement."[139]

It is not clear exactly when Philipp and Christoph began helping the Nazi leaders with introductions. As noted earlier, Philipp reportedly helped Göring gain entrée to Mussolini in the mid-1920s while the latter was in Rome following the failed Beer Hall Putsch. Hitler had named Göring "Plenipotenziario" of the Nazi Party with the express function of raising money in Italy. Göring had approached aides to Mussolini and asked—some say "demanded"—2 million lire to help the fascist counterparts in Germany. According to reports, Philipp helped Göring briefly meet with *Il Duce*—a quick introduction but not long enough to count as an official audience.[140] Göring was appreciative of Philipp's efforts but still regarded the rejection by Mussolini as humiliating. While the specifics of this episode remain unclear, there were more reliable accounts by the early 1930s of Philipp helping make Hitler and his associates socially acceptable. Goebbels's diary entry noted at the beginning of this chapter, where he recounted the evening with the Hessens at the Dirksens in Berlin, was the first of many reports of their work together—efforts that often involved socializing. One week after the party at the Dirksens, Philipp joined Goebbels, his sister Maria, and Ritter von Epp on an excursion to the Nikolasee in the suburbs of Berlin—"*sehr nett!*" [very nice!] as Goebbels described it in his journal.[141] The propaganda minister also spent time with Philipp and Mafalda during a June 1933 trip to Rome. The prince helped arrange audiences for him with King Vittorio Emmanuele and Mussolini, and then worked to create a positive lasting impression. Toward the end of the visit Philipp told Goebbels "that the king and Mussolini were completely enthused about [him]." The propaganda minister appeared charmed; he added, "I spoke with Princess Mafalda. "*Liebes Ding!*" (dear thing!).[142] Two weeks later they reconnected back in Berlin. This time they met at Hitler's residence in the old Reich Chancellor's palace on the Wilhelmstrasse, the heart of the government quarter. Actress-filmmaker Leni Riefenstahl joined the group, and they socialized late into the night. Goebbels remarked tersely in his journal, "Very nice. Late to bed."[143]

Hitler and the other Nazi leaders were not always accepted with open arms by the traditional elite. Even though most party leaders were not the uncouth ruffians as some have sought to portray them, most were also not particularly polished or adept at navigating high society. That is why Göring, and to a lesser extent, Rudolf Hess and Joseph Goebbels, were especially important as liaisons with aristocrats. Berlin society correspondent Bella Fromm recorded one telling episode in her diary: dated 30 March 1933, she described an evening at the Palais of Prinz Friedrich Leopold von Preussen: "[Hitler] was no awe-inspiring personality. He gave no impression of dignity. He was indifferent to whom he talked or which group he joined. He was self-conscious and inferior in attitude. He did not know what to do with his hands. . . . Hitler's eagerness to obtain the good

Hitler and Göring amid Nazi high society in the late 1930s.

graces of the princes present was the subject of much comment. He bowed and clicked and all but knelt in his zeal to please oversized, ugly Princess Louise von Sachsen Meiningen, her brother, Hereditary Prince George, and their sister, Grand Duchess of Sachsen Weimar. . . . Prince Ratibor-Corvey . . . is one of the best paying members of the party. [His daughters,] the young princesses, reacted with a proper show of pleasure to his hand kissing and his piercing glance."[144] This passage suggests that social acceptance was a struggle for Hitler and most other Nazi leaders. While they were ultimately successful, the wooing of the old elite and the creation of a Nazi high society was a process that was at times arduous. Even Prince Philipp would occasionally put his Nazi patrons in their places socially: At one gala dinner at the Italian Embassy on 27 May 1933, when Göring was presented with an award—the Order of St. Mauritius—which was pinned to his "new snow-white uniform," Philipp commented to Bella Fromm, "[I]f this goes on, Goering will soon have to pin the medals to his rear."[145] Yet derogatory comments of this kind were uncommon for Philipp and Christoph, and the support for Nazi leaders exhibited by the Hessens and most other princes proved crucial to the transformation of German society during the Third Reich.

Hitler and the Nazi leaders sought acceptance from the traditional elite for a number of reasons. In broad terms, they possessed totalitarian aspirations and wanted to dominate all elements in society; their strategy, if only partly conscious, entailed infiltrating the upper strata. They also viewed high society in practical terms and conceived myriad ways in which the elites could help their cause. This included turning to members of the nobility as sources of information. Bella Fromm used the phrase "Nazi society spy" to describe Baroness Wally von Richthofen and maintained that she was, "another of these female informers. . . . She entertains on a lavish scale in her elegant Potsdam home, paid for by the Gestapo. 'She gets a high salary in return for her confidential information about the diplomatic corps,' said Austrian Minister Tauschitz."[146] Martha Dodd (1908– 90), daughter of U.S. Ambassador William Dodd (who was in Berlin from 1933 to 1937) was both a socialite and a spy (ultimately for the Soviets).[147] Prince Friedrich Franz von Mecklenburg, to take a later example, when stationed at the German Embassy in Copenhagen during the war, had an appointment within the SD (the Security Service).[148] One should not overestimate the importance of the cloak-and-dagger thinking among the Nazis in wooing nobles. A simpler, more common-sense explanation is that much of the previous political leadership came from this strata and that it retained too much power to be ignored. Finally, there were advantages in terms of foreign policy. The Nazi leaders recognized the international contacts of the traditional elite. They usually turned to German-born nobility to take advantage of their relationships, but on occasion, Hitler and other top Nazi leaders would meet in person with foreign aristocrats. The Mitford sisters (Unity and Diana) and Diana's husband, the British Union of Fascists leader Sir Oswald Mosley, for example, provided useful information and held some potential in terms of future geopolitical developments. Diana and Sir Oswald Mosley were married in a clandestine ceremony at Goebbels's ministerial residence in Berlin in October 1936; Hitler was present as a guest, and during the luncheon that followed at the Goebbels's villa on Lake Wannsee, Diana provided "a blow-by-blow account of a scandal still known to a small circle: the new King of England was obsessively in love with an American Wallis Simpson, who was about to divorce her second husband."[149] At another meeting, a luncheon at Hitler's apartment on the Prinzregentenstrasse in Munich where among other guests he invited the Mosleys, English-born Winifred Wagner (daughter-in-law of the composer), and the Duchess von Braunschweig (the Kaiser's only daughter), Hitler and Sir Oswald "outlined an agreement" for the peaceful cohabitation between Germany and Britain.[150]

Prince Philipp was in Berlin when the Nazis came to power on 30 January 1933, although he played no significant role in Hitler's appointment. The same cannot be said for a number of aristocrats. President von Hindenburg's son, Oskar von Hindenburg, entered into the picture, meeting with Hitler on 22 January at Ribbentrop's Berlin-Dahlem residence. As

Henry Ashby Turner noted, "What passed between Hitler and Oskar von Hindenburg on the evening of January 22 has long been the subject of speculation. It has often been suggested that Hitler threatened to blackmail the younger Hindenburg or his father unless he was named chancellor."[151] The speculation about blackmail centers on a state subsidy to the Hindenburgs that enabled them to purchase their estate, and the fact that the estate was put in the son's name, a measure clearly intended to evade the payment of death duties. While Turner appears correct in dismissing the theory of blackmail, noting that "Hitler would have realized that such crude methods might well backfire in the case of the Hindenburgs, with their aristocratic hypersensitivity to questions of honor," it is not implausible that the Nazi leader gave unspecified assurances about the family's future.[152] At the same time Hitler was negotiating with the Hindenburgs, Göring contacted Otto Meissner, the president's chief of staff, and "gave Meissner to understand that a Hitler cabinet would eventually move to restore the monarchy, an obvious attempt to curry favor with Hindenburg, who made no secret of remaining a convinced monarchist even while serving as republican head of state."[153] The aged president was surrounded by a group of mostly noble advisors—many of whom belonged to the exclusive, hundred-year-old *Herrenklub* (Gentlemen's Club), a venue for political speeches and networking. Many such individuals had access to Hindenburg and encouraged him to appoint Hitler as chancellor—even if they naively believed that the Nazi leader could be controlled. Historian Gerhard Weinberg observed that after the Nazis' setback in the November 1932 election, when they suffered a four percentage-point drop from the July 1932 poll and were losing momentum, Hitler "was again rescued, this time by a small coterie around President von Hindenburg.[154]

It is not clear whether Prince Philipp was actively lobbying those around Hindenburg during the critical period prior to Hitler's appointment as chancellor on 30 January 1933, but he was certainly present in Berlin, in regular contact with Nazi leaders and lending moral support. Goebbels thought enough to comment in his journal on 5 February 1933, "briefly spoke with Philipp v. Hessen. . . . [he] is beside himself with joy."[155] Later in the month, on 27 February, the night when the Reichstag burned, Putzi Hanfstaengl recalled that he, Prince Philipp, and Prince Auwi were all staying with Göring in the palace of the Reichstag president.[156] They all raced over to see the parliament engulfed in flames and watch as Hitler fulminated against the Communists and other enemies of the Reich.[157] Philipp's proximity to the Nazi leaders during the dramatic events of the seizure of power helped forge tighter bonds. His relationship with Göring, in particular, developed during this period. In April 1933, for example, they traveled to Rome: they visited museums, met with Mussolini, and had an audience with King Vittorio Emmanuele.[158] In the first half of 1933,

Philipp became part of Göring's entourage. The Prussian minister president used him as part of the spectacle he created. While Goebbels preferred to consort with actors and cultural figures, Göring chose to exhibit his social connections (while feeding his own ego). But in the theater politics of the Third Reich, the princes were mesmerizing actors, and no other Nazi leader could assemble such a dazzling cast.

Hermann Göring arrived at an idea that would make even greater use of the support offered by the Princes of Hessen. Prince Christoph, as will be discussed in greater detail shortly, went to work for Göring in the Prussian state ministry right after the seizure of power. Prince Wolfgang was engaged as county commissioner for the area around Bad Homburg, one of the wealthiest areas in all of Germany that has long been favored by Frankfurt's business elite. Wolfgang was part of the administration of the Prussian ministry of the interior—that is, a local official, but one that had considerable authority. Although much of his work focused on the county's budget (especially debt management), he was also responsible for a range of issues concerning housing, taxation, and civic affairs.[159] Prince Richard also found a place in the Nazi state, although not specifically within Göring's bailiwick. Richard, who joined the Nazi Party and the SA in 1932, was enthusiastic about organizational matters involving the party, and spent the summer of 1933, for example, working to help stage the party rally at Nuremberg.[160] An expert on roadways and traffic issues, Prince Richard played a role in the construction of the German *Autobahnen* and became a general in the National Socialist Drivers' Corps (Nationalsozialistische Kraftfahrer Korps), where he headed the Motor Group Hessen. The NSKK was established as a special unit of the SA on Hitler's birthday in 1931 (20 April); its aim was to put private automobiles at the disposal of the party in order to transport members and to provide a courier service. "The creation of the NSKK was initially prompted by electioneering and propaganda considerations, which later were superceded by military goals."[161] Göring, however, had much grander plans for Philipp.

Toward the end of March, Göring called Philipp and asked if he would become the Oberpräsident (governor) of the province of Hesse-Nassau. Göring evidently had previously offered the position to Prince Auwi as well as similar posts in Hanover, Brandenburg, and East Prussia, but the Hohenzollern prince had turned him down.[162] After the war, Philipp claimed that "I immediately declined the offer, since I had no ambitions in this direction and not the slightest trace of desire to leave my home in Rome, in which I led an extraordinarily happy life with my family."[163] While this statement should be interpreted as a postwar attempt to minimize his responsibility for events during the Third Reich, it is accurate in so far as Göring approached him and offered him the post. Göring then called him to a second audience in the middle of April and reiterated the request—this time, in Philipp's words, "he asked in a very pressing way."[164] Göring also explained that he was in a difficult position: that the two main Gauleiters in the region, Jakob Sprenger and Karl Weinrich (1887–1973), aspired to the same position and neither of them was suitable. Göring said he wanted "a personality that did not hold a party office, knew the province well, and offered him a guarantee that the office would be administered according to a purely state [-oriented] point of view."[165] Philipp claimed that he turned him down again—saying that his position had not changed—that his "freedom was too valuable to trade for a high position in the state."[166] Mafalda was also opposed to him accepting the appointment—primarily because she did not wish to live in Germany. Göring became agitated and upon Philipp's departure said that he did not consider the answer final and asked the Prince to think it over some more. Philipp discussed the matter with his family: "I also spoke with my father and he said to me, 'I understand your views, but if you think that you could do it, it might be in the best interest of your homeland (*Heimat*). You could do a lot of good and avoid a lot of unhappiness, in case the unforeseen comes about.' "[167]

Philipp met with Göring a few days later for a third discussion about the governorship, and this time the Prussian minister president had changed his tactics: "He appealed to my sense of duty with regards to the people (*dem Volke*).[168] Göring added, "the German *Volk* has decided for Hitler with an overwhelming majority; an appointment from him is just like an appointment that would come from the people."[169] Philipp added, "he knew of my love for the *Heimat* from which I come and wanted to give me the singular opportunity to be engaged for their benefit. At my disposal would be a staff of the best experts who would advise me and work with me, so that I would quickly adjust to my new obligations and tasks. Should some kind of difficulties develop with the Gauleiters, I could be assured of his fullest support. However, I had to decide immediately, since he wanted to report to Hitler on the same day."[170] Philipp concluded, "with a heavy heart I decided to sacrifice my freedom for my *Heimat* and agreed."[171] This version of events, of course, raises issues concerning sources. Or more specifically, how accurate was Prince Philipp's account during his denazification trial? The answer varies from episode to episode and subject to subject. In this case, the general outlines ring true: Göring recruited Philipp, and more radical elements in the party had designs on the post (there were even some protests about Philipp's appointment from within the SA).[172] But the thoughts ascribed and the wording comprised part of the prince's postwar legal defense strategy.

Prince Philipp, who like his brothers had no legal training or experience with public administration, formally assumed the position as Oberpräsident on 15 June 1933.[173] He displaced the incumbent, a conservative named Dr. Ernst von Hülsen, but there was considerable continuity at the

Oberpräsidium: the vice-president Kurt Jerschke (1872–1948), who had been a Landrat there for thirteen years, stayed on until he retired in 1937, and he was succeeded by Dr. Ernst Beckmann (1893–1957), a professional civil servant but also a Nazi Party member since 1933.[174] Indeed, the vice-president did much, if not most, of the work of the Oberpräsident. Philipp had a representative function, as well as considerable authority, but the local Gauleiter, although a strictly party position, possessed more power.[175] Philipp was also appointed to the Prussian Staatsrat—a body that advised Prussian Minister President Göring and included industrialist Fritz Thyssen, Field Marshal von Mackensen, Admiral of the Fleet Erich Raeder, and later Albert Speer.[176] This council met so infrequently—approximately three times in 1934 and then less often in subsequent years—that Philipp had difficulty remembering it during postwar interrogations.[177] Yet early on, the council put him in proximity to a number of influential individuals and made him feel part of the elite governing strata. Among the topics the council discussed were corporatism, legal reforms, and the National Socialists' vision of the future.[178] Another position held by Philipp was that of Reichstag deputy. Philipp, like his distant relation Prince zu Waldeck, was a deputy in the rubber-stamp parliament that had been created by the 23 March 1933 Enabling Act.[179] While Philipp's influence in the Reichstag was minimal, the fact remains that he was the "highest ranking administrative official in the province."[180] As the chief of staff of Italian Foreign Minister Ciano noted after visiting Philipp in Kassel for several days in 1936, "The prince, blond and in a brown uniform with a swastika band around the arm, sauntered through the city like a landlord (*Hausherr*) who had just come back into money."[181]

After the war, Philipp noted that his was a "state office and not a party office"; however, because of the origins of his appointment, it would be more appropriate to categorize it somewhere in the middle.[182] The ambiguity is suggested by the address of his office in Kassel: the Oberpräsident's headquarters were at Adolf Hitler Platz Nr. 6—although this matter was clearly beyond Philipp's control and is more symbolic than anything else (nearly every German city had a Hitler Platz).[183] Perhaps the act that most symbolized the National Socialist characteristics that were part of the office was the manner in which Philipp marked the advent of his governorship. On 7 June 1933, a grand ceremony took place at the Red Palace on the Friedrichsplatz in Kassel, where he was sworn in by Göring personally.[184] The event was accompanied by a celebration in memory of heroes (*Heldengedenkfeier*). Philipp and Göring then made a "propagandistic trip through Hessen" together in an open car—in the view of some, "so that [Philipp] could publicly register his close connection to National Socialism."[185] The two men drove from Kassel to Frankfurt as crowds cheered them. The inauguration culminated when they arrived at the famous

Prince Philipp and Princess Mafalda at his swearing in as Oberpräsident in Kassel in June 1934.

central square in Frankfurt—"*im Römer*"—the historic city hall where the Holy Roman Emperors had traditionally been selected. It was a scene similar to the Day at Potsdam: a synthesis of feudal and National Socialist images. But the latter was clearly predominant. As one observer later noted, "Prince Philipp von Hessen was undoubtedly an active member during the founding years of the party, and he undoubtedly owed his position as Oberpräsident to his active membership in the party."[186]

Hermann Göring also took care of Prince Christoph, appointing him first secretary (Oberregierungsrat) in the Prussian state ministry in May 1933. This very general title obscured his true activities. His son, Rainer von Hessen, believes that it hinted to the start of his work for Göring's Forschungsamt. Among Göring's positions at this time were the posts of Prussian minister of the interior and the chief of the police. Historian Robert Wistrich has noted, "as the creator of the Gestapo (with Rudolf Diels), Göring together with Himmler and Heydrich set up the first concentration camps for political opponents, showing formidable energy in terrorizing and crushing resistance."[187] Göring sought to create his own police and intelligence network, and Christoph played an important role in this clandestine project. As a member of the SS, Prince Christoph duly requested and received Himmler's permission—granted personally by the Reichsführer-SS (as evidenced by his initials, the double "HH" on the notice)—to work in the Prussian state ministry for the interior.[188] Yet the FA was so secret that in the summer of 1933, when Reinhard Heydrich, then working for the Munich police, started to implement an order from Himmler to create a technical office that would monitor communications for the entire Reich, he was shocked to find out that such an office already existed.[189] Heydrich and Himmler were among the very few who knew of the FA's existence, and they worked hard to bring it under their control.

At the beginning of his tenure in the Prussian state ministry, Christoph worked as the personal aide (*persönlicher Referent*) for one of Göring's state secretaries, Pilli Körner (1893–1957). The latter had began his career in the Third Reich in the Prussian justice department—a position where he had influence over the Gestapo and other police agencies. Previously, Körner had served as Göring's chauffeur and driven him about in an ostentatious Mercedes. The two had grown close—for example, Körner had driven Göring to the funeral of Carin Göring in Sweden in October 1931. Körner parlayed this friendship into considerable influence. In April 1933, Körner assumed the position of Göring's personal aide and became the first supervisor of the Forschungsamt.[190] Later, he assumed a top position in the Four-Year Plan office that oversaw economic policy making, and in 1939, became Göring's personal secretary.[191] Throughout the Third Reich, Pilli Körner would be supportive of Christoph, as well as a friend of Philipp. In the case of Christoph, there was a strict hierarchy: Christoph worked for Körner, and Körner reported directly to Göring. But Christoph and Körner, like Philipp and Wolfgang, were all devoted members of Göring's administration. After the war, Körner told Nuremberg prosecutor Robert Kempner, "I would not say anything bad about Göring."[192]

After two years of quiet work with Pilli Körner under the guise of a staffer in the Prussian state ministry, Christoph moved into a more important position when Göring offered him an opportunity to serve as the chief of the Forschungsamt (provisionally, or "*kommissarische*" at first). The circumstances surrounding the appointment remain mysterious—why choose a prince, a dilettante when it came to intelligence matters and someone who did not have a university degree, to head this very technical intelligence operation? Indeed, by the highly regularized practices of the German civil service, it was nothing short of astonishing that an individual without a university degree would rise to the post of *Ministerialdirektor*. Even the manner in which the position opened up has given rise to rumor.

Reception in Berlin. From right: *Göring, Pilli Körner, Prince Philipp von Hessen, and unidentified man in February 1936.*

While Körner initially oversaw the budget and staffing, the more direct supervisor and the actual head of the Forschungsamt had been Hans Schimpf, who was a long-time acquaintance of Göring's and had previously been a naval cryptological liaison to the Abwehr (then the central agency for all German intelligence).[193] On 10 April 1935, Schimpf shot one of his mistresses and then apparently took his own life in Breslau. Yet there were also reports that he was killed by a Czech agent. At the time, his death was presented as a "motor accident." The circumstances surrounding his death have never been conclusively resolved.[194]

The most likely scenario is that Hans Schimpf was murdered by Himmler and Heydrich. Even though Himmler (and therefore Heydrich) succeeded in wresting the Prussian Gestapo from Göring in April 1934 and then creating the first unified national police agency in July 1936, the FA remained outside its orbit. Göring eventually lost the FA to Himmler and the SS, but only in March 1945.[195] Heydrich had approached Hans Schimpf in 1933 and asked him to work for him and Himmler—without Göring's knowledge.[196] Schimpf had rebuffed this overture, "but it was not," in the words of author Günther Gellermann, "the last attempt of the high ranking SS leader to get his hands on the Forschungsamt."[197] Heydrich evidently tried to blackmail Schimpf and make use of his extramarital affairs: the FA chief had no desire to divorce his wife, and this made him especially vulnerable. The appearance of Schimpf and a mistress dead in a Breslau hotel room remains what the Germans call a *Krimi* (murder mystery), with the English connotations of the word quite appropriate, as it is likely that his demise involved foul play.

The alacrity in which Göring replaced Schimpf with Prince Christoph is itself quite striking: Christoph's appointment as office chief (*Amtsleiter*) occurred the day after the bodies were discovered (11 April 1935). Göring derived numerous benefits from the appointment: Christoph already knew the ropes at the FA and would not have to be trained. Christoph was a member of the SS and, as of 1934, was a member of the personal staff of Reichsführer-SS Himmler. The appointment, therefore, could be construed as a conciliatory gesture on Göring's part (this, at a time when he was forced to give up oversight of other police agencies, including the secret police or *Geheime Polizei* in Prussia). Göring also believed that he could rely on Prince Christoph's personal loyalty—just as he could Prince Philipp's. Furthermore, Christoph did not have boundless personal ambition that would cause difficulties for Göring: among other indications, the appointment coincided with the high point of his equestrian ambitions, and he strove to preserve time for his riding. Indeed, correspondence within the family suggests that he had some misgivings about taking on the new assignment: on 12 April 1935, Sophia wrote Christoph's mother, "he had lunch with Göring & they have talked it all over. But one awful fact is that Chri can't possibly leave now that he has just been named, so all our pleasant plans turn into nothing."[198] Christoph, then, was something of a reluctant figurehead at the FA: with his limited political experience and technical knowledge, he relied on professionals—most notably, Gottfried Schapper, who had been one of the founders of the FA and then succeeded Christoph as the agency's manager.[199]

Christoph, Philipp, and Wolfgang all assumed their first posts in the Nazi state as a result of Göring's patronage. The concerted efforts of the future Reichsmarschall raise the question posed by the chair of Philipp's denazification trial: with so many "senior experienced experts" who could have done the job as Oberpräsident, why did Göring want Philipp? Or, for the Forschungsamt, why Christoph? (Wolfgang, with his background in banking, as a county commissioner is more comprehensible.) The answer is that Göring appreciated their social connections, and they had useful skills—linguistic abilities and considerable intelligence. He certainly realized that princes could be politically useful. And, they would be beholden to him personally. Rainer von Hessen believes that his parents had a relationship based on dependency and that Göring "liked to show who was the boss."[200] Regardless, the Hessens joined him in an array of undertakings. For example, Philipp and Christoph, at ages thirty-nine and thirty-four respectively, became reserve officers in the Luftwaffe in 1935—the year

that an air force with explicit military purposes was created (in contraven-
tion of the Treaty of Versailles). Philipp even wore the uniform of a
Luftwaffe officer at the funeral of his father in 1940. While Philipp actually
never served in the Luftwaffe and did little more than show himself in a
flashy uniform, Christoph entered in September 1935 as an "officer candidate" of the reserve. He finished his basic training in October 1935 as a
noncommissioned officer and took part annually in reserve exercises, until
promoted to lieutenant in 1939. The choice to wear a Luftwaffe uniform
reflected the brothers' loyalty to Göring, although Christoph also saw an
opportunity to fulfill his longstanding ambition of military service.[201]

The bonds that initially tied Göring and the princes together did not
endure throughout the Third Reich. Christoph became increasingly
critical of his chief—although cordial social visits continued even after
relations had frayed. Philipp and Göring's friendship suffered even greater
strains. Philipp's lawyer maintained after the war, "the initially completely
friendly relationship . . . cooled because of a growing mistrust."[202] Still,
Philipp and Göring were on good terms until about 1939. The foreign
minister until 1938, Baron Constantin von Neurath (1873–1956), noted
for example, "that Philipp stayed in Göring's house whenever he was in
Berlin."[203] While it is doubtful that Philipp stayed *chez* Göring on every
visit, the notion of them breakfasting together or staying up late with
snifters of brandy and discussing current events presents a striking image.
Equally extraordinary is that Prince Christoph and Princess Sophia were at
the head table at Göring's wedding with the actress Emmy Sonnemann
(1893–1973) in April 1935—with Sophia seated in a place of honor within
arm's length of Hitler (the witness) as well as the bridal couple. Among the
298 guests were Prince Auwi, the Duke von Sachsen-Coburg-und-Gotha,
the Prince and Princess zu Wied, Gustaf Gründgens, Reinhard Heydrich,
and Martin Bormann.[204] Later, just after the 1936 Olympics had concluded, Philipp, Mafalda, and their children were invited to Carinhall.
Mafalda warned the children about the lions, which the Görings kept as
pets: "during the last visit, one of the cubs leapt on me and tore the sleeve
on my leopard-skin coat."[205] Hermann and Emmy Göring periodically
invited the Hessens to the Opera—such as on 11 January 1936, when the
two couples, glittering with medals and jewels, sat in what had once been
the royal box. The Görings evidently derived great pleasure from consorting with the Hessens: as Emmy Göring noted in her postwar memoirs,
Prince Philipp, Prince Christoph, and Princess Sophia were "three people
whom Hermann especially cherished."[206]

The second man of the Reich clearly enjoyed consorting with princes: he
had planned to represent Germany at the coronation of King George VI in
May 1937 and had been invited to stay at Londonderry House, the opulent
home of the seventh Marquis of Londonderry (the former secretary of state

The wedding of Hermann and Emmy Göring in April 1935. On the far side *of the table: Hitler, Emmy Göring, and Hermann Göring; on the* near side *is Princess Sophia and General Field Marshall August von Mackensen.*

for air who had been a guest of Göring in both 1936 and 1937).[207] But as the event approached, plans went astray. The British ambassador Sir Eric Phipps noted that he "received a telegram reporting a meeting in England of 3,000 people under the chairmanship of 'a Quaker and Liberal Member of Parliament,' at which an insulting resolution against himself had been passed." Phipps and his wife, who discussed the matter with the Görings in their box at a gala ball, noted how peeved and disappointed he was: "General Goering greeted me coldly, and did not thank me for coming to his expensive ball or for our visit."[208] The Germans, after receiving feedback from the British, ended up sending as official representatives Foreign Minister von Neurath and Reich Minister for War, Field Marshal von Blomberg.[209] Among the German high nobility in attendance were several members of the Hesse-Darmstadt family, including Grand Duke Ernst Ludwig, his son Prince Georg Donatus, and the latter's wife, Princess Cécile.

Prince Philipp and Göring often traveled with one another, experiences that had implications for the prince's future role in the Reich's foreign affairs. He accompanied Göring on a tour of the Balkans in 1934, a trip that took them to Belgrade, where they visited Philipp's cousin, Yugoslav

Regent Prince Paul, and to Athens, where they met with the Greek leaders, including Prime Minister Eleftherios Venizélos (1864–1936). This likely presented difficulties for Philipp: Venizélos was an ardent critic of the monarchy and had helped lead the ouster and exile of Philipp's relatives, his aunt Sophie (born Princess von Preussen (1870–1932) and her husband King Constantine I (1868–1923). The main purpose of the trip, however, was for Göring to become acquainted with Balkans leaders. Göring, however, sought special responsibility among Nazi leaders for the region, and this was part of his effort to establish credibility. Göring appeared more interested in wrapping up the official business quickly and heading to the Greek Islands. One reason for the 1934 trip, after all, was to celebrate his engagement to Emmy Sonnemann.[210] Göring, Philipp, and the entourage therefore devoted much of the trip to leisure: they visited the classical sites at Mycenae and old Corinth, and then toured several islands on a yacht.[211] The following year, in late spring 1935 (six weeks after his marriage), Göring organized his "honeymoon" trip, where he and Emmy were joined by Philipp and others in the entourage. This excursion went through Bulgaria, where they met with the new monarch Boris III (Philipp's brother-in-law), to Belgrade (Philipp brought "two beautiful Augsburg silver *cache pots*" to Paul as presents from Hitler), and then to Poland and Hungary.[212] Philipp was then sent on to Athens, where he participated in ceremonies relating to the restoration of the Greek monarchy: Venizélos had been ousted by General Kondylis, and after a referendum, King George II (1890–1947) was restored to the throne (he ruled until 1947).[213] The trips that Philipp took with Göring were part business and part pleasure, but they helped cement their bond and made Philipp feel as though he was playing a meaningful role in world affairs.

Philipp recognized Göring's patronage with his own acts of generosity. One of Philipp's secretaries at the Oberpräsidium testified, "the files labeled '*Staatsrat*' were completely empty. The only thing I can remember is a communication about the withdrawal of funds for the birthday present of Reichsmarschall Göring."[214] The Görings visited the Hessens' home on Capri during a 1937 trip—dining together, along with Italian Crown Prince Umberto—as they ate alfresco on rocky cliffs overlooking the sea. The private correspondence of Philipp and Christoph with Göring evidently did not survive the war, but both brothers enjoyed a personal relationship with the Nazi leader. The American intelligence service in 1945 also believed that there were business connections between the Hessens and the Reichsmarschall, and reported huge land purchases in conquered Poland as an example.[215] One of the briefing documents used by his American interrogators in 1945, for example, stated, "What were the circumstances of Hesse's acquisition of estates in Poland and other occupied territories? Who was instrumental in making possible such acquisitions?" The

Lunch alfresco in Capri, January 1937. Prince Philipp and Emmy Göring (with backs to viewer), *Hermann Göring, and Italian Crown Prince Umberto.*

summaries of these interrogations make no mention of Philipp's answers to these questions and the allegations remain unproved.[216] The ostensible benefits accrued by Philipp and Christoph in return for their loyalty to Göring did not come primarily in material form but by way of their official positions and their access to the corridors of power.

4

A Place in the Reich:
Princely Careers in the Nazi State

As the experiences of Philipp and Christoph attest, the years 1933 to 1937 marked the pinnacle of the Nazi-princely alliance. After that, Hitler and most of his top leaders exhibited a radicalism—as well as a megalomania—that fostered an antiaristocratic outlook. Yet during the years after the Nazis' seizure of power, there were numerous princes, and even more aristocrats, who supported Hitler. The traditional elite remained powerful in certain spheres: in the armed forces, for example, 21.9 percent of the officers were members of the nobility in 1935 (although the figure declined during the military buildup prior to World War II and then during the war due to losses).[1] The persistence of the old elite in the military can be seen in the list of attendees when Hitler addressed the heads of the *Reichswehr* (armed forces) on 3 February 1933. Among the Reich Chancellor's audience were five barons, including Baron Kurt von Hammerstein (chief of the army staff) and Baron Hans von Seutter von Lötzen (general of a Gruppenkommando in Kassel).[2] Three years later, with Berlin in its most festive mode for the 1936 Olympic games, future Foreign Minister Joachim von Ribbentrop hosted a gala at his Dahlem villa. The guest list included the Prince and Princess von Hessen and various Princes von Preussen, but also Himmler and Heydrich, among other Nazi leaders.[3] The Germans were flush with ever-increasing confidence (and winning the most medals at the Berlin games didn't hurt), and the old and new elite mingled solicitously. That Prince Georg Donatus von Hessen-Darmstadt and his wife Cécile took the fateful step and decided to join the Nazi Party in May 1937 was yet another sign that the Nazi leaders continued to court members of the high aristocracy right up into the war.

Elsewhere in the burgeoning Nazi state apparatus, other princes also found their patrons. Even Joseph Goebbels, long identified with the so-called left-wing of the Nazi Party (the more socialistic faction led by the Strasser brothers) engaged Prince Friedrich Christian zu Schaumburg-Lippe (1906–83) in the newly created Reich Ministry for People's Enlightenment and Propaganda. As of April 1933, the prince was an upper privy councilor and the Reich Minister's adjutant.[4] In May 1933, the prince arranged for Goebbels's involvement in the book burning in the main square of the Berlin University on Unter den Linden. Goebbels delivered his infamous "Fire Speech" (*Feuerrede*), as books written by Jews, Marxists, and other declared enemies were committed to the pyre by zealous students and members of the SA.[5] Schaumburg-Lippe also associated himself with the left wing of the Nazi Party and stressed the socialist element in the Nazi ideology in his speeches and writings.[6] Somewhat ironically, Schaumburg-Lippe, by his own admission, came from one of the wealthiest princely houses in Germany: he himself lived in a villa on the Rhine near Bonn where he employed several servants.[7] To take another example, Carl Eduard von Sachsen-Coburg und Gotha, who had no specific patron, was also among the wealthiest aristocrats in Germany. A grandchild of Queen Victoria, he was educated in both England and Germany—at Eton College and then the Lichterfelde Cadet Academy (he was older than the Princes of Hessen and so did not overlap).[8] A prominent leader of the DNVP and a supporter of the Harzburg Front as of 1931, he joined the Nazi Party in May 1933, around the same time he was appointed to the post of Reich Delegate for German Automobile Affairs. Duke Carl Eduard became a member of the Reichstag and held the rank of a general in both the SA and the NSKK. As of 1934, he was also president of the German Red Cross. Sent by Hitler to England in 1936 to meet with the new King Edward VIII, he attempted to foster better Anglo-German relations. He was received at the Court of St. James and at Buckingham Palace.[9] Even after the king's abdication, Carl Eduard remained in the UK and sent Hitler regular reports. In March 1940, he made a high profile visit to the United States: the president of the German Red Cross elicited protests in Chicago and Washington, with his propagandistic utterances only fanning the flames (he was quoted in the *Chicago Daily Times* as saying, "most of the evacuated Poles are being taken care of adequately and given a chance to start small farms or return to their old occupations in territory surrounding Warsaw").[10] Such missteps were reminiscent of his attending the 1936 funeral of King George V in, what Diana Mosley described, as "a Nazi uniform."[11]

There were, of course, tensions between the old and new guard. Prince Philipp experienced them as Oberpräsident of the province of Hesse-Nassau as he frequently clashed with the local Gauleiter. In the mid-1930s Prince Philipp became increasingly frustrated by the competitiveness of the Nazi bureaucracy and spent more time in Rome with Mafalda at the Villa Polissena. His presence in Rome created new career opportunities as he became involved in diplomatic approaches to Fascist leaders, and then later, helped Hitler acquire artworks for the Führermuseum. Philipp reached the apogee of his political influence in the late 1930s, although his relationship with Hitler flourished well into the war before foundering. Like his brother, Prince Christoph was dispirited by the internecine battles in the Nazi government—especially the rivalry between Himmler and Heydrich on the one hand, and Göring on the other. He sought a way out in 1939 and appealed to Göring to let him enter active service in the Luftwaffe. But beginning in 1935, the year that Christoph became head of the Forschungsamt, he himself was a powerful force in the Third Reich.

Christoph's Career in the Nazi State

During the period that Prince Christoph managed the Forschungsamt, it turned into one of the most powerful agencies in the Third Reich. The Forschungsamt can be compared in certain respects to the National Security Agency in the United States. While it does not have the public visibility of the CIA or the FBI (indeed, experts talk of a "policy of anonymity," and President Truman's 1952 directive creating the agency was kept secret for decades), the National Security Agency evolved into the largest and most important information gathering agency in the country.[12] The FA's effectiveness is conveyed by the fact that in the postwar period, as West German politicians debated amnesties for former Nazis and the renewal of pensions, they initially proposed extending these benefits to all civil servants, except for members of the Gestapo and employees of the Forschungsamt.[13] Göring's intelligence agency played a central role in many historic events: aside from the Röhm purge, perhaps most notably during the Anschluss. The agency's transcripts of telephone conversations where Hitler schemed to take over Austria were so extensive that they were used as evidence at the International Military Tribunal (IMT) at Nuremberg.

The FA employed more than 6,000 experts, making it "the most capable and precise information collecting agency in the world [at that time]."[14] Each day FA employees intercepted on average 34,000 domestic telegrams and 9,000 from abroad.[15] They did not, however, intercept mail: this task was carried out by other agencies, including the Reichswehr.[16] Historian David Kahn has noted, "The Forschungsamt's information came strictly from telecommunications: a brief venture into espionage failed ignominiously, and no further attempts were made."[17] They also did not have police authority or active agents, and instead, communicated information to other state agencies and ministries. D. C. Watt wrote, "the job of the Forschungsamt was, in the jargon of the intelligence agencies, purely 'passive': to collect and record information in accordance with general and specific requests made to it by other German Government agencies."[18] One report from the U.S. Counter Intelligence Corps (CIC) dated September 1945, provides a synopsis of the FA: "The Forschungsamt was founded in May 1933 in Berlin on the Behrenstrasse [in the building occupied by the] Danat Bank. In 1934 it moved across the street and from there to the Schillerstrasse. The name *Forschungsamt* is a cover-title for an independent signal intelligence organization. . . . The FA retained its status independent of all other German intelligence agencies throughout [most of] the war."[19] Despite eventually becoming part of Himmler's empire, the agency was under Göring's control throughout most of the Third Reich. The information it gathered gave Göring a distinct advantage over his rivals in the Nazi state and partly explains his remarkable effectiveness as he was officially appointed Hitler's successor in 1939 and given the unprecedented title of Reichsmarschall.

The competition between Göring and Himmler was of fundamental importance to the history of the Third Reich, and their rivalry had unavoidable consequences for their employees. Although the Reichsführer-SS managed to pry the Gestapo away from Göring in 1936, and in doing so unify both the ordinary and political polices, he did not get the upper hand more generally until well into the war.[20] Indeed, in the 1930s Göring's empire was unsurpassed among subleaders. Certain differences in style characterized the two camps. Reinhard Heydrich, for example, reflected this split when he told the head of research in the Forschungsamt, "you are a bourgeois who wishes for objectivity. You must learn to think state-politically [and] subjectively!"[21] Göring tended to be more concerned with wielding power and his worldview was more cynical. On the other hand, to say that the FA staffers were not ideological is misleading. Gottfried Schapper, for example, who stood out among the leaders within the agency, has been characterized as "a Jew hater" (he had initially joined the Nazi Party as early as 1920).[22] A 1945 study of the agency by U.S. historians noted, "The majority of the prewar employees and officials, especially of the Berlin FA, belonged to the SS."[23] Indeed, the FA initially had its own SS company, *Haus-Sturm*, that existed from 1934 to 1938. This enabled staffers, including Prince Christoph, to remain in the SS, while keeping them apart from other SS units. According to the CIC report, "at the

Prince Christoph von Hessen at his desk at the Research Office (Forschungsamt) of the Reich Air Ministry, 1934. He wears his SS uniform.

request of several members of the FA who had been old time SS members (Prince of Hessen, Schols), the *Sturm* was dissolved in 1938 as it was felt that the spirit in which the SS duties were discharged were not in conformity to SS standards. All members were given the opportunity of joining other SS units but it appears that relatively few availed themselves of this privilege."[24] If anything, this 1938 decision speaks to the increasingly nonideological orientation of Prince Christoph. One estimate is that 50 percent of the FA staff belonged to the NSDAP, which shows a general proclivity to support the Nazi regime, but also that party membership was not a requirement.[25]

Regardless of whether there was a political litmus test, FA staffers performed work of an ideological nature as they monitored the telecommunications of Socialists, trade unionists, church leaders, and others perceived as enemies of National Socialism. The FA also eavesdropped on other government agencies, including the RSHA (Reich Security Head Office) and Heydrich himself.[26] According to one of Hitler's adjutants, Fritz Wiedemann, the Forschungsamt even recorded conversations in the Reich Chancellery: in 1938, Wiedemann had discovered that someone named Gottfried Kell had compiled a dossier about him, and that some of the information could only have been obtained by spying on him in his Reich Chancellery office. Wiedemann contacted Heydrich and asked discretely if the SS-Gruppenführer could determine Kell's identity. When Wiedemann learned that Kell worked for the FA, he wrote to Göring's aide, General Karl Bodenschatz (1890–1979), and asked his old friend (*lieber* Bodenschatz) if he could speak to his chief and order a halt to the eavesdropping in the Reich Chancellery.[27] It is not known whether this request achieved the desired results. Others targeted by the FA included Wiedemann's close friend, Princess Stephanie zu Hohenlohe, Franconian Gauleiter Julius Streicher (1885–1946), Unity Mitford (1911–48), and Goebbels's romantic interest, actress Lida Baarova (1914–2000).[28]

The Forschungsamt had very elaborate security procedures. Every piece of paper was numbered and registered: "the German bureaucracy ruled here, German thoroughness to its ultimate conclusion."[29] For example, the staffers divided their subject matter alphabetically: *A* was for telephone; *B* for wireless; *C* for radio broadcasts; and *D* was for teletype and telegrams. "The telephone wires were tapped at the main exchange of the local post office and the wire tap run to the FA office." "The interceptors, upon the lighting of a small bulb, cut into the conversation by depressing a small lever. When necessary (particularly long or technical conversations), a wire-type recorder could be employed."[30] Indeed, they not only pioneered this technique of silent interception but also were among the first to utilize tape recorders. The intelligence was then passed on to analysts for evaluation and sorting in the appropriate archive (with reports often sent via pneumatic tubes).[31] The results of the analysis, the reports on brown paper or *braune Meldungen*—had to be returned to the FA: one of the few FA documents to survive concerns Christoph writing to the adjutant of the Führer in June 1938 following up on FA messages that had not been returned. In an internal FA memorandum of February 1938, Prince Christoph wrote, "The work of the FA will have both point and profit only if its secrecy is safeguarded by every possible means. Inadequate security will result in the enemy taking precautions, and our sources drying up."[32] All recipients of these reports then, were required to sign a written oath swearing secrecy under potential punishment of death: at least one person (a friend of Abwehr chief Wilhelm Canaris) was found guilty of revealing secrets and executed.[33] Prince Wolfgang added, "since my brother, like all employees of the office, was bound by an oath of silence, he never spoke about his activities in family circles."[34]

Officials at the Forschungsamt pursued both domestic and foreign intelligence. For the latter, they focused on intercepting communications of diplomats, journalists, and businessmen (there was extensive economic espionage).[35] Accordingly, the FA employed a staff of code breakers with foreign language skills.[36] Later, during the war, the FA established offices outside Germany: in Copenhagen, Paris, Amsterdam, Brussels, Prague, Sofia, Riga, and other cities—all with considerable native personnel.[37] Among the intercepts were British plans for the invasion of Norway in April 1940 and the Churchill-Stalin correspondence of 1942.[38] The agency kept an elaborate archive to record its findings. There were actually three special archives: one called a *"Personenarchiv,"* which was organized according to the subject who was being watched; one called the *"Sacharchiv,"* which corresponded to subject; and the third called the *"Pressearchiv,"* which housed a collection of newspaper articles and correspondents' reports. The three archives were cross-referenced by way of a massive card file.[39] In a sense, the Forschungsamt was a bureaucratic computer. In the late 1930s, Göring's intelligence agency began to make use of the first computers, incorporating "the metallic syncopation of Hollerith technology" in their sorting operations.[40] By 1942, the FA archives reportedly contained records on more than three million people.[41]

The Forschungsamt was a coldly efficient operation—part of the machinery that buttressed the totalitarian state. At times, the FA even eavesdropped on Philipp—notably on the calls he made from Rome to Germany. Christoph alerted Philipp and other family members about the regime's capabilities in a general way. Princess Sophia recalled his warning: her husband said that ". . . I must be extremely cautious and discreet about my opinions and views, as all foreign wives were being watched and shadowed. He even advised me to only talk about politics with my sisters and cousins, if we were out of doors and out of ear-shot of other people."[42] Christoph had helped establish such a powerful surveillance apparatus and implemented such rigid procedures that members of his family could not completely elude the grasp of the FA. Granted, the security complex in the Third Reich did not compare to certain other regimes, such as the German Democratic Republic's secret police "Stasi," in terms of the number of agents or technical capability, but the FA was nonetheless a formidable operation.[43]

The FA has remained an underappreciated organization in the Third Reich for several reasons. The elaborate security procedures of the agency were a key factor, but more generally, there was an almost complete destruction of its documents. This began when the British dropped incendiary bombs on the FA headquarters on the Schillerstrasse on 22 November 1943, and culminated with the shredding of surviving documents at war's end before employees evacuated Berlin for St. Gilgen in Austria, Flensburg near the Danish border, and other places of refuge.[44] The Allies were not even sure the agency existed until well after VE–Day.[45] The importance of espionage during the Cold War also militated against a public treatment of the FA's wartime work. The Nazis' intelligence methods, like their network of human assets, were important to all the Allies, who in turn guarded the information they gathered. CIC special agents James Olsen and Harvey Gutman recommended that "a policy should be established defining whether or not personnel of the FA fall within the Automatic Arrest Category, . . . as do the members of the SD, Abwehr, and Gestapo."[46] This never happened, and few Forschungsamt officials were ever apprehended.[47]

There were many members of the nobility in the Forschungsamt—especially those stationed abroad, who frequently posed as diplomats. In a CIC list of "key personnel of the attaché section," five of the eleven were nobles (based on the "von" in their names).[48] This might be attributed to several factors. First, Prince Christoph may have recruited friends and acquaintances. It also helped that Göring favored members of the nobility. Aristocrats would more often have the language skills that were vital to this work. And, as noted above, during the Third Reich, as now, a linkage existed between diplomacy and espionage, and aristocrats have traditionally excelled with regards to the former. Indeed, during the Third Reich, the Foreign Ministry continued to employ many nobles.

Although it is not possible to obtain precise figures because so many personnel files were destroyed during the same November 1943 bombing raids that damaged the FA headquarters, historian Hans-Adolf Jacobson has calculated that "the majority of the high ranking officials (*Beamten*) came from aristocratic circles."[49] It was also not uncommon to find elite members of society in other countries involved in intelligence-related activities. There was almost a tradition in Great Britain where the upper classes offered their services to MI-6: the Duke of Hamilton (1903–73), for example, who was to play a role in Rudolf Hess's mission to Scotland in 1941, worked for British intelligence in the mid-1930s.[50] Even in the less class-conscious United States, it is telling that President Roosevelt turned to Vincent Astor and other social elites for intelligence work in the 1930s. FDR's cohorts, which constituted themselves as "The Club," were in part "adventure-seeking dilettantes," but they were also useful and provided the president with considerable information that was of value. In a manner suggestive of Prince Christoph's activities, Vincent Astor was a director of the Western Union Cable Company and "ran the risk" by intercepting cable traffic in violation of U.S. law.[51]

It is striking that Göring entrusted the Forschungsamt—the agency that gave him a decisive advantage over rival subleaders—to Pilli Körner and Prince Christoph. The former, as noted, was like a son to him. The latter also clearly elicited a sense of trust. Perhaps this grew out of Göring's long-standing ties to the Hessens, going back to his school days, or perhaps it grew out of his views regarding aristocrats and their traditional code of honor. That Christoph's brother was Oberpräsident under Göring was probably also a factor in the decision: both princes were part of a strategic alliance with him. Ultimately, with an agency as powerful and important as the Forschungsamt, it came down to personal relationships as far as Göring was concerned. This is perhaps most evident with regard to the Röhm purge of June 1934. In "Operation Hummingbird," as it was called, Göring worked hand-in-hand with Himmler to attack certain leaders of the SA and eliminate various other opponents. Through Forschungsamt intercepts, Göring discovered the hostile and disrespectful views toward him held by Ernst Röhm. The SA chief would refer to him as "that pig Göring" and "*Herr Reaktion*," and call Göring's future wife, Emmy Sonnemann, "Göring's sow." Röhm was also overheard talking about "the day when this friend of the big bosses would be swept out of the way and the future aims of the National Socialist revolution would be fulfilled."[52] Because Hitler was a longtime friend of Ernst Röhm—the head of the Brown Shirts was one of the few to use the familiar "*du*" form when addressing him—Hitler was initially reluctant to act against him. Even after learning about Röhm's ambitions to combine the SA, SS, and armed forces, and place them under his command as minister of defense, Hitler attempted to resolve the situation through negotiations—or at least, to give Röhm another chance to become compliant. It was the intercepts that Göring obtained from the FA that convinced Hitler to move against Röhm. Other victims in the purge also lost their lives because they were implicated in the intercepts: A cable sent by French ambassador in Berlin André François-Poncet, for example, discussed a meeting between Röhm, ex-chancellor General von Schleicher, and former Nazi Gregor Strasser, where the three men told the French ambassador of an imminent "change of regime." Schleicher and Strasser were among the approximately two hundred who were murdered in the Night of the Long Knives.[53] Göring, then, used the Forschungsamt to wage his personal battles. Many observers—both at the time and subsequently—have also seen the Night of the Long Knives as having a social component. Röhm had argued for a "second revolution" that would topple the regnant establishment and distribute wealth more evenly: his demise was applauded by President von Hindenburg, many aristocratic army officers, and a significant section of the "landed elites."[54] There is considerable validity to this interpretation, but there were also noble victims (at least fifteen), and class was not the primary factor in the purge.[55]

Aside from helping provide the crucial evidence that induced Hitler to turn against his paramilitary chief and others, it is not clear what role Prince Christoph played during the purge. As his mother, Landgravine Margarethe noted in a letter to her husband shortly after the fact, "one faces so many riddles." But, she added, "Chri called me early on Sunday & said that he spent the entire day yesterday with Hermann [Göring], and that was ceaselessly interesting. Everything has been put in order again, but not until the last moment. Hermann & Himmler had a fabulous achievement, and apart from Hitler, we have these two men to thank greatly."[56] In other words, while Himmler and the SS carried out the arrests and killings in Bavaria, Christoph remained alongside Göring, as he orchestrated the purge in Berlin. Göring consulted FA reports as he decided the fate of individuals. He had managed to throw "a cordon around Brown Shirt headquarters" in the city center, and he himself assumed the role of judge. As Leonard Mosley wrote:

> Göring was brisk and efficient. He had a long list in his hand, for he had long since worked out just who among the Brown Shirts were the most dangerous to the regime or who were the most degenerate. He jogged at a trot from room to room, where the Brown Shirts had been assembled, and with a stubby finger he would point among them, saying, "Arrest him . . . arrest him . . . no, not him, that character skulking behind . . . and him . . . and him. . . ." The arrested men were taken down to the trucks and driven away to Lichterfelde.[57]

The Lichterfelde Cadet Academy had been transformed into barracks of the SS-Leibstandarte and was the site of many of the executions on the 30 June. SS marksmen shot the victims from a distance of seven yards, ostensibly so as not to miss. However, this resulted in large holes in the victims' chests, and "the wall behind soon became festooned with bleeding flesh which no one thought to hose away between executions."[58] In the words of historian Robert Koehl, a kind of "mixed court martial" preceded the executions, and the tribunal consisted of mostly SS leaders as well as Göring.[59] Although Christoph was a member of the SS, and had been promoted less than two weeks earlier from SS-Captain (Hauptsturmführer) to SS-Major (Sturmbannführer), there is no evidence that he was present at Lichterfelde during the executions. Many mysteries continue to surround the Röhm purge: the participants in the Night of the Long Knives took an oath of secrecy and relevant documents were systematically destroyed; no one has even been able to arrive at an exact number of those killed. Prince Christoph's precise role in the purge also remains unclear. Yet Rainer von Hessen regards Christoph's involvement in the Röhm purge as the most troubling episode in his father's career. He noted, "I was shocked when I read the letter of my grandmother and realized where he was, how caught up he was, in the events of June 1934."[60]

By remaining at Göring's side, Christoph demonstrated a toughness and loyalty that recommended him for the position as head of the FA. Indeed, considering that his three surviving brothers were members of the SA, Christoph's reliability was proven beyond a doubt (Landgravine Margarethe had noted "poor Richard is most crushed, as he feels deeply that this is a blow for the SA").[61] Prince Christoph therefore became the manager of arguably the most effective intelligence agency in the Third Reich and an operative of Göring's. The powerful Nazi would put a large "G" next to an application to tap a line, and this was all that was needed to proceed. Besides the hands-on involvement of the number-two figure in the Third Reich, the FA is remarkable for its evolution into a weapon of the murderous dictatorship. Early in 1933, the Emergency Decrees signed by President Hindenburg that followed the Reichstag fire had legalized the tapping of phone lines (for reasons of national security). But the FA superceded its original purpose and grew into an instrument that permitted the Nazi leaders to implement their increasingly malevolent policies.

Despite the important post held by Christoph, he did not exhibit a marked sense of personal ambition. One sign of this was the manner in which he continued to pursue his interests in sports; this, at a time when he gradually assumed more authority over operations on the Schillerstrasse. Indeed, his father objected to his mother that she supported Christoph's sports aspirations at the expense of his professional responsibilities. At least his interest in sports helped him meet expectations in the SS, of which he was still a member. Himmler strongly encouraged athletic activity among SS members: Generals Heydrich, Prince zu Waldeck, and Philipp Bouhler, for example, headed SS programs for fencing, horseback riding, and motor sports respectively.[62] Riding, in particular, as a symbol of the nobility, was appropriated by the SS. Shortly after the Nazi seizure of power, Himmler arranged for the riding associations in the main breeding areas (including East Prussia, Holstein, and Hanover) to be absorbed into his organization.[63] The entire German equestrian team for the 1936 Olympics was comprised of members of the SS (the *Reiter-SS*). Christoph nearly earned a spot on this team (a remarkable feat considering his other responsibilities), but he came up short in a crucial qualifying competition in Budapest. For Himmler, Heydrich, and other SS leaders who shaped the organization, horses offered a way to communicate multiple messages: to emphasize martial values, to confirm assumptions about race and breeding, and also a means of appearing noble and elite. Even certain concentration camps, such as Buchenwald, had equestrian facilities.[64] The image of the imposing Prince Christoph, dressed impeccably in his SS uniform, and sitting atop a horse, was indeed a potent symbol. Fashion historian Irene Günther makes the point, "The male uniform, particularly the all-black clothing of the SS, to most [is] a symbol of social control, ruthlessness, and evil. . . ."[65] Although this is exaggerated in the case of Prince Christoph, his status as an SS officer and his keen enthusiasm for sports intersected in significant ways and helped shape his persona. His SS file is filled with reports of his athletic activities: for example, in July 1937, he sent an account of his performance in a three-day mountain race (*Mittelgebirgsfahrt*), where his

Prince Christoph riding in the 1930s and wearing an SS uniform.

car failed on him eighty meters before the finish due to a break in the differential.[66] Prince Christoph effectively transformed service in the SS into participation in sporting events. It was nonetheless notable that the head of the spy agency could pursue these interests and serve as a reservist in the air force—all this, while his family steadily grew.

Philipp's Career during the Third Reich

After accepting the position as Oberpräsident in June 1933, Philipp moved into "the residence of his ancestors" in Kassel.[67] It was a new experience for him. Even though he came from the most illustrious family in the region, the ten years he had spent in Italy made him a virtual outsider. Philipp recalled later that "upon taking office as Oberpräsident he was unknown to the German public and himself counted as a 'new citizen' of the province."[68] He introduced himself to the population largely by way of public ceremonies and cultural events. In terms of the former, he built on the trip in the open car he made with Göring on the occasion of his inauguration by attending a variety of functions—sometimes attired in his SA uniform, such as the ceremony to make local Gauleiter Karl Weinrich an honorary citizen of Kassel.[69] Yet Philipp preferred to gain visibility by way of opening exhibitions and attending the theater. He was genuinely enthusiastic about attending cultural events and put real effort into planning—for example, inviting Richard Strauss for a two-day visit in 1937 when one of the composer's operas was performed in Kassel.[70] As Franz Ulbrich, the head of the Kassel State Theater, noted, "in the personal inter-actions with my actors—he gladly participated in both our official and unofficial celebrations."[71] Ulbrich and other observers also attached significance to the fact that Philipp preferred sitting in the "intendant's box" rather than the "official box." That is, he preferred to sit up close to the stage—but in a less visible place—so that he could concentrate on the performance.

Despite a certain shyness and unremarkable oratorical abilities, Prince Philipp became a popular figure in the province. He had advantages from the outset because of the glamour and prestige he brought to the post. He also had the benefit of a Nazi-controlled media, which was always com-plimentary. Later, Gauleiters Sprenger and Weinrich gave orders limiting the press coverage devoted to the Oberpräsident, but at the outset, Prince Philipp received only glowing notices. One report on a public reception in 1933 is typical: "the news that the Prince of Hessen would be Oberpräsident was greeted everywhere with great joy, and at the installation, all of Kassel was on its feet."[72] He also appealed to many contemporaries because he appeared to balance a commitment to both National Socialism and to tradition.

One episode involving a crucifix sculpted by Expressionist artist Ernst Barlach is telling. Since 1931, the modernist piece stood prominently above the altar in the Church of St. Elisabeth in Marburg. When Philipp paid a visit in late spring 1933, he was reported to have said, "he wanted to take care that such stuff was removed from the new Reich."[73] After the war, the prince's critics used this as an example of his Nazi views: the majority in the Nazi Party detested modernist art and associated it with the dreaded Weimar Republic, and Barlach was a particularly visible target because of his war memorials, which many considered subversive because they did not glorify death.[74] Philipp's role in the Marburg episode is not clear cut. First, it is far from certain that he impugned Barlach's art in the ideological terms cited above. Second, Philipp personally provided a replacement for the Barlach crucifix: "a valuable Gothic cross of Italian origin" that came from the thirteenth century, making a very valuable donation indeed.[75] And third, his intervention was consistent with his appreciation of art history. The Church of St. Elisabeth, according to Philipp, was the oldest Gothic church in Germany. He claimed that the nineteenth-century restoration of the church had constituted "a very strong attack" and that he was simply trying to return it to its "original appearance."[76] Dr. Bleibaum, the provincial curator of Hesse, also observed that this was "the burial church for his ancestors."[77] Yet, Philipp was most likely also conscious that his actions would please many Nazi colleagues; his interest in art and art policy was so great that he could hardly have been unaware of the debate over Expressionism that raged in the 1930s (and other Barlach sculptures, most notably his memorial in the Magdeburg cathedral, elicited attacks from veterans' groups and a number of right-wing associations prior to its removal in 1934). Philipp's principle impulse was art historical, and thus he acted according to his own tradition-bound tastes. Another mitigating factor was that the Barlach altar was not destroyed (as were many other works by the modernist artist). Philipp claimed that he arranged for the Barlach altarpiece to be stored in the provincial Building Inspectorate (Hochbauamt). The clergy of St. Elisabeth maintains today that it was hidden in the rafters of the medieval church, thus saving it from destruction. Regardless, the Barlach crucifix was returned to its place above the altar in 1945.[78]

Throughout his tenure as Oberpräsident, Philipp sponsored projects on a more traditional, princely basis, as compared to state-backed initiatives —although the line was often blurred. In the mid-1930s, for example, he played a decisive role in the creation of the Landgrave Museum, as he transformed sections of his family's eighteenth-century Palais Bellevue into a public gallery. While this was part of an effort to turn Kassel into the "city of art in Prussia" (*Kunststadt Preussens*), it also entailed a conscious effort to rekindle the museum tradition of his ancestors—notably Landgrave Frederick II, who had established the Fridercianum.[79] (Interestingly, with Kassel now hosting the quadrennial *Documenta*, arguably the most important exhibition of contemporary art in the world, these ambitions have been partly realized.) Of course, the prince's tastes lay in an entirely different direction. One conservation expert recalled, "since [Philipp] himself had an important collection of Greek sculptures, after the creation of the Landgrave Museum he made them available as loans next to the paintings from his family property."[80] Working with the director of the state art collections Professor Kurt Luthmer, Philipp combined his own collection with objects of the state museums and the Kurhessische Hausstiftung to realize, in the words of his nephew, "what seemed the dream of a historical synthesis."[81] The Landgrave Museum featured elaborate stuccowork, imposing gilt mirrors, and period furniture. Philipp's father, Landgrave Friedrich Karl, donated a valuable meter-high coat-of-arms from the Hesse-Kassel family that went into the so-called throne chamber. The current head of the Kassel Painting Gallery, Dr. Bernhard Schnackenburg, noted that at the time the Landgrave Museum was sometimes regarded as "unscholarly" and as an obvious attempt to glorify the

A section of the Schloss Belvedere complex in Kassel, before Prince Philipp transformed it into the Landgrave Museum in the mid-1930s.

Hesse-Kassel family (there had been a contemporaneous veiled critique along these lines in the *Frankfurter Zeitung*). But in Philipp's defense, the museum was opened in stages. The fully envisioned project was never realized because with the advent of war most objects, including Philipp's collection of antiquities, were placed in storage.[82]

A concern for culture had been inculcated in Philipp as part of his aristocratic upbringing. Historian James Sheehan has commented on the importance of culture for princes that dates back centuries: "Like the military uniforms the princes began to wear and the state papers over which they labored, their role as patrons of public culture was part of a structural transformation in the way dynastic authority was exercised and imagined. But this new involvement in the public sphere was also a natural extension of the prince's traditional role as a patron of the arts, as well as of the court's traditional function as a means to communicating values to its own members and to the world at large."[83] Prince Philipp's concern for culture

The Landgrave Museum after its refurbishment. Prince Philipp had worked as an interior decorator in the 1920s, specializing in projects that featured a grand, old-world aesthetic.

coincided with the efforts of Hitler, Göring, Goebbels, and the other Nazi leaders, who also stressed the importance of the arts for the New Reich populated by "superior" Aryans. Philipp did not cloak his cultural interests in this racist mantle: he left that to other Nazis. But during the May 1935 "celebratory inauguration" of the first part of the museum, where Prince Philipp handed the keys of the museum over to Reich Education Minister Bernhard Rust (with both making the *Heil Hitler* salute as part of the ceremony), Philipp commented in his address that "realization of the museum represented the execution of an order from the Führer."[84] Philipp's devotion to art therefore provided a means to build bridges to Hitler, Göring, and other leaders.

The question naturally arises, what kind of Nazi was Philipp? Postwar American and German investigators could not come to agreement on this point, as they ventured a range of opinions. One CIC document included

The Görings and the Hessens (Mafalda is on the far right) *in the Görings's box at the Opera Ball in 1936.*

the opinion that he was "a complete adventurer and not a convinced Nazi."[85] Others, including the anti-Nazi manager of the Hessische Hausstiftung, Heinrich Lange, testified that he was "reserved politically."[86] Philipp himself told his American captors, "[he] had joined the movement for idealistic reasons."[87] He added that he was a "positive Christian" and "opposed the Nazi antireligious campaign."[88] There is an element of truth to all these views. With regards to the first, Philipp was clearly ambitious and sought to play a prominent role of representation—a position he believed at some level was due to him by birthright. Rainer von Hessen notes, "he was motivated rather by vanity to play a traditional public role in the style of his ancestors rather than by political ambition."[89] This understanding of Philipp perhaps underestimates his wish to wield influence: to leave his mark on the world and be taken seriously by those with power. It is easy to understand how these qualities would be construed as adventurism. His reticence was also a notable quality. Philipp, like many princes, possessed a certain reserve—a coolness or distance. It was part of his dignified demeanor. Prince Philipp was far from a firebrand; he would not give passionate speeches like Hitler or launch into oratorical flights like Goebbels. Especially outside the family, he tended to behave in a calm and collected manner, and this was consistent with the aristocratic tradition of self-control.[90]

There is considerable truth in his statement that he was an idealist. Of course, one would call him naïve, but especially during the years prior to the war, he embraced views and aspirations that merit this term. Philipp, for example, frequently expressed concern for workers. He noted: "I didn't think about dictators, but about countries . . . and about workers, where my heart really lies. The dubious position of the worker in Germany was the main reason I was interested in the NSDAP."[91] Significantly, he began his tenure as Oberpräsident with a visit to a local mine, where he delivered a speech to the miners. Although both his remarks and the journalistic accounts had a propagandistic ring, they emphasized the prince's idealistic impulses regarding workers: "The prince and the men who accompanied him exhibited a lively interest in the mine located there, and an animated discussion offered the opportunity to discuss many important questions. In the process, the employees came up out the mine so that they could use the encounter to present their concerns and wishes. The prince exhibited a warm understanding for the plight of the miners and promised to work energetically for an improvement of their condition."[92] His behavior here is reminiscent of the well-known contemporaneous statement of Prince Auwi: "whether worker or prince . . . we are all a great community of victims."[93] Philipp also noted in his testimony before the denazification board, "The party was supposed to create a platform where all strata and classes of the German *Volk* could find common and constructive cause without regard to their political past. The main goals of the domestic policy was the creation of work and bread."[94] Of course, these sentiments were consistent with traditional trope of an empathetic and humane nobility—and Philipp himself would publicly express the corollary "that higher birth does not offer greater rights but only greater responsibilities. . . ."[95] While Philipp believed such ideas—and they perhaps explain his membership in the SA—there were clear limits to the extent to which he was prepared to go to actualize them. Philipp feared radical workers and talked of "protecting Germany from the threatening chaos—Bolshevism."[96] His lawyer noted in 1947, "after the Bolsheviks in Russia hideously murdered many of the closest relatives of the concerned party, he endeavored to protect his native homeland from the same fate."[97]

A key element in Philipp's naïve idealism was the faith he placed in Adolf Hitler. All who knew Philipp—and even he himself—recognized the great admiration he felt for the dictator. Kurt Jerschke, the vice-president in Kassel, used the word "admiration" (*Bewunderung*) regarding Philipp's views and described Philipp returning from one meeting with Hitler and saying, "The Führer again has great ideas."[98] The prince certainly subscribed to the "Führer principle" (*Führerprinzip*) and early on pledged loyalty to Hitler. After assuming office in June 1933, he sent Hitler a telegram that read, "Reich Chancellor Adolf Hitler. I hereby report with complete obedience for the assumption of the office of Oberpräsident of Hesse-Nassau and give praise to my new leader (Führer) to whom I will remain steadfastly loyal. Philipp von Hessen."[99] Dr. Jerschke added, "he was at that time (1933–37) surely and in good faith convinced of the lofty qualities of the 'Führer.' "[100] After the war, Philipp acknowledged that Hitler had perpetrated horrible crimes, but he still expressed sympathy for the dictator, noting "he himself had never seen any but the best side of the Führer, who may perhaps have been in some way insane and who in his view, was given an altogether inordinate amount of injections."[101] Here he referenced the injections of hormones and other substances prescribed for Hitler by Dr. Theodor Morell. Like many others who have sought to defend Hitler, he pointed to quack medicine to explain the dictator's turn to more radical and irrational policies (note that the most authoritative biographer of Hitler, Ian Kershaw, has discounted the impact of these "medicines," pointing to lifestyle, diet, stress, and congenital weaknesses as more important factors in explaining his deteriorating physical condition).[102]

Philipp had frequent and direct access to Hitler to a greater extent than most of the dictator's closest associates—Bormann, Goebbels, and a few others excepted. Philipp noted, "I always had access to Hitler if I wanted it. I was rejected only once in awhile. Unfortunately, I had no influence in a political sense. Where I had influence, it was very slight. I can only say, that Hitler evinced a benevolent attitude—except a few times—and remained that way."[103] The question arises as to why it was that Philipp had such access to Hitler. The chief denazification board judge characterized the relationship between Hitler and Philipp as "of a special kind. . . . Although not a true 'National Socialist' in the narrow and real sense—as both Philipp and Hitler recognized, there was a special political trust and human benevolence on the part of Hitler that ostensibly went so far that the Prince von Hessen was for years perhaps the *only* German—notwithstanding very few exceptional cases—who had access to Hitler at any time! And this at a time (before and after the unleashing of the war) when many Reich Ministers had to wait six to nine months before they were permitted an audience."[104] One might compare the relationship of Philipp and Hitler to that of the dictator and Albert Speer. The architect turned armaments minister noted in court at Nuremberg, "If Hitler had any friends, then I would have been one of them."[105] As mentioned earlier, historian Lothar Machtan asserts that from 1938 until 1942, Philipp, next to Speer, was "Hitler's closest friend in terms of a foremost unpolitical relationship."[106] While one can dispute this claim—Bormann, Goebbels, Göring, or other associates may have been even closer—the friendship between Philipp and Hitler was very important to both men. It is striking, for example, that Hitler traveled to Kassel in June 1939 to visit Philipp and Mafalda, and that Philipp

Hitler, Prince Philipp, and Princess Mafalda in Kassel, 1939.

had a kind of open invitation to the Führer headquarters during the war.[107]

The Führer and the prince were so close that their relationship has elicited speculation about mutual homoerotic inclinations. Lothar Machtan has argued in a recent book that Hitler was homosexual, with active physical relationships in his youth and in the early 1920s.[108] Machtan does not believe that Hitler and Philipp had an actual physical relationship—they met in 1930, and it would have been virtually unthinkable for the up-and-coming politician to consort in this way with a prince (no less the son-in-law of the king of Italy). But, as noted earlier, Philipp had homosexual affairs. Machtan believes that the homosexual inclinations of both Philipp and Hitler proved central to their relationship. Many critics have been skeptical of Machtan's thesis about Hitler's sexuality—and indeed, it is extremely difficult, if not impossible, to prove any assertions about this aspect of Hitler. One encounters similar obstacles with regards to Philipp's comportment during the Third Reich: it is not clear if he continued to have same-sex liaisons. The reasons for him to conceal any such behavior are numerous and obvious.[109] At most, then, one can talk of a homoerotically charged relationship between Hitler and Prince Philipp, and note, as does Machtan, that Philipp was "captivated" by Hitler. One can also imagine that there was something more generally about National Socialism that had an attractive homoerotic element for Philipp. Historian Elizabeth Heineman has provided a useful overview of the scholarly literature linking sex and fascism, noting, "Wilhelm Reich linked the rise of fascism to the repression of sexuality in a patriarchal and capitalist society. Erich Fromm and Max Horkheimer saw authoritarian-masochistic tendencies within the family as a breeding ground for fascism."[110] Heineman goes on to discuss the work of Klaus Theweleit and, more specifically, his book *Male Fantasies*, where Theweleit examined the violent fantasies of *Freikorps* members, and the homoerotic bond that existed among many in these early Weimar paramilitary organizations.[111] The SA as a homosexual milieu, led by the Storm Troopers' leader Ernst Röhm, whose sexual proclivities were something of an open secret, has also attracted considerable scholarly attention. While such considerations are speculative in the case of Philipp, it is likely that he was aware of sexual political issues: As a member of the SA who was well-acquainted with Ernst Röhm, the 1934 purge would probably have caused some alarm; and with his past, as well as present associations (like Eddie von Bismarck), he most likely would have feared blackmail from Himmler and Heydrich, who compiled dossiers as a means of enhancing their own power. Philipp knew that he must be careful about sexual matters and try to avoid making himself ever more vulnerable to rivals and critics.

Despite Prince Philipp's special relationships with Hitler and Göring, he was plagued by an interminable struggle with the region's two Gauleiters. Jakob Sprenger of Hesse-Nassau, the primary authority in the southern part of the province (above all, Wiesbaden and Hanau), had the additional advantage of a state post as Reichsstatthalter (regional leader). Karl Weinrich of Kurhessen farther north, who lived in Kassel, only held the party post of Gauleiter, but he was nonetheless a formidable rival. Weinrich served as Gauleiter since 1927 and led an influential faction of local Nazis that included the later notorious people's court president, Roland Freisler.[112] Another competitor appeared in 1939, when Fritz Sauckel (1894–1946)—himself a Gauleiter in Thuringia—was appointed to Reich defense commissioner for the military district of Kassel.[113] This was a classic case of the Nazi "polyocracy"—or the divide-and-rule philosophy that was consciously exploited by Hitler. As discussed earlier, even Göring availed himself of it when he leveraged Philipp into accepting the position as Oberpräsident by threatening to give the position to Sprenger or Weinrich. Despite the transparency of this strategy, the competition of the Gauleiters plagued Philipp in profound ways for over a decade. As Philipp reported in a July 1945 interrogation, "The Gauleiters often interfered in matters which were no concern of the party at all. . . ." They had different plans for administrative reform (e.g., Sprenger wanted to unite Nassau with the territory of the historic Grand Duchy Hessen, while Philipp sought to merge Nassau and Prussian Hesse). This conflict was exacerbated by an administrative reform undertaken by Göring and other Nazi leaders: the 15 December 1935 "Law Concerning the Expansion of the Authority of the Oberpräsident" dissolved many of the communal assemblies in the provinces (in the case of Hessen, most notably Kassel and Wiesbaden) and transferred authority to the office of the Oberpräsident.[114] This was part of the Nazi policy of *Gleichschaltung* (coordination), as well as the above-mentioned divide-and-rule strategy of the top leaders. But the result was that Philipp gained greater power in Hessen, and this entailed authority over a range of state facilities, including the sanitarium at Hadamar, and this was to involve him more directly in the criminal programs of the regime.

A more fundamental reason for the rivalry stemmed from the deep and mutual personal animosity that existed between the Oberpräsident and the Gauleiters. Philipp, for example, described Sprenger as a "dishonest and unscrupulous man . . . [who] was hated throughout the Gau"; while Weinrich was simply "stupid."[115] Philipp's son Heinrich recalled that Sprenger "was a man with no scruples, and his name itself had a threatening ring to it" (there was a pun in this statement: the German word "*sprengen*" means to blow up).[116] The antipathy of the Gauleiters and the Oberpräsident was more acute than most rivalries in the Third Reich, and moreover, it was widely known within party and governmental circles. As one observer noted, "an open secret was the almost adversarial approach of the Gauleiters against the Oberpräsident."[117]

Generally speaking, the Gauleiters (as compared to the government administrators in the Nazi "dual state"), were more radical in their anti-Semitism, more inclined to promote the Nazi Party and its loyalists, and more violent. The combatants waged battles over a host of matters. For example, a typical incident involved a confident of Gauleiter Sprenger by the name of Fritz Bernotat (1890–1951), the Landrat (provincial official) in Kassel after 1937 who tried to take control of the District Administration in Wiesbaden. Bernotat, like Sprenger, was a radical Nazi (joined the party in 1928 and was also a member of the SS).[118] Bernotat's maneuvering in Wiesbaden elicited an "energetic" response from Prince Philipp, who went to the Reich minister of the interior and "requested an extensive disciplinary review against Bernotat."[119] Not surprisingly, Minister of the Interior Frick had a difficult time adjudicating between the two sides and no decision about the dispute was ever rendered. These battles generally ended in a stalemate, but they were not insignificant. Philipp recalled, "the entirety of my efforts up until my final defeat went to preserving and defending the administrative and territorial structure of the province and to weakening as much as possible the pernicious influence of the Gauleiters."[120] Philipp worked against his more repressive and anti-Semitic cohorts.[121] One of Philipp's assistants noted that the "struggle with Gauleiter Sprenger" peaked during the early part of the war; and that Philipp "always strongly adhered to the state line in stark opposition to the party course."[122] He was not alone in this respect, and one found conflict of this kind throughout the Reich.

The rivalries were not solely about issues but were very personal in nature. Sprenger, according to Philipp, "was and remained his most bitter opponent" until Sprenger's suicide in 1945.[123] Sprenger had given orders to the local press not to report on Philipp's activities, and this, he claimed, "left him as good as unknown in the rest of the Reich."[124] Philipp and the Gauleiters also appealed to their allies in an attempt to garner support. Sometimes these alliances broke down along lines that were unexpected. Karl Wolff, for example, who was a high-ranking SS officer, appears to have sided with Philipp, as he stated after the war, "the objective and correct thinking prince was mostly in the right."[125] Propaganda Minister Joseph Goebbels, however, was pulled in the other direction, as revealed in his journal entry of 23 November 1935: "Consultation with Weinrich. He is having an in-house fight (*Hauskrach*) with Prince Philipp. Yes, the princes. Not for us. Unfortunately, they're a weakness of Göring's."[126] These feelings eventually became mutual. Although Philipp and Goebbels enjoyed good relations from their meeting in early 1931 until well after the seizure of power, they grew ever more critical of one another. One of Philipp's colleagues noted after the war that Philipp "always spoke about Hitler with great respect, but he rejected other party members, like Himmler and Goebbels."[127]

Philipp became so frustrated by the Gauleiters' opposition that he contemplated resigning his office in 1936. There was a gradual buildup to this moment. Previously, he attempted to "document" his oppositional behavior, such as not going to "party assemblies in the province."[128] Philipp then approached Göring. He professed to be concerned about three subjects: (1) the intensifying persecution of the Jews; (2) the growing oppressiveness—he observed, "the restrictions on freedom were constantly increasing"; and (3) the "personal politics of the Gauleiters."[129] Göring, according to Philipp, listened patiently and then responded by adopting the tactic he had used back in 1933. He told him that as a "successor only Gauleiter Sprenger would come into question." This, then, for Philipp, presented what he called a "conflict of conscience."[130] In this account of his career Philipp made staying on as Oberpräsident sound like noblesse oblige. He did, however acknowledge having been outwitted by Göring, recalling, "The chess move was undoubtedly sophisticated; it did not miss its mark. . . . I [also] had my loyal colleagues and all the people in the province who had placed their trust in me and hoped for me to deliver them from the mercy and displeasure of my worst opponents."[131] Philipp claimed he had some sense of foreboding: "[I]f I didn't want to be a traitor and coward, I had to hold out longer, even though there was no doubt that it had to end in catastrophe for me sooner or later."[132] He concluded, "I therefore asked Göring to regard my attempted resignation as though it never happened and returned to Kassel with a heavy heart."[133] His lawyer used another metaphor, as he compared Philipp to "a physician in the presence of a devastating plague who must act by staying at his post without regard for his personal fate rather than fleeing to safety, so long as he might possibly help and heal."[134] This account, while undoubtedly embellished to serve Philipp's defense, is accurate in presenting the prince's misgivings in the mid-1930s—and the mounting frustrations that came with the regional post.

It was easier for Prince Philipp to endure the Gauleiters' opposition and hold on as Oberpräsident because he gradually assumed new responsibilities involving German foreign policy that kept him away from the tensions and conflicts in Hesse-Nassau. As of 1936, Philipp assumed the role of liaison (*Verbindungsmann*) between Hitler and Mussolini. This posting, of course, did not come out of the blue but was based on years of performing similar services for German and Italian elites. For example, an article on Prince Philipp from the mass market magazine *Berliner Illustrierte Zeitung* of June 1933 was titled "Intermediary between Germany and Italy."[135] At the time, he was Honorary President of the German-Italian Society. This organization had "aims and activities . . . of a purely social nature. There were lectures, concerts, performances by Italian guest artists and opera companies."[136] The society, which was based in Berlin, had about fifteen hundred members and was largely funded by Adolf Hitler Fund from the German Economy—an association comprised mostly of industrialists who made donations so that the dictator had added discretionary funds.[137] More importantly, of course, Philipp had remarkable (and even unparalleled) familial connections linking Germany and Italy.

Hitler recognized the usefulness of back-corridor communications and used princes for this purpose on several occasions. As noted earlier, he turned to Duke Carl Eduard von Sachsen-Coburg und Gotha in 1936 in order to approach the latter's cousin, the new British monarch Edward VIII, and explore the possibilities of a meeting (with an eye on a rapprochement between the two countries).[138] Hitler and other Nazi leaders saw fit to mobilize the princes as part of his strategic effort to change the international system and the balance of power, with an ostensible commitment to seeking alliances with Britain and France, among others. These views are evident, for example, in the letters Hitler sent Lord Rothermere

(1868–1940) between December 1933 and December 1935. Additionally, in 1934, Reichsleiter Alfred Rosenberg, head of a Nazi Party Foreign Policy Office, turned to Prince Gottfried zu Hohenlohe Langenburg, "in order to discuss drawing closer to the English royal house."[139] Prince zu Hohenlohe-Langenburg, who was married to Princess Margarita (Christoph and Philipp's sister-in-law), was the son of Alexandra Louise of Great Britain (1878–1942), a cousin of King George V. While little came of his mediation, a memorandum from Rosenberg expresses the prince's willingness to offer his assistance. In 1938, Princess Stephanie zu Hohenlohe-Waldenburg-Schillingsfürst (no direct relation to Prince Gottfried, she was born Steffi Richter in Austria and of Jewish ancestry), also worked to cultivate influential contacts in the United Kingdom. Princess Stephanie had a close relationship to Fritz Wiedemann, one of Hitler's adjutants, and saw Hitler frequently. The dictator had arranged for her to receive the "Aryanized" (or confiscated) Schloss Leopoldskron of theater impresario Max Reinhardt in Salzburg, and she was often a guest at the Obersalzberg. She also had numerous contacts in Britain and was close to Lord Rothermere. Her mission failed, however, when Himmler told Hitler about her Jewish ancestry. This precipitated a vitriolic denunciation from the dictator: Wiedemann was sent to San Francisco as German General Consul, and she moved first to the U.K., then to the United States, and finally to Switzerland.[140]

In another instance where a prince tried to foster better Anglo-German relations, Prince Ludwig von Hessen-Darmstadt worked closely with Ambassador Ribbentrop in London from 1936 to 1938. Previously, Prince Lu had been affiliated with Ribbentrop's Nazi Party agency for foreign policy (the Büro Ribbentrop). He became more active in 1936, when Ribbentrop appointed the prince honorary cultural attaché at the German Embassy in London.[141] His tenure overlapped briefly with Prince Otto Christian von Bismarck (a good friend of the Duke of Windsor), who was stationed there from 1928 to 1936.[142] Prince Lu had impressive social contacts: he was a cousin of the dukes of Windsor and Kent, and had sat for portraits by photographer Cecil Beaton (1904–80), who was known for his work with British society figures. Shortly after the arrival of Prince Ludwig in London in early 1937, the Mountbattens even threw a "special family party" at their spectacular home on Park Lane (Brook House), where the new King George VI and Queen Elizabeth were "to welcome their German cousin."[143] The story goes that Hitler was so piqued about the abdication of Edward VIII and the treatment that Edward and Wallis Simpson had received, that he forbade Prince Ludwig from attending. Regardless, Prince Lu worked to foster better Anglo-German relations prior to his departure from London in May 1938.[144] After the war, his aunt, Victoria Milford Haven, with King George VI's explicit blessings, wrote on

Relaxing at Schloss Wolfsgarten near Darmstadt in 1937: from the left, "Aunt Onor"
von Hessen-Darmstadt (rear left), Prince Christoph (reclining), Princess Sophia
(seated in chair), Edwina Mountbatten (on the blanket), Victoria Milford Haven
and Patricia Mountbatten (on the lounge chair). Prince Christoph's BMW
automobile stands in the background.

"Lu's" behalf during his denazification trial and testified that when he "was here in England in 1936 his greatest desire was for peace and goodwill between Germany and England. . . ."[145]

Among English peers, the Duke of Westminster traveled to Berlin in order to meet the leading personalities of the Third Reich (he had a special interest in being received by Göring) and to learn more about the "current Germany." This trip came on the heels of the Windsors' much publicized excursion in October 1937.[146] Lords Londonderry, Lothian, Rothermere, and Beaverbrook all had audiences with Hitler and Göring.[147] Oftentimes, aristocratic avocations provided the pretext for visits: Lord Halifax (1881–1959), who was Master of the Middleton Hounds in Yorkshire, attended the International Hunting Exhibition in Berlin in October 1937 and then went to shoot foxes in East Prussia with Göring.[148] In July 1938, King George VI accepted Göring's invitation to join the German Hunting Brotherhood (Deutsche Jägerschaft)—another case where a royal tried to forge better Anglo-German relations.[149]

Hitler's most extraordinary scheme to utilize royals to promote Anglo-German relations involved the centuries-old notion of a dynastic marriage of alliance. For this plan, he turned to Her Royal Highness Viktoria Luise, Duchess von Braunschweig und Lüneburg and Princess von Preussen (perhaps more easily recognized as the ex-Kaiser's only daughter). She and her husband, Prince Ernst August, Duke von Braunschweig, had met with Hitler on a number of occasions and discussed, a ". . . *rapprochement* between England and Germany."[150] Prince Ernst August had also been an English peer until being stripped of his titles and honors in March 1919—a result of having fought for Germany during World War I.[151] In her memoirs, Princess Viktoria Luise wrote:

> It was after this sojourn in England [in 1934–35] that we received an astounding demand from Hitler, conveyed to us by von Ribbentrop. It was no more nor less than that we should arrange a marriage between [our daughter] Friederike and the Prince of Wales [later Edward VIII]. My husband and I were shattered. Something like this had never entered our minds, not even for a reconciliation with England. Before the First World War it had been suggested that I should marry my cousin [the Prince of Wales], who was two years younger, and it was now being indicated that my daughter should marry him. We told Hitler that in our opinion the great difference in age between the Prince of Wales and Friederike alone precluded such a project, and that we were not prepared to put any such pressure on our daughter.[152]

Princess Friederike (1917–81), after securing the assent of King George VI, ended up marrying Prince Paul of Greece (1901–64) in January 1938. But it is illuminating that Hitler turned to a time-honored strategy for achieving a foreign policy goal and striking that he did so in such a clumsy and unsuccessful manner.

Hitler viewed royals not only as a means of building bridges to the British but also as pawns in a grander kind of chess game. For example, he viewed the 1937 marriage of Prince Bernhard zur Lippe to Princess Juliana (1909–2004), the daughter of Queen Wilhelmina of the Netherlands, as an opportunity to forge closer ties between the two countries. Furthermore, in the late 1930s both King Carol II of Romania (1893–1953) and Yugoslav Regent Prince Paul paid successive state visits to Germany and the United Kingdom. Prince Paul and his wife Princess Olga were invited to Berlin in early June 1939, and they followed this up in July with a visit to the U.K., where they were guests in Buckingham Palace. The Nazi leaders pulled out all the stops to court the Yugoslav Regent: a pro-Yugoslav propaganda campaign preceded the visit, followed by a series of formal dinners, a visit to the Berghof, and an impressive display by the Luftwaffe (reportedly, "For seven nights in a row, Olga sat alongside the Führer at dinner"— although this appears a slight exaggeration).[153] It helped that both Paul and Olga spoke excellent German and were welcomed by their extended family. Prince Philipp helped entertain his cousin and participated in a number of the functions. He joined the Yugoslav royals for the final two days of the trip when they stayed at Göring's Carinhall estate (during one black-tie

Prince Paul of Yugoslavia, Prince Philipp von Hessen, and Ribbentrop at Potsdam, June 1939.

dinner, Göring appeared, in Philipp's words, as "Wilhelm Tell" with "powdered hair, white breeches, a full shirt, a jeweled belt, and hanging from it, a dagger" while Emmy dressed in "full Croatian national costume").[154] Prince Christoph and Sophia also spent time with Paul and Olga: there was a "family lunch" on 2 June 1939 at the Palais Bellevue, which served as the lodgings for the Yugoslav guests during the state visit. According to the notes of the Infante, Alphonso of Spain, the guests included Christoph and Sophia, as well as her sisters Margarita and Theodora (as well as their husbands), and the Toerrings.[155] While the discussion of politics was usually avoided during family visits, the relationships were not unimportant. There have been suggestions that both Count Toerring and Philipp helped win over Prince Paul to the German side, but if so, they were only part of a much larger equation.[156] Ultimately, the Germans' courtship evidently paid off; on 20 March 1941, Paul announced he was prepared to sign the pact whereby Yugoslavia would enter the Axis. King Carol II of Romania proved more impervious to the entreaties of the Germans and was forced out by Prime Minister Ion Antonescu in September 1940 in favor of his son, Prince Michael (b. 1921), who helped bring Romania into the Axis the following November.[157] Hitler devoted considerable time and energy to playing this "royal game" in the late 1930s and early 1940s: Philipp von

Hessen, as the German prince whom he trusted most, therefore had an opportunity to help formulate and execute this grand strategy.

Other Princes: A Range of Options

German princes as a whole were much more supportive of National Socialism than has generally been recognized. While families often included members with heterogeneous views, one can discern patterns among the *Fürstenhäuser*, with certain houses more or less supportive of Hitler's regime. The Nazis earned support from princes for a range of policies and statements: their radical anti-bolshevism; their positions surrounding princely property; their vague but still encouraging utterances about a restoration; and their revival of the military, which also suggested a more assertive posture in international affairs. Certain houses, like that of Hesse-Kassel, embraced National Socialism with almost undiluted enthusiasm. The Houses of Lippe and Schaumburg-Lippe, with eighteen and ten members in the party respectively, would offer other examples of almost consistently fervent supporters. If one moves along the spectrum toward an oppositional stance, one would place the Hohenzollern somewhere in the middle but still firmly in the pro-Nazi camp. The former rulers of Bavaria, the Wittelsbach family, and the deposed emperors of Austria-Hungary, the Habsburgs, occupied positions further along the continuum. The reasons for the divergent views about National Socialism varied by family and by individual. But with regard to the Wittelsbach and the Habsburg families, it is significant that they represented separatist tendencies, and this was anathema to Hitler's vision of a unified Germany. In the case of the Habsburgs who remained in Austria, they were almost immediately targeted by the Nazis after the Anschluss and were scarcely given the opportunity to arrange a modus vivendi with the new regime.

Since the end of World War II, the Hohenzollern have frequently endeavored to give the impression that they were anti-Nazi, that they considered Hitler and his cohorts to be déclassé, dangerous, and politically illegitimate. This was possible for several reasons—the foremost being that the head of the house, former Kaiser Wilhelm II, was so arrogant and sharp-tongued that he made a number of statements denigrating the Nazis. He was dismayed by the killings that accompanied the Röhm purge and thought Kristallnacht to be an act of "gangsterism."[158] And because Wilhelm II never obtained what he sought—a return to the throne—he was to retain a marked ambivalence about the Third Reich. After the war, family members also attempted to distance themselves from the regime. Crown Prince Wilhelm began the process immediately after his capture by French troops in May 1945: " 'The German people have behaved like idiots. First they followed Ebert, then Hindenburg, then Hitler. This war has been madness. . . . I saw [Hitler] two or three times and each time I told him he was making a mistake. I especially warned him about persecuting Catholics and Jews, but Hitler really hated the Jews.' "[159] A closer examination of the Hohenzollern during this period shows, however, that they were generally supportive of the Nazi regime and that they maintained good relations with Hitler and other leaders well into the war years. While they did not go so far as the Hesse-Kassel or Schaumburg-Lippe families in supporting the Nazi regime, they were not so far behind.

The support for Hitler shown by the Hohenzollern before the seizure of power and the manner in which many family members joined Nazi organizations constituted an important symbolic gesture that was highly visible in Germany in the early 1930s. As noted earlier, Prinz August Wilhelm, fourth son of the Kaiser and an SA major general (Obergruppenführer) was the single most important early supporter from the royal ranks. He joined the Nazi Party on 1 April 1930, and helped bring many other aristocrats, including several of the Hessen princes, into the Nazi fold.[160] SS-General Karl Wolff testified after the war, "The only one truly active in the party was Prinz August Wilhelm, called Auwi. One had naturally made inroads in

Kaiser Wilhelm II and his six sons, 1912.

these circles, in order to use them as advertisements and publicity for the NSDAP. One frequently invited them to larger assemblies and rallies and gave them an appropriate place where they could be seen by all.[161] The first part of Wolff's statement is not quite accurate, especially if one considers branches of the Hohenzollern family: Prince Franz Josef von Hohenzollern-Emden (1891–1964), for example, from the southern and Catholic branch of the Hohenzollern (Sigmaringen) family, was an official in the Nazi Party's colonial political office, as well as a member of the SS.[162] But Prince Auwi stood out. Like Prince zu Schaumburg-Lippe, he was given the title of "national speaker" (*Reichsredner*), and he proved effective in this respect: in June 1931, Prince Auwi came out with the oft-quoted phrase, "Where a Hitler leads, a Hohenzollern can follow."[163] The prince clearly had personal ambitions that he thought the Nazis would help him fulfill: shortly before the Nazis' seizure of power, he told Putzi Hanfstaengl, "I shall make a point of keeping in with Hitler as much as possible myself. . . . After all I am the best horse in the Hohenzollern stable."[164] Although Auwi was elected to the Reichstag in early 1933, and then appointed to the Prussian Staatsrat the following July, these were not positions where he wielded much power.

That he never held an important post in the Nazi state is a testament to his general ineptitude. Auwi did possess some intellectual ability. Within the immediate family, he was called "the artist," and he evinced an interest in art and music (he was a passionate collector of antiques, porcelain, and etchings).[165] Prince Auwi also possessed a certain charm: the young "White Russian" émigré Princess Marie Vassiltchikov (1917–78) recalled one dinner at the Schaumburg-Lippes' in Berlin in March 1940 where "in front of the fire, Prince August-Wilhelm . . .—a man in his sixties—told many amusing stories about earlier days."[166] But a more representative judgment was offered by the ex-Kaiser's *Hausminister* Wilhelm von Dommes, who judged him as "ceaselessly dense, horrifically superficial, and soft."[167] Auwi also did not possess reliable political instincts: despite being close to Hitler and Göring at the time the Nazis came to power in 1933–34, he was sufficiently unaware about internal party dynamics that he gave a speech in Osnabrück on 24 June 1934 praising SA-chief Ernst Röhm—that is, less than a week before the murderous purge.[168] Auwi, like his older brother, Crown Prince Wilhelm, was interrogated by the Gestapo in the days that followed the purge—Hitler and others wanting to make sure that there was no response from those sympathetic to the SA—but little came of the inquiries.[169] Auwi's career fortunes subsequently declined: after 1935, his speeches received scant attention in the state-controlled press. Hitler and most other leaders, however, continued to tolerate the prince throughout the 1930s.[170] He was promoted to SA-Obergruppenführer in November 1938; awarded the "Golden Party badge" in January 1939; and retained access to a range of top leaders: for example, when Count Moltke had difficulty securing a permit to visit the ex-Kaiser in Doorn in 1940, he enlisted Prince Auwi, who went to speak with Reinhard Heydrich and Gestapo-chief Heinrich Müller about the matter. [171]

Despite his extensive network of relationships, Prince Auwi gradually elicited more direct and consequential attacks from critics within the party. He had earlier been forced to defend himself on charges that he had falsified his low party number and that he had been complicit in over-throwing his SA-chief Ernst Röhm, but these allegations had not stuck. More serious problems emerged as a result of his speaking too freely. In September 1942, the prince was denounced by several party members after he criticized Dr. Goebbels for his extravagant lifestyle. This led to rebukes not only from the propaganda minister (Prince Auwi's boss in his position as a "national speaker") but also from party leaders such as Martin Bormann. The alienation from Goebbels was most damaging to his career. He was dropped as a *Reichsredner*, received a ban on speaking in November 1942, and was essentially abandoned by Hitler.[172] He accepted his fate —writing a formal response to the sanctions from his Villa Liegnitz in the Sans Souci palace complex in Potsdam—but it left him depressed: in the words of his sister Duchess Viktoria Luise, "it hit him hard, his disappointment about the way things went politically."[173] The final years of the war entailed limitations on his freedom—even a kind of house arrest—although he was permitted to move to Kronberg in early 1945, where he spent the last phase of the war with the Hessens.

Auwi's older brother, Crown Prince Wilhelm, was also out on the cam-paign trail for the Nazis before 1933—often wearing a brown SA uniform. Wilhelm initially joined the SA's motor division, where he was under the command of his cousin, Duke Carl Eduard von Sachsen-Coburg und Gotha. Later, like several of the Hessen princes, he was active in the NSKK, where he too would participate in Nazi Party–sponsored motor races. He had taken the important step of backing Hitler against the incumbent von Hindenburg in the presidential 1932 election, and Hitler was most appre-ciative.[174] This, as one observer noted, entailed, "turning against his milieu, against own circle at this time."[175] He had also used his influence in 1932 to help rescind a government ban against the SA and SS. Wilhelm's own political views were not as radical as most Nazis: he was a great admirer of Italian fascism (enjoying a successful meeting with Mussolini in 1928) and a key member of the right-wing Stahlhelm before it was absorbed into the SA in 1934. Some authors have suggested that Wilhelm did not support the Nazis and was manipulated by the new leaders: for example, he was photographed in his Stahlhelm uniform in 1934, but because it was manda-tory for Stahlhelm members to include a swastika as part of their dress, the photo gave the false impression that he was a party member.[176] Regardless,

Crown Prince Wilhelm and Göring at reception at the Aero Club in the House of the Flyer, February 1936. Philipp von Hessen is on the far right.

the fact remains that he was in an SA unit (and was close to Röhm, whom he gave a fine horse as a gift), and that he developed cordial relations with Hitler and Göring (the latter had stood under Wilhelm's command during World War I).[177] It helped that two of Wilhelm's sons joined the NSDAP: Prince Wilhelm (1906–40) and Prince Hubertus (1909–50). Hitler and Crown Prince Wilhelm met periodically in the mid-1930s and participated together in various public ceremonies (e.g., the "heroes memory celebrations" in Berlin in March 1935 and 1936). They also carried out a cordial correspondence that included reciprocal birthday greetings and notes of condolence: Wilhelm, for example, wrote Hitler (*"Mein Führer und Reichskanzler"*) in 1936 upon the death of longtime aide Julius Schreck.[178] Letters of congratulation concerning the Anschluss and the major military victories followed: on 25 June 1940, for example, Wilhelm wrote Hitler on the occasion of the German triumph over France and the Benelux countries. He began by praising Hitler's "inspired leadership" and concluded with, "In this hour of the greatest historical importance, I extend my hand to you in complete admiration as an old soldier and a German.

God protect you and our German Fatherland. *Sieg Heil!*"[179] This and several of Wilhelm's other telegrams were published in Germany—steps that sent clear messages to monarchists, among others.[180] These telegrams expressed such enthusiastic support for Hitler that certain aides of the Kaiser (Dommes and Ilsemann), who felt great loyalty to the family, maintained after the war that the missives were drafted by the crown prince's secretary, and that Wilhelm did not know about them beforehand.[181] Yet it seems highly improbable that these aides, sensitive to protocol and symbolic gesture, would have written the German dictator on their own. Defenders of the family sometimes offered versions of events that are at odds with contemporaneous documents. For example, in 1936 Hofrat Albrecht Berg wrote to Frau von Dirksen, wife of the German Ambassador to London: in this ten-page missive, Berg noted how well he knew the crown prince and then chronicled Wilhelm's support for Hitler ("the deep, positive position of the crown prince to the Führer"); he concluded with the observation that the relationship was currently especially strong "because the crown prince now views and recognizes the racial question from the perspective of the Führer."[182]

This is not to say that Wilhelm did not at times experience conflict with the Nazi regime: he was chastised by the NSKK-leader Adolf Hühnlein in mid-1936 for sending Mussolini a telegram congratulating him on a successful conclusion to the Abyssinian campaign—the telegram, which was published in the Italian press, was viewed as interfering with German foreign policy (the Germans were officially neutral at this point). In response to Hühnlein's rebuke, Wilhelm resigned from the organization.[183] In 1938, he became alarmed by the Sudeten crisis and wrote to British Prime Minister Chamberlain and Queen Mary, among others, expressing his anxieties about war (telling the former, "all my best friends from youth fell in the world war").[184] But, as suggested above, when war came, Wilhelm sought to do his duty as an officer and felt elation after German victories. The Nazi leaders, however, kept him on the sidelines, and that is where he remained for the duration of the war.

The ex-Kaiser also made a concerted effort to preserve cordial relations with Hitler, as he wrote a number of letters expressing praise and support for Nazi policies. He had ambivalent feelings about the regime. On the one hand, he objected to the violence and was critical of his son Auwi, whom he regarded as so incautious that it imperiled the House of Hohenzollern. In 1935, the Kaiser asked Auwi to "finish with his National Socialism," noting that "his fanaticism was almost pathological."[185] Yet despite expressing reservations about the Nazis, Kaiser Wilhelm expressed sympathy for many of Hitler's views. He supported the idea of a revitalized and remilitarized nation, and he himself espoused anti-Semitic views. The leading biographer of Kaiser Wilhelm, John C. G. Röhl, concluded, "It is difficult to come to any other conclusion than Kaiser Wilhelm II was a staunch anti-Semite, and that anti-Semitism formed a central element of his outlook on the world."[186] In 1940, Wilhelm wrote his sister, Landgravine Margarethe, "The hand of God is creating a new world & working miracles. . . . We are becoming the U.S. of Europe under German leadership, a united European Continent." He added, approvingly, "The Jews [are] beeing [*sic*] thrust out of their nefarious positions in all countries, whom they have driven to hostility for centuries."[187]

Wilhelm II's correspondence with high-ranking Nazi officials communicated a similar and fundamentally supportive position. One of the most striking documents is Wilhelm's communication to Hitler in the wake of the German victory over Poland in September 1939. It was penned by his adjutant, General von Dommes, who wrote "His Majesty the Kaiser and King Wilhelm II has followed the triumphal campaign of the German eastern Army with passionate interest (*mit heissem Herzen*). He went on to express the Kaiser's admiration of the Blitzkrieg—the modern weapons, the operational strategy, and the "unsurpassed courage of the troops." The letter noted that the House of Hohenzollern "remained loyal" and that nine Prussian princes (one son and eight grandchildren) were stationed at the front. It concluded "because of the special circumstances that require residence in a neutral foreign country, His Majesty must personally decline to make the aforementioned comment. The Kaiser has therefore charged me with making a communication."[188] Indeed, Wilhelm II stayed in regular contact with Hitler through General von Dommes, who represented the family in Germany. In spring 1940, for example, Dommes approached the Reich Chancellery to inquire whether the Kaiser could return to Germany if the British occupied Holland (Reich Minister Lammers took a "wait and see" approach to this request).[189] This was followed by a 17 June 1940 telegram, directly from the Kaiser, congratulating Hitler on military success in France.[190] Hitler responded politely on 25 June.[191] The relationship between Kaiser Wilhelm II and Hitler was certainly complicated and ambivalent, and one can select examples to argue either for alienation or acceptance. While there was a cooling of relations between the Hohenzollern and the Nazi leaders that became increasingly evident in the late-1930s, both sides took steps to prevent a complete break. For example, when an article by a journalist named W. Burckhardt appeared in the international press in December 1938, quoting the Kaiser as saying, "All attempts in history to achieve world domination have failed"—a formulation that provoked headlines such as "Ex-Kaiser Says Hitler is Doomed to Failure"—Wilhelm II not only sent Hitler a letter assuring him that the interview was a fabrication but arranged for aides to threaten legal action; this induced the sponsoring paper (*The Daily Telegraph and Morning Post* in London) to offer an "unreserved withdrawal and apology."[192] On the other side, when the Kaiser's grandson—also named Wilhelm—fell in battle on the Western Front in late May 1940, Hitler promptly arranged for Reich Minister Lammers to send a respectful note of condolence to the family.[193]

The Germans' great military success in the early phase of the war gave rise to rumors of some official role for the Hohenzollern. One British Foreign Office memorandum from July 1941 noted that the Russian tanks were proving formidable, but that, "The Germans were now, however, confident that the battle was more fluid and that they could make progress towards their main objectives, namely Leningrad, Moscow and Kiev. The Germans contemplate setting up an Emperor in Russia, who would be, it was thought, the third son of the late Kaiser [*sic*], Louis Ferdinand. They intend to garrison and occupy Russia west of the Volga."[194] It is evident that the British officials were not very well-informed (Louis Ferdinand was Crown Prince Wilhelm's *second* son and quite disaffected from the Nazi regime—he left the Armed Forces in December 1941). But rumors of various kinds of restoration-schemes and make-shift monarchies proliferated in British Foreign Office reports. In the case of Prince Louis Ferdinand, who developed contacts with members of the German resistance, these rumors persisted well into 1944, as some regarded him as an alternative to Hitler as head of state.[195]

One should avoid painting the entire picture in one color, and there were indeed some variations among the Hohenzollern in terms of family members' relationships to the Nazi regime. Prince Eitel Friedrich von Preussen, although once a member of the right-wing Stahlhelm who signed an oath of loyalty to Hitler in early 1934, remained unimpressed with the Nazis, as was his younger brother, Prince Adalbert von Preussen (1884–1948), who moved to Switzerland in the 1930s.[196] Cambridge-educated Prince Friedrich von Preussen (1911–66), the fourth son of Crown Prince Wilhelm, was also living abroad and distanced himself from the Nazis. As a British Foreign Office report from March 1941 noted, "the best of the young Hohenzollern [Friedrich] is interned in England, having been brought back from an internment camp in Canada. It has been suggested that he should be released to work on the land, which he himself desires to do, but the Home Office are not yet willing to agree to this course. Little is heard of the other two brothers, and there has been no indication of any revival for the Hohenzollern among Germans."[197] Friedrich distanced himself from Hitler's regime and married Lady Brigid Guinness just after the war in 1945. When the Hohenzollern princes stood in opposition to the Nazis, the favored approaches were either flight, or more commonly, a kind of "inner emigration" where they retreated from public life. When discussing the idea of resistance and joining an organized movement, Crown Prince Wilhelm warned his son Louis Ferdinand in early 1943, "Hands off! Don't get involved!"[198] Wilhelm feared the consequences not only for the royal house but also for the future of Germany. Despite the growing mistrust between the Hohenzollern princes and the Nazi leaders—especially during the latter stages of the war—neither side ever broke completely with the other.

At times, Hitler and his subordinates were unsuccessful in their attempts to court princes. This was the case with Crown Prince Rupprecht von Bayern (1869–1955), the head of the House of Wittelsbach after the death of his father, Ludwig III (1845–1921), who had been the last ruling king of Bavaria and was forced to abdicate in 1918. Crown Prince Rupprecht, whom Golo Mann described as "a clever man," had remained in Germany after World War I and had never renounced his rights to the Bavarian throne.[199] Rupprecht opposed the Weimar Republic and "pushed for a constitutional, social monarchy with universal suffrage."[200] But he was never seduced by the extreme right wing. Early on, while the Nazis were still a local political phenomenon in Munich, Hitler had sent Ernst Röhm to see Rupprecht in an attempt to win him over to the cause. Röhm, who had attended the prestigious Maximilian-Gymnasium in Munich, and trained as a *Fahnenjunker* (cadet) in the Prince Ludwig Regiment of the Bavarian Infantry (later rising to the rank of captain), had also been a General Staff officer in Ritter von Epp's *Freikorps* volunteer brigade. While nothing came of this initial approach to win Rupprecht over to the Nazis, Röhm returned to see him in early 1923. In a remarkable scene, the thickset paramilitary chief approached Rupprecht and, "As Count Soden, an eyewitness reported, he made the request very forcefully and then finally, fell to one knee to beseech him." Count Soden added, "such theatricality was, all things, the surest way to be dismissed fast and short."[201] The Nazis could never entice the Wittelsbach prince with vague assurances of a restoration because that would have furthered Bavarian separatist tendencies. There was also evidently a personal antipathy between Hitler and Prince Rupprecht: the German dictator confided to Prince Auwi "that he couldn't stand Rupprecht von Bayern" (and this evidently pleased Auwi, who thought this would be "very advantageous for the Hohenzollern").[202]

In 1932, as the Depression approached its most critical phase, a remarkable coalition of political parties encouraged the Bavarian Crown Prince to offer himself as a bulwark against the Nazis. One plan that attracted considerable support was to make Rupprecht *Staatskommissar* of Bavaria and give him dictatorial powers. Even many SPD members of the Reichstag and postwar Bavarian Minister President Wilhelm Hoegner supported this plan. But Hindenburg's appointment of Hitler as Reich Chancellor—a legal move—thwarted the unconventional Bavarian scheme.[203] The early years of the Third Reich proved difficult times for Bavarian monarchists, and some, like journalist Baron von Aretin, were temporarily imprisoned as political prisoners.[204] After 1933, Rupprecht expressed his reservations about the dictator in numerous ways: he refused to allow Wittelsbach residences, such as the Leuchtenberg Palace in the heart of Munich, to be adorned with swastika flags on festive occasions, and he would not permit the family Schloss in Berchtesgaden to be put at Hitler's disposal for special guests. In the summer of 1934, Rupprecht had lunch with King George V in London and talked about "reasonable rearmament." The summary of this meeting in British Foreign Office reports has him telling the British king that he "remained convinced that the Führer was insane."[205] In 1935, he told British Ambassador Eric Phipps that he continued to believe that a restoration of the monarchy was possible.

Matters came to a head in 1939 when the Wittelsbach were associated with a resistance plot surrounding Baron von Harnier. The Gestapo confiscated many of their properties, including Schloss Leutstetten near Lake Starnberg just outside Munich, the main residence of the royal family. Crown Prince Rupprecht left Germany for Italy in December 1939, and his wife and children followed shortly thereafter. As the guests of King Vittorio Emmanuele, they lived there undisturbed until 1944, although they were not permitted to return to Germany.[206] Rupprecht stewed and schemed during this exile. In 1942, the British Consul General in Zurich reported on "the ex-crown prince of Bavaria, who normally resides at Florence, and who is not allowed to enter Germany." The diplomat noted, "The ex-crown prince, who is described as mentally very active (he is mainly interested in art), appears to favor a kind of political subdivision of Germany after the war, possibly a monarchic union between South Germany and what is left of Austria."[207] The idea entailed not only a union of Bavaria and Austria-Tyrol as one state, but the Rhineland with Hanover as another and Schleswig, Mecklenburg, Brandenburg, Saxony, and Posen combining to form a buffer state against Russia. In May 1943, the British received a memorandum by Prince Rupprecht in which he "envisage[ed] the complete defeat of Germany [and . . .] apparently hope[d] for the Crown, not only of Bavaria, but of the whole of the country."[208] The Wittelsbach prince concluded his memorandum by noting, "I have the intention and am committed to returning immediately to my homeland if the current regime steps down—something that has been denied me for three years. With the centuries-long tradition of our dynasty and my own authority, I hope to protect [Germany] from chaos."

In the wake of the 20 July 1944 plot to kill Hitler, Rupprecht feared for his safety and went underground in Florence. Taking refuge in the home of an Italian colonel, he eluded the German authorities until the British entered the city at the end of August 1944. However, his wife, Princess Antonia (1899–1954), and their children were arrested on Hitler's personal orders and interned. After staying in a series of hospitals and other temporary lodgings, they were sent to the concentration camp at

Oranienburg-Sachsenhausen. Rupprecht's eldest son, Duke Albrecht von Bayern (1905–96), his wife and their four children, were also arrested—this time, in German-occupied Hungary in October 1944—and sent to the same camp near Berlin.[209] As the Soviets approached in early 1945, they were transferred first to the Flossenbürg camp in northern Bavaria, then to Dachau near Munich, and finally sent on with guards into the Tyrol, where they were liberated by French troops. The crown prince remained in Florence and returned to Germany in November 1945 (flown in by a special airplane put at his disposal by General Eisenhower).[210] The American occupation authorities were not prepared to consider a restoration, but they treated him graciously. Rupprecht nonetheless had to content himself as a private, albeit extremely popular, citizen of Bavaria. As one journalist wrote with a certain hyperbole, "Rupprecht's popularity reached its high point after 1945, although with his reserved manner, he was never pushy. He was the focus of an adulation that extended not only to monarchists, but to all who saw in themselves something Bavarian." He continued to advocate a constitutional monarchy and estimated that he had the support of between 60 and 70 percent of the Bavarian public. When Rupprecht died at age eighty-six in 1955, he was treated as a deceased monarch, with more than 50,000 people visiting Schloss Nymphenburg to view the coffin and pay their respects. The ceremonies went on for days and included a state funeral at the Ludwigskirche in Munich, where the Bavarian government, all Bavarian bishops, as well as selected representatives of the Bundestag were in attendance.[211] German historian Max Spindler expressed the predominant popular sentiment in 1961 when he described Rupprecht as "uncrowned, and yet a king."[212]

The German princes, like any sizeable group, represented a variety of outlooks and endured a range of experiences. One should not ignore these differences. Yet one can also discern certain similarities—indeed, tendencies that often transcended national boundaries. It is worth recalling David Cannadine's observation that "Aristocracy is a recognizably supra-national phenomenon."[213] One commonality is the sense of decline that many members of the nobility perceived in the twentieth century. The overthrow and murder of the Romanovs, the end of the Hohenzollern and Habsburg empires, and the rise of social democratic parties contributed to a pessimistic and nostalgic worldview. Even Winston Churchill in the first installment of his autobiography, *My Early Life*, published in 1930, exhibited considerable wistfulness about the idea of a vanished age.[214] This nostalgia, so pervasive among members of the high aristocracy, made them more vulnerable to the blandishments of the Nazis and fascists. Nazi Germany, with its melding of the old and new elite, offered an exciting notion of "reform" for many of these disillusioned nobles. Novelist Kazua

Ishiguro communicates how seductive such notions could be in his evocative work, *The Remains of the Day*, as his pro-Nazi character Lord Darlington remarks, "Other great nations know full well that to meet the challenges of each new age means discarding old, sometimes well-loved methods. . . . Look at Germany and Italy. . . . See what strong leadership can do if it's allowed to act. None of this universal suffrage nonsense there. If your house is on fire, you don't call the household into the drawing room and debate the various options for escape for an hour, do you?"[215] Many aristocrats who supported the Nazis subsequently wished that they had indeed explored the other options.

5

Roles in an Increasingly
Radical Regime

In a quest for meaningful service to the "new" Germany, Philipp and Christoph, like a host of other princes and nobles, became involved in the Nazis' programs, leading eventually to territorial expansion and ethnic cleansing. Among the questions that arise are: To what extent were they involved, and did they contribute to Hitler's program wittingly or unwittingly? As liaison between Hitler and Mussolini, for example, Prince Philipp helped solidify the Axis alliance, and in the process, set the stage for World War II. On the domestic front, Philipp acceded to the request of officials in the Reich Interior Ministry to take over the Hadamar sanatorium, where thousands deemed mentally or physically handicapped were murdered by gassing. He was also in a responsible position as Oberpräsident of Hesse-Nassau when the province's Jewish inhabitants —most notably those in Frankfurt (the second largest Jewish community after Berlin in Germany)—were persecuted. Many were subsequently deported to the ghettos and death camps in the East.[1] Prince Christoph, as an espionage chief, was concerned with monitoring operations on both domestic and foreign fronts. The open question about his career, as noted in the introduction, is why the operational chief of the country's most important signals intelligence agency would be permitted to become a regular member of the Luftwaffe. The incongruity of this move is a factor that contributed to the rise of legends: most notably, that he participated in the bombing of Buckingham Palace in an attempt to kill his cousin, King George VI.

Writing this history presents many challenges. These include: (1) determining what happened; (2) ascertaining whether the princes participated in these events; and (3) understanding why they acted the way they did. These fairly straightforward questions defy easy answers. The picture is clouded further by archives that remain closed and by a voluminous record of exculpatory statements that emerged in postwar trials. Ascertaining why individuals acted in the manner they did is never easy—and the challenge is compounded by the very ambiguity of their actions noted above. Yet certain patterns emerge. Philipp and Christoph, like many of their cohorts, placed great faith in Hitler and the idea of a new and revived Germany (free of Bolshevism and disorder). They expressed tremendous bitterness about the onerous Treaty of Versailles and saw their efforts as redressing this injustice. Princes rarely thought exclusively in terms of individual nations—as one would expect with their familial ties and peripatetic lifestyle. What started as a wish for the rehabilitation of Germany among the community of nations evolved into a growing acceptance of the vision of Hitler: a new order secured by a *Pax Germania*. Moreover, the class-conscious princes were motivated by a concern for their collective social standing. Their careers in the Third Reich were meant to secure a position of power in a rapidly evolving world.

Philipp at the Center of Nazi Foreign Policy in Italy

A fundamental question surrounding Prince Philipp's role as liaison between Hitler and Mussolini concerns his influence in the realm of foreign policy. Was Philipp merely a messenger or did his views and his actions affect the outcome of world historical events? Contemporary observers are split in their opinions about his importance. Certainly all have acknowledged the active and decisive role played by Hitler when it came to German foreign policy; yet many still believed that Philipp and other subordinates also shaped this history.[2] One German official, for example, noted shortly after the end of the war, "without the involvement of the prince, the foreign political rise of Hitler, and in particular, the emergence of the 'Axis' might not have come about."[3] Others, however, saw Philipp as a kind of window dressing. Ernst von Weizsäcker (1882–1951), state secretary in the Foreign Ministry, testified in 1947, "The prince had a representative function and as such he was more or less exploited by the party leadership, as well as by Hitler himself. There can be no talk, however, of his own political negotiations."[4] Both positions contain elements of truth, and indeed, there is also an area of overlap between them.

One way to assess Philipp's importance to German foreign policy is to clarify the role he played. The prince operated in Italy outside of the

Mussolini strolls with Prince Philipp at Carinhall.

customary diplomatic channels. This was not entirely unusual in the Nazi state: previously, Hitler had used both Joachim von Ribbentrop and Alfred Rosenberg as alternatives to the Foreign Office. Ribbentrop himself later noted in his memoirs, "Hitler distrusted the Foreign Office and its staff."[5] The German dictator therefore nurtured these rivals to official diplomats —a strategy, he reckoned, that enhanced his power and gave him a broader range of options. Foreign Minister von Neurath described Philipp as a kind of special envoy (he called him an *Agenten*), and emphasized that the prince did not answer to the Foreign Office. Von Neurath explained, "he received his instructions directly from Hitler or Göring, such as they were."[6]

Prince Philipp, however, endeavored to maintain good relations with members of the Foreign Office. He appeared to get on well, for example, with many German diplomats in Italy, including ambassadors Ulrich von Hassell and his successor Hans Georg von Mackensen (although historian Elizabeth Wiskemann claims that Philipp aspired to become German ambassador to Rome and hence "joined the chorus against" von Hassell that led to his ouster in January 1938).[7] More certain is that Philipp did not like von Neurath's successor as Foreign Minister, Joachim von Ribbentrop. Walter Schellenberg (1910–52), an intelligence operative who worked for Himmler and Heydrich in the RSHA, went so far as to say that Prince Philipp had "a bad relationship with Reich foreign minister Ribbentrop."[8] One of the reasons for the strained relationship, of course, was that the prince stood outside the foreign minister's authority. Philipp was also quietly dismissive of the latter's ability (it did not help matters that Ribbentrop had purchased his aristocratic title). Of course, many other Nazi leaders shared this view of Ribbentrop (Göring told Prince Paul of Yugoslavia in 1939 that Ribbentrop was "conceited" and an "idiot").[9] Still, Philipp and Ribbentrop coexisted—and often worked toward common goals. It is telling that Princess Mafalda reported to her secretary, "[T]he diplomatic representatives of the Reich have created unpleasant situations through their tactless conduct and the prince had to 'iron out' these mistakes."[10]

The origins of Prince Philipp's involvement in foreign affairs lay, of course, in his network of contacts, starting with his royal relations. In addition to his Italian in-laws, there were influential cousins whom he tried to win over for the Nazi regime. Indicative of these efforts was the letter he sent to Prince Paul of Yugoslavia in January 1935, shortly after Paul had assumed the regency in the wake of the murder of King Alexander I in Marseilles in October 1934. Philipp wrote:

> Goering, in who's [*sic*] house I am staying for a few days came back greatly impressed from the funeral + his stay in Belgrade. He was full of admiration for you + all he had seen + spoke in the most enthusiastic way about it to Hitler + to me. You have made a good friend in him which pleases me very much because you can always rely on his loyalty. His greatest wish is that you should come here as soon as you have got a chance so Hitler + he can show you the new Germany + would be able to prove their friendship.[11]

This kind of cheerleading for the Third Reich outside of official channels —the letter above was scribbled hastily in pencil and delivered by an unnamed party who was traveling to Belgrade—did not generate immediate dividends, but it was welcomed by the Nazi leaders. Previously, in December 1933, Philipp had provided reports to Hitler on talks he had held with French ambassador to Germany André François-Poncet on the issue of German rearmament. Even though the French ambassador was sympathetic to the German position (he indicated a willingness to permit Germany's armed forces to grow to 250,000—well above the 100,000 specified in the Treaty of Versailles), Philipp's intervention yielded no discernible results. Indeed, Philipp's efforts provoked a rebuke from Reichswehr Minister Werner von Blomberg, who objected to the involvement of "private persons" in such matters.[12]

Philipp was far more effective in Italy. Relations between Germany and Italy remained unsettled until the mid-1930s. The first meeting between Hitler and Mussolini on 14 June 1934 had gone badly, with Hitler "ill at ease" and Mussolini unimpressed by his counterpart. In his memoirs, Putzi Hanfstaengl recalled some of the other difficulties: "The two regimes, although similar in nature, were on opposite sides of the diplomatic fence. Italy was still one of the victorious allies, and Nazi intrigues in Austria, in an area which Italians considered the nerve center of their southern European sphere of influence, were a constant source of friction between the two countries."[13] Mussolini viewed Hitler as an upstart, and Hitler in turn retained a host of resentments he associated with the more senior dictator —starting with the perceived lack of support given during the *Kampfzeit* preceding the seizure of power. Bilateral relations deteriorated still further in the summer of 1934 after the assassination of Austrian chancellor Engelbert Dollfuss. Mussolini, who had been sympathetic to the Austro-Fascist leader (and viewed Italy as the protector of Austrian independence), suspected that Hitler was behind the plot.[14] The situation was ripe for mediation, and a number of Nazi officials, including foreign press attaché Putzi Hanfstaengl, endeavored to make their mark here.

Prince Philipp also perceived an opportunity with regard to the faltering German-Italian relations. After all, he had previously helped Göring in his approaches to Mussolini, and his connection to the Italian royal family provided him with a unique advantage. He enjoyed warm relations with both Mussolini and with Count Ciano, the latter who became foreign minister in 1936. It helped that Il Duce could speak German (he learned the language as a young man), that Ciano spoke English, and that Philipp was generally proficient in Italian.[15] Already in the autumn of 1934, Philipp had induced Hitler to entrust him preliminary discussions with the Italian leaders regarding Austria. At the time, British ambassador to Italy, Sir Eric Drummond, the Earl of Perth (1876–1952), reported to the British Foreign Office that "[his] French colleague" had information that Philipp was a "secret German emissary" and was helping "make every possible effort to ameliorate Italian-German relations."[16] Although Philipp's influence on foreign policy peaked between 1938 and 1940, he had prepared the groundwork during the previous years. While Philipp generally tried to improve bilateral relations on a day-to-day basis, there were four important instances where Philipp reported to Mussolini as Hitler's personal representative: the Anschluss, the Sudeten crisis, the occupation of rump-state Czechoslovakia, and the invasion of Poland.[17]

Philipp also helped organize Hitler's state visits to Italy. Perhaps the most important of Hitler's trips to Italy occurred in early May 1938—that is, shortly after receiving Mussolini's support for the Anschluss. On this occasion, the huge German contingent, which included Party leaders such as Himmler, Goebbels, and Hitler Youth Leader Baldur von Schirach, required four special trains. The trip featured "endless galas, receptions, and banquets, the expensive presents and imposing decorations."[18] It also involved, in the words of SD agent Walter Schellenberg, the arrest of "over six thousand suspicious persons" as the Italians placed them in "preventive

Meeting at the Berghof: Ciano talks with Himmler (back to viewer), as well as Hermann and Emmy Göring; Prince Philipp is caught in the reflection of Heinrich Hoffmann's photograph on both the left and the right.

custody."[19] Philipp accompanied Hitler on a tour of the Colosseum in Rome and helped plan many of the events, including a banquet with King Vittorio Emmanuele and Queen Elena.[20] The prince also took steps during the visits to remedy any awkward and antagonistic feelings that arose. One observer recalled, "Hitler comported himself with regards to the king and the royal family in an arrogant and haughty way. His entourage, for example, had forced their way into the royal garden without permission and demanded to be served by the royal kitchen. Similar incidents always repeatedly occurred on visits of the Italian Queen to Germany."[21] Philipp was relatively successful in his efforts as a liaison and organizer. Years later, during the war, Hitler reminisced fondly about the May 1938 trip, "The enchantment of Florence, Rome, Ravenna, and Siena or Perugia, how beautiful is Tuscany and Umbria. Every palace in Florence or Rome is worth more than all Windsor Castle."[22] This was also the trip where the dictator visited the Uffizi Gallery in Florence—an experience he claimed that galvanized his plans for the *Führermuseum* at Linz.

As important as these state visits were—and they did facilitate the two nations coming together in the series of agreements that culminated in the Pact of Steel of May 1939—they built upon the negotiations that were hammered out during periods of crisis. None was more important for bilateral relations than the arrangement arrived at in March 1938, when Mussolini reversed a long-standing policy and permitted Austria to be absorbed by the German Reich. The chair of Philipp's denazification board described this shift as being of "world historical importance."[23] On two occasions—21 May 1935 and on 11 July 1936—the Nazi regime had confirmed the inalienable right of the Austrian state to exist as sovereign and independent.[24] But Hitler clearly abandoned such assurances starting in early 1938. Though he proceeded by way of intimidation and brute force—most notably, the incursion on 12 March—it was necessary to prepare the way diplomatically and induce Mussolini to abandon his role as the de facto protector of Austrian independence. The postwar denazification tribunal called Italy's response "of decisive importance for the execution, result, and success of the planned attack."[25]

Although Hitler focused on a solution to the Austrian situation in the wake of his meeting with Austrian chancellor Kurt von Schuschnigg (1897–1977) on 12 February 1938—ratcheting up the pressure on the Austrian government via propaganda, organizing the indigenous Nazi forces in Austria, and preparing the German army—he initially failed to secure the support of Mussolini.[26] This was more easily said than done; relations between the two dictators were still uncertain, with each mistrusting the other. Recently declassified documents from the Vatican archives, for example, have revealed that Mussolini advised Pope Pius XI in early April 1938 (that is, less than a month after the Anschluss) "that it would be worthwhile with Hitler . . . to adopt more forceful measures, for example, excommunication."[27] Mussolini still thought himself the senior statesman among fascist leaders and often contemplated checking the increasingly powerful German dictator. Relations were not improved by the absence of a German ambassador in Rome: the Anschluss took place during a three-month interlude between the dismissal of von Hassell in January 1938 and the arrival of von Mackensen later in the spring. Furthermore, Foreign Minister Ribbentrop, who was appointed in February 1938, did not get along well with his counterpart Ciano. Foreign Office state secretary von Weizsäcker, noted, "Each of them looked down upon the other."[28] Philipp was therefore called upon to smooth over some very rough patches. On 18 February, in the wake of Hitler's meeting with von Schuschnigg at the Berghof, he went to see Ciano in Rome: the Italian foreign minister "read a lecture in what the Nazis might have called the English governess fashion," protesting the lack of consultation regarding events in Austria.[29] On 11 March, the day before the climactic invasion, Hitler realized that he had yet to communicate directly with Mussolini and negotiate this very delicate proposition. This was most likely an intentional decision: Hitler did not want to reveal his plans too early or provide Mussolini with an opportunity to coordinate any diplomatic resistance. While the German dictator had not yet decided on formal annexation, he was intent on an incursion by the army and intended to strike the next day.

Hitler summoned Philipp, who was then in Kassel. Coincidentally, Philipp was planning a trip to Rome in the next few days, so he was prepared to leave on the eleventh if Hitler so wished. Of course, Hitler so wished, and he ordered a plane to bring the prince to Berlin. Because Philipp had so much luggage—he was transporting flowers for his mother-in-law's residence in the royal palace—he asked for a special airplane and received a *Kuriermaschine* (express plane).[30] Hitler later learned of the extravagant requisition and was so upset that this provided "grounds for lasting friction." While the annexation of Hitler's homeland to the German Reich hung in the balance, Philipp was transporting flowers from Schloss Wilhelmshöhe in Kassel to Italy so that his family's "garden could thereby be planted."[31]

The plane made an intermediate stop in Berlin, and Philipp was taken by a car to the Reich Chancellery. The prince was made to wait for two-and-a-half-hours before Hitler saw him. As Philipp entered the dictator's office, Hitler was just finishing signing an oversized letter, and there were instruments nearby to seal it with red wax. Hitler provided Philipp with only a cursory explanation, remarking that there was no time for a "detailed briefing," but he added that the letter said all that Mussolini needed to know.[32] Philipp's job was to convince Mussolini that "the entire question is purely a German matter in which he did not want to intervene."[33] That afternoon, Philipp took the large, wax-sealed letter that Hitler had penned to Mussolini and departed on his special plane. He endured terrible weather as storms battered the plane, but he delivered the letter to Mussolini at the Palazzo Venezia that night. The missive summarized the negotiations between Hitler and Schuschnigg, and recounted Hitler's efforts "to establish peace and order once again."[34] The letter also mentioned German plans to invade and included an apology "for the rushed nature of this letter and the form of this communication."[35] Philipp had instructions from Hitler to call him immediately with the results ("he feverishly waited for Mussolini's answer"), and Philipp did so at 10:25 p.m.[36]

Because the call was routed through the German Embassy in Rome in the Villa Wolkonsky—an effort to achieve a secure line—the connection was poor, and Philipp had to yell and repeat himself in order to communicate with Hitler. The two men spoke for only four minutes, but the conversation was memorable. The Forschungsamt recorded the text of their conversation, and because it was reproduced and circulated to certain government ministries, it is one of the few documents from Prince Christoph's agency that survived the war. The transcript, which was entered into evidence at the International Military Tribunal at Nuremberg on 29 November 1945, included the following passages:

> PHILIPP: Il Duce has taken the entire matter in a very friendly manner. He says I should send very friendly greetings to you. . . . Then Mussolini said that Austria was a done deal.

HITLER: Then please tell Mussolini, that I will never forget it.

PHILIPP: *Jawohl!*

HITLER: Never, never never. It can be as he wants. I am now also ready to enter into an entirely new agreement with him.

PHILIPP: *Jawohl!* That's what I said to him.

HITLER: If the Austrian matter is now then cleared out of the way, I am prepared to go through thick and thin—it's all the same to me.

PHILIPP: *Jawohl, mein Führer!*

HITLER: You can tell him again, I really want to thank him from my heart. I will never, never forget this. I will never forget this.[37]

Philipp's denazification panel also reviewed this transcript and opined, "He was charged with leading highly important diplomatic discussions with a government chief of an allied state who was a personal friend."[38] Philipp, of course, took another view. He recalled, "I was very unpleasantly disturbed by this assignment, since neither did I know the contents of the letter I was transmitting, nor had I been briefed on the political precedents. Thus I was not in the position to answer Mussolini's eventual questions."[39] Philipp's lawyer Fabian von Schlabrendorff (1907–80) added that the prince was an "administrative official who unexpectedly was entrusted with a special diplomatic mission to Mussolini, seemingly because Hitler thought he could use for his purposes the social position, and above all, the reputation of the concerned party in Rome due to his familial relations to the Italian royal house."[40] His denazification board did not place much credence in this attempt to mitigate responsibility and ruled that while Philipp may not have seen the letter, he knew "its general content and motive, sense and purpose, of the transmitted message."[41] Historian John Wheeler-Bennett, in his official biography of British king George VI, noted that "Philip of Hesse had been pressing Mussolini for some time to give just this assurance, but he did not succeed in getting it unequivocally until the night of March 11, the very eve of the German annexation of Austria."[42] This interpretation, then, dismisses Philipp's claim that he was only a messenger and suggests a more central role for the Prince in shaping the two countries' bilateral relations. The most plausible rendition of events combines the two versions: Because the prince saw Mussolini on a regular basis and because German-Austrian relations had been a thorny issue for some time, it is almost certain that Philipp pushed for the Italian leader to give his German counterpart a freer hand; but the invasion itself developed as a plan only in the days prior to the *Einmarsch*, and it is unlikely that the prince had been making explicit requests for support in this undertaking during the previous weeks. The fact remains, however, that Philipp had contributed in a significant way to Hitler's first act of aggression against a foreign nation—an act that led down the slippery slope leading to World War II. Or, as Ian Kershaw has written in his biography of Hitler, the Anschluss suggested that the German dictator "could do anything he wanted."[43]

Hitler began to rely less on professional diplomats in the wake of the successful annexation of Austria, and accordingly he continued to use Philipp to keep Mussolini apprised of the rapidly changing situation. Some five months after the Anschluss, the Sudeten crisis moved to the fore when Hitler ordered the local Nazi leaders to agitate more vigorously (supposedly on behalf of the approximately three million ethnic Germans that lived in the crescent-shaped region in the northwest of Czechoslovakia). The situation appeared grave, and war seemed a possibility even before 15 September 1938, when British prime minister Neville Chamberlain and Hitler met at the Berghof (they also held a follow up meeting a week later at Bad Godesberg near Bonn). During the first week of September, Mussolini and Ciano had turned to Prince Philipp and requested information about the German demands regarding the Sudetenland. Philipp traveled to Berlin and met with Hitler, who on the fourth or fifth of September dictated a "lengthy memorandum" that Philipp brought back to Rome. Even though "the Führer only reiterated his general views and provided no clue to his actual plans," Philipp was securing his place in the Nazi foreign policy apparatus.[44] On 10 September 1938, Philipp met with Ciano in Rome and raised the issue of a military pact between Italy and Germany—a subject that Philipp had previously broached with Mussolini.[45] In the wake of Hitler and Chamberlain's meeting on 22 September at Bad Godesberg near Bonn, Philipp was once again dispatched to Rome to brief the Italian leaders.[46] Later, in October 1938, Philipp called on Ciano to explore a proposal that was the brainchild of Göring: a four-power pact between not only Germany and Italy but also Britain and France (allied against the Soviet Union). While little came of this discussion, Philipp contributed to the creation of both the Pact of Steel and ultimately, the Axis alliance.[47] Several weeks later, in the wake of the Munich Conference, Hitler and Mussolini concluded a protocol that articulated plans for mutual support, a copy of which Philipp hand delivered to Mussolini. Philipp later testified, "I received this assignment from Hitler personally."[48]

Or course, the drama and tragedy surrounding the German takeover of the Sudetenland culminated with the Munich conference of 29–30 September 1938. With Mussolini personally present, Philipp's services as a liaison were not needed. But the Prince was nonetheless close at hand; on the morning of the twenty-ninth before the conference begun, he had traveled with Hitler to Kufstein on the old German-Austrian frontier to meet with Mussolini and travel on the train up to Munich.[49] The pictures of the actual conference taken by Heinrich Hoffmann show Philipp huddling with Göring, Himmler, Ernst von Weizsäcker, and other members of the German entourage. Philipp was there mostly as window dressing:

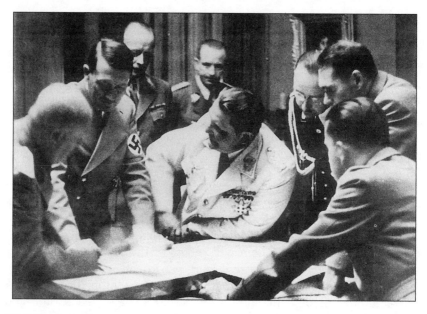

The Munich Conference in September 1938: from left, Mussolini, Hitler, Prince Philipp, Otto Dietrich (Reich Press Chief), Göring, Himmler, Hess, Ciano.

as Hitler and the other leaders personally shaped the actual agreement. But Philipp had the opportunity to play a bit part on the world stage, and was visible in the newsreel footage and the still-photos that circulated around the globe (usually standing a step back from the principals).[50] He also had the opportunity to celebrate that night with Hitler and Mussolini at a gala dinner: Chamberlain and Daladier declined the invitation and retired to their hotel rooms.

In the wake of the agreement—the culmination of the policy of appeasement—Philipp joined Hitler on a tour of the newly acquired territory: 11,000 square miles where 2.8 million Sudeten Germans and 800,000 Czechs resided. An official in the Oberpräsidium recalled that Philipp "had visited the Sudetenland together with Hitler after its occupation."[51] One can only imagine Philipp's enthusiasm for Hitler at this point. Even American journalist William Shirer recalled, "No one who was in Germany in the days after Munich, as this writer was, can forget the rapture of the German people. They were relieved that war had been averted; they were elated and swollen with pride at Hitler's bloodless victory. . . . Within the short space of six months, they reminded you, Hitler had conquered Austria and the Sudetenland, adding ten million inhabitants to the Third Reich and a vast strategic territory which opened the way for German domination of southeastern Europe. And without the loss of a single

German life! With the instinct of a genius rare in German history, he had . . . forced [Europe] to bend to his will."[52]

With the German invasion of rump-state Czechoslovakia on 15 March 1939, Philipp was again deployed to placate the Italians. The strategy differed this time because there was no plausible justification of the invasion. On two previous occasions—11 March 1938 and 26 September 1938— Hitler had made public assurances concerning the territorial integrity of Czechoslovakia.[53] The strategy this time was to act first, and then, only after the fact, have Philipp justify, explain, and if necessary, apologize. The Italians received no prior notice as Wehrmacht troops began crossing the frontier on 15 March 1939. That morning, Philipp requested a meeting with Mussolini and Ciano, explaining that it was an urgent matter. Philipp proceeded to the Quirinal Palace, where he met the Italian leaders. There is disagreement over exactly what transpired. Ciano reported in his diaries that Philipp informed them of the invasion verbally; while Philipp maintained after the war that he delivered another letter from Hitler and was therefore only a courier.[54] But the letter never turned up in either Italian or German archives; and the denazification board, which investigated the matter, could see no reason why Mussolini would have concealed such a document from his son-in-law, the foreign minister. Ciano, of course, was not around to testify after the war, having been hanged in Verona in 1944. In all likelihood, both Ciano and Philipp were partly right and partly incorrect: there was almost certainly a letter from Hitler to Mussolini that Philipp had delivered (Foreign Office state secretary von Weizsäcker wrote to German ambassador to Italy von Mackensen on 11 March that this would be the plan); but Philipp did more than simply hand over the document.[55]

Philipp recalled the events as follows: "As I arrived in Rome at that time, I was expected by Mussolini. We were alone. I handed him the relevant letter, which was in an envelope. It was not especially extensive. Mussolini took note of it and had a very serious expression on his face. He said relatively little."[56] Philipp said they did not discuss the document; he personally had not read it and Mussolini raised no questions. Il Duce simply folded the document and placed it in the jacket pocket of his suit and escorted Philipp to the door. At that moment, Count Ciano entered and Philipp heard him say that "he had heard that Mussolini was looking for him. He was playing golf and as a result could not come earlier."[57] Mussolini then said, "The Prince von Hessen has come from Berlin with the following communication" and then told Ciano the contents of the document.[58] Ciano asked if Mussolini had any orders, and the latter said no, not at the moment. Ciano then escorted Philipp to his car, at which point Ciano noticed that his own official car wasn't there; Philipp therefore gave him a lift in his. They drove to Ciano's villa, the Palazzo

Chigi, where, Philipp presumed, he went to his office and made the entry in his diary.[59]

Prince Philipp tried to conciliate the Italians in the wake of the German invasion of 15 March. He reportedly told Mussolini and Ciano, "With the completion of the operation, twenty German divisions were available for action 'tomorrow, if necessary' on another front in support of Axis policy."[60] While the Axis alliance was not yet fully in place, Philipp was helping work toward the Pact of Steel and trying to mollify the Italians. Count Ciano noted in his diaries, "I find [Mussolini] dissatisfied with the message and defeated. He does not want the press to report on the visit of the Prince von Hessen. 'The Italians will just laugh at me. Every time Hitler occupies a country, he sends me a message.' "[61] Ciano also noted that he personally was not convinced by Philipp's arguments—that is, the official German line. He wrote, "The Führer tells us that he acted because the Czechs would not withdraw their troops and because they remain in contact with Russia, and because they mistreated Germans. These justifications may be enough for Goebbels's propaganda, but when one speaks to us, one should spare us such nonsense."[62] Ciano added, "Our mistake was to talk too much with them."[63] Ironically, this is what Hitler sought to avoid and helps explain why he sent Philipp on these short-notice briefing missions. As Luftwaffe adjutant to the Führer Headquarters Nicolaus von Below noted in his memoirs, "Hitler always notified his allies *post festum*, but Hitler preferred their resentment to the greater evil of risking their loquacity."[64] Officially, the Italians gave the Germans their "unreserved approval for the 'liquidation of Czecho-Slovakia.' "[65] Phillip in turn told Mussolini about "the gratitude of the Führer for the unmistakable Italian support" and remarked that their support would "free up twenty divisions for other undertakings that would benefit the Axis."[66] According to Ciano, this would be the last German move for some time: "Hitler let Mussolini know that it would be better to wait a couple more years until he had a hundred Prussian divisions at his disposal, because he intended to embark on a great undertaking."[67] Philipp received clear indications of Hitler's geopolitical aspirations and appeared to be supportive of the Nazi foreign policy at this point. Granted, he was almost palpably naïve: concerning the invasion of Czechoslovakia, he said, "I proceeded in good faith, [believing] that the attacks on the ethnic Germans took place and that they were the reason for the invasion."[68]

As Philipp continued his involvement in international relations, he adhered to two constants: the belief in the effectiveness of royal relationships, where those with titles worked to preserve their influence, and the importance of peace between European powers, especially Germany and Britain. Prince Philipp, like many other princes, often took steps to conceal his efforts to advance these agendas. For example, he wrote the new regent of Yugoslavia, Prince Paul, in January 1935: After advising him on how to deal with Hitler and Göring—and mentioning that he was writing from Carinhall—he concluded this very informal letter, written in English, with the words, "Please destroy this letter after you have read it."[69] While one letter does not prove the existence of a network of princes, it is consistent with other information attesting to how the traditional elite continued with their efforts to preserve their influence—which they viewed as most likely happening on a German-dominated Continent. Their vision was more likely to be realized if there was no active fighting between Germany and Britain, and Philipp, like a number of other princes, took steps that he hoped would help keep the peace. Prince Auwi, for example, went to see his cousin, King Leopold III of Belgium (1901–83) in Brussels in January 1939 with the idea of forestalling a war.[70] In another instance, Prince Max Egon von Hohenlohe-Langenburg (1897–1968), as J. K. Roberts in the British Foreign Office noted in July 1940, "was very active as an intermediary with Göring and other so-called moderate Germans before the Munich agreement. He also sent a message in favor of peace talks last December, when Mr. Dalherus was also active."[71] Prince Max Egon von Hohenlohe-Langenburg was in Madrid in early 1941 and met with British Ambassador Sir Samuel Hoare: he suggested that Göring head an interim government that would be prepared to conclude a peace agreement.[72] And Albrecht Haushofer (1903–45), a professor of political geography at the University of Berlin who sought to facilitate a meeting between Rudolf Hess and the Duke of Hamilton, wrote to Deputy Führer Hess on 19 September 1940 about "a settlement between the Führer and the British upper classes."[73] While Haushofer was pessimistic about concluding this pact, it is striking that he contemplated a rapprochement between elites.

The most important meeting between German and British princes prior to the outbreak of World War II took place in Florence on 1 July 1939, on the occasion of the wedding of Princess Irene (1904–74), the daughter of Constantine I, the king of Greece, to Prince Aimone Roberto di Savoia-Aosta, the Duke of Spoleto (1904–48), the cousin of the Italian king who had long harbored thoughts of harnessing fascist support to succeed Vittorio Emmanuele.[74] While the Duke of Kent was ostensibly sent to represent the British royal family and extend the traditional courtesy accorded to individuals from such illustrious families on special occasions, much more was going on behind the scenes. The wedding occurred after the German invasion of rump-state Czechoslovakia—the "last straw" in Chamberlain's appeasement policy—and after the British had given assurances to Poland in case of a German attack. With war looming, the governments of Europe were jockeying for position, and the British aimed, among other goals, to keep the Italians out of any future conflict. One reason to send the Duke of Kent was to improve relations with the Italian king, and hope that he could use his influence in the desired way. The Duke's trip, which involved relations between ruling houses, would have been within the conventional boundaries observed by royals. But the Florentine wedding entailed more than this.

King George VI had such a strong desire to avert war between Britain and Germany that he felt it appropriate to utilize a royal emissary for this cause. Historian Tom MacDonnell observed, "George VI was haunted by the memory of the Great War, and he had been an enthusiastic supporter of Chamberlain's appeasement policies. Repeatedly he had offered to make his own appeal to Hitler, sharing with his brother the Duke of Windsor the idea that kings and princes still had a meaningful part to play in diplomacy, as if nothing had happened to the map of Europe since 1914 when the Continent had been the private domain of royal cousins."[75] He therefore turned to his younger brother, whom he trusted completely and who had excellent contacts in many nations. In 1934, the Duke of Kent had married Princess Marina of Greece and Denmark (1906–68): one of Marina's sisters, Olga, was the wife of Prince Regent Paul of Yugoslavia, and another, Elisabeth (1904–55) (known as "Woolly") lived in Munich. Woolly had married Count Karl Theodor zu Toerring-Jettenbach (1900–67), a member of the ducal Wittelsbach family who possessed a large fortune and an imposing home, Schloss Winhöring, which the Kents often visited. (Note that the Duchess of Kent and the Countess von Toerring were first cousins of Princesses Sophia and Cécile von Hessen as well as good friends.)[76] Count Toerring also apparently evinced some sympathy for the Nazis, although he was not a Nazi Party member and exhibited considerable refinement (he possessed a superb collection of modern art).[77] While visits to Marina's sisters often provided the pretext for trips, there were other excursions in the 1930s: the Duke of Kent, for example, had traveled to Poland in 1937—ostensibly on the private invitation of Count Potocki, but, as a contemporaneous journalist noted, "the 'private' journeys of members of the English Royal House in fact have been quite often equivalent to discreet political missions."[78] The Kents, as well as the Toerrings and Prince Albrecht von Bayern, were visiting Paul and Olga at the latter's summer residence at Brdo in late summer 1939 when war broke out.[79] Later, in July 1940, the Duke of Kent went to Portugal to meet dictator Antonio Salazar in an effort—successfully in this instance—to keep Portugal neutral in the event of war.[80] While it is unclear precisely what he sought to accomplish during these trips to the Continent in the 1930s, a remark made by his brother, George VI, to Canadian prime minister Mackenzie King and President Roosevelt in a well-lubricated late-night exchange on 1 June 1939 is revealing. According to the Canadian leader, "the King spoke very frankly about how the Germans for many years past had been spying on England. Gave his own experience and said his own family relations in

Wedding photo of the Duke and Duchess of Kent sent to Prince Christoph and Princess Sophia, 1934.

Germany had been used to try and spy and to get particulars from other members of the family. . . ."[81] It would appear then, the King was using royal relationships in an effort to prevent a war and that the Duke of Kent was a pawn in the appeasement game played at the time.

"Georgie Kent" and Philipp von Hessen had evidently met earlier in the year in Rome (although Philipp did not mention it in his postwar accounts).[82] In any case, the Duke of Kent and Prince Philipp were well acquainted. In a recent interview, Prince Philip, Duke of Edinburgh, commented, "There was a tremendous amount of contact between the two."[83] Both, for example, had attended the funeral of King Alexander I in Belgrade in October 1934 after the Yugoslav monarch had been assassinated in Marseilles.[84] The Duke of Kent and his brother Edward (then Prince of Wales) had traveled to Belgrade to represent the family, while Philipp and Hermann Göring were among the Germans present.[85] In July 1938, the Duke of Kent and Prince Philipp met at the funeral of Queen Marie of Romania, which took place in Bucharest. Queen Marie (1875–1938) was born a British princess, the daughter of Prince Alfred, Duke of Edinburgh and Grand Duchess Marie Alexandrovna—that is, a granddaughter of Queen Victoria and Tsar Alexander II. She had married King Ferdinand von Hohenzollern-Sigmaringen in 1893, and her funeral, which entailed her body lying in state for three days in Bucharest before being taken to Curtea de Arges to be buried among the graves of the Romanian monarchs, drew royals from all over Europe.[86] The Duke of Kent and Prince Philipp therefore had ideal opportunities to hold discussions in both July 1938 and July 1939: a royal funeral and a royal wedding.

King George VI and Prime Minister Chamberlain evidently discussed what the Duke of Kent would say when he traveled to Florence. Indeed, the king's plans went farther than this. His official biographer John Wheeler-Bennett noted that Prince Philipp von Hessen

> was believed still to retain the Führer's confidence. Why, therefore, thought the King, should Prince Philip not be employed to good purpose? "Do you think it would be possible go get him over here," he wrote to Mr. Chamberlain [on 3 July 1939] & to use him as a messenger to convey to Hitler that we really are in earnest? He asked the Prime Minister to talk the idea over with [Foreign Secretary] Lord Halifax, and to communicate the result to him personally.[87]

It is striking that King George VI would have considered Prince Philipp as a liaison; yet the two men were acquainted (they had met as children and very likely at the wedding of Paul and Olga of Yugoslavia back in 1923, where "Bertie," the future king, had served as best man.).[88] Yet Chamberlain and Halifax wanted to constrain the royals because the situation in Europe was too complicated and unsettled to entrust negotiations to amateurs such as the Duke and the Prince (at that moment the British were also trying to bring the Soviets on board in a coalition against Germany). The prime minister considered it essential that he and the professional diplomats speak for the United Kingdom and "dismissed a suggestion by the King that they use Philipp of Hesse, a royal relation."[89] Wheeler-Bennett concluded that "in deference to [Chamberlain and Halifax's] views, the King did not press it."[90] But the Duke of Kent and Philipp nonetheless held discussions in Florence, and the former took the appropriate steps of consulting with professional diplomats before embarking on the journey. The Foreign Office, for example, vetted the toast he was to give to the newlyweds at the wedding banquet held in the Pitti Palace, so as to convey just the right message (ostensibly to avoid recognition of King Vittorio Emmanuele as emperor of Ethiopia and King of Albania—both conquered by Mussolini's forces).[91] Chamberlain and members of the Foreign Office evidently continued to believe that they had impressed upon the duke the need for a limited role. This understanding is borne out, indirectly, by the report written by a British diplomat on the wedding, which says a great deal about the public ceremony, and nothing about consultations with influential foreigners. The British consul wrote of the lavish festivities, noting "during the two days of the wedding festivities Florence was *en fête* . . . the central parts of the town were beflagged . . . [and] the Florentines gathered to gaze on and applaud the procession of carriages."[92] It is striking that while the Duke of Kent and Prince Philipp carried on substantive discussions at the wedding, the British diplomat writing to the foreign minister reported on, in his words, "the pomp and jubilation" (he even included a precise listing of royals in attendance, which covered several pages).[93] The diplomat appeared to have no inkling about the exchanges between the Duke of Kent and Prince Philipp.

Prince Philipp later offered his own account of the discussions that took place at the wedding in Florence. He recalled after the war: "in a last attempt to avoid the catastrophe that stood before us I had a conversation with my cousin, the Duke of Kent in the summer of 1939, in the course of which he indicated a way, according to his personal opinion, that the worst perhaps could be avoided."[94] According to Philipp's denazification lawyer von Schlabrendorff, they discussed the "tense situation in Europe" in general, and Danzig more specifically.[95] The Duke of Kent communicated the view that England would regard a German attack on Poland as a "casus belli." The duke "wanted us to proceed with no illusions. Besides that, he said 'an important point is Ribbentrop as Foreign Minister is a perpetual insult to England and conflicts will always come as long as this man is Foreign Minister. I was also of his opinion and saw the danger of Ribbentrop's politics."[96] The wine-salesman turned foreign minister elicited negative reactions from most aristocrats because of his radical and hawkish views, but also because of his pompous manner and nakedly ambitious social aspirations. Contemporaries, for example, seemed to relish the story that the Fellows at Eton had rejected his son for admission to the school.[97]

One can only speculate about the frankness of the discussion between Philipp and the Duke of Kent. For Philipp to confide (as he claimed after the war) that he viewed Ribbentrop as dangerous constituted an incautious statement, and, by Nazi standards, verged on the treasonous. If true, it indicated a strong trust in the Duke of Kent and suggested that Philipp's first loyalty was to royal relations. And conversely, as noted above, it was bold for a British royal to circumvent established diplomatic and political procedures, and communicate to the Germans what acts would precipitate a war. According to the established practices of the British constitutional monarchy, this was not the purview of the royals. In this instance, his discussions directly contravened the instructions of the prime minister. Even more striking, but also far more speculative, is the idea that King George VI and the Duke of Kent continued to push for a negotiated peace through 1941: after his capture in Scotland, Rudolf Hess repeatedly requested to see the king, and several authors have argued that the British royals were active members of an anti-Churchill "peace party" in the United Kingdom.[98] Of course, such charges have been vehemently denied by British officials, and at the time in 1941, Hess's "requests to see the King were regarded by the authorities as proof of his madness."[99] While theories of the royals' involvement in wartime peace negotiations cannot be proven with the available documentation, they are not inconsistent with the pattern established in the 1930s.

Because Chamberlain had not sanctioned the Duke of Kent as an official representative, this effort to secure peace had dim prospects for success. Hitler, at least, appeared to ignore the message communicated to him and did not regard the Duke as a spokesman for Great Britain. After the Florentine wedding, Philipp returned to Germany and requested a meeting with Hitler in order to tell him what he had learned. He was not granted an audience until 23 August, when he was invited to the Berghof. It was already evening when the Führer received him. But Philipp gave his account and "told Hitler everything."[100] He reported that "an attack on Poland would be the beginning of a world war. England would enter this war. Such a war would end in catastrophe for Germany and Europe." Yet, as he noted later, "Hitler threw this warning to the wind."[101] Hitler said to him: "Now I want to tell you something. I have already indicated that you are coming to a decisive moment in the history of the world."[102] This proved an accurate statement: Ribbentrop was in Moscow, negotiating with his counterpart Molotov and with Stalin. As Hitler made this comment, the telephone rang and Ribbentrop was on the line. The two men spoke for about ten minutes. When Hitler hung up the phone, he explained that the pact with the Soviet Union had been signed.[103] Hitler opined the pact "with Russia means that it would be senseless for England to enter into the coming war, [especially] after Germany freed up its back in the East through the treaty."[104] In hindsight, Philipp recognized that he was sunk by the German-Russian nonaggression pact, but he maintained, "despite that I made a constant effort after the outbreak of war for a call to reason; I was not successful, however, and Ribbentrop also opposed me with fierce resistance."[105] Ribbentrop, like Hitler, remained skeptical of Philipp's assertion that an attack on Poland would bring England into the war. Ribbentrop retorted that the British were too "decadent" to fight.[106] The Duke of Kent's message, despite coming from the heart of Buckingham Palace, was not taken seriously.

Prince Philipp continued to push for a negotiated peace with England even after the German attack on Poland and the British declaration of war. The prince met with Hitler again after the end of the Poland campaign in the fall of 1939, this time at the Führer Headquarters at Zoppot, a seaside

Meeting at the Kehlstein teahouse atop the Berghof: Prince Philipp, Ribbentrop, and Hitler.

resort on the Baltic. They again spoke in the company of Ribbentrop. Philipp later claimed that he argued for a peace initiative aimed at Great Britain; Ribbentrop countered that it was an inappropriate time for such an offer. Philipp recalled, "Hitler said, 'you know, we have now actually achieved what is most important. We have vanquished Poland [and] Danzig is again German. I am now inclined really to extend the hand of peace, a success that is perhaps conceivable.' But Ribbentrop replied to Hitler, 'I can say to you that by doing so, you will destroy all that you have achieved. One will regard you as weak and the entire world will laugh at you.'"[107] At this time, in October 1939, Hitler requested that Philipp go to Mussolini and deliver an update on the situation.[108] Philipp claimed that he begged off, telling Hitler that would entail being "utilized for tasks that did not correspond to his views."[109]

Philipp, in fact, not only continued to foster communications between Hitler and Mussolini but remained in contact with British assets. While he may have been discouraged, he continued to be an active interlocutor during the "Phoney War" or *Sitzkrieg*. Swedish physician and writer Dr. Axel Munthe (1857–1949), a neighbor of the Hessens in Capri and author of a best-selling autobiography *The Story of San Michele* (a book dedicated to Mafalda), sent a telling report to the British Foreign Office on

10 May 1940. Munthe and Philipp had just lunched at the Villa Svezia in Rome, and Philipp informed him that he "was now the official personal courier between Hitler and Mussolini for the conveyance of written and verbal messages. He travels between the two capitals about once a week."[110] Significantly, Munthe's report to the British government was labeled "Special Distribution and War Cabinet." The report stated that "Hitler did not wish Italy to enter the war as he can do without her. . . . In his opinion (Hesse's) Italy would not come into the war unless it spread into the Balkans." Philipp was also reported as saying that Hitler was "one of the greatest men of all time"; that he thought "the war would be over in favor of Germany by next spring"; and that Mussolini "was in the best of health and spirits" (except for some insomnia). Another report, this one unsigned, but evidently from the British ambassador in Rome, was dated 30 May 1940 and addressed to foreign secretary Viscount Halifax: it claimed Philipp as the source of a rumor that King Vittorio Emmanuele was contemplating abdication and flight to the United States because "Mussolini is the complete master of Italy."[111] This communication was also passed on to King George VI. Philipp was clearly not the most reliable source of information, and he had little effect on limiting the spread of the conflict, but he nonetheless continued his behind-the-scenes efforts.

Philipp's views in many ways mirrored those of Italian foreign minister Ciano, who wanted to limit the escalation of war in 1939 and 1940. Indeed, Philipp and Ciano, who also met frequently, would not only represent their masters but also pursue their own, rather less bellicose, agendas. Philipp, it seems, tried to gain the foreign minister's trust by providing a great deal of information. For example, in their meeting in Rome on 14 November 1939, Ciano claimed that Philipp informed him that the German attack on the French would begin soon, and not through Holland and Belgium (again, his reports were not always accurate). He also offered an account of the Venlo affair where Walter Schellenberg and agents from the RSHA nabbed, in Philipp's exaggerated words, the "Chief of the British Intelligence Service" (the Germans actually seized two senior British agents). Finally, Philipp told the Italian foreign minister about the assassination attempt made against Hitler on 9 November in the Bürgerbräukeller in Munich: Philipp reported that "those responsible were to be found among [Ernst] Röhm's old friends."[112] On 8 February 1940, Philipp again met with Ciano —this time, in the presence of Mussolini. The purpose of the discussion was to arrange a meeting between the Il Duce and the Führer. The two dictators had not met face to face since the Munich Conference in September 1938—an intercession that only magnified the importance of the role played by Philipp. Ciano told Philipp privately that he did not like the idea of a summit because "if the Duce meets up with the Germans, he always exceeds himself."[113] Ciano feared that Mussolini would express himself in a very "bellicose" way and promise to fight on the side of Germany. Hitler, of course, hoped to nurture such sentiments, and this was the reason he requested Philipp to arrange for the meeting: the aim of which was to bring Italy into the war, and coordinate an attack on France. This presented a predicament for Prince Philipp, who feared a wider war in Western Europe—especially one involving the three countries with which he had such close ties: Germany, Italy, and the United Kingdom. To this end, he supported Ciano in trying to delay the meeting between Hitler and Mussolini. In Philipp's audience with Il Duce on 8 February 1940, they discussed both political and military issues but came to no agreement on a course of action.

In attempting to reconstruct Prince Philipp's views at this critical juncture, one must be wary of the accounts he gave after the war. Philipp claimed that he returned to Hitler and took advantage of this unresolved situation, reporting that Mussolini did not consider it a good time to meet. Philipp also recalled that this tactic pleased Ciano very much. When the Italian foreign minister heard what Philipp had done, he shook the prince's hand and said, "you did that well."[114] Yet other Nazi leaders were convinced that Philipp was working to bring the Italians on board for the upcoming fight. Joseph Goebbels noted in his diary for 19 April 1940: "Prince Philipp von Hessen flies to Rome. He is supposed to try to expedite matters there and change somewhat the minds of the aristocracy."[115] While Philipp did not want to see Germany and Italy launch an invasion of France and the Benelux countries, he was conflicted in his loyalties. Accordingly, his efforts failed, and Hitler and Mussolini met at the Brenner Pass on 18 March 1940 where they firmed up the Axis.[116] Italy joined Germany as an active combatant on 10 June 1940 when Mussolini ignored the advice of Ciano and Field Marshal Badoglio and declared war on the French.

Philipp, of course, was not only the liaison to Mussolini but also to King Vittorio Emmanuele. The king had also counseled Philipp to keep Hitler and Mussolini apart during the Sitzkrieg that followed the Polish campaign, and Philipp's bold steps were evidently partly determined by his father-in-law's influence. Within German leadership circles, Prince Philipp became known as an advocate for the Italian royal family. For example, the adjutant of the famed SS-Lieutenant-Colonel (Standartenführer) Otto Skorzeny, reported how his chief was once in the Führer Headquarters during the war in the presence of Prince Philipp. Skorzeny uttered remarks that were critical of the Italians and their war efforts. Another SS officer present pulled Skorzeny aside and said that he should watch his words because Philipp "was present, and that the son-in-law of the Italian king was known to stand on the side of the king, and that he could inform the king about this conversation."[117] A German aide stationed in Italy recalled that Mussolini, after his rescue by the Skorzeny commando, commented, "that various circles in Italy were always against the war. He meant above all else the royal house and a certain circle around the king (the crown prince's Party). . . . I mean also the Prince von Hessen, who often visited his relatives, the king and the crown prince."[118] Indeed, Philipp's efforts to keep Mussolini and Hitler apart in the first half of 1940 may well have been discovered by the two leaders, and may have contributed to his harsh treatment during the latter part of the war.[119]

In attempting an assessment of Philipp's importance as player in German foreign affairs, one must acknowledge a complex and at times even contradictory record. While he helped facilitate the early expansionist initiatives, he recognized in 1939 the implications of a wider European war and took steps to prevent this kind of conflagration. Philipp, in the words of Karl Wolff (Himmler's liaison to the Führer Headquarters), "was one of the few state officials after the outbreak of the war who regularly had free access to the Führer"; however, he nonetheless had limited influence.[120] One associate of Philipp's also recalled asking what Hitler had said of the war; "The prince explained to me that Hitler didn't speak with him at all about these things, and that he himself also as a rule didn't ask, since they always conversed only about art and cultural matters."[121] Of course, Hitler was not known to engage in dialogues with any of his associates: Albert Speer and other close observers testified as much.[122] In comparison to others in Hitler's inner circle, Philipp measured up quite well. Karl Wolff concluded, for example: "It was established that whenever something was going on, the Prince of Hessen, as a valuable liaison, would be used, and as such, he was competent. . . . The prince was a highly regarded man in the circles of the Führer Headquarters."[123] Philipp, then, gave the appearance of loyalty to Hitler well into the war, as he surreptitiously balanced his divided loyalties between Germany and Italy, as well as between the internationalism associated with his royal relatives on the one hand, and the Nazis' quest for hegemony on the other. The chair of his denazification board rightly acknowledged, however, that the scales were tipped in favor of Hitler and the Nazis' goals, as he wrote, that Philipp "fulfilled the foreign policy assignments given to him in a manner loyal to the directions of the Führer until at least early 1943. If these did not meet the ultimate expectations of Hitler, especially hindering the overthrow of Mussolini and the fall of Italy, then circumstances were more powerful than him."[124]

Peace Among Princes

As "the gathering storm" took shape across Europe in the late-1930s, Winston Churchill was in the minority in advocating a hard-line against German demands. Indeed, among the elite in both the United Kingdom and Germany, the idea of appeasement proved extremely attractive. Events in the 1930s provided a basis for such thinking, starting with the pro-German attitude of nearly all members of the British royal family. True, World War I loomed large in the minds of the British royal family, and most members were not as positively disposed toward the Germans as during the years before 1914. Kenneth Rose has noted with regard to King George V, "not until 1935 could he write to a German cousin, the Grand Duke [Ernst Ludwig] of Hesse, 'That horrible and unnecessary war has made no difference in my feelings for you.' "[125] But relations between English and German royals had rebounded to a considerable extent in the mid-1930s. Furthermore, as historian Andrew Roberts notes, "It was correctly considered axiomatic that another war would spell doom for the British Empire. The royal family, which had watched the stock of monarchies diminishing after European wars, had acquired highly developed antennae for survival."[126] But there were other factors at play. One should not underestimate the impact that the Russian Revolution had on this generation of royals and princes: besides the political revulsion they felt, and the horror of knowing that the Romanovs were brutally murdered at Yekaterinburg, there was an added element of guilt (especially for the British) because George V had not provided sanctuary to his cousins and saved them: "Prime Minister Lloyd George himself advised King George to decline the Romanovs' arrival in order to buy popularity among leftist England at the price of his own relatives' lives."[127] Whether or not they were fully conscious of the political expediency that underscored the decision, the murders at Yekaterinburg provided the single most traumatic moment in the minds of most European royals and helped produce an intense, almost visceral hatred of bolshevism. For the Hessens, there was added dimension that the tsarina was a cousin from the Hesse-Darmstadt branch.

If the British royal family in the nineteenth century was effectively German, this did not change much in the new century. King George V, who ruled from 1910 to 1936, had married a German Princess, Mary of Teck (1867–1953)—the mother of Edward, the Duke of Windsor (1894–1972) and his younger brother, the future king George VI. Indeed, most in this generation also spoke flawless German and remained close to German relations, especially members of the Hesse-Darmstadt family. As noted earlier, a steady stream of German princes traveled to the United Kingdom to win over the British royal family, including Prince Ludwig von Hessen-Darmstadt, Prince Gottfried zu Hohenlohe-Langenburg, Princess Stephanie zu Hohenlohe, Prince Adolf von Mecklenburg, and Prince Otto Christian von Bismarck, among others. While George V appeared to vacillate in his views about Germany (some historians regard him as staunchly anti-Hitler while other argue that he "clearly took an extreme stand over

George, Duke of Kent, in the 1930s.

appeasement"), his sons, Edward VIII and George VI, were notably supportive of a rapprochement—with Edward VIII apparently the most sympathetic to the National Socialists.[128]

A key member of the British royal family who evinced a deep concern for Anglo-German relations was the youngest surviving brother, Prince George, the Duke of Kent—although so little is known about him that all assertions must be regarded as tentative. Many observers take the dearth of information about the duke as an indication of his pro-Nazi views. Indeed, the Duke of Kent has become a kind of magnet for proponents of conspiracy theories. One website, for example, includes the observation that there have been "a series of actions that seem to point to a massive concerted cover-up at [the] governmental level. . . . Today researchers find a wall of silence surrounding the subject. . . . It seems that George, Duke of Kent, must have committed some action that the establishment considered shaming or offensive, and have resolved to keep the truth from the public for two generations."[129] In order to advance their theories, they seize upon telling elements of his biography. For example, the Duke of Kent spoke excellent German, and as noted earlier, he made frequent trips to Germany and the Continent.[130]

The Duke of Kent, like his wife, professed great interest in the Nazis, although he himself was known as "the democratic duke" because of his concern for workers and his penchant for inspecting factories. Still, it is telling that Prince Ludwig von Hessen-Darmstadt scribbled the following notes in 1938 at the end of his tenure at the German Embassy in London: "Duke of Kent. Very German friendly. Clearly against France. Not especially clever, but well-informed. Entirely for strengthening German-English ties. His wife is equally anti-French."[131] While the Duke of Kent's views about National Socialism remain murky, it is likely that he was unenthusiastic about the ideology (save for the anti-bolshevism), but nonetheless made an effort to help the British and German governments come to an understanding. Ian Kershaw has shown in his biography of Lord Londonderry that a desire for accommodation with Germany did not always entail support for National Socialism.[132] Among the accessible letters from the Duke of Kent, one gains the impression that he eventually felt a strong antipathy toward the Nazis but that such sentiments took time to develop. On 5 December 1939, for example, he wrote to his cousin and brother-in-law, Prince Paul of Yugoslavia about Prince Friedrich von Preussen, who was then in London: "I saw Fritzi, who said he couldn't fight for Nazis, etc. I think he is wrong as he is in the army. He should have gone back + they would have given him other work. Now I doubt he can ever go back to his country again."[133] This suggests that he did not initially see the fight against National Socialism as a moral issue. But by July 1940 he wrote Prince Paul, "what a hell of a world we live in, with evil pushing its way everywhere."[134]

As noted earlier, the Duke of Kent took steps in the summer of 1939 to prevent war and met with his cousin Prince Philipp in Rome and Florence to this end. At this time, he evidently also sought to arrange a direct, face-to-face meeting with Hitler—a plan that apparently "had the support of the king" (but evidently not Chamberlain and Halifax).[135] Frederick Winterbotham, the head of British air intelligence, wrote in his memoirs about the Duke of Kent meeting regularly with Baron William de Ropp, a Baltic-born British citizen who was, according to him, Nazi leader Alfred Rosenberg's envoy and a kind of "liaison" with the British royal family. While the full story of these meetings is not known—Winterbotham even excised the chapter on the de Ropp-Kent meetings in the second edition of the book—it is fair to say, "the Duke of Kent obviously had very real influence on political events. He was uniquely placed to act as an intermediary between high ranking Nazis and the movers and shakers of British society for the betterment of Anglo-German relations, an opportunity he seemed to relish."[136]

Many of the nonroyal British elite were also sympathetic to the idea of an Anglo-German alliance. Historian John Lukacs noted, "In Britain, (unlike almost anywhere else in Europe), there were many members of the aristocracy who, at least before May 1940, expressed their rather definite sympathies for Hitler—or, at least for the then-Germanophile inclinations of Chamberlain. Such tendencies were shared by members of the royal family and, what was more important, by high civil servants of considerable influence."[137] While it is an exaggeration to label the British prime minister "Germanophile," his willingness to grant concessions to Hitler could give this impression. This was the case for many in the so-called Cliveden set, who were not so much pro-Nazi as opposed to war. The clique, which was associated with the Berkshire manor house west of London, featured media sensation and Tory MP Nancy Astor; she and her associates brought tremendous attention to this position, with both the British and American media obsessed with the "Cliveden set." The Astors and their friends made it easier for others to adopt more pro-Hitler views.[138] But again, they were far from alone among the British elite. After meeting Hitler at the Berghof in late-summer 1936, former British prime minister David Lloyd George called him "the greatest living German" and "the George Washington of Germany."[139] Nearly every British leader who met personally with Hitler came away impressed by his "sincerity and reasonableness"—and this included Lords Londonderry, Lothian, Beaverbrook, Rothermere, and Allen of Hurtwood, among others.[140] Events like the "Anglo-German Fellowship Dinner" of December 1937, where the guest of honor was the Duke von Sachsen-Coburg und Gotha (president of the German-English Society in Berlin), attracted the Earl of Glasgow and Viscountess Snowden, who joined the Ribbentrops and Prince Friedrich von Preussen, among others.[141] In May 1940, foreign secretary Lord Halifax—who was also present at the aforementioned dinner—"was deluged with letters from a number of the nation's grandest aristocrats imploring him to return to appeasement," and he himself favored accommodation with Hitler well into May 1940, supporting the idea of enlisting Mussolini to secure a "general European peace."[142] Halifax was a "close friend" of King George VI, who, among others in the British royal family, strongly favored him over Churchill as Chamberlain's successor.[143]

The full extent of pro-accommodation sentiment is difficult to gauge because most appeasers eventually recognized the malevolence of the Nazis and altered their positions, and also because many prominent figures of the time later culled their papers or sequestered them. John Lukacs has remarked on this, noting how figures such as Lord Halifax and R. A. Butler weeded their correspondence and notes.[144] But the fact remains that many elite endorsed the idea of accommodation with Germany and did so with class interests in mind. As the then aspiring British Labour politician A. L. Rowse noted, "The Tories connived at sacrificing their country's interests for their class interests."[145] Of course, such thinking extended to a significant number of Americans: members of what one might call the Anglo-American transatlantic elite. Here one thinks of U.S. ambassador to Britain Joseph Kennedy (1888–1969) and his pro-appeasement sentiments. Winston Churchill was especially remarkable because he was a member of this elite who came out against the Nazi government so early and so forcefully.[146]

There was also a significant constituency in Britain who expressed even stronger pro-Nazi sentiments than the establishment figures noted above. John Lukacs is correct in stating that "extreme elements—such as the Mosleyites, British Fascists, Germano-maniacs, obsessive anti-Semites, and so on—were without considerable influence."[147] But these "extremists" often captured the popular imagination. Albert Speer, for example, recalled that Unity Mitford "even in the later years of international tension persistently spoke up for her country and often actually pleaded with Hitler to make a deal with England. In spite of Hitler's discouraging reserve, she did not abandon her efforts through all those years. Then, in September 1939, on the day of England's declaration of war, she tried to shoot herself with a small pistol in Munich's *Englischer Garten*. Hitler had the best specialists in Munich care for her, and as soon as she could travel, sent her home to England by a special railroad car through Switzerland."[148] The attractive and "well-born" Miss Mitford was a staple of the British press. Members of one group called "The Link," who were also decidedly pro-Nazi, also attracted considerable media coverage. The organization itself published a magazine called *The Patriot*, and its leader was a distinguished naval veteran, Admiral Sir Barry Domville.[149] The group had close ties to the charismatic Oswald and Diana Mosley. This helped give rise to wild rumors, some that have persisted—including sympathy for "The Link" on the part of members of the British royal family and their households.[150] Sir Oswald and Lady Diana Mosley, as well as Admiral Domville, did in fact have remarkable social connections. Sir Oswald had met Philipp von Hessen in Rome in 1932 when "Mosley was trying to get in with Mussolini and was seeking funds from the Italian leader."[151] But, as suggested above, Mosley's influence had declined markedly in the latter portion of the decade as a result of his wildly incautious statements and the rowdy misbehavior of the members of the British Union of Fascists. The pro-German segment of the British elite had found other avenues for accommodation with the Nazis besides Mosley and "The Link." Domville and the Mosleys were imprisoned by British authorities early in the war.

Most of the British elite eventually recognized the malevolence of the Nazis and rallied to become patriotic supporters of Churchill's government and its uncompromising anti-German position, but the question is *when* that occurred. While there was no one single moment of recognition, and there were certainly vicissitudes in Anglo-German relations throughout the 1930s, an important transformation occurred from May to August 1940: from the time of the British Expeditionary Forces' travails in France through the Battle of Britain, when the RAF fought off the powerful Luftwaffe.[152] In particular, the attack on the British Isles—with bombs landing on native soil—steeled resistance to the Germans and made the idea of accommodation increasingly untenable. This development, however, should not obscure the fact that there was considerable support among British leaders for a negotiated peace through much of that summer. Lord Halifax continued to urge dialogue through Italian mediators into June, and there was talk of bringing David Lloyd George into the government (to quote John Lukacs, "Lloyd George was, to put it simply, a defeatist").[153] Historian John Costello noted in the early 1990s, "Newly declassified records show how close Britain came to the brink of making peace with Germany in June 1940. If the British had joined the French in accepting Hitler's reasonable terms—as diplomatic logic and military circumstance argued in the wake of Dunkirk—Churchill's administration would have fallen and the Second World War would never have become a global conflict."[154] Many influential observers, including Joseph Kennedy, perceived the Luftwaffe as "invincible," and were inclined to accept the "right" kind of German peace offer.[155] There was also the fact that Leopold III, King of the Belgians surrendered his country's army on 28 May, stating to his ministers just before the capitulation, "The cause of the Allies is lost. . . . There is no reason for us to continue the war on the side of the Allies."[156] Interestingly, the Belgian king allowed himself to be interned at Laeken Castle in Brussels and endured a relatively comfortable existence for most of the war.[157] He was even granted an audience with Hitler at the Obersalzberg in November 1940. This and the other circumstances described above made the idea of a negotiated peace seem far less outlandish than most recognize today.

Given the attractiveness of a peace accord in the early phase of the war, a number of questions emerge. Did British and German princes play significant roles in the negotiations? Were there efforts undertaken by the Duke of Windsor or by Prince Philipp von Hessen? How did the princes fit into the plans and hopes of the Nazi leaders? What does this history tell us about princes as a group (or a caste)? And why has this subject given rise to so many conspiracy theories?

To address the first of these questions, yes, a number of princes did endeavor to play a role mediating a peace deal. As noted earlier, a key factor in the early Anglo-German peace discussions was in the form of Prince Max-Egon von Hohenlohe-Langenburg, a "German prince, Spanish landowner, and Liechtenstein citizen who excelled in back-room discussions."[158] Prince Max-Egon was a member of the financial-industrial Circle of Friends of the Reichsführer-SS and an SD agent who worked closely with Walter Schellenberg (he was on the latter's list of agents as

No. 144/7957).[159] Prince Max-Egon worked to negotiate a peace between Germany and the U.K.: in September 1939, he sent Göring a long memorandum about how this might be obtained ("Roosevelt might still be prepared to mediate, but it will soon be too late").[160] The prince also had extensive dealings with the Vatican, "which frequently used him as a channel of communication for warning messages to the Third Reich."[161] Prince Max-Egon's efforts to secure a peace continued through most of the war (historian Heinz Höhne argues that as an owner of vast estates in Central Europe he was primarily motivated by financial interests). He had extensive contact with British ambassador to Spain, Sir Samuel Hoare (an appeaser), who was, during the early years of the war, "the prime target for German peace feelers."[162] But it is striking that one finds Prince von Hohenlohe-Langenburg in combination with certain figures—Hoare, Göring, Schellenberg—all of whom were to explore the possibilities of a negotiated peace.

Of course, efforts to secure an armistice were not confined to princes. With the multifaceted (or "polycratic") Nazi state, there were initiatives in many branches of government aimed at negotiating an Anglo-German peace accord. Andrew Roberts is accurate with his amusing observation, "There were so many amateur and professional contacts between the protagonists in the various neutral countries that one is left with the impression that it must have been hard to get to the bar in any Swiss café during the Phoney War for all the spies discussing peace terms with one another."[163] One notable effort was made by Dr. Ludwig Weissauer in Scandinavia.[164] Trained as a lawyer, and possessing considerable international experience, Weissauer became an agent of the Reich Security Head Office (RSHA) and traveled to both Finland and Sweden in an attempt to advance discussions concerning an armistice. More specifically, he utilized intermediaries to contact British officials in Stockholm in September 1940 and continued communications through 1942. Similar efforts were made by Swedish industrialist Birger Dahlerus, who was active starting in August 1939 as he met with Göring and others in an attempt to forestall a wider war.[165] Various agents of the Abwehr, the counterespionage branch of the armed forces headed by Admiral Canaris (1887–1945), also engaged British representatives: a Cologne banker Baron Waldemar von Oppenheim traveled to Sweden on various occasions in 1942 for such purposes, and Canaris himself purportedly met with the head of British intelligence, General Sir Stewart Menzies and OSS chief William Donovan in Spain in 1943.[166] Even the king of Sweden, Gustaf V, offered to serve as a mediator (an idea vetoed by Churchill, who believed he had deserted Finland and Norway and was "absolutely in the German grip").[167] Certain members of the German opposition to Hitler, such as Carl Goerdeler, also had contact with the British and explored peace terms. Princes were among those who endeavored to negotiate a peace deal, but the efforts extended to a broader range of elites. Understandably, elites tended to have more extensive international contacts and the resources to travel abroad for such purposes, and therefore predominated among the protagonists in these negotiations.

The circumstances surrounding the Duke of Windsor and Prince Philipp regarding a peace accord are more difficult to ascertain. It is not even clear whether they met after the onset of hostilities, or whether they communicated with one another, although certain authors have maintained this was the case.[168] Many other mysteries surround the two men. It is helpful to step back and look at the bigger picture before exploring the issue of contact between the duke and the prince. The Germans certainly put great stock in the Duke of Windsor and his ability, once back on the throne, to deliver a negotiated peace. To that end, they embarked on "Operation Willi," where the Germans would meet with the duke on the Iberian peninsula and arrange the restoration. The crucial issue here is actually not whether the Windsor plot was viable. That is highly doubtful. What is important is whether Nazi officials believed in the scheme. This appears to have been the case. One reason for this, in historian Gerhard Weinberg's words, is that "Hitler, like many other Germans, exaggerated the importance of the king's role in determining British policy."[169] Moreover, there was the widespread perception that the Duke of Windsor was so pro-German that it would pay off to take steps to place him on the British throne. Historian Martha Schad wrote, "already in January 1936, the king [Edward VIII—later Duke of Windsor], shortly after ascending to the throne, communicated to Hitler through his relative, Duke Carl Eduard von Sachsen-Coburg und Gotha, that he regarded an alliance between Great Britain and German as politically necessary and this even extended to a military pact that would include France. Thus, he wished to speak personally with the Reich Chancellor as soon as possible, whether it be in Great Britain or Germany."[170] Schad notes that Edward's abdication was seen not only in Germany but also in certain circles in Britain and the United States as "a behind-the-scenes conspiracy to remove the Nazi-friendly king."[171] Ambassador Ribbentrop reported to Hitler "that the whole marriage question was a false front that [Prime Minister] Baldwin had utilized to get rid of the king because of the latter's pro-German views."[172] Even the *New York Times* included the observation after the Windsors' 1937 German tour that the duke "demonstrated adequately that the Abdication did rob Germany of a firm friend, if not indeed a devoted admirer, on the British throne."[173]

The Duke of Windsor appeared to have ambivalent feelings about returning as monarch or regent. While he had chafed under the demands of the royal schedule, he longed to play a meaningful role in his country's history and hoped to be asked back as a peace-maker. He would never have condoned a plan that involved assassination, but, in the case of a tragic accident and the death of his brother, he might have felt compelled to do his duty and return to the throne. In this calculation and the likelihood that Edward would have pushed for peace between the U.K. and Germany, the Germans' plan was plausible. This gave them a geopolitical reason to commit regicide. They didn't know whether the British people or the civilian government would embrace Edward (which was doubtful), but it seemed possible. Furthermore, there were indications that many of the British people were tired of war and pessimistic about the future course of the conflict. The Duke and Duchess of Windsor seemed to invite specu- lation about plots from all quarters: American intelligence agencies, for example, later explored the idea that the Germans would try to kidnap the Duke of Windsor and trade him for Rudolf Hess, who remained impris- oned after his May 1941 flight to Scotland. Both sides were therefore imag- ining fantastic schemes involving the Windsors.[174]

The Duke of Windsor convinced the Nazi leaders that he was both pro-German and pro-appeasement. There was considerable history to support this notion. He had frequently traveled to Germany, and this included educational trips just before and just after World War I (July 1913 and January 1919). During these excursions, he spent time with German relations; in 1919, he "was billeted with the Kaiser's sister"—a reference to the visit he paid to Princess Victoria von Schaumburg-Lippe in Bonn.[175] The duke spoke fluent German and continued to correspond with family members *auf deutsch* throughout the 1930s. Indeed, he sometimes referred to German as his *Muttersprache* (mother tongue) and, according to Diana Mosley, "remembered as a child [how] the older members of the royal family waited until the English courtiers were no longer in the room, and then comfortably lapsed into German."[176] He often received German princes while in England, even though, as was the case of Prince Wilhelm von Preussen (son of the crown prince) and the Hereditary Grand Duke von Mecklenburg in 1933, he took care that "their names will not appear in the court circular" (the latter was a Nazi and member of the SS).[177] Significantly, these German relations, including "Charlie Coburg," would address him in the familiar *du* form—even after he had been king.[178] Just prior to the Windsors' October 1937 trip, the Duke von Sachsen-Coburg wrote his cousin—addressing him in English but writing in German— "Dear David! I hear that you are coming to Germany. . . . I naturally would be delighted if you could take this opportunity to see me; perhaps I could introduce you to a couple of interesting personalities whom you otherwise wouldn't meet during your trip."[179] On 19 October 1937, the Coburgs hosted "an elaborate dinner party" for the Windsors at the Grand Hotel in Nuremberg, with over a hundred guests in attendance, including "many of the aristocrats with whom the duke had hob-nobbed during his father's

The Duke of Windsor (center) with German Labor Front leader Dr. Robert Ley (left) inspect SS troops in October 1937.

funeral and jubilee" (it is not clear if any Hessens were present).[180] The Windsors' sympathies even found expression in their choice of transportation: when they departed the Continent for the United States in late 1937, they opted for the German liner *Bremen*—a decision that prompted a long letter from Winston Churchill, where he unsuccessfully pleaded with them to travel on the *Normandie*—"to pay a compliment to France, which after all is the country to whom our fortunes at the present time are bound up."[181]

The duke and duchess confirmed this pro-German image during their German tour in October 1937. This visit, which was paid for by the German government, included an inspection of a Nazi training school for aspiring political leaders at Burg Crössensee in Pomerania, where an SS band played the British national anthem. The duke and duchess also paid a visit to Hermann Göring's estate, Carinhall, where they had tea with the second most powerful man in the Reich, who showed them his burgeoning art collection. Ribbentrop hosted a dinner for them at the gourmet restaurant Horchers in Berlin, where they also had an opportunity to meet Joseph and Magda Goebbels, who were deeply impressed by the royal couple (Goebbels gushed in his diaries "The duke is wonderful—a nice, sympathetic fellow who is open and clear and with a healthy understanding of people. . . . It's a shame he is no longer king. With him we would have entered into an alliance.").[182] On 22 October 1937, the Windsors had a private audience with Hitler at the Berghof in Obersalzberg.[183] One of the reporters who was present when Hitler escorted the couple to their car after tea noted, "the Duchess was visibly impressed with the Führer's personality, and he apparently indicated that they had become fast friends by giving her an affectionate farewell. [Hitler] took both their hands in his saying a long goodbye, after which he stiffened to a rigid Nazi salute that the Duke returned" (the duke made the Nazi salute on several occasions during the trip, some caught by the newsreels).[184] Hitler's translator, who was there for the duchess, recalled that as the Windsor's car took them down the mountain, the dictator remarked, "she would have made a good queen."[185] The Windsors were thrilled that Hitler addressed the duchess as "Royal Highness," a title denied her in Britain.[186] After departing Berchtesgaden for Munich, the Windsors spent the final evening of their trip at the home of Rudolf and Ilse Hess, who hosted an intimate dinner party for fourteen people, including Nazi officials from the German Labor Front and the Party Headquarters (Gauleitung).[187] There is no extant record of what transpired at the Hess's home in the Harlaching neighborhood in the southern section of Munich, but it is striking that the duke and Hess, both future advocates of a negotiated peace, had the opportunity to spend the evening together and review the Windsors' tour. It is also worth recalling that, in the words of John Parker, "when the Duke and Duchess of Windsor visited Berlin in 1937, Göring ordered him [Prince Christoph] to tap their phones, as happened with most visiting politicians, important businessmen, and so-called guests of the Third Reich."[188]

Members of the British government struggled to manage the public relations, but they had no control over the situation from the start. King George VI's private secretary Sir Alexander Hardinge noted just prior to the trip, "Eden had discussed the matter with the Prime Minister, and it was agreed that nothing could, of course, be done to stop the contemplated tour."[189] Thereafter, reports from the Foreign Office communicated in sober terms what was transpiring. The British ambassador's report, for example, which was rather sketchy, still included telling passages such as: "before going to *Herr* Hess's dinner party, H.R.H. received in the hall of the hotel [the Vier Jahrzeiten] *Herr* von Yorry, previously Master of Ceremonies to the Grand Duke of Mecklenburg, who was a personal friend of His Majesty, the late King George V and who had known the Duke of Windsor for many years. *Herr* von Yorry . . . is now a Kreisleiter in the NSDAP" [a district leader of the Nazi Party].[190] Occasionally, the reports were more panicky, such as that of the British consul in Dresden who wrote in November 1937:

> Germans here were much puzzled about the reasons for the tour which many of them attributed to the Duke's supposed strong pro-Fascist sympathies. This belief was strengthened by the words which H.R.H. is alleged to have used to sum up his impressions of the tour, and which was rendered by

Dr. Ley to a recent meeting of the German Labor Front in Leipzig as follows: "I have traveled the world and my upbringing has made me familiar with great achievements of mankind, but that which I have seen in Germany I had hitherto believed to be impossible. It cannot be grasped and is a miracle; one can only begin to understand it when one realizes that behind it all is one man and one will."[191]

As the British consul duly noted, there was some doubt as to whether the duke uttered these words, but his report is nonetheless indicative of the concerns of British government officials.

The Duke and Duchess of Windsor's pro-German sympathies were so plainly evident that the subject attracted the interest of intelligence agencies around the world. One September 1940 report to FBI director J. Edgar Hoover noted: "for some time the British Government has known that the Duchess of Windsor was exceedingly pro-German in her sympathies and connections and there is strong reason to believe that this is the reason why she was considered so obnoxious to the British Government that they refused to permit Edward to marry her and maintain the throne."[192] The FBI file contains numerous reports that Wallis Simpson was fervently pro-Nazi. It even includes documents stating that the Duchess was believed to have had a sexual relationship with Joachim von Ribbentrop when he was German ambassador to the Court of St. James between August 1936 and January 1938.[193] During his tenure as ambassador in London, Ribbentrop made the extraordinary gesture of sending Mrs. Simpson seventeen red roses every morning, and this gave rise to much talk among contemporaries.[194] The matter surfaced, couched in polite language, in the House of Commons debate about the abdication of Edward, when a left-wing MP named Willie Gallagher suggested that Mrs. Simpson's "social net" extended to "a certain government and the ambassador of this foreign government."[195] While the rumor about the duchess and Ribbentrop is quite outlandish —and indeed, most serious scholars of the Windsors such as Hugo Vickers reject the notion of a physical relationship—it has retained a remarkable durability and continues to appear in both popular and scholarly articles.[196] Less uncertain is that many observers at the time suspected the Windsors of pro-Nazi sympathies: the British Foreign Office "carefully screened the red boxes of documents it sent to Fort Belvedere"; the security services dispatched agents to observe Wallis Simpson and many of her friends; and even President Roosevelt "ordered covert surveillance of the duke and duchess in 1941."[197] The Windsor couple continued to travel in pro-German circles right up until 1 August 1940, when they sailed from Lisbon on the SS *Excalibur* so that the duke could take up the appointment as Governor of the Bahamas. It is likely that certain incautious statements were of use to the German government. But part of the explanation for this may have been because, as an FBI agent noted, "The Duke is in such a state of intoxication most of the time that he is virtually *non compos mentis*."[198]

Author Martin Allen goes much further than this, arguing in his controversial book, *Hidden Agenda*, that the duke spied for Hitler, especially in the critical phase in late-1939 and early-1940 prior to the Battle of France.[199] According to Allen, the duke made inspection tours of the French army's front line positions, including the Maginot line, and provided reports of troop deployments not only to the British (French-British cooperation not being what it should have been), but also to the Germans. The link between the duke and the Nazis, according to Allen, was wealthy American industrialist Charles Bedaux (sometimes spelled Bedault), who was a close friend of the Windsors. Bedaux had loaned them his home, chateau Candé in France, for their wedding in June 1937, and he was almost certainly a Nazi intelligence asset: he knew Göring personally and had many German business contacts.[200] Martin Allen goes so far as to argue that the Duke of Windsor provided Bedaux with the crucial information about the French deployment, that this information, when passed on, induced Hitler to take the bold move and invade France through the poorly defended Ardennes forest, and that this is the primary explanation for the stunning Nazi victory in May–June 1940. It is a devastating indictment: the Duke of Windsor was not only a traitor but the main reason for the German victory in the West and all that came with it (occupation, the Battle of Britain, and the persecution of Jews in these regions, among other developments). But it is an interpretation without firm evidence, and many critics think Allen has exaggerated the extent of the Windsors' treasonous actions.[201]

The issue of whether the Windsors engaged in treason is closely related to Bedaux's actions and intentions. If he spied for the Germans, then they were far more likely to have aided him. As Michael Bloch has noted, "Bedaux has received bad press from historians." Indeed, the majority of authors view Bedaux as a German asset. Peter Allen, for example, notes that "the British Government . . . knew by September 1940 that Bedaux was a German agent, for the Americans then passed on the evidence"; he adds that Bedaux was arrested in 1942.[202] Michael Bloch is an exception, noting that Bedaux had been posthumously "absolved by the French authorities" and given an award in the Legion of Honor.[203] Still, it is difficult to regard Bedaux as an entirely benign individual. Bloch himself acknowledges "that [Bedaux] committed suicide in an American prison in 1944, while awaiting trial on charges of wartime collaboration. . . ."[204] It appears that Bedaux had pro-Nazi sympathies and took steps to enlist the Duke of Windsor in a scheme to bring "world peace": a polite way of saying that they favored Western accommodation with Nazi Germany. Bedaux involved two Americans in his plan—Colonel Oscar Solbert, a senior executive at Eastman Kodak, and Thomas Watson of IBM—and their idea was to have "the Duke head up and consolidate the many and varied peace movements throughout the world. . . ."[205] Again, this rhetoric of peace and reconciliation was a front for pro-Nazi sentiment, and occasionally the correspondence between the Windsors, Bedaux, Solbert, and Watson reveal this thinking: as Bedaux wrote to Solbert, starting his letter with, "I am authorized to speak for H.R.H. the Duke of Windsor. . . . The first step must be to determine to what extent, in all places, with all due regard to differences in racial mental qualities and racial degree of civilization advancement, the practical maximum in the rights and comforts attendant to life has been given to and enjoyed by the laboring classes."[206] Invoking race, the way he did, and using populist rhetoric, were signals that would have been clear to others with pro-German views. Bedaux was wooing the Windsors—loaning them his chateau and hatching political plans—starting in the spring and summer of 1937 (at a time, as his correspondence revealed, when Bedaux spent most of this period based in Berchtesgaden, not far from the compound of Nazi leaders). Charles Bedaux, a world-renowned industrial efficiency expert, had met Göring (head of the Four-Year Plan, among other titles), Robert Ley of the German Work Front, and other Nazi leaders who made economic policy. While Michael Bloch characterizes Bedaux as a "naïve idealist, who sincerely wished to promote the Duke as a world statesman who might help solve the problems of the Depression and avert war," there are compelling reasons to see him as a more sinister figure.[207]

It is still an open question whether the Duke of Windsor unconsciously influenced the course of World War II. The Battle of France in May–June 1940 remains a conundrum for historians because of the Germans' unexpectedly decisive victory. The Western Powers actually had an advantage in terms of armaments: 13,974 artillery pieces versus 7,378 in the Wehrmacht. France and Britain possessed 3,524 tanks as compared to the Germans' 2,439. The Western Powers had 4,460 military aircraft versus the 3,578 in the Luftwaffe. Recent scholarship suggests that there may not even have been a gap in quality. Anglo-French planes, for example, shot down more of their German counterparts in the six-week conflict, and in recent simulations of the Battle of France run on sophisticated U.S. Army computers, the Allies invariably win. Clearly, the Germans gained an advantage through dramatically superior strategy and execution. The questions that would logically follow center on whether either espionage or indiscretion contributed to this superiority and whether the Windsors were the source of any intelligence.

While Martin Allen assembles a great deal of information to establish that the Duke and Duchess of Windsor were sympathetic to the Nazis, and that they befriended the treacherous Charles Bedaux, he is unconvincing in arguing about the duke's *conscious* efforts to help Germany win the war. The extant evidence—an indeterminable amount has been concealed by the British royal family and various governmental agencies in several countries—suggests that the duke and duchess were responsible for a variety of lesser sins against Britain. One lesser sin may have come from unguarded conversations on the part of the Windsors, both with friends and with members of their staff. The duke was indeed engaged to review French troops and study the Maginot Line, and the Windsors did meet with Bedaux after the inspection tours.[208] But Martin Allen and others over-argue the case. The British government had concerns about the duke's reliability and "as the war began to look more serious and German attacks were expected [in the autumn of 1940 the Duke of Windsor] was increasingly deactivated and sent to places where there was even less information to be obtained which could be of use to the enemy."[209] In the case of the duchess, whom some see as more likely to communicate sensitive information to Bedaux and others sympathetic to the Germans, it is important to recall that she had even less concrete and specific information—the knowledge that makes up military intelligence. World War II authority Gerhard Weinberg believes that a member of the Windsors' staff was leaking information.[210] But again, the quality of this intelligence must be doubted.

Another of the duke's sins was to lead the Germans to believe that he sought to return to the throne and would work to achieve a negotiated peace. Both Edward and Wallis sincerely believed that he was more suitable for the position than his stuttering younger sibling. One must keep in mind Edward VIII's tremendous popularity in Britain as monarch: in July 1936, when a man in a crowd was arrested after pointing a gun at him, the press was abuzz from this assassination attempt, with a writer in the *Edinburgh Scotsman* opining, "King Edward is beyond question the most popular man in the realm."[211] Lord Louis Mountbatten later described his close friend as a "spell-binder" and recalled in a tribute on the occasion of the duke's death, "that whenever he went into any gathering of people in any walk of life, in any country in the Commonwealth, his charisma, his magic always worked."[212] German officials therefore had grounds to think that Edward was the best man for the job, especially after the commencement of the war. The private secretary to King George VI, Sir Alexander Hardinge, wrote a memo in July 1940 titled "Report from Informant in Close Touch with [former foreign minister] Neurath's Entourage," which suggested as much: "Germans expect assistance from Duke and Duchess of Windsor, latter desiring at any price to become Queen."[213] The most damaging aspect of this scenario, then, was that the Germans continued to think that a plot was feasible, and accordingly, put Nazi agents in motion.

The German's efforts to restore the duke to the throne came to a head in July 1940—after the fall of France on 22 June but prior to the aerial assault on England that began on 14 August and marked the highpoint of the Battle of Britain. On 19 July 1940, Hitler delivered a speech before the Reichstag that he titled, "A Last Appeal to Reason"; the text, which called for a negotiated peace, was, according to Lord Louis Mountbatten, "dropped from German aircraft all over England [in] August 1940."[214] It is not clear why Hitler held off so long in bombing England, but a compelling interpretation is that he still hoped for a negotiated peace.[215] This would also be a consideration in his decision not to prosecute the attack on the British Expeditionary Force at Dunkirk in May—although again, his thinking here is not entirely clear. Because Hitler wished to avoid the difficult if not impossible task of vanquishing the British by military means, it is logical that he would look to the Duke of Windsor as one way of pursuing the negotiated peace. A year before, on 29 August 1939 (just days prior to the outbreak of hostilities), the duke had sent Hitler a telegram from the Cap d'Antibe, where he pleaded for peace; and Hitler had responded to him on the same day saying that "with regard to England, it was [his] wish to avoid a new war between our two people."[216] It is also telling that during the war, the duke's residence in Paris, his personal property, and even his bank account were all preserved by German occupation authorities; as one writer noted, "whether he was aware of it or not, the Duke of Windsor was Hitler's puppet-king in waiting."[217]

How exactly the Germans were going to utilize the Windsors was not entirely clear. A report to Foreign Minister Ribbentrop by German ambassador to Spain Eberhard von Stohrer (1883–1953) identified one scenario they envisioned: "According to reports available to the Minister, the decision will very quickly go against England and the English Government and King will soon be forced to leave the country. From the Bahamas, where the Duke would be in the power of the English Government (even if he should settle in Canada), he would not be free to intervene. This would be possible only from a neutral country. Accordingly, a return to Spain is advisable."[218] Ribbentrop himself wrote at the end of July 1940 to the German ambassador in Lisbon, Baron Oswald von Hoyningen-Huene (1885–1956), "Germany truly desires peace with the English people. The Churchill clique stands in the way of such a peace. Following the rejection of the Führer's final appeal to reason, Germany is determined to compel England to make peace by every means of power. It would be a good thing if the Duke were to hold himself in readiness for further developments. In such case Germany would be prepared to co-operate most closely with the Duke and to clear the way for any desire expressed by the Duke and Duchess."[219] It is fitting that such a vague plan would be overseen by Ribbentrop: the foreign minister was known for fuzzy thinking. One can well imagine Ribbentrop taking on the Windsor assignment without any clear idea of how he was going to achieve his objective of restoring the duke to the British throne. Ribbentrop's plan was to keep the Duke of Windsor in a neutral country and await whatever advantageous circumstances might arise. Well into the summer of 1940, Ribbentrop was told that the duke "believed severe bombing would persuade his country to sue for peace and . . . [he was] convinced that if he had remained on the throne war could have been avoided."[220]

It is worth noting that the idea of "regime change" through intelligence agents was common to both sides during the war. After Yugoslav prince regent Paul signed a tripartite pact with Germany and Italy in Vienna on 25 March 1941, the British Special Operations Executive (SOE) carried out one of its first initiatives when it ousted Prince Paul and his wife, Princess Olga, on 27 March.[221] The British plan was to replace Prince Regent Paul with the seventeen-year-old Peter II (1923–70). John Parker writes, "Paul and Olga were taken into custody and whisked out of the country immediately to Greece; from Athens they were moved on to internment in Africa."[222] This coup d'état was approved by British king George VI, who was approached by Hugh Dalton of the SOE. Churchill announced that with the crowning of the new monarch, Yugoslavia "had found its soul."[223] Of course, the plan proved unsuccessful. The Germans responded by pounding Belgrade with a brutal bombing attack that began on 6 April (Operation Punishment). King Peter II and his government fled into exile

Hitler seated between Prince Regent Paul of Yugoslavia and Princess Olga at a banquet in Berlin, June 1939.

(moving into Claridge's Hotel in London and then later to the United States where he struggled with many personal problems).[224] This operation, based on the idea that a change of kings would determine the side on which a nation would fight, spelled the end of the monarchy in Yugoslavia: after the war, Tito established a Communist government.

The German plot to kidnap the Duke of Windsor was eventually entrusted to Walter Schellenberg, the SD agent and RSHA department chief who made a name for himself with the Venlo affair in November 1939 (the kidnapping of British intelligence agents in the Netherlands). Citing Hitler's authority, Ribbentrop sent Schellenberg to the Iberian peninsula on 24 July in order to track the Windsors and induce them to cooperate with the Germans.[225] While one must be wary of Schellenberg, who was known to lie, there is a great deal of truth in his account of the Nazis' efforts to woo the Windsors in Spain and Portugal in the summer of 1940. He tells of the foreign minister of Spain meeting with the Windsors, and passing on the details of the conversation to the German ambassador Eberhard von Stohrer, where "the Duke . . . had expressed himself as 'against Churchill and the war.'"[226] The duke said as much to Alexander Weddell, the American ambassador to Portugal. Or, as John Costello noted, "The Duke was freely holding forth on his belief that the correct course for the British government was to seek a compromise peace with Germany. He made a point of delivering his defeatist views to anyone who would listen, including the representatives of foreign governments. . . . Such subversive statements would have been unforgivable for any British citizen. When they were promulgated from the lips of a former King who made no secret of his pro-German sympathies, it was tantamount to treason."[227]

The Windsors' statements provoked the Nazis to take increasingly bold steps. The Duke of Windsor balked at the appointment to the Bahamas, which he considered beneath him, and this delayed his departure from Lisbon in July 1940, thus giving the Germans more time to scheme. A cat-and-mouse game developed between the Germans and British. While Prime Minister Churchill ordered the duke to report to his post as governor or possibly face a court martial, Ribbentrop tried to lure the Windsors to Spain by using an old friend of the duke's as an intermediary, Falangist leader Duke Don Miguel Primo de Rivera (1904–64). Rivera encouraged them to come to Spain as the duke "might yet be destined to play a large part in English politics and even to ascend to the English throne."[228] The Germans tried to convince the duke that the British were preparing to assassinate him, and Schellenberg went so far as to go "to the Windsors' villa [at Cascais north of Lisbon and] lurk in the shadowy grounds after dark" in order to alarm the Windsors and their security detail.[229] The Germans evidently also tried bribery: Ribbentrop testified at Nuremberg that he had offered the duke 50 million Swiss francs (about $12 million at the time) if he would assert his claim to the British throne (the duke denied this through his lawyer in 1956).[230] In the midst of this drama, the Duke of Kent wrote to Prince Paul of Yugoslavia in a letter dated 17 July 1940:

> My brother has behaved disgracefully + to accept to be governor of a small place like that is fantastic. But they [the Duke and Duchess] are both terrified of returning here + thank God they haven't (I did my best to stop it, as he would surely have caused trouble) + W. C. [Churchill] didn't want him back.[231]

The letter from Kent suggests a belief that the duke and duchess had nurtured the Germans' hopes. In any case, Churchill won out when he sent the duke's long-time friend Walter Monckton (1891–1965) down to see him on 28 July.[232] The duke and duchess appeared to have become alarmed by all of the intrigue, and the Germans' increasingly desperate and heavy-handed efforts. Still, on 1 August 1940, the day they departed Lisbon, the duke reportedly told his Portuguese host that he could return on short notice via airplane and "arranged a code word by which he could be recalled when sentiment in Great Britain changed and he was required to take his part in peace negotiations"; this information was duly reported to Ribbentrop by Ambassador Baron Hoyningen-Huene and is preserved in the German Foreign Ministry archives.[233] Subsequently, once in the Bahamas, the Windsors appear to have become alerted to the Nazi threat and behaved in a less pro-German manner.

There have been persistent rumors that Prince Philipp played a role in the events surrounding the Duke and Duchess of Windsor in Portugal in the summer of 1940. Two authors of recently published books stated in print that Philipp traveled to Lisbon in July 1940 in order to meet with his cousin. But in collegial and frank exchanges, they both acknowledged that they lacked any firm evidence for these statements and retracted the assertions.[234] Author Charles Higham has also maintained that the Duke of Windsor was the victim of a blackmail plot in Paris in 1938 that involved papers stemming from Prince Philipp, and that the two men sustained contact into the war years.[235] Higham's primary source for the blackmail plot is the diary of Constance Coolidge, a prominent American socialite and friend of the Windsors. Coolidge specifically mentions Prince Philipp and his involvement with these sensitive documents. However, because the alleged documents that formed the basis for the extortion have never been located, this episode remains shrouded in mystery and constitutes another attempt to link the two men that falls short.

There are reasons why so many authors posit scenarios whereby the Duke of Windsor and Prince Philipp would meet in an attempt to secure peace between their two countries. This does not mean that they met;

it is only an effort to explain the sources of the rumor. Göring clearly orchestrated some behind-the-scenes efforts to explore a negotiated peace: he utilized Prince Max-Egon von Hohenlohe-Langenburg; he had earlier tried to cultivate British aristocrats such as Lord Londonderry; he had the Forschungsamt engaged in intelligence work (tapping the phone line of British ambassador to Berlin Nevile Henderson, among others); and he occasionally postured as a kind of alternative to Hitler.[236] Andrew Roberts noted that British foreign minister Lord Halifax (who held the post until December 1940), "was willing to offer inducements to what he called 'the Göring tribe' for a reasonable peace and seems to have stuck to [Sir Alexander] Cadogan's line that the principal war aim was the personal removal of Hitler and his replacement with someone who could make a trustworthy peace."[237] Because Philipp was part of "the Göring tribe," because both he and the Duke of Windsor each wanted a negotiated peace and undertook independent efforts to secure an accord, and because of the familial ties linking the two men, there is a strong temptation to make the leap and posit direct interaction.

So what does one make of theories positing face-to-face negotiations between Philipp and the Duke of Windsor? The short answer is that it is improbable that they met during the war. Considering that Prince Philipp never turned up in other documents from "Operation Willi" and that the matter never emerged in his denazification trial, it is unlikely that he was in Lisbon in 1940. This does not mean that they did not attempt to play some other kind of role in pursuit of a negotiated peace. Philipp's twin, Prince Wolfgang, stated in 1979 in an article that appeared in *The Sunday Times* of London that the Duke of Kent served as an intermediary between Prince Philipp and the Duke of Windsor; while Wolfgang may have been referencing the 1939 wedding between Princess Irene of Greece and the Duke of Spoleto in Florence, he may also have had other interactions in mind.[238] It is also not improbable that Prince Philipp had written communications with the Dukes of Kent and Windsor after the outbreak of war in September 1939. Just because there were no meetings does not mean that Philipp and his cousins did not try to work for a negotiated peace. One can reflect more generally on Walter Schellenberg's observation that he made during a postwar interrogation: "in Great Britain espionage is considered to be an occupation for gentlemen of high social standing, whereas in Germany the worst and most corrupt elements are recruited as agents."[239] That said, we now know that German princes were involved in behind-the-scenes negotiations and information gathering, and that Göring, Ribbentrop, and even Hitler thought them potentially useful. While Germany did not have the same tradition as Britain in terms of the involvement of social elites in intelligence work, it was not as clear-cut as Schellenberg suggests.

Christoph and Legends

Despite repeated claims that Prince Christoph played a role in a plot to kill British King George VI, there is no conclusive evidence for such assertions. Indeed, it is questionable whether there was ever such a plot. But because Buckingham Palace was bombed nine times during the early years of the war, there appears to have been conscious intent on the part of the Germans.[240] The dearth of relevant archival records has helped fuel speculation: combing through the extant documents from Luftwaffe bases in western France and the Low Countries that are housed in the Federal Archives Military Branch in Freiburg does not resolve issues about targets or the personnel involved. There are other factors that have led people to believe in the theory of attempted intrafamilial regicide: one concerns the plausibility of Christoph's motives for attempting to kill the king; another involves the circumstantial evidence; and finally, there is the view among certain contemporaries that Prince Christoph was complicit in the plot. One thing, however, is clear: Christoph was not on any plane that attacked Buckingham Palace. Nonetheless, a consideration of the questions posed above provides one way for thinking about Christoph and his career in the Third Reich, and demonstrates how legends are formed.

In terms of motivation, a key question is whether Christoph fervently believed in National Socialism. One source of information about Christoph's commitment to National Socialism is his personal SS file. For decades, it was housed in the U.S.-controlled Berlin Document Center, a repository known for its "dramatic ability to unmask former Nazi participants who have gained political and cultural power in the postwar world."[241] It was evident that for many years the German authorities did not want control of the archive because the awkward secrets it contained would implicate many who occupied prominent places in government and society. Since the 1990s, this has been less of an issue: the files have been administered by the German Federal Archives and are generally accessible. The prince's dossier begins with documents about his ancestry—a precondition for membership in the SS. Christoph duly provided a family tree (*Ahnennachweis*), which was not difficult to procure, considering it was printed in various reference books.

More interesting documents in the file reveal his membership in the Lebensborn Association (often translated as the "Well of Life Society").[242] This SS organization, which offered "welfare assistance to SS families having a large number of racially valuable children," was best known for its program to breed a "master race" (*Herrenvolk*) by way of unions between SS men and racially suitable women.[243] Striving to implement a counterpart to the SS-led program of ethnic cleansing, Lebensborn officials embarked on a program to take children with desirable physical characteristics from their families in Central Europe and raise them as "Aryans."[244] As historian Larry Thompson has noted, "racial purity was an obsession with Himmler. . . . He believed that not only physical attributes but character traits, such as loyalty, determination, courage, and a sense of honor, could be biologically transmitted . . . [and viewed] the SS as the racial nucleus from which Germany could replenish an Aryan inheritance now dangerously diluted through generations of race-mixing."[245] The extent to which Prince Christoph subscribed to such views is unclear: "Himmler required all *hauptamtlichen Führer* [officers attached to any one of the then four SS main departments] to join the society and make monthly payments to it. Membership for the rest of the SS was encouraged but remained voluntary."[246] Yet in January 1939, only 8,000 of the 238,000 men in the SS belonged to the society, which indicates that membership was intended for those with a special commitment to the SS and its goals.[247] Larry Thompson added, "The SS membership should have known of the Lebensborn's function, inasmuch as a procedural announcement explaining how, when, and where to apply to admittance to the maternity homes appeared in the *SS-Befehlsblatt.*"[248] Christoph's donations to the Lebensborn are themselves not proof that he subscribed to a radically racialistic, and hence, anti-Semitic worldview. But his membership in the organization, like his position as an SS officer, nonetheless suggests support for the Nazis' racial program.

Other documents in Prince Christoph's SS file also indicate that he was a member in good standing, and that accordingly, he would subscribe to the corps' radical ideological orientation. In 1936, he signed an affidavit that he had never belonged to a Free Mason's lodge, and one memorandum noted that he had received a death's-head ring (*Totenkopfring*) to go along with the one on his SS cap.[249] The Death's Head Division of the SS, which was created later, oversaw the concentration and death camps; but early on, the death's-head insignia was part of the SS uniform. The prince, as was customary for a high-ranking SS officer, also received many gifts from Himmler that had ideological significance. One, for example, was the *Julleuchter*, a candelabra used to celebrate the Nazis' pagan Christmas.[250] Another document from an officer in the security police dated January 1939 reads:

> On the occasion of a report by SS-Gruppenführer Heydrich to the Reichsführer-SS, [Himmler] ordered that SS-Standartenführer Prince von Hessen receive the honorary dagger of the SS. Since the Reichsführer-SS had charged SS-Gruppenführer Heydrich with its conveyance to SS-Standartenführer Prince von Hessen, I would ask you to send the dagger here.[251]

This note, written in Nazi bureaucratese, reveals that the prince was on the radar of both Himmler and Heydrich at a crucial time just before World

Prince Christoph von Hessen in his SS-uniform (with the death's-head emblem on his cap). The photograph comes from his SS file in the German Federal Archives.

War II. Another clue concerning his views about National Socialism is the naming of his eldest son, who was born in 1937: while he turned to family tradition to select a first and second name (Karl Andreas), the third name was "Adolf"—a clear reference to Hitler meant to pay homage to the dictator.

Prince Christoph's career within the SS was marked outwardly by success. He was repeatedly promoted—on six occasions up until his final rank as colonel (Oberführer) in June 1939. He excelled in the skills tests and had no difficulty earning the badges for sports (including riding). It is also significant that Prince Christoph's SS appointment after July 1934 was on the Personal Staff of the Reichsführer-SS—one of the many branches of his burgeoning empire, but notable because Himmler controlled it more directly, as compared to delegating it to a subordinate.[252] Christoph's son Rainer offers a plausible interpretation of this: when Prince Christoph explained that his duties at the Forschungsamt prevented him from fulfilling his obligations to his regular SS unit, Himmler, who wanted to keep him in the organization, found an alternative and brought him onto his Personal Staff. The Reichsführer-SS thought that the prince might be useful to him—in terms of Himmler's ambitions to take over the Forschungsamt, but more generally, because the dashing prince and expert sportsman fit the SS ideal. Christoph, in turn, probably considered it beneficial to be a member of the SS. The Berlin Document Center file shows Christoph as a dutiful officer. He would seek permission from his SS superiors to travel abroad: for example, he wrote to the Personal Chancellery of the Reichsführer-SS in October 1937 asking for permission to travel to England "in order to make good on an invitation" and received an affirmative response in return. However, for reasons never specified he did not make the trip (Sophia went alone to see family, including Queen Mary, on several occasions in the mid-1930s). Christoph also requested and received a "holiday pass" for a four-week trip to Italy in 1938.[253] He also never ceased to pay his SS dues. On the other hand, there is no indication that he was ever on the SS payroll.[254]

The reality of Christoph's SS career may have been more at odds with the outward success suggested in his file. His son Rainer believes that Christoph became disaffected from the organization as early as 1934. Because Himmler often accepted nominal membership in the SS (and used "honorary" appointments to establish links with prominent individuals), it was not uncommon for an officer to have limited involvement with the black corps; an honorific appointment would not necessarily find expression in the personnel file, which would still list the customary gifts and contain copies of correspondence on birthdays and anniversaries. While not clear to what extent Christoph distanced himself from the SS, it is certain that he pulled back from the activism of the early 1930s but did not resign or cease involvement altogether. It rings true when Rainer recalls that Christoph never brought home the decorations and gifts he received from Himmler.[255] At the time he received the dagger from General Heydrich in early 1939, he evidently harbored gradually increasing misgivings about the SS and his work at the Forschungsamt. Prince Christoph appears to have been torn by conflicting emotions in the mid-to-late 1930s. This found expression in health problems: he suffered from an ulcer, sinus infections, and periods of emotional collapse. In March 1936, his wife Sophia had written his mother from the Italian Alps, "Chri has got his strength back . . . but mentally he isn't what he should be. He gets fits of depression & then of restlessness & he is worried about it & can't understand that his nerves don't improve quicker. . . . Dr. Krüger warned us not to be surprised at anything, considering he is recovering from a nervous breakdown. . . ."[256]

Although motivation is difficult to deduce in the absence of auto-biographical statements, Christoph made career decisions in the late 1930s that arose from his growing antipathy toward Himmler's black corps. While he apparently retained sympathy for certain tenets of the SS (including the notion of an elite corps and an appreciation of discipline), and he may have feared the consequences of trying to resign his position, he also became aware of the organization's malignant objectives. When Reinhard Heydrich was assassinated by Czech partisans and died in June 1942, Landgravine Margarethe wrote that both Philipp and Christoph were "greatly relieved through the death of a certain dangerous and cruel man. Chri said it was the best news he had for a long time."[257] As noted above, he was acutely aware that Himmler and Heydrich sought to control the Forschungsamt: yet a complete break with the SS leaders might undermine what leverage he had with them. With the outbreak of war, other agencies also sought to encroach on the Forschungsamt's monopoly on signals intelligence—and indeed, this is what transpired: as historian D. C. Watt noted, "The exigencies of military intelligence demanded a vast increase in the monitoring of military radio traffic; at the same time, the Foreign Ministry, the Reich Security Headquarters and Himmler, Heydrich and Schellenberg invaded the field . . . [and] the Post Office emerged from passive co-operation with the Forschungsamt to active competition."[258] Christoph evidently felt tremendous pressure in his position at the Forschungsamt: "According to statements from Prince Christoph's friend Michael Graf Soltikow. . . . It was friction with the Gestapo that induced the prince to volunteer as a Major [*sic*] in the Luftwaffe in 1939."[259] It is not clear what caused this friction—whether there was a crisis of conscience as the regime grew more radical and genocidal—or whether it was the continuous attempts of Heydrich and Himmler to take over the FA (which the latter ultimately did in 1945).

One must go back to the more fundamental question of why Christoph opted for service in the Luftwaffe in September 1939. It is nothing short of astonishing that Göring permitted the head of his intelligence agency to become a common soldier. This is a matter that certain family members still cannot understand today: Landgrave Moritz asked, "How was it, that at a time when the necessities of war required each to do his duty, that Göring would allow his seasoned director of the FA go off to join an ordinary Luftwaffe unit?" There are a number of possibilities—and they are not mutually exclusive. One is to note the great respect accorded to front-line service during World War II. Most of the Nazi leaders, including Göring, came of age while fighting in World War I. For them, combat was an honorable undertaking, and one consistent with the tenets of the Nazi ideology. Deputy Führer Hess approached Hitler when the war broke out and asked to join the Luftwaffe (the request was denied), and even Reinhard Heydrich, the number two in the SS hierarchy, volunteered as a pilot and saw active service on the Eastern Front.[260] With the romanticized notion of flying as something heroic and chivalric, there was an added draw for members of the nobility. Just as Baron Manfred von Richthofen (1892–1918) gave rise to this image during the Great War, figures like Prince Heinrich zu Sayn-Wittgenstein (1916–44) contributed to a similar perception during World War II. A major in the Luftwaffe, Prince zu Sayn-Wittgenstein was credited with shooting down eighty-three Allied planes—a record for all Night Fighters in the war (one website refers to him as "*le prince de la chasse de nuit*").[261] He became the head of Night Fighter Squadron Two (based in the Netherlands) and intercepted mostly English bombers as they crossed on raids in Germany. He shot down six bombers in one memorable and highly publicized sortie in January 1944, before falling victim himself several weeks later.[262] One story about Prince zu Sayn-Wittgenstein, for example, entailed his racing to an airfield during a British attack and jumping into the cockpit while still wearing his dinner jacket; he then proceeded to fight off the invaders.[263] One would speculate then, that Christoph felt he could not endure the pressure applied by the SS leaders, but by formally retaining the post as head of the FA, he helped out Göring by not creating an opening that would invite even more intrigue. Christoph, according to one theory, sought to take the valiant and traditional way out of trying circumstances—by becoming a soldier.[264] With his strong interest in flying, his relationship to Göring, and his long-standing membership in the Luftwaffe reserve, the choice of what branch of the military to join was straightforward.

Some writers have viewed Christoph in a different light—and more specifically, as bitter and vengeful with regard to the British: besides E. H. Cookridge's unsubstantiated charge that Christoph was intent on avenging the death of his older brother Prince Maximilian, author Sarah Bradford maintained that Christoph "had frequently been heard declaring how much he would like to bomb Buckingham Palace."[265] Like Cookridge, Bradford does not offer a source for this alleged statement. Those who knew Christoph, including his nephew Moritz and brother-in-law, Prince Philip, Duke of Edinburgh, dismiss charges of an anti-British animus. It bears reiterating that Christoph frequently wrote to his mother and wife in English. The assertions of Cookridge and Bradford do more to explain the origin of the legend of Christoph's involvement in the bombing of the British monarch than they do to clarify his worldview. Christoph was certainly a German nationalist, a fervent anti-Communist, and someone with a love of the military. He apparently saw himself as a kind of modern-day incarnation of a knight (or so he was portrayed posthumously in a poem by his cousin Prince Ludwig von Hessen-Darmstadt). One can draw out other likely beliefs—for example, that he would subscribe to the notion of a New Order, where Europe would be under German hegemony and be governed by fascist precepts, and that this geopolitical vision extended to the Hitlerian notion of alliance between Germany and the United Kingdom, where the former would control the Continent and the latter permitted to keep most of its empire.[266] Ironically (or at least in opposition to what Bradford and Cookridge argue) it is this likely support for an Anglo-German entente that gives rise to another source of the legend.

While the idea of an alliance between Britain and Germany is often associated with Rudolf Hess—largely because of his support for the Haushofers (who advocated an agreement) and his failed 1941 mission to Scotland, which he hoped would lead to a negotiated peace—Göring and his circle also embraced the concept with great enthusiasm. Author Hugh Thomas, while viewed with skepticism by most scholars because he advanced the argument that the person who landed in Scotland, was tried in Nuremberg, and then imprisoned at Spandau was not the real Rudolf Hess—includes some careful research in his book. Thomas notes, "The idea of flying to make peace may have been inspired originally by Goering, who told Hitler just after England had declared war on Germany, 'We must fly to Britain and I'll explain the position.' Hitler told him that such a move would be useless, but that he could try if he wanted, and for some time, it was rumoured that Goering would indeed make the attempt."[267] While it is unlikely that Hitler ever entertained the notion of sending Göring to Britain, the Reichsmarschall and his circle indulged in geopolitical fantasies about an Anglo-German alliance. Even Hitler is alleged to have told Unity Mitford in late-August 1939, "After appeasement would come neutrality, in the penultimate stage of that full Anglo-German cooperation. . . ."[268]

It is also conjectural to posit a connection between "Operation Willi" and the bombing of Buckingham Palace. Some believe that had George VI been killed, the Duke of Windsor would have had another opportunity (especially because Princess Elizabeth was fourteen years old in 1940). But this view is naïve: it is highly unlikely that the British would have interfered with the proper and legal line of succession (she would most likely have succeeded with the Duke of Gloucester as Regent). The most one can say is that some contemporary observers, including German officials, did not comprehend the minimal chances of the duke to ascend to the throne. It is worth noting that during the period between the Windsors' departure from Lisbon on board the S.S. *Excalibur* on 1 August and the bombing of Buckingham Palace on 13 September 1940, there continued to be machinations on the part of the Germans with regard to the Windsors. Historian John Costello wrote that "on 15 August, the day the Windsors reached Bermuda [on the way to the Bahamas], the German ambassador in Lisbon received notice that 'Willi' might yet be willing to play a part in Hitler's peace offensive."[269] Costello suggests the possibility that the duke, or perhaps even British intelligence, intentionally kept the Germans on the hook in August/September 1940 as a way of sustaining their hopes for a negotiated peace. This would have induced Hitler to hold off on an all-out invasion and given the British more time to rearm and train sorely needed

RAF pilots. But even if this latter scenario is true and the overtures were no longer genuine, the Germans would not have known this and would have retained the wish to install a new monarch.

The British royal family and the Hessens today exclude the possibility that Prince Christoph bombed his cousin George VI. Prince Philip, Duke of Edinburgh, communicated the following to the author through his press secretary: ". . . There is no truth whatever that Prince Christoph bombed Buckingham Palace. In 1940, the Prince was not a qualified pilot, and he was stationed at the western front undertaking missions in the Netherlands and France. Furthermore, neither the King nor Queen were in Buckingham Palace at the time of the bombing, and none of the bombs hit the building."[270] He revised this statement in an interview to acknowledge the presence of the king and queen during at least one raid, but remained steadfast in his belief that his brother-in-law played no role in the attack. Rainer von Hessen also rules out his father's involvement. He notes that the entries from his father's service record show clearly that from mid-November 1939 through July 1941 he held a staff position in the *Generalkommando* of the Second Flying Corps. At the time in question, he did not even have the training to participate in flying missions. Furthermore, Rainer points out, Prince Christoph so wanted to fly that he immediately wrote home about his experiences later in the war when he finally had an opportunity to participate in missions. All of this, Rainer von Hessen says "certainly does not minimize his share of responsibility in the strategic planning of the devastating terror raids on Dutch and British cities, in the course of which thousand of civilians were killed."[271] Rainer von Hessen's substantive arguments go a long way to clarifying matters with regard to the raid. Prince Christoph was not flying the plane that buzzed the Mall and bombed the palace. Because the ME 110 typically utilized a navigator, it is not beyond the realm of possibility that he was in the plane; but Christoph at that time was not even trained as a navigator. The only possibility—and this too is speculative—is that Christoph helped plan the attack in his capacity as a staff officer.

This latter scenario would point to the possibility that Christoph combined both military and intelligence assignments. Because of the destruction of FA documents at war's end, it is difficult to determine whether he continued to do intelligence work during the war. Certain clues point toward a sustained role in the FA: for example, he kept a personal assistant there who handled some of his correspondence.[272] Additionally, Christoph's superior and friend, Pilli Körner, wrote Reich finance minister Count Schwerin von Krosigk in November 1940 "that the Reichsmarschall places great importance on the fact that the head of the Forschungsamt Prince von Hessen is at the front, where he has had an indispensable post as an officer since the beginning of the war. . . . I would therefore ask you to see to the matter yourself, in accordance with the wishes of the Reichsmarschall."[273] While an intriguing document, the context of Körner's letter casts doubt about the statement: it was written to request higher pay for the acting director of the FA (Gottfried Schapper)—one commensurate with the job he was doing—and was meant more as a justification of the better wages than a commentary about Christoph's real mission. Nonetheless, Christoph continued to return to Berlin on a regular basis, which suggests that he retained contact with colleagues at the Forschungsamt and kept informed of intelligence activities. The precise nature of his involvement with the FA during the war therefore remains unclear: even his brother Prince Wolfgang could not shed light on the matter; he remarked, "since my brother like all employees of the Forschungsamt was bound by an oath of silence, he never spoke about his activities within the family."[274]

So, what did Prince Christoph *do* during the war? After training as a reserve officer with the Luftwaffe regiment in Kassel from 1935 onward, he volunteered for active service once war broke out in Poland in September 1939. This was not dissimilar from his brothers Wolfgang and Richard: both pulled strings to join the Army (they were forty-four and thirty-nine respectively) and participated in the occupation of Norway that began in April 1940.[275] Christoph was promoted fairly quickly at first, but then more slowly: from his initial appointment as corporal to lieutenant in October 1939, to first lieutenant on 1 May 1940, and to captain on 1 September 1940; but his next jump, to major, did not come until April 1943.[276] His military career was clearly unconventional in certain respects. It had started in a typical manner. In October and November 1939, Christoph was in Bad Kreuznach in the Palatinate at a Luftwaffe commando center. He then moved on to Bad Homburg, near Frankfurt (and Kronberg), to the staff of the Second Flying Corps headed by General Bruno Loerzer (1891–1960), where he was stationed from January to May 1940. Loerzer was a highly decorated pilot during World War I (forty-four air victories and a recipient of Pour le Mérite) and a good friend of Hermann Göring. The latter had made him Reich Air Sports Leader in 1935. In short, Loerzer, like Christoph, had very close ties to the Reichsmarschall.[277]

During the period leading up to the Battle of Britain, Prince Christoph was transferred to Luxembourg, where he remained through the end of June 1940. While stationed at the Bergfeld base, Christoph carried out staff work. He wrote Sophia on 13 May: "It really is interesting work and '*selbständig*' [independent], which I like. To know how everything is planned and then to wait until you hear the success is thrilling. . . ."[278] Christoph also enjoyed an expedition to Paris just after the capitulation: he wrote how the city was "rather empty. . . . Only German military cars en masse. The people are very depressed but polite and correct. . . . Paris certainly is a beautiful town. We lived in the Grand Hotel, *auf Kosten der Wehrmacht* [at the expense of the Armed Forces], but there was no breakfast. So we had breakfast in a café and lunch and dinner at the Ritz where of course all the '*Bonzen*' [bigwigs] live. . . ."[279] On the 10th of July, General Loerzer took Christoph to meet with Foreign Minister Ciano, who was on tour in Belgium. Christoph wrote, with a vagueness appropriate for a letter during military operations, how they "then accompanied him to all the famous places on the coast he went to see. It was very interesting to see all the stuff the English left behind during their glorious retreat. . . . Fancy I saw England quite clearly without glasses!"[280]

Christoph evidently excelled at the staff work he performed. He was awarded the Iron Cross (second class) by General Loerzer personally on 15 May—a medal usually given for acts of bravery. Yet in his case, it appears that he was recognized for his work helping plan the bombing of Rotterdam and Eindhoven. The Luftwaffe obliterated the city center of Rotterdam on 13 May, where the bombs killed nearly a thousand civilians and left 78,000 homeless. It is generally regarded as a notorious and gratuitous act of aggression—most notably, because it "was a prelude to warfare conducted against the civilian population as well."[281] Christoph was likely responsible for helping identify targets. While his part in the strategic planning of the air raids cannot be dissociated from the rest of the general staff, it bears mentioning that these raids constituted a notably radical measure at the time ("for years—even after the war—it was believed that 30,000 persons had perished in the attack").[282] There is no evidence that Christoph was troubled by the attacks on civilian targets. His letters home at the time reflect his high spirits: he wrote Sophia on 21 May, "We are in a little summer Schloss about 25 km north of Lotti's Capital [Luxembourg, with a reference to the monarch, Grand Duchess Charlotte (1896–1964)]. And soon we will move on towards the West. . . . What do you say to our success? Isn't it marvelous! I wonder what will happen next?"[283]

In the wake of the capitulation of the Netherlands on 15 May 1940, Christoph came home to Germany: he saw his father for the last time in Kassel on the twenty-second and then headed to Berlin, where he presumably conferred with his colleagues at the Forschungsamt. Christoph then returned to active military service in June, when he was assigned to the Luftwaffe base at Mariakerk in Belgium, not far from Ghent. He was deployed in the department that tracked enemy movement in the general staff of the Second Flying Corps.[284] His office was housed in a "pretty little chateau," although he lived "in a little villa" five minutes away and traveled between the two by bicycle.[285] Throughout the summer of 1940, Christoph did not seem especially taxed by his work. Although he would occasionally complain of fatigue, most of his letters home concerned trips to the beach and shopping expeditions in Brussels. Yet his work became more interesting as the Battle of Britain came to a head. On 2 September he wrote Sophia, "I'm afraid there is no leave to be expected just now because the air force is just very much engaged as you know."[286] On 9 September he described how "The other day I saw Göring; there was no opportunity to talk. He only asked how I was and then after a few minutes called me back to ask how old I am and then said he was going to make me a captain. It was during the first big attack on London. Yesterday Loerzer took me with him again to where Göring is and it was most interesting again for me. The attacks on London must have been quite colossal!"[287] Christoph, like all soldiers, clearly left a great deal out of his letters—including the topics of conversation when he sat in on the meeting with Göring and Loerzer. But they well may have discussed the bombing of Buckingham Palace: Göring personally had taken over direction of the Blitz on 7 September.[288] In any deliberations about these plans, Christoph would have played a subordinate and consultative role. The decision to attack the British King would have been made at a level well above Prince Christoph's rank.

In early September 1940, Christoph was transferred to a Luftwaffe base at Boningues les Calais, just a few kilometers inland from the Channel coast.[289] It was near enough to England that, in Christoph's words, "sometimes English batteries shoot over the Channel."[290] He added that the British bombed them "several times every night . . . and drop bombs all over the place." The Germans, in turn, launched operations against the United Kingdom from Boningues. Luftwaffe records show that sorties originated from this base at Boningues in September and that among their targets was the city of London, some two hundred nautical miles away. This was a time when the raids occurred frequently, and the city was bombed by German planes from dozens of bases—not just Boningues. Among the planes that were sent off from Boningues were Messerschmidt 110s.[291] It is therefore possible that one of the planes that departed from Boningues attacked the palace and that Christoph played a role in planning the attack.

The episode then becomes even more complicated because there were multiple attacks on Buckingham Palace. On Monday, 9 September, the palace was struck and a bomb lodged in the Regency room just below the king's study. It exploded at 1:25 a.m. on 10 September: while there were no casualties, a number of windows in the palace were shattered, including those to George VI's study. Several days later, on 13 September, the Luftwaffe struck again and hit Buckingham Palace with six bombs.[292] The bombing that came closest to claiming the life of the king occurred midday on 13 September. As King George VI later recounted:

> We were both upstairs with Alec Hardinge talking in my little sitting room overlooking the quadrangle. . . . All of a sudden we heard an aircraft making

a zooming noise above us, saw 2 bombs falling past the opposite side of the Palace, & then heard 2 resounding crashes as the bombs fell in the quadrangle about 30 yards away. We looked at each other & then we went out into the passage as fast as we could get there. The whole thing happened in a matter of seconds. We all wondered why we weren't dead. Two great craters had appeared in the courtyard. The one nearest the Palace had burst a fire hydrant & water was pouring through the broken windows in the passage. 6 bombs had been dropped. The aircraft was seen coming down the Mall below the clouds having dived through the clouds & had dropped 2 bombs in the forecourt, 2 in the quadrangle, 1 in the Chapel & the other in the garden. There is no doubt that it was a direct attack on the palace.[293]

One can draw several conclusions from the reports of the bombing. First, the British monarch was fortunate to survive the 13 September assault. John Wheeler-Bennett noted, "The fact that the palace had been bombed was, of course, known, but the imminence of the peril to the King and Queen was kept a close secret, and not even the Prime Minister was informed."[294] Indeed, if the windows to his study had not been blown out on the 9–10 September raid and he had been in usual quarters, the consequences may have been more serious. Second, in the words of the bomb assessment officer (and consistent with George VI's perceptions), "There can be little doubt that Buckingham Palace has been deliberately selected for attack."[295] The raid on 15 September, which involved more than one plane, would underscore that the Germans intentionally attacked Buckingham Palace and that the bombing was not a spontaneous act of a rogue plane. It may have been the Germans' intention to send a message to the British about their vulnerability, rather than to demolish the palace or even to kill the king.

Another reason for the legend of Christoph's involvement is that King George VI voiced suspicions that one of his relations was involved in the attack. Sarah Bradford noted, "despite the Queen's public declarations of being glad to be able to look the East End in the face, he was privately furious and outraged at what he suspected to be an attack upon himself by a member of his own family. As an airman himself, he was well aware of the difficulty of executing a bombing raid on a specific building in good visibility, let alone in the daring or dangerous manner in which this particular raid had been executed, by diving through the rain clouds and flying low under the cloud, aiming straight up the Mall at the heart of the Palace. To him, the affair suggested a detailed local knowledge."[296] George VI apparently also suspected his second cousin from Spain—who was a general in the Spanish air force and a member of the House of Sachsen-Coburg und Gotha.[297] Sarah Bradford, as noted earlier, also supports the theory that it was a relative of the king who participated in the mission: in her words, "a more likely candidate as the royal bomber would have been . . . Prince

Christopher of Hesse, a Nazi pilot in the Luftwaffe."[298] Recognizing that Christoph was not a pilot, one must conclude that she is also unable to provide compelling evidence on the subject of who attacked Buckingham Palace. But for several decades (a contemporary of King George VI, Lord Lambton is another who argues for Christoph's involvement), Christoph's participation in one of the raids has remained an enduring legend.[299]

There are clearly fundamental problems with such renditions and the most one can say is that Christoph may have helped plan an attack. But it is significant that the issue even arises: it says something about his career in the Third Reich and about the consequences of a dearth of source material. It also says something about the manner in which people attempt to fill in gaps in the historical record (with their imagination). Perhaps one can say little more than Holocaust historian Raul Hilberg and observe, "the rumor in itself is always a fact."[300]

Philipp as the Führer's Art Agent in Italy

Philipp served Hitler in Italy not just by representing him in discussions with Mussolini and King Vittorio Emmanuele but also by locating and purchasing artworks earmarked for the *Führermuseum* to be located in Linz. Philipp and Hitler had long shared a passion for art, and Philipp was well informed about the Special Project (*Sonderauftrag*) Linz: the creation of a cultural mecca in Hitler's adopted hometown, with the gargantuan museum as its centerpiece. Philipp had accompanied Hitler during a tour of Italian museums in 1938 when the dictator reportedly became inspired to undertake the project. The crystallizing experience for Hitler with regard to the Führermuseum had been a visit to the Uffizi in Florence. This was an excursion that Philipp had helped coordinate. Philipp subsequently played a leading role with regard to Special Project Linz, especially after autumn of 1940 when he became an active procurer of paintings.[301] The Führermuseum became one of Hitler's most important projects; he devoted innumerable hours during the war to architectural plans for the museum and was in close contact with the architects, Hermann Giesler, Roderick Fick, and Albert Speer. He discussed virtually every acquisition with professors Hans Posse and Hermann Voss, the directors of the planned museum, as well as with selected agents such as Karl Haberstock and Prince Philipp. Even at war's end, when Hitler was confined to the Berlin Bunker, he had a special room that housed a model of the Linz complex and would spend hours there engrossed in his fantasies.

Hitler's May 1938 state visit to Italy had featured the acquisition of an important sculpture, Myron's *Discus Thrower*, for which the German dictator paid the equivalent of $327,000. Frederic Spotts recounted:

Hitler, Himmler, and Prince Philipp inspect antiquities at a museum in Kassel, 1939.

This second-century Roman marble copy of a Greek bronze original was one of the best surviving statues of the ancient world. Discovered in Rome in 1781, it belonged to the Lancellotti family on whose property it had been found. Although Ludwig I of Bavaria had tried to purchase it early in the nineteenth century, it was not until 1937 that it went up for sale. The Metropolitan Museum tried to get it for New York, the Berlin State Museums wanted it for Berlin, and Prince Philipp of Hesse had his eye on it for Hitler.[302]

Spotts suggests that Prince Philipp's bid for the statue was "turned down," but he also notes that "what happened has been an object of speculation." More certain is that Hitler requested that Mussolini let him inspect the sculpture during the May 1938 trip and that the two men viewed it—with Philipp tagging along—on the second day of the state visit. Hitler made a personal plea to Il Duce, and it was left to the subordinates to iron out the details. "Two weeks after that Foreign Minister Ciano informed Italian officials that the export had been authorized 'in view of the personal interest of the Reich Chancellor.' "[303] Philipp, who was very knowledgeable about ancient art, expressed views about the piece that evidently influenced Hitler; and the prince followed up by helping arrange the special dispensation for export. The *Discus Thrower* was displayed prominently in the Munich Glypthothek, a fine trophy for both Hitler and Philipp in their own ways: the dictator marketed the piece to the German public as a gift from Il Duce, "a dividend of the Rome-Berlin Axis," while Philipp regarded it as tangible evidence of his work for Hitler in Italy. After the war, the Italians viewed the sculpture in symbolic terms as well and demanded its return.[304] The Americans did so amid considerable controversy in 1948, and today it is exhibited in Rome in the Museo Nazionale Romano Palazzo Massimo delle Terme.[305]

Because Hitler acquired many works by way of plunder—including, of course, the seizure of art from Jewish victims—a key question is whether Philipp was also involved in unlawful expropriations. The answer is no. But he came very close to complicity in the Nazis' plundering. For example, one component of the looting operation involved effecting the "return" of cultural objects that had been taken from German lands during the previous centuries. The *Rückführung* program, which was headed by Propaganda Minister Goebbels, entailed the compilation of lists of targeted works in France, the Benelux countries, and later in Eastern Europe. Philipp played a role in organizing this program. On 8 November 1941, German ambassador to Rome Hans Georg von Mackensen circulated a secret order to high ranking German officials, including the SS chief of Rome Herbert Kappler, in which he reported:

> Prince Philipp von Hessen visited me today and told me that during his recent visit to the Führer Headquarters several days ago the Führer issued an order which was communicated to [Italian] Education Minister Bottai. The Führer is prepared to hand over to the Italians all the artworks taken by the French from Italy in so far as they are located in occupied France. He has requested that the Italians provide a list of such works. Prince Philipp declared that Minister Bottai received this information with the greatest joy and would work on providing the requested list.[306]

The *Rückführung* program was never implemented in the manner originally envisioned (the decision was made to wait until peace treaties were concluded before artworks changed hands, and these treaties were never drafted), but the Goebbels-led initiative clearly reflected the intent to redistribute Europe's cultural patrimony by use of force. It was part of a larger strategy: if the Germans provided their ally with works in France and other defeated nations, then the Italians would hopefully respond by lifting export restrictions—or so claimed the head of Italy's postwar restitution program, Rudolfo Siviero, in his memoirs.[307]

While the expropriations of artworks from Jews in Hessen provided instances where the prince was proximate to plunder, it was his purchases in Italy on behalf of Hitler that induced Allied investigators to place him on a list titled, "Individuals Involved in Art Looting."[308] One can debate both the ethical and legal implications of his activities as a buyer for Hitler, but it seems fair to say that Philipp fell into a kind of gray area of complicity in the

Nazis' art plundering program. By working in Italy in the years up to 1943, Philipp stayed away from the worst of the Nazi depredations in France, the Netherlands, and of course, Eastern Europe; these were the areas where the plundering commandos ran amok (one scholar estimated that in France "one-third of the art in private hands was pillaged by the Nazis").[309] Philipp was opposed to the brazen plundering carried out by the Nazi regime. Christoph's wife Princess Sophia recalled, "during the war we met once in Kronberg and there he expressed his anger about the 'transporting' of artworks from outside Germany to Reich territory and declared that the Party people had 'sticky fingers,' a fact that would come back to [haunt] Germany and would be regarded as a black mark."[310] Philipp was predisposed against the Nazis' policy of "securing" art because of his own family's history. In January 1807, Baron Denon had preyed upon the Hessen collection on behalf of Napoleon, who was in the process of transforming the Louvre into a symbol of France's imperial power in Europe (Denon selected 299 especially valuable paintings for the Louvre on this trip, although the *Kurfürst* lost other works to the French during this period).[311] This historical precedent to the Nazis' *Kunstraub* was—and remains—etched into the consciousness of members of the Hessen family. In a letter to the author, Philipp's nephew, Rainer von Hessen, described the history of the Napoleonic looting of the family art collection, adding, "the most valuable pieces of the Hesse-Kassel painting collection that Napoleon gave to his first wife as a gift, was sold to Tsar Alexander I and are still located today in the Hermitage in St. Petersburg."[312]

While Prince Philipp was not directly plundering artworks, certain questions arise concerning his involvement in the Nazis' *Kunstpolitik* during the war. The first centers on the issues of remuneration and profit from his work as an art agent for Hitler and the Führermuseum. Members of the American Art Looting Investigation Unit, who examined documents relating to Philipp's acquisitions in Italy for Hitler, noted with regard to two transactions in early 1941, "the differences [in the prices listed] relate to mark-ups in the prices paid and indicate that someone may have been padding the expense account for personal profit."[313] The markups identified here amounted to nearly one-third the purchase price. They added about Philipp, "Not averse to doing a little business in art."[314] While these charges are more credible than others levied by other American intelligence agents that Philipp joined Göring in reaping handsome profits through the acquisition of land in Poland, conclusive documentation is missing in both instances.[315] Other Nazi art experts who acquired works for Hitler took commissions, so it would not have been out of the ordinary or illegal. Self-enrichment would have been a matter for the denazification courts, which in principle sought to strip opportunists of the profits made during the Third Reich, but the matter was never even raised at Philipp's trial. This may have been because Philipp was so adept at concealing the details of the transactions he brokered: the American investigators cited above, for example, "deciphered . . . receipt forms which underlay the completed forms and on which the pressure of the pencil [had] left legible traces."[316] In other words, the suspicious (if inconclusive) documents had gone missing.

Another possible link between Philipp and the Nazi plundering operations was his bank account in the Netherlands, at the "Aryanized" bank of Lippmann, Rosenthal & Co.[317] There were actually two banks by that name: a conventional merchant bank on the Nieuwe Spiegelstraat that had been "Aryanized"; and a new but separate LIRO on the Sarphatistraat that had been established to process the assets plundered from Dutch Jews. Philipp and Mafalda had a bank account at the former.[318] German tax investigators determined in 1943 that Philipp had a bank account there worth RM 49,000 ($20,000) and that he had failed to report it on his taxes. Philipp and Mafalda's account was evidently opened back to the mid-1930s when the LIRO was a rather ordinary merchant bank. Indeed, as a well-known Jewish bank, one could even argue that the account revealed a general absence of anti-Semitic sentiment (there were non-Jewish establishments that would have provided alternatives). After the war, Philipp reported that he had RM 37,746 there in 1935 (and RM 59,404 in 1940).[319] The sums deposited there provided them with foreign currency that was not subject to the strict currency controls of the Nazi state.[320] This would have enabled them to buy goods outside of the Reich without filing for the difficult-to-obtain foreign currency. In other words, they may have engaged in currency smuggling. It would be a stretch to say that Philipp and Mafalda profited from this bank-turned-plundering institution, but they did reap benefits from this financially healthy institution. Their LIRO account is perhaps a fitting symbol of their obliviousness as they continued to patronize this problematic establishment after it had been Aryanized. It is also an indication of how complicated and opaque their financial dealings had become.

Despite Philipp's distance from the most egregious of the Nazis' plundering operations, there were still important political and ideological implications to his art collecting efforts on Hitler's behalf. For starters, his exertions brought him closer to Hitler and put him in a position of trying to elicit the approbation of the Führer. Beginning in the fall of 1940 Philipp helped Hitler buy at least ninety works, including paintings by Tintoretto, Titian, Lotto, Pannini, Tiepolo, Veronese, Canaletto, Rubens, and others.[321] This created a dynamic whereby the prince would traverse Italy looking for prized pieces, and then report back to Hitler—or to Dr. Posse—about what he had found. Allied investigators noted that "in June 1941, Posse's special purchasing account at the German Embassy in Rome was made over to Prince Philipp von Hessen and the sum of 13,200,000 lire (1,650,000

Reichsmarks or $660,000) was deposited there.[322] The prince, therefore, did not need Posse by his side in order to make purchases. The ninety-some works, although but a fraction of the over eight thousand paintings acquired by Hitler, nonetheless represented tremendous effort for one individual, especially when one considers the extraordinarily high quality of the pieces.[323] This harvest of artworks drew the two men closer, as they would discuss acquisitions and future plans. But it also put Philipp in a more subordinate position. A prince had been transformed into an art dealer, or perhaps one might say, a procurer. It was a paradoxical situation: Hans Posse, for example, would address letters to him as "Your Royal Highness!" while Philipp chased after the works.[324]

At times, Philipp was caught in between the competition between Hitler and Göring, for whom he earlier assisted in the pursuit of artworks.[325] Both leaders hoped to acquire a painting then attributed to Leonardo da Vinci, *Leda and the Swan*. Philipp, who had grown closer to Hitler personally by the outbreak of war, naturally helped him buy the piece, with the deal closing in June 1941 for 10.5 million Lire ($520,000). Göring's primary art agent, Walter Andreas Hofer, was bitterly disappointed by the outcome; one can only imagine the reaction of the Reichsmarschall, and this undoubtedly cooled relations between Prince Philipp and Göring.[326] But Philipp had made up his mind about his primary allegiance: in late May 1941, he even sent Martin Bormann a gift, a sketch by the nineteenth-century artist Friedrich Stahl, in what appeared to be an effort to put himself in the good graces of the increasingly powerful gatekeeper to Hitler (the present was not accepted, since Bormann's aide, Walter Hanssen, wrote back that the Reichsleiter, "without exception does not accept gifts intended for himself personally, but as always intends them for public purposes").[327]

In snapping up valuable works in Italy, Philipp also expressed approbation for Hitler's project. His participation in the effort to collect art was akin to Dr. Posse, the venerable director of the Dresden Painting Collections, agreeing to oversee the construction of the Führermuseum: both men helped confer respectability to the undertaking. Posse's involvement represented professional or scholarly acceptance, while Philipp's denoted a combination of social (that is, aristocratic) and personal approbation. It is striking that the Nazi leaders as a group employed so many aristocrats in their art plundering campaign: to take other examples, SS-Major Baron Eberhard von Künsberg (1900–45) was one of the most prodigious plunderers in France and the Soviet Union; Baron Kurt von Behr (1894–1945) was one of the leaders of the ERR in France (and oversaw the *Möbel-Aktion*, or the seizure of French Jews' furniture); and Prince Franz zu Sayn-Wittgenstein (1901–74) was part of an army photographic team in France, connected to the *Kunstschutz* (art protection) unit—a relatively innocuous position but sufficient to warrant his inclusion in an OSS's list of "individuals involved in art looting."[328] The deployment of nobles in the plundering bureaucracy in part stemmed from their knowledge of art and of foreign lands, but such appointments also reflected the Nazi leaders' efforts to make them complicit in the programs of the regime.

Issues of social class certainly came into play as Philipp scoured Italy for suitable works. The prince was told by Hitler to use his social connections to open doors to the great Italian collectors. One sees this played out in many of the purchases: the so-called da Vinci *Leda and the Swan*, mentioned above, came from the Spiridon family and Hans Memling's stunning *Portrait of a Man in a Black Cap*, was sold by the Corsini family; in both instances, the sellers were Italian aristocrats. Other nobles approached by Philipp on behalf of Hitler in Italy included Prince del Drago, Prince Barbarini, Count Paolo Labia, Prince Massimo, Princess Emila Ourousoff, Count Lazzaroni, Count Robilant, and Countess Luisa Traine.[329] Without Philipp, even someone as respected as Dr. Posse would not have been granted access to these collectors.[330] Philipp used his other aristocratic contacts to scout for works; even his friend Count Eddie von Bismarck helped him in this regard.[331] The process then was that Philipp would locate and photograph the works, and then send the results to Posse. The professor would often inspect the works himself on tours of Italy, but occasionally Philipp acquired works for Linz on his own. This was the case with the Memling, which one scholar described as "perhaps the grandest prize" of Hitler's Italian acquisitions. Philipp convinced Prince Corsini to sell the portrait and then saw to the ancillary matters of payment (between 5 and 6 million Lire) and an export permit.[332] As these works left the possession of old aristocratic families and became the property of Nazi parvenus, a message was being sent: the old guard was being supplanted, and this was a material form of expression. Philipp, with his divided loyalties, chose National Socialism over social class.

Notably, however, Philipp did not sell his own family's works or pressure his cousins to do so: for example, there were attempts in 1934 to transfer the great Holbein *Madonna* to the Landesmuseum in Darmstadt, but the head of the House of Hesse-Darmstadt, Grand Duke Ernst Ludwig, successfully preserved the family's ownership. Later, Hitler's primary dealer, Karl Haberstock, persisted in his attempts to acquire the Holbein *Madonna* from the grand duke's son, Ludwig, but to no avail. Prince Ludwig's secretary, Wilhelm Wirth, responded to an October 1941 offer from Haberstock —one that included the possibility of payment in property rather than money. Wirth noted tersely, "all inquiries of this kind are futile and we beg you to inform your prospective purchaser accordingly. *Heil Hitler!*"[333] Philipp also acknowledged after the war that his cousin Prince Ludwig had been pressured by Göring to relinquish Cranach's *Portrait of the Prince of Saxony*: the Reichsmarschall had called him on the telephone and "asked for the picture in a manner such that Ludwig could not refuse."[334] While postwar American investigators believed that Prince Lu had given up the picture (and that Goering had not paid anything for it), the Hessen family records indicate that they had never relinquished the Cranach (it remains in the collection today)."[335] In general, it is fair to say that Philipp helped preserve the Hessen collections against the encroachments of the Nazi leaders.

One finds a number of instances where Nazi leaders acquired artworks from princes in exchanges that reflected the new balance of power. Prince Johann Georg, Duke von Sachsen, for example, sold Hitler forty-two exquisite German drawings in 1940. The prince was a longtime patron of the Dresden Painting Gallery and a friend of Hans Posse, who had overseen the museum since 1911. This collection of drawings by artists such as Moritz von Schwind, Wilhelm Leibl, and Adolph von Menzel was, in Posse's words, "one of the last important collections of great German graphic art of the early nineteenth century."[336] Hitler and Posse were thrilled to obtain them from the Saxon royal family. Another, even more dramatic example involved Antoine Watteau's masterpiece *La Danse*, which Hitler acquired from Crown Prince Wilhelm von Preussen. This charming painting, which had been in the family's possession since Frederick the Great acquired it in the late eighteenth century, was so cherished by the Hohenzollern that the Kaiser took it with him to Doorn when he went into exile. After the ex-Kaiser's death in 1941, his son permitted Hitler to have it, and art dealer Karl Haberstock brokered the deal. Whatever reluctance Crown Prince Wilhelm might have felt, the painting would henceforth be part of the Führermuseum, a monument to the dictator. The form of payment was also symbolic: while the official price was RM 900,000, Hitler allegedly permitted the crown prince to receive payment in the form of a land grant (a parcel of property previously designated Reich hunting forest).[337] This gesture had feudal connotations—much like a king offering land to a vassal. In this case, the person in the subordinate position was a prince who would have been emperor had the monarchy not been abolished. It is unlikely that such symbolism was lost on the Hohenzollern or other princes—a caste ever sensitive to such matters. Just like the other princes who sold to Hitler, Göring, and other Nazi elite—and this included Baron von Frankenstein, the Duke of Oldenburg, and the Prince von Schaumburg-Lippe—the Nazi leaders used art instrumentally to articulate the new social relations as they amassed their collections.[338]

Prince Philipp's efforts in Italy helped send other, more ideological, messages. The Führermuseum was intended to be an expression of German hegemony in Europe: the most militarily and economically powerful nation on the Continent would also possess the greatest cultural resources.

When it came to cultural treasures, this was a zero-sum game. One nation's gain was another's loss. Mussolini and the Italians were aware that the Germans' cultural aspirations represented a threat to them: they passed a law prohibiting the export of artworks deemed national treasures in December 1939 and then strengthened the provisions in 1942.[339] Philipp used his connections to Mussolini and other Italian leaders in order to secure export waivers for the works he acquired for Hitler. He reported after the war that there were only two occasions when his requests for an export permit was declined, although he did not provide specifics.[340] Mussolini personally intervened on a number of occasions in order to permit pieces to leave Italy. Most often, the works were of Germanic origin—such as Hans Makart's triptych, *The Plague of Florence.*[341] The symbolic message was not lost on contemporaries. Mussolini even elicited criticism for such moves from nationalistic Fascist compatriots—Ciano and the minister for education and culture Giuseppe Bottai, for example.[342] While Philipp had no direct connection to the Makart triptych, the Americans after the war returned to Italy many of the works Philipp helped Hitler acquire because they deemed the transactions in violation of Italian export laws. Mussolini, like Prince Philipp, had known exactly what he was doing. They had both used art to communicate their political views and allegiances.[343]

Christoph in the Soviet Union, North Africa, and Sicily

While mysteries remain surrounding Prince Christoph's varied experiences in the early years of World War II, his career proved eventful since he was deployed on all of the major fronts while periodically returning to Berlin to keep apprised of developments at the Forschungsamt. The FA had shifted the focus of its activities to war-related espionage. As Joseph Goebbels wrote in his journal in the spring of 1942: "Lecture about the work of the Forschungsamt. . . . Above all, they have succeeded in deciphering most of the enemy codes, so that today we can monitor part of the telegram traffic between Ankara and London or Moscow and London. . . . One can draw from the intercepts an entire series of important conclusions. Above all, one must keep this work extraordinarily secret, or else one will obviate the results."[344] Christoph would have been aware of this shift in the work of the agency; his mother, the Landgravine wrote his brother Richard in October 1940, that "Pilli [State Secretary Körner—his superior in the Prussian State Ministry] wants to have Chri back; there is so much that is new to sort out. But will Chri really go?"[345] Christoph, however, refused all offers to return to the more administrative intelligence post as he exhibited a clear preference for service in the Luftwaffe. Furthermore, there is no evidence showing that Christoph combined secret assignments for the Forschungsamt and the Luftwaffe.

Prince Christoph and the Second Flying Corps were transferred to the Eastern Front in June 1941, prior to the attack on the Soviet Union.[346] He first played a role in the planning, as he worked from a train that headed east. On 8 June he was in Posen in the General Government, but he did not remain there long as the train pushed east, stopping only for supplies. A note to Sophia on 20 June, a day before the attack, explained "we have been working very hard the last days, but all is satisfactory. . . ."[347] He could not communicate the nature of his work because the attack on the Soviet Union was of the highest secrecy. Earlier in the month, he had written to Sophia, saying, "If you should not have any letters for some time don't be worried. You can guess the reason."[348] But his letters gradually became more expressive as he pushed eastward with the invading German forces: by 28 June he was at Brest-Litovsk, and by 5 July 1941 he was in Minsk, where he remained through August. This posting in Belarus was near the front, hundreds of miles into the Soviet Union. One letter from Sophia to Christoph's mother from 3 August 1941, is indicative of the news she received from him: she wrote that Christoph was "camping close to the Dnieper in tents and had very little water to wash in. Things were going very well, but he thinks it'll take some time still as the country is so huge and the fighting so hard."[349] Christoph also wrote that he had managed to be transferred to a "fighting squadron" (*Kampfgeschwader*) that was under the command of General Loerzer. In one dangerously blunt letter to Sophia after the transfer, he noted that the colonel, who had operational command of the squadron (von Chamier), "offered to take me already a year ago, only that swine our '*chef*' [Göring] wouldn't let me go. But now at last I've succeeded. I'm delighted to be rid of that b[loody] staff, the people got on my nerves so terribly."[350] Christoph undoubtedly knew that his mail might be intercepted and read, but he could always explain away the disparaging reference to Göring by his eagerness to fight. That was a sentiment that the Reichsmarschall would likely have understood. Still, the phrasing was incautious and conveys Prince Christoph's fervent desire to see active duty.

Although he rarely stated it explicitly in his letters, it is likely that Christoph was ideologically committed to the murderous invasion, as was the great majority of the officers in the German Armed Forces. His decision to give up staff work for active combat might be understood in this light. He would also occasionally use terms such as "bolshies," although there was no explicit racism in his letters.[351] Of course, the documentary basis for determining the extent of his racism is largely missing: his official papers were destroyed, and his personal correspondence with Sophia was not a place to discuss his racial views. This leaves some ambiguity about his thinking regarding the ideological war in the East. While Christoph was engaged in aerial missions, as distinct from fighting taking place on the ground, he was also a member of the German armed forces, which, as historians now know, was deeply complicit in crimes in the East.[352] As historian Richard Vinen noted, "for Germany, the war in the east was an ideological one (against communism) and a racial one (against Slavs and Jews) as well as a war between nations. This was not just a concern for Nazi theoreticians. The attack on the Soviet Union was desperately important to the aristocrats who composed a large part of the upper reaches of the German officer corps, because their own estates lay in the east. At the beginning of the century, Theobald von Bethmann Hollweg had told his son not to plant oak trees on the family's Prussian estate because 'the Russians will be there before they mature.' Now Germany was fighting to remove the Russian threat from her border forever; defeat would ensure that Bethmann Hollweg's prophecy came true."[353] While Christoph was not a Junker, his family connections to the Hohenzollern and the time he spent in East Prussia during his youth made him sensitive to the perspectives of many aristocrats in eastern Germany.

After a brief stint in Belgium and the Netherlands in August 1941, where he underwent further training for active combat, Christoph returned to the U.S.S.R. in the autumn of 1941. He had passed through Kronberg on his way east and seen his family, including his youngest son, Rainer (b. 1939). Princess Sophia, with good reason, was "sad and anxious" for Christoph because he was preparing to take part in flying missions for the first time.[354] The prince was sent to the region of Wjasma-Gradina, where he was in the Third Flying Division of the Third Fighter Squadron—part of the Central Army Group (*Mitte*) under the command of General Field Marshal Fedor von Bock that pushed toward Moscow. While the autumn rains slowed the advance—Christoph commented on "the famous stream of mud" [the road in a town he was based]—General Heinz Guderian led the Panzers as they thrust eastward through Wjasma. This was tough fighting: Field Marshal von Bock's Army Group assumed the main burden of the attack as the Germans launched Operation Typhoon in October and November 1941.[355] Christoph was flying reconnaissance missions and working as an "active observer." He had also received training in bomber protection strategy and flew as a fighter escort. In late October, he was stationed at Witebsk, the site of a great battle between the Wehrmacht and Red Army. By 25 November, he had already made eighteen missions over enemy lines (*Feindflüge*).[356] A week later, the Germans had reached the outskirts of the Soviet capital, where their advance was halted in one of the turning points of the war.[357]

Prince Christoph, however, was called back from the Eastern Front on 22 November 1941 as a result of orders prohibiting princes from participating in combat. This was an early manifestation of what became known as the *"Prinzenerlass,"* or the decree that limited the roles that princes could play. The Nazi regime gradually, and somewhat haphazardly, marginalized the princes, and this was a first step (more on this below). Christoph's surprise and anger at the decision was captured in a 25 November 1941 letter to Sophia:

> Why did Welfi [Prince Welf Heinrich von Hannover] have to leave the army?. . . . I'm most frightfully annoyed and angry, because since the 22nd I'm not allowed to fly anymore! There was the most terrible excitement amongst all of *vorgesetzte Dienststellen* [superiors] because suddenly there came an *Anfrage* [inquiry] by telephone from Berlin in the name of Göring *angeblich* [supposedly] asking whether I had been flying here, and, if so, how this was possible, because it was forbidden for me! You can imagine my feelings. I did 18 *Feindflüge* [flights over enemy territory] which was thrilling and most interesting and suddenly it's forbidden. I've never heard of such a thing. I've firmly made up my mind to make my way till Göring if necessary, to find out, what is at the bottom of this. So here I am now, sitting indoors all day long. It's simply maddening. . . .[358]

Prince Christoph had engaged in a long struggle to participate in active combat and was bitterly frustrated when permission was rescinded.

Well into 1942, it was common for princes to push for the opportunity to fight for Nazi Germany. The case alluded to by Prince Christoph, where the son of the Kaiser's daughter Viktoria Luise, Prince Welf Heinrich von Hannover (b. 1923), was released from the Army, elicited strong protests from the young Hannoverian prince and also inquiries from more senior family members. Princess Viktoria Luise even turned for assistance to her cousin, Prince Philipp von Hessen. Philipp wrote her:

> On 21 February [1942] I had an audience with Hitler at Headquarters and had an opportunity at the end to speak to him alone. I told him quite frankly that I'd heard there was a decree in existence which stipulated that Princes were no longer to be allowed to join the army and this gave me great cause for anxiety concerning my sons. He answered "A decree in such a form does not exist and your sons can naturally become officers at any time. I must, however, refuse entry into the army of the sons of Royal Houses who have either verbally or by their actions opposed the National Socialist State or me."[359]

In all likelihood, Hitler was still angry at the Hohenzollern family for not cooperating with his plans for the ex-Kaiser's funeral: when Wilhelm II had died in Doorn the previous June, Hitler had wanted to organize a state funeral in Potsdam (in Viktoria Luise's words "He want[ed] to use this opportunity to walk behind the German Kaiser's coffin in front of the whole German people and the world, to show them he is the legitimate successor").[360] The restrictions on princes serving in the armed forces often resulted from sentiments of a very general and at times irrational nature. A process of marginalization and increasing mutual mistrust, however, had begun.

The measures aimed at limiting the role of princes were applied haphazardly and inconsistently. For example, among Christoph's cousins, Prince Friedrich Karl von Preussen was an officer in the Sixth Army that advanced in the south toward Stalingrad; Prince Georg Wilhelm von Hannover (b. 1915) was a general staff officer with the Second Panzer Group under the command of General Guderian and fought at Smolensk and Kiev; Prince Ernst August von Hannover served in another Panzer group under General Erich Hoepner; and Prince Ludwig von Hessen-Darmstadt was posted to the Eastern Front on the staff of General Blaskowitz, but "eventually managed to escape the main thrust of the war."[361] He was not dismissed from the Wehrmacht until 30 December 1943, a measure ordered from the Führer Headquarters by chief of the Supreme Command of the German armed forces, General Field Marshal Wilhelm Keitel himself.[362] One Nazi Party document from early 1944 listed thirty-nine members of princely houses that had been dismissed from their positions in the armed forces, including ten from various branches of the Hohenzollern family, and also members of the Hannover, Habsburg, and, of course, Hessen families.[363] The same report listed seventeen princes who were permitted to stay on at their posts: most from very illustrious families—Sachsen-Coburg und Gotha, Schaumburg-Lippe, and Waldeck, although the only Hohenzollern to keep his position was Prince Alexander Ferdinand von Preussen, son of Prince Auwi. These lists were not exhaustive and appear to have been a work in progress.

Prince Christoph, however, remained in the Luftwaffe, although he had the relatively good fortune to be transferred away from the Eastern Front in December 1941, just prior to the Red Army's powerful counteroffensive —an attack that almost resulted in the destruction of the German Central Army Group in early 1942. Christoph was ordered to a new assignment in Sicily, and he had the opportunity to return to Kronberg and see his family prior to departing for Italy. While on the way to the southern theater in January 1942, Christoph stopped in Rome to see Philipp and Mafalda. It was a short visit, and there is no record of what they discussed. Christoph then moved on to Taormina, a Luftwaffe base in Sicily, where he again held a staff position with the Second Squadron. Suffering through another ban from flying combat missions, he moaned that Taormina was "the most dull place I've met for a long time."[364] Still, it was not all bad news for him

Christoph (center) *with comrades at Luftwaffe base in Southern Italy, 1943. The officer on the* left *is Colonel von Maltzahn.*

personally: Göring gradually reemerged and made efforts to re-establish contact with Christoph and his family. In early March, the Reichsmarschall awarded Christoph an Iron Cross First Class (which elicited the reaction, "I am very pleased. No other news from here. This place is just as bloody as ever").[365] Later in the month, when Sophia and Landgravine Margarethe were invited to the Görings in Berlin, the Reichsmarschall offered an explanation for Christoph being consigned to noncombat duty: "[H]e could not make an exception for him not being at the front, since he had first heard from his frontline pilots—and then immediately forbidden it regardless of all risks—that if such a man [as Christoph] was captured there, they [the enemy] would not only make boundless propaganda, but also turn to unheard of methods in order to obtain information—injections, etc. One had examples of things being said by people who would never say such things under normal circumstances. The Führer himself had ordered that [Göring's] nephew could not remain at the front because of his name."[366] With Christoph's background in intelligence work, the risk was all the greater (akin to Allied officers who knew about top-secret ULTRA decryptions falling into enemy hands).

Göring, however, did grant Christoph's request to transfer back to an active squadron—albeit, in a nonfighting capacity—and by April the prince had joined Fighter Squadron Fifty-three under the command of Colonel (Baron) Günther von Maltzahn that was based in Comiso, Sicily. The unit fought hard against the British on Malta through much of 1942. Christoph carried out staff work, focusing on weapons procurement. While this frustrated him, he enjoyed good relations with other members of his squadron and relished the camaraderie. He wrote his wife from Comiso in June 1942, just after he finished a three-week leave at Kronberg, "that he had arrived safely and was suffering under horrible heat, siroccos and sand, that forced its way into the room. [But] he was received very warmly by his comrades."[367] Christoph had few illusions about the course of the war: he knew that the entry of the United States had left the Axis overmatched. But his letters reflected a positive attitude: in June 1942 he wrote, "Isn't it wonderful Tobruk being taken again, none of us thought of that possibility and now they have reached the Egyptian frontier."[368]

Much of 1942 was indeed pleasant for Christoph. In September his mood was bolstered by the visit of his brother-in-law, Crown Prince Umberto ("Beppo"), who arranged a meeting near Christoph's base at Donnafugata. Christoph recalled, "he had only come to see me and thought that I lived in the place, which by the way is a kind of *castell*, rather impressive with a glorious view on the sea which is far off. We sat alone for a short hour, he asking questions . . . and all the rest of his officers consisting of general, colonels, etc. remained out on the terrace with the German officers. I was in shorts and he most beautifully dressed."[369] Later in the month, Christoph traveled to Corfu to inspect an airfield: he reported back to Sophia that Mon Repos, the villa where she was born, was occupied by the Italian governor, but that "the island looks beautiful." He wrote home of a pet dachshund that he had inherited from a fellow officer: "Boobie"— "being a real *Dackel* he does anything but obey"—was eventually shipped to Sophia at Kronberg. And at year's end, he paid a visit to the Villa Polissena, where he spent more time with Mafalda: "Muti," as she was called, was "particularly nice and friendly," and they played cards and "talked incessantly." As he departed, Christoph was the beneficiary of "a most elaborate parcel of food for the journey, just fancy," a gift from Queen Elena.[370]

Prince Christoph's situation became more precarious beginning in December 1942, when he was transferred to Tunisia. He wrote on 28 December in a note that reflected his continued good morale, "The American bombers come here now and then and drop their bombs. We gave them a jolly good licking the other day. It's great fun after the dull time in Comiso."[371] In February, he tracked the German defeat at Stalingrad ("things are looking rather nasty after the disaster in Russia"), but remained upbeat: "The attack in the South has been successful so far. Unfortunately, I don't think we can do much more for the present. The Americans were beaten thoroughly and soundly, that is for sure, and they did not show much skill or fighting spirit! Their big bombers with four engines are quite remarkable, and there is nothing we have to be compared with them, I am sorry to say. However, we are doing quite well so far."[372] In fact, Christoph

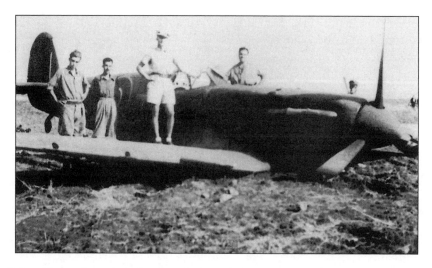

Prince Christoph stands on the wing of a downed British plane in North Africa, 1943.

was witnessing the gradual defeat of Rommel and the Afrikakorps, which ultimately capitulated on 13 May 1943. It is telling that just after the German defeat at Stalingrad in February, Christoph switched from English to German in his letters home to his wife and mother. One senses that he detected a different climate among the Nazi authorities—one in which his writing in a language of Germany's enemies might be construed in a negative way.

Christoph remained the number two officer in the squadron—under Colonel von Maltzahn—and they moved about North Africa in an attempt to fend off the Anglo-American forces. Stationed in numerous cities and towns, including Kairouan, Sidi bou Said, Ras el Djebel, and La Sebala near Tunis. Christoph described the Germans' gradual encirclement by the enemy, writing on 17 April, "[H]ow long it will last is difficult to say and it depends entirely on the enemy. It can come to an end very quickly or perhaps last still weeks longer. Don't worry, my Petson. I'm doing very well. And everything comes as it should come."[373] Christoph remained in North Africa near Tunis into May 1943—sleeping in a tent and trying to bolster his comrades, but also struggling with the overwhelming conditions (in his words *"Alles ist so nutzlos!"*). He and the others had been told to hold on and fight until "the bitter end." But then suddenly, on 5 May, as the British and American tanks approached the German positions, they were told to evacuate. Shortly thereafter, he recalled, "the last weeks were a strain day and night. The thunder of guns came ever closer and the bombs fell during the day or at night or both; over the long run it was unpleasant."[374] After battling their way past the city of Tunis (and the massive force of Allied tanks deployed there), and enduring repeated air attacks, they undertook an evacuation of the African Continent. Christoph got on one of the last planes from his squadron to escape back to Comiso in Sicily. As he noted, "at Stalingrad, one discovered the possibility of cutting out a dividing panel from the rear of an ME 109, which permitted—with the greatest effort —one additional passenger to be squeezed in. We did that two days ago and yesterday with great success."[375] Upon landing in Italy, Christoph sent a telegram to his brother Philipp, asking him to call Sophia and tell her about his escape.

Despite feeling fortunate to survive, Christoph had few illusions about what awaited him and his compatriots. Indeed, there was increasing bitterness in his letters: "it was certainly a good feeling as we flew back in Europe, but I could not rid myself of the bitter and disappointed feeling that it had come to this."[376] More specifically, he could not understand why the German troops were not removed from North Africa at an earlier point, when valuable men and materiel could have been saved: "That Tunisia was not to be held was nothing new to all clear thinking men already last December. . . . Why we sacrificed all of these worthy, courageous people —instead, as the English had demonstrated at Dunkirk, pull them out and therein win a victory for England and perhaps save 100,000 men— no one understands."[377] While on leave at Kronberg, from 29 May until 28 June, he took the opportunity to draft a will.[378] As an intelligence chief and a Luftwaffe officer with front-line experience, he had a much better-than-average sense of what the Allies' future attacks would entail, and his thinking, sometimes expressed in a reckless manner in his letters, reflected what would at that time be regarded as "defeatist" thinking. His sense of foreboding was borne out. This leave in the early summer of 1943 was to be the last time he saw his family.

Christoph headed back to the front in Sicily at the end of June 1943. On the stretch from Munich to Rome, he was on the same train as Mafalda and had the opportunity to join her in the Italian royal railroad car ("very pleasant and comfortable" as he wrote Sophia).[379] This plush Pullman was used to transport members of the Italian royal family, as well as dignitaries (Hitler included). The contrast with his subsequent posting was striking. Back in Comiso, he had to reckon with the Anglo-American invasion of Sicily, which came on 10 July. The Allied bombing that was part of the "softening up process" resulted in his lodgings suffering a direct hit, but Christoph maintained a distinct sangfroid, writing to Sophia, "one can now see the heavens through the ceiling but nonetheless it's now cooler!"[380] Christoph continued to do staff work, and for several weeks was assigned to General Adolf Galland and his number two, Colonel Günter Lützow. But he returned to his squadron later in July and took command when

Colonel von Maltzahn contracted malaria. Christoph appeared a cool commentator as the battle progressed up the boot of Italy: "[T]he entire landing operation of the English was carried in an enormously deliberate but paradigmatic way. I have to grant them credit. Now they are bombing us out of all of our positions."[381] By August, Christoph and his squadron were holding out in the hills above Naples, sheltered, as he noted in a letter to Sophia, in "a monastery high up on a hill with the most beautiful view over the town towards Vesuvius and over the gulf towards Capri." He added, "if only one could enjoy it."[382]

One interesting footnote to his subsequent deployment in southern Italy is that he would have opposed his brother-in-law, Prince Philip of Greece. His wife Sophia noted after the war, "We have reason to believe that at one time during the Allied invasion of Sicily my brother and my uncle [Philip and Lord Louis Mountbatten] were fighting on the same sector of the island where my husband was serving."[383] Christoph and the future Duke of Edinburgh had been well acquainted, although the age difference of nearly twenty years militated against a close friendship. Philip had attended Christoph and Sophia's wedding as a nine-year-old boy. They were also together at the funeral of the Darmstadt relations in November 1937, which was followed by Philip's visit to Berlin the following year, when he stayed with his sister and brother-in-law. During the war, Prince Philip knew that Christoph had enlisted in the Luftwaffe, but while serving on HMS *Valiant*, he was unaware that his brother-in-law was fighting nearby on the Italian peninsula. Still, he remembers hearing of Christoph's death prior to war's end.[384] Philip's mother, Prince Alice, his sister Sophia, and a number of the other princesses provided a conduit of information and used travel and letters to keep the extended family connected.[385] Along these lines, and with a sense of aristocratic understatement, the Duke of Kent noted in a letter to his cousin, Prince Paul of Yugoslavia in March 1942, "We have heard through Luise [the sister of Louis Mountbatten and wife of the Swedish crown prince] of our various relations abroad. Most of the men seem to be in the East. That can't be pleasant."[386]

Prince Philipp, T-4, and the Holocaust

While the allegation of complicity in the Röhm Purge of 1934 stands out among the charges that one could level against Prince Christoph, the counterpart for Philipp would center on the killing facility at Hadamar in the province of Hesse-Nassau. The Hadamar sanitarium was part of the network of six killing centers used in the T-4 program: the initiative ordered by Hitler in October 1939, and backdated to 1 September to coincide with the start of the war, that murdered those individuals deemed having "a life unworthy of life." This operation was run jointly by the

Führer's Chancellery (located on Tiergartenstrasse 4 in Berlin and hence T-4) and the Reich Interior Ministry. Over seventy thousand individuals were killed, and many of the personnel who carried out the executions later played prominent roles in the murder of Jews and other victims in the East.[387] The T-4 program was supposedly halted in August 1941: as word of the killings leaked out to the German public and a number of clergy denounced the measures in their sermons, public knowledge was transformed into public pressure, and Hitler ordered a cessation to the killings. But the murders actually continued, and "at least 3,000–3,500 additional patients were killed at Hadamar [alone] after the T-4 program had ended."[388]

The killings at Hadamar began in late 1940—that is, well before Philipp signed a contract placing the sanitarium, formally known as the Provincial Healing and Care Facility Hadamar, at the disposal of the control of the Reich Interior Ministry.[389] In the words of U.S. investigators after the war, "after he facilitated the use of this sanitarium, about 10,000 mentally ill people were exterminated"[390] In 1946, Philipp was charged with murder in a Frankfurt court—although the charges were later dropped. His role in making Hadamar available to the T-4 program also loomed large in his denazification trial: a copy of the contract bearing his signature is still to be found in the Spruchkammer files. Both German and American authorities struggled with several key questions regarding this contract: What did Philipp know and when did he know it? Did he actually agree with the program or did he take steps, like many other Germans, to oppose the T-4 killings? The answers that emerge from the postwar investigations provide a disconcerting account of how an official can be co-opted, how a lack of inquisitiveness can lead to personal involvement, and how restrained protest would prove essentially useless. The royal tradition of helping the ill and handicapped could not counterbalance the pressure exerted in the opposite direction.

Prince Philipp had many opportunities to ascertain the danger faced by the mentally and physically handicapped in Germany, even prior to his signing the transfer of Hadamar on 15 February 1941. Philipp himself maintained that he was in Italy at this time, purchasing paintings for Hitler, and that in carrying out his responsibilities as an administrator in Hessen, he signed papers in far too perfunctory and uncritical a manner. Yet the signs were there. He would have known, for example, about the regime's program of forced sterilization, which dated back to the July 1933 Law for the Protection of Hereditary Health and resulted in involuntary procedures on over three hundred thousand Germans.[391] Indeed, Philipp as Oberpräsident issued an order in July 1935 that aimed to stifle criticism of clergy who were speaking out against the sterilization law.[392] Hitler stated as early as 1935 that if war broke out, he would initiate a program of euthanasia "for the incurably insane."[393] Later, T-4 officials applied the forced sterilization measures ushered in by the July 1933 legislation to a number of patients at Hadamar.

Not only would Philipp have known about the law and resulting measures, but a member of the extended Hessen family was subjected to forced sterilization. Philipp's distant relation, Prince Alexis von Hessen of the Philippsthal-Barchfeld line (1907–39), suffered from epilepsy and lived in Schloss Philippsthal. The unfortunate young prince was sterilized (*Unfruchtbarmachung*) on 27 September 1938.[394] Alexis's brother, Prince Wilhelm, was a member of the SS and accordingly had to complete forms about his family history and hereditary diseases. Prince Alexis's condition caused problems for Prince Wilhelm, and his SS file is filled with a voluminous correspondence, including reports to Himmler personally. The documents, which were collected by the SS Race and Settlement Head Office as part of their investigation into whether Alexis's condition was due to a "hereditary illness" (*Erbkrankeit*), suggest that the Hessens communicated among themselves in an attempt to share information and resolve the matter.[395] Members of the Hesse-Philippsthal family maintained —and continue to do so to this day—that there was no hereditary illness in the family, and that Prince Alexis's condition was caused by a fall from a horse as a child.[396] The SS officials appeared skeptical that one could contract epilepsy from an accident. The decision to sterilize Alexis was made on 6 July 1938 by the Hereditary Health Court (*Erbgesundheitsgericht*) in Kassel, the city that was the seat of Philipp's office and where he was so well connected. According to procedures, there were two weeks to appeal this decision.[397] It is not clear whether Prince Philipp knew about the sterilization of Alexis; but in that there were requests from the SS for information about the health of the extended family and because the court decision was rendered in Kassel, Philipp most likely would have been informed of the measure. While forced sterilization was not nearly as drastic as murder, it still served as an indication of measures undertaken by Nazi medical personnel in sanatoriums and clinics. Even if Hadamar had been the site of "only" forced sterilizations, Philipp's preparedness to hand it over to the Reich Ministry of the Interior would have raised questions for postwar legal authorities. The files from the period show that Prince Alexis died on 22 October 1939 in Berlin; the cause of death was not given.[398]

It was also significant that many of the key personnel who carried out the killings at Hadamar previously conducted similar operations at the Grafeneck Castle near Stuttgart. Grafeneck, or "Facility A" as it was called within the T-4 program, was the site of nearly ten thousand killings from October 1939 until December 1940, whereupon the "personnel were transferred to the newly fitted-out facility at Hadamar."[399] The influx of personnel and the transfer of this operation would have been difficult to conceal from the governor of the state. Hadamar became operational as a killing center in December 1940, "thus becoming the sixth and last killing center" in the T-4 program.[400] It featured a gas chamber disguised as a shower room and a crematorium, both located in the basement of the main building. Historian Henry Friedlander noted, "Signs on the road leading to Hadamar warned that the danger of epidemics prohibited entry, but the chimney's smoke and the smell made local inhabitants aware of the nature of the operation."[401]

So how did it come about that Philipp signed the contract in February 1941 that transferred Hadamar to the T-4 authorities? He later reported that an official responsible for state hospitals in the province of Hesse, Landrat (administrative counselor) Fritz Bernotat, came to him and made a presentation, explaining that Hadamar would be taken over by a charitable organization by order of the Ministry of the Interior. This would involve a transfer agreement. Philipp told him, "I will sign it, but I really want to know how the facility will be used."[402] Landrat Bernotat responded by giving what Philipp called a "curious answer": he knew why they wanted to rent it, but "on order of the Ministry I may not say because it is a special task (*Sonderauftrag*)."[403] Philipp claimed that he then wrote the Reich Minister of the Interior Wilhelm Frick asking to be informed about plans for Hadamar, but that he received a response that was "surprising and unexpected." Frick provided a decree signed by Dr. Leonardo Conti (1900–45), the Reich Physicians' Leader, saying "the requested explanation could not be given because it concerns a secret order of the Reich government."[404] Philipp maintained that he also filed a complaint against Bernotat because he would not give him information, but that the Ministry of the Interior responded by supporting Bernotat and reiterated that the matter must be kept quiet: it was on a need-to-know basis, and that Philipp, even as Oberpräsident, did not qualify.[405] Philipp recalled, "I tried everything to get rid of Landrat Bernotat. Later everyone feared him. So far as I know, B[ernotat]. continued to murder, even after the matter was long concluded."[406] This portrait of Bernotat is consistent with the testimony of others. He was, according to Henry Friedlander, "a Nazi Party and SS member of long-standing, [who] terrorized the hospital staffs and imposed the most radical form of euthanasia on his domain."[407] After the war, Bernotat escaped justice, living under an assumed name while operating a tobacconist's shop near Fulda; he died of natural causes in 1951.[408]

The questions surrounding the timing and extent of Philipp's knowledge, as well as the nature of his response, form a kind of complex knot that is difficult to untangle. As noted above, Philipp and his lawyers claimed after the war that when he signed the contract in February 1941, "he did not know what measures were intended for the Hadamar facility."[409] Yet Philipp also admitted that the "euthanasia" program was "an open secret" as of early-1940.[410] There were clerical protests of the T-4 program dating back to May–June 1940: e.g., Protestant pastor Paul Gerhard Braune, and Bishop Count Clemens von Galen (himself a member of the Westphalian aristocracy), "had detailed information about the euthanasia program in July 1940."[411] After the war, Philipp realized that it was untenable to argue he knew nothing about what had transpired at Hadamar and acknowledged gradually growing "suspicions"—but he refused to be pinned down as to when these developed.[412] He related how these suspicions gradually jelled into a more definitive awareness as he heard rumors of other killing centers from "various locales in Germany."[413] Philipp also recalled: "I also received several letters, among others, from a colleague in my administration, whose child faced the danger of falling victim to this facility."[414] Friedrich Marggraf, a low-ranking civil servant in the provincial government, wrote Prince Philipp and asked the Oberpräsident to intervene on behalf of his son, whom he knew was in danger of the T-4 program. Philipp did not intervene and the boy "perished in the Hadamar gas chamber."[415]

The spring of 1941 saw mounting protests against the so-called euthanasia program, with Cardinal Michael Faulhaber and Bishop Clemens von Galen standing out among the courageous clergy. Around the same time, the renowned Protestant pastor Fritz von Bodelschwingh wrote to Prince Philipp and asked for his support in opposing the T-4 program.[416] Philipp was finally induced to act. He traveled to Berlin to speak with those overseeing the T-4 program. In his postwar depositions, Philipp was unable to assign a precise date for this intervention—the closest he could come to giving a date was "at the end of the beginning of the year" (*Spätfrühjahr*); however, the meetings certainly preceded the 24 August 1941 "suspension" of the T-4 program. (As noted earlier, killings, especially of children but also of adults via "wild euthanasia"—involving an overdose of narcotics —continued after this date but at a slower pace than before.)[417] Philipp's protest also predated Bishop von Galen's public declarations—or at least his famous homilies on the subject of "euthanasia" delivered between 13 July and 3 August 1941. To his credit, Prince Philipp spoke bluntly to those implementing the program. Philipp went to Berlin to see Reichsleiter Philipp Bouhler (1899–1945), the chief of the Führer's Chancellery and head of the T-4 program. They met at the Reich Chancellery. Philipp demanded that the orders be retracted and the killing be stopped—at a minimum, within the province of Hesse. He added, "I was Oberpräsident and I would later have to bear the responsibility."[418] Bouhler reportedly offered two responses: one was that Philipp "bore no responsibility for incidents in Hadamar and that there were good reasons for the measures in question."[419] The other comment from the chief administrator of the T-4 program was that he could do nothing—that this was up to Hitler.[420]

Prince Philipp claimed that he went to Hitler on the same day and "asked him to step in."[421] The two men spoke alone (*unter vier Augen*) in the Reich

Chancellery. Philipp told him about the rumblings among the people about the "killing of the mentally ill (*Geisteskranken*) and that it was troubling his conscience.[422] Hitler reportedly responded, "that the program was definitely necessary since other countries had already carried it out. The war forced him to do it. It was not feasible for people to be fed with the largest rations when they no longer knew whether they lived or not."[423] He also described how Hitler "spoke at great length, as was his custom, and in a manner that precluded the possibility of making one's objection in detail, where upon he made it clear that he felt the measures were justified—or at least, he would not intervene to stop them."[424] Hitler also reportedly said, "My dear prince, what you say here is quite correct and I can understand your point of view. But in this case, you must trust me more than you trust yourself. I have already determined that you do not have enough toughness (*Härte*) for war."[425] Hitler emphasized, "Prince, you must be tougher (*härter*)."[426] As Philipp's appeal fell on deaf ears, he then asked that Hitler lift his exemption from active military service and permit him to join the army. It was quite common for individuals to report that their response to learning of the Nazis' criminal programs was to request a transfer to active service: Bruno Lohse, for example, an art historian who worked for the art plundering agency the ERR in France, went to Göring and asked to be transferred to a combat unit.[427] These requests, it seems, were rarely granted, which raises questions about the sincerity of the subjects' desire to go to the front. And few noticed how illogical it was for individuals, upon deciding that they could not work for a murderous regime, to then choose to fight and thereby try to sustain it. For those who perceived themselves as having honor, there was a knee-jerk reaction to join the army. In the case of both Philipp and Lohse, the question became moot because neither was transferred to military units. "Hitler turned down [Philipp's request on the grounds] that in war, everyone must tough it out at their assigned posts."[428]

The prince's involvement with the T-4 program reveals complexities and challenges faced by an official committed to the regime, but not necessarily to its murderous policies. Philipp fell somewhere in the gray area of complicity. He himself later tried to put his efforts in the best possible light. Philipp believed that his protests were ethical and that he paid a price for them. He noted in December 1947, for example, that "I had the impression that after my conversation with Hitler concerning the facility, that he was more inaccessible to me."[429] He added, "I tried everything possible to help avoid the worst. That I didn't have more success isn't due to me. . . ."[430] One observer of his denazification trial underscored this argument, writing, "he went to the Führer with his complaints about the numerous political murders in the Röhm affair and against the systematic murder of the mentally ill in the Hadamar sanatorium."[431] Yet despite this explanation,

Philipp faced an "investigation process concerning murder," a charge filed by the chief attorney in the Landgericht Frankfurt am Main in May 1946. The Greater Hessian Minister of Justice accused Philipp of having "played a decisive role in the killing of mentally ill in the healing and care facility of Hadamar. . . . It must be accepted from the results of the investigation to date, that the former Oberpräsident was informed about the purpose of the undertaking."[432] The most plausible assessment regarding Philipp's role in the T-4 program, one that bridges the gap between the Hessen Minister of Justice's charges and Philipp's defense, posits that the prince should have known in February 1941 that handing over Hadamar to the Reich Ministry of Interior would usher in a program of systematic murder in his province; that he was subsequently compelled to voice opposition to the program; but that he was not sufficiently courageous to go public with his views or take some other consequential step. Philipp, like so many others, showed a lack of "civic courage." One is reminded of the observation of Holocaust scholar Victoria Barnett, who noted that "the stance of local residents [who lived near the Mauthausen concentration camp] was to accept the camp as an unpleasant but unchangeable reality. Accordingly, they arranged their lives and psyches—and their ethics—so they did not have to deal with what was going on there."[433] It is probably not coincidental that in the wake of Philipp's trip to Berlin in spring 1941, he spent much more time in Italy and devoted himself to art purchases for Hitler.

Another serious charge leveled against Philipp concerned the treatment of Jews in Hessen. The large Jewish community had been one of the most prominent in Germany. Jews played an especially important role in the Frankfurt's cultural life—for example, Hermann Weil, a Jewish grain merchant, endowed the Institute of Social Research at the university (the famed "Frankfurt School") that featured Theodor Adorno, Herbert Marcuse, Max Horkheimer, Walter Benjamin, and Gershom Scholem, among others.[434] Kassel had a smaller Jewish community: about three thousand people in 1933 or 1.8 percent of the population.[435] Irrespective of the size of the Jewish communities, members suffered ever-increasing discrimination, including, of course, the Nuremberg Laws of 1935 and steady economic marginalization (including the loss of property and businesses through Aryanizations). Philipp was well aware of the escalating persecution and appeared to find it unsettling. After the war, he even attempted to present himself as a veritable philosemite. Philipp remonstrated that he had tried to help Jews and suggested four areas where this occurred: first, regarding local government officials, especially in the wake of Kristallnacht; second, with respect to propaganda and culture; third, by helping individuals whom he knew; and fourth, by approaching Hitler and other top leaders in an attempt to influence policy. The fact remains that his efforts failed: of the approximately 58,000 Jews in Hessen in 1933, only 600 lived there in 1945.[436] The question arises—just as with Hadamar—could he have been as well intentioned as he later claimed and yet been so ineffectual? The answer, taking into account the exculpatory nature of the statements in the denazification files, is yes, and that in itself is telling.

With regard to his efforts to influence other officials in Hessen, the two critical events were the pogrom of November 1938 and the deportations from Frankfurt and Kassel, which occurred in 1941 and 1942. The former entailed the burning of many of the region's synagogues and Jewish community buildings as well as the abuse and incarceration of many Jewish residents.[437] In Kassel, for example, the violence started in the evening of 7 November—the day that Herschel Grynszpan burst into the German Embassy in Paris and shot diplomat Ernst vom Rath—when a group of young Nazis broke down the doors of the Great Synagogue on the Königsstrasse and torched the building. The violence continued until peaking on the ninth, the day vom Rath actually died. On 10 November, 258 Jewish males were taken from their homes in Kassel and detained in the barracks of the Eighty-third Infantry Regiment; they were subsequently shipped off to Buchenwald.[438] Additionally, Jews in Hessen suffered many symbolic indignities, such as when, in the wake of Kristallnacht, many were forced to march through the streets with placards around their necks featuring denigrating slogans. Philipp was not in Hessen on the night when mobs rampaged, burned, and murdered; he, like Gauleiter Weinrich and others, had been in Munich for a meeting of old fighters that commemorated the failed Beer Hall putsch on 9 November 1923. Philipp was conscious of the pogroms and also received a firsthand report from Mafalda when he returned from Kassel on 10 November.[439] Philipp in turn commented to the Wiesbaden government chief and SA-Major General Friedrich Pfeffer von Salomon (1892–1961), another aristocrat, "that he did not wish to see something like that again."[440] Philipp later claimed that he told von Salomon to bring those responsible for the pogrom to justice.[441] This, of course, scarcely happened, but Philipp could point to the arrest of the party district leader in Hanau who was charged with theft: so far as he knew, the Hanau official had received "a very heavy sentence in prison."[442]

After the war Philipp emphasized other symbolic actions he undertook as Oberpräsident to defend the civil rights of Jews. For example, in the wake of the pogrom, an ordinance was passed that prohibited Jews from riding the streetcars of Frankfurt. This elicited a protest from the local Oberbürgermeister because of the lost revenue and other economic consequences that would arise when this important means of transportation was blocked. Philipp supported him, and together they took the matter to authorities in Berlin.[443] Philipp did not prevail in this or most battles involving policy, but he at least put other officials on notice that he opposed the persecution of Jews. A Jewish physician who treated the prince and his family, Dr. Rohrbach, recalled, "I became aware of great tensions, those on the side of the Gauleiters who threatened to neutralize the prince, especially because of the rejection of the prince concerning the [prejudicial] treatment of the Jews. It might be mentioned that I repeatedly treated Princess Mafalda in Rome. Socially I didn't find any anti-Semitism whatsoever in the court circles."[444] Individuals such as Gauleiters Sprenger and Weinrich knew that they would have to reckon with Philipp as they pursued a more radical Jewish policy.

Nonetheless, brutal persecution took place right under Philipp's nose. The orders issued in Berlin, such as the 12 November 1938 decree prohibiting Jews from entering theaters, concerts, and museums, were implemented in Hessen.[445] A local SS leader in Kassel, Captain Klingelhöfer, began making plans for the deportation of Jews from the city and its environs in early 1940 (although Polish Jews had been forcibly resettled starting in the autumn of 1938).[446] He counted 3,000 Jews in the district (*Regierungsbezirk*).[447] The actual deportations began on 9 December 1941, when 463 local Jews were sent to Riga, where they were put in a ghetto. Two subsequent transports, making three in all, left from the Hauptbahnhof in Kassel on 7 September 1942. Before the transports left the train station, the affected Jews were assembled at a staging area in a school on the Schillerstrasse, right in the heart of downtown. Very few survived the resettlement because the Riga ghetto was soon liquidated. After the Kassel Jews were sent to the East, non-Jews from the surrounding environs moved into their vacated homes. Kassel was a small enough city that these events could hardly go unnoticed—certainly not by the Oberpräsident. Indeed, Philipp was evidently informed by the Gestapo about the "organizational aspects" of the deportation a day after the main transport left Kassel in September 1942.[448] The local authorities compiled lists, identifying each person prior to the deportation. The local tax office also kept precise records of the property that was seized.[449] The state then sold the real estate and household goods belonging to the victims.[450]

Philipp also claimed to have intervened with Hitler for specific individuals—"partially with and partially without success."[451] He recalled, for example, having helped the brothers Weinberg—although he did not know what had happened to them at the time of his denazification trial. In fact, one brother made it to Italy but subsequently died, and the other (Arthur) was sent to Theresienstadt, where he perished in 1943. Naturally, most of those whom Philipp assisted were prominent and wealthy. He helped Herbert von Marx, the younger brother of one of his best friends as a youth. Herbert von Marx, who came from a patrician Jewish family, grew up in Frankfurt and served in the same regiment as Philipp from 1914 to 1918. As the situation for Jews became more dire in 1938, Philipp intervened with the police president and told von Salomon that he would be held responsible for Marx's safety. He then told Marx to leave Germany, which the latter did. Philipp also helped him preserve part of his property.[452] Herbert von Marx wrote a note from the United Kingdom in 1946, stating simply: "This is to certify that Prince Philipp of Hesse has assisted me several times during Nazi rule and helped me getting out of Germany in December 1938."[453]

When Prince Philipp intervened to help people who were vulnerable to racial discrimination, he tended to do so for personal acquaintances —either other elites or those who served them. One case, for example, involved Baroness Marion von Goldschmidt-Rothschild (1902–73), whom Philipp helped protect.[454] The second wife of Baron Albert von Goldschmidt-Rothschild (1879–1961), Baroness Marion's mother was a Jewish noble (von Essen) and her father Christian. She was already divorced from her husband, Baron Albert von Goldschmidt-Rothschild, when the most serious difficulties began in the late 1930s. Philipp later recalled that Gauleiter Sprenger was particularly interested in the matter and had imprisoned her. According to the baroness's lawyer, Ferdinand de la Fontaine, she was held by the Gestapo without charges (but evidently kept in some "clinic under strict observation").[455] Philipp later testified that she was held "out of suspicion of taking flight."[456] Philipp was contacted by de la Fontaine while in Rome; he immediately went to Berlin in an attempt to arrange her release and evidently discussed the matter with Hitler. Whether this intervention alone resolved the matter is unclear, but the baroness was set free in May 1940.[457] Prince Wolfgang also helped the family: in his capacity as Landrat in Bad Homburg, he protected the nearby home of Baroness Marion's brother-in-law, Rudolf von Goldschmidt-Rothschild (1881–1962), when his villa in Königstein was threatened with an arson attack by the SA.[458] Another telling incident took place in Italy after Mussolini enacted the anti-Semitic racial laws in 1938. Philipp approached Foreign Minister Count Ciano in September of that year on behalf of the Italian queen: "The king and queen, he said, were indignant because their Jewish doctor, Stukjold, had been expelled. Ciano did not fail to see the irony in this approach. He pointed out that Hitler would hardly approve of a mission of this nature being entrusted to the prince, a German, and a Nazi. 'He turned pale,' Ciano said."[459]

In Philipp's denazification file, multiple witnesses describe instances where Philipp supposedly intervened to help Jews, but one effect was to show how much Philipp must have known about the crimes of the regime. Virtually all of the Rothschilds' assets in Frankfurt were seized or subject to forced sales: to take one example, Maximilian von Goldschmidt-Rothschild (1843–1940), the father-in-law of Marion, was compelled to sell the Rothschild-Palais, a 13.5-acre park, and his art collection comprising

1,400 works all to the city of Frankfurt at well below market value.[460] There were many other instances of persecution that were rendered in contemporary documents in extremely vivid terms, such as Oberpräsidium vice-president Kurt Jerschke describing how Kassel police president von Kottwitz came to him to report the murder of another Jewish lawyer named Dr. Max Plaut (1888–1933). The latter was beaten to death by SA men in Kassel in March 1933 (before Prince Philipp assumed office), and the widow had created a problem because she photographed the corpse and the bloody room (the murder attracted international attention even without the photographs). There was fear that her life was also in jeopardy. Jerschke got her out of the country (leaving the pictures behind), and Philipp, he said, supported this solution. But the episode suggests that Philipp had clear knowledge of the persecution.[461]

Prince Philipp would have been cognizant of varying kinds of persecution perpetrated by the regime, beginning with concentration camps in Hessen. While the province did not contain any of the large notorious camps associated with Nazi rule, there were smaller facilities, dating back to the "wild concentration camps" of 1933 when the SA locked up opponents in local jails, city halls, schools, or whatever building was available.[462] Subsequently there were the camps Breitenau and Osthilfen. Although these were closed down in the 1930s, other camps sprang up. SS officer Werner Best got his start overseeing camps in Hesse as a Special Commissar for Police Affairs. Regarding the persecution in the East, Philipp stated after the war that "he did not have firsthand knowledge of German atrocities in Poland, but he had known a tough SS-man by the name of Max Henze (1899–1951), who had been police president in Kassel and was transferred to Poland (he became police president in Danzig in 1940). Henze had returned, he said, completely broken by what he had been forced to do and witness there. Henze himself was extradited to Poland in 1945 and tried for war crimes. Philipp later maintained that he believed "Reinhard Heydrich was responsible for the introduction of the worst brutalities into concentration camps and the final responsibility therefore rested with Himmler."[463] Philipp's comments here are analogous to those concerning Hadamar: while they convey his opposition, they also reveal knowledge of the persecution.

In a manner similar to his protests against the T-4 program, Philipp went to the highest authorities to discuss the mistreatment of Jews, but to no effect. The prince claimed that he protested to Hitler about the Jewish policy in 1937 or 1938 and that Hitler had responded, "He would see what he could do. [But] in order to keep a free hand, [he said that] he must discuss everything with Bormann."[464] Philipp maintained his faith in Hitler, just as he did in certain other leaders. For example, with regards to Kristallnacht, he defended SA chief, Viktor Lutze, whom he believed was "energetically against" such events. This help explains Philipp's continuing commitment to National Socialism: Hitler and others, in his view, remained honorable and committed to laudable goals, while certain leaders, such as the local Gauleiter in Hessen, hijacked the party for their own purposes. Certainly, some Nazi leaders behaved like gangsters in their interactions with him. On one visit to Bormann, Philipp saw a file with the title, "The Pro-Jewish Activity of the Prince von Hessen."[465] As he explained, Bormann was holding a file—fingering it—and he intentionally turned it around so that Philipp could see its title. Philipp said, "I noticed that this was done quite intentionally . . . ," and added, "I believe that the entire record on my part concerning Jewish matters was registered by Bormann."[466] These kinds of tactics, which included not only threats to Philipp, but also the prospect of a more malignant party radical replacing him, by and large neutralized the prince.

The general ineffectiveness of Prince Philipp in his efforts to mitigate the persecution of Jews did not obscure the fact that the Hessens knew that terrible things were happening in Poland and the East. Although it is unlikely that they were informed of the gas chambers, their wide-ranging connections in the party, state, and society would have brought knowledge of the shootings (and over a million Jews were killed in this way—making the regime's genocidal intentions very clear). Just as Philipp kept the account in the banking house of Lippmann, Rosenthal, and Co. after it was Aryanized, he continued to hold his post in the Nazi state through 1942, the most murderous year of the Holocaust.

Princes, the SS, and the Holocaust

The SS was a magnet for aristocrats.[467] Indeed, there are too many to list here. But to offer one indication of this phenomenon, a cursory glance at the SS roles reveals the membership of over seventy barons (*Freiherrn*), ranging from the influential Karl von Eberstein (1894–1979), who served as Himmler's chief of staff, and rocket scientist Wernher von Braun (1912–77) to Günther von Reibnitz (1894–1983)—the father of Marie-Christine von Reibnitz, the current Princess Michael of Kent.[468] One might also recall the princes noted earlier, which included members of the Houses of Hohenzollern, Mecklenburg, Thurn-und-Taxis, Lippe, Braunschweig, and Auersperg.[469] While several members of the high aristocracy had appointments that were largely honorific, others were leading figures in the SS. The fact remains that Himmler, while holding ambivalent views about aristocrats, conceived his order as "a new knighthood" and liked to surround himself with nobles.[470] He told one meeting of the Circle of Friends of the Reichsführer-SS, "to fulfill its mission, the SS required as members the best elements of society, 'genuine military tradition, the bearing and breeding of the German nobility, and the creative efficiency of the industrialist, always on the basis of racial selection.' "[471] The Reichsführer-SS conceived his order as a *Blutadel* (blood nobility) and drew upon the resources and traditions of the aristocracy.[472]

Heinrich Himmler had been raised in proximity to princes. His father had served as a tutor for the Wittelsbach family—having been an employee of Prince Arnulf von Bayern and supervisor of his son, Prince Heinrich.[473] Putzi Hanfstaengl, who was also a student of the senior Himmler, described him as "a terrible snob, favoring the young titled members of his class and bearing down contemptuously on commoners."[474] The future Reichsführer-SS spent his youth in a staunchly pro-Wittelsbach milieu (the family even moved to Landshut in 1913—"the administrative seat of the Wittelsbach dukes" with an *Altstadt* whose style one historian described as "mediaeval splendour").[475] Prince Heinrich von Bayern agreed to serve as Heinrich Himmler's godfather.[476] In 1917, Himmler received 1,000 Marks as a gift from the chamberlain of his late-godfather—Prince Heinrich having been killed in battle the previous year—that Himmler used to pay his way into the elite officers training program of the First Bavarian Infantry. Indeed, the young man reported for training at Regensburg on 1 January as a *Fahnenjunker* (officer trainee—a word with strong aristocratic connotations).[477] While Himmler did not remain a monarchist—especially after Prince Rupprecht refused to support the Nazis in the failed Beer Hall Putsch of 1923 (Himmler had helped man the barricades at the War Ministry in Munich)—he continued to admire many aspects of aristocratic life, including the connectedness to history, the martial heritage, and the sense of honor and duty. He created a pseudoknightly order at a castle called the Wewelsburg, made plans for an ideological school in Schloss Grünwald near Munich (the birthplace of, in his words, "Ludwig der Bayern, a great German Kaiser"), and exhibited a fixation with the founder of the Saxon dynasty, King Heinrich I ("the Fowler") (875–936)—a conqueror of the Slavs.[478] On the anniversary of the king's death, Himmler would visit what he believed was his tomb in the Quedlinburg Cathedral "and at the stroke of midnight in the cold crypt of the cathedral, Himmler would commune silently with his namesake. . . . He became so obsessed by his hero that he gradually came to regard himself as a reincarnation of the king."[479]

Himmler also realized the usefulness of aristocrats: the respect they often commanded in Germany and the resources they could frequently commit to the cause. Even before the Nazis came to power, one of Himmler's closest colleagues, Baron Karl von Eberstein (1894–1979), "traveled the country recruiting for the SA and SS" and helped land, among others, Reinhard Heydrich.[480] Baron von Eberstein, who had the extraordinarily low SS number of 1,386, became the police president of Munich in 1936 and remained a force in the Bavarian capital until 20 April 1945, when he was fired—because of defeatism—from all his posts (including general of the Waffen-SS) on orders of Martin Bormann.[481] Eberstein was sacked at a time when Himmler was meeting with Count Folke Bernadotte (1895–1948): the Swedish prince (who had "left" the royal family after marrying without the king's consent). Bernadotte was the vice-president of the Swedish Red Cross who worked toward the end of the war to rescue concentration camp inmates and to negotiate an armistice between Germany and the Allies.[482] Himmler did not remain enamored with the traditional aristocracy as a whole throughout the Third Reich. Indeed, he turned on the princes as a caste during the latter part of the war. Historian Gerald Reitlinger argued that it was the replacement of the relatively more genteel Karl Wolff as his chief aide by the more radical Hermann Fegelein in April 1943 that "marked an important change in the character of Himmler's court."[483] Reitlinger added, "Wolff was a relic of the days when the SS was considered the respectable section of the Party suitable for the sons of princes."[484] Despite the gradual shift, it is important to recognize the linkages between the SS and the aristocracy. In order to do this, it is helpful to examine several important figures.

Hereditary Prince Josias von Waldeck und Pyrmont, who had an extraordinary and varied career, enjoyed an especially close relationship with Himmler. The eldest son of the last ruling Prince in Waldeck (Prince Friedrich abdicated in November 1918), the nephew of the king of Württemberg, and a close relation of the Dutch queen, Josias was badly wounded in World War I (including a victim of a gas attack) and highly decorated (receiving the Iron Cross First and Second Class).[485] He later volunteered for the Freikorps, where he fought in Upper Silesia in 1919. Waldeck joined the Nazi Party in 1929 and the SS in 1930. He had married one of the sisters of Grand Duke Nikolaus von Oldenburg (1897–1970)— while the Grand Duke's first wife was Waldeck's sister, Princess Helene (1899–1948). The Grand Duke von Oldenburg's two sisters married SS-Major Prince zu Schaumburg-Lippe and an SA-Colonel von Hedemann, making this a tight-knit circle of aristocratic Nazis.[486] During his first year in the SS, Waldeck became the chief of Himmler's Personal Staff.[487] Later, in 1933, he became the aide-de-camp of SS General Sepp Dietrich (1892–1966), who also headed up Hitler's personal security. That same year Waldeck was promoted to Major General (Gruppenführer)—part of his precipitous rise in rank. He also had a brief appointment as a counselor in the Foreign Office in 1933 and held a seat in the Reichstag throughout the Third Reich. As of 1935, he headed the SS division in Fulda, putting him in close proximity to Philipp von Hessen (both were based in Kassel). Indeed, in Kassel, he created a "Bureau for the Germanification of Eastern Peoples," which promoted the idea of SS-directed settlements in Eastern

Prince Waldeck und Pyrmont at the SS training camp at Döberitz near Potsdam in 1933.

Europe.[488] In 1939, Waldeck was appointed the Higher SS and Police Leader of Weimar, and in this capacity, he had supervisory authority over the concentration camp at Buchenwald. The prince was also a general of the Order Police (*Ordnungs-polizei*)—appointed by Hitler personally in April 1941. The Order Police, as Christopher Browning and others have shown, played a central role in the Holocaust.[489] Waldeck, while never commanding one of the murderous units, was also made a general of the Waffen-SS in July 1944.

Waldeck was severe, hard-driving, and ambitious. To cite several (among numerous) examples: he oversaw an execution commando at the Stadelheim prison near Munich during the Röhm Purge in June 1934, where he helped murder a number of former comrades; and then, on 12 March 1938, the day of the German invasion of Austria, he wrote to Himmler—addressing the letter to the *"Reichsführer-SS persönlich"*—requesting to be deployed to Austria. [490] He noted that he had once been the leader of an SS division in Austria and wanted back where the action was. In November 1938, Waldeck's SS unit in Arolsen was one of the first to launch attacks on local

Jews during the Kristallnacht pogrom. Joseph Goebbels, who coined the euphemistic phrase, gave his inflammatory speech in Munich on 9 November—the night when the violence peaked; but by then, Waldeck's troops had already destroyed the local synagogue and a number of Jewish businesses, having embarked on a rampage during the night of the seventh (and, as noted earlier, there were violent acts that evening in Kassel, where Waldeck also had an office). Waldeck, like Philipp von Hessen, was in Munich at a meeting of party leaders and later claimed to have telephoned back to Arolsen and ordered his men to refrain from violence, but the leading scholar of the pogrom in Hessen, Wolf-Arno Kropat, doubts the veracity of this statement.[491] Considering the culture of discipline in the SS and Prince zu Waldeck's overbearing demeanor, it is hard to believe that his troops would have acted against his orders. Much more trivial, but nonetheless revealing, was the grievance filed against him in September 1941 when a subordinate accused him of "damaging his honor": Waldeck had reportedly castigated the man for "moaning" about his duties in a Luftwaffe flak unit, and said to him, "In my eyes, you are a *Schwein!*"[492] In this instance, Waldeck's sharp tongue led to a 1941 trial in an SS court in Munich. Later, in 1942 Prince zu Waldeck sacked Buchenwald commandant Karl Otto Koch and his notorious wife Ilse because of their embezzlement of over RM 700,000 in valuables from the camp. Waldeck arranged for them to be transferred to the death camp at Maidanek and then subsequently had them put on trial.[493] Koch was found guilty of corruption and executed at Buchenwald just days before the camp was liberated by the Allies. While there has been a debate among historians about Waldeck's direct responsibility in carrying-out the sentence, there is no doubt that the contemporaneous evacuation of the camp—where Waldeck oversaw the Germans' efforts to conceal the horror of the site by shipping off inmates—resulted in thousands of deaths.[494] Some inmates were sent on forced marches, while others were put in sealed trains where they languished during the final days of the war in Europe; on one transport to Flossenbürg that was supposed to last eighteen hours, only 300 of the 3,105 on board survived after days without provisions. It is a gross under-statement to say that Waldeck exhibited little compassion.

While the prince was responsible for persecution on a vast scale, he still considered himself principled and disciplined. Scholars now generally reject the charge made by Buchenwald inmate and historian Eugen Kogon that Waldeck himself was brazenly corrupt.[495] But this is not to say that he did not profit handsomely from his position in the Third Reich. The manner in which he did so is in itself significant. It concerned the Waldecks' princely property, which, in a manner similar to the Hessens, had been transferred to a foundation in the 1920s. For certain properties, such as the castle (*Residenz*) in Arolsen, the Princes zu Waldeck had only the right of use: they paid only a quarter of the upkeep costs, while the state paid the rest.[496] Prince zu Waldeck wanted to change this; especially as of 1938 when the Nazi government passed legislation that provided for the dissolution of trusts and foundations.[497] He therefore turned to another Nazi legal initiative: hereditary farms (*Erbhöfe*). Intended as a way to protect peasants and small farmers from the voracious expansion of modern agro-businesses, Erbhof-status both protected a property and limited the owner's ability to sell it. The Nazis conceived of the Erbhof as a program for small landowners and imposed limits on the size of the holdings (between 18.5 and 212 hectares, around 46–524 acres) that could receive this designation. It was part of their "blood and soil" ideology. There were loopholes in the law: when the property had been owned for 150 years, and when the applicant was a "worthy German." To simplify a complicated story, Prince zu Waldeck arranged for the property in the Waldeck Foundation— including over 5,000 hectares (12,350 acres) of farmland and forests—to be declared an Erbhof.[498] This came about when Himmler intervened on his behalf with Reich Minister for Nutrition and Agriculture (and also SS Race and Settlement Head Office chief) Richard Walther Darré.[499] This was similar to Göring and Chief of the Reich Chancellery Hans Lammers intervening in 1938 in an attempt to secure an Erbhof for Prince Wilhelm von Preussen, the eldest son of Crown Prince Wilhelm.[500] What is so strik- ing is how Waldeck secured his financial status—the estate was valued in 1938 at over RM 1.7 million, making him an extraordinarily wealthy man—and how he couched it in ideological terms.[501] According to Nazi law, an Erbhof was limited "only to a person of German or related blood," and it permitted the owner to call himself a "peasant" (*Bauer*).[502] Clearly, it was in vogue for princes to cloak themselves in the Nazis' populist as well as "blood and soil" rhetoric.

Prince zu Waldeck was publicized as a kind of role-model for the SS. As noted earlier, he was made head of the SS office for riding (he held the title *Leiter des Deutschen Reitsports*), and, like Prince Christoph, he frequently competed in international competitions in his SS uniform. Just after the Anschluss in the spring of 1938, Waldeck inquired whether he could serve on the police unit that would accompany Hitler to Rome: his aide wrote the request to Himmler, noting that the proposal would be welcomed by SS-General Sepp Dietrich and Oberpräsident Prince Philipp von Hessen, and he added that Waldeck would be in Rome from 24 April to 5 May com- peting in an international riding competition.[503] Himmler wrote back that he could not assign Waldeck to the police detail because the Italians were taking charge of security, but that it would be no problem to invite the prince to other functions during the Führer's visit in May.[504] Waldeck was a visible figure in the entourage that was photographed by the press during the state visit. He fit the SS ideal in many other ways too: not surprisingly,

Waldeck and his wife had five children, which would earn the latter the Mother Cross in gold, the highest award for bearing children for the Reich.

Prince Waldeck was one of Himmler's favorites, and the Reichsführer-SS made special efforts to take care of him. They used the familiar form of address (one of Himmler's few *Duzfreunden*), and the Reichsführer-SS sent numerous gifts, not only to Waldeck but to his family: Himmler was godfather to the prince's only son, Volkwin (today known as Wittekind), to whom he sent a regular stream of presents and notes.[505] In March 1943, Himmler ordered that Waldeck be awarded the Military Service Cross with Swords—the highest award granted to Higher SS and Police Leaders. Himmler's aide wrote back that Waldeck had already received the award the previous year (for service as part of civil defense).[506] Waldeck in turn venerated Himmler and made every effort to honor his SS chief. This included giving Himmler a new train car—a *Salonwagen* at the meeting of SS leaders in Posen in the autumn of 1943—the conference where Himmler made the infamous remarks about the Holocaust.[507] Giving similar speeches before the Gauleiter and Reichsleiter on one day, and the Higher SS and Police Officials shortly thereafter, Himmler informed these powerful figures about the regime's genocidal program—an act that eliminated any chance of plausible deniability and, in a sense, tied these leaders even more closely to the regime (the operable concept being that knowledge brings with it responsibility).

Waldeck's experiences during the war took a toll on him. In January 1944, SS General Udo von Woyrsch (1895–1982) wrote Himmler and explained how the Prince was suffering from serious eye problems and that "he must constantly smoke and evidently appears shaken." Woyrsch asked Himmler to intervene—to prohibit Waldeck from smoking and to take better care of himself.[508] Yet Waldeck survived the German defeat. He was captured by General Patton's forces at Buchenwald on 13 April 1945—the day the camp was liberated—and he faced two trials in the postwar period.[509] The first was the so-called Buchenwald trial, which was conducted by the Americans at Dachau. On 14 August 1947, Waldeck was sentenced to life in prison and incarcerated at Landsberg am Lech in Bavaria. He subsequently underwent a denazification trial back near his home in Hesse —more specifically, in Fritzlar-Homberg. Because he had already been sentenced to life in prison, it appeared that it was his property that was at stake (as well as the historical record, since the entirety of his career and not just his activities in connection to Buchenwald were considered). Utilizing the five-tier scale of the denazification system, with Category I as a main offender and Category V as exonerated, the court placed Waldeck in Category II as "burdened" (*belastet*) and seized 70 percent of his property (among other sanctions).[510] The verdict was rendered on 17 September 1949; but by 29 November 1950, Waldeck had been released from prison

—one of the first to benefit from American High Commissioner John J. McCloy's amnesty program. In July 1953, he received an amnesty from the Hessian Minister President that resulted in a huge reduction of his fine, whereby he paid less than half the original sum and remained a very wealthy man.[511] Although he was investigated on several occasions in the late 1950s and early 1960s in connection to the Buchenwald camp complex, the murder of civilian workers, and the Röhm Purge, there were no serious consequences. Prince zu Waldeck lived out his life in the Federal Republic until his death in November 1967.[512] He passed away in his castle, Schloss Schaumburg near Diez an der Lahn, at the age of seventy-two. His son, Prince Wittekind zu Waldeck und Pyrmont (b. 1936), then a Lieutenant Colonel in the German armed forces, succeeded him as head of the house.[513] In 1993, Wittekind gave his second child the name Josias—a family name, to be sure, but also that of his very problematic father. And, as noted at the outset of this book, the family has kept its archives closed to scholars.

Another member of the high aristocracy who rose within the Nazi state was Hereditary Prince (*Erbprinz*) Ernst zur Lippe (1902–87). Like Waldeck und Pyrmont, he was a distant relation of the Hessens: his mother was born a princess of Hessen-Philippsthal-Barchfeld. As noted earlier, the Lippe family, like the Hessens, joined the Nazi Party in great numbers. Ultimately, eighteen members of the House of Lippe joined the NSDAP. Among the princely families, it was often the case that when several members joined the Nazi movement, others followed. In the case of the Lippe clan, it was significant that Princess Marie Adelheid zur Lippe was an early enthusiast. A highly unstable woman who married two Princes von Reuss between 1920 and 1927—one was Heinrich XXXII (whom she divorced) and the other Heinrich XXXV (thereafter she used the name Princess Reuss zur Lippe)—she was a convinced Nazi who embraced "blood and soil" notions with great enthusiasm.[514] It bears mentioning that some states "provided an over proportionally high percentage of later Waffen-SS officers": including Hesse-Nassau and nearby Lippe in north-central Germany, but also Schleswig-Holstein, East Prussia, Bavaria, Berlin, and Munich.[515] Indeed, Protestant agrarian centers tended to be "secure strongholds of the National Socialists" from 1930 onward.[516]

Like Philipp von Hessen and many other princes who gravitated to the Nazi Party, Prince Ernst zur Lippe was a veteran of World War I. He had been a Lieutenant of the Sixth Westphalian Infantry Regiment that was commanded by his father, Prince Leopold IV. Prince Ernst joined the NSDAP in May 1928 and served as a party functionary. He also joined the SS, where he held the rank of Major. The Prince zur Lippe soon found a post on the staff of Reich Peasant Leader Richard Walther Darré, who also headed the Race and Settlement Head Office (RuSHA).[517] "The functions of the RuSHA concerned basic issues of SS ideology: the 'alignment of the SS in terms of race,' issues dealing with peasants and settlements, 'clan cultivation' (*Sippenpflege*), and instruction."[518] Darré and Himmler were both inflexible ideologues and the former, whom one scholar described as "independent-minded," was dismissed by the Reichsführer-SS as head of the RuSHA in 1938.[519] Darré nonetheless retained the post of Reich Minister for Nutrition and Agriculture and pursued his vision of a peasant-based utopia, and Prince zur Lippe continued to aid him. Darré was particularly notable for "helping prepare the spiritual soil for the NS policy of 'Living Space,'" and Prince zur Lippe, as his personal assistant (*Referent*) worked closely with him. His sister Princess Marie Adelheid zur Lippe was also a member of Darré's staff and wrote several heavily ideological tracts, including *Nordische Frau und nordischer Glaube* (1934).[520] Because Darré suffered a gradual decline in influence—it was not only Himmler who helped marginalize him but also Göring (whose Four-Year Plan office sought to maximize efficiency and hence clashed with the pseudo-romantic "blood and soil" ideas)—the Lippes lacked a viable power base.[521] Darré retreated to his hunting lodge on the Schorfheide outside Berlin—not far from Göring's Carinhall. Prince Ernst, however, maintained his SS affiliation up through 1945.

Prince Ernst zur Lippe and his family were most notable for the zealousness of their belief in National Socialism. Another relation, Prince Bernhard zur Lippe-Biesterfeld (1911–2004), who had a series of titles during his lifetime, culminating in Prince of the Netherlands when he married Queen Wilhelmina's daughter Juliana in 1937, joined the SA, the National Socialist League for Air Sports, the NSKK, and was a member of the SS.[522] Employed by I. G. Farben in Paris in the 1930s, Prince Bernhard was reportedly recruited by the Nazi intelligence services and engaged in industrial "espionage on behalf of the SS."[523] Whatever loyalties he had to Hitler clearly dissipated: in 1936, he renounced his German nationality during a "chilly meeting" with Hitler, and he agreed with Dutch Queen Wilhelmina in opposing "the Führer [who] was keen to treat the wedding as the alliance of two countries. . . . Hitler responded by trying to stop his relatives [from] attending the ceremony."[524] In 1940, Prince Bernhard helped the Dutch royal family escape to Great Britain, and from 1942 to 1944 worked for the Royal Air Force (on at least one occasion overcoming Queen Wilhelmina's ban on his participation in active combat by flying under an assumed name). While General Eisenhower did not trust him enough to grant him access to Allied intelligence, Queen Wilhelmina made him Commander of the Netherlands armed forces in 1944, and the following year, he accepted the German surrender at Wageningen.[525] Other members of the family remained loyal to the Nazi regime. For example, Prince Carl Christian zur Lippe-Weissenfeld was an SS-Major and the country commissioner (Landrat) in Silesia up until his death in 1942. His sister, Princess Christine was married to Dr. Wilhelm von Oswald, an SS-Major who served on the Personal Staff of the Reichsführer-SS.[526] His distant cousin, Prince Stephan zu Schaumburg-Lippe, who was a German diplomat stationed in Buenos Aires during the War, also held a position as an SS-Major.[527]

The princes who had SS affiliations tended not to play active roles in the killing operations. Of course, one does not need to go very far down the social ladder to find killers. One can point, for example, to Erich von dem Bach-Zelewski: an SS-General, Higher SS and Police Leader for the center section of the Eastern Front, and chief of the anti-partisan units. Bach-Zelewski stemmed from a noble milieu: his father had owned an estate in Pomerania, and the future SS leader was raised there. Still, he proved to be about as murderous almost as any figure in the SS. According to historian Christian Gerlach, "In mid-July 1941 Bach-Zelewski had asked Himmler if they could carry out a liquidation operation in Polesje. After a visit to Baranovitchi on 31 July, Himmler issued this radio message on the morning of 1 August: 'Express order of the RF-SS. All Jews must be shot. Drive Jewish women into the swamps.' By mid-August, the brigade had murdered at least 15,000."[528] Bach-Zelewski personally demonstrated mass shootings to Himmler in Minsk on 15 August 1941.[529] Gerlach notes, "We can thank former Higher SS and Police Leader of "Russia Center" Erich von dem Bach-Zelewski for his confession in the Nuremberg trial for the Himmler statement [regarding plans to decimate the Soviet population by about 30 million people]. Bach-Zelewski neglected to mention, however, that the plans called for the death of 20 million people in his region alone."[530] A Munich denazification court sentenced him to a ten-year prison term in 1951. In 1952, he came forward and admitted that he was indeed a mass murderer. He was tried again for murder in 1961, during which he affirmed, "I am still an absolute Hitler man."[531]

Aristocrats were all over the spectrum in terms of their position to the Nazi regime: from opponents in exile, such as Prince Rupprecht von Bayern, to SS radicals like Prince zu Waldeck. But there was indeed a special connection between the SS and aristocrats. Himmler had noted, "[W]e want to create an upper class for Germany, selected constantly over centuries, a new aristocracy, recruited always from the best sons and daughters of our nation, an aristocracy that never becomes old."[532] While Himmler never completely disavowed the idea that the aristocracy was susceptible to degeneracy due to inbreeding (and this perception became more marked toward the end of the Third Reich), his fundamental conception of the traditional elite was a positive one. Most members of the nobility had ancestry that conformed to SS ideals, and Himmler appropriated many ideas from the fighting, chivalric, and exclusionary noble classes. Certain authors have nonetheless sensed the contradictions in the SS leader's think-ing. Heinz Höhne remarked, "For years the Imperial Guard of National Socialism had preached the law of selection on racial and biological grounds; now, however, the SS began to lure into its ranks sections of the population possessing qualities which appeared in no dictionary of Nazi racial philosophy—prestige, money, and an aptitude for command born of generations spent in positions of authority."[533] Be that as it may, Himmler found ways to resolve such contradictions. In 1938, 18.7 percent of the lieutenant generals (Obergruppenführer); 9.8 percent of the major generals (Gruppenführer); and 14.3 percent of the brigadier generals (Brigadeführer) were members of the aristocracy.[534] Among the Higher SS and Police Leaders, eight of forty-four stemmed from the nobility (*Oberschicht*).[535] While it is an exaggeration to use the phrase that was "popularly bandied about after the war that the SS was 'at times almost a nursing home for princes,'" there were organic ties between the nobility and Himmler's elite—the consequences of which were indeed sometimes murderous.[536]

6

Miscalculation and Misfortune

While Princes Philipp and Christoph grew increasingly disenchanted with the Nazi regime as the war progressed, they never lost faith in Hitler or initiated measures intended to bring about an end to the regime. It may well have been that in 1943—the time when more resistance groups coalesced and aristocrats in particular took the lead in opposing Hitler— the princes were simply not in a position to participate. Nonetheless, the Hessens' experiences illustrate the steadily increasing tensions that developed between the Nazi leaders and the aristocracy. What had once been a solid relationship developed a crack, which in turn expanded into a fissure and then, in 1944, into a complete break. At an earlier point it would have been misleading to conceive of the Nazi elite and aristocrats as mutually exclusive groups; but as the regime grew increasingly radical (aggressive in its foreign policies, violent in its persecution of enemies, and intolerant of dissent), more aristocrats became disaffected. This process was gradual and complex—and involved thousands of individuals, each with their own specific experiences—but it can best be characterized as follows: members of the nobility undertook what might be described as minor acts of opposition, where they countered specific policies but did not seek to topple the regime. Hitler and his cohorts became increasingly alarmed—some would say paranoid—and in refusing to countenance any resistance, they struck back with measures aimed to limit the influence of aristocrats. Hitler began with princes, issuing decrees prohibiting them from occupying positions in the state, the party, and the armed forces. In the wake of the noble-led July 20 assassination plot, the Nazi leaders moved beyond legalistic measures and subjected aristocratic resisters to the kind of vicious ad hominem attacks for which Hitler and his cohorts have become known. This open break, which led to the deaths of hundreds of aristocrats, played out gradually. Class warfare did not develop overnight.

There was little indication at the outset of the war that the Nazi leaders would embark on this antiaristocratic campaign. Nobles, including many princes, suffered no discrimination in terms of military appointments and many of them held high-ranking posts. Among the early war casualties were princes from the Hohenzollern, Ratibor-Corvey, and Saxon dynasties. The Nazi leaders also continued with customary practices regarding feudalistic medals and commendations; there is in fact a voluminous correspondence in the German Foreign Office files about the bestowal of such awards, the implications for protocol, and the feelings of those involved. One episode, for example, involved Prince Philipp, who told Foreign Minister Ciano on 6 February 1940 that "Göring was more than ever incensed at Italy, and especially at Ciano." "That won't keep me awake," Count Ciano wrote, "The real reason must be sought in the Collar of the Annunciation given to von Ribbentrop when he expected it for himself. He will calm down when he gets his."[1] Göring did receive his honor ("the Collar had to be returned to the monarch upon the death of the holder, and it carried with it the right to be considered the cousin of the king"—at least as a style of address). Hitler, in kind, bestowed similar awards—such as the German Cross in Gold—on Italian Crown Prince Umberto, Ciano, General Franco, and other leaders whom he found sympathetic.[2] While Prince Philipp sometimes played a role in the deliberations that preceded these awards, the more important point is that the Nazi leaders still engaged in practices associated with the traditional aristocracy and that their negative outlook did not develop until Germany's military fortunes suffered a noticeable decline.

The friction that developed between the Nazi leaders and members of the nobility grew out of disillusionment on both sides. There are several reasons why nobles in particular became alienated from the Nazi regime and returned to the idea of constituting a distinct group. The first and most obvious reason was that they had long viewed themselves as a separate and superior group (or caste). Although many aristocrats—and even princes like the Hessens—embraced the Nazis' notion of a cohesive racial community (*Volksgemeinschaft*), few could overcome centuries of history within a decade. Moreover, the tremendous pressures brought about by total war showed that these traditional views had persisted. Aristocrats were also more likely to speak out and believe that they were justified in circumventing certain Nazi measures: for example, receiving information from abroad and sustaining contact with family members living in countries with which

Germany was at war. These attitudes grew out of long-standing social and political practices. Philipp, for example, recalled just after the war, "initially I had the impression that [Hitler] appreciated my openness; however later, and especially during the war, I often had the feeling that I was treading on thin ice."[3] While it would be an exaggeration to say that princes were raised to speak truth to power, they, as a group, possessed the self-confidence to speak with greater openness to the Nazi leaders and to embrace specific policies that were at odds with those of the regime. Certain gestures also sent messages to the Nazis: Prince Friedrich von Mecklenburg had joined the SS against the will of his father back in the early 1930s; in 1943, the Mecklenburg family council voted that he would be passed over as heir and instead his younger brother would inherit the family property.[4] For the oldest princely family in Germany to prohibit an eldest son from becoming head of the family because of his loyalty to National Socialism constituted an unambiguous gesture. Finally, one must keep in mind the broader context: princes were but one of many groups targeted by an increasingly totalitarian regime. Anyone viewed as undermining the war effort—pacifists, defeatists, and homosexuals—suffered more from 1943 to 1945 as the regime grew increasingly malignant and lethal.[5] With regard to the latter, RSHA chief Ernst Kaltenbrunner, who was to play a leading role in pursuing princes, was "keen to start the *forcible* castration of all homosexuals" in 1943 and pushed, albeit unsuccessfully, for the Reich Justice Ministry "to issue a special decree in order to give some legal cover."[6]

The tribulations of the Hessens in the latter half of the war represent a microcosm of the experiences of many German aristocrats. Philipp's opposition to the regime on certain points—even if done privately—and the blame he received as a result of Mussolini's overthrow in July 1943 led to his incarceration. Yet many nobles would be persecuted for other reasons. He was relatively fortunate compared to other family members. While these tragic events were specific to the Hessens, they were part of a larger scenario. It was not only many princes but many aristocrats who suffered in the process that began in the late-1930s, peaked in the period after 1943, and then played out in the postwar period.

The Roots of Aristocratic Opposition

Princes were more likely than members of other segments of society to engage in behavior that the Nazi leaders would consider oppositional. As noted above, this partly stemmed from assumptions with which many were raised. They were accustomed to speaking their minds; family wealth (and often not being dependent on a specific job) would contribute to this spirit of independence. Another reason that princes would express views on specific subjects that differed from those held by Nazi leaders related to their traditional areas of purview. There were certain spheres, such as art and music, and also church affairs, where princes had long played leading roles. The generation who reached their mature years during the Third Reich had been raised with the expectation that it was appropriate to assert themselves in these areas. Of course, this sowed the seeds of a struggle with the Nazi leaders because culture and religion proved of paramount importance in the quest to establish a totalitarian state: the Nazis would brook no rivals for people's loyalties.[7] The Hessens clashed on a number of occasions with Nazi authorities with regard to culture and religion. But it was a balancing act, as they attempted to remain loyal, dependable servants of Hitler and Göring, while asserting themselves in these areas. This balancing act was such that they never crossed over into the camp that actively sought a change of regime, but, as indicated in the discussions concerning the T-4 program and anti-Jewish measures, it was sufficiently significant to warrant consideration as a kind of opposition.

While Prince Philipp recognized the Nazi leaders' interest in culture —as noted earlier, this was an area in which he bonded with Hitler—he failed to comprehend the limits of his power in this sphere. Artist Arno Breker reported that he and Philipp tried in 1937 to prevent the opening of the *Degenerate Art Exhibition* and that they approached counselors in Bernhard Rust's Reich Ministry for Science, Education, and Culture hoping to block the traveling show that defamed modern art. Breker recalled that they were unsuccessful "because the exhibition was occupied by an SS unit and Hitler himself was present on the day of the opening."[8] It is unclear whether Philipp and the Nazi sculptor believed they could actually stop the show—an impossibility considering its importance to Hitler and its high visibility—or whether they simply wanted to go on record as opposed to this initiative. It is also uncertain how energetically they intervened on behalf of the defamed art. Philipp had never demonstrated enthusiasm for modern art or music; in fact, this had been a chief complaint of Siegfried Sassoon in the early 1920s. The British writer had noted that Philipp "thinks I am wrong to tolerate Gauguin and Van Gogh and Stravinsky."[9] Prince Philipp most likely opposed the vulgar spectacle of the *Degenerate Art Exhibition*, but it is unlikely that he carried his protest very far.

Another source of friction with the top Nazi leaders stemmed from church affairs. Philipp managed a few victories on the local level regarding religious institutions, but his involvement had costs as Hitler and Bormann, among others, became aware that he held divergent views in this sphere. Aristocrats and the various churches had long traditions of mutual support, and this applied even to Philipp, who was personally not very religious.

Still, he would publicly participate in Protestant services, as had long been customary for nobles. When his father Friedrich Karl died, Philipp, Christoph, and the other siblings participated in a "publicly celebrated service in the church of St. Martin's in Kassel."[10] Philipp later recalled, "I have never attended church on a regular basis, either before or after 1933. What struck me especially was the continued battle against the church by the radical parts of the party during the war."[11] The church for him was more important as a symbol—of culture, tradition, family identity, and the political climate—and not a matter of sincere faith.

This concern for tradition with regard to the church found expression in numerous ways. For one, Philipp believed in continuity. In the 1930s, for example, he expressed apprehension about the division (*Zersplitterung*) of the Protestant church. This was a response to the purging of the German Evangelical Church to converted Jews after 1933, and the emergence of the German Christians, whose adherents sought to reconcile Christianity with National Socialism (and in doing so, make the religion racist and baldly ideological).[12] The transformation of the Evangelical Church had prompted theologian Karl Barth (1886–1968) and Berlin pastor Martin Niemöller (1892–1984), among others, to found the Confessing Church (*Bekennende Kirche*), which was critical of the regime. Philipp referred to this emergence of rival institutions as "a danger" in a way that was reminiscent of traditionalists' anxieties before and during the Reformation.[13] Like his ancestors, Philipp also helped by donating art and money to churches; most notably, he gave many artistically valuable pieces to the church of St. Martin in Kassel and to the St. Elisabeth Church in Marburg (these gifts were sometimes publicly acknowledged with plaques). Growing out of his interest in interior design, Philipp offered advice about the restoration of old churches.[14]

Philipp's efforts to preserve tradition and help local churches found clearest expression in the way he fought against the seizure of property belonging to monasteries. Here he defended both Protestants and Catholics from the encroachment of party radicals. Philipp had not always defended the churches: in 1935, he had issued an order concerning the "intensification of the church struggle" that aimed to subdue clerical opposition to the sterilization laws and the Hitler Youth, among other Nazi initiatives.[15] But by 1940, he perceived the attacks on the churches as having gone too far and intervened to help oppose the confiscation of the Frauenberg cloister in Fulda. Philipp recalled an exchange with Hitler in 1940: "I told him that I thought it was entirely wrong to proceed against the church at this time," and that he asked for "peace with the churches" (*Kirchenfrieden*).[16] Philipp described how Bormann proceeded to enter the room and take notes. Hitler then responded in a manner that surprised the prince and said "all attacks against both confessions should be stopped

—also against the cloisters and other church institutions."[17] When Philipp said he hoped it would be as Hitler had ordered, Bormann responded "I can say under oath, that I have always been against the persecution of the church." Philipp later admitted, "I believe that he lied completely."[18] This meeting in 1940 did result in the rescinding of an order to confiscate the Frauenberg cloister; however, it had no discernible effect on church policy more generally as the attacks continued.[19] The basis of Philipp's intervention was local politics—that he was helping his constituents. The chief of monuments protection in the province of Hesse-Nassau, Dr. Friedrich Bleibaum, noted, "above all, the prince tried to neutralize in a positive way the multifaceted policies of the Gauleiter that were hostile to culture and the church."[20]

Philipp's foray onto the grand stage of church affairs also came about through his dealings with Pope Pius XII, and although his role here did not involve resistance to the regime's policies, the agreement he attempted to broker might have softened the Nazis' stand regarding the Catholic Church. In that sense, one sees Philipp trying to alter the course of the Nazi leaders. Count Ciano reported in January 1940 that Philipp repeatedly told him that he was very close to negotiating a modus vivendi between the Reich and the Holy See; it is not clear what the Pope would have given up in exchange for softer antichurch line from the Nazis.[21] Presumably, the Germans would have limited attacks on Catholic clergy (Polish clerics were already suffering tremendously at this point) in exchange for silence about German actions. Philipp later boasted that "I could count a notable church-political success at the beginning of the war as I succeeded in inducing Hitler to issue a decree that ordered the ending of the struggle against the churches and its organs."[22] But this was also the period when Pius XII made "efforts to mediate between the British and the German opposition to Hitler in 1940. . . ."[23] It is unlikely that Philipp played a role here or was in contact with representatives of the two sides: he almost certainly would have found a way to bring such information into evidence in his trial to help exonerate him.[24] Rather, it appears that Philipp played a more conventional role for him as Hitler's representative and tried to broker a deal involving greater mutual tolerance between the church and the Reich.

Unfortunately, the Vatican's refusal to open its archives for this period and Philipp's reticence after the war on his dealings with Pius XII leave this history very sketchy. In his denazification trial, Philipp offered that "Pope Pius XII placed special trust in me and personally charged me with an important mission. I don't think it right that I give information about the purpose or nature of this mission without his special approval."[25] The chairman of the panel initially pursued the matter by noting that there were no documents explaining the nature of the discussions between Philipp and Pope Pius XII, and asked whether an explanation was forthcoming. After acknowledging "the delicate nature of the affair," Philipp's lawyer elaborated, "The defense took up negotiations before the denazification trial [to enter into evidence information about Philipp's dealings with the Pope]. The Vatican answered 'no' to this question. [Philipp] was not given permission [to discuss his interactions with church leaders]. In consideration of the fact that the Holy Father Pope Pius XII led these negotiations personally, the Vatican asks to take distance from a consideration of this question."[26] If this prolix officialese was not enough to obscure the issues at stake, the prosecutor and Spruchkammer chairman did their part: the former by declaring that the meetings between Philipp and the pope "had nothing to do with politics" and the latter by ruling that "the chamber intends not to inquire into this complex of questions."[27] Prince Philipp's mission to the Vatican remains shrouded in mystery. Suffice to say that his relationship with Pope Pius XII provided additional grounds for Nazi leaders to view him with suspicion.

There is no evidence that either Philipp or Christoph moved from trying to influence the Nazi leaders on specific issues to a more general form of resistance, but their disillusionment started to build during the war. Philipp's protests on the range of issues noted earlier suggest his growing unease. And, as discussed earlier, his approach to Göring in 1937, where he discussed tendering his resignation as Oberpräsident, indicates a change of heart.[28] Princess Sophia offered another telling anecdote: "Before the outbreak of the war, on the occasion of going to the theater in Berlin, the Prince [Philipp] said to me as he saw Dr. [Hans] Frank, later to serve as the governor of Poland, that he couldn't stand this man, that he was a horrible person. [Philipp] often condemned the dark side of the Party— that is, the ambition [and] greed of certain leading people."[29] Christoph appeared to express his disaffection by abandoning his powerful office in the Forschungsamt in order to serve in the armed forces. There was also the letter mentioned earlier, where Landgravine Margarethe wrote her son Prince Richard and reported that both Christoph and Philipp were "greatly relieved through the death of a certain dangerous and cruel man."[30] Philipp later maintained, "My human goal was resistance in my province against the two Gauleiters. I tried everything in Italy to undermine this regime, and I must add that I was a solitary fighter. I had no help from any quarters. I hear today how many people were against the [regime]. No one was there for me, even though I was publicly oppositional."[31] While one must treat such statements skeptically and understand that they were made in an attempt at self-exculpation during a denazification trial, there is truth to the notion that Philipp and Christoph gradually became disaffected with the regime.

This leads to an interesting counterfactual question whether the brothers would have joined the July 20 conspiracy had they been in a position to do so. The issue is worth exploring because it speaks to the steadily increasing disaffection of nobles during the war—in particular, after 1942. The July 20 plot was, among other things, a gesture on the part of the aristocracy—an attempt by individuals who had maintained an element of class-consciousness. Among the prominent conspirators were the following members of the nobility: Count Claus von Stauffenberg (1907–44), Count Ewald von Kleist-Schmenzin (1890–1945), Werner von Haeften (1908–44), Albrecht Ritter Merz von Quirnheim (1905–44), Erwin von Witzleben (1881–1944), Adam von Trott zu Solz (1909–44), Ulrich von Hassell (1881–1944), Henning von Tresckow (1901–44), Count Helmuth James von Moltke (1907–45), Count Wolf-Heinrich von Helldorf (1896–1944), Count Friedrich Werner von der Schulenburg (1875–1944), and Count Peter Yorck von Wartenburg (1904–44).[32] This list, of course, does not include all nobles who joined the plot. As noted earlier, Prince Louis Ferdinand von Preussen, exhibited a willingness to lend his support, and Crown Prince Wilhelm's former adjutant, Count Heinrich Dohna-Schlobitten (1882–1944) was not only arrested but also hanged.[33] Even Prince Philipp's close friend Eddie von Bismarck had grown disaffected from the Nazi regime; he deserted the Wehrmacht and fled to Switzerland in January 1944 (and his brother Gottfried was a conspirator). Historian Hans Mommsen has noted, "the standout role of members of the aristocracy, namely, in the military opposition, is further evidence that national conservative resistance emanated primarily from a social foundation, one based on simultaneous pre-political fields of communication in opposition to the grasp of nazification."[34]

One could also imagine certain ideological affinities between the Hessens and the resisters. Many of the July 20 plotters believed in "revolution from above": Hans Mommsen elaborated, their "plans for a new order relied extensively on neoconservative and corporatist ideas of the Weimar period, in particular going back to Spengler's model of a 'Prussian socialism.' For a number of the conspirators . . . the Prussian tradition represented a central motive for the decision to join the resistance."[35] The idea here is that there would be a coherent social order without unrest—notions not unattractive to the Hessen princes. And, according to one of the conspirators, Fabian von Schlabrendorff, resistance leader Dr. Carl Goerdeler "favored a monarch as head of the new German state. He preferred the inherited to the elective monarchy as a guarantee for the continuity of the state" (but left the issue as to the choice of monarch until a later date).[36] Indeed, a number of members in Goerdeler's circle expressed interest in a restoration, including Prussian Finance Minister Johannes Popitz, former chief of the Army General Staff Ludwig Beck, and Ambassador Ulrich von Hassell.[37] Furthermore, in that Count von Stauffenberg, among others, came from South German aristocracy, there was geographic diversity among the July conspirators. What was crucial to them was retaining a sense of German honor and decency. The Nazis' genocidal programs represented a clear transgression. Countess Marion von Dönhoff has suggested that many of the conspirators had firsthand experience of atrocities in the East and that this moved them to act.[38] The Hessen brothers' wartime service kept them away from the most murderous regions; but with Philipp's awareness of Hadamar and Christoph's participation in Operation Barbarossa, they were hardly uninformed on lookers. In that Philipp and Christoph possessed a sense of honor and decency and had knowledge of the regime's genocidal policies, they were candidates for participation in the aristocratic opposition.

This notion of networks raises the question of Philipp's and Christoph's contacts prior to 1943. They knew several of the key members among the July 20 conspirators. Philipp, for example, was well acquainted with Ulrich von Hassell, who had been German ambassador in Rome until 1938. Von Hassell tried to use his international contacts to secure a peace with Britain and the United States, and he worked closely with Goerdeler and General Beck, among the conspirators.[39] A figure one might compare to Philipp in terms of social contacts and a range of options is Crown Prince Rupprecht of Bavaria, who moved between various residences while in exile in Italy and established contact with the British government through secret channels. Rupprecht even used confidants in the Vatican to pass along a policy paper to the British where he argued openly for the restoration of Wittelsbach dynasty.[40] There were individuals in the Hessens' social orbit who undertook a much more active, if sometimes self-serving, oppositional role.

Were the Hessens perceived as such loyal Nazis—as so close to Hitler and the other top leaders—that they were never approached by Stauffenberg and the other conspirators? The foremost authority on the July 20 plot, Peter Hoffmann, stated that Philipp's and Christoph's names came up among the plotters, but that there was no agreement to go forward and approach them.[41] The Hessen princes would likely have been attractive to the conspirators in certain respects: with the princes' family ties and contacts in the intelligence world, they offered some hope in working toward a negotiated peace with the Western Allies (a goal of most conspirators). Yet up through autumn 1943, the period when Philipp and Christoph lost their ability to join the resistance, Philipp was viewed as too close to Hitler to approach, and Christoph, with his relatively low-ranking staff position in the South, was too unimportant (and he was, after all, still a member of the SS).

The most that one can say with regard to the Hessens is that a general awareness about the nature of the Nazi leadership appears to have coalesced in mid-1943. Princess Sophia wrote to her grandmother Victoria in May 1945, "Since 2 years my eyes have been opened & you can imagine what feelings one has now about those criminals."[42] When asked about whether he had ever considered assassinating Hitler—he did have direct access to him in the Führer Headquarters—Philipp responded, "the thought occurred to me that perhaps I would have the chance to free Germany. This opportunity did not present itself through 1943. We must always think how it was in 1943. We may not do this with the following years in mind. If I had retained my freedom for longer, it is entirely possible that I would have come to this decision. Then I would have done it and carried it out by myself. Unfortunately, my fate was sealed in 1943 and I no longer had the chance."[43] The Frankfurt Court of Appeals that considered Philipp's case after the war noted, "the men of 20 July 1944 had also initially participated in the Hitlerian war policies with great enthusiasm (*vollen Herzen*). . . . It is not to be excluded that the concerned party, if he had possessed freedom, would have belonged to this circle or at least supported them."[44]

To be sure, these reflections are speculative. The denazification board, for example, which was more concerned with actual deeds, was quite unimpressed at Philipp's commitment to resistance.[45] One might also consider his behavior in light of the observation made by philosopher Karl Jaspers (1883–1969), when he wrote a December 1945 letter "that a change of heart brought about by a switch to the anti-Nazi camp has to be judged by the motives that underlie it." Jaspers then singled out three crucial dates that might be used as benchmarks in evaluating a supposed "change of heart": 1934, 1938, and 1941. "To my way of thinking," he concluded, "a change of heart that postdates 1941 is virtually meaningless—and indeed means very little unless it occurred decisively after the events of June 30, 1934 [the Röhm purge]." 1938 was no doubt a reference to the November pogrom.[46]

Philipp and Christoph, of course, continued to believe in National Socialism after Jaspers's cutoff dates. Philipp, for example, contacted Nazi Party officials in January 1941 to inform them that he had lost his "small golden honorary badge of the Nazi Party member" and requested a replacement.[47] The Hessen princes continued to work and fight for Germany—and hence for the Nazi regime—as long as they had the freedom to do so. And indeed, this was part of their character: loyal to their country, self-sacrificing in certain ways, and bound by oaths of allegiance (which were required in the armed forces, let alone in the SS). Landgravine Margarethe, made a significant remark about Philipp after the war, "the prince was never a conspirator; he was conscious of his duty and attempted to carry out his assignments in the interest of the Fatherland."[48] Rainer von Hessen adds, "this is correct and precludes any involvement in the 20th of July."[49] Furthermore, mindful of the courage and sacrifice of the July 20 conspirators, he counsels caution and modesty when reflecting on his father's and uncles' behavior: out of respect for the true resisters, one must draw a clear line between the Hessens and the actual members of the resistance.

The Nazis Wage Class War

It was the Nazi leaders, of course, who first turned on the princes and aristocrats. One striking feature of this conflict was the failure on the part of most nobles to comprehend the Nazi leaders' views about their social class. The National Socialists, with their populist roots and talk in the early years about a social revolution, had articulated antiaristocratic ideas for decades. More specifically, there were a range of views among the Nazi elite about the nobility: some, like Joseph Goebbels and Robert Ley were disposed against them or conflicted in their feelings; others, like Göring, Hess, and Himmler, were more positive. Hitler, as shown earlier, exhibited marked ambivalence: while he pursued certain aristocrats and tried to exploit them, he was not averse to tapping into a tradition of antiaristocratic sentiment, and would do so on occasion.

The Germans suffered significant military setbacks in the war in late 1942 and 1943, and these misfortunes helped ratchet up the pressure that contributed to the attacks on nobles. In the West, the ULTRA decryption device reached its peak of usefulness: in December 1942, Allied code-breakers overcame a period of relative blackout that had begun in February, when the Germans added a fourth rotor to the Shark Enigma machines used by the navy; the Allies' breakthrough had disastrous consequences for the German U-boat and littoral forces.[50] The losses in the navy became so great that German high command became convinced that there were spies in their midst (and launched major counterintelligence missions). In the autumn of 1942, a spy ring, the "Red Orchestra," led by high ranking intelligence officer Harro Schulze-Boysen (1909–42)—a great-nephew of Admiral Alfred von Tirpitz—was discovered operating in Göring's Reich Air Ministry. Investigations were conducted both by Göring's agents and by the SS, and this involved placing "Luftwaffe officers and officials under close surveillance."[51] A "European-wide network was exposed," and it included a number of aristocrats, including Arvid von Harnack (1901–42) in the German Economics Ministry, and Rudolf von Scheliha (1897–1942) in the Foreign Ministry. Ultimately, some 130 members of the Red Orchestra were arrested, of whom sixty were executed (some, like Schulze-Boysen, on Hitler's personal orders). The French Résistance also grew into a more effective force at this time. In short, the Allies' intelligence initiatives provoked suspicion among Nazi leaders—a fear of subversives that bordered on paranoia—and some of this anxiety was directed at nobles. Additionally, most Nazi leaders began to realize in 1942 and 1943 that the war in the East was not going to be won quickly but would require an unprecedented commitment from the German population. This led certain government leaders to question whether nobles would sacrifice themselves for the cause. One must also factor in the psychic toll taken by the Holocaust. These were the most deadly years of the genocide. Although incalculable and varying among Nazi leaders, the murder of millions of civilians weighed on their minds and contributed to this heightened pressure. It is probably not coincidental that Hitler, Himmler, and many other top Nazis experienced acute health problems around this time. The mounting pressure induced them to act upon ideas that had been developing for years.

In light of events that transpired during the war, the roots of the Nazi leaders' anxieties about the princes can be discerned quite clearly. Prior to 1942, these sentiments most often played out in a symbolic manner. Princess Peg von Hessen-Darmstadt, reported, for example, that Gauleiter Sprenger of Wiesbaden prohibited public expressions of grief and official ceremonies in the wake of the airplane crash of November 1937 that claimed the lives of five members of the Hesse-Darmstadt family. He was motivated purely by a desire not to generate more sympathy for the family. Sprenger, however, could not halt observances in Darmstadt. The city was, in fact, consumed with symbols of grief (black flags), and the public came out in large numbers to watch the funeral procession featuring Lord Mountbatten and an array of princes.[52] Explicitly antinoble propaganda took many forms. Fabian von Schlabrendorff, Philipp's lawyer at his denazification trial (as well as an aristocrat and July 20 conspirator), noted, "the princes von Hessen-Kassel and therein their heirs in the family from which the concerned party stems, have been attacked and defamed as enemies of the people for political reasons in the most varied ways in a series of literary and historical works from the eighteenth century until the end of the Third Reich."[53] He added that the Nazis "had always brought up these historical untruths and falsehoods," and cited as an example "the promotion of the rise of the Frankfurt-based Rothschild family through the Hessen princes," which he called "a downright inexhaustible source of National Socialist attacks"; and indeed, the archives in Darmstadt contain denunciations about the Hessens and the Rothschilds, including one sent to Gauleiter Sprenger in 1934.[54] While Schlabrendorff exaggerated the frequency of such attacks in an attempt to help his client, there were occasions, more numerous during the later years of the Third Reich, when fervent Nazis would turn to these shibboleths.[55]

Despite the long tradition of aristocratic service in the military, the Nazis became more mistrustful of this caste with the advent of the war. A key element in the widening riff, ironically, was the princes' valor in war. More specifically, two Hohenzollern princes fell in battle, and the

Nazi leaders were threatened by the public response. The first of the Hohenzollern to fall was the Kaiser's grandson, Prince Oskar von Ruppin (1915–39), who died at the end of the first week of fighting during the invasion of Poland. The following spring, on 23 May 1940, Prince William (1906–40), the eldest son of Crown Prince Wilhelm, was shot in the lungs and stomach while taking part in the French campaign. He died shortly thereafter and more than fifty thousand people turned out at Potsdam for his funeral.[56] Historian Giles Macdonogh noted that this "was enough of a display of monarchical enthusiasm to disturb Hitler."[57] Lutz Graf Schwerin von Krosigk (1887–1977), who received his title through adoption in 1925 and served as Reich Minister of Finance from 1932 to 1945, later reported: "Monarchical demonstrations at the funeral for the eldest son of the crown prince, who fell in the war, compelled Hitler personally to issue a prohibition of members of the earlier ruling houses from serving in the German army."[58] More precisely, as Princess Marie Vassiltchikov noted in her diary from 10 June 1940, "all German royal princes have been debarred from frontline duty and at best are still 'tolerated' in staff jobs. Adolf does not want them to distinguish themselves and thereby acquire 'unhealthy popularity'—for all have shown themselves to be good soldiers."[59]

Actually, it took some time for Hitler to act on this impulse, but the process of limiting the military involvement of the princes had started. In 1941, two anonymous American newspaper correspondents reported, "The deaths of two Hohenzollern princes at the Front led to a brief flare-up of popular sympathy towards the House. Following this all other members of the Hohenzollern family were withdrawn from exposed positions. Prince Louis Ferdinand, who had been acting as a blind-flying instructor, was retired from the Service and is now managing the family estates in Silesia. The ex-Crown Prince keeps very much in the background and seldom appears in public."[60] The thinking of the Nazi leaders regarding the Hohenzollern quickly moved beyond military matters. Schwerin von Krosigk, in describing their removal from positions in the armed forces, noted, "The protest of the Crown Prince remained ineffectual. The Gestapo had the suspicion that the Crown Prince had circumvented certain foreign currency restrictions and taken part of his property to Switzerland."[61] Here one sees clearly how the Nazis' anxieties about the princes gaining popular support—and hence dividing the loyalties of the German people—began to feed off stereotypes and perceptions associated with nobles: that they had international connections, that they hid away property, and that they gravitated toward neutral Switzerland (many of these charges were also frequently levied against Jews). The fear that became paramount among Nazi leaders during the war was that the princes were insufficiently loyal and patriotic: with their international connections, the princes could not be counted on to put Germany first. As with most stereotypes, there was an element of truth. But the Nazis, of course, magnified the threat as they turned on the nobility.

It was after the turning of the tide in 1943 brought about by Allied victories at Stalingrad and North Africa that antiaristocratic sentiment in the regime became more pronounced. Even those Nazi leaders who had previously evinced sympathy for princes became more hostile. Heinrich Himmler exhibited his guardedness already in 1942: in February, he wrote to Heydrich from the Führer Headquarters about reports concerning the "circles of reaction" and how the matter needed attention; in August, he issued an order that all "members of princely houses needed his personal approval before joining the SS."[62] While Himmler was an incorrigible micromanager who would have always signed off on any prince joining his organization, the fact that he issued the August order from his field headquarters sent a message of warning. After a 1943 meeting with Mussolini, an observer reported: "On point four Himmler became agitated and held forth at length on the evils of the corrupt internationalist, Jew friendly monarchy and aristocracies in general. As to Philipp of Hesse, no doubt he had been of service to Nazism but his 'double nature' came out in his double identity, general in the SA and in-law of the antifascist Italian monarchy."[63] Just as Philipp came under suspicion, Christoph and other family members also had growing concerns about their positions in the Third Reich. Back in June 1942, Christoph had approached Göring to discuss his status; this followed an earlier meeting between Landgravine Margarethe and Princess Sophia with the Reichsmarschall. The Landgravine reported in a letter that "[Christoph] is very skeptical about all H. [Göring] told Tiny & [the Landgravine] in Berlin & not at all convinced that he has not been put in *einen Topf mit den anderen* [a pot with the others]."[64] Landgravine Margarethe voiced the concern spreading through the family about the Nazi leaders' suspicions of the princes—and did so, apparently with unintentional irony, in a mixture of German and English.

A crucial event in the gradually escalating war against the princes came on 19 May 1943, when Hitler issued the "Decree Concerning Internationally Connected Men."[65] This decree was not published in the press or advertised in the state-controlled media: the Nazis had not yet proclaimed an open class war. But it stipulated that princes and others with international ties—nearly all of whom were aristocrats—could not hold positions in the party, state, or armed forces. Word of Hitler's order spread rapidly, leading some to believe that the Nazis had conclusively turned against the old elite. Author Anthony C. Brown wrote of "a large group of persons whom Hitler called contemptuously the Purple International, or the *"Gesellschaftsklasse,"* members of various first families or persons of social or political prominence in their native countries, all of whom Hitler considered to be enemies."[66] In fact, the decree was not as indiscriminate as the passage above would suggest and did not entail the automatic firing of nobles. Certain nobles continued unimpeded in their positions up until the end of the war.

Hitler ordered all branches of the Nazi bureaucracy to compile a record of individuals with "international contacts"—a chart listing their ties to foreign lands (often by way of a spouse)—and then he himself made the decision whether the person in question was to be "retired."[67] In the case of Prince zu Schaumburg-Lippe, his superior, Goebbels, had an initial discussion with Bormann on 20 December 1943, where he attempted to obtain a waiver. Hitler's secretary had doubts about the prince and refused to grant the dispensation. Goebbels was forced to go directly to Hitler to request his "further deployment in the Propaganda Ministry."[68] Goebbels vouched for his aide, explaining that he was the "holder of the golden badge of honor and a trusted National Socialist" and Hitler, in January 1944, ruled that the May 1943 decree did not apply to the prince.[69] Schaumburg-Lippe retained his post until 17 July 1944, when he also relinquished his commission in the SA-Standarte Feldherrnhalle. Later, the prince blamed Bormann for the May 1943 decree: he said of Hitler's secretary, "in his deepest depths, he's a Marxist."[70]

Because the decree provided a legal basis for dismissing individuals, it also made them eligible for certain benefits. Legalistic and bureaucratic practices persisted in curious ways during the Third Reich, and this often included pensions for those who were sacked. Indeed, Prince Philipp received his pension from 25 January 1944—the official date of his "retirement"—until the end of the war in May 1945, despite the fact that he was languishing in solitary confinement in a concentration camp. Of course, not all victims of this campaign received such benefits. Some noble victims were treated much more severely than others. Philipp was fairly fortunate: he was not one of those who was dismissed right on the spot after the 19 May 1943 decree. When Philipp was officially terminated on 25 January 1944, the document featured, what one writer called a *Grosse Reichssiegel* [great Reich seal] and notably contained the signatures of both Hitler and Göring. There was often considerable formality that accompanied the campaign to disempower the old elite.[71]

As noted earlier, the dismissal and arrest of Mussolini by King Vittorio Emmanuele in the summer of 1943 alarmed the Nazi leaders, who perceived a similar threat in Germany. Goebbels was moved to expound on "why there can be no twenty-fifth of July" [Mussolini's overthrow]: "the enemy who calculated on a 'Badoglio experiment' in Germany misjudged the '*innere Machtverhältnisse*' [internal distribution of power]. The reasons why there would be no twenty-fifth of July in Germany were (1) the Führer

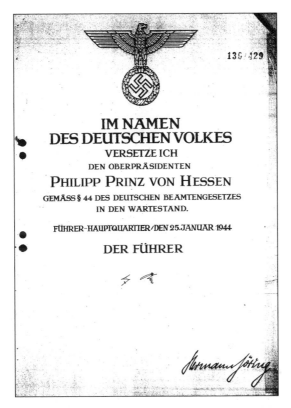

Document formalizing the dismissal of Prince Philipp von Hessen as Oberpräsident of Hesse-Nassau, signed by Hitler and Göring at the Führer Headquarters, 25 January 1944.

was at the head of the country; (2) Kings 'only occur in fairy tales and musical comedies'; (3) Germany is a <u>republican</u> '*Führerstaat.*' "[72] Goebbels went so far as to launch a propaganda campaign designed to prove that there was no parallel between Italy and Germany.

The next major increase in antiaristocratic sentiment came in the wake of the July 20 plot. Hitler and a number of other Nazi leaders were inclined to view the failed assassination attempt as an event with deeper implications: not only had providence saved the Führer but the treachery of the aristocracy was thrown into dramatic relief. Hitler ordered Kaltenbrunner to implement the kith-and-kin reprisals (*Sippenhaft*), whereby the head of the RSHA unleashed his agents—not only the Gestapo but also a special task force—that pursued and incarcerated many of the family members of the conspirators. In the wake of the July plot, Hitler had "stated that he did not regard the regulations for passing sentence as sufficiently wide to cover so grave a crime, which not only greatly endangered the Head of State, but also the security of the population and state during the very difficult conditions of war. Thus, in addition to the perpetrator of the crime being arrested his relations were also held responsible and arrested."[73] This was not some secret "night and fog" measure: a Führer order concerning Sippenhaft was published in the press and regarded as part of the German legal code.

Various kinds of offenders were pursued under the rubric of Sippenhaft. The first group to be arrested were the relatives of those who played an active part in the July 20 plot. This entailed some three hundred people. They were sent to concentration camps—although some were released after a short period after the intervention of connected individuals.[74] The kith-and-kin reprisals were also invoked in cases where German soldiers deserted to the Soviet side or when POWs were shown to provide the enemy with valuable information: the family of German Sixth Army commander, Field Marshal Friedrich Paulus (1890–1957), was incarcerated after he joined the National Committee of a Free Germany that worked with the Soviets against the Axis.[75] Heinrich Himmler, in a speech held in Posen several weeks after the 20 July 1944 assassination attempt, compared the plotters to soldiers who had betrayed the country. Not surprisingly, he cast his remarks about Sippenhaft in racial terms and turned to ancient Germanic history, noting, "you need simply to consult the Germanic tales. . . . The man who perpetrated treason has bad blood and the blood of traitors must be exterminated."[76]

The Sippenhaft provision was therefore utilized to arrest aristocrats related to the plotters who had not committed an explicit act of treason. The Wittelsbach, for example, had twelve family members sent to concentration camps (this is similar to the ten members of the Stauffenberg family and eight from the Goerdeler clan who were imprisoned at Buchenwald).[77] While the head of the house, Crown Prince Rupprecht von Bayern, had gone into hiding in Italy in June 1944, Hitler personally ordered the imprisonment of his wife, Crown Princess Antonia, and their children as *Sippenhäftlinge* (prisoners due to kinship).[78] To this day, historians dispute the precise number who perished in Nazi custody: there were reports after the war that five or six thousand aristocrats had died as a result of reprisals, and this number was cited by certain contemporaries, such as Fey von Hassell, who was a Sippenhäftling because of her father's involvement in the July 20 plot.[79] More recent scholarship by Peter Hoffmann indicates that the toll was much lower—probably in the order of several hundred.

Regardless of the number of nobles killed after July 1944, there is no doubt about the vastly increased mistrust of the Nazi leaders toward the traditional elite. Robert Ley railed against the "blue-blooded swine" who were to blame for the assassination plot. The SS newspaper, *Das Schwarze Korps*, attacked the *"blaublütige Schweinehunde und Verräter"* (adding "traitors" to Ley's formulation).[80] In a speech published in Joseph Goebbels's newspaper, *Der Angriff*, Ley fumed, "Degenerate to their very bones, blue-blooded to the point of idiocy, nauseatingly corrupt, and cowardly like all nasty creatures—such is the aristocratic clique which the Jew has sicced on National Socialism. . . . We must exterminate this filth, extirpate it root and branch."[81] The most extreme comments were reported by Himmler's physician, who quoted a diatribe by the Reichsführer-SS:

> There will be no more princes. Hitler gave me the order to finish off all the German princes and to do so immediately. He suggested that the most important of them should be charged with espionage and high treason, others with committing sexual perversions. The People's Court will thereby sentence them to death. Goebbels wants the hangings to take place in Berlin before the Imperial Palace. The princes should be herded on foot down Unter den Linden. The German Work Front will provide the necessary personnel, who will spit on them and in this way give expression to the anger of the nation. We will prove that the princes are responsible for the destruction of German cities through the Allied air forces. We will blame the defeat in the East on them. The property of the princes will be divided between party members and Old Fighters.[82]

In a certain sense, an unfocused rant such as this was less dangerous than allegations directed against specific individuals. Oftentimes, Nazi leaders suspected members of the nobility of treason when there was little or no evidence. Hitler, for example, reportedly remarked, "the Crown Prince [Wilhelm von Preussen] is the actual instigator [of the July 20 plot]."[83] In fact, as we now know, Wilhelm had refused any involvement. In the wake of Stauffenberg's assassination attempt, it was nonetheless possible for certain aristocrats to retain their freedom and, less often, their official posts; but they were swimming against the tide in very treacherous waters.

The Arrest and Concentration Camp
Experiences of Philipp and Mafalda

Prince Philipp continued to serve as Oberpräsident of Hesse-Nassau through the spring of 1943 processing the paperwork that came with the post, but his relationship with Hitler started to deteriorate in April 1943 when he provided the Führer with an honest assessment of the situation in Italy.[84] The two met alone at Schloss Klessheim near Salzburg. Philipp had prepared carefully for the meeting—rather like an ambassador about to deliver a situation report. He had sought out Crown Prince Umberto and asked him for his opinion about conditions in Italy. Umberto responded that the situation was dire (Axis forces surrendered in North Africa on

12 May 1943) and that Italy needed a competent expert to head the government, not a Fascist.[85] This is ultimately what happened when Field Marshal
Badoglio succeeded Mussolini. Philipp recalled: "In Schloss Klessheim
near Salzburg in April 1943 I made one last push with Hitler, in which
I opened his eyes in an unembellished way to the catastrophic situation
in Italy, the untenable position of Mussolini in his own country, and, what
seemed to me to be the unavoidable military and political collapse."[86]
Philipp told Hitler of Crown Prince Umberto's views and argued for a
negotiated peace, although he did not specify whether this was exclusively
with the Western Allies. He also described the meeting as tense, "threatening to take a dramatic turn." After more than two hours of discussion,
Hitler "dismissed him in an extremely cool and terse manner" and Philipp
returned home to Kassel that same evening.[87] Up until that point, Hitler
had relied mostly on Hans Georg von Mackensen, the German ambassador
to Rome, for reports on the situation in Italy: the ambassador, according
to former SD agent Wilhelm Höttl, was "primarily responsible for the
false impressions in Berlin. . . . He bombarded the Foreign Ministry with a
series of soothing telegrams."[88] Philipp later regarded this April 1943
meeting as both "the dramatic high-point of his resistance" and the turning
point in his relations with Hitler.[89] Up until that point, the prince believed
that he could speak with Hitler in a relatively frank and direct manner.

Hitler grew markedly more anxious and radical in early- to mid-1943.
By August, to take one example, he had sacked Wilhelm Frick as Reich
minister of the interior and replaced him with the architect of the genocide,
Heinrich Himmler. Indeed, certain scholars have observed that Hitler's
physical condition declined in 1943—that he almost suffered a breakdown
after the debacles in Stalingrad and North Africa. Physician and historian
Fritz Redlich, who studied Hitler's medical history, noted how in May 1943
"Hitler complained of increasingly severe pains, first in the region of the
transverse colon, later all over the abdomen."[90] Redlich added, "Some attacks
lasted for days. Hitler and [his personal doctor Theo] Morell strongly
believed that the gastrointestinal symptoms were caused by adverse events
and upsets, particularly with Hitler's general staff."[91] Furthermore, the
dictator suffered from serious cardiovascular problems and had an oxygen
apparatus placed in his sleeping quarters. As Hitler became more anxious
and mistrustful in mid-1943, it affected not only his physical condition but
also his relations with associates.

With regard to Philipp, Hitler demanded that he be watched more
carefully. Albert Speer, who remained a key member of Hitler's inner circle,
recalled:

> Hitler [later] boasted that he had begun suspecting early in the game that
> Prince Philipp was sending information to the Italian royal house. He himself

had kept an eye on him, Hitler said, and ordered his telephone conversations tapped. By methods such as these it had been discovered that the prince was passing number codes to his wife. Nevertheless, Hitler had continued to treat the prince with marked friendliness. That had been part of his tactics, he declared, obviously delighted with his gifts as a detective.[92]

Even though Philipp remained loyal to Hitler, these were dangerous times for the prince.

Philipp found himself in a dire situation not just because he had alienated Hitler, but because he had lost the support of Göring. This had occurred gradually. In June 1939, Philipp's cousin Prince Paul of Yugoslavia met with Göring in Berlin and recorded in his notes that the Reichsmarschall 'warns me against Ph. [Philipp], who is too Hitlerian.'[93] Philipp himself recalled an incident in 1940 when a meeting was scheduled to mediate the conflict between the Oberpräsident and Gauleiter Sprenger in Hessen. Göring had promised Philipp that he would attend and represent his interests. While Frick, Sprenger, and an aide of Bormann's from the party chancellery were present, Göring failed to show or send a representative. Philipp took this as a sign of the Reichsmarschall's waning support.[94] In this instance, the prince claimed he experienced a "defeat" that was "total," and was brought to realize that his once friendly relations with Göring had deteriorated. Landgravine Margarethe later recalled, "I know that the prince and Göring had been befriended for a long time, but after this point, the friendship cooled off markedly."[95] Already in December 1939, Göring's sister Olga had told Ulrich von Hassell that Philipp, "had markedly lost his position and got on Göring's nerves and that Göring would no longer permit him to stay with him, but would put him up in the Reich president's palace."[96] Philipp later observed that "I had only reasons of foreign policy to thank that my removal was delayed until 1943."[97]

Philipp perhaps exaggerated the degree to which he and Göring were alienated. He was, after all, invited to Carinhall in January 1942 to celebrate Emmy Göring's birthday. Three months later, Emmy Göring telephoned the Landgravine and Princess Sophia and invited them to an intimate luncheon with her husband and only two other guests. Landgravine Margarethe reported that the Görings were "completely charming to us and of comforting cordiality."[98] But tensions remained between Philipp and Göring. A key reason was Philipp's work for Hitler acquiring paintings in Italy: this made Göring envious and sparked suspicions of disloyalty. Landgravine Margarethe wrote her son Richard on 15 February 1942 about a recent visit by Philipp, where he reported that on a trip to Berlin "Goring had completely ignored him." Philipp, however, did manage to get Göring on the phone and after exchanging "all possible pleasantries," they talked about the artworks that Göring would like to acquire.

However, in the Landgravine's words, "he [Göring] actually was a little angry with the O. P. [Oberpräsident—Philipp] because various objects to which he attached importance were now in the hands of 'Ini' [Hitler]!!!" She added, "I have always thought that a certain envy for what Ini had received through the O. P. played a role in H's [Göring's] peculiar behavior."[99] Even with the cooling of relations between Göring and Philipp, the fact remains that the Reichsmarschall himself had suffered such a decline in his fortunes in 1943—with the Luftwaffe's increasingly dismal performance standing out as a primary factor—that even if so disposed, he would have had difficulty saving Philipp or other threatened family members.

At the end of April 1943, Hitler ordered Philipp to report to the Berchtesgadener Hof—the hotel near the Berghof—and await further instructions. Karl Wolff, who was an eyewitness, noted, "this was the beginning of an incarceration that lasted several months and was thereby veiled."[100] Philipp was told that he was needed for "special tasks," and kept close at hand as Hitler moved between Munich, Königsberg, and the *Wolfsschanze* (Wolf's Lair) near Rastenburg and the Masurian Lakes in East Prussia, where one year later the July 20 bomb exploded. Philipp was permitted to leave Hitler's headquarters on two occasions subsequent to the Klessheim meeting: the first was in June 1943, when he returned to Italy and met with members of the Italian royal family. Crown Prince Umberto was even more pessimistic this time, saying, "the situation in April 1943 and the current situation in June 1943 are comparable, except for the difference that in April, it was a quarter to twelve and now it's five minutes before twelve."[101] The second leave was to visit his family, which he did for the last time on 20 July 1943. One of his sons—Heinrich, the second oldest—was ill and was undergoing an operation on his leg in Rome.[102] It was the last time Philipp was to see Mafalda. His visit with his wife and children in Rome was cut short after two days when, on 22 July, he was "urgently recalled to the Führer Headquarters and he was brought there by a special plane."[103] King Vittorio Emmanuele was to sack Mussolini on 25 July—when he had the dictator arrested in the Villa Savoia and transported to prison in an ambulance—and rumors were already flying about the week before.[104] This precipitated panicky communications between many of the top Nazi leaders, including Himmler, Bormann, and Ribbentrop.[105]

Philipp remained under this remarkable form of house arrest. Karl Wolff later testified, "before his internment he was kept in the most honorable form for weeks in the Führer Headquarters. . . . He couldn't leave the Führer Headquarters because the Führer had to have him at his disposal for special projects. He was therefore already interned before the Badoglio betrayal came about; upon which he was nabbed."[106] It was indeed a curious picture: the prince following Hitler about on the specially armored Führer trains and remaining on hand at the Wolfsschanze. Another witness testified, "that [Philipp] was . . . frequently ordered to Hitler in the night, who used these opportunities to hold lectures about God and the world."[107] Prince Heinrich recalled that the family received periodic phone calls from Philipp in the period after 25 July, but noted that "it was clear that he couldn't speak openly."[108]

Philipp, of course, was a kind of hostage, or pawn in the chess match that Hitler played with the Italian king. As Hitler endeavored to rescue Mussolini—which an SS commando did from atop a mountain in the Gran Sasso—and prevent the defection of an ally, he tried to use Vittorio Emmanuele's son-in-law to generate leverage. Nuremberg prosecutor Robert Kempner noted, "the prince was more or less connected to the policies of the Italian royal house."[109] Princess Peg von Hessen-Darmstadt observed after the war, "Relations with his in-laws, that is, the Italian monarchy, were good and heartfelt."[110] Philipp was once again to be Hitler's secret weapon in Italy. Mussolini encouraged Hitler to pursue this tactic. He had long believed he could manipulate the Italian royal house, telling the Reichsführer-SS in the 1943 conversation mentioned earlier, "My dear Himmler, you will see that the Crown will abstain from undertaking anything serious against me. As you see, Fascism and National Socialism have analogous possibilities."[111] Himmler shared the view that the royal connections could be utilized for some gain and encouraged Hitler to exploit Philipp.

There is a dearth of credible evidence that Philipp worked toward the overthrow of Mussolini or that he sought to alter the status of Italy as a combatant nation. Granted, there were plots afoot against the dictator at court. Historian Robert Katz noted, "The plans to bring down the Duce were all in place. They had been deftly constructed by the minister of the royal household, a Genoese duke and master of intrigue named Pietro d'Acquarone. The King had held himself strategically aloof from the plotters, positioned to repudiate them should they fail."[112] RSHA agent Wilhelm Höttl put Crown Prince Umberto's wife, Marie-José, at the center of the plot.[113] But Philipp, it appears, was outside the circle of con-spirators. Indeed, his brother Christoph wrote Sophia on 17 September, without knowing exactly what was transpiring: "What an unpleasant situation for Phli [Philipp]. You and I were quite right about why he was kept so carefully away [from the royal family]."[114] One might argue that he was "defeatist" in his thinking—and this was a favorite charge of the Nazis, partly because it could be so vague and difficult to refute. But the prince continued to support Mussolini and offered advice to Hitler with the intent of salvaging the position of the Italian dictator. On the other hand, he was sympathetic to Vittorio Emmanuele's views and perhaps insufficiently critical of the decision to arrest Mussolini. Whatever his true inclinations,

Philipp gave rise to rumors and suspicion. Fabian von Schlabrendorff, for example, then stationed on the Eastern Front, recalls one episode involving his fanatically Nazi commander, General Hans Krebs (1898–1945), in early autumn 1943: "Hitler had told [Krebs] that Prince Philipp von Hessen had been under suspicion for a long time. For this reason, he had held him for weeks at the Führer Headquarters in order to make a game between him and the royal family in Italy impossible. . . . Prince Philipp von Hessen had always been a defeatist. He had repeatedly turned against his Gauleiter and filed complaints against them."[115] While some of these allegations had elements of truth, as a whole they constituted a misrepresentation of Philipp's loyalties.

The most compelling evidence of Philipp and Mafalda's "betrayal" at best leaves open the question of opposition. Their son, Prince Heinrich, reported having found one page of notes in an address book that belonged to Mafalda. These notes consist of eleven sets of numbers and attached short phrases, such as:

> 1: The king will soon be there
> 119: I am afraid
> 169: We're off.
> 221: Forward
> 222: But nothing.
> 224: It is peace!

Prince Heinrich himself concludes that this code is indecipherable and that the matter remains a mystery.[116] The most compelling interpretation is that the couple, who remained devoted to one another throughout their marriage, may well have communicated through a numerical code but that the intent was not treasonous. They were well aware of the surveillance taking place. Notably, Christoph had told all family members to be careful. He had instructed them to hold political conversations outdoors and never inside. In early 1943, the Germans had undertaken a vast expansion of espionage activities in Italy, with Wilhelm Höttl heading up the efforts of the RSHA.[117] There was also the family tradition of code words (recall "Ini" for Hitler). And the situation in the summer of 1943 had clearly become tense and uncertain. Mafalda even withdrew her jewels from the bank and buried them in the garden of the Villa Polissena.[118] But just because they may have been exchanging information in a concealed manner does not mean that they were helping plot the overthrow of either Mussolini or Hitler. The person who probably knew Philipp best, his friend Eddie von Bismarck, remarked in February 1944, "Sometimes we would speak alone and when it came to the political situation of our country, the situation would be somewhat unpleasant, since I could find nothing good in Nazism and the prince would not tire of praising it."[119] Granted, this remark may well have been intended to help Philipp, but even he, Philipp, denied assisting in the overthrow of Mussolini in his postwar denazification trial.

Prince Philipp was arrested on Hitler's orders at the Führer Head-quarters in Rastenburg on 8 September 1943, the day of Italy's surrender. This occurred, according to Philipp, "because of the suspicion of the cooperation of the Italian royal family with the overthrow of Mussolini."[120] This belief in the betrayal of the House of Savoy was actively propagated by the Nazis in the media, including numerous articles in the Nazi Party paper, *Der Völkische Beobachter*, and was one reason for the sharper antimonarchist tone that prevailed in the last years of the Third Reich (the 10 September edition of the paper, for example, featured the headline, "Thus the Liar-King Betrays the *Duce*").[121] Franz Ulbrich, the general intendant of the theater in Kassel recalled another remarkable element of this campaign: he blamed Gauleiter Weinrich for the "shameful poster hung by the thousands in Kassel in the autumn of 1943; in particular, there were numerous posters placed on the [Hessens'] Palais on the Schöne Aussicht [Bellevue], which were directed against the Italian royal house."[122] The arrest of Philipp was also striking because of the location of where it occurred and the personal involvement of Hitler. One had to go back to the Röhm purge in 1934 to find a target of the Nazis who had been so proximate to Hitler just prior to meeting his fate. According to the former military attaché in Rome, General Enno von Rintelen, "Prince Philipp was incarcerated in the Führer Headquarters after he dined with Hitler. The incarceration was carried out by an SS-Gruppenführer just as the prince sought to leave the Führer-barracks."[123] The dinner and ensuing conver-sation with Hitler had not ended until the early hours of the morning. Philipp recalled that he was arrested in Hitler's name and that two SS men escorted him to the "guest bunker" where he was kept in the dark, both literally and figuratively.[124] Von Schlabrendorff added: "The command to come to the Führer Headquarters and his arrest there immediately after a conversation with Hitler at four or five in the morning [induced Philipp to consider this] a personal felony on the part of Hitler. For the first time it was clear to him how Hitler had acted."[125]

The following night, Philipp was secreted out of the Führer Headquarters —evidently unseen by others—and transported to the Gestapo facility in Königsberg in the northeast of the German Reich.[126] After a short interlude there, he was transferred to Berlin, and more specifically, to the RSHA headquarters on the Prinz Albrechtstrasse. Philipp was met there by SS-Major General Heinrich Müller, the head of the Gestapo. He recalled that Müller "cynically led me to understand that the Prince Philipp von Hessen who had existed until now was to be regarded as dead and that all memory of him had to be extinguished. In his place, there would now be a *Herr*

Wildhof, whom [Müller] could only but urgently advise to never say a word about his past, his person, or his family, and under no circumstances was he to enter into political discussions; violations could have consequences of a very serious nature. . . . Besides that, all indications of my name on my clothes and such were removed and my papers were sealed."[127] Actually, Müller first wanted to give him the name of Weinberg, "because this was the name of a [Jewish] family [with] which I was acquainted in Frankfurt."[128] But the prince convinced him to permit the name of Wildhof—a name used both by his father and his twin, Wolfgang, when they wanted to travel incognito (the name came from favorite hunting grounds in Hessen near Offenbach). Philipp later testified, "I chose this name for the simple reason that if something should happen to me, my family would always know it was I."[129] The prince later portrayed his fate like a character in an Alexandre Dumas tale: a noble deprived of identity and unjustly imprisoned by a tyrant. Indeed, his fate was not without drama.

    Philipp was stripped of his membership in the Party and the SA, and also prohibited from displaying Nazi Party badges and honors. He was also dismissed as an officer of the Luftwaffe through an order signed by General Loerzer on 16 October 1943.[130] And, as noted earlier, Hitler and Göring dismissed him as Oberpräsident on 25 January 1944.[131] He was subsequently replaced as Oberpräsident in Hessen by SS Major General Karl Gerland, who also took over Gauleiter Weinrich's post after the latter was sacked due to his cowardly behavior during the 22 October 1943 air raid (Gerland was such a convinced Nazi that he raced to Berlin in April 1945 to help hold off the Red Army, where he then went missing and was presumably killed).[132] With the Nazi regime becoming more malignant after 1943, it is striking that Philipp did not face a worse fate. Even Gestapo chief Heinrich Müller treated him with a certain consideration. Within hours, Müller had the prisoner "Wildhof" sent off to southern Germany. Escorted by five criminal police dressed in civilian clothes the prisoner arrived at the Flossenbürg concentration camp near Regensburg in Bavaria under the cover of darkness.[133] The facility, which opened in March 1938, would hold some 65,000 inmates all told (most of them political prisoners), including many prominent figures, such as ex-Austrian chancellor Kurt von Schuschnigg and his wife, various members of the Wittelsbach dynasty, and a number of the July 20 conspirators (notably pastor Dietrich Bonhoeffer, Admiral Wilhelm Canaris, and General Hans Oster).

    As Philipp sat in a truck heading southeast toward the notorious camp in northern Bavaria, he recalled struggling to understand why he had met this fate. Philipp "had always believed that no one could be put into a concentration camp without a good reason. I, however, was locked up without any grounds being given."[134] He was not alone in this regard, as the Nazis imprisoned many without notifying them of the specific reasons.

Little did Philipp realize at the time that his captors were also uncertain of the charges.[135] After the war, Philipp himself was still searching for an explanation: "It is more likely that [Gauleiter] Sprenger and others might have caused his arrest. Sprenger had systematically been collecting evidence against the prince to build up a case against him: for example, that the prince was opposed to the party, that he had sabotaged Sprenger's efforts, that he used to have Jewish friends in Frankfurt, etc."[136] In that Sprenger aspired to succeed Philipp as Oberpräsident in 1944, the Gauleiter almost certainly did what he could to hasten the downfall of the prince. But other high-ranking Nazis also showed little sympathy for the prince. Philipp later reflected on being abandoned by Göring, who was now "too busy."[137] He also noted that "I, through my openness, elicited the irreconcilable hatred of Himmler and Bormann."[138] Goebbels exhibited personal animosity toward Philipp even prior to Hitler's orders for arrest in September 1943: on 10 August, the propaganda minister recorded in his diary, "The Führer is firmly convinced that Prince Philipp von Hessen was fully informed of the measures planned by the king [of Italy]. He is an unfaithful traitor. Once upon a time he couldn't praise Il Duce enough to high heaven, now he can't do enough to damn him to hell. He would do the same with us given an opportunity."[139]

The belief that Philipp had perpetrated some kind of "national treason" induced Hitler to order Himmler to launch an investigation. In October 1943, Himmler in turn charged Higher SS and Police Leader Prince zu Waldeck with carrying out a "house search" of the Hessens' residences.[140] Philipp's remote relation was ordered to dig up dirt on him. Waldeck and his men immediately searched Palais Bellevue in Kassel. A dozen Gestapo men arrived at 6:30 a.m. and roused the Hessens' secretary Adelheid Fliege from her bed. They also went through her parents' house nearby. SS-Brigadier General (Brigadeführer) Johannes Harnyss, who was on the staff of Prince zu Waldeck, later recalled that in October 1943, he overheard his chief telephone an inspector of the Security Police and order a sweep. Waldeck reportedly said, "search until you find something, and if you don't find anything, then make something up."[141] Fräulein Fliege recalled, "the house search of the residence of the Prince was a very thorough undertaking. They opened everything. Twelve people were involved. They also took papers."[142] Some of the correspondence was in Italian and Fräulein Fliege "later had to come to the Gestapo in order to translate the letters."[143] Fliege reported that most were "family letters or letters from friends or offers from art galleries in Italy," and that they were destroyed in "the great attack on 22 October 1943."[144] After the war, Philipp labeled his cousin, Prince zu Waldeck, a "declared enemy."[145]

Prince zu Waldeck seized upon the charge of homosexual activities as grounds for Philipp's incarceration. Philipp's lawyer Schlabrendorff noted that "in order to give an additional pretext for the imprisonment of the concerned party, it was the intention of circles within the Secret Police (Gestapo) to propagate the untrue rumor of the homosexual inclinations of the concerned party as grounds for his delivery to a concentration camp."[146] Adelheid Fliege provided more detail—an account she heard from one of the Hessens' servants named Fritz Hollenberg, who himself had a harrowing experience. Waldeck wanted Hollenberg to testify against Philipp—that he was anti-Nazi and a homosexual. Before that, Hollenberg had been with Mafalda in Rome. Hollenberg was told to pack their possessions for transport to Germany. He prepared fourteen cases—some valuable furniture, fur coats, and so forth. The cases were sent to the Prince Albrecht Strasse Palace. "The fourteen cases were said to be confiscated and the name of the prince where marked was to be changed."[147] Fliege continued, "The servant Hollenberg did this and was received at the appointed place in Berlin. But he protested and subsequently spent two months in the cellar of the [Albrechtstrasse] Palace and then eleven months in a concentration camp. He was let out in order to report to the front, and before doing so, he came by and told this to me."[148] Philipp himself recalled, "the objects that belonged to my wife and me located in our home in Rome that were of value were packed and transported off on orders of the Gestapo. Their whereabouts is unknown."[149] While there is a certain irony that Philipp, a cog in the Nazis' art plundering bureaucracy, became a victim of looting, the larger point would be that the Nazis almost always availed themselves of the opportunity to steal.

Philipp was incarcerated in the Flossenbürg concentration camp from 12 September 1943 until 15 April 1945 in conditions he described as "a hermetical concealment from the outside world."[150] While this was a slight exaggeration, his postwar attorney Fabian von Schlabrendorff, who later was also in Flossenbürg as a result of his involvement in the July 20 plot, testified, "the prince was watched especially closely. He could not receive any letters nor write any letters. . . . He was in solitary confinement in Flossenbürg. He sat in the special bunker (*Sonderbunker*) of the concentration camp, which is where I was also brought. The cell of the prince, as I remember, lay immediately next to the guard room of the Sonderbunker."[151] Some qualifications need to be made to this description. First, he was permitted to send letters to Himmler and Hitler, which he did on a number of occasions (not surprisingly, he never received responses). Second, he was told of the fate of his brother Christoph in November 1943.[152] And third, he had some small degree of human contact—mostly with the guards, and with the camp commandant, SS-Major Max Koegel (1894–1946), who would visit him once a month. Toward the end of his time in the camp, Philipp also had the opportunity to talk with the Schuschniggs as well as with Schlabrendorff. In general, however, he was cut off from the other inmates, and even most of the guards did not know his true identity. His isolation was due more to his previous political position than his social rank: as Joseph Goebbels noted, "due to state political reasons, he must be kept in security; after the weeks that he spent at the Führer Headquarters, he learned so much that he could be extraordinarily dangerous to us."[153] In spite of this isolation, Philipp was a privileged prisoner: he continued to wear his civilian clothes (when he was arrested and transported from Rastenburg, the guards brought his three suitcases and toiletries kit); he was housed in a double cell that included a wash basin, a table, and a window; and he ate the same food as the SS guards, rather than the meager rations given to other prisoners. His SS captors even built a wooden-fence enclosure outside his cell where he could sit in the sun. He could peer through cracks in the fence and catch glimpses of the camp, even though others could not see in and recognize him.[154]

Philipp described living "in an atmosphere of death." He elaborated, "the hangings, for example, took place only a few paces from my cell on a small gallows, and the corpses on carts went by my window daily to the crematorium."[155] He recalled that he "could hear off and on a soft cracking, something like a soft shot being fired," which turned out to be executions in the distance.[156] All told, some 30,000 of the 100,000 prisoners that passed through Flossenbürg between 1938 and 1945 died, with the final year of the war standing out as far and away the most lethal.[157] Philipp mostly sat in his cell day after day and looked out his window at the "transport of the corpses" (*Leichentransporte*).[158] Despite his preferential treatment, there was a great deal to endure in terms of harsh conditions and fear. Schlabrendorff, speaking more as a witness than a defense attorney, praised Philipp: "in the dangerous moments of the evacuations from the various camps, when we were frequently close to being shot or hanged, the prince, in contrast to many other prisoners, never betrayed a trace of fear. He always remained steady and cool."[159] This came from a member of the resistance who himself barely survived the July 20 reprisals: Schlabrendorff was tried before the *Volksgerichtshof* (People's Court) in Berlin, and faced notoriously severe president Roland Freisler, a radical Nazi. The defendant, however, was saved from Freisler's judgment when an American bomb struck the courtroom and killed the judge (who was found dead clutching Schlabrendorff's file).[160] After the war, Philipp remarked, "if someone had told me earlier of the conditions and methods that prevailed in a concentration camp, I probably would have had that person brought to a concentration camp for spreading propagandistic lies."[161] While Philipp exhibited a sense of black humor here and attempted to show that he was not aware of conditions in the camps prior to his arrival in one, he also sought to communicate in a relatively understated way the shockingly harsh conditions that are now well known.[162]

Princess Mafalda had a different and ultimately more tragic experience. On 8 September 1943, Princess Mafalda was in Sofia, Bulgaria, where she was attending the funeral of her sister Giovanna's husband, King Boris III, who died under mysterious circumstances. Many believe that he was assassinated by Axis sympathizers, while others maintain that the king committed suicide, the result of increasing pressure from Hitler. King Boris had visited at the Führer Headquarters in Rastenburg on 15 August 1943, where he also saw his brother-in-law Prince Philipp.[163] Hitler endeavored to induce Bulgaria to make a greater contribution to the Axis war effort, and this resulted in a contentious, and indeed "stormy meeting."[164] While Boris had brought Bulgaria into the Axis in 1941, he had not declared war on the Soviet Union and would not send troops to the Eastern Front. In September 1943, a week after his return to Sofia, the forty-nine-year-old king fell into a coma from which he never emerged (the official cause of death was "stress and a heart condition").[165] Because Mafalda was present in the Bulgarian capital, visiting her sister Queen Giovanna, she attracted the

King Boris of Bulgaria and Hitler descend the steps of the Berghof on the Obersalzberg after a 7 June 1941 meeting.

suspicion of certain Nazi leaders—and Hitler and Goebbels in particular. The propaganda minister articulated a conspiracy theory in blunt terms in his diary entries. On 11 September 1943, he fulminated, "The Führer intends to transmit to Prince Kyrill the findings of the German doctors on the poisoning of King Boris, which he believes was in all likelihood inspired by the Italian court. For it is very suspicious that Princess Mafalda, the greatest bitch (*grösste Rabenaas*) in the entire Italian royal house, was on a visit to Sofia four weeks before King Boris's death." He added, "the Führer again related how often he had warned Il Duce against the monarchy and the aristocracy, but Il Duce was too trustful. He must now pay for it dearly. The monarchy thanked him in a manner that he certainly had not expected." Finally, Goebbels recounted how, "the Führer once more expressed his conviction that Princess Mafalda was the trickiest bitch (*geriebenste Aas*) in the Italian royal house. He thought her capable of having expedited the journey of her brother-in-law Boris to the hereafter. It was also possible that the plutocratic clique administered poison to Mussolini, for Mussolini's illness too, was somewhat mysterious."[166] Of course, in light of Princess Mafalda's rather gentle nature and her loyalty to her family, this theory is ludicrous. There would be no compelling reason for her to murder her brother-in-law. Goebbels's diaries attest to his growing paranoia and were part of his calculated effort to use King Boris's death as a means of turning Hitler against the Hessens. That Hitler was plagued by fears of being poisoned was probably not lost on the calculating propaganda minister.

Like others, Princess Mafalda had been surprised by the capitulation of Italy. It had occurred while she was in Sofia. Not certain what to do, she decided to return to Rome, and this entailed an extremely taxing journey: first to Budapest, then to Vienna, and down to Venice, and finally to Rome. The princess was tracked the entire time by the SS, with reports sent directly to Himmler, including her mode of transportation—an "Italian special plane"—and times of departure (The SS agents did, however, lose track of her for a time).[167] She arrived back home in Rome "broken in body and soul" on 21 September and took refuge in the Vatican, thanks to the help of Monsignor Giovanni Montini (1897–1978), the future Pope Paul VI.[168] Three of her children were waiting for her there. After the flight of King Vittorio Emmanuele and Queen Elena—who had initially escaped to an estate of the pope, and then moved on to establish a headquarters in Brindisi in the South—the children had been taken in by Monsignor Montini, who put his magnificent residence adjacent to the Sistine Chapel at their disposal.[169] The Vatican, a sovereign entity as confirmed by the Lateran Accords of 1929, was respected by the Germans and therefore not occupied. Early in the morning on the following day, Mafalda received a message from the German Embassy. It said that her husband had called and urgently wanted to speak with her, and that she should proceed to the embassy in order to make this call. Because this was the only way to arrange a secure line, such steps had been taken in the past. According to SD agent Wilhelm Höttl, Ambassador Mackensen, in an attempt to prevent reports at odds with his own, had gone "so far as to ban all telephone communication with Germany, with the exception of his own private line."[170] In other words, it was plausible that one would need to go to the German Embassy to make a call of this kind and Mafalda therefore left her refuge in the Vatican.

As Mafalda approached the Villa Wolkonsky—until 8 September the German Embassy but now reconfigured as the German military headquarters in Rome—an SS-officer from the Afrikakorps emerged from a waiting car and told the princess, "Your husband called and said that he will soon arrive at the air field here in Rome and that he wanted to speak with you there."[171] The SS officer asked her to step into the car, which she did, and together with two other SS men, they headed for the Rome airport. At the terminal, the SS guards took her to a room where two other women were waiting. He left the ladies alone. When Mafalda tried to leave the room to get some breakfast, one of the women told her, "you may not leave the room."[172] At this moment, according to what Philipp later learned from witnesses, Mafalda knew she had become a prisoner.[173] Of course, the airplane supposedly carrying Prince Philipp never arrived. But another one did, and Mafalda was told to get on board. She was accompanied by the woman who had told her she couldn't leave the room in the terminal. In the account given by Philipp, that includes details and areas of concern one might expect from a distraught spouse, he noted, "without breakfast, only lightly dressed [in a silk suit], the princess had to set out on her air journey."[174] Mafalda's secretary added that she took only a "a small bag."[175] These observations, of course, also speak to the luxuries the royal pair were accustomed to, and also the nature of air travel in the 1940s before the advent of climate-controlled cabins, when planes flew at lower altitudes and often presented difficulties for the feint of heart. Mafalda was told that she would be taken to Munich where she would meet her husband. But this didn't happen and the plane continued north to Berlin, where it landed at the Tempelhof airfield, a monument to the Nazis' aeronautical ambitions.

The plane of Princess Mafalda was met by Gestapo agents, who escorted her to their offices near Lake Wannsee. She was kept at the Gestapo branch office for fourteen days, and the treatment was fairly harsh. There was, for example, no bed. The authorities interrogated her repeatedly, although the records have evidently not survived.[176] On about 20 October 1943, she was taken to the Buchenwald concentration camp, placed in a specially isolated barrack, and held under the name "Frau von Weber."[177] (Note that the Nazis retained the aristocratic prefix.) Deeply confused, Princess Mafalda cried incessantly. She was not permitted to receive mail and was led to believe "that her husband was dead, and thought the entire day about her children."[178] She heard rumors that Philipp had been shot—and indeed, the authorities only tried to increase her fears: "Already upon her arrival [at the Gestapo office] at Berlin-Wannsee, the princess was addressed as a widow."[179] Interestingly, she was permitted to write letters, and this she did in profusion—almost every day. She wrote to her parents, her in-laws, and of course, in an attempt to maintain a glimmer of hope, to Philipp and the children. But camp officials intercepted all her missives and none ever reached the intended recipient. She also wrote, according to an SS officer named Johannes Harnyss, "to people whom she had once known (Hitler, Himmler, Kaltenbrunner, and so forth)."[180] There is no trace of these letters to Nazi leaders in the archives or any evidence that she ever received an answer.

Mafalda and Philipp's three youngest children had been escorted from Rome to Germany. In late September 1943, they had left the Vatican for the Villa Polissena, where they remained for several weeks, as they waited to join their parents in the North. It is notable that the official charged with overseeing their trip to Germany was SS Lieutenant Colonel Herbert Kappler (1907–78), the head of police and Gestapo operations in Rome (and in Wilhelm Höttl's words, " a mere creature of Heydrich").[181] Kappler had just tracked the imprisoned Mussolini to the Gran Sasso, which he did in late-August prior to Mussolini's rescue on 12 September. Subsequently Kappler was a key, if ambiguous, figure in the persecution of Rome's 12,000 Jews: he extorted a ransom of fifty kilograms in gold from them and was later complicit in the March 1944 massacre of 335 Roman men and boys in the Ardeatine Caves—an act of retaliation in response to an attack by members of the resistance.[182] Kappler was a sinister figure who cast a shadow over the fate of the Hessens during the autumn of 1943. In early October, while still waiting at the Villa Polissena, Prince Heinrich was astonished to see his uncle, Prince Christoph, who arrived in his Luftwaffe uniform. Heinrich was pleased to see his uncle, whom he adored, and after exchanging news, Christoph told him to pack a suitcase with personal belongings. He would return the next day to pick up the bags and then take them by airplane to Germany, thereby reducing their load as the children headed north by train.[183] Christoph departed and a comrade named Dreiffke from the Luftwaffe came and picked up the luggage (which had been packed with valued possessions). After a difficult journey on crowded trains, escorted by an SS officer, the children made it back to Kronberg to be with their grandmother.

Princess Mafalda's experience in Buchenwald was so extraordinary that it would scarcely be credible as fiction or film. The primary authority in the concentration camp was Prince zu Waldeck. Her husband's distant relative and familiar acquaintance was the Higher SS and Police Leader of Weimar, and therefore was the foremost local power. Prince zu Waldeck would make regular inspections of the camp. Johannes Harnyss, the former aide of Waldeck, who himself ended up a prisoner in Buchenwald due to insubordination, took it upon himself to arrange one meeting between the prince and princess. Harnyss requested to see Waldeck, who consented and came to the barracks where both Harnyss and Mafalda were housed. Harnyss described how "as [Waldeck] came in I didn't converse with him. I told him that I had reconsidered. As he left the room, the princess was standing before him. She was dressed very badly. He knew that the princess was in the same barracks. He looked her up and down and then went out. The princess did not speak to him. But he must have recognized her, as he himself had said, he was often with Prince Philipp von Hessen as a guest."[184] Another observer added with regards to Waldeck, "he had no sympathy for the indescribably distressed woman."[185]

Mafalda was lodged in the special "I-Barracks" (short for "Isolation Barracks") that were located near an armaments factory, the Wilhelm-Gustloff-Works. She was housed with other prominent prisoners in Buchenwald that included former Austrian chancellor Kurt von Schuschnigg, industrialist Fritz Thyssen, and later six members of the family of Count von Stauffenberg.[186] Her more immediate neighbors included former Social Democratic Reichstag deputy Dr. Rudolf Breitscheid and his wife, as well a Jehovah's Witness, and the above-mentioned Johannes Harnyss.[187] The group pledged to one another that should one of them make it out, they would communicate to loved ones and friends what had happened.[188] In the summer of 1944, Mafalda did receive word that her four children (then aged between four and eighteen) were alive and well. But all appeals to see them or hear from them were denied by Prince zu Waldeck.

The I-Barracks stood in a particularly dangerous place near the Gustloff factory, a facility that had been constructed just outside the perimeter of the camp. The Americans attacked the factory on several occasions, and the prisoners were not given refuge in bomb shelters. On 24 August 1944, shortly before noon, the bombs fell again. According to reports, three struck that part of the camp: one went astray and hit the I-Barracks, which immediately caught fire. Another bomb fell outside the barracks and hit the covering under which Mafalda and several others had taken refuge. Approximately four hundred prisoners were killed, including Rudolf Breitscheid, who died instantly. Princess Mafalda was gravely wounded and buried beneath rubble. Burning walls had collapsed around her, and she was up to her neck in debris.[189] Even though she was soon rescued, her left arm had been burned. According to Harnyss, who witnessed the events, it had "burned almost to the bone."[190] Mafalda received medical help in a building that had hitherto housed the camp brothel (Himmler had ordered its creation in the summer of 1943). For this reason, a rumor spread after the war that Mafalda had been housed in the brothel—with suggestions (entirely unfounded of course), that she had been forced to work there.[191] The princess and other severely wounded were cared for, and in this case, she was given injections to ease her pain. The arm, however, became infected, and the decision was made to amputate. This was done by the camp physician, Dr. Schiedlausky. The procedure did not go well, however, and Princess Mafalda started bleeding profusely. Frau Breitscheid, who was there with her, recalled, "The princess was very collected and brave," and said, "she was not so badly injured. Then, after the treatment, she never regained consciousness."[192] Mafalda died from loss of blood during the night of 26–27 August 1944.[193] Some questioned whether the amputation was necessary, and in hindsight it was certainly the wrong decision.[194]

Rumors of Mafalda's death began to spread at the end of 1944. Her secretary in Kassel, Adelheid Fliege, heard some of these reports. This prompted Mafalda's sister-in-law Sophia and others in the family to attempt to learn more. Despite their concerted efforts, definitive word did not come until after the end of the war. Philipp found out while in custody of the Americans. At that time, he was interned with a number of other prominent figures while the Americans tried to determine a course of action. One of them was pastor Martin Niemöller, who had also been imprisoned in several Nazi camps. It was in the internment facility at Niederdorf near the Czech border that Niemöller broke the news to Philipp about Mafalda's fate. Niemöller tried to console Philipp. As he noted, "At this time I was also his spiritual adviser (*Seelsorger*)."[195] The children also learned of their mother's fate in different and difficult ways: "Prince Heinrich, the second son of the prince, first received the news about the death of his mother on [20 April] 1945, and that was when he heard it on the radio [in a broadcast by the Allies]."[196] The young prince initially believed, or wanted to believe, that this broadcast was Allied propaganda.

It is indeed remarkable that Hitler kidnapped the daughter of the king of Italy, his one-time ally, and placed her in a notorious concentration camp. To this day, the German dictator's motives remain murky. Journalist William Ellinghaus speculates that he may have held her hostage in the hope that she would afford him some leverage at a critical point; or alternatively, that she knew something special.[197] But the most likely explanation was that it was an act of revenge against someone whom Hitler felt had betrayed him. If one accepts this reason, a subsequent question arises as to whether Mafalda actually did something to provoke such reprisals? As with Philipp, was she innocent of these charges? Or did she play any role in the overthrow of Mussolini? There is indeed the possibility that Philipp and Mafalda had engaged in genuinely treasonous behavior as far as Hitler was concerned. Philipp's postwar lawyer noted, "that the concerned party could maintain up until the end his clandestine contact with a large segment of the opponents of Fascism in Rome."[198] But Philipp was unable to provide further information about his ties to anti-Fascists. More likely is that Hitler was upset that King Vittorio Emmanuele (like the kings of Greece and Norway earlier), had escaped from his control when he fled in September 1943.[199] Mafalda, like Philipp, was arrested for symbolic and strategic reasons, rather than as a result of any specific act of resistance. It also did not help that Hitler was lukewarm about her personally (as opposed to Philipp): the dictator reported to his generals in a conference held in May 1943, "What do I care about Mafalda? . . . . Her intellectual qualities aren't such that she would charm you—to say nothing of her looks."[200]

Although the Germans responded to the Italians' defection to the Allied side with a distinct harshness with regard to the Italian armed forces, they were less severe in their treatment of the Italian royal family—Mafalda excepted. As von Schlabrendorff noted after the war, "other members of the Italian royal house were treated fundamentally differently after the fall of Mussolini and his wife. Another son-in-law of the king, Count Calvi, was appointed commandant of Rome by the Germans."[201] Count Calvi di Bergolo was a general and the chief of the Italian "Bersaglieri-Regiment," which had remained loyal to the Axis.[202] Still, he was eventually removed by the Germans and sent north to the Reich, where he was kept under relatively benign house arrest in Munich.[203] To take another example, Mafalda's younger sister, Princess Maria, along with her husband, Prince Luigi di Bourbon-Parma, were arrested on 13 September by the Gestapo at their house near Cannes and sent along with their three children to a villa in Mecklenburg in northern Germany. They were permitted to have servants; they lost only their "freedom of movement."[204] Hitler and the other top Nazi leaders went after those Italian royals whom they thought had particular influence on the king. Philipp, the liaison, and his wife, were treated the most harshly. But their experiences must be put in the broader context of the Nazi reprisals. Infuriated by what they perceived as a betrayal by key allies, the brutality of the German response to Italian defection in September 1943 is a relatively little-known aspect of World War II. In "Operation Axis," German army units forcibly subdued Italian soldiers who followed Bagdolio's orders and defected from the Axis. While some 650,000 Italian soldiers were taken into captivity, there were also instances of murderous retribution: on the Greek island of Cephalonia, the Italians actually fought with the Germans; when they finally surrendered, they were summarily executed. On Corfu, after resisting the Wehrmacht for three days, seven thousand Italian soldiers who had capitulated were gunned down.[205] What happened to Philipp and Mafalda was but just one manifestation of the anger felt by many Germans. Historian Susan Zuccotti noted, "The poor Italian military performance before the armistice, Badoglio's betrayal of the Axis alliance, and the subsequent strength of the Italian anti-Fascist Resistance transformed Nazi contempt for their ally into profound distrust and hatred."[206] There can be little doubt that Hitler himself issued the orders concerning Mafalda: the princess experienced the dictator's rage on a personal level.

Christoph's Death

At the same time Philipp and Mafalda were struggling with their initial phase of their incarceration in concentration camps, Christoph's plane crashed in Italy. It is remarkable that he continued to serve in the German Luftwaffe in the wake of the May 1943 Decree Against Internationally Connected Men (also known as the "Princes Decree" or *Prinzenerlass*). This fact in itself suggests that he was still viewed as a Nazi stalwart. His twin, Richard, had been forced to resign his post in the Wehrmacht in January 1943, and his elder brother Wolfgang was dismissed from his unit in Finland a short time later (although Wolfgang was able to retain his post as Landrat in Bad Homburg).[207] That Christoph was still serving in the wake of Philipp and Mafalda's arrest in September 1943 is all the more remarkable. But well before this, he sensed trouble for the family. As Landgravine Margarethe wrote her son Prince Richard in November 1942, "Chri takes a terribly pessimistic view of the future, in all that concerns us personally. . . ."[208] By July 1943 Christoph himself commented, "At the moment I see a lot of worries for the future. It was all recognized too late."[209]

Prince Christoph was able to spend a considerable amount of time in Germany during the war because of his continued involvement with the Forschungsamt. He was on leave from the agency, and as director-on-leave, still concerned about operations. One theory, supported by his son Rainer, was that Göring maintained Christoph's formal appointment as director in a conscious effort to keep the agency out of the hands of the SS. Because the head of the agency was an SS officer, it would have been awkward for Himmler to assert control. Rainer adds, "my father—or his name—might have helped Göring in his rivalry with Himmler." As noted earlier, after the German capitulation in North Africa in May 1943, Christoph returned to Germany for a month—although he mostly stayed with his family at Kronberg. For an officer in the Luftwaffe, he spent an unusual amount of time in Germany. But there is paltry evidence to suggest that he combined intelligence and military work. Rainer von Hessen has spoken with his father's former comrades in the Luftwaffe, and none of them had the slightest idea of his post at the Forschungsamt, or of his rank in the SS. Furthermore, the recently discovered correspondence between Christoph and his wife Sophia do not reveal any special operations. These letters indicate that Christoph used the Forschungsamt as an excuse for travel back to Germany but usually only in cases of great emergency.

Once the German forces had been forced out of Sicily and were back on the mainland, Christoph was recalled to his squadron. The members of Fighter Squadron Fifty-three were also gradually pushed northward from the port of Brindisi to the hills above Naples, and then later on to Castel Gandolfo, not far from Rome. Christoph's letters from this period suggest certain concerns. First, he appears to be a committed soldier: he expressed the hope that the Italians would hold on until winter, and also wrote that he and his comrades were "going to fight our way through and they'll get all they have asked for, since we are here!"[210] Christoph also exhibited loyalty to Germany and expressed his anger about the Italian royal family members "abandoning" their German ally: in mid-September he wrote, "What do you say to the king? Really I think he must be quite gaga, or he is the biggest

Prince Christoph (right) and Italian Crown Prince Umberto (center) at Donna Fugeta in southern Italy, 1943.

scoundrel that ever lived."[211] However, he could also appear moderately critical of the Nazi regime, taking exception on occasion to poor decisions made by "*die Führung*" [the leadership]. These sometimes blunt and pessimistic statements are remarkable because he knew that it was likely that his letters would be intercepted and read by government agents.

Above all, Christoph appeared most concerned about his family and kept in contact with various members during the critical period between August and October 1943. He remained in touch with Mafalda, which was made easier by their geographical proximity in Italy. He visited her in Rome on 8 August, where they discussed the unsettled situation. Sophia kept him informed about events in Germany: in August, she reported on Wolfgang's forced departure from the armed forces, and there were exchanges about the predicament of Philipp, including the ominous remark made by Christoph in a 7 September letter: "I quite agree about what you say concerning Phli. I have also had the same idea and I'm quite convinced it is so, but he does not seem to have found out for himself yet!"[212] Christoph's sense of foreboding proved accurate, as his brother was arrested the following day at the Führer Headquarters. At the end of September, after both Philipp and Mafalda had been incarcerated, he returned to the Villa Polissena; as he wrote to Sophia, "I've been trying to get this beastly mess in Phli's house in order and hope to manage to get some of the most valuable things away."[213] This was the moment when he visited his nephews Heinrich and Otto and niece Elisabeth and told them to prepare to leave for Germany. But before he could make travel arrangements, SS-Lieutenant Colonel Herbert Kappler phoned Heinrich at the villa. He explained that he had been charged with transporting the children to Frankfurt. The entire family was struggling to find information about Philipp and Mafalda: Princess Sophia had written to Christoph on 17 September, telling him that "Wolf has got no further information about Phli. Yesterday he wanted to ring up the *Führerhauptquartier*."[214] It appears that he held off making the call, realizing that his intervention with Hitler would only increase the danger. The family knew no more in early October, as Christoph and the children prepared for their respective departures.

During the crisis precipitated by the Italian abandonment of the Axis, Christoph experienced conflicting emotions. On the one hand, he remained a staunch supporter of the German war effort and felt committed to his comrades in the Fighter Squadron. On the other hand, he was dismayed by the Prinzenerlass, frustrated by the limitations placed on his own role in the conflict, and increasingly critical of the German leadership. The overriding emotion, however, was fear for his family. He realized that the Nazi regime had turned against them and that his relations were in grave danger. While he may have used his status, including his positions as an SS officer and nominal head of the Forschungsamt, to secure a meeting with Rome Gestapo chief Herbert Kappler, it is far more likely that he thought the best way to ascertain the location of Philipp and Mafalda was to head to Germany. This is where the decision about the imprisonment had been made, and this is where his highly placed connections were located. He most likely would have sought out Pilli Körner in Berlin, who in turn would open the door to Göring. On 19 September, Christoph wrote Sophia that he was trying to return to Germany, "As a reason I shall say I must see to the 'Amt' [Forschungsamt], as they are moving. Perhaps we'll manage it."[215] Meanwhile, he arranged to ship some of Philipp's boxes north to Germany with Baron von Maltzahn.[216]

Although there has been considerable conjecture about Christoph's intentions and destination when he departed from the airport near Rome on 7 October, recently discovered documents show that he was flying back to the Fighter Squadron's home base in Mannheim.[217] It is not clear whether he utilized the ploy that he mentioned to Sophia—claiming to have urgent business at the Forschungsamt—or whether he himself was recalled to Germany (perhaps in some version of the Prinzenerlass): one of Christoph's comrades later testified that the prince "was ordered to leave his squadron and therefore Italy and to report for reassignment in the territory of the Reich."[218] His son Rainer believes the most likely scenario is that his father was able to use the FA as an alibi: that Christoph intended first to travel to Mannheim, then to visit the family in Kronberg to obtain an update on the situation, and then to head to Berlin to see what could be done. Many questions still remain about the flight. What is certain is that the prince and his pilot, Wilhelm Gsteu, checked the weather conditions repeatedly before commencing their journey and that they embarked in a twin-engine light staff transport, a Siebel 204. At 5:30 p.m. the plane ploughed into a 1,000-meter-high mountain near Monte Collino in the Apennine Mountains, thirty kilometers southwest of Forli in Romagna (not far from Ravenna) and was completely destroyed, so much so that the bodies were not found until two days later.[219] The search party, which had difficulty reaching them, buried Prince Christoph and Gsteu in the cemetery in nearby Forli in a section reserved for German soldiers.

The circumstances surrounding the crash remain mysterious. Major Bennemann, in the letter cited above that gave Mannheim as the destination, explained that the summit of the mountain was obscured by fog and that there was a "deterioration in the weather" after the initial takeoff.[220] Yet why would an experienced pilot like Gsteu fly so low in foggy conditions (and at that time of year, in the twilight of dusk)? Why would he not take precautions and fly at a higher altitude? Why, on a flight heading in a northwesterly direction, would one be flying due east? The most direct route from Rome to Mannheim would have been to head straight north. Furthermore, observers saw the plane traveling in the region of the Apennine

Mountains in a southwesterly direction: that is, it appeared to be circling back in the opposite direction just before the plane struck the mountain.[221] Does the low altitude and inexplicable course speak to a failure of the instruments? If yes, were they sabotaged? These questions defy conclusive answers. As Prince Philip, Duke of Edinburgh noted of his brother-in-law's death, "No one has explained it."[222]

The broader circumstances at the time of the crash leave doubt that it was caused solely by weather and human error. If Christoph had returned to Berlin, he would have learned of the fate of Philipp and Mafalda because this top secret information would have come up in eavesdropping operations and been included in intelligence reports. This would have created an unacceptable situation for Hitler, Himmler, and other top Nazi leaders. Granted, the question arises, why not send Christoph to a concentration camp like Philipp and Mafalda? Admiral Canaris, an even more powerful spy chief, was later put in a camp. The answer, if one were to follow this line of thinking, would lie in the Germans' brutal occupation of northern Italy in the period that followed Badoglio's defection from the Axis. Indeed, a particularly notorious SS regiment had moved into Rome and the surrounding areas and was undertaking the arrest and deportation of Roman Jews.[223] The Germans had occupied Rome with 10,000 troops on 16 September; seized the gold in the Italian state bank and shipped it to Germany on the twenty-first; and SS officer Kappler received the order to seize the 8,000 Jews in Rome and liquidate them.[224] Amid this rapid radicalization, it would not have been inconceivable for an order to be given to "take care of Prince Christoph." His cousin, Lord Louis Mountbatten, believed that "Hitler, distrustful of his loyalty, had killed him by a bomb planted in his aero-plane."[225] While it is impossible to prove that Christoph was murdered by an act of sabotage, it is notable that this theory has retained a certain credence within the family and among those who work for them.

Airplane crashes during World War II have provided a ripe field for conjecture. There are similar rumors, for example, surrounding the death of the Duke of Kent. His Sunderland flying boat crashed in northern Scotland on the Duke of Portland's estate in August 1942 while en route to Iceland, where he was to inspect RAF forces. The mysterious death—the plane was reliable and flown by an experienced pilot, Wing-Commander T. L. Moseley—has provoked a number of observers to suspect both foul play and a secret mission to arrange a negotiated peace.[226] One theory even has it that the plane was supposed to stop and pick up Rudolf Hess, who was allegedly kept in a house at Loch More, "perhaps to take him away to freedom and a possible peace deal between Britain and Germany."[227] But this speculation enters into the realm of the outlandish—certainly in comparison to the far more likely notion that Prince Christoph was killed by an act of sabotage. It bears mentioning that observers have long spe-culated about the murder of a number of high-ranking figures in Nazi Germany: from Field Marshal Walther von Reichenau, who supposedly died of a stroke in January 1942, to Reich Minister Fritz Todt, who perished in a plane crash in February 1942, and General Eduard Dietl, one of the leaders of the Norwegian Campaign, whom Prince Wolfgang suggested may have had his plane sabotaged in 1944.[228] Gerhard Weinberg, one of the deans of World War II historians, believes that the death of Reich Minister Todt stands out as the only likely murder among this group (the stated cause of death—the accidental deployment of the self-destruct mechanism—is insupportable because Todt's plane did not have this feature). Weinberg also notes that during World War II more planes were lost to accident than were shot down. In other words, more died not because of enemy action but because of human error and the failure of technology.[229]

The news of Christoph's death spread quickly among Nazi leaders, but there was little in the way of public acknowledgement. The Reich Air Ministry circulated bulletins to many quarters. That is how Himmler, for example, learned of the fatal crash. On 13 October 1943, a high-ranking aide to Himmler took the call and made both a written and verbal report. Granted, he reported the wrong date of death (11 October). And in an SS document dated 3 November, the date of 12 October was listed. Author Günther Gellermann raises the question whether there is significance of these errors but concludes that it cannot be answered.[230] The silence in the press was also striking, but explained largely by the "Princes Decree." Previously, it would have been news when a prince, a nephew of the Kaiser, perished during active service. But the antiroyal campaign that was under-way precluded any sympathetic media coverage. The Nazis were not going to provide the same publicity that had attended the death of the Hohenzollern prince in France in May 1940. Instead, Princess Sophia placed a conven-tional notice with relevant dates and place of death in the *Völkischer Beobachter*, making her husband seem like an ordinary solider who had fallen in the line of duty.[231]

Christoph's wife Princess Sophia and their children were living at Schloss Friedrichshof at Kronberg at the time of Christoph's death. Her grandmother, Victoria, Marchioness of Milford-Haven, then in the United Kingdom, wrote to her former lady-in-waiting Nona Kerr on 16 October 1943, "Poor dear Tiny [Sophia], she loved her husband & had been so anxious about him ever since he was in Sicily. . . . I am so sorry for Mossie too; this is the 3rd son she has lost in war, the eldest two in the last one & now her favourite in this one. This is now the 7th relation of mine who has lost his life flying."[232] Sophie's mother Princess Alice joined her in Kronberg, which provoked another observation from Victoria in a letter to Lord Louis Mountbatten: "Luckily they both have good nerves as they are so near Frankfurt, which has lately not been a pleasant neighborhood."[233] Indeed, Frankfurt was continuously bombed by the British and Americans, and even Kronberg, which sits on a hill overlooking the city, was not immune. In October 1944, a British incendiary bomb struck the chapel that served as a family crypt.[234]

Even though Christoph had been disaffected from the SS, he had formally remained an officer. Himmler ordered an aide to visit Christoph's widow in November 1943. More specifically, he ordered the overseer of the Wewelsburg castle (the medieval castle that Himmler created as a spiritual base for SS leaders), General Siegfried Taubert to make an unannounced visit to Sophia and the family in order to "sniff around."[235] Taubert penned a remarkable report to Himmler, dated 30 November 1943, about his visit to Schloss Friedrichshof.[236] He noted that Sophia was staying with her mother-in-law, the Landgravine, along with many other family members, including the children of Philipp and Mafalda. Taubert had not seen the twenty-nine-year-old princess in six years and "was astonished by her terrible appearance; she has become thin and looks to be suffering a great deal, probably because she is expecting her fifth child." (The other children were ages ten, eight, six, and four).[237] After Christoph's death, Sophia gave birth to a daughter, Clarissa, on 6 February 1944. The princess and Taubert talked about the old times of Christoph's SS unit as well as the crash. Princess Sophia and Landgravine Margarethe comported themselves in a cautious manner—after all, they were still deeply concerned about Philipp and Mafalda, and they themselves felt vulnerable. They did not articulate suspicions about a plot to kill Prince Christoph—or not any that Taubert included in his report. They played along with Taubert, accepting with "nervous laughter" the "absurd" gift of a promise of an extra ration of bean-coffee, which, they later recalled, never arrived.[238] Still, they sent "heartfelt greetings to the Reichsführer-SS and Princess Christoph [Sophia] extended special thanks to the Reichsführer-SS for his concern."[239] Taubert's report includes marginalia from Himmler dated 26 March 1944, showing that he had a personal interest in the von Hessen family.

Sophia and the Landgravine scrutinized General Taubert's comments and found certain formulations suspicious: at one point, Taubert mentioned that "we at the Wewelsburg Castle hear nothing about this [plane crash] and other similar things."[240] It was the last part of that sentence—"other similar things"—that raised questions. What kind of similar instances were there? Taubert, family members believed, had said a few words too many. Of course, this in no way demonstrates the complicity of the SS in the death of Prince Christoph, only that family members viewed Himmler's agents with suspicion. In October 1943, Prince Richard was informed by Reichsleiter Martin Bormann that he was also "completely intolerable" in the armed forces and simultaneously released from his post as a general of the National Socialist Drivers' Corps (NSKK).[241] When combined with the disappearance of Philipp and Mafalda and the fatal crash of Prince Christoph's airplane, a readily apparent pattern formed in the minds of most family members. Prince Richard commented shortly after the war, "looking back from this vantage point I might point to three incidents that are closely connected by temporal proximity"—the subtext of this statement being that the connections were more than a matter of timing.[242]

In the wake of Christoph's death, the family's main concern had become the fate of Philipp and Mafalda. Already in mid-October 1943, Prince Wolfgang had traveled to Berlin and called on Pilli Körner to ask about the fate of his brother and sister-in-law. Körner explained that he could not say anything, whereupon Wolfgang asked to see Göring. Körner replied "God no! The Reichsmarschall is not reachable. Everything is chaotic here. It is best to do nothing, otherwise you will only endanger your family."[243] Sophia therefore decided to contact Emmy Göring to see if she could help with information. The wife of the Reichsmarschall responded that she did not know where Philipp and Mafalda were, but that her husband did, and he "was not permitted to speak about it."[244] Emmy Göring tried to be reassuring, saying that her husband was supposedly looking for a villa for Mafalda, and that when he found one, he would contact Sophia and she could bring the children there. When General Taubert visited the following month, Sophia and the Landgravine told what they had learned, and Taubert reported, "Göring could only say provisionally that Princess M. and her husband were doing well."[245] Taubert also observed that despite the assurances that he and the Görings had given, "both ladies are wracking their brains" (*zerbrechen sich den Kopf* or literally, "breaking their heads") because they could not understand why the whereabouts of Philipp and Mafalda was being kept so secret.

Cast into a state of anxious ignorance regarding Philipp and Mafalda, the rest of the family worked to console and support one another. This was especially the case for the women in the family. Princess Alice, Sophia's mother, for example, visited Kronberg in the spring of 1944: she wrote her son, Prince Philip, "I went to Tiny, who is so brave when she is with her children and us, being her usual self and making jokes but her hours in her room alone are hardly to be endured. . . . I never suffered after 'the accident' [the 1937 Hesse-Darmstadt family air crash] as I did those three weeks with Tiny and I certainly will never forget them as long as I live. Her children are perfectly adorable, you would love them, and the new baby is too sweet for words."[246] Alice was able to travel back and forth from Greece to Germany while Greece was under Nazi occupation, but this situation ended in October 1944 and Alice was left in Greece, cut off from Sophia and her other daughters. Most family members, however, headed to Kronberg.

War's End for Philipp

In mid-April 1945, Philipp's year-and-a-half of "harrowing solitary confinement" in Flossenbürg came to an end, but that did not mean freedom.[247] The Nazi government ordered his transfer from Flossenbürg to Dachau, and this was accomplished by way of a green police transport wagon—or in Berliner jargon, a *Grüne Minna*. He was accompanied by von Schlabrendorff and several other prominent prisoners, and from then on, had contact with others until liberated. After the war, certain witnesses who saw him in Dachau came forward and related their impressions of Philipp: one priest characterized him as "deeply religious"—which was peculiar considering his own self-characterizations.[248] Another inmate thought he "seemed to have taken the hard lot of imprisonment with manly bravery."[249] Nonetheless, while in Dachau, Philipp suffered an attack of faintness, and thereafter was badly treated by the camp authorities.[250] But he was fortunate not to remain in Dachau for long—he was there for only ten days. The first of the Nazis' concentration camps had been flooded with prisoners —a number coming from camps in the East like Auschwitz—and the overcrowding, combined with an acute food shortage, made it a terribly lethal place: over a hundred people died there each day, "with fully half of all documented deaths in the camp occurring in the last six months before liberation."[251] He had also been fortunate to avoid execution at Flossenbürg, unlike Dietrich Bonhoeffer, Wilhelm Canaris, and Hans Oster, who, on 9 April 1945, "had been led out naked to the gallows" and killed by slow strangulation.[252] Philipp was clearly aware of the danger he faced: as Canaris's biographer Heinz Höhne noted, "Prince Philipp von Hessen, another inmate, saw the dead man's clothes lying in a heap in the guardroom, together with Canaris's final choice of reading material, Ernst Kantorwicz's biography of Emperor Frederick II. . . ."[253]

Philipp, like many of the prominent prisoners, was transferred quickly and repeatedly from camp to camp. To take another example, Fey von Hassell recalled being in Poland, East Prussia, Württemberg, Dachau, and then several camps in the Alps—all in an eight-month period. She ended up in the same group as Prince Philipp in the South Tyrol, in a town called Villabassa (known in German as Niederdorf).[254] They, the prominent, were guarded by SS men who moved them about in trucks in an effort to avoid enemy units. While the British Foreign Office described the 120–30 prisoners as being in a "concentration camp" (they placed it at the nearby town at Dobbiaco), this obscures the way the prisoners were kept in transit.[255] Among the illustrious prisoners were former Austrian chancellor Kurt von Schuschnigg (who had been in Buchenwald with Mafalda), Hjalmar Schacht, Prince Friedrich Leopold von Preussen, the son of Admiral Horthy (deposed Regent of Hungary), ex-French premier Léon

Blum, Prince Xavier de Bourbon-Parma, Fritz Thyssen, Dr. Josef Müller (a confidant of Pope Pius XII and head of the Bavarian Catholic Party), Countess Nina Schenck von Stauffenberg and several of her family members, as well as members of the Goerdeler family. Indeed, there were a large number of children and siblings imprisoned as part of the Sippenhaft measures. The stress of incarceration and constant relocation forged bonds among the prisoners: Philipp even became acquainted with certain British prisoners, including Captain Sigismund Payne-Best, one of the intelligence officers captured by Schellenberg in November 1939 in the Venlo affair.[256] While Philipp made at least one friend while imprisoned with the prominent, he was viewed with a certain trepidation by others. He was known to have been a Nazi and a friend of Hitler's and Göring's. Fey von Hassell remarked in an understated way, "I was surprised to encounter Prince Philipp of Hesse in that particular crowd."[257] An element of pity entered in to the way people viewed him because of Mafalda's tragic fate. Certain other prisoners had learned of her death before Philipp did: Fey von Hassell recalled, "I did not have the heart to tell him of her sad end. I just shook my head, leaving the unpleasant task to someone else."[258]

While the prisoners were better treated than those in other camps, they had their own harrowing experiences. Fey von Hassell reported the general sense of fear among the prominent prisoners as the convoy of buses crisscrossed the Alps. They were in one of the last parts of the Reich to be conquered, and rumors were rife that fanatical Nazis would establish an "Alpine redoubt" to continue the fight—by way of guerilla tactics if necessary.[259] Anthony Cave Brown wrote about vague orders to kill them "if it seemed they would be liberated by the Allies." He continued, "at last they came to Villabassa, a village in the north Italian Dolomites, where it seemed that [the SS-Second Lieutenant (Untersturmführer) Edgar] Stiller must at last execute his order. The party was surrounded in the hills above by red-kerchiefed Partisans, and the advance guard of the U.S. Army was in the valley below. But Stiller did not execute his orders. Payne-Best offered him life, liberty, and a little gold if he could delay. This he did. . . ."[260] While it is unlikely that Payne-Best would have had access to gold after five years in German custody, and the role of the partisans remains unclear, there was a dramatic conclusion to the imprisonment of the *Prominenten*: regular units of the German Army confronted the SS guards and forced them to hand over the prisoners. This encounter was fraught with danger and could have turned deadly. However, the SS units gave way to the German soldiers, who in turn surrendered to American units in the region on 4 May 1945.[261] World War II ended in Europe several days later.

Because there were so many British inmates, His Majesty's government took an active interest in interviewing and processing the illustrious prisoners (their liberation was front-page news in British papers on

8 May 1945).[262] One report from G. W. Harrison of the Foreign Office read:

> I have said we would deal with the famous separately. I don't think we can deal with these people on an individual basis, but must try to classify them. . . . I suggest our reply might be: we consider high military officers and officials should be held for the time being, especially those like General Falkenhausen who may be required as war criminals; it will also be desirable to hold temporarily political (Schacht) and social (Prince Frederick of Prussia, Prince Philipp of Hesse) figures. The rest can, so far as we are concerned be returned to Germany subject to intelligence requirements.[263]

This memorandum elicited a response from John Wheeler-Bennett, then working for the Political Intelligence Department in the Foreign Office in London, who agreed with Harrison's suggestions, and noted explicitly, "I would also be in favor of holding Prince Frederick Leopold of Prussia and Prince Philipp of Hesse. The rest could well be returned to Germany after interrogation."[264] The British made a list suggesting fates for different prisoners; for Schacht, Philipp, and a few others, they recommended that they "be held as prominent political figures and might, for convenience sake, eventually be transferred to the [Supreme Headquarters Allied Expeditionary Force's (SHAEF)] special camp. The remainder should be carefully screened. . . ."[265]

Philipp was transferred to a series of facilities set up by the SHAEF, starting with one near the High Command in Naples. All the prominent figures from the group were sent there. In Fey von Hassell's words, "The Allies wished to know exactly whom they were freeing and whom they might detain."[266] The von Stauffenbergs and von Schuschniggs were released immediately. Philipp continued to be held with the other German officers and political figures on the nearby island of Capri—not far from the house that he had owned with Mafalda. One can imagine Philipp in these familiar environs, reflecting back on better times. At least he was afforded nice accommodations, as Philip and the other internees were quartered at the Hotel Paradiso Eden, "a beautiful spot, up in the village of Anacapri, with splendid views over the blue Mediterranean."[267] It was an intriguing place to hold interrogations; perhaps reflecting the hope that it would put the prisoners in positive, cooperative frames of mind (it also had the practical advantage of being so near to headquarters). The Americans focused on affairs in Italy, including information pertaining to the communist threat, the Vatican, and former Nazis trying to flee.[268] After officials in Capri were done with him, Philipp was sent to another interrogation center across the Continent at Chateau de Chatenay near Paris.[269] But this also proved temporary, and he ended up in ASHCAN (Allied Supreme Headquarters for Axis Nationals) on 6 July 1945. ASHCAN, which was located in the

Palace Hotel in Mondorf-les-Bains, Luxembourg, held fifty-two high-ranking figures from the Nazi regime and the military; in the summer of 1945, this included Göring, Speer, and Ribbentrop, among others.[270] They were treated fairly severely; as one American observer reported, "civilians in this camp, which has the perhaps not inappropriate code name of 'ASHCAN,' have had their neckties, belts, suspenders and shoe laces taken away in order to prevent attempts at suicide."[271] Prince Philipp therefore endured more questioning—this time by Counter Intelligence Corps (CIC) units—as they pursued investigations of potential war criminals.[272] This would be the last time that Philipp would see Göring face to face. There is no extant record of their conversations, and one can only imagine what the prince said to the man who had been so instrumental in enlisting him to the Nazi cause and then abandoned him after 1943.

The frequent transfers continued, and Philipp was sent back to Germany: first, in August 1945, to Wiesbaden, where he was housed in the Villa von Bergen with other prominent prisoners (including Dönitz, Ritter von Epp, and Schwerin von Krosigk). In early autumn, he was transferred to the Counter Intelligence Corps Camp 96 at Allensdorf near the Hessian university town of Marburg, and then on to a camp called Butzbach (the site of a state prison). The Allies' facilities clearly represented a dramatic improvement over what he had experienced before war's end. Although the Butzbach camp did not compare to the hotel in Capri, it at least featured art exhibitions, including one where "handicrafts by the prince [were] exhibited."[273] Still, Philipp was sorely disappointed to go from incarceration by the Nazis to "internment" by the Allies. He was permitted, for example, to write only one letter per month.[274] In early 1946, he was sent to an internment camp at Darmstadt, where he was to remain with only a few short breaks for almost two years.

The Americans arrived at Kronberg on 29 March 1945 and began the process of determining the fate of those still in the Schloss. The first troops present were members of an African-American tank-repair unit (whom the estate manager Lange described as *Kolonialtruppen*); they occupied the stables in the Marstall.[275] Other soldiers from General Patton's Third Army followed; on 12 April they ordered that Friedrichshof be cleared out, which largely entailed moving out the metal collections company, an operation that had been deemed essential to the war effort and had been relocated there from Frankfurt late in the war. On 19 April 1945, the Americans ordered the Hessens out of not only Schloss Friedrichshof but also the cottage and all the neighboring buildings in the park. Landgravine Margarethe, Princess Sophia, and the others—including the many children (four from Philipp and Mafalda and five from Christoph and Sophia)—were "given the customary notice that they must leave . . . in four hours and could only take with them food and clothing."[276]

This order created a dilemma and the Landgravine, who was quite ill with "double pneumonia," refused to vacate the premises. When she refused to leave her upstairs bedroom in the cottage, an American soldier overseeing the handover reportedly responded, "If that old girl does not come down at once, I'll go up and shoot her."[277] The Landgravine relented, and after an odyssey in several houses in the neighborhood, she looked to move to the house occupied by Heinrich Lange, just beyond the grounds of the estate. Even though she owned the house, this proved difficult because Lange had given refuge to another homeless family, and he himself refused to leave (the fact that Lange had been opposed to the Nazis and saw that the time of reckoning had come may also have entered into the dynamic). Emotions were charged for all involved, in particular Landgravine Margarethe and Princess Sophia. Lange recalled, "Princess Christoph became very agitated and declared in tears that she bore responsibility for these measures, since the [adult] princes weren't there."[278] Previously, on 7 April 1945, representatives of the CIC arrived and arrested Prince Auwi, who as of February had left Berlin and taken refuge with his cousins. On the twelfth, the Americans had arrested Prince Wolfgang (both he and Auwi were sent to a series of internment camps).[279] The Landgravine and Sophia therefore ended up relying on the help of neighbors and friends, including the Kiep family, whose young son Walter Leisler Kiep, became a prominent political figure in the Federal Republic. The Hessen matriarchs and the children were therefore dispersed to a number of different homes.

For the Hessens, giving up Schloss Friedrichshof, a place so tied to their identity and with so many memories, was a bitter experience. Even before they left, discovering the African-American troops roasting their peacocks on a rotisserie over a spit soured their mood. According to Landgrave Moritz, the Americans also burned papers they found, as they ignited a bonfire in the courtyard.[280] This would have been highly irregular and a violation of standing orders, which aimed to preserve documents as evidence against Nazis and war criminals. There is no doubt that the American troops ravaged the Hessens' wine cellar and also immediately began taking "souvenirs," but the intentional destruction of documents remains difficult to confirm.[281] It bears mentioning that Prince Heinrich recalled burying all the "political books" in March 1945.[282] It is not inconceivable that the family also took steps to conceal sensitive papers. Subsequently, Schloss Friedrichshof was turned into an American officers' club.

Many members of the House of Hesse suffered losses during and after the war. Philipp's twin brother Wolfgang, who was nominally in charge of the House in Philipp's absence, lost his wife, Princess Marie-Alexandra, when she and seven other women who were aid-workers for the NS-Frauenschaft were killed in a bomb attack on Frankfurt on 29–30 January 1944. The cellar in which they had taken refuge collapsed under the weight of the building, rendering Marie-Alexandra scarcely recognizable. Wolfgang's uncle, Landgrave Alexander Friedrich, also had his Frankfurt home destroyed in October 1944.[283] The latter, the blind composer, died on 26 March 1945; his funeral was disrupted by advancing American troops when the cortege and mourners were forced to the side of the road to make room for the tanks.

In terms of other property damage, Schloss Rumpenheim, near Offenbach on the Main River where Philipp was born and which he described as "charming" (*wunderhübsches*) was bombed out in 1943.[284] Schloss Fasanerie near Fulda, now rebuilt and the site of the family museum and archives, was struck and badly damaged by American bombers, who mistakenly believed rumors that the Germans had concealed a munitions factory there. Most of the two-hundred bombs that were dropped missed the Schloss and landed in the park, but all the windows were blown out and the roof was largely destroyed.[285] The Church of St. Martin in Kassel, which held the tombs of the ruling Landgraves of Hessen was also destroyed—obliterating the graves as well.[286] Most of the Landgrave Museum in the Palais Bellevue complex was also destroyed in the 22 October 1943 raid that killed over six thousand people in Kassel (Prince Heinrich was in the shelter of the Palais, while Prince Moritz was serving on a flak battery outside the city—both witnessed the devastation as 444 British Lancaster bombers turned the streets into a sea of liquid phosphorous).[287] Some of the Hessens' art was also plundered—that is, aside from the thefts from Schloss Friedrichshof. The Hesse-Darmstadt branch had taken a great deal of property to their Silesian castle Fischbach, which was overrun by the Soviet Red Army. The conquerors managed, for example, to carry off Peter Paul Rubens's painting of Tarquinius and Lucretia, and it has remained in a Russian repository for more than half a century. It is part of what the Germans call *Beutekunst* (trophy art) and is the subject of ongoing negotiations between German and Russian authorities.[288] Beyond the Soviets' depredations, the Hesse-Darmstadt family lost a great deal more than this: most notably, in the words of their friend Tatiana Metternich, "The city of Darmstadt and the Hessian Schloss in its middle with its valuable collections was totally destroyed shortly before the end of the war."[289] The Neue Palais, where Prince Philipp had lived while at university, was also among the family's properties flattened by the RAF.[290] The Princes von Hessen-Darmstadt had believed that their ties to the British royal family would help protect the city (and they later pondered what might have happened if Lord Louis Mountbatten had not been stationed far away in Burma). But they too quickly recognized that such hopes had been naïve; Commander Sir Arthur Harris and his colleagues fine-tuned their fire-bombing techniques on the hitherto unscathed city.

The aftermath of the 22 October 1943 RAF bombing raid on Kassel, where more than six thousand residents of the city perished.

With regard to other branches of the family, Prince Wilhelm von Hessen-Philippsthal-Barchfeld, an SS officer and cousin of Philipp and Christoph, died in combat on the Eastern Front on 30 April 1942.[291] While he was somewhat older than a typical combatant—thirty-seven when he fell in action with Seventh Company at Wyasma in the Soviet Union—he was clearly vigorous and had spent two years with a motorcycle regiment attached to the notable Second Panzer Division. This division had participated in the invasions of Poland and France (they were the first to reach the Atlantic and helped encircle the Anglo-French forces at Dunkirk); subsequently, they fought in Greece and Romania.[292] Prince Wilhelm received the Iron Cross in June of 1940. While we know little of his wartime experiences, he participated in intense fighting on several fronts: the Second Panzer Division had advanced to within twenty-five kilometers of Moscow before being driven back by the Red Army's counteroffensive. Prince Wilhelm and his motorcycle regiment were part of Army Group Center in the spring of 1942; stationed about 150 kilometers east of Moscow. Because Hitler had ordered the major German offensive to take place in the South—the push into the oil-rich areas of the southern USSR—the lines around Moscow were relatively quiet at this time. The dangers in the area, however, remained considerable: one wartime diarist recalled his experiences in the region west of Moscow at the time Prince Wilhelm fell in the spring of 1942: in Minsk, he "saw much war suffering"; their train was attacked by partisans; and in the town of Rzhev, "dirt, misery, hunger and typhoid were there."[293] Prince Wilhelm's son, Prince Hermann von Hessen, writes that his father died during an attack; in other words, despite the absence of a major offensive, the Germans were still attempting to push the front eastward. Prince Hermann also notes that his mother, Princess Marianne, was widowed at age twenty-nine with three children under the age of ten.[294]

The Hohenzollern also suffered greatly during and after the war. Besides the deaths of the ex-Kaiser's grandsons, Princes Oskar and Wilhelm (who fell in combat), the Kaiser's second oldest son, Prince Eitel Friedrich, died of an illness at his villa in Potsdam on 8 December 1942: he was just fifty-nine. Hitler had prohibited a funeral with military honors (the generals and other officers attended in civilian clothes).[295] The Kaiser's widow, Princess Hermine, was captured in 1944 by the Red Army in Silesia. She had moved to the East after her husband's death and "perished in poorly explained circumstances in Frankfurt an der Oder in 1949."[296] Historian Giles Macdonogh noted, "she was the only one [of the family] to be caught in the East, but both Auwi and the crown prince [Wilhelm] died, their spirits broken by their experiences of internment."[297] Auwi, according to his sister Viktoria Luise, spent four years in a total of thirty-three different places of confinement; he died on 25 March 1949, his health weakened by his imprisonment as he lost weight and strength.[298] Crown Prince Wilhelm, who was captured by the French, had also become a pathetic figure, as a French general noted when the prince complained about the lack of "acceptable dwelling places." General Jean de Lattre de Tassigny reportedly responded, "You have lost above all, monsieur, the sense of dignity. After the collapse of your country . . . you have no other interest than your own comfort, the house of your idle hours, and the woman of your pleasures. You are to be pitied, monsieur, that is really all I have to say to you."[299] Wilhelm survived into the postwar period by "selling one picture after another from the possession of the Prussian royal house." He took up with a younger woman, a hairdresser named Stefi Ritl, at times living in a villa in Switzerland and at times in a five-room house near the Hohenzollern *Burg* in Hechingen.[300] But his comportment elicited "shock and dismay" among many family members and royal observers.[301] The last Hohenzollern crown prince died at age sixty-nine in June 1951.

Many of the German princely families suffered greatly during World War II. They endured a series of blows that they perceived as an almost sustained assault. But the start of their misfortunes was not 1933, as has often been maintained. While certain princes were at odds with the Nazis from the outset of the Third Reich, they were a distinct minority. Rather, significant mutual disaffection with the Nazi regime began during the war. There was no one event or action that signaled the advent of this process; rather there were a series of decisions that combined to form a critical mass. Early on, one can point to the Germans' assault against princes and aristocrats during the conquest of Poland. The expropriation of property and the rhetoric of class warfare, while grounded in a desire to eradicate Polish national identity (and sovereignty), contributed to certain ideas and stereotypes that were developed in the broader struggle against princes. (It is worth noting that, to this day, many of the accoutrements of the Polish royal family, including most of the royal insignia embroidered into pillows or the backings of furniture, have never been recovered. They were ripped out by German troops as they conquered the country.[302]) Similarly, though not in as destructive manner, the Dutch royal family had most of its property seized upon a directive from Reichskommissar Arthur Seyss-Inquart.[303] Clearly, the struggle between princes and the Nazi leaders evolved and intensified with time. The mistrust of Hitler and his cohorts was the key factor in this growing enmity. If the Nazis had not turned against the princes, the vast majority, with their traditions of loyalty and honor, as well as their strong antipathy to Bolshevism, would have fought until the bitter end.

One irony is that the decrees that removed princes from the army, state, and Nazi Party—measures that they usually viewed as discriminatory— also helped many survive. These policies actually offered the princes a measure of protection in that they avoided combat during the period when German losses soared. This, however, was small consolation. Many were utterly devastated by the experiences of being declared traitors, suffering vilification in the Nazi press, enduring incarceration, discovering the destruction of their property, undergoing the conquest of their country, and then being viewed by the Allies as a root cause of this catastrophe. Although most princes would fall somewhere in the gray zone between innocence and culpability in terms of what transpired during the Third Reich, many also indisputably experienced great hardship.

7

Postwar Justice:
Denazification and (Partial)
Dispossession

Prince Philipp's difficulties continued after the end of hostilities. In the spring of 1945, he had "been promptly arrested" by the Americans because, as the former governor of Hesse, he had ranked as number 53 among the most wanted Nazis.[1] After a tour of various Allied interrogation centers, he was sent to a series of Allied internment camps, culminating in early 1946 with the civilian internment enclosure at Darmstadt—a facility that housed a number of other important (but still second-rank) officials from the Third Reich, including Prince Auwi, former Kassel Gauleiter Karl Weinrich, and, until his escape in July 1948, SS-commando Otto Skorzeny. All told, Prince Philipp was in twenty-two different camps, his brother Wolfgang reported.[2] Philipp continued to be periodically interrogated by the Counter Intelligence Corps, as well as IMT prosecutor Robert Kempner (1899–1993). The Americans' treatment of him varied: on the one hand, the prince was again a privileged prisoner and permitted periodic furloughs to visit his four children and family; yet, on the other hand, the interrogations involved brusque and challenging questions where the quiet and sensitive man was often browbeaten. The Americans held him responsible for a range of events: including helping bring Hitler to power, convincing Mussolini to accept the Anschluss, and facilitating the murders at Hadamar. Philipp went through denazification at a court convened inside the Darmstadt internment camp. He mustered considerable support, with letters on his behalf from figures such as Martin Niemöller, Hitler's adjutant Julius Schaub, Foreign Ministry state secretary and ambassador to the

Vatican Dr. Ernst von Weizsäcker, and Walter Schellenberg, the chief of the SD intelligence division who attempted to woo the Windsors.[3] Philipp faced various serious charges as the prosecutors requested that he be classified as a "major offender"—Category I. At the same time, a criminal court in Frankfurt was collecting evidence on the charge of murder in connection with his authority over the Hadamar sanatorium.

To add to Philipp's troubles, during his incarceration, the Americans had occupied his family's castle at Kronberg near Frankfurt and turned the magnificent Schloss into an officers' club. Being forced out of Friedrichshof had been a traumatic experience for family members, but most had reassembled at Wolfsgarten near Darmstadt to stay with Prince Ludwig and his wife, Princess Peg. They were joined here by other refugees, including a number of aristocrats from the East who had fled the advancing Red Army (Paul and Tatiana Metternich arrived after abandoning their castle in Bohemia).[4] Princess Cecilie von Preussen (1917–75), the youngest daughter of Crown Prince Wilhelm, also took refuge there, where she was to meet her future husband, an American Monuments, Fine Arts, and Archives officer, who came to investigate the theft of jewels from Schloss Friedrichshof.[5] Kronberg was the repository of many kinds of valuables—especially because the family had consolidated property there from other residences damaged or threatened by war. The British were particularly interested in the letters between the Hessens and the British royal family, and sent not only the Royal Archivist Sir Owen Morshead to secure documents at war's end but also art historian/spy Anthony Blunt. There was little abatement in the drama of the Hessens' lives from the Third Reich to the early postwar years.

Philipp as Prisoner of the Americans

Prince Philipp, like many other former Nazi officials, was initially uncertain about how he would be treated by the Allies. For starters, interrogators varied widely in terms of their expertise and temperament. Philipp's son Heinrich recalled one episode in 1945: An American asked the castellan at Schloss Adolphseck near Fulda, What's the name of this place? When the castellan responded that he was at Schloss Adolphseck, the American queried, "Adolf, because of Adolf Hitler?" The castellan explained "no, the Schloss belonged to the Princes of Hessen"; to which the American asked, "Hess—as in Rudolf Hess?"[6] The Hessens, then, knew early on that the arrival of the Allies would bring difficulties. Later, as Philipp sat in his tent in the Darmstadt camp, he could envision very different paths and outcomes. He was fairly certain that he would not be included in the trial of the major war criminals by the IMT; he had not achieved such stature in the

Nazi regime. But it was disconcerting to be repeatedly interrogated by American prosecutor to the IMT Robert Kempner. Philipp also knew that plans were afoot for the subsequent trials in Nuremberg: of the Foreign Office, industrialists, *Einsatzgruppen* leaders, Hadamar employees, and so forth. It was not inconceivable that he would face a trial in a highly visible—and humiliating—venue. At the other end of the spectrum, he imagined quick exoneration and release; the Americans would certainly realize that he had been opposed to many Nazi policies and that he and his wife had suffered terribly.

He was given hope for the second option by the relatively lenient treatment he received in the Darmstadt camp, although this was a huge and in many ways bewildering facility—especially once it was transformed from a POW camp to a civilian enclosure in February 1946.[7] His twin-brother Wolfgang estimated that there were approximately twenty thousand inmates there at one point, and he described how former SS men formed a kind of self-proclaimed police force that imposed order.[8] When Philipp arrived at the Darmstadt camp in 1946, he was weak and demoralized, and the cold of the winter caused him great difficulty. But he soon rallied, in part thanks to the presence of Wolfgang, their cousin Prince Auwi, and certain friends, including Carl Radl, a former subordinate of Otto Skorzeny who had helped spring Mussolini in 1943.[9] One person who served time in Allied captivity and knew the prince recalled, "especially striking was that in the camps Allensdorf, Butzbach, and also Darmstadt, the prince was often with painters, sculptors, and other artistic types, with whom he cultivated contact. The prince said that in the future he wanted only to be involved with the arts. My impression was that it would make him happy if in the future he could be active as a patron of the arts."[10] In the Darmstadt camp, the inmates were given musical instruments, which they used to perform concerts, while others staged operettas and plays. However surreal it was to see former members of the SS dressed in drag singing the female parts of *The Merry Widow*, it helped pass the time and lift Philipp's spirits.[11]

There were continual efforts to arrange Prince Philipp's release. One document from the U.S. CIC noted how Prince Lu and Princess Peg were "very active in attempt to free Philipp from U.S. internment, [as] was Ulrich Noah, friend of family and frequent guest at Wolfsgarten."[12] A fellow inmate in Darmstadt recalled in 1946, "I can remember that at the beginning of this year, a high-ranking officer of the American military government, who supposedly came upon the intervention of the king of England, spoke with the prince in a visit that lasted almost two hours, in contrast to customary practices."[13] Queen Elena of Italy also wrote on behalf of her son-in-law, asking the Americans to release him if only as a courtesy to his children.[14] The Bishop of Limburg echoed this plea for leniency because of the children: "After the death of his wife, Princess

Mafalda in the concentration camp, I would especially like to support the release of the father in the interest of the children, who have had to suffer fearful conditions."[15] Pastor Martin Niemöller also weighed in and tried to help, writing an appeal from Schloss Büdingen in Hesse.[16]

Philipp's situation, however, was hardly dire. His cousin, Princess Peg, noted at the time, "In the civilian internment enclosure in Darmstadt, it wasn't so bad." He could walk around as he pleased. He was permitted in late 1945 to visit his children and other family members for a "one day holiday from incarceration."[17] He received similar consideration the following Christmas in 1946, when he enjoyed an eight-day furlough to visit his family at nearby Schloss Wolfsgarten.[18] The children were faring as well as could be expected: Moritz spent the difficult postwar years working on a farm, and Heinrich pursued his school diploma (Abitur) in Biberstein near Fulda. The younger two remained with Prince Lu and his wife Peg.[19] Because of his family and friends, Philipp had reason for optimism. One of the judicial boards reviewing his case met in August 1946 and the three judges unanimously ruled, "release from incarceration is recommended."[20] His brother Richard was let out of an internment camp in Bavaria in the summer of 1946 and his twin, Wolfgang, was released on their fiftieth birthday, 6 November 1946.[21]

Despite these encouraging signals, Philipp remained interned by the Americans. A 20 December 1947 appeal on Philipp's behalf from his attorney von Schlabrendorff elicited a response three days later from the director of the military government in Hesse, James Newman, "I find it difficult to overlook the benefits which this man derived from 13 years of undeviating pro-Nazi activity and consider an emotional appeal on his behalf today. To my mind comes instead, the thought of the countless men, women, and children, who as a result of that war will never be able to enjoy another Christmas. I can find no justifiable reason for granting your request. The case of Prince Philipp of Hesse will be handled in its proper time in accordance with the procedure applicable to all internees at the Darmstadt camp."[22] Newman, like many among the occupation forces, believed it important to establish an administration that functioned according to the rule of law and avoided preferential treatment.

It had quickly become clear to Philipp that he was viewed by the Allies as knowledgeable about, and thus possibly implicated in, the crimes of the Nazi regime. While held in the Darmstadt camp, Philipp was required to appear as a witness in a series of trials. For example, he was called as a witness at the Flossenbürg trial, which was held in the American-occupied camp at Dachau in June 1946.[23] The most remarkable aspect of Philipp's testimony was not that he reported on the executions of Admiral Canaris, Dietrich Bonhoeffer, and others who had been killed near his cell, but that he appeared as a witness for the defense—and in particular, three SS guards

whom he had encountered there. He recalled, for example, a guard named
Mohr whom, he claimed, "always treated me well. Mohr always showed
a friendly conduct towards me and proved himself to be a good natured
man with a good heart."[24] Later, he testified, "I saw prisoners working on
the slope of the hill. These people worked extraordinarily slowly. And I saw
that once in a while, very seldom, they were incited to work. But there were
no forms of coercion, no assault and battery used to make them work."[25]
While Philipp admitted that he heard the crack of guns during executions
and that he frequently saw corpses dragged by his window, all the guards
he encountered appeared to be decent, and indeed friendly, souls. It was
curious, remarkable testimony. One can only speculate as to his reasons
for his sympathetic feelings toward his captors. He had undoubtedly come
to appreciate that he was a special prisoner and had not endured physical
suffering comparable to other inmates. Perhaps more importantly, at the
time of the trial, he was an inmate in the Darmstadt camp and was facing
a judicial inquiry of his own—both denazification and a murder charge
stemming from his role regarding the Hadamar facility. One can imagine
that he viewed himself as a good person caught up with malevolent associates and that this gave rise to sympathies for these guards, people whom
he thought had also been placed in a difficult environment. Whatever the
motivation behind his views, the prince's comments astonished observers.[26]
His testimony also appeared to lack credibility: two of the guards were
sentenced to death, and the third received a twenty-year sentence—harsh
verdicts indeed.

     While Prince Philipp's testimony at the Flossenbürg trial was surprising
and in many ways generous with respect to his former captors, he faced a
different situation when called as a witness in the Hadamar trial. As noted
earlier, a court in Frankfurt had initiated an investigation into his role in the
T-4 killings, and he was no longer recalling his time spent as a prisoner.
After all, in theory, Philipp as Oberpräsident "retained ultimate responsibility for state institutions under his jurisdiction," and this included
Hadamar.[27] With three of the seven defendants in the first Hadamar trial
of 1945 having been sentenced "to be hanged by the neck until dead," the
seriousness of his situation was not lost on Philipp.[28] While Philipp did
not testify in the first Hadamar trial, which occurred in Wiesbaden, he
was questioned in subsequent proceedings—especially in connection with
the Hadamar trial held in Frankfurt in the spring of 1947. Philipp appeared
in court on 6 March 1947—again having been transferred from the
Darmstadt internment camp—and he told of his ignorance while signing
the transfer agreement in February 1941. He also reported his protests to
Reichsleiter Bouhler and his conversation with Hitler.[29] The authorities
by and large believed him and assigned responsibility to others, including

Fritz Bernotat, who was tried in absentia. Separate charges against Philipp in connection with Hadamar were not pursued.

Another interesting episode occurred when Philipp gave testimony against his former rival, Gauleiter Karl Weinrich, who faced a denazification trial in 1949.[30] Philipp had a long history of differences with the defendant, and this testimony was an opportunity to voice many of his grievances. But it was not only an opportunity to make sure that Weinrich received fittingly harsh punishment; it was also a chance for Philipp to show that he opposed the party radicals and their actions during the Third Reich. In short, Philipp gave damning testimony about Gauleiter Weinrich, especially with regard to personal corruption and the persecution of Jews.[31] On 1 February 1950, a German court declared Weinrich to be a major offender and sentenced him to seven years imprisonment in a labor camp (although he was released by state authorities on 31 October of that year). In the scheme of denazification in the Federal Republic, this constituted severe punishment.

In the spring of 1947, at the outset of his denazification trial, Philipp was called to Nuremberg to be interrogated as part of the so-called Wilhelmstrasse trial of Nazi Foreign Ministry officials. German-American jurist Robert Kempner carried out the questioning, and the transcripts of their sessions were subsequently entered into evidence at Philipp's own trial.[32] At times, the exchanges were very pointed. Kempner, for example, responded to the claim by Philipp, that he was just a messenger who on two occasions passed letters on to Mussolini. Kempner challenged him, "Listen, Prince Philipp, the son-in-law of the king of Italy is no mere courier." When Philipp protested, "but it really was so," Kempner responded, "do me a favor and don't say—like *Herr* Lammers—that I was only a postman. A great-grandson of Queen Victoria is no postman. A nephew of [Kaiser] Wilhelm II is no postman."[33] When Kempner finished the last of the May 1947 sessions, he provided the prince pencil and paper and instructed him to write an essay, "[H]ow I gradually recognized the criminal nature of the Hitler regime's domestic and foreign policies." He added, "I would like you to write it from another point of view. In the denazification trial you have marshaled a great deal of evidence in your defense. I don't want that. . . . I want it from an educated man, viewed historically. Free yourself from the defendant's complex."[34] Philipp wrote the account, although he continued to be defensive, and there was nothing new in this rendition of events. Despite the spirited exchanges where neither side conceded much, Kempner found Philipp to be sympathetic and suggested as much in the books he published later.[35]

Regardless of his somewhat preferential treatment in the Darmstadt camp, Philipp was often miserable. One contemporary referred to him as, "the problem child of the camp doctor"; and added, "he was in the sick bay and the hospital on many occasions. I had the impression that he suffered extraordinarily in body and soul from the years of incarceration."[36] Princess Peg von Hessen-Darmstadt noted after visiting him that Philipp "outwardly looks well and seems unchanged . . . , but the death of his wife under such gruesome circumstances have greatly shaken him inwardly, if not fully ground him down. A freedom-loving artistic nature, of course, suffers from years-long imprisonment more than that of an average person."[37]

With all his troubles, Philipp exhibited minimal interests in politics. Indeed, he refused to discuss politics with others in the camp. This may have been part of his effort to gain his release, because the question of whether he would be a political threat was one of the first posed by Allied authorities. However, Philipp never again involved himself publicly in politics. When German authorities were investigating Philipp, and contemplating his release, they concluded, "almost all questioned sources and people have answered no to the question whether the release of the prince today [1946] would stand in the way of the political development in Germany and in the affairs of the Allies."[38] As was the custom in the denazification trials that took place in western Germany, numerous people provided *Persilscheine*: statements where they testified to the concerned party's commendable behavior and political harmlessness (the word came from the best-selling laundry detergent in Germany, *Persil*, and offered a wordplay on "*reingewaschen*" or being "washed clean"). Despite these interventions by a range of influential friends and family members, and the widespread feelings of sympathy for a man imprisoned by both the Nazis and the Allies, Philipp did not receive an early release. A retired provincial court president named Dr. Karl Anton Schulte was appointed as trustee of the Hessen property. A former member of the Center Party, Dr. Schulte was allegedly tough on members of the family: Prince Heinrich, for example, claimed that he was given only one room in Schloss Adolphseck in which to live and to paint (even though the castle contained over a hundred), and that he was forbidden to set foot in other parts of the residence or to entertain guests.[39] Schulte told him to stop being so lazy—that he should get a real job—and expressed the opinion that the Hessische Hausstiftung should be nationalized. The Hessens were prohibited from disposing of any of their assets and even had to request funds, including pocket money, from Dr. Schulte. In September 1946, Schulte entered a statement to the board in charge of Prince Philipp's denazification: "if one considers today the large number of those incarcerated in the American internment camps, among whom are thousands who had comparatively low-ranking and unimportant positions . . . one must say that the release of Philipp would not be understandable."[40]

Prince Philipp's Denazification

In January 1947, eight tribunals operated in the Civilian Internment Enclosure (CIE) 91 in Darmstadt. Those bodies were responsible for "denazifying" some five thousand internees according to a document contemporaneous with the start of Prince Philipp's case.[41] The 5 March 1946 Law for the Liberation from National Socialism and Militarism had put the West Germans in charge of denazification, and they, in turn, provided the personnel for panels (Spruchkammer). The Americans, who retained supervisory authority, were eager for the trial to commence and made specific requests "that the Prince of Hesse be tried immediately."[42] On a more general level, the Americans initially tried to keep a watchful eye on the Germans as they embarked on a review of fellow nationals—a vigilance that dissipated within several years. In this specific case, the Americans monitored the proceedings carefully and indicated a concern that the illustrious local prince might get off with inappropriately lenient treatment.

As it turned out, there was little reason to be concerned about an overly lenient denazification trial. The German prosecution filed charges placing him in the highest category of offenders: on the five-tiered scale, with one being the most severe and five signifying exoneration, the prosecution sought to place him in Category I as a "major offender" (*Hauptschuldiger*). They pointed to his posts and honors—Oberpräsident, SA-Obergruppenführer, bearer of the Golden Party Badge, and so forth— as well as his activities both on the domestic and foreign policy fronts.[43] Their rationale for the weighty charges also cast an eye to the future, as the prosecutors alluded to his "radical right wing tendencies and bearing."[44] But they were perhaps most conscious of his social status and what this meant for the establishment of National Socialism, noting, "The fact that he, as a member of the once ruling Hessen princely house and direct descendent of the earlier ruling Prussian and British ruling houses, as well as a member of the Italian royal house, has given him very high visibility and meant that he must take care to act with special restraint and caution."[45] Furthermore, Philipp's trial, despite taking place largely out of public view in an internment camp, was covered in great detail in the local press. Authorities placed advertisements in local newspapers, including the *Hessische Nachrichten* in Kassel, asking people to come forward if they had any evidence concerning the prince.[46] While this did not qualify as a show trial, the authorities were aware that it provided an important opportunity to send messages to the citizens of Hesse as they attempted to overcome twelve years of National Socialism and make the transition to democracy.

Philipp's surviving brothers, Princes Wolfgang and Richard, were treated more leniently but also subjected to denazification trials. Prince

Richard, who had been released from an internment camp after thirteen months incarceration, was initially placed in Category III (lesser offender) in August 1948 but had his sentence reduced on appeal to Category IV (fellow traveler) in May 1949.[47] Prince Wolfgang, who much to his astonishment was released on his fiftieth birthday in November 1946, went before the local denazification board near Kronberg in June 1948.[48] On 15 June 1948, he was placed in Category V—that is, completely absolved of responsibility. According to the 5 March 1946 Law for Liberation from National Socialism and Militarism, Category V entailed demonstrating "active resistance to the N.S. rule of violence and resultant personal disadvantages."[49] This judgment was very generous for someone who had been the county commissioner, let alone a member of the Nazi Party and SA. The public prosecutor immediately challenged the ruling: just as defendants could appeal sentences they believed were excessively harsh, so too could prosecutors pursue what they perceived as miscarriages of justice. On 24 July 1950, the Central Appeals Chamber in Hesse, which was based in Frankfurt, suspended the initial judgment of June 1948. In principle, this denied Wolfgang of the right to say he had been placed in Category V. But a 30 November 1949 law for the federal state of Hesse ruled that a new hearing would take place only when there were grounds to believe that the concerned party would be placed in Category I or II (that is, deemed a major offender or offender).[50] It was clear that Prince Wolfgang would not qualify in this regard, and so the case was closed. He was free to move on with his life.

Prince Wolfgang's twin brother, Philipp, was not to get off so easily. There were numerous challenges involved with investigating Prince Philipp. The deferential treatment he elicited from many commoners created one obstacle, but more significant was the destruction of the relevant documents. For example, the building of the Oberpräsidium in Kassel had been obliterated by Allied bombs and very little of his official correspondence survived. The investigation that had followed the arrest of Philipp and Mafalda in September 1943 also appears to have contributed to the disappearance of documents: some papers were seized while others may have been removed or destroyed by employees of the prince and princess. Finally, Philipp had often made a conscious effort not to leave a paper trail: this may have been one of the consequences of having a family member who worked as an intelligence operative, and was to be expected in light of some of the sensitive matters with which he was involved.

Philipp mounted an impressive defense, a strategy that started with his choice of a defense attorney, Fabian von Schlabrendorff, who was not only competent but also had a sterling reputation as a member of the resistance.[51] As noted earlier, Philipp and Schlabrendorff met in Flossenbürg in April 1945.[52] Schlabrendorff, like Philipp was moved to a series of camps, including Dachau, Innsbruck, and Niederdorf. The two became close in the Innsbruck facility, and "since this time had spoken daily."[53] After the war, Schlabrendorff became an assistant to General William J. Donovan (1883–1959), an attorney then working for the prosecution at the IMT at Nuremberg.[54] Schlabrendorff therefore had perfect credentials for Philipp's purposes. While the relationship between the resister and the former Nazi was evidently not without tensions, they kept their differences well concealed.

Like many Germans, Philipp represented himself as a member of the resistance. He wrote one of the denazification oversight officials, the Hessian Minister for Political Liberation, in October 1947—before the verdict—"that he was imprisoned in September 1943 on the grounds of his criticism and his resistance to a series of Nazi measures."[55] Philipp argued that before that, he had just been a messenger (*Bote*).[56] He and his lawyer petitioned for him to be placed in Category V for those completely exonerated. Furthermore, he asked that the costs of the trial be borne by the state.[57] Philipp's was an aggressive defense that sometimes stretched the boundaries of historical accuracy.

Philipp's denazification trial reached a climax between 15 and 17 December 1947, when the public hearing took place in the Darmstadt Camp. Dr. Hans Quambush chaired the five-member board, and he took the lead in interrogating Philipp and the other witnesses. The trial, which lasted twenty-five hours over three days, was structured according to themes: background, including family history; activities as Oberpräsident; involvement in foreign affairs; and attempts at resistance. Philipp was the first to testify. He began with a sober and familiar account of his family history, noting, for example, that his mother was the only living sister of Kaiser Wilhelm II. But the questions gradually became more intense as he was asked about the T-4 program, the persecution of the Jews and his role in the Anschluss, among other challenging topics.

A parade of witnesses came before the board—seventeen in all—and they were often very emotional. For example, Anne Aubel, an old friend of the prince and princess, argued for the popularity of Philipp and the injustices he had suffered: "the population would feel deeply wounded if the prince was not released now. If the prince should remain incarcerated longer, I have been charged by the city of Kassel to provide surrogates in order to get him out. He has such a blessed effect that all would be imprisoned for him. I also put myself at your disposal to enter the work camp for him."[58] Most of the witnesses were sympathetic to Philipp and gave testimony in which they tried to support him. This was not uncommon for such trials: one understands why denazification boards have been commonly associated with whitewashing (the aforementioned *Persilscheine*). At least the board considered a significant amount of evidence—much of it written testimony. For example, reports were submitted by seven individuals who were previously in the Foreign Ministry. All told, the trial and subsequent appeal generated more than a thousand pages of documentation—an invaluable source for historians now housed in the Hessian Central State Archive in Wiesbaden (the central repository of the province's denazification files).

The verdict for Prince Philipp was rendered on 17 December 1947. The five-member board placed him in Category II, which labeled him as "burdened" or offender. The penalty included: (1) a sentence of "two years forced labor" in a work camp; 2) the forfeiture of 30 percent of his property; (3) a ban on holding public office in the future; (4) the loss of any public funds, pensions, or rents; (5) the loss of voting rights; (6) a prohibition from joining a union or professional association; (7) a five-year ban on certain professions, including that of teacher, priest, editor, or radio announcer; (8) restrictions on where he lived and stayed; (9) the loss of all honors, concessions, and privileges; and (10) the loss of the right to have a vehicle.[59] With regard to the two years already spent in the work camp, the judges ruled that "the political incarceration after 8 May 1945 will be counted in."[60] In other words, he was let off for time served.

The board was not only tough but also seemed to have a genuine animosity toward Philipp. The justification of the verdict included lines such as

> With his complete repudiation and total obliviousness of the mentality of other people, he was in all earnestness filled with madness: With regards to foreign governments, he thought he could push through the same clumsy ruses and use the brutally violent methods with which he successfully deceived an honorable people. With all his evil instincts that gave rise to inexpressible suffering, he proved at the end how deep a people can sink if they have been robbed of their freedom.[61]

They added that his experience in a concentration camp and the "tragic death of his wife in a concentration camp caused him to endure extraordinary suffering," but that this had no mitigating effect on his sentence.[62] The board acknowledged that he did some good: "in conjunction with his wife, he tried to remain upstanding and practice the principles of tolerance and humanity in his official and personal spheres of influence." Furthermore, they concluded that his "personal lifestyle was morally unobjectionable." For these reasons they did not put him in Category I as a "major offender."[63]

The denazification process included the right to appeal. Most defendants availed themselves of this right, and Philipp was no exception: he filed an appeal of the sentence with the Frankfurt Court of Appeals in early

1948. The Courts of Appeals, although staffed by professional jurists, had a reputation for leniency.[64] Philipp decided to use a different attorney: he was not entirely satisfied with Schlabrendorff (not surprising considering the verdict). Philipp therefore turned to Ferdinand de la Fontaine, who, as noted earlier, also represented various members of the Rothschild family. While de la Fontaine took the lead filing briefs, Schlabrendorff continued to be supportive and assumed a more prominent role as a witness—using his reputation as a member of the resistance to assist his client and friend.[65] Ferdinand de la Fontaine offered some new arguments: for example, he maintained that in early 1941, when the contract for the Hadamar facility was signed, Philipp "at that point in time was very often traveling on assignment from Adolf Hitler and was abroad"; he added, "these trips abroad of the concerned party had nothing to do with politics, but came about because he had received at that time the assignment to inspect art objects in Germany and Italy." Philipp and de la Fontaine, as noted earlier, also revealed for the first time the role of Crown Prince Umberto in the toppling of the Fascist regime. In the first trial, Philipp remained close-lipped regarding his confidential discussions with Umberto in 1943, when the latter had revealed that the Italian royal house had lost confidence in Mussolini. His initial reticence presumably was because the Italian royal family had just been deposed and was in the precarious position of settling its legal status (one that resulted in a prohibition of the king and male heirs from setting foot in the country). De la Fontaine noted, "the concerned party has withheld an account about the two conversations with Crown Prince Umberto in consideration of [the latter's] position, but he finds himself now forced to report on the entire matter; he now believes that it can only contribute to the honor of Crown Prince Umberto that at that time he proceeded in this way and did all that he could for the peace and well-being of the Italian people." For Philipp to have taken Umberto's message to Hitler, de la Fontaine, argued, constituted an act of real courage that "could have cost him his freedom or even his life."[66]

Philipp's appeal engendered another tough battle and meant that the prince had to respond to more challenging questions. But at least he had been released from the Darmstadt internment camp and could rely on family and friends for support. His appeal was opposed by the Hessian Minister for Political Liberation, a Social Democrat who wrote to the prosecutor and said that it was wrong to exonerate Philipp and put him in Category V, "because not one single case of active resistance has been provided."[67] This official, who was mandated to pursue justice on behalf of victims of the Nazi regime, argued that it was Philipp's role in foreign affairs, in forging the Axis, that made him so problematic.[68] He argued in a subsequent report from March 1948, "The efforts [represented in] the appeals papers to portray in a positive light the effects of the concerned party on foreign policy is . . . only a hopeless battle against . . . the facts."[69] Despite his opinion, the appeal—as was often the case with denazification trials—improved the fortunes of the prince. On 10 February 1949, the Frankfurt Court of Appeals ruled that Prince Philipp's deeds during the Third Reich warranted his placement in Category II, but that the manner in which he and his family were victimized—"the demonstrable political persecution through the Nazi rule of violence and the suffering that Hitler had brought on the concerned party and his family"—were mitigating factors and he was therefore declared "less burdened" and placed in Category III (lesser offender).[70]

The five-person panel, who was joined by the public prosecutor and the clerk in signing the appeals verdict, also amended the sentence in other ways. Philipp now had one year "probation" in which he could not work as a proprietor or executive. He was still prohibited from holding positions as a teacher, priest, editor, writer, or radio commentator. And he was obliged to pay a fine of DM 20,000 to a restitution fund, which was calculated as approximately 10 percent of his property. He was also held responsible for the costs of the trial, which were assessed at the amount of DM 200,000—an extraordinarily large figure but one that reflects a long and difficult investigation.[71] This latter sum was so high that Philipp's lawyer de la Fontaine wrote the court in July 1950 saying, "the payment of the entire amount [200,000] is not possible."[72] As was often the case with denazification trials, the authorities negotiated a settlement: Prince Philipp agreed to pay DM 36,568, which included the DM 20,000 fine, plus court costs and interest.

Philipp's estate was very confused at the time of his denazification and appeal, and determining his net worth proved a highly challenging undertaking. His father, Landgrave Friedrich Karl, had died in a sanatorium in Wilhelmshöhe near Kassel on 28 May 1940, and his uncle, Landgrave Alexander Friedrich, had passed away on 26 March 1945; Philipp had inherited a portion of each man's property. As the trustee for the Kurhessische Foundation wrote, "in both cases the deliberations about the inheritance had not concluded . . . and questions of a legal nature still need to be clarified."[73] The information about Philipp's assets provided by his staff to investigators at the end of 1946 showed that his total worth had grown precipitously during the war, from approximately RM 416,000 in 1940 to RM 686,000 by war's end.[74] While these numbers appeared suspiciously low—there is no mention of the family's jewels, or what might have been his share, for example—the fact that he was paying a fine of RM 36,568 against total assets of over RM 600,000 shows that Philipp fared much better in the appeals process than the one-third penalty levied after the original trial. As noted earlier, the Americans had initially placed the property of the Kurhessische Hausstiftung under trusteeship according to Military

Law 52 and the Law of Liberation, and this property included, according to a 1947 report, the "most valuable artistic treasures in the province," five castles, forests, and other properties.[75] With the conclusion of the appeals process, the trusteeship over the family property was removed, and Dr. Schulte resigned his office.[76] The RM 36,568 that Philipp paid in fines and court costs therefore represented a sum about which he earlier could have only dreamed.

The penalties meted out to the Hessens by the denazification authorities were comparable to those of the other members of the high aristocracy. Prince Auwi went through a Ludwigsburg Spruchkammer and, in a judgment rendered in May 1948, lost 40 percent of his property; but he was let off for time served, which amounted to two-and-a-half years in a work camp. Duke Carl Eduard von Sachsen-Coburg und Gotha was sentenced as a "fellow traveler" in June 1948 but had to pay what one commentator called "a large atonement payment," which left him impoverished during his last years in Coburg.[77] Prince Friedrich Christian zu Schaumburg-Lippe was incarcerated for seven months at Nuremberg, where he was housed in the Palace of Justice near Prince Philipp for a period. After being interrogated by Robert Kempner and others, he was sent off to the nearby internment camp at Hersbruck in Bavaria. He spent several years in captivity (moving between several camps) before going through denazification. The judicial proceeding resulted in a significant fine, which in turn compromised his standard of living in the postwar period. Schaumburg-Lippe

Prince Auwi at his denazification trial in the Ludwigsburg Internment Camp, near Stuttgart, 1948. His attorney, Dr. Emmy Dreier, pleads on his behalf.

benefited from an amnesty law of 27 July 1950, but he had endured five years of hardship (in his memoirs he compares American internment facilities unfavorably to Nazi concentration camps).[78] For the princes in general, the fines were higher than was the norm for the general population. The punishments were initially harsher because both the Allies and the indigenous German authorities in the West sought to send a message about the pernicious influence of the old elite. Viewed as autocratic, illiberal, and militaristic, German aristocrats were identified as playing key roles in "the German catastrophe" in the twentieth century. Thus, one saw a number of initial verdicts concerning princes in the denazification process that were quite severe by the standards of the day. These punishments, however, usually did not withstand the appeals process and legal wrangling that played out during the subsequent years.

In the case of Philipp von Hessen, West German authorities spent the five years after his relatively successful appeal trying to collect the fines. Palais Bellevue, one of the few structures to survive the forty bombing raids launched by the Allies against Kassel, had been seized back in June 1947.[79] Up through September 1950, the city of Kassel received the proceeds from the rent, which amounted to DM 5,000 per year until 1955. At that point, Philipp owed only DM 10,000 on the original fine, and this was negotiated away by Philipp's lawyer de la Fontaine. His attorney noted a law passed in October 1951—the Second Law for the Conclusion of Political Liberation in Hessen—which stated that for individuals placed in Categories III, IV, and V in the denazification scheme, their debts for fines and court costs were absolved when the amount was less than DM 2,000. This was part of the process in the early years of the Adenauer regime that gradually granted amnesties to former Nazis. Prince Philipp benefited from this trend in various ways: In 1950, he used a provision in the 30 November 1949 law in the state of Hesse to petition that his sentence be reduced still further, and this was granted: Philipp was ultimately placed in Category IV as a fellow traveler.[80] While West Germans' perceptions of the Third Reich in the 1950s were deeply complex and at times contradictory—an awareness of history and postwar trials existed alongside the suppression of memory and the creation of myths—few citizens remained committed to the prosecution of former Nazis.[81] The Western Allies facilitated this because they sought Germany as a partner in the intensifying Cold War. Philipp's attorney therefore claimed that his client needed to pay only DM 8,000, with the remaining DM 2,000 being forgiven.[82] This strategy worked: DM 5,000 came from that year's rent on Palais Bellevue, and Philipp paid the remaining DM 3,000 in mid-1955.[83] The foot-dragging that Philipp and his lawyers exhibited in paying off the already light fine suggested an unrepentant attitude. Prince Philipp continued to view himself as a victim throughout the postwar period.

The Morshead-Blunt Mission to Retrieve Royal Documents

One of most persistent rumors haunting authors in regard to the Hessens concerns the removal of royal documents from Schloss Friedrichshof in Kronberg in the summer of 1945. A number of authors, mostly British nationals, view this episode as an attempt on the part of members of the House of Windsor to remove papers that would expose the ties binding the British royal house to the problematic Hessens. More specifically, they believe that these documents would elucidate the Duke of Windsor's pro-Nazi activities. Two authors, Kenneth Alford and Martin Allen, initially advanced this theory in the greatest detail, but they have been joined more recently by the team of Lynn Picknett, Clive Prince, and Stephen Prior, who earlier wrote a controversial book about Rudolf Hess's mission to the U.K. With regard to the purportedly incriminating documents at Kronberg, one could characterize these authors as being in the "cover-up camp."[84]

After the Americans seized Schloss Friedrichshof in the spring of 1945, King George VI charged Royal Archivist Sir Owen Morshead with removing the letters from Empress Friedrich to her mother, Queen Victoria, to the safekeeping of Windsor Castle. King George VI believed these items should be temporarily placed in the Royal Library, and they apparently secured the permission of Landgravine Margarethe to remove the papers —at least as a temporary measure. Major Anthony Blunt, who had just succeeded Kenneth Clark as surveyor of the king's (and later the queen's) pictures, also appeared on the scene. Until war's end, Blunt was a member of British Intelligence—the counterintelligence branch, MI-5. The authors in the cover-up camp suggest that Blunt's mission to the Continent in August 1945 took advantage of his background in espionage.

With regard to Schloss Friedrichshof, Martin Allen claims that because U.S. authorities denied Blunt access to the castle, he surreptitiously circumvented the guards one night and removed two crates that included papers from the Duke of Windsor—documents, he maintains, that chronicled the Duke of Windsor's treasonous activities. Allen posits that the two crates were removed from the castle's upper floor (a doubtful assertion because the library, which housed Queen Victoria's letters, is located on the ground floor) and then taken to "the British zone before the American authorities discovered what had been done."[85] Allen writes, "Ultimately Blunt was revealed as a traitor who had spied for Russia, and he in turn was protected by the royal family lest he reveal the details of the secret mission he had undertaken at the end of the Second World War."[86]

A more recent effort to make sense of these allegations has been taken up by Miranda Carter in her biography of Anthony Blunt. Carter accepts elements of cover-up camp's rendition, but concludes that the implications are less damning for the British royals. Carter acknowledges that Morshead and Blunt were ordered "to find the relevant papers . . . to get the permission of seventy-three-year-old [Landgravine] Margaret of Hesse . . . and to take the papers back to England."[87] She identifies the main concern as "4,000 letters from Queen Victoria to her eldest daughter, the Empress Fredrick of Germany." Carter describes how Blunt and Morshead flew to Frankfurt on 3 August, how Blunt was especially valuable because he spoke German, and how he was able to identify a wider range of papers found in the library at Kronberg. Carter adds, "Margaret required more 'delicate handling.' She had lost three sons in two world wars and now felt 'rancorous hatred' toward England. Morshead nevertheless persuaded her that the letters would be safer at Windsor, and she signed an agreement. Morshead returned to England the next day; Blunt stayed on an additional day for his mysterious 'military business.' The letters were later returned in 1951."[88] Indeed, Landgravine Margarethe wrote Queen Mary, widow of King George V, on 15 October 1951 "to ask whether you think Bertie [the king] would allow me to have my grandmother's letters back."[89] After a special crate was constructed, they were sent in December. The red leather volumes remain to this day in the possession of the Hessische Hausstiftung, housed at Schloss Fasanerie in a special fire-proof and steel-encased room.

Miranda Carter, however, complicates this straightforward explanation of the Morshead-Blunt mission. She cites an interview with Anthony Blunt from 1979, where he admitted to having been blocked by an "American woman officer in charge of the castle," and then sneaking into Kronberg to take the papers.[90] This hardly sounds like the aboveboard agreement with the Landgravine described above. Carter suggests one way to reconcile the various stories: "another version of the story, told by the espionage writer Chapman Pincher, claims that, having been refused entry, Morshead and Blunt went off to see [Landgravine] Margaret of Hesse, who directed them to a back entrance. They broke in at night, found their treasure, and withdrew."[91] This version would feature the British operatives and the Landgravine conspiring to circumvent the uncooperative Americans. Rainer von Hessen, in contemplating this scenario, remains unconvinced and warns against even this "watered-down" conspiracy theory. Supporting his interpretation is a 6 August 1946 memorandum by U.S. colonel John Allen about the contents of Schloss Friedrichshof, where he noted "on 3 August 1945, however, the Victoria letters were officially received by Sir Owen Morshead and Major A. F. Blunt for transfer to Windsor Castle, England."[92] Although almost one year after the Morshead-Blunt mission, the Americans acknowledged the transfer and did not point to any irregularities.

Morshead's mission was hardly a top-secret operation. He wrote up an anecdote-filled account for the king's private secretary, with vivid descriptions of the flight over to Germany and back, as well as his efforts to charm the Landgravine into handing over the documents for safekeeping. Someone in the British royal administration scribbled a note that his account, after editing a few specific sentences, would be perfect for *The Sunday Times*. The account, despite appearing to convey ulterior motives, is a useful one. It shows that Morshead knew the Hessens personally. It also exhibited his rather flamboyant style. Upon arriving in Hesse, when he first went to Wolfsgarten to speak with Prince Lu, Princess Peg, and Princess Sophia, he showered them with gifts—"vitamin preparations, toilet paper, soap, tea, coffee, matches" and so on—including chocolate. His chatty account is also notable for the scant reference to his traveling companion. Blunt is mentioned just twice—and then, without reference to his mission or without explaining his specific tasks.[93]

Anthony Blunt was in Schloss Friedrichshof in August 1945. The current head of the House of Hesse, Landgrave Moritz, remembers the visit because it was his birthday (6 August). A more interesting question is why Blunt was there. Morshead noted in his report:

> In this narrative I have, for simplicity hitherto said nothing of my colleague Anthony Blunt, Surveyor of the King's Pictures. He is serving during the war in Military Intelligence, and since he had in any case to go out to Germany on business I had brought him with me, for agreeable companionship and because his German is excellent. But he took no part in the diplomatic side [discussions with the Hessens]; I used to liberate him whenever I was engaged with the Family, because he did not know any of them (being new to the Household), and because I felt it might frighten them to have an English officer present.[94]

Blunt's presence could also be justified because Friedrichshof contained some valuable paintings that were linked to the British royal family. Blunt duly compiled an inventory. It is also likely that members of the British royal family worried that there might be incriminating documents at Friedrichshof and sent the adroit Blunt to help find out. But there is no way of knowing the extent to which they worried about such documents or whether Blunt found anything.

Similar circumstances surrounded Blunt's trip to Schloss Marienburg in Lower Saxony near Hanover. This castle belonged to the Princes von Hannover. Because Prince Ernst August von Hannover, the son of the Duke von Braunschweig, was close to members of the Nazi regime, there was concern that some of the documents (e.g., Queen Mary's letters to the Duke von Braunschweig) were of a sensitive political nature and also might reveal pro-German sentiment from British royals. But again, there was a good reason for Blunt to travel there: in this case, the fear that valuable cultural property would fall into the hands of the Soviets (the ironies abound—if it was not enough for a Communist to become a courtier, a Soviet spy was now charged with keeping royal property out of the hands of the Red Army). Blunt apparently traveled to Marienburg after leaving Kronberg—that is, in August 1945. In that British monuments officer Felix Harbord had just overseen an evacuation operation from Schloss Marienburg that had been concluded on 23 July 1945, it is not clear that Blunt was overseeing the primary evacuation effort: rather, it appears that he carried out the mop-up work—one final check, as it were.[95] Nonetheless, during the August 1945 trip and in at least three subsequent expeditions to the Continent for King George VI, Blunt evidently brought back royal property.[96] For example, he is reported to have retrieved "treasures from the royal house of Hannover, including an extremely valuable twelfth-century illuminated manuscript and the diamond crown of Queen Charlotte, wife of George III."[97] Blunt also visited the deceased ex-Kaiser's estate in Doorn in order to secure objects that had come from Wilhelm's mother (Empress Friedrich), grandmother (Queen Victoria), and other British royals. Miranda Carter acknowledges the dicey nature of the retrieval effort, as documented by British government officials at the time: "The Foreign Office was extremely worried that if it was discovered that the British Crown was engaged in 'evacuating'—if not actually smuggling—archives and objects from Germany, it would look extremely bad when Britain was lecturing its Allies on the subject of war looting."[98] While the British could maintain that their actions were security measures and had nothing to do with looting, the acts of removal still appeared suspect. Very little information about Blunt's missions has been released: while it may be for this reason—that his efforts contravened Allied restitution policy—one consequence has been to fuel conspiracy theories.

The king and his court officials evidently requested that Blunt help maintain the secrecy of his mission, and they rewarded him accordingly. Blunt was knighted in 1956.[99] Later, although identified as a spy in 1964, he was permitted to continue as Surveyor of the Queen's Pictures (until 1972) and as director of the Courtauld Institute (until 1974). He was not exposed publicly until 1979, when Prime Minister Thatcher made a statement in the House of Commons and his knighthood was annulled.[100] But Blunt remained reticent about his trip to Kronberg at war's end. Peter Wright, the former MI-5 officer who wrote the controversial exposé *Spycatcher*, recalled asking "Blunt about his travels to Germany in 1945, when he had visited the Hessen home. At this point Blunt immediately became very aggressive, and said nastily, 'Now this isn't on. You know you're not supposed to ask me that!' Thus we have the clear intimation that before his interrogation [by Wright], Blunt had *already* been briefed about the subjects Wright was allowed to ask about, and more importantly, those he was *not* supposed to ask. A strange way to conduct an interview of a spy, and this says to me that the Royal Family had more to cover up than merely the Duke of Windsor's machinations."[101] Peter Wright added in *Spycatcher* that before interviewing Blunt, he was briefed by Sir Michael Adeane, the queen's private secretary, who told him "you may find Blunt referring to an assignment he undertook on behalf of the Palace—a visit to Germany at the end of the war. Please do not pursue this matter. Strictly speaking, it is not relevant to considerations of national security. . . . Although I spent hundreds of hours with Blunt, I never did learn the secret of his mission to Germany."[102] When Blunt cut a deal with British Intelligence in 1964, there may also have been an element of blackmail, where Blunt leveraged his knowledge from the mission to Germany.

In all likelihood, Blunt was instructed to keep a lookout for any incriminating documents involving the Duke of Windsor or the royal family. Certain retainers around the royals expressed the belief that there were files in Germany that needed to be secured. In autumn 1945, for example, Sir Alexander Hardinge noted the king's response to the recently unearthed files of the German Foreign Office concerning the Duke of Windsor ("the Marburg File"): "King [George VI] fussed about the Duke of Windsor's file and captured German documents."[103] Blunt then, offered a perfect cover. Because he was the new Surveyor of the King's Pictures, he could be said to investigate the circumstances surrounding the artworks of a family member (Empress Friedrich). Of course, one should note that Blunt did not, in fact, remove any paintings (he merely compiled a list of the thirty-one English works that had belonged to the empress).[104] The question arises, if Morshead secured the empress's letters, why would Blunt have left her pictures? Some of them were quite valuable, including family portraits by F. X. Winterhalter. One answer, but not the only one, is that Blunt merely sought a pretext to search for incriminating correspondence. That he had no real intention to safeguard art at Friedrichshof is also reenforced by Morshead's claim that Blunt just came along for the ride—on his way to other missions in Germany. If his mission was to secure Empress Friedrich's artworks, it is odd that he traveled in such a haphazard and spontaneous manner. Blunt's visit to this castle of royal relations who were high-ranking Nazi officials most likely reflected a concern that there might be incriminating documents *chez* Hessen.

This, then, leads to further questions: were there any papers and did Blunt find them? The first of those questions goes to the heart of this book. Was there a royal connection at play in the 1930s and 1940s where members of the Windsor family and Philipp von Hessen cooperated in an attempt to avert a war? The evidence suggests yes. Adding to the likelihood of a correspondence is the number of actors involved: on the British side alone, one has the Duke of Windsor, the Duke of Kent, and King George VI (who had suggested to Chamberlain that Philipp von Hessen be utilized as a conduit to Hitler). In alluding to scenarios discussed earlier in this book, *The Sunday Times* in 1979 featured an article on the Duke of

Kent that noted, "George VI had every reason to believe that the Hesse archives might contain a 'Windsor file,' because Prince Philipp of Hesse had been an intermediary, via the Duke of Kent, between Hitler and the Duke of Windsor, a fact confirmed to *The Sunday Times* last night by Prince Wolfgang of Hesse."[105] Recall too, that the British and Hessen princes were approximately the same age and that they were cousins. Among royals, cousins have a very special familial relationship—typically much closer and warmer than among nonroyals. There was a conscious effort by elders to cultivate connections among disparate family members. It therefore would have been very surprising if Prince Philipp von Hessen never communicated with his British cousins.

Despite all the theories—and the Picknett, Prince, and Prior team even cite a source, code-named "Phoenix," who claims to have traveled with Blunt in August 1945 and to have actually seen the Windsor documents —it is most likely that Blunt did not find the Windsor-Hessen correspondence at Kronberg.[106] That any such letters went directly from Friedrichshof to the Round Tower at Windsor is most unlikely. The Americans arrived on 29 March 1945—that is, months before Blunt—and any incriminating papers would most likely have been removed for safekeeping before those first units of GIs rolled up the long drive to the Schloss. Furthermore, it would have made more sense for the Dukes of Windsor and Kent to have sent letters to Prince Philipp at his homes in Kassel or Rome. It is possible that papers in the former were incinerated in Allied bombing raids: as noted earlier, this was the case with most of Prince Philipp's official papers when the Oberpräsidium building was demolished in October 1943. However, because the Palais Bellevue remained largely unscathed, some documents may have survived there. In Rome, the Villa Polissena remained a secure sanctuary. After the war Philipp and his son Heinrich lived in the family home. It is possible that Windsor-Hessen letters were stored at that location. Yet recall also that Philipp had told his cousin Prince Regent Paul of Yugoslavia to destroy a letter he had sent. Philipp, it seems, was prepared to eliminate sensitive materials. In short, while Blunt was successful in securing valuables at other locations in Germany and the Netherlands, he almost certainly came up empty-handed looking for a Windsor file at Kronberg.

With regard to the correspondence in the other direction—Prince Philipp von Hessens' letters to the Windsors—there is a strong likelihood that anything that existed has by now been eliminated. The Duke of Windsor would have every reason to destroy any such letters—even during the war. Documents that survived would have been subjected to subsequent vettings: for example, after death of the Duchess of Windsor in 1986, the trustee of the estate, Maitre Suzanne Blum, culled letters. Royal Archivist Pamela Clark acknowledged that certain letters were removed by the duchess's agents before coming to Windsor Castle.[107] Ms. Clark also stated that the Royal Archives contain relatively few papers relating to the Duke of Kent; she maintains that his sudden death prevented the careful organization and preservation of his papers (one of the advantages of surviving to old age is the opportunity to put one's affairs in order). Again, perhaps his spouse, Marina, preserved the papers, and they may have been passed on to their children after her death in 1968. However, astonishingly few of the Duke of Kent's papers are accounted for. Even many of the documents belonging to those who were close to the British royal family during the 1930s and 1940s have been kept out of the hands of researchers: some of the documents regarding the royal family in the papers of Sir Walter Monckton in the Bodleian Library at Oxford University, for example, are classified until 2037.[108]

Contact during the Third Reich between members of the British royal family and German officials has been a sensitive subject for many who seek to preserve the monarchy. Winston Churchill, for example, endeavored at war's end to cover-up evidence concerning the Duke and Duchess of Windsor's interactions with German officials. A group of Allied historians based in Marburg after the war charged with examining German archives had discovered documents relating to the Duke of Windsor. These included: "telegrams from German officials recording meetings with [the Duke of Windsor] in Lisbon in 1940; a reference to Hitler's attempts in the 1930s to use the former Kaiser as an intermediary with the Windsors; and an account of a visit to England in 1936 by one of the Hesse family."[109] (This latter reference may concern a trip made by Princess Sophia—a visit, of course, without significance for international relations.) On 26 August 1945, after reading extracts from captured German Foreign Ministry files, Churchill wrote Prime Minister Clement Atlee, "I earnestly trust it may be possible to destroy all traces of these German intrigues."[110] Indeed, "when the so-called Windsor file [from the German Foreign Ministry] was discovered in 1945, Churchill found it so distressing that, out of sentimental regard for the Duke of Windsor, he called for it to be expunged from the historical record."[111] He was not able to do this (largely because the Americans microfilmed the documents before handing the originals over to the British), yet he continued to object to their declassification in the years that followed.[112] In 1953, when Churchill was again prime minister, he wrote to President Dwight Eisenhower in an attempt to delay the publication of the Windsor documents: Churchill sought an embargo "for at least ten or twenty years."[113] Even though he did not get his way and many of the documents were published in the 1950s, Churchill's attitude toward the captured German documents suggests a certain mindset among the British establishment regarding the Windsors' sensitive documents. Because many relevant archives are not accessible, it is not possible to answer all of the questions raised by the Blunt-Morshead mission. Of course, the British royal family could help discourage the conspiracy theories by providing greater access to the papers in the Royal Archives.

Thefts from Kronberg Castle

The Hessens' difficult years after 1945 were compounded by the theft of the family members' jewelry from Kronberg in 1946. This was not an insignificant case of pilfering, but one of the greatest jewel heists of all time. Valued at over £2 million at the time, the collection included a number of exceptionally precious pieces: "nine diamond-studded tiaras containing hundreds of diamonds, . . . another bracelet contained 365 large diamonds . . . one diamond wristwatch glittered with so many gems that it was difficult to see the time-telling hands. . . ."[114] "The jewels of the house of Hesse—those belonging to Prince Richard, Prince Christoph, Princess Mafalda, Princess Sophia of Hannover, Prince Wolfgang, and his wife, Princess Marie-Alexandra—and other property belonging to Margarethe, the Landgravine of Hesse, were individually wrapped in secure brown paper packages that also contained lists of the contents and the names and addresses of the owners."[115] Additionally, Prince Auwi had delivered some of his valuables for what he thought was safekeeping. It was common for well-to-do Germans to bury their valuables at war's end. In the year 2000, a milk canister containing valuable silver was unearthed at an estate belonging to the Bismarck family in the town of Stendal in Sachsen-Anhalt.[116] As the Red Army pushed westward, the last owner, Eddie von Bismarck, had arranged for valuable pieces and family heirlooms to be concealed below ground. Because the family was driven out (and the Soviets and GDR made it impossible to return), the treasure remained undiscovered for more than fifty years. In the case of Kronberg, after seeing a Frankfurt bank obliterated by bombing in 1943, Prince Wolfgang moved the family jewels out of the Deutsche Bank branch on the Rossmarkt and took them to Friedrichshof. He arranged for a special zinc-lined box to be constructed, and once filled, it was taken to the cellar and buried in a hole that was concealed by an expert stone mason.[117]

The threat to the treasures came from both the invading Allied armies and the local population. The Western Allies had regulations prohibiting the seizure of art and cultural property, and this extended to jewelry. Especially in comparison to the Soviet's "trophy brigades," they were restrained and law-abiding. Yet American policy permitted the occupation forces to utilize assets belonging to the Nazi Party and its leaders.[118] This provision naturally gave rise to some ambiguity and affected the Hessens, as it was unclear how one should categorize them. Additionally, both the Soviets and the Western Allies exhibited an animus toward princes, especially the Hohenzollern. For example, a report that appeared in February 1946 noted that "the war department today took custody of the seven tons of Hohenzollern silverware which the army's 175th regiment captured at the Elbe River in Germany and carried to Baltimore as war booty. . . . Howard G. Peterson, assistant war secretary, will decide whether the regiment should be permitted to keep the silverware as a trophy. . . . Because it was taken in combat from troops, the war department has wavered over the question of whether it was war booty."[119] At the end of 1946, the War Department had still not decided what to do with the silver (counting it as reparations charged to Germany was a leading option), and the fate of the settings, each marked with an imperial crest, remains unclear.[120] But returning the silver to the Hohenzollern did not appear among the options under consideration.

Besides the officially sanctioned seizures, the invading Allied troops also exhibited what one might euphemistically call individual initiative. Those with valuable property, such as the princely families, were particularly vulnerable to theft. There is much truth to historian Günter Bischof's observation that "the American soldiers took 'souvenirs' and those in the Red Army took 'loot.'"[121] But Bischof's remark is meant as a wry understatement: there was a great deal of "souvenir" collecting on the part of U.S. forces, and the Hessens were again representative in terms of losing valuables albeit exceptional in terms of the scale. In the province of Hessen, as a whole, the castle of Büdingen, which was a repository for valuable paintings and other cultural treasures, was plundered by American troops, as was Schloss Eppstein near Wiesbaden and the castle in Hochstadt.[122]

The Americans' expropriation of property at Kronberg escalated gradually. There were reports of the July 4 celebration in 1945, for example, where "dolls, harmonicas, stockings and dresses taken from the castle were distributed to U.S. military units as prizes at parties, bingo games, and so forth."[123] Later, much of the family silver and many of the china services, as well as commemorative swords, medallions, and other historic objects began to disappear, as the visiting troops helped themselves to the Hessens' treasures. Prince Heinrich, for example, recounted losing the three gifts he received from his godfather Kaiser Wilhelm II: a gold cigarette holder, a gold bowl, and a gold pocket watch.[124] A number of sculptures and paintings, including one picture listed as a "school of Rubens," also disappeared in the autumn of 1945.[125]

But far more important was the theft of the Hessen jewels by Captain Kathleen Nash, Major David Watson, and Colonel Jack Durant. On 5 November 1945, they entered the basement of the Schloss and discovered the more recently bricked-in enclosure that stood out from the older masonry, and this in turn led them to the jewels and other treasure in the strongbox. While they gave as their explanation that they had been searching for wine—and indeed, they found 1,238 bottles of fine vintages in the enclosure (some dating back to 1834), author John Parker suggests that they were looking for documents connecting the Hessens to the Windsors (Nash, after all, had interacted with Morshead and Blunt in August).[126] While this specific goal seems questionable (why would it have taken several months to act?), the American officers almost certainly hoped to find more than fermented grapes.

Although word of the discovery leaked out to American personnel at Kronberg, Nash and her accomplices said nothing about the quantity or value of the jewels. The three American officers who unearthed the Hessen jewels were friends, with Nash and Durant involved with one another romantically, and this contributed to the conspiracy. Captain Nash took the boxes containing the treasure to her room and locked herself away for a day, issuing orders that she was not to be disturbed. The estate manager Heinrich Lange subsequently made inquiries and asked for a receipt; he was told by Nash that the jewels were safe and that he should tell the Landgravine. While Landgravine Margarethe was "disturbed," she did not pursue the matter, "trusting the word of an officer of the U.S. Army."[127] Captain Nash left Kronberg in February 1946 without having been made to account for the jewels. The Hessens became fully conscious of the theft in early 1946 when Princess Sophia was preparing to remarry: she was engaged to Prince Georg Wilhelm von Hannover and wanted to wear some of her jewelry at the wedding scheduled for 23 April at Schloss Salem near Lake Constance.[128] The U.S. authorities were gracious about the request and permitted Princess Sophia and Landgravine Margarethe to return to Schloss Friedrichshof, where, after meeting with Captain Nash's successor, they learned that the jewels were indeed missing.[129] The Hessens filed a claim that in turn precipitated an investigation. This then led to the meeting and burgeoning romance of the Monuments, Fine Arts, and Archives officer, Lieutenant Clyde Harris (1917–58), and Princess Cecilie von Preussen, when he came to conduct interviews at Wolfsgarten.[130] But this was the silver lining in what were very difficult experiences for the Hessens. A biographer of Prince Philip, Duke of Edinburgh, noted how the April 1946 wedding "was the first time he had seen his sisters for seven years. They had wept and hugged. . . . Now the cry was for a different reason": the discovery of the jewel theft.[131]

Both the detective work and the trial were notable because of the manner in which American authorities pursued the case. American officials quickly determined that Nash, Durant, and Watson were the main suspects and tracked them to the United States. Military police rushed to find them and apprehended Nash and Durant one day before they left the army (and hence the jurisdiction of the military police). This expedited the judicial process. Nash and Durant were returned to Germany in the summer of 1946, where they faced a trial before a military court in Frankfurt. This trial was also a landmark in the occupation of the American zone, as U.S. authorities made a conscious effort to show that they governed by the rule of law and would prosecute their own nationals. The press swarmed around the trial, and it made front-page news. The theft was even discussed during deliberations in the Senate, as at least one senator used the episode to criticize the comportment of U.S. troops in Germany.[132]

The trial itself, which began during the summer of 1946 in Frankfurt, was highly theatrical, with the recovered jewels displayed on a massive fourteen-meter-long table that was covered with red velvet. Imposing and armed MPs stood guard. The Hessens were again represented by the resistance hero von Schlabrendorff, and Prince Auwi joined the Landgravine to testify about his property.[133] They were required to identify every piece and testify under oath to whom it belonged. The defense tried to discredit Prince Auwi's statements because he had been such a visible supporter of the Nazis, but "the court ruled that membership in a political party was no proof of a lack of credibility for a witness."[134] Considerable attention was also paid to "a large Nazi emblem in solid gold (although the press did not report its owner)."[135] The Landgravine, who knew a great deal about jewelry, distinguished herself with her testimony, telling the history of many individual pieces. Another issue was about the designations "crown jewels" (*Kronjuwelen*) and "family jewels" (*Familienschmuck*) and whether they were one and the same (the Hessens rejected the term "crown jewels," stating they were personal property). The government of the Land Hesse was interested in this question because it pertained to the issue of whether the theft concerned state assets.[136] Philipp was brought from his cell in the Darmstadt internment camp in order to testify: he made it clear that the owners were the Hesse-Kassels, as opposed to the Darmstadt branch, and also managed to fit in short visits with family members.[137]

The trial, which lasted nearly a year, concluded in July 1947. The defense offered by Nash, Watson, and Durant, was that the owners were "either dead, SS members, or ardent Nazi Party members and as such the property would never be returned to them."[138] This thinking did not reflect U.S. policy, although there was an element of truth to it because the top Nazi leaders, including certain members of the SS, had their property seized. The three accused also explained that they had been cognizant of the other thefts at Kronberg, and that "souvenir" taking was so commonplace among GIs that they themselves did not do anything out of the ordinary. Rationalizations aside, this was a jewel theft—and a fairly crude one at that. They removed the diamonds and other gems from the settings—thereby greatly reducing the value—but making the jewels easier to fence.

Landgravine Margarethe and Princess Sophia identify family jewelry at the Frankfurt trial of three members of the U.S. armed forces, July 1946.

Because many of the pieces stemmed from the eighteenth century, their dismemberment was especially regrettable. Nash and Durant had taken some of the valuables to Switzerland and lived extravagantly in a grand hotel on Lake Lucerne as they tried to sell the treasures. Certain dealers, who were suspicious of U.S. army personnel with such precious stones, took a pass and refused to buy. But Nash and Durant managed to hawk some of their loot, and they smuggled the remainder stateside. This incriminating information came out at the trial and led to a guilty verdict, with all three sentenced to jail terms of between three and fifteen years.

Even after the successful prosecution of the three American officers, the Hessens were denied custody of the recovered jewels. The valuables were sent to Washington DC, where they were to be the subject of a civil trial (the Frankfurt trial was the criminal procedure). Certain observers thought they might be seized and counted against war reparations. One of the American attorneys who had participated in the Frankfurt trial, a Major Robinson, offered to represent the Hessens—for a fee of 25 percent of the jewels' value. After lengthy deliberations in the family, they decided to accept his offer. The U.S. government decided in 1951 to return the jewels to the Hessens.[139] They were flown back to Frankfurt on a special plane and presented to the family on 9 May 1951. The Hessens were again not able to take the objects; they first had to settle up with Major Robinson. Because two vastly different appraisals were received, the deliberations continued;

Robinson won out, and the higher figure was utilized. He evidently selected the most valuable objects and returned to the United States. The Hessens received their share on 1 August 1951. Prince Wolfgang estimated that they recovered only 10 percent of what had been stolen—although this figure has been contradicted by others who have maintained that they lost considerably less.[140]

Certain missing pieces surfaced gradually in the postwar period, such as a sword, medals, and gold coat buttons that the grandson of an American GI discovered in the late 1990s. Dr. David Hartley, a physician from Parkesburg, Pennsylvania, wrote the German Embassy in Washington with information about his grandfather, Major Joseph Hartley, who was an officer in the Special Services Unit of the U.S. Army. Hartley had helped set up the officers' club at Kronberg and had, according to his grandson, "removed some 'souvenirs' from the castle that belonged to the House of Hesse."[141] These included some nineteen valuable objects, including "a dual portrait bracelet of gold, turquoise, and pearl with the pictures of Albert and Victoria; the inscription reads 'to our daughter' Victoria from her affectionate parents, Albert and Victoria, Xmas 1856"; a gold broach with an inscription "*Salve*, From Albert, 14 April 1857" (a gift to his wife, Queen Victoria); and a set of gold buttons with the Finnish coat of arms given to Friedrich Karl after he was selected to be king of Finland in 1918.[142] Major Hartley died in 1964 and left the objects to his son, who kept them in a safe-deposit box. This was a common fate for valuable war loot taken by American soldiers: Joe Tom Meador, a GI who removed medieval objects from the Quedlinburg Cathedral, kept them in a safe deposit box in Texas until his death (these objects, worth millions of dollars, subsequently went back to Germany in the mid-1990s after his heirs collected a "finder's fee").[143] Major Hartley's grandson decided to donate the objects he had inherited and turned to Yale University to see if they wanted them. The curators at Yale, however, quickly recognized that the objects "were most likely stolen." They encouraged the Hartleys to do some research and try to return the items to the proper owners. The German Embassy referred Dr. Hartley to the German Historical Institute in Washington, DC, and there, a talented art historian named Dr. Cordula Grewe did some sleuthing. Using the National Archives in College Park, Maryland, Grewe ascertained that the objects came from Kronberg and helped broker the return. The objects were sent back to Landgrave Moritz in July 1999, and he placed them on display at Schloss Fasanerie, where most of the family's treasures are currently displayed. Landgrave Moritz also wrote Dr. Hartley with an invitation to visit the Schloss and the exhibit, noting, "I would be very happy to show you around to return a bit of your family's kindness."[144] The current head of the House of Hessen added, "I think it is a noble gesture of your father's to want these historical pieces returned to their true owners. This attitude is extremely exceptional, since up to today only four foreign officers have returned 'souvenirs' which they helped themselves to or got from the officers in charge of the Kronberg castle officers' club who disposed of our collection quite freely. More than 1,000 items are still on the missing list."[145] Clearly, the recovery of objects stolen from Friedrichshof will continue to be the work of generations to come.

Feeling Victimized

The theft of the jewels by members of the U.S. Army, and the fact that not all of the treasures have been recovered, contributed to feelings of victimization on the part of the Hessens. These days, family members are very stoic about their fate, behaving in a way that one might expect from an august and wealthy dynasty. But they are also cognizant that their family, like all princes in Germany, suffered a decline in their fortunes and power during and after World War II. The punitive measures initiated by the Nazis were compounded by the Allies' occupation policies, which stressed democratization. The Allies viewed the princes in mixed terms: with respect (and awe for their wealth) but also with a suspicion that they had contributed to the illiberal system that had given rise to Hitler and the Nazis. The Allies targeted Philipp more because of his associations with National Socialism than because of his princely status. But after he had gone through denazification and paid his dues, they were determined to render him just another wealthy German citizen in the postwar order.

On an individual basis, the Americans who made up the postwar occupation forces had more varied and complex relationships to the members of the German princely families. Very telling in this regard is a letter sent to the *Times Literary Supplement* in September 1956 by a former GI named Parker Lesley concerning Landgravine Margarethe:

> The pretext for this shabby treatment [by the Americans] was, of course, that her sons had been high in the party hierarchy and (through an ugly revival of old animosities) that she herself was a sister of the last Kaiser. But may I point out that she was not persecuted by *some* Americans, a small group in the Military Government detachments at Frankfurt and Wiesbaden, to whom she eventually became "Tante Mossy": a welcome guest, oftentimes a candid and friendly adviser, and a source of unique recollections and historical reminiscences.[146]

Lesley goes on to tell how the Americans assisted with the reburial of the remains of King Friedrich Wilhelm I of Prussia and Friedrich II (the Great). He recalls asking "Tante Mossy" whether it had been "dignified and appropriate," to which she replied, "even my own people could not have done better." Clearly flattered by this remark, Lesley remarked, "I am sure that no other American ever received such a compliment from a *königliche und kaiserliche Hoheit*."[147] The solemn, respectful ceremony was a key factor, according to her grandson, in her giving up her "private war" (*Privatkrieg*) against the Americans.[148]

Konrad Adenauer and the leaders of the Federal Republic also exhibited an ambivalent policy with regard to princes—and aristocrats more generally. On the one hand, the West German leaders shared in the Americans' belief that the traditional elite had shown itself unfit to continue as a ruling caste and sought to create a new national identity distinct from that associated with the Hohenzollern and Prussia (autocracy, militarism, and the like). Historian Giles Macdonogh noted with regard to the former imperial family, "There was to be no sympathy for the Hohenzollerns in post-war Germany either. Officially, there is none today."[149] Yet on the other hand, Adenauer and other leaders were in need of laudable figures to hold up as examples of "good Germans." Because of the role of aristocrats in the resistance and because certain princes were also members of the capitalist economic elite, there were compelling figures from this milieu who were suitable for recognition and praise.

The association of aristocrats with the notion of the "good German" remained complex during the early postwar period. Count von Stauffenberg, for example, who had been gravely injured while serving his country and then sacrificed himself in an attempt to overthrow Hitler, was also viewed by some as a traitor. Yet the positive—some would say hagiographical—tendencies won out, and by the early 1950s, there was scarcely a German child who was not exposed in school to the story of his death, where his last words before being executed were "long live Germany!" Just as West Germans cultivated the myth that the Holocaust had been perpetrated by a small gang of SS criminals—a myth recently debunked in books such Christopher Browning's *Ordinary Men* and Daniel Goldhagen's *Hitler's Willing Executioners*—so they created the notion of the "good German": someone who was cultured, principled, respectful of tradition, patriotic, and self-sacrificing.[150] Stauffenberg and the other July 20 conspirators fit the bill—if not perfectly, then satisfactorily. By 1954, in a speech to mark the tenth anniversary of the assassination plot, President of the Federal Republic Theodor Heuss expressed gratitude to the "Christian aristocracy of the German nation" for its sacrifice; he also used phrases such as "upris-ing of the conscience" (*Aufstand des Gewissens*) that became associated with the resisters.[151] Historian Theodore Hammerow described the transform-ation regarding public opinion of the July 20 plotters with the phrase, "through martyrdom to beatitude."[152] Because the "saints in the making" were largely aristocratic, it helped them endure other kinds of negative images (such as the militaristic Junkers) that held currency at the same time. The legacy of aristocrats and their role in German society in the postwar period is complicated, and remains, in certain ways, unresolved today.

8

Rebuilding a Life:
Schloss Fasanerie, Financial Viability,
and Burdens of the Past

M any princes in the postwar period tried to lead more private lives, but
this was not always easy. For those who owned castles and estates in
rural areas and small towns, they could not help but stand out among the
local population. The villagers would always be cognizant of the princes,
and many exhibited enthusiasm for traditional customs with feudal associations. Turning out for weddings in great numbers was but one example.
Certain princes remained visible by opening their grand homes to the
public. They benefited from the income—operating an estate has always
been an expensive proposition—and they served a useful civic function by
giving something back to the locals in the form of tourist revenue. This
would be a version of what might term "the Neuschwanstein phenomenon."
"Mad" King Ludwig's castle, which was so expensive to construct in the
nineteenth century that it, and his other building projects, precipitated
charges that Ludwig was bankrupting the Bavarian state (and helped lead
to his ouster as monarch) today attracts millions of visitors and has paid
for itself with tourist revenue many times over.

Additionally, some princes, like aristocrats in general, were much sought
after as members of corporate and philanthropic boards. Many West
Germans evinced considerable respect for individuals with titles. In certain
ways, the mindset was similar to that in the Weimar Republic when Hitler
used the princes to enhance gatherings of Nazi supporters (although
clearly, "Bonn is not Weimar").[1] Aristocrats have had a long history serving
on boards: already at the turn of the nineteenth century, "the younger

generation sought or accepted positions in board rooms which assumed a gentlemanly air, thereby furthering the amalgamation of the notables of land and capital only in the ruling but also the governing class."[2] Certain fields, the art world and publishing houses, for example, have often featured members of the nobility in leadership roles: today, the head of the German branch of Sotheby's is Count Heinrich von Spreti (and the managing director is Duke Philipp von Württemberg). At one show of nineteenth-century art from Germany, Austria, and Hungary, as featured in *Bunte*, Count von Spreti was joined by the Prince and Princess zu Hohenlohe-Langenburg and Princess Elisabeth zu Sachsen-Weimar.[3] There are myriad reasons for the over-representation of aristocrats in the art world: notably, they often possess the social connections to secure consignments and court customers.

Yet the status of princes shifted in the postwar period, as they no longer exerted political influence as a caste. There was little support for a restoration in either the Federal Republic or the German Democratic Republic. The political hegemony of princes, and aristocrats more generally, was conclusively broken by the Nazis and the Allies. The Soviets played a central role in this process, first in the form of the Red Army, and then through the Soviet Military Administrative District, which occupied the eastern zone of Germany. Historian Richard Vinen wrote, "Soviet victory meant extinction for the Junkers."[4] Furthermore, of the 8,827 German nobles studied by Norman Naimark, 6,448 were killed in World War II (4,948 in combat); several hundred were killed after 1945 by captive foreigners who had been working on their estates; around 500 died in detention; and another 500 or so committed suicide.[5] The threat represented by the Red Army and civilians intent on revenge induced many to flee to the West. Many aristocrats in the East, including the Hohenzollern, lost a considerable amount of property, and this too undermined their political clout. Crown Prince Wilhelm's palace in Potsdam, Cecilienhof, became the Soviet military headquarters in the GDR.[6] Most Junker property was nationalized as part of the so-called agrarian reforms launched by the Soviets at the start of the occupation: one writer estimated that "estates amounting to 2,700,000 hectares [about 6,669,000 acres] were distributed to 320,000 families"—figures that convey the vastness of the old elite's holdings.[7] Those nobles driven from their homes in the East maintained a certain degree of political activity via the mutual aid organizations they formed. The Institute for German Aristocratic Research (Institut für Deutsche Adelsforschung), offers one example, because it has served as a pressure group for the interests of the nobility; it has kept track of families who had been displaced and offered a venue for publishing the histories of these individuals.[8] But neither this nor any other organization could alter the fundamental historic realities that confronted the princely families.

The struggles of the traditional nobility to find popular acceptance also became manifested in the fate of the Hohenzollern's urban palace, the Stadtschloss, in Berlin. Indeed, the palace's fate signifies the predominant view toward royalty that prevailed in communist East Germany. A structure that dated back to the fifteenth century, the palace was steadily expanded and remodeled so that it surpassed even Versailles in size.[9] It featured a number of notable rooms, including the grand Alabaster Salon, which had been used for the wedding of Friedrich Karl and Margarethe back in 1893, and the royal stables designed by Ernst von Ihne (the architect of Friedrichshof). Wilhelm II made the palace his primary residence. Later, in 1897, he placed right outside its gates a lavish, expensive, and hence controversial monument to his grandfather, Kaiser Wilhelm I.[10] The palace therefore served as a potent symbol of the monarchy, and it remained just that because the Nazi regime basically ignored it and let the building, including its Baroque masonry, deteriorate.

Like nearly all structures in Berlin, the palace was badly damaged during the war, but it was far from unsalvageable. Its meter-thick walls and sandstone facade, as well as the cupola, remained largely intact in 1945. Yet in 1949, the nascent government of the German Democratic Republic permitted the Soviets to shoot an epic film, *The End of Berlin*, and "to add realism to their battle scenes, the filmmakers brought several functioning artillery pieces with them and began firing live shells at the palace walls."[11] Rumors of the impending destruction of the palace began to circulate: preservationists did what they could to try to save the structure (for example, searching for a letter by Lenin where he praised its architecture), while the government made its case by advertising the 50-million-mark estimate for its repair. The chairman of the Central Committee of the East German Communist Party, Walter Ulbricht, announced the decision on 2 July 1950: he "felt little nostalgia for the emperor's last home" and issued the decision to raze the structure.[12] Because the decision was so controversial, Ulbricht ordered the destruction to be expedited, and many other building projects were temporarily halted so that workers could concentrate on the palace: "demolition began in September 1950 with crews working in three shifts."[13] The coup de grace, which entailed some 10,000 kilos of dynamite, took place on 14 October 1950. Quite remarkably, the site of the royal palace remained vacant for over twenty years: it was only in 1973 that GDR leader Erich Honecker announced that the Volkskammer, or People's Parliament, would occupy the site, and the resulting Palace of the Republic was erected from steel and glass (and asbestos). The Palace of the Republic also featured a restaurant, a theater, and a bowling alley in the basement. It became a popular locale for East Germans and one of the most recognizable symbols of the GDR. When the Berlin Wall fell, suggestions to demolish the Volkskammer precipitated objections from many East

Germans, who saw this as a kind of cultural imperialism perpetrated by the "*Wessies*."[14] Today, there is a Society to Promote the Imperial Palace, led by an aristocratic Hamburg businessman named Wilhelm von Boddien. The Society has raised several million dollars to fund the reconstruction of the royal palace (they used some of these funds to erect a full-dimension canvas replica). Others fought to refurbish the Palace of the Republic and managed to secure an order to halt the destruction in 1995.[15] While the ultimate fate of the structure remains in doubt, the debates that have raged over the two palaces that have occupied the site reveal the strong emotions attached to history and its symbols in Germany. The movement to restore the Stadtschloss is in itself revealing; a sign that antiroyal sentiment dissipated in the late twentieth century.

Despite a more limited political role, some princes resurfaced to be highly visible figures in the Federal Republic. Others, of course, have chosen to lead more inconspicuous and ordinary bourgeois lives. But those who are attracted to the limelight and who play up to it—either by cooperating with the media or fighting with them—are favorite subjects of popular society and gossip magazines. The German public, like its counterpart in most other European countries, seem fascinated with the royals' looks and glamour, and alternatively with their scandals and woes. Responding to an insatiable demand for royal gossip: magazines such as *Bunte*, *Gala*, and *Neue Revue* have thrived for years. They are not noticeably different from period-icals such as *Monarchy* magazine and *Royalty* in the United Kingdom, *Point de Vue* and *Paris Match* in France, *Hola!* in Spain, or *Gente* in Italy, among many others. A host of Internet websites tracking European royals has also come into existence.[16] Modern media has increased the public exposure of many princes as compared to the 1950s and 1960s, when there were fewer outlets. In light of the popular press, it is easy to understand why many princes choose to pursue more private lives. But it is not that straightforward: many princes continue to take great pride in their lineage and status, and make efforts to preserve their special place in society.

Philipp, Schloss Fasanerie, and Other Memorials

Upon emerging from both Nazi and American incarceration in January 1948, Philipp focused on rebuilding his life.[17] He had no desire to return to the home in Kassel that he and Mafalda had shared. As noted earlier, he transferred ownership of the Palais Bellevue to the city in exchange for relief from his fines and court costs. In 1959, the house was transformed into a museum devoted to the history of the Brothers Grimm (who had lived in Kassel while they compiled their famous fairy-tale collection in the first decades of the nineteenth century); the museum remains open to this day. Philipp initially chose to move into a tower that was part of the castle at Kronberg, the medieval Burg that Empress Friedrich had restored at the same time she built Schloss Friedrichshof. The half-timbered tower was actually a nineteenth-century English princess's notion of what a German castle should look like. The U.S. Army continued to occupy Schloss Friedrichshof until 1953, and many of the other Hessen properties were either too damaged by bombs to inhabit (including Schloss Fasanerie and Rumpenheim), or too expensive to maintain. Philipp therefore lived modestly—albeit within a stunning fortress featuring soaring ramparts—as he occupied a tower that is now referred to as the *Prinzenturm*.

The fortress at Kronberg continued to serve as the burial site of the family, but it required reconstruction because it too had been struck by Allied bombs. Philipp's first project was to restore the graves and adjoining chapel, which lay just below his rooms in the Prinzenturm. He repaired the small chapel with its medieval sculptures but left the long nave of the structure—what had previously been the choir—in the open air without a roof. The high stone walls were partially rebuilt, and vines soon climbed this shell of the old church, giving the place the look of a Caspar David Friedrich painting. That this was Philipp's first undertaking after he had emerged from incarceration says something about his feelings of loss, memory, and also heritage. Landgravine Margarethe also came often to pay her respects to family members before her death in January 1954, when she too took her place in the fortress cemetery.

Philipp devoted himself to this monument to death and family tragedy. In 1951, he arranged for Mafalda's remains to be transferred from Weimar, the city closest to Buchenwald (a notable gesture for the communist German Democratic Republic), to the family crypt at Kronberg.[18] A larger-than-life bronze bust of the princess was placed there, soon to be joined by other plaques donated by Italian royalists. Even though the Savoys were forced out in a 1946 plebiscite (Vittorio Emmanuele abdicated in favor of his son Umberto, but the latter's reign lasted less than two months), a sizeable royalist movement persevered in the Italian Republic. King Umberto II never formally abdicated prior to his death in 1983, and his sister, Princess Mafalda, remained a beloved figure and a symbol of a tragic, bygone era. Associations like the Gruppo Cavour di Genoa would visit her grave on the anniversaries of her birth and death, carrying the proverbial torch. Such fervently monarchical sentiments help explain why male members of the House of Savoy were prohibited from setting foot in Italy until a 2002 ruling by the European Court of Human Rights induced the Italian parliament to amend the constitution.[19]

Philipp also undertook the restoration of the family Schloss Adolphseck in Eichenzell (near Fulda), now bearing its original name "Fasanerie." (Considering Prince Heinrich's anecdote, one is led to wonder whether the

American soldier's confusion of the castle's name with Hitler's first name might have contributed to the change of name after 1945?) The Americans, for reasons that remain unclear, had bombed the eighteenth-century Schloss in October 1944. Philipp oversaw its reconstruction and concentrated the art collection of the Hausstiftung in the structure, which is now a museum. He had apparently conceived this plan for Fasanerie during the war, and thought about it a great deal during his years of imprisonment.[20] The reconstruction of the actual structure lasted until 1959; and although individual rooms were opened to the public as early as 1951, Fasanerie was not complete as a museum until 1972. Featuring some sixty exhibition rooms, it contains paintings, furniture, and porcelain largely from the eighteenth and nineteenth centuries as well as what "some experts regard as the finest private collection of antiquities in Germany."[21] Schloss Fasanerie counts as one of the most beautiful baroque castles in Hessen. Princess Sophia had noted about Philipp, "His sense of taste with regard to interior decorations and presentation as applied not only to homes, but also to gardens is especially impressive. . . ."[22] Sophia's son Rainer von Hessen called Fasanerie "Philipp's *Gesamtkunstwerk*" (total work of art).[23] One guide recalled how Philipp would visit the public rooms of the castle at night in order to move or remove objects—the latter usually for purposes of restoration. After an embarrassing incident, where the guide lectured a group on a picture she thought stood behind her (and then discovered the visitors were staring at a blank wall), she learned to be more cautious and check to see if Philipp had made any nocturnal alterations.[24]

Philipp was in many ways a changed man. He had grown bitter, more cynical, and less inclined to live a public existence. Granted, he continued to receive positive, respectful notices in the local press on his birthday. He also made small gestures that earned him goodwill: in the 1960s, he decreed that all students studying classical art would have unlimited free admission to Schloss Fasanerie for study purposes. It was clear, however, that this was a chastened man who had retired from public life to devote himself to his art collection.[25]

After the war, Philipp and his twin brother, Wolfgang, formed a kind of partnership as they oversaw the family foundation (Kurhessische Hausstiftung). Wolfgang, who had a background in banking, focused on financial matters and was the business manager of the family foundation; Philipp, on the other hand, concerned himself with more artistic projects. Wolfgang had remarried: in 1948: he wed Ottilie Moeller (1903–91), a longtime friend who had owned a fashion boutique in Frankfurt. Even though he continued to be a formal, rather old-fashioned gentleman, he was changing with the times. While his choice of spouses was not as remarkable as that of Princess Cecilie von Preussen, who relocated to Amarillo, Texas, after marrying American soldier and interior designer

Prince Philipp von Hessen in 1955, studying architectural plans for Schloss Fasanerie.

Clyde Harris, it became more common for princes to enter into matches that were not "*ebenbürtig.*" The 1949 meeting between Clyde Harris and Crown Prince Wilhelm, where they discussed a possible betrothal, is revealing: Harris explained that he was not a rich man but that he "could feed her" and that "she would lead a very simple life as Mrs. Harris in Amarillo."[26] That the crown prince offered no objections (and that nourishment should enter into the discussion) speaks to the changed fortunes of many princes. The postwar period, of course, was a time of readjustment for many princely families, including the Hohenzollern and the Hessens, as they rearranged their considerable property to be more in line with the changed circumstances.

By the late 1950s it became evident that it was necessary to restructure the estates of the House of Hesse, and this meant selling certain properties and finding ways for others to generate revenue. A great concern was Schloss Friedrichshof, which was a massive drain on resources. In earlier times of economic difficulty, the family simply shut up the representational rooms in the castle, covered the furniture, and moved to the kitchen wing of the house and to a cottage in the park. After the Americans vacated the premises in 1953, the family resorted to a variation of this tactic: the Landgravine continued to live in the estate manager's cottage, where she remained until her death in 1954, while Prince Wolfgang promoted the idea of turning Schloss Friedrichshof into a luxurious hotel, which occurred after a thorough renovation in 1954. The picturesque castle, with its half-timbered sections, wood paneling, and stained-glass windows, became a favorite meeting place for the Frankfurt business elite as well as for a fashionable international clientele. The family kept certain rooms for private purposes, including Empress Friedrich's quarters, which still have most of the authentic furniture as well as pictures that she herself painted (outside the family, only the manager of the hotel has the keys to her rooms). Friedrichshof emerged as a remarkable amalgamation of hotel, family home, and museum; one therefore finds parts of the family patrimony, such as paintings by English painters J. M. W. Turner and Sir Joshua Reynolds, in the piano bar. In another attempt to generate revenue from the inheritance, the surrounding grounds were leased to a golf club (in Germany, the sport is very expensive by American standards). In short, constant financial "restructuring" has been required to maintain the family patrimony.

Besides transforming certain residences into hotels (Wolfgang's former home in Frankfurt became what is arguably the city's finest hotel, the Hessischer Hof), another major initiative of the Princes von Hessen was their vineyard in the Rhineland. While this enterprise did not stem from one of the family's traditional domains (the estate had long been in the Metternich family), it is nonetheless closely linked to their recent history.[27] In the wake of the theft of the Hessen jewels from Friedrichshof, and the failure of the Hessens to recover all the objects, the German government provided them with financial compensation. It is curious that the money did not come from the United States, whose nationals—and indeed, military personnel—committed the offense, but instead from the Federal Republic. The Hessens took these funds and invested them in a fifty-acre estate specializing in Rieslings. The Weingut Prinz von Hessen did well in the 1960s and helped Wolfgang, Philipp, and others, put the family back on sound financial footing. Family members have taken an active part in marketing the product.

While Philipp retreated from public life, he was nevertheless the "head of the House of Hessen" from 1940 until his death in 1980. This meant that he "received under the designation 'primary agent' a fully dominant position; without an election he was a member of the board [of the Kurhessische Hausstiftung]; and he received by far the largest part of the disposable income from the various designations."[28] Despite this power, he remained a reserved, even self-effacing man. He continued to divide his time between Germany and Italy.[29] He spent summers in Germany, focusing on his collection of ancient art. He returned to Rome, to the Villa Polissena, during the winter, where he could enjoy the warmer climate and build his collection further. It is fair to say, however, that while Philipp cultivated his interest in classical art and archeology, he repressed his own more recent history. His son, Landgrave Moritz, recalled that they never discussed events during the Third Reich or Mafalda's tragic fate: "It was simply too painful for him," he said.[30]

Moritz's younger brother, Prince Heinrich, also remained deeply affected by his mother's death. A talented artist, known as Enrico d'Assia in Italy, he was perhaps most proud of his set design for a production of *Turandot* at the Roman opera in 1965. Puccini had dedicated the opera to Mafalda, and for the Prince to win an award—the "Silver Mask"—was a particularly emotional moment for him (the then twenty-nine-year-old Zubin Mehta had conducted the orchestra).[31] Heinrich and his siblings later inherited the Villa Polissena in Rome, and like their father, they kept certain rooms unchanged.[32]

Philipp maintained friendships with many other princes, including the Duke and Duchess of Windsor, whom he visited at their home just outside Paris. The Windsors also grew much closer to Sir Oswald and Lady Diana Mosley in the 1950s and 1960s. Among the common denominators was not only aristocratic birth (including a familial link on Diana's side to the duke), but also once-sympathetic views about National Socialism.[33] Mosley, who signed his letters to the duke using the familiar, "Tom," wrote in January 1963, "May I with great respect congratulate you on the conclusion, clarity, and dignity of your reply to recent attacks, and on the course with which you stressed the true patriotism of striving to avert the catastrophe of a second world war."[34] Both the Mosleys and the Windsors lived in elegant exile in France (their country homes were separated by only a few miles).[35] Others in this circle of, some might say, tarnished nobility included members of the Bismarck family: for example, Countess Mona Bismarck (widow of Eddie), remained a good friend of Philipp's, and she also had a Paris home.[36] This cohort remained largely unpolitical—or at least with regard to the public sphere. But Philipp, like the Mosleys, continued to elicit sympathy from certain extreme right-wing quarters: a biographical reference work edited by Dr. Gerhard Frey, a well-known leader of the German radical right, stated that Philipp had "not received restitution (*Wiedergutmachung*) for his imprisonment in a Nazi concentration camp, in an Allied concentration camp, for the murder of his wife, or for the seizure of his property."[37] Philipp's difficult history provided an opportunity for the extreme right to advance its agenda of relativizing Nazi crimes and emphasizing the Germans' suffering (or in their eyes, victimization).

Philipp died in Rome in October 1980, just short of his eighty-fourth birthday. His body was transported back to Kronberg, and after a service in the chapel of the Burg, was placed in the family cemetery next to Mafalda's.[38] When Philipp died, there was considerable coverage in the local press—just as there had been articles on him on the occasion of his sixtieth, seventieth, and eightieth birthdays (usually with the same photo— the prince never appeared to age!). Within the towns in Hessen where the family had residences, Philipp elicited positive sentiments and nostalgia. He was viewed as a grand and kind seigneur, and certain myths surrounding him took hold. The Castellan of Kronberg, for example, talked about his "*Kriegsgefangenschaft*" (being a prisoner of war) after 1945—a euphemistic term, and one tinged with images of victimization.

His son Prince Heinrich authored a volume of memoirs that romanticized the past. The title, which one would translate as "The Crystal Chandelier," captures the sense of deep pathos in the book.[39] Prince Heinrich opens by reflecting on the chandelier that was in the Villa Savoia in Rome where he was born; how it reminds him of 8 September 1943, when he was forced to flee. He then describes how the building was taken over by the Egyptian state and used as its embassy. Not wanting this relic of a bygone era, "this last witness of family life," to endure the ignominy of dust and cobwebs, he writes how he induced the superintendent to let him remove it. He then took it next door to his home in the Villa Polissena and hung it in his bedroom. Perhaps less benign is Heinrich's whitewashing of history, where, for example, he claims that Prince Philipp was initially categorized by the denazification board as being in Category III (lesser offender) and then being placed in Category IV as a "fellow traveler."[40] Prince Heinrich did not report the initial findings of the board that placed his father in Category II (offender). Nor did he hint at the long and contentious appeals process. Instead, he suggested that his father was like the vast majority who went through denazification and placed in Category IV (there is a reason historians talk about the "fellow-traveler factory").[41] The omissions made by Prince Heinrich appear to be no mere oversight (he cites a specific date for the Category III ruling) and reflect an effort to whitewash the past.

Christoph's Legacy and the Burdens of the Past

In certain ways, the family of Prince Christoph faced greater challenges than that of Philipp, and in certain ways they were in a more advantageous situation. The challenges began with Christoph's more problematic career during the Third Reich: as an SS officer and director of a Nazi intelligence agency, his was a difficult past to overcome. Furthermore, his widow Sophia was left at war's end with five children without a home of her own. More advantageous, however, was that Christoph did not have to experience the two-years forced internment faced by all SS officers or go through denazification. Author John Parker argued that "if Christopher had survived he would have been brought to trial at Nuremberg. This in turn would undoubtedly have killed off the Mountbattens' aspirations to marry the future Queen of England to their most eligible bachelor."[42] While Christoph would not have been regarded as sufficiently high ranking to be included in any of the Nuremberg trials (his more visible and high-ranking brother Philipp was not), and the second part of Parker's formulation is a gratuitous counterfactual, Christoph would have faced some measure of justice. His immediate superior and friend, Pilli Körner, received a prison sentence of fifteen years, of which he served ten.[43] (After his release he moved to the Tegernsee in Bavaria but died two years later.)[44] Christoph's death meant that he avoided a denazification trial and the confrontation of the past brought about by the process.

There was, in fact, a posthumous denazification trial involving the estate (*Nachlass*) of Prince Christoph, which took place in Berlin between 1950 and 1953. The purpose was to determine whether Princess Sophia and their five children were entitled to their shares of the inheritance; property belonging to individuals placed in Categories I and II was subject to seizure by the state. The trial concerning Prince Christoph's estate did not entail an in-depth investigation of his record; from the extant documentation, it appears that the prosecution did not call any witnesses. And, of course, Christoph could not be cross-examined. The defense counsel produced supportive statements from several Luftwaffe comrades, including the highly decorated Baron von Maltzahn. The verdict rendered in March 1953 is that Christoph would not have been in Categories I or II, and that it was impossible to place him in Category III as a lesser offender; for this to occur "some profit was necessary," and this had not happened.[45] The judge ruled that there would be no subsequent trial to levy a fine, and all restrictions on Prince Christoph's estate were thus lifted. His heirs received their inheritance (for the children it was evenly apportioned), even if the sums were modest.

Princess Sophia faced a situation in some ways analogous to her brother-in-law Philipp in that both had lost spouses and had children to raise. But she was able to remarry and provide for a more conventional family environment. On 23 April 1946, she married Prince Georg Wilhelm von Hannover (b. 1915), who became the headmaster of the Salem School near Lake Constance in 1948 after having finished his studies in Göttingen as a doctor of law. Previously, on 22 March 1946, the groom's father, Ernst August Duke von Braunschweig, in following a provision dating to the reign of King George III in the eighteenth century, "formally applied" to his cousin, King George VI, for his consent to the marriage (the Duke signed the request, "Your Majesty's affectionate Cousin"—customary wording among royals.)[46] The king was notified by the Lord Chancellor that "in view of the fact that a state of war still exists between Great Britain and Germany, His Majesty is advised that the case is not one in which it is practicable for His consent to be given in the manner contemplated by the Act."[47] Indeed, "in view of the Duke's technical enemy status it would be difficult for His Majesty to send any written reply to his letter, or even an intimation that there is no objection to the marriage as far as His Majesty is personally concerned, since any intimation of this kind might later on lead to an argument as to whether such personal consent was effective, which would be very embarrassing."[48] A small army of royal officials, diplomats, and legal experts—as well as Foreign Secretary Ernest Bevin—weighed in. The sum of their wisdom resulted in no formal response from George VI, but a behind-the-scenes communication of his "personal" approval and best wishes. Despite the awkward situation (made more so because Ernst August von Braunschweig had exhibited sympathy for the Nazis), certain of the king's advisers commented that the Duke of Brunswick had "done the correct thing in applying to His Majesty."[49] Queen Mary also expressed her pleasure that the "pretty little widow Tiny" had found a new husband.[50] She wrote to Sophia's mother, Princess Alice, "[Sophia] has 5 children, so they will need a large house! They seem delighted."[51] Sophia's younger brother, Prince Philip, managed to slip back into Germany to attend the wedding and brought, in addition to the traditional wedding gifts, provisions sent by other family members. Sophia and Prince Georg then had two sons and a daughter. While she received an inheritance when her father, Prince Andrea, died in 1944, and more money when her grandmother Victoria passed away in 1950, these sums were not great.[52]

Another aspect of the difficult postwar years was the awkward situation created by her deceased husband's support for National Socialism and the fact that her brothers-in-law had been officers in the Wehrmacht. Neither Sophia nor any of her sisters were invited to the 1947 royal wedding of their brother to then Princess Elizabeth: "The war so recently ended was far from forgotten [Britain still had rationing] and it was deemed politically insensitive that they should come. . . . Palace advisers did not want Princess Elizabeth's groom tarnished by innuendo in the press. Philip's sisters considered it a necessary sacrifice that they would make for him. But they felt doubly hurt when invitations were sent to Queen Helen of Romania and her sister, the Duchess of Aosta, since Romania and Italy had been Hitler's chief allies in the war."[53] Although this view reflected a lack of understanding of the Hessens' involvement with the Nazi regime, there is no denying the hurt feelings. Princess Sophia, for example, wrote to her uncle "Dickie" (Louis Mountbatten), "It is not very easy, I assure you, to make the press (who interview us continually) understand & they keep insisting that we must be estranged, which only makes a difficult & humiliating position even more unpleasant."[54] The German connection

—and more specifically the Nazi connection—may have been one of the factors that militated against the use of the Mountbatten name for the royal family in the United Kingdom. This had been very important to Louis Mountbatten, who "within days of the King [George VI's] death [in February 1952], had boasted to Prince Ernst August of Hannover that the House of Mountbatten now reigned in England."[55] Winston Churchill, who had returned to office as prime minister, became involved in the deliberations about this matter; he "prevailed upon the Queen to declare that the reigning family should continue to be styled the House of Windsor, which declaration was made on 9 April 1952. This decision was disappointing, if not rather more than that, to Dickie."[56] In fact, as noted earlier, Prince Philip's surname prior to adoption by his uncle Lord Louis Mountbatten was Schleswig-Holstein-Sonderburg-Glücksburg, and this should have been the name of the British ruling house. But as one author quipped, "it sounded too much like Borussia Mönchengladbach's back four to be passed off as typically British" and the matter was handled in a manner reminiscent of 1917.[57]

Despite the difficulties faced by Sophia and other members of the Hessen family in the early postwar years, they still managed private visits to the British royals (despite foreign travel being impossible for most Germans until the early 1950s). In 1948 Sophia was the first of Philip's sisters to visit, bringing two of her daughters to the relatively secluded estate on Windlesham Moor in Surrey where Philip and Elizabeth resided until Elizabeth became queen. Philip's other sisters came later that summer, prompting author John Parker to write, "if the German faction had felt troubled about being left out in the cold at the wedding, normal family relations were now resumed."[58] The visit, however, took place privately, "without a whisper in the British newspapers."[59] Somewhat analogously, King George VI reached out to Prince Paul of Yugoslavia, who while regarded by many as a kind of quisling after caving to Hitler in 1941, "was welcomed and treated by the King and Queen, and later by Queen Elizabeth II, as a friend, a royal prince, and a Garter Knight."[60] With regards to his German relatives, the Duke of Edinburgh traveled back to Germany on a regular basis, sometimes under the auspices of his work as honorary regimental commander for forces stationed there. He was particularly fond of hunting invitations that his relations organized for him on their various estates.[61] Although the German and, indeed, Nazi connections of the Duke of Edinburgh's family remained a sensitive subject, time improved matters. When Queen Elizabeth's coronation took place on 2 June 1953, Sophia and her sisters were permitted to attend the ceremony in Westminster Abbey: their mother, Alice, "sat in the royal box behind the Queen Mother and the royal princesses. With her were her three daughters and their husbands."[62] Still, it is a telling symbol that Queen Elizabeth II and Prince Philip did

Prince Philip, Duke of Edinburgh, Princess Margaret ("Peg") von Hessen, Prince Moritz, and Princess Sophia von Hessen-Hannover at the opening of the Jugendstil rooms in the Darmstadt Schlossmuseum, 1981.

not make their first state visit to Germany until May 1965—twenty years after the end of the war.[63] When asked about the long interval between the war and this state visit, the Duke of Edinburgh quipped with a certain sarcastic humor, "It was quick"; but he then added more seriously, "it took some time . . . before there was a sort of relaxation. It wasn't outright hostility [to the Germans]. There were a lot of people who had suffered seriously. I think they would have been upset if we had done it earlier. I mean, even now, with the Emperor Hirohito's funeral, there is considerable anxiety here by veterans. So it lasts quite a long time."[64]

The process of "mastering the past" proved challenging for many members of the Hessen family. Prince Christoph's twin, Prince Richard, who at war's end had been interned by the Americans at a camp in Moosburg in Bavaria, became a great believer in "Moral Rearmament." This religiously tinged philanthropic movement, which had been founded by Lutheran clergyman Frank Buchman in 1938, had its European headquarters in Caux near Montreux on Lake Geneva. It offered a new ethic that would replace nihilism and communism. Adherents believed that every person had a good core and should be accepted for who they are.[65] Richard shared this experience with ex-king Michael of Romania, the son of his cousin, Queen Helen (born Princess of Greece and Denmark) (1896–1982). They used a kind of didactic theater to articulate their message and were very successful in the

1950s and 1960s. For Prince Richard, Moral Rearmament helped him with his conscience after World War II.

Most members of the Hessen family took decades before they confronted the difficult history associated with the Third Reich. In the 1980s, Prince Christoph's son Rainer induced his uncle, Prince Wolfgang, to set down his memories. For the older generation, Prince Wolfgang was typical: as his nephew Rainer noted, "He did not want to speak about the Third Reich and was inclined to view the past with considerable self-pity."[66] Because of Rainer's gentle prodding, the book featured some useful material, but it was hardly an objective study. In certain respects, it offers an example of what Marcus Funck and Stephan Malinowski have called "the strategic use of autobiographical memory"; but because the book was published privately (only seventy copies were produced), the intended audience consisted of family members and friends, and not the general public.[67] The prince nonetheless offered a selective history of his and other family members' experiences. For example, in his treatment of his own denazification trial, Wolfgang noted that he had been placed in Category V—among those who were exonerated.[68] He said nothing of the fact that the public prosecutor immediately challenged the ruling and that an appeals court had suspended the judgment.[69] In fact, Wolfgang ended up in a kind of limbo. From the vantage point of the mid-1980s, he could not rightly say that he had been exonerated: this distinction had been taken away from him by the appeals court, and thus his omission must be considered a misrepresentation. Prince Heinrich then set down his recollections of his parents and his experiences as youth in a 1992 book, first published in Italian. But Heinrich was so emotionally involved with the subject that he lacked the necessary distance for reflection, which indeed found expression in this elegant but uncritical book.

Emblematic of the Hessens' view of the recent past is the disposition of the family archives, housed at Schloss Fasanerie. As stated in the introduction to this book, access to the family archives containing private letters and papers from the twentieth century is usually not granted to scholars. Documents in private archives do not fall under the federal and state laws that regulate access in Germany. The family has a legal right to keep these files closed in perpetuity. The Hessens have nevertheless adopted a policy whereby they make accessible papers of generations above grandparents of living family members. Occasionally, they make an exception to this policy: they informed me, "On the basis of personal acquaintance and growing mutual confidence, an exception was made given the scholarly nature of your work and the importance of helping explore the National Socialist period."[70] Much of the credit goes to Landgrave Moritz, the head of the House. The Landgrave clearly has a keen interest in this history: it is telling that he visited the German Federal Archives in 1991 and ordered his father's records from the Third Reich (the former Berlin Document Center file)—as indicated in the ledger attached to the file.

Within the Hessen family, the real force for openness is Rainer von Hessen, a historian himself who has worked on earlier periods of the family's history.[71] Rainer has been unfailingly supportive of my research: he made available letters and photographs in his possession and spent a great deal of time discussing the many challenging issues. For him, investigating this history is not just a scholarly project but also a very personal one. In late 2003, for example, letters from his father to his mother were found in her home in the Bavarian Alps. They had been stored in the cellar and were found by one of her daughters, as she helped to clear the house after Princess Sophia's death. These letters astonished her family. Rainer commented, "She kept them all and either must have forgotten about them or didn't want anyone to see them during her lifetime but thank God she didn't destroy them! I went there immediately to rescue the treasure. . . . Christoph becomes alive again, and I start to get to know my father."[72] There is then, a profound interest in history on the part of the Hessens —and many other aristocrats. It constitutes a fundamental part of their identity and often elicits strong emotions.

Royals in Postwar Germany

To be a prince or princess again became fashionable in the 1990s. While it may be fair to assert that being a royal was never out of fashion (except in the midst of a revolution), one can discern fluctuations in the fortunes and public perceptions of the traditional elite. Tracking the changes in their status is an imprecise and somewhat subjective enterprise. Fortunes vary according to individual, to family, and perhaps even to region. It is striking, for example, to witness the popularity of the Wittelsbach in Bavaria: at a 2003 birthday fete for the head of the dynasty, Duke Franz von Bayern (b. 1933), and several other family members, none of the 3,100 guests invited to Schloss Nymphenburg in Munich declined the invitation. Local Bavarian television devoted seven hours of live coverage to the event, much of it focusing on the receiving line.[73] While the Wittelsbach family has been popular throughout the postwar period, there is something telling about a remark made by one royal (who requested anonymity) that before German reunification in 1990, few of her cohort used aristocratic titles (although they would keep the "von" in their names); yet subsequently "it became the thing to do." While the immediate postwar period proved exceptionally trying for many princely families, these dynasties that often stretched back to feudal times exhibited a capacity for survival and revival.

The nadir of German royals' fortunes in the twentieth century came in the years after 1945. The Americans implemented their plan of the "four *D*s": denazification, demilitarization, decartelization, and also democratization. Princes appeared antithetical to the last of the *D*s, and perhaps several of the others. Indeed, to the four *D*s one could add an unofficial fifth: "defeudalization." The British also often shared such sentiments: many associated the German monarchy with a tradition of militarism that led to World War I and contributed in some fundamental way to National Socialism and World War II.[74] Among the Western Allies, there was also a lingering concern that Germans might advocate a return to a monarchy after 1945. In the East, within the Soviet Military Administrative District, the Soviets opposed aristocrats for both ideological reasons (symbols of a bygone feudal era) and for practical political reasons (threats to their rule). Princes and other aristocrats were therefore among the millions who fled their homes in the East—the "*Vertriebene*" (those driven out)—and started again in the Federal Republic. This is a history captured in memoirs, such as those by Countess Marion von Dönhoff, the well-known editor of the weekly periodical, *Die Zeit*. But many royals in both the East and West suffered difficulties in the immediate postwar period. It is perhaps an apt symbol that members of the Schaumburg-Lippe family needed to sell their residence in Bonn and that it became the first residence for Chancellor Konrad Adenauer. To take another of many examples, Hereditary Prince Ernst zur Lippe, the first of his family to join the Nazi Party and the former aide to Reich Peasant Leader Darré, was reduced to a decidedly nonaristocratic existence, working for the electricity firm AEG and then for a Berlin hotel.[75]

Somewhat astonishingly, a royalist movement regenerated itself in the early postwar period. Leading proponents of a restoration convened in Marburg, Hesse, in 1952, in order to discuss their strategy. In the words of John Röhl, "They decided against founding a political party. Instead, they launched a campaign to popularize the pretender, Prince Louis Ferdinand of Prussia. Funds were raised, an organization created with a card index listing all monarchist supporters and sympathizers, statesmen and parliamentarians of all party and religious affiliation were approached in the hope of winning them over to the cause." They also contacted representatives of other princely houses in Germany, with the request that they back the Hohenzollern as the monarch. In light of the views of the victorious powers, not to mention the majority of the German population, Röhl added, "These proposals demonstrated [a] breathtaking lack of realism."[76]

Strong antiaristocratic sentiments continued to prevail in West Germany in the 1960s and 1970s, fueled, in part, by left-wing protesters who opposed the Vietnam War and were generally critical of "the establishment." Lord Louis Mountbatten's biographer Philip Ziegler offers one example, as he discusses his subject's attachment to Wolfsgarten:

In 1973, it seemed as if this most sacred of all his places of pilgrimage might be threatened. The left-wing Hessian government was bent on making life impossible for owners of private property. They told Princess Margaret [Peg] that she would have to take down the wire fence around her park so that anybody might freely wander through it. She pointed out that the fence was not there to keep the public out but to keep in the mentally and physically handicapped children to whom Wolfsgarten was now largely devoted. She won that battle, but the war went on.[77]

While Ziegler exaggerates the Hessian officials' animus against property owners, he captures very effectively the perceptions of many members of princely families at this time, who often felt embattled and unfairly put upon. Even Princess Peg's philanthropic work was not without complications.

John Wheeler-Bennett noted about George VI, "At the King's birth [1895], there were twenty reigning monarchs in Continental Europe. At his death [1952], there were but seven (Norway, Denmark, Sweden, Holland, Belgium, Luxemburg, and Greece)."[78] Clearly, an epochal shift occurred in this span of years. But the trajectory was not a straight or predetermined line. Indeed, subsequent to Wheeler-Bennett's tabulation, one country (Greece) abandoned its monarchy, while another (Spain) rejoined the monarchical ranks. By the year 2000, nine countries in Europe counted themselves as some form of monarchy (Monaco and Liechtenstein included)—one sign of the royals' persistence. To take another example, Prince Hans Adam II, the sovereign of Liechtenstein, threatened to resign unless he was given more power; and a referendum in March 2003 gave him more authority in his country than any of his counterparts. He now has the power to dismiss governments, approve judicial nominees, and veto laws.[79] More often, princes have worked within democratic systems as ordinary, if prominent, citizens. Members of the Habsburg family have been active in European politics, particularly since 1961, when Archduke Otto (the son of the last Austrian Kaiser) renounced his claims to the thrones of Austria, Hungary, Bohemia, and other lands that once made up his family's empire. This move enabled him to return to Austria. He and his son, Karl von Habsburg (b. 1961), have both been members of the European Union Parliament in Strasbourg.[80] Their pan-European vision, frequently found among members of the high nobility, has contributed to the resurgence of princely families. At times, it is not always clear that politicians are princes. Free Democratic Party member and current vice-president of the Bundestag Hermann Otto Solms bears the name Prince zu Solms.[81]

Another sign of the resurgence of princes appears in the claims for property in what was formerly Communist-dominated Eastern Europe. While these claims are not limited to princes, they and myriad aristocrats were in the forefront of a movement seeking the return of billions of dollars of ancestral property after the collapse of Communism (there were some 2.5 million pieces of property confiscated either by the Nazi state or by the GDR).[82] Among the princely families that have claimed property are the Schwarzenbergs and Lobkowiczes in the Czech Republic, and the Potockis and the Lanckoronskis in Poland.[83] A number of German aristocrats of Junker heritage have also contemplated claims in the East. However, to date, members of dispossessed Junker families have not recovered property in reunified Germany. In the Czech Republic, approximately forty castles (from the more than five hundred confiscated by the postwar Benes Decrees) had been restituted by July 2003, and this has given claimants all over Europe reason to hope that the trend might continue in other countries.[84] These property claims, some believe, lie at the heart of a September 2004 resolution by the Polish parliament that demanded compensation from the Germans for World War II losses; according to one interpretation, this resolution represented a kind of preemptive strike. A more important point, however, is that in the wake of the collapse of Communism and the Soviet empire, and with the reunification of Germany, many aristocrats, including princes, felt emboldened. Just as many Germans began to feel more patriotic, so too did it become more common for members of the nobility to feel a greater sense of familial pride.

This is not to say that members of princely families have not faced distinctive challenges. Resentment and mistrust continue, especially in Europe. To take two specific, but suggestive, examples: when American attorney Stuart Eizenstat took on members of Habsburg family as clients in a suit against the Austrian government for damages incurred during the Third Reich, one Austrian historian queried why Eizenstat, a prominent advocate for Holocaust victims who had held a number of important posts in the U.S. government, "would use his reputation and good name to help these reactionaries?" There is also the recent incident where Princess Michael of Kent attracted controversy and negative press for allegedly uttering a racist remark—reportedly telling African Americans in New York, "you need to go back to the colonies." One writer commented, "Just think about it. A German-born British aristocrat—whose father was in the Nazi SS—in the United States telling African Americans who have been here for centuries to 'remember the colonies' "?[85] Both comments—about the Habsburgs and Princess Michael—have elements that are unfair: the Habsburgs were generally quite pro-Jewish and anti-Nazi, and Princess Michael cannot be blamed for the actions of her father. But these episodes indicate that the past—and in particular the National Socialist past—remains a sensitive topic. It is perhaps understandable: there is the widespread perception that princely families have not been completely forthcoming regarding this history.

Conclusion:
Understanding German Princes
in the Twentieth Century

"Why did you pick on the Hessens?" were the first words he uttered, as we moved to take our seats on two perpendicular sofas that formed the sitting room in his study, formerly King George VI's library.[1] Taken aback by this good but very direct question from Prince Philip, Duke of Edinburgh, I ventured that it was because they were both emblematic of the German princes during the Third Reich and, at the same time, exceptional. As I started to explain that many German princes had joined the Nazi Party, he responded, "They did not!" I could see that this was going to be rough going. I then responded that the Nazis kept very good records, and that one document I had found in the German Federal Archives contained a list of 270 members of princely families who had joined the Nazi Party (see appendix 1).[2] While it was difficult to provide an exact percentage, it appeared that about a third of the princes eligible to do so had joined the NSDAP. Prince Philip listened attentively. It was as though we were in a boxing match, and after being pushed to the ropes, I had managed a straight jab that helped stabilize the situation. I then elaborated, but about the latter part of my opening formulation, which I sensed he found less objectionable. The Princes of Hessen were exceptional: few in their cohort rose to such high-ranking positions in the Nazi state, or had such dramatic lives. Prince Philip responded, "I wouldn't generalize in that case—if you are going to lump it [the history of the Hessens] together with all the other families."

Contrary to the advice of His Royal Highness, this book has indeed lumped the Hessens in with a number of other families. In many ways,

Philipp and Christoph von Hessen were representative of others in their station throughout much of the twentieth century. But they must also be viewed as unique individuals, with distinctive and indeed complex personalities. There have also been many moments when the temptation to judge has presented itself; and this temptation has sometimes proved difficult to resist. However, the overriding objective has been to present the lives and careers of the princes in a balanced way: to be simultaneously critical and empathetic. As one combines the approaches just noted, it is fair to say that Prince Philipp and Prince Christoph von Hessen, like many members of the high aristocracy, faced monumental challenges as they experienced events and transformations of epochal importance. The world into which they were born at the turn of the last century seems like something out of a fantasy—and even more so when one considers what followed: world wars, National Socialism, and the Holocaust. One is reminded of a journalist's comment regarding their cousin, Princess Viktoria Luise ("the Kaiser's daughter"): "I ask myself what sort of horrible type I would have become if my father had been able to make me the gift of a Regiment of Prussian Life Guards Hussars on my confirmation."[3] Princes Philipp and Christoph were born with extraordinary privilege and great expectations. They were almost destined for disappointment.

The world into which they were born was a confusing one, and even for scholars today it retains insoluble complexities. Historians continue to debate whether the traditional aristocratic elites preserved their predominant status through the Great War, or whether they had already been forced by the proponents of modernity (including the bourgeoisie) to relinquish control in the political, economic, social, and cultural spheres. Arno Mayer's thesis about "the persistence of the old regime" remains controversial. As Eckhart Franz has noted, "The question of whether and to what extent international dynastic relations were still politically relevant in the age of the national state had actually been resolved at the latest with the outbreak of the First World War and with the end of the Romanovs."[4] While this may be true, this does not mean that the royals did not continue to attempt to utilize their influence. Professor Franz adds, "In as much, I have . . . my doubts whether one really believed in the Berlin of 1939–1940 that one could influence British policies with aristocratic relations: the Hohenzollern (as compared to the Hesse-Darmstadt relations) were already *personae non grata* in England since 1914 and would lead nowhere. Indeed in this light, Philipp's role with regard to Italy was the exception."[5]

Prince Philipp was exceptional—in his role as interlocutor between the German and Italian regimes, in his position as the highest-ranking prince in the German state administration, and in his close relationship with Hitler—but he and his brothers were in many respects also exemplary. They were conditioned by their upbringing. As Goethe once noted, "man is unable to free himself from the impressions of his youth."[6] They retained a sense of duty and even honor—even if it is difficult to accept the idea that an SS officer-turned-intelligence-operative (Christoph) was an honorable person. But it is telling that three of the four brothers who had survived World War I requested appointments in the armed forces in 1939 (Philipp was the exception here, and even he later broached the subject with Hitler). While the desire to join the armed forces did not grow solely out of their quasi-feudal upbringing—there were other factors at play, including, perhaps, responding to the intensifying political problems—they were raised to believe in a fighting nobility.

Most princes of their generation also continued to value public service. Granted, there were some among them who retreated to their castles and managed their properties (more often, the heads of houses—that is, the eldest siblings who inherited the castles as well as the means to keep up a more traditional lifestyle). Yet for many princes, there was the notion, the ideal toward which they strived, that they should be public figures and contribute their considerable leadership skills to society. Princess Peg von Hesse-Darmstadt said of Philipp in 1946, he is "a great idealist, very gentle and never brutal. . . . He is not a fanatic or a propagandist, and also not an egotist [but rather] a poor speaker, very modest and steps reluctantly into the lime-light."[7] Despite personal qualities that might militate against a role in politics and public life, Philipp stepped forward and did what he believed was his duty. The princes of Hessen, like many of their cohorts, were "tradition-bound men."

Regardless of the extent to which the power of the traditional elite had eroded in the years prior to 1914, the Great War and the events of 1918–19 that transformed Central Europe had a great impact on the princes. Certain responses to these epochal events were endemic to members of their caste. A disillusionment with politics (both the imperial and republican varieties), was just one of many *ressentiments* that frequently took hold. This disillusionment was to have a marked effect on their subsequent behavior. The defeats suffered during and after World War I taught them how to retreat into a private sphere, to "lie low" and protect their interests as best they could. By 1942, when it was clear to many of the princes that things had gone terribly wrong, the most frequent response was somewhere between a conspiracy of silence and the cowardice of acquiescence. Among the princes, only Louis Ferdinand von Preussen and Gottfried von Bismarck played anything approaching an active role in the July 20 resistance. Granted, Hitler and most of the other top Nazi leaders had grown mistrustful of the princes to such a large extent that by 1944, very few were in a position to act against the regime. They had missed their opportunity.

The area where some had acted most boldly, albeit unsuccessfully, concerned a negotiated peace between the British and the Germans. The extent of the efforts by certain princes to broker such a settlement remains shrouded in mystery. The British royal family, above all, exhibits the greatest discomfort with this history. But there is little doubt that most princes sought to avoid hostilities: they did not want to fight against family members on the opposite side; they did not wish to see lives sacrificed (their own included); and they thought that another protracted war would lead to results similar to those brought on by World War I (a further loss of influence and a decline of monarchical rule). While the extent to which there was a "network" is highly debatable (most royals today would dispute the term and find it too conspiratorial), certain princes hoped to utilize familial and social connections as a means of facilitating negotiations. Hitler himself believed in the existence of these connections. In the 1930s, he tried to exploit them for geopolitical reasons when he sought alliances with Great Britain, Yugoslavia, Bulgaria, and Romania, among others. But his growing paranoia during the war led him to view these ties in a different light.

Were the princes victims during the Third Reich? The most compelling answer to this question would exclude them from the primary groups of victims (Jews, Communists, Sinti and Roma, homosexuals, and Jehovah's Witnesses, among others); but it would also recognize that some princes suffered and lost a great deal. A central reason to omit them from a list of victim groups is that too many princes supported the Nazis. This in itself distinguishes them from other victims. The alliance that the princes formed with Nazi leaders had resulted in material and political gains for many princes. Prince Philipp had never held political office (and scarcely a real job) before 1933; suddenly, he was the highest-ranking state official in the province of Hesse-Nassau. Prince Christoph had not completed his university course; by 1935 he was the manager of one of the most powerful intelligence agencies in the world. While Philipp and Christoph were exceptional in terms of the meteoric ascent of their careers after 1933, many other princes were complicit in their own ways. Even if they were not SS generals like Prince zu Waldeck, many found lesser degrees of confraternity with the Nazis: state dinners with King Carol of Romania or Prince Paul of Yugoslavia; ready access to Reinhard Heydrich or Hermann Göring; and assurances that their vast property holdings would remain untouched. These were some of the benefits accrued by the princes in return for their political support. While these princes were drawn to the Nazis for reasons of both affinity and utility, the latter was invariably present. Of course, the Nazi leaders turned on them. But the relationships that existed up until the early years of the war preclude the inclusion of princes among the victims of National Socialism.

The princes ultimately lost their predominant position in Germany, and this process played itself out during the Third Reich and in the early postwar years. While there was a great deal of continuity in the position and influence of princes in the years stretching from the turn of the century up through 1940s, the years that followed were characterized by rupture and change. The Röhm purge of 1934 had put a halt to a "second" or a "social" revolution that some Nazis had sought after the seizure of power, yet Hitler and his cohorts carried out just that kind of revolution a decade later. The "Decree Against Internationally Connected Men," the "kith-and-kin" measures aimed at the July 20 conspirators (but also others who were merely suspected of being unreliable), and then finally the devastating defeat at the hands of the Allies, all contributed to the decline of the caste. The Allies continued the work of the Nazis in this regard (yet another irony). Soviet land seizures east of the Elbe and the occupation policies of the Western Allies oftentimes brought dislocation, the loss of property, and a loss of credibility. While the denazification trials did not always render harsh verdicts and punishments, they served to discredit many of the princes who had collaborated with the Nazis. Furthermore, the prevailing view among the British and Americans—that an anachronistic feudal elite had contributed in a fundamental way to the "German problem" of the twentieth century—helped buttress the movement to curtail the influence of princes. Ralf Dahrendorf noted back in the 1960s that while the traditional elite retained some power, especially on the local level, they were no longer in a position to threaten the democracy that prevailed in the Federal Republic (that is, if they had wanted to do so).[8] The decline of the princes as a caste comprised part of the modernization process that transpired in mid-century Germany, and provides an instance when over-arching structures connect the pre-1933 period to the Third Reich to the postwar period.[9]

This study has shown that the princes, as a group, were resilient and oftentimes opportunistic. Accordingly, many found ways in the postwar period to preserve their wealth, even if it required dramatic measures. Turning one's Schloss into a hotel, for example, constituted a challenging exercise in "changing with the times." The history of the German princes in the postwar involved accommodation with the new political culture, the creation of lives more private (and bourgeois), and at the same time, the maintenance of networks founded upon birth and influence. The princes remain with us and, as a whole, they enjoy greater popularity now than at any time since the end of World War II. It may help that with the collapse of the Soviet Union, there are fewer communists around who agitate against them. Also working in their favor is our celebrity-obsessed culture, which features a media that has grown to meet an almost insatiable demand to know more about the "rich and famous." The princes have evolved and adapted; many have now become adroit at managing public perceptions of them (but there are still a few notable exceptions). As historians gradually shed light on the history of the princes during the Third Reich, it will be interesting to see how royals respond to potentially damaging revelations. The current generation of the princes of Hessen are to be commended for their willingness to confront this difficult past. To permit an outsider (and not only a nonroyal but a non-German) to study the lives of their parents and grandparents has certainly presented challenges. But this was the point: if they were to come to terms with this difficult past, it would be best to have an outsider, someone with distance and perhaps greater objectivity, write the history.

And so, to conclude, what does this outsider make of Princes Christoph and Philipp von Hessen? In many ways, of course, they were products of their environments. Christoph, for example, was always most comfortable on country estates. He loved the animals and the rural culture, and sustained a dream of a life as a kind of squire. He also evinced a high regard for the military and martial values. One cannot underestimate the impact that World War I had on him—or his inability to serve in the army during the Weimar Republic. While there is no certain explanation for his joining the SS in 1931, his wish to serve in a (para-) military unit—to play an active role in fighting Communists and to share in the discipline and camaraderie of the undertaking—was a key factor. Prince Christoph was arguably the most psychologically complicated of the Hessian princes. His nervous breakdown in 1936 offers one indication, as does the stunning decision in 1939 to leave the important post as director of the Forschungsamt in order to become an ordinary soldier in the Luftwaffe. Christoph exhibited paradoxical qualities: extroverted, charming, and with a great sense of humor, he also adored his wife and children, and remained close to his family. His nephew Prince Heinrich recalled Christoph as "a highly sympathetic man, whom I loved very much because of his humorous manners. He was athletic and always cheerful."[10] But Christoph simultaneously possessed a dark side: his secretive work as an intelligence operative, where he monitored "enemies" of the Third Reich, made him a part of the surveillance system, and his contact with Göring, Himmler, Heydrich, and other Nazi leaders put him near the heart of the malevolent regime. He appears to have experienced a gradual recognition regarding the nature of his work: the transfer to active military service, while hardly an act of resistance, constituted an act of ethically motivated detachment from the regime. Like his brothers Wolfgang and Richard, he believed that the only honorable way to serve his country during a war was fighting in the armed forces, and his estrangement from Göring grew notably when he was forbidden to fly in late-1941. Christoph's death in October 1943 occurred as he attempted to assist family members. His death, much like his personality, remains enigmatic. But one must live with such mysteries and acknowledge the limits of understanding.

Prince Philipp von Hessen also possessed paradoxical qualities. Despite his impeccable manners, his multilingual charm, and his general worldliness, he would be an individual quite alien to most readers. One need only look at the portrait of him executed by Philipp de László in 1920, where the young prince is rendered in a Renaissance costume.[11] Although clearly intended to convey his aristocratic station (one thinks of similar portraits by Pontormo in the sixteenth century and later by F. X. Winterhalter in the nineteenth), the painting raises all sorts of questions: is he meant to be a Medici-like patron, a Machiavellian prince, or a modern-day intellectual who is making a comment about a life founded on illusions and quasi-theatrical roles? That the young man represented in this portrait became a high-ranking official in the Third Reich—and a friend of Göring and Hitler—accentuates the paradoxes of his personality. Philipp von Hessen clearly had his positive qualities. It speaks well of him that he had such a close relationship with an artist like Siegfried Sassoon, who had very high standards and was hypercritical. Princess Mafalda adored Philipp, and he, like Christoph, remained close to his family. Philipp interceded to help Jewish friends during the Third Reich and spoke out on behalf of members of the clergy, who saw their churches threatened. When the threat of war became apparent, he advocated negotiation and diplomacy. And yet, Philipp failed in so many ways: the province that he helped govern, Hesse-Nassau, saw its Jewish community persecuted and then decimated; he himself played an instrumental role in the forcible takeover of Austria and the creation of the Axis alliance; and he did not openly protest the murder of thousands of disabled individuals at the Hadamar sanitarium. Up until the time of his imprisonment in 1943, Philipp remained devoted to Hitler—a sign of his naïveté but also an indication of more problematic views. Subsequently, he was unable to engage his past in a direct and honest way. It was too painful for him. The loss of his wife and brother, as well as his experiences in twenty-two Nazi and Allied camps, overwhelmed him.

The history of the princely houses during the Third Reich was one of decline: gradual, irregular, and delayed, but decline nonetheless. While a critical moment in a vast and complex process, 1918 did not completely eradicate the power of the feudal elite. Yet even before World War I, there was a general awareness among contemporaries, and especially aristocrats, that the *ancien régime* was in its death throes. To take one example, Winston Churchill exhibited what historian David Cannadine suggests was "perhaps, an excessively apocalyptic view of the decline and fall of Churchill's own caste, the British aristocracy, though on the basis of his family experience it is easy to see why he felt and wrote as he did."[12] Cannadine also notes Churchill's nostalgia for the "social structure that had existed in his youth [which he regarded] as the best of all possible worlds."[13] Philipp and Christoph von Hessen, like many German princes, shared this nostalgic

Portrait of Philipp von Hessen by society artist Philipp de Laszlo from the early 1920s.

perspective: they were among the privileged members of their generation who had childhood memories of "the enchanted garden" of the long nineteenth century that stretched until World War I.[14] They were also the ones to experience the great decline. True, the princes proved resilient—even again after 1945. But the most recent renaissance in no way constitutes a revival of the old order. The wealth and power of certain princes, like their visibility in the mass media, are overwhelmed by other forces in the modern world. The princes no longer lie at the heart of the predominant political, economic, or cultural systems. The Nazis, through the class war they launched after 1941 and through their defeat at the hands of the Allies, helped carry out a revolution. In a sense, one can say that as a result of World War II, German royals finally lost their Reich.

Appendix 1

High Nobility in the Nazi Party

Title	Family Name	Christian Name	Birth Date	Nazi Party Nr.	Date of Entry
Count	Adelmann	Hans Heinrich	14 Jun 1911	2917661	1 May 1933
Duchess	v. Anhalt	Edda Charlotte	20 Aug 1905	4843880	1 May 1937
Duke	v. Anhalt	Joachim Ernst	11 Jan 1901	7267717	1 Nov 1939
Princess	v. Anhalt	Marie Aug.	10 Jun 1898	3452693	1 May 1934
Prince	v. Auersperg	Eduard	7 Apr 1893	8417015	1 Apr 1940
Count	v. Baudissin	Klaus	4 Nov 1891	1055622	1 Apr 1932
Count	z. Bentheim	Wilhelm	9 Jun 1883	266338	
Prince	z. Bentheim und Steinfurt	Eberwyn	10 Apr 1882	1102733	1 May 1932
Prince	z. Bentheim und Steinfurt	Karl	10 Dec 1884	5194927	1 May 1937
Princess	z. Bentheim und Steinfurt	Luise	2 Sep 1891	1105324	1 May 1932
Prince	z. Bentheim-Tecklenburg	Adolf	29 Jun 1889	5135969	1 May 1937
	v. Blumenthal	Friedrich	11 Aug 1884	5876751	
	v. Boeckmann	Hans-Fritz	7 Dec 1884	1029285	1 Apr 1932
	de Bruyn-Ouboter	Otto	23 Dec 1907	483014	1 Mar 1931
Prince	v. Buchau	Wilhelm	21 Apr 1881	5517921	1 Apr 1938
	v. Bülow	Ilsabe	27 Oct 1916	7777343	

Prince	z. Castell-Castell	Carl	8 May 1897	3417319	1 May 1933
Count	z. Castell-Castell	Georg	12 Oct 1904	2988003	
Countess	z. Castell-Rüdenhausen	Clementine	30 Jan 1912	3133896	1 May 1933
Countess	z. Castell-Rüdenhausen	Frieda	18 Jul 1882	3437961	1 May 1933
Count	z. Castell-Rüdenhausen	Hubert	12 Feb 1909	1137513	1 Aug 1932
Prince	Clary	Alfons	12 Mar 1887	8106186	1 Nov 1940
Princess	Clary	Ludwine	15 Aug 1894	8227451	1 Nov 1940
Prince	v. Croy	Anton	6 Jan 1893	2845352	1 May 1933
Prince	v. Croy	Max	12 Jun 1912	6452903	1 Dec 1938
Count	v. Donnersmarck	Henckel	12 Mar 1890	8704550	1 Apr 1941
Count	z. Erbach	Eberhard	23 Aug 1922	7834138	1 Sep 1940
Hereditary Count	z. Erbach-Erbach	Alexander	16 Sep 1891	5937007	1 May 1937
Prince and Count	z. Erbach-Schönberg	Alexander	12 Sep 1872	4497486	1 May 1937
Princess and Countess	z. Erbach-Schönberg	Elisabeth	6 Sep 1873	4497486	1 May 1937
Hereditary Prince	Erbach-Schönberg	Georg Ludwig	1 Jan 1903	3496777	1 May 1933
Hereditary Princess	z. Erbach-Schönberg	Marie Margarethe	25 Dec 1903	5931846	1 May 1937
Prince	z. Erbach-Schönberg	Wilhelm Ernst	4 Jan 1904	1170298	1 May 1932
Count	z. Erbach-Fürsternau	Eugen	13 May 1923	8651490	1 Sep 1940
Prince	Fugger-Babenhausen	Friedrich Karl	19 Mar 1874	1078044	1 May 1932
Count	Fugger-Glött	Hans Karl	4 Aug 1916	2258441	1 Oct 1934
Count	Fugger-Glött	Josef Karl	19 Mar 1874	1078044	1 May 1932
Princess	z. Fürstenberg	Irma	19 May 1867	4006133	1 May 1937
Prince	z. Fürstenberg	Joachim	28 Jun 1922	8631900	1 Sep 1941
Hereditary Prince and Landgrave	Fürstenberg	Karl Egon	6 May 1891	8543545	1 Jan 1940
Prince	z. Fürstenberg	Max	31 Mar 1896	3454652	1 Jun 1934
	Habsburg-Lothringen	Heinrich	27 Aug 1908	8766361	1 Jan 1940
	Habsburg-Lothringen	Heinrich Ferdinand	13 Feb 1878	6346998	1 May 1938
Count	v. Harrach	Wichard	6 Mar 1916	7032904	1 Nov 1938
	v. Hedemann	Sophie Charlotte	2 Feb 1879	306888	25 Jun 1930
Prince	v. Hessen	Alexis	8 Jun 1911	1184026	1 Mar 1932
Prince	v. Hessen	Christoph	14 May 1901	696176	1 Nov 1931

Hereditary Grand Duchess	v. Hessen	Cécile	22 Jun 1911	3766313	1 May 1937
Landgrave	v. Hessen	Friedrich Karl	1 May 1868	4814689	1 May 1938
Hereditary Grand Duke	v. Hessen	Georg	8 Nov 1906	3766312	1 May 1937
Prince	v. Hessen u. b. Rhein	Ludwig	20 Nov 1908	5900506	1 May 1937
Landgravine	v. Hessen	Margarethe	44 Apr 1872	4814690	1 May 1938
Princess	v. Hessen	Marianne Wilhelm	23 Aug 1913	4628851	1 May 1937
Prince	v. Hessen	Philipp	6 Nov 1896	418991	1 Oct 1930
Prince	v. Hessen	Richard	14 May 1901	1203662	1 Aug 1932
Prince	v. Hessen	Wilhelm	1 Mar 1905	1187621	1 May 1932
Princess	v. Hessen	Viktoria Cécile	26 Oct 1914	3515493	1 May 1933
Prince	v. Hessen	Wolfgang	6 Nov 1896	1794944	1 Apr 1932
Princess	v. Hessen u. b. Rhein	Marie Alexandra	1 Aug 1902	7900128	1 Jan 1940
Prince	v. Hessen u. b. Rhein	Richard	14 May 1901	1203662	1 Aug 1932
Prince	v. Hessen u. b. Rhein	Wolfgang	6 Nov 1896	1794944	1 Apr 1933
Prince	z. Hohenlohe	Albrecht	9 Sep 1906	1234146	1 Aug 1932
Princess	z. Hohenlohe	Alexandra	22 Apr 1901	3587919	1 May 1933
Prince	z. Hohenlohe	Carl	20 Oct 1905	1359811	1 Nov 1932
Princess	z. Hohenlohe	Hella	25 Feb 1883	5637217	1 May 1937
Princess	v. Hohenlohe	Lahmann Mariella	31 Aug 1900	1331054	1 Sep 1932
Prince	z. Hohenlohe	Rudolf	1 Dec 1903	3508258	1 Jan 1936
Princess	z. Hohenlohe-Langenburg	Alexandra	1 Sep 1878	4969451	1 May 1937
Prince	z. Hohenlohe-Langenburg	Ernst	13 Jun 1863	3726902	1 Apr 1936
Prince	z. Hohenlohe-Bartenstein	Friedrich	3 Sep 1910	1891373	1 May 1933
Hereditary Prince	z. Hohenlohe-Langenburg	Gottfried	24 Mar 1897	4023070	1 May 1937
	z. Hohenlohe-Langenburg	Jrma	4 Jul 1902	4453767	1 May 1937
Prince	z. Hohenlohe-Langenburg	Karl	1 Dec 1903	6580922	1 Dec 1938
Prince	z. Hohenlohe-Langenburg	Konstantin	11 Sep 1893	6580933	1 Dec 1938
Hereditary Princess	z. Hohenlohe-Langenburg	Margarita	18 Apr 1905	4453768	1 May 1937
Princess	z. Hohenlohe-Langenburg	Viktoria	21 Oct 1914	6510492	1.12.38

Prince	z. Hohenlohe-Oehringen	August	28 Apr 1890	5371558	1 May 1937
Prince	z. Hohenlohe-Oehringen	Kraft	16 Mar 1892	1787117	1 Jul 1933
Prince	z. Hohenlohe-Oehringen	Max-Hugo	25 Mar 1893	2151756	1 May 1933
Prince	z. Hohenlohe-Schillingsfürst	Alfred	31 Mar 1889	6294978	1 May 1938
Prince	z. Hohenlohe-Waldenburg	Karl-Friedrich	31 Jul 1908	3409977	1 May 1933
Prince	v. Hohenzollern	Albrecht	28 Sep 1898	3289751	1 Jan 1934
Princess	v. Hohenzollern	Ilse Margot	28 Jun 1901	3280752	1 Jan 1934
Prince	v. Hohezollern-Emden	Franz Josef	30 Aug 1891	3765580	1 Apr 1936
Hereditary Prince	v. Isenburg	Franz Ferdinand	17 Jul 1901		
Prince	v. Isenburg	Karl Ferdinand	20 Feb 1906	810958	12 Dec 1931
Princess	v. Khenvenhüller-Metsch	Ida	6 Apr 1914	2459436	
Countess	v. Khenvenhüller-Metsch	Leopoldine	23 Feb 1913	2459700	
	v. Khenvenhüller-Metsch	Marianne	16 Jun 1911	2459689	
Prince	v. Khenvenhüller-Metsch	Sigismund	26 Jul 1873	766388	
Princess	Kinsky	Mathilde	24 May 1900	6566899	1 Nov 1938
Dr.	v. Lanzenauer	Alois Hähling	4 Oct 1903	2787702	1 May 1933
Prince	z. Leiningen	Ennich	18 Jan 1866	3416656	1 May 1933
Prince	z. Leiningen	Hermann	4 Jan 1901	3416657	1 May 1933
Prince	z. Leiningen	Hesso	29 Jul 1903	5265063	1 May 1937
Princess	z. Leiningen	Jrene	17 Jul 1895	3159362	1 May 1933
Hereditary Prince	z. Leiningen	Karl	13 Feb 1898	4852615	1 May 1937
Hereditary Princess	z. Leiningen	Maria	20 Jan 1907	5162615	1 May 1937
Princess	z. Leiningen-Nesselrode	Maria-Luise	31 Jul 1905	5265065	1 May 1937
Prince	z. Lippe	Ludwig	27 Sep 1909	479952	1 Mar 1931
Prince	z. Lippe	Bernhard D.	29 Jun 1911	2583009	1 May 1933
Princess	z. Lippe	Elisabeth	27 Oct 1900	1334759	1 Oct 1932
Hereditary Prince	z. Lippe	Ernst	12 Jun 1902	88835	1 May 1928
Prince	z. Lippe	Ferdinand	16 Jul 1903	4533031	1 May 1937
Princess	z. Lippe	Franziska	14 Dec 1902	6153171	1 May 1938
Princess	z. Lippe	Hedwig-Maria	29 Dec 1903	674238	1 Oct 1931

Princess	z. Lippe	Johanna	15 Jun 1894	621441	1 Sep 1931
Prince	z. Lippe	Karl Christian Joachim	21 Oct 1889	461527	1 Feb 1931
Prince	z. Lippe	Klodwig	27 Sep 1909	479952	1 Mar 1931
Prince	z. Lippe	Kurt	5 Mar 1855	292948	1 Sep 1930
Prince	z. Lippe	Leopold Bernhard	19 May 1904	891529	1 Feb 1932
Count	v. Lippe	Otto	4 Jul 1904	868756	1 Jan 1932
	v. Lippe	Rolf	4 Jan 1912	4320380	
Princess	z. Lippe	Sophie	9 Apr 1857	565619	1 Jun 1931
	v. Lippe	Walther	7 Apr 1878	3723952	
Prince	z. Lippe-Biesterfeld	Ernst-Aschwin	13 Jun 1914	5854038	1 May 1937
Princess	z. Lippe-Biesterfeld	Franziska	14 Dec 1902	6153171	1 May 1938
Prince	z. Lippe-Weißenfeld	Christian	12 Aug 1907	5164799	1 May 1937
Prince	z. Lippe-Weißenfeld	Kurt-Bernhard	4 Jul 1901	7218152	1 Oct 1939
Prince	z. Löwenstein-Wertheim	Alban	14 Aug 1892	2523598	1 May 1933
Hereditary Prince	z. Löwenstein-Wertheim-Freudenberg	Alfred Ernst	19 Sep 1924	9175410	27 Sep 1942
Prince	z. Löwenstein-Wertheim-Freudenberg	Wolfgang	25 Nov 1890	1151047	1 May 1932
Hereditary Grand Duke	v. Mecklenburg	Friedrich-Franz	22 Apr 1910	504973	1 May 1931
Count	z. Münster	Albrecht	4 Jul 1911	179794	
	v. Oldenburg	Herta	2 Apr 1897	2451986	
Hereditary Grand Duke	v. Oldenburg	Nikolaus	10 Aug 1897	4085803	1 May 1937
	v. Papperheim Rothenstein	Gottfried	18 Sep 1858	1136048	
	v. Platen	Günther	2 Feb 1893	2437730	
Countess	Praschma	Elisabeth	16 Jan 1895	2127639	1 May 1933
Prince	v. Preußen	Alexander-Ferdinand	26 Dec 1912	534782	1 May 1931
Prince	v. Preußen	August-Wilhelm	29 Jan 1887	24	1 Apr 1930
Prince	v. Preußen	Franz	15 Dec 1916	2407422	1 Apr 1935
Count	v. Rechberg	Albert Germanus	29 Nov 1912	5365380	1 May 1937
Prince	v. Reuß	Heinrich	26 May 1921	7089148	1 Sep 1939
Prince	v. Reuß	Heinrich XIV	13 May 1895	2199219	1 May 1933
Prince	v. Reuß	Heinrich XVII	22 Sep 1892	3127378	1 May 1933

Hereditary Prince	v. Reuß	Heinrich XXVII	13 Dec 1897	4418345	1 May 1937
Prince	v. Reuß	Heinrich XXXIII	26 Jul 1879	3603963	1 May 1935
Prince	v. Reuß	Heinrich XXXV	1 Aug 1887	3018157	1 May 1933
Prince	v. Reuß	Heinrich XXXVI	10 Aug 1888	1190474	1 May 1932
Princess	v. Reuß z. Lippe	Marie Adelheid	30 Aug 1895	237553	1 May 1930
Prince	v. Reuß-Plauen	Heinrich	28 Mar 1890	912977	1 Feb 1932
Princess	v. Reuß-Plauen	Huberta	14 Apr 1889	912978	1 Feb 1932
Count	v. Reuttner	Josef	12 Sep 1886	119692	1 Mar 1929
Count	Reuttner v. Weyl	Josef	6 Aug 1911	1571971	1 Apr 1933
	v. Rhoden	Wolrad	27 Sep 1900	1706849	
Prince	Rohan	Alain	26 Jul 1893	7240414	1 Apr 1939
Prince	Rohan	Karl	9 Jan 1898	6234513	1 May 1938
Princess	Rohan	Marie	29 May 1899	6172795	1 May 1938
	v. Rosenberg	Marianne	3 Nov 1862	739936	
Duke	v. Sachsen-Altenburg	Ernst	31 Aug 1871	4868932	1 May 1937
Prince	v. Sachsen-Coburg	Heinrich	4 May 1900	300354	1 Sep 1930
Duke	v. Sachsen-Coburg-Gotha	Carl-Eduard Herzog	19 Jul 1884	2560843	1 May 1933
Prince	v. Sachsen-Coburg-Gotha	Ernst	25 Feb 1907	196633	15 May 1930
Hereditary Princess	v. Sachsen-Coburg-Gotha	Feodora	7 Jul 1905	1037967	1 Apr 1932
Prince	v. Sachsen-Coburg-Gotha	Hubertus	24 Aug 1909	7213588	1 Oct 1939
Princess	v. Sachsen-Coburg-Gotha	Irmgard	27 Jan 1912	1560711	1 Mar 1933
Hereditary Prince	Sachsen-Coburg-Gotha	Johann	2 Aug 1906	1037966	1 Apr 1932
	v. Sachsen-Coburg-Gotha	Leopoldine	13 May 1905	1453322	7 Mar 1933
	v. Sachsen-Coburg-Gotha	Rainer	4 May 1900	300354	20 Sep 1930
Princess	v. Sachsen-Meiningen	B. Margot	22 Jan 1911	898841	1 Mar 1932
Prince	v. Sachsen-Meiningen	Bernhard	30 Jun 1901	898842	1 Mar 1932
Prince	v. Sachsen-Meiningen	Georg	11 Oct 1892	2594794	1 May 1933
Princess	v. Sachsen-Meiningen	Klara	31 May 1895	525333	1 May 1931
Prince	z. Salm	Philipp	31 Mar 1909	809056	1 Jan 1932
	z. Sayn-Wittgenstein	Elena-Helene	3 Apr 1883	5023552	1 May 1937

Prince	z. Sayn-Wittgenstein	Friedrich-Theodor	17 May 1909	2657640	1 May 1933
Princess	z. Sayn-Wittgenstein	Helene	3 Apr 1883	5023552	1 May 1937
Princess	z. Sayn-Wittgenstein	Lucy	3 Jul 1898	233688	1 May 1930
Prince	z. Sayn-Wittgenstein	Otto	11 Jun 1878	933028	1 Apr 1932
Prince	z. Sayn-Wittgenstein	Stanislaus	23 Sep 1872	5023553	1 May 1937
	z. Sayn-Wittgenstein	Walburga	31 Jul 1885	3657537	1 May 1935
Prince	z. Sayn-Wittgenstein	Wolfgang	13 Mar 1887	233687	1 May 1930
Prince	z. Sayn-Wittgenstein-Berleleweg	Gustav Albrecht	28 Feb 1907	8811942	1 Oct 1941
	v. Schaumburg	Eva-Sophie Frelin	20 May 1923	8717300	
	v. Schaumburg	Friedrich	26 Oct 1877	1078106	
Princess	z. Schaumburg-Lippe		11 Nov 1903	3681097	1 Aug 1935
	Schaumburg-Lippe	Albrecht	17 Oct 1900	6308702	1 May 1938
Princess	z. Schaumburg-Lippe	Alexandra	29 Jun 1904	144005	16 Aug 1929
	Schaumburg-Lippe	Franz Josef Adolf Ernst	1 Sep 1899	6189085	1 May 1938
Prince	z. Schaumburg-Lippe	Friedrich Christian	5 Jan 1906	95146	1 Aug 1928
Princess	z. Schaumburg-Lippe	Ingeborg-Alice	20 Jul 1901	309345	1 Oct 1930
Prince	z. Schaumburg-Lippe	Max	28 Mar 1898	3018293	1 May 1933
Prince	z. Schaumburg-Lippe	Stephan	21 Jun 1891	309344	1 Oct 1930
	Schaumburg-Lippe	Walburgis	26 Mar 1906	7965863	1 May 1938
Prince	z. Schaumburg-Lippe	Wolrad	19 Apr 1887	3681098	1 Aug 1935
Schenck	z. Schweinsberg	Erika Ruth	19 Mar 1919	8050030	
	v. Schendel	Alice	2 Jul 1882	2025765	
Duke	v. Schleswig-Holstein-Glücksburg	Friedrich	23 Aug 1891	4420347	1 May 1937
Duchess	v. Schleswig-Holstein-Glücksburg	Maria Melita	18 Jan 1899	4082979	1 May 1937

Princess	v. Schönaich-Carolath	Edelgard	16 Jul 1891	2595872	1 Aug 1935
	v. Schönaich-Carolath	Emma-Elisabeth	28 Jan 1906	3133897	1 May 1933
Prince	v. Schönaich-Carolath	Gustav	9 Nov 1894	2595791	1 Aug 1935
Prince	v. Schönaich-Carolath	Hans-Georg	3 Nov 1907	179045	1 Jan 1930
Princess	v. Schönaich-Carolath	Margarete	31 Jan 1877	1734918	1 Apr 1933
	v. Schönberg	Angela	15 Aug 1906	2994628	
	v. Schönberg	Bernhard	26 May 1882	739973	
	v. Schönberg	Friedrich	23 Oct 1903	4295690	
	v. Schönberg	Georg	11 Jul 1886	1378781	
	Schönberg	Hansvon	8 Nov 1893	2446485	
	v. Schönberg	Hendrick Camp	18 Jul 1887	261606	
	v. Schönberg	Joachim Diener	1 Apr 1900	295694	
Dr.	v. Schönberg	Karl Heinrich Diner	1 Jun 1903	295586	
	v. Schönberg	Margitta Diener	17 Nov 1906	295693	
	v. Schönberg	Martha Camp	25 Jul 1896	1134739	
	v. Schönberg	Withold (?)	22 Jul 1923	8690208	
	v. Schönburg	Adolf	8 Dec 1923	8642244	1 Sep 1941
	v. Schönburg	Agathe	6 Apr 1888	7673861	1 Jun 1940
Prince	v. Schönburg	Alexander	28 Jul 1888	3355000	1 Mar 1934
Hereditary Count	v. Schönburg-Glauchau	Karl	26 Jul 1899	2424643	
	v. Schönberg-Pötting	Hedwig	11 Dec 1894	4525276	
	v. Schönberg-Pötting	Horst	5 Feb 1915	2991554	
	v. Schönberg-Roth	Elisabeth		5805833	
	v. Schönberg-Roth	Joseph	1 Sep 1873	3724553	
Count	v. Schönborn	Erwin	6 Oct 1877	5120815	1 May 1937
	v. Schönborn	Karl	15 Oct 1916	2359389	1 Mar 1935
Prince	v. Schönburg Waldenburg	Georg	18 Nov 1908	5279173	1 May 1937
Count	v. Soden	Julius	11 Feb 1897	5162633	1 May 1937
Prince	z. Solm-Braunfeld(s?)	Alexander	5 Aug 1903	4355672	1 May 1937
Prince	z. Solm-Braunfeld	Ernst August	10 Mar 1892	2760968	1 May 1933

Prince	z. Solm-Braunfeld	Franz	8 Jun 1906	8155637	1 Jul 1940
Prince	z. Solm-Braunfeld	Georg Friedrich	13 Dec 1890	5932079	1 May 1937
Hereditary Princess	z. Solms-Hohensolms	Gertrud	29 Aug 1913	8822878	1 Jul 1941
Count	z. Solms-Laubach	Ernstotte	8 Nov 1890	5393731	1 May 1937
Count	z. Solms-Laubach	Georg Friedrich	7 Mar 1899	1648153	1 Apr 1933
Countess	z. Solms-Rödelheim	Anna Hedwig	26 Apr 1909	5863425	1 May 1937
Countess	z. Solms-Rödelheim	Viktoria	12 May 1895	5577815	1 May 1937
Count	v. Starhemberg	Georg	10 Apr 1904	6899883	1 Dec 1938
Prince	z. Stolberg-Rossla	Christoph-Martin	1 Apr 1888	4338904	1 May 1937
Hereditary Prince	z. Stolberg-Rossla	Heinrich-Botho	13 Dec 1914	4342482	1 May 1937
Prince	z. Stolberg-Stolberg	Wolf-Heinrich	28 Apr 1903	1888358	1 May 1933
Countess	z. Stolberg-Wernigerode	Magdalene	5 May 1875	5519716	1 May 1937
Count	v. Strachwitz	Alfred	8 Aug 1898	875539	1 Dec 1931
Countess	v. Strachwitz	Erna	12 Jul 1876	1684727	1 Apr 1933
Countess	v. Strachwitz	Gabriele	3 May 1902	1076347	1 May 1932
Count	v. Strachwitz	Hyazinth	30 Jul 1893	1405652	1 Dec 1932
	Sulkowski	Edgar	1 Dec 1905	6290786	1 May 1938
	Sulkowski (Sulkowska) geb. Prinzessin v. Lichtenstein	Ilse	8 Jul 1910	6375671	1 May 1938
	v. Tettau	Anni	1 Dec 1877	4391762	
	v. Tettau	Ilse	4 Sep 1892	4524908	
Countess	v. Thun-Hohenstein	Eugenie	22 Oct 1895	7072881	1 Apr 1939
Count	v. Thun-Hohenstein	Hans	9 Apr 1884	7072882	1 Apr 1939
Prince	v. Thun und Hohenstein	Franz-Anton	17 Dec 1890	6555631	1 Dec 1938
Princess	v. Thun und Hohenstein	Franziska	2 Apr 1893	6465380	1 Dec 1938
Princess	v. Thurn und Taxis	Eleonore	25 Jan 1877	8094564	1 Nov 1940
Prince	v. Thurn und Taxis	Friedrich	21 De 1871	6557197	1 Nov 1940
Prince	v. Thurn und Taxis	Hans	28 Jun 1908	6807114	1 Dec 1938

Prince	v. Thurn und Taxis	Georg	26 Apr 1910	6433313	1 Nov 1938
Countess	v. Uexküll-Gyllenband	Alexandrine	30 Jun 1873	2645280	1 May 1933
Count	v. Uexküll-Gyllenband	Friedrich	27 Jul 1885	877593	1 Feb 1932
Count	v. Uexküll-Gyllenband	Friedrich	17 Aug 1914	3432899	1 May 1933
Countess	v. Uexküll-Gyllenband	Inge	16 Fen 1918	5514443	1 Sep 1937
Prince	v. Urach	Albrecht	18 Oct 1903	2738311	1 Oct 1934
Countess	Waldburg-Wolfegg	Franziska	18 Jun 1913	6597984	1 Dec 1938
Hereditary Prince	z. Waldeck	Josias	13 May 1896	160025	1 Nov 1929
Hereditary Princess	z. Waldeck-Pyrmont	Altburg	19 May 1903	161001	1 Nov 1929
Princess	z. Waldeck und Pyrmont	Margarthe	22 May 1923	8562493	1 Sep 1941
	v. Wallis	Hugo	12 Apr 1910	2104321	
Count	v. Wedel	Clemens	15 Oct 1866	8180740	
Count	v. Wedel	Haro Burchard	26 Jull 1891	982599	10 Feb 1932
Count	v. Wedel	Karl Erhand	7 Nov 1898	3159078	1 May 1933
	v. Wedel	Lipold	2 Jan 1890	1911321	
Countess	v. Wedel	Pauline	7 May 1881	8180804	
Princess	z. Wied (verehel. Frfr.von Scholtheim)	Benigna Victoria	23 Jul 1918	7685745	1 Jul 1940
Princess	z. Wied	Gisela		855946	1 Jan 1932
Princess	z. Wied	Pauline	19 Dec 1877	1732487	1 Apr 1933
Prince	z. Wied	Viktor	7 Dec 1877	856879	1 Jan 1932
Prince	z. Windisch-Grätz	Friedrich	7 Jul 1917	6261799	1 May 1938
Prince	Wittgenstein	Gustav-Albrecht	28 Feb 1907	8811942	1 Oct 1941
Princess	Wittgenstein	Sidon-Maria	11 May 1877	1232998	1 Aug 1932
	v. Woedtke	Alexander	2 Sep 1889	294710	1 Sep 1930
	Wolfskehl v. Reichenberg	Luitpold	20 Jan 1879	3440525	1 May 1933
	Wolfskehl v. Reichenberg	Sophie	28 Feb 1892	3439099	1 May 1933
Princess	Wrede	Carmen	28 Mar 1904	3208974	1 May 1933
Princess	Wrede	Edda	28 Mar 1904	3208975	1 May 1933
Countess	Zeppelin-Aschhausen	Elisabeth	10 Sep 1904	7669883	1 Jun 1940
Count	Zeppelin-Aschhausen	Friedrich Hermann	4 Nov 1900	3727267	1 Apr 1936

Appendix 2

Geneological Tree of the Princes von Hessen-Kassel in the Twentieth Century

Landgrave Alexander Friedrich (1863–1945)
m.
Gisela Freiin Stockhorner (1884–1965)

Landgrave Friedrich Karl von Hessen (1868–1940)
[Son of Landgrave Friedrich Wilhelm (1820–84) and Princess Anna von Preussen (1836–1918)]
m.
Landgravine Margarethe von Preussen (1872–1954)
[Daughter of Kaiser Friedrich III (1831–88) and "Kaiserin Friedrich" (Victoria of Great Britain: 1840–1901)]

Friedrich Wilhelm (1893–1916)

Maximilian (1894–1914)

Landgrave Philipp (1896–1980)
m.
Mafalda of Savoy (1902–44) (Daughter of King Vittorio Emmanuele III)

Landgrave Moritz (b. 1926)
m.
Tatiana zu Sayn-Wittgenstein-Berleburg (b. 1940)–divorced 1974

Heinrich (Enrico d'Assia) (1927–99)

Otto (1937–98)

Elisabeth (b. 1940)

Wolfgang (1896–1989)
m.
1. Marie Alexandra von Baden (1902–44)
2. Ottilie Möller (1903–91)

Richard (1901–69)

Christoph (1901–43)
m.
Sophia of Greece and Denmark (1914–2000)

Christine (b. 1933)
Dorothea (b. 1934)
Karl (b. 1937)
Rainer (b. 1939)
Clarissa (b. 1944)

Notes

Introduction

1. Lothar Machtan, statement to author, Bremen, Germany, 24 July 2002.
2. Speer, *Inside the Third Reich*, 399.
3. Ian Kershaw includes three mentions of Prince Philipp in *Hitler: 1936–1945*, 76, 78, 600; and Joachim Fest mentions him once in *Hitler*, 546. Philipp is not even listed in the reference work by Erich Stockhorst, *5000 Köpfe*.
4. *Almanach de Gotha: Annuaire Généalogique, Diplomatique et Statistique.*
5. The notion of "the second rank" is a broad and, in a certain sense, subjective category. Yet it is also a useful construct for historians. See Petropoulos, "History of the Second Rank," *Contemporary Austrian Studies* 4:177–221.
6. Reif, *Adel im 19. und 20. Jahrhundert*, 2.
7. Bundesarchiv Berlin (BAB), Sammlung Schumacher, R. 187/400, "Aufstellung derjenigen Parteigenossen, die Angehörige fürstlicher Häuser sind." See also Malinowski, *Vom König zum Führer*, 570.
8. Kater, *Doctors under Hitler*, 54–59. For the nobility as a whole, Malinowski reports that fewer than half joined the Nazi Party, although he notes that a precise determination will require more research. See Malinowski, *Vom König zum Führer*, 574–75.
9. Note that Arno Mayer himself acknowledges that his book is polemical and that he attempts to provide sharper definition to a social phenomenon. Mayer, *Persistence of the Old Regime*. See also Cannadine, *Aspects of Aristocracy*, 9.
10. Macdonogh, *Last Kaiser*, 458. See also Louis Ferdinand Prince von Preussen, *Im Strom der Geschichte*, 282.

11. BAB, Sonderakte 4 in the research files of the former Berlin Document Center (BDC), "Erlass des Führers über die Fernhaltung international gebundener Männer in Staat, Partei, und Wehrmacht," 19 May 1943. See also Rebentisch, "Persönlichkeitsprofil und Karriereverlauf," *Hessisches Jahrbuch für Landesgeschichte* 33:304.

12. Ley, "Gott schutz den Führer," *Der Angriff* (23 July 1944).

13. Papers of Rainer von Hessen (hereafter RvH), Abschrift: "Was Himmler seinem Arzt sagte. Aus dem Artikel der *Sunday Express*, London, 30 March 1947."

14. Wheeler-Bennett, *Nemesis of Power*, 685, n3. Wheeler-Bennett cites a report that states that "5,000 [nobles were victims] of whom 2,000 were officers," but regards these figures as inflated. He himself compiled a list in that book's appendix D of about 160 who perished in the reprisals for the July 20 plot.

15. Dahrendorf's argument is summarized by P. Baldwin, "*Historikerstreit* in Context," in *Reworking the Past: Hitler*, 16. Dahrendorf, *Gesellschaft und Demokratie in Deutschland*, chap. 25.

16. Schmeling, *Josias Erbprinz zu Waldeck und Pyrmont*, 13.

17. Interview with Heinrich von Schuschnigg, *Profil* 22 (24 May 2004): 37.

18. Prince Michael of Greece, "Case for Kings," *Vanity Fair*, September 2003, 410.

19. Muggeridge, ed., *Ciano's Diary, 1939–1943*, 194.

20. See, for example, Friedlander, "Der deutsche Strafprozess als historische Quelle," in *Keine "Abrechnung": NS-Verbrechen, Justiz und Gesellschaft in Europa nach 1945*, eds. Kuretsidis-Haider and Garscha. See also Niethammer, *Die Mitläufer-fabrik.*; and Frei, *Karrieren im Zwielicht*.

21. Rainer von Hessen to author, 2 December 2003.

22. Ruck, *Bibliographie zum Nationalsozialismus*. The only work specifically concerning princes is the three-page article by Preradovich, "Regierende Fürsten im Dritten Reich," *Deutschland in Geschichte und Gegenwart* 2 (1981):28–30.

23. Gerlach, "Men of 20 July," in *War of Extermination*, eds. Heer and Naumann, 127–45.

24. See Dönhoff and R. von Weizsäcker, "Wider die Selbstgerechtigkeit der Nachgeborenen," *Die Zeit* 11: 63; and Dönhoff's letter in *Die Zeit* 15 (5 April 1996): 70. Also, communication of Christian Gerlach to author, 8 February 2005.

25. M. Allen, *Hidden Agenda*, 295–96.

26. See, for example, Bradford, *George VI*, 324. E. H. Cookridge claims that Christoph "took part in the Blitz air raids on London," although he does not mention Buckingham Palace. Cookridge, *From Battenberg to Mountbatten*, 243.

27. Keil and Kellerhoff, *Deutsche Legenden*.

28. Maier, *Unmasterable Past*, 121.

29. Among other works, see Gellately, *Backing Hitler*.

30. This photograph of the Counts von Stauffenberg and Stefan George continues to be published: see *Der Spiegel* 29 (12 July 2004), 47.

31. Postwar perceptions of the aristocracy were clearly very complex: many members of the Social Democratic Party, for example, would not have viewed the notions of "aristocracy" and "good Germans" as synonymous. For a

deft treatment of memory in the early postwar period, see Reichel, *Erfundene Erinnerung*. See also Frei, *1945 und Wir*, 129–44: in particular, his chapter "Erinnerungskampf. Der 20. Juli 1944 in den Bonner Anfangsjahren."

32. Malinowski, *Vom König zum Führer*, 573–74. See also Enigl, "Der Adel und die Nazis," *Profil* 22 (24 May 2004): 35.

33. Royals were clearly in a minority even among the nobles: while there is no precise number of nobles, historians, using the *Almanach de Gotha* as a foundation, place the number of German nobles at between sixty thousand and one hundred thousand in the 1920s. Taking a middle number of eighty thousand, nobles would have comprised approximately 1.5 percent of the German population (as compared to about 1 percent of the population for Europe in general—although certain countries, such as Poland, had higher concentrations). Malinowski, *Vom König zum Führer*, 34. See also Hoyningen-Huene, *Adel in der Weimarer Republik*, 17–19.

34. Kater, *Nazi Party*, 27.

35. Malinowski, *Vom König zum Führer*, 574–78.

36. The Deutsche Forschungsgemeinschaft project is titled "Elitenwandel in der Moderne" and includes Heinz Reif and Stephan Malinowski, among others. Other recent collections on the German nobility include, Conze and Wienfort, eds., *Adel und Moderne*; and G. Schulz and Denzel, eds., *Deutscher Adel im 19. und 20. Jahrhundert*.

37. As an example of a more focused study, see the outstanding work by Eckart Conze, *Von Deutschem Adel. Die Grafen von Bernstorff im zwanzigsten Jahrhundert*, 16. He offers a sophisticated discussion of the merits of a biographically based history, citing Martin Broszat, Joseph Schumpeter, and others. Stephan Malinowski argues that the Counts von Bernstorff constitute but one type among the nobility. Malinowski, *Vom König zum Führer*, 26.

38. Gallus, "Biographik und Zeitgeschichte," 40–46.

39. Remy, *Heidelberg Myth*, 4.

40. Ian Kershaw quoted in Richard Evans, *Coming of the Third Reich*, xx.

41. Hessisches Hauptstaatsarchiv Wiesbaden (HHStAW), Spruchkammer file of Prince Philipp von Hessen, HHStAW, 520 D-Z, Nr. 519563, statement of Dr. Franz Ulbrich, 16 December 1947.

42. HRH Prince Philip, Duke of Edinburgh, interview with author, Buckingham Palace, 3 March 2004.

43. See more generally, Petropoulos and Roth, eds., *Gray Zones*.

44. Kershaw, *Making Friends with Hitler*; Nolte, *Three Faces of Fascism*; Rezzori, *Memoirs of an Anti-Semite*; and Eatwell, *Fascism*.

45. Malinowski, " 'Führertum' und 'Neuer Adel' " in Reif, *Adel und Bürgertum in Deutschland II*, 173–212.

46. Malinowski, *Vom König zum Führer*, 564.

CHAPTER I

1. Reif, *Adel im 19. und 20. Jahrhundert*, 1. See also Lieven, *Aristocracy in Europe, 1815–1914*, xiv.

2. *Almanach de Gotha*. See also Huberty, *L'Allemagne dynastique*; and BAB, R 43 II/286, "Zusammenstellung der Namen, die von den Mitgliedern der ehemals regierenden und der ihnen der früheren Gesetzgebung gleichgestellten deutschen Fürstenhäuser geführt werden," (n.d.) 1938.

3. The sovereign princely houses are as follows: (1) Hohenzollern; (2) Wittelsbach; (3) Hannover; (4) Württemberg; (5) Hessen; (6) Mecklenburg (including Mecklenburg-Strelitz and Mecklenburg-Schwerin); (7) Lippe; (8) Schaumburg-Lippe; (9) Sachsen (the Wettin but also Sachsen-Meiningen, Sachsen-Altenburg, and Sachsen-Weimar-Eisenach); (10) Sachsen-Coburg und Gotha (although related to the Sachsen House, it also stood alone as a ruling house, for example in Bulgaria); (11) Baden; (12) Braunschweig-Lüneburg (Guelph); (13) Waldeck; (14) Reuss; (15) Schleswig-Holstein-Sonderburg-Glücksburg; (16) Holstein-Oldenburg; (17) Schwarzburg; and (18) Anhalt.

4. Reif, *Adel im 19. und 20. Jahrhundert*, 5.

5. These gradations are explained in the *Almanach de Gotha*.

6. See also Montgomery-Massinberd, ed., *Burke's Royal Families of the World*.

7. See http://home.foni/net/~adelsforschung1/blattoo.htm.

8. Rainer von Hessen to the author, 4 November 2002.

9. Information from website http://pages.prodigy.net/ptheroff/gotha/hesse.html. Note that some members of the Hessen family would be royal by way of marriage to foreign royals. This would have been the case of Prince Philipp after his marriage to Princess Mafalda, but he already warranted the title after the deaths of older brothers made him the heir. See Fromm, *Blood and Banquets*, 88.

10. The Hesse-Philippsthal branch of the family was not a ruling house, although they were permitted to use the title of Landgraf. While counting as a princely family (*standesherrliche Familie*), its members were not quite at the same niveau as the Kassel and Darmstadt lines and rarely married into the ruling houses. See Philippi, *Haus Hessen*; and Heinrich Prinz von Hessen, *Kristallene Lüster*, 227.

11. HStAD (Hessisches Staatsarchiv, Darmstadt), 024 53/8, Ministerialrat Hesse to Oberregierungsrat Dr. Oppler, 5 August 1946.

12. John Wheeler-Bennett noted, about Prince Philipp von Hessen, "He had thus the curious distinction of being, on his father's side, a great-great-great grandson of George II of England, and also of George III on his mother's side." Wheeler-Bennett, *King George VI*, 396.

13. Shaw, *Royal Babylon*, 284. See also Strandmann, "Nationalisierungsdruck und königliche Namensänderung in England," in Wende, ed., *Veröffentlichungen des Deutschen Historischen Instituts London*, 69–91; Vickers, *Alice*, 127; and K. Rose, *Intimate Portraits of Kings, Queens and Courtiers*, introduction. A fascinating treatment of the subject is in the Broadlands Archives, MB1/Y18, report of Lord Louis Mountbatten on the change of names, n.d.

14. Macdonogh, *Last Kaiser*, 47. Rainer von Hessen, "Einführung," in Rainer von Hessen, ed., *Victoria Kaiserin Friedrich*, 15–19.

15. Eilers, *Queen Victoria's Descendents*. The royals' ties spread likes spoke from a wheel; and if there is a center to this wheel, it would be Queen Victoria. The family tree for her relations on the Internet extends to over a hundred pages,

and there is an entire volume devoted to the subject titled *Queen Victoria's Descendents*.

16. Vickers, *Alice*, 47. See also Macdonogh, *Last Kaiser*, 250–52. Note that Otto von Bismarck in the third volume of his memoirs referred to Wilhelm II in a manner meant to be pejorative as "Coburg-English" and not Hohenzollern. See Aronson, *The Kaisers*, 255.

17. HHStAW, 520 D-Z, Nr. 519.563, "Freilassungsantrag Philipp Prinz von Hessen," n.d.

18. Schmitz, "Adel in Deutschland," *Stern*, 24/2001, 214.

19. Tsarina Alix from the Hesse-Darmstadt family, the mother of the hemophiliac heir, "dwelt morbidly on the fact that the disease is transmitted through the mother and that it was common in her family." See Lincoln, *Romanovs*, 632. Note that the brother of the future Dukes of Windsor and Kent, Prince John (1905–19) was also epileptic (and kept out of public view). Shaw, *Royal Babylon*, 303. More generally, see Röhl, Warren, and Hunt, *Purple Secret*.

20. Wolfgang Prinz von Hessen, *Aufzeichnungen*, 9. Christian IX's wife was Princess Luise Wilhemina von Hessen-Kassel (1817–98), and Christian IX's mother was also a Hessian princess. The idea of interconnectedness among European royals is advanced even further in Farago and Sinclair, *Royal Web*.

21. Prince Michael of Greece, "Case for Kings," 400.

22. Vickers, *Alice*, 55.

23. http://www.royal.gov.uk/family/philip.htm.

24. Vickers, *Alice*, 55. Philip retained his Greek citizenship until 1947 when he gave it up to become a British subject.

25. For a discussion of the political implications of dynastic expansion, see Ferguson, "Das Haus Sachsen-Coburg und die europäische Politik des 19. Jahrhunderts," in Rainer von Hessen, ed., *Victoria Kaiserin Friedrich*, 27–48.

26. Cookridge, *From Battenberg to Mountbatten*, 1–10.

27. P. Ziegler, *Mountbatten*, 22.

28. The wife of George VI ("the Queen mother"), Lady Elizabeth Bowes-Lyon, was similarly not from the high aristocracy. For a comparison of Princess Diana and "Sissi," see Sinclair, *Death by Fame*, 94.

29. Macdonogh, *Last Kaiser*, 447.

30. Cookridge, *From Battenberg to Mountbatten*, 135.

31. Vickers, *Alice*, 16.

32. *Funk & Wagnalls Standard Desk Dictionary* (New York: Funk & Wagnalls, 1977), 423, s.v. "morganatic."

33. Prince Michael of Greece, "Case for Kings," 400.

34. Reif, *Adel im 19. und 20. Jahrhundert*, 1.

35. For sweeping a history of the Hessen family, see Philippi, *Haus Hessen*.

36. Sheehan, *Museums in the German Art World*, 36–37.

37. Showalter, *Wars of German Unification*, 49, 112; and Pflanze, *Bismarck and the Development of Germany*.

38. See Wolfgang Prinz von Hessen, *Aufzeichnungen*, 10. More generally, see Friderici, *1866: Bismarcks Okkupation und Annexion Kurhessens*.

39. Wolfgang Prinz von Hessen, *Aufzeichnungen*, 11.

40. Mayer, *Persistence of the Old Regime*, 26.
41. Miller, "Schloss Fasanerie. 50 Jahre Museum der Hessischen Hausstiftung," in Franz and Lachmann, eds., *Das kulturelle Erbe des Hauses Hessen*, 161–70.
42. Heinrich Prinz von Hessen, *Kristallene Lüster*, 112–15. Letters of Alexander Friedrich von Hessen are at Washington State University in Pullman, WA, in the papers of the conductor Hans Rosbaud.
43. Wolfgang Prinz von Hessen, *Aufzeichnungen*, 22.
44. Schloss Rumpenheim "was known for decades as the preferred meeting place of the related royal houses of the families of Hessen, Denmark, England, Russia, Greece and Battenberg"—indeed, turn-of-the-century German Reich chancellor Prince Bernhard von Bülow complained about the "Rumpenheimer Clique." Röhl, "Die Kaiserwitwe als Kritikerin der Persönlichen Monarchie Wilhelms II," in Rainer von Hessen, ed., *Victoria Kaiserin Friedrich*, 210.
45. Rainer von Hessen, "Friedrichshof: 'A Country Home.' Der Witwensitz der Kaiserin Friedrich in Kronberg (Taunus)," in Franz and Lachmann, eds., *Das kulturelle Erbe des Hauses Hessen*, 123–30.
46. Fulford, *Friedrichshof*, 8.
47. Heinrich Prinz von Hessen, *Kristallene Lüster*, 107.
48. Wolfgang Prinz von Hessen, *Aufzeichnungen*, 24.
49. Sheehan, *Museums*, 170.
50. Cuneliffe-Owen, "Wolfgang of Hesse: A Rich, Royal Twin."
51. HHStAW, 520 D-Z, Nr. 519.563, Itemized Schedule of Property, June 1946. HStAD, 024 53/9, [author's signature illegible], "Denkschrift über die Behandlung des Vermögens der Kurhessischen Hausstiftung," 24 August 1947. The more notable of the Hessens properties were Gut Hof Eich (Kreis Gelsenhausen); Hofgut Rumpenheim bei Offenbach; Wald-und-Deichgut Hessenstein (Kreis Plön); Gut Panker; Gut Friedrichshof; and Gut Schmoel.
52. HStAD, 024 53/9, [author's signature illegible], "Denkschrift über die Behandlung des Vermögens der Kurhessischen Hausstiftung," 24 August 1947.
53. HHStAW, 520 D-Z, Nr. 519.563, Itemized Schedule of Property, June 1946.
54. The Hessens' real estate holdings were valued at RM 16.29 million minus the mortgage and capitalization of RM 6.94 million. Ibid., "Real Property and All Interests Therein," June 1946. Brigitte Hamann multiplies by a factor of thirty-three to translate 1938 values to their present-day equivalent. See Hamann, *Winifred Wagner*, x.
55. Reif, *Adel im 19. und 20. Jahrhundert*, 93.
56. HHStAW, 520 D-Z, Nr. 519.563, Itemized Schedule of Property, June 1946.
57. Cannadine, *Aspects of Aristocracy*, 183; Mayer, *Persistence of the Old Regime*, 19.
58. HHStAW, 520 D-Z, Nr. 519.563, "Inventory of Castles and Jewelry," n.d.
59. Ibid., Klageschrift of Hessisches Staatsministerium, 22 October 1947.
60. Ibid., Grosshessisches Staatsministerium, Öffentlicher Kläger bei der Spruchkammer, memorandum, 27 March 1947. See also ibid., Spruchkammer Protocol of Prince Philipp, 15–17 December 1947, 20: statement of Karl Anton Schulte. No figures were provided for 1945. The income was based on total wealth of RM 416,000 in 1940 and RM 686,000 in 1944 (although

this sum evidently excluded much family property—including the Hessen jewels).

61. Spielvogel, *Hitler and Nazi Germany*, 183; and Bajohr, *Parvenüs und Profiteure*, 235.

62. HHStAW, 520 D-Z, Nr. 519.563, Grosshessisches Staatsministerium, Öffentlicher Kläger, memorandum, 27 March 1947. More generally, J. Eckert, *Der Kampf um die Fideikommisse in Deutschland*.

63. HHStAW, 520 D-Z, Nr. 519.563, statement of Ernst Ebert, 11 March 1947.

64. Ibid., "Real Property and All Interests Therein," 30 June 1946.

65. Courcy, *1939: The Last Season*, 142.

66. HHStAW, 520 D-Z, Nr. 519.563, statement of Adelheid Fliege, 8 July 1946.

67. Ibid., statement of Heinrich Lange, 12 June 1946.

68. Reeves, "A Nation of Servants," *Hartford Courant*, 28 December 2002, A9.

69. Schmeling, *Waldeck*, 15. She notes that "over 90 percent of the population, like the princely family, belonged to the Evangelical Lutheran church."

70. Ibid., *Waldeck*, 14.

71. HHStAW, 520 D-Z, Nr. 519.563, statement of Heinrich Lange, 12 June 1946.

72. Ibid.

73. Cuneliffe-Owen, "Wolfgang of Hesse: A Rich, Royal Twin."

74. Vickers, *Alice*, 274.

75. Röhl, *Wilhelm II*, 651.

76. Huldén, *Finnlands Deutsches Königsabenteuer*, 198–200.

77. Singer, *Göring*, 22.

78. Rainer von Hessen, interview with author, France, 19 July 2002.

79. PRO, FO 372/2162, Colonel Clive Wigram to Mr. Lloyd Thomas, 14 August 1925. A question is raised here whether Prince Philipp should be "Royal Highness" or "Highness"; the aides refer the matter to the king. Philipp, as heir to head of the house, was entitled to use the former, but this was not known by the aides, who thought the Hessens were overstepping their position.

80. Wolfgang Prinz von Hessen, *Aufzeichnungen*, 18.

81. Röhl, *Wilhelm II*, 496–98.

82. Prince Louis Ferdinand von Preussen quoted in Fenyvesi, *Royalty in Exile*, 73–74.

83. Cuneliffe-Owen, "Wolfgang of Hesse: A Rich, Royal Twin."

84. For the letters from Landgravine Margarethe, including some on the stationery of Buckingham Palace, see HStAD, Grossherzogliches Familienarchiv (GF), Abt. D 24/5.

85. See the website "Historical Boys' Clothing," at http://histclo.hispeed.com/royal/ger/royal-gerw20c.htm. As the children got older, there was a marked preference for sailor suits.

86. James, ed., *"Chips,"* 111, entry for 15 August 1936.

87. HHStAW, 520 D-Z, Nr. 519.563, statement of Princess Margaret von Hessen-Darmstadt, 22 June 1946.

88. Ibid., Spruchkammer Protocol of Prince Philipp, 15–17 December 1947, 10.

89. Ibid., statement of Princess Margarete von Hessen-Darmstadt, 22 June 1946.

90. Crown Prince Rupprecht von Bayern (1869–1955), for example, received a private education. Weyerer, "Bestattet wie ein König," *Süddeutsche Zeitung* 178 (4 August 2000).

91. John Wheeler-Bennett noted that Kaiser Wilhelm II spoke "'guttural but fluent' English, which was spiced with such words as 'topping,' and 'ripping.'" See Macdonogh, *Last Kaiser*, 457. In contrast, King Vittorio Emmanuele and Queen Elena spoke French with one another—at least during meals. Heinrich Prinz von Hessen, *Kristallene Lüster*, 23.

92. "A Brief History of Bexhill on Sea," at www.kingoffa.e-sussex.sch.uk. The German school stemmed from the arrival of Hannoverian troops, who were based there from 1804–14.

93. Wolfgang Prinz von Hessen, *Aufzeichnungen*, 26.

94. Steiner, *In Bluebeard's Castle*, 5–6.

95. HHStAW, 520 D-Z, Nr. 519.563, statement of Princess Margaret von Hessen-Darmstadt, 22 June 1946.

96. Geheimes Staatsarchiv Preussischer Kulturbesitz (GStAPK), Rep. 62 III, Nr. 10, Prince August Wilhelm to Dr. Presber, 9 February 1919. For other memories of visits to the Hohenzollern in Potsdam, see Wolfgang Prinz von Hessen, *Aufzeichnungen*, 28. See also Machtan, *Kaisersohn*.

97. Wolfgang Prinz von Hessen, *Aufzeichnungen*, 28.

98. Ibid., 151. Also, Landgrave Moritz von Hessen, interview with author, Kronberg, 22 July 2002.

99. Royal Archives, Windsor Castle (RA), Court Circular for 1914, 128.

100. Wolfgang Prinz von Hessen, *Aufzeichnungen*, 39.

101. For lack of enthusiasm about the war, see Ferguson, *Pity of War*, 174–211; and Verhey, *Spirit of 1914*, 46–57, 89–96. Verhey makes special reference to Hesse—and in particular, Darmstadt.

102. Mann, *Deutsche Geschichte*, 573, 578.

103. HHStAW, 520 D-Z, Nr. 519.563, Response of Prince Philipp's attorney Fabian von Schlabrendorff to Spruchkammer Darmstadt, 21 November 1947. See also Brose, *Kaiser's Army*, 35, 172.

104. Wolfgang Prinz von Hessen, *Aufzeichnungen*, 27.

105. Hessisches Staatsarchiv Marburg (HStAM), 401/02, Nr. 18, Dr. von Helms in the Reich Interior Ministry to the Oberpräsident of Hessen-Nassau, 7 June 1944.

106. HStAD, GF, D 24, Nr. 57/7, Prince Philipp to Grand Duchess Eleonore von Hessen und bei Rhein, date illegible (1914); and ibid., 10 June 1917.

107. Schwarzmüller, *Zwischen Kaiser und "Führer,"* 155.

108. BAB (formerly BDC), Prince Philipp's "Partei Karte," n.d. He won the Iron Cross First and Second Class, Hessian Cross of Courage, and the Austrian Cross of Service. Granted, this was a man who took his medals and awards seriously; like many nobles, it was part of his stock and trade. Philipp was awarded, among other medals, the War Decorations of Brunswick, Saxon-Meiningen, and Schaumburg-Lippe; the Honor Award of the German Red Cross; the Medal in Commemoration of 13 March [the Anschluss]; the Medal in Commemoration of 1 October 1938 [annexation of the Sudetenland]; the War Service Medal First Class; the Royal Italian St. Mauritius- and Lazarus

Order; the Royal Egyptian Mohammed-Ali-Order; the Great Cross of the Royal Greek Order of the Confessor; the Royal Yugoslavian Karadjordje-Star First Class; and the Great Cross of the Royal Bulgarian Order of St. Alexander. Many of these were clearly ceremonial decorations.

109. Landgrave Moritz von Hessen, interview with author, Kronberg, 23 July 2003.

110. HStAM, 401/02, Nr. 18, Dr. von Helms in the Reich Interior Ministry to the Oberpräsident von Hessen-Nassau, 7 June 1944. Wolfgang Prinz von Hessen, *Aufzeichnungen*, 159.

111. Hessische Hausstiftung (AHH), Prince Philipp to Landgravine Margarethe, 5 and 6 September 1918.

112. Funck, "The Meaning of Dying," in Eghigian and Berg, eds., *Sacrifice and National Belonging*, 44.

113. Friedrich Wilhelm Prinz von Preussen, *Das Haus Hohenzollern*, 232.

114. Wolfgang Prinz von Hessen, *Aufzeichnungen*, 42.

115. Hoyningen-Huene, *Adel in der Weimarer Republik*, 20.

116. Ibid., 21.

117. Offiziervereinigung "Alt 81," eds., *Das Königlich Preussische Infanterie-Regiment*, 14.

118. Rainer von Hessen, interview with author, France, 19 July 2002. Wolfgang Prinz von Hessen, *Aufzeichnungen*, 44–46.

119. Cooper (Viscount Norwich), *Old Men Forget*, 90–91.

120. Cookridge, *From Battenberg to Mountbatten*, 243. See also Wolfgang Prinz von Hessen, *Aufzeichnungen*, 55–62.

121. For the letter of Baron de la Grange of 19 March 1915, see Wolfgang Prinz von Hessen, *Aufzeichnungen*, 60–61.

122. Cuneliffe-Owen, "Wolfgang of Hesse: A Rich, Royal Twin."

123. HHStAW, 520 D-Z, Nr. 519.563, statement of Landgravine Margarethe von Hessen, 15 July 1946.

124. Wolfgang Prinz von Hessen, *Aufzeichnungen*, 87.

125. Ibid., 90.

126. Cookridge, *From Battenberg to Mountbatten*, 243.

127. BAB, NL 1470/37, Prince Friedrich Christian zu Schaumburg-Lippe to Robert Kempner, 3 April 1980, and Hans Boberach to Robert Kempner, 27 June 1980. There was talk in 1940 of making the Duke von Sachsen-Coburg the King of Norway. See Irving, ed., *Breach of Security*, 157. Note that I am aware that the quality of David Irving's research has been called into question, and I cite his work with trepidation. None of my arguments or conclusions rests upon his writings. See Richard Evans, *Telling Lies About Hitler*.

128. PRO, FO 371/17758, Sir Eric Phipps to Sir Orme Sargent, 13 January 1934.

129. PRO, FO 371/29783, Sir Ronald Campbell to Foreign Office, 10 July 1941.

130. Wolfgang Prinz von Hessen, *Aufzeichnungen*, 103. Preussen, *Haus Hohenzollern*, 238.

131. Ibid., 99–110. See also Heinrich Prinz von Hessen, *Kristallene Lüster*, 107.

132. Huldén, *Finnlands Deutsches Königsabenteuer 1918*, 161.

133. Hardinge letter quoted in Wolfgang Prinz von Hessen, *Aufzeichnungen*, 106.

134. Ibid., 23.

135. Ibid., 24.
136. Heinrich Prinz von Hessen, *Kristallene Lüster*, 226–27.
137. Rainer von Hessen, interview with author, Kronberg, 23 July 2003.
138. Tuchman, *Guns of August*, 15, 17.
139. Whalen, *Bitter Wounds*, 31.
140. Wolfgang Prinz von Hessen, *Aufzeichnungen*, 163.

CHAPTER 2

1. Mann, *Deutsche Geschichte*, 643, 666.
2. Nelson, *Soldier Kings*, 442.
3. Cannadine, *Aspects of Aristocracy*, 136, 222.
4. Eatwell, *Fascism*, 209.
5. Moseley, *Mussolini's Shadow*, 6–7; Fromm, *Blood and Banquets*, 221. The phrase "immoderate consumption of lovers" is made in direct reference to Ciano's wife, but Fromm implies similar behavior on his part.
6. Cannadine, *Aspects of Aristocracy*, 3, 70–72.
7. Bosworth, *Mussolini*, 142.
8. Hoyningen-Huene, *Adel in der Weimarer Republik*, 21.
9. Conze, "Adel und Adeligkeit," in Reif, ed., *Adel und Bürgertum in Deutschland II*, 278. See also Kessler, *Diaries*; and Easton, *Red Count*.
10. Nelson, *Soldier Kings*, 442. Note that Wilhelm was most upset that he was also forced to relinquish the Crown of Prussia. He later maintained that he understood the need to step aside as Kaiser, but it was inconceivable that he would cease to be king. See also, Kohlrausch, "Die Flucht des Kaisers," in Reif, ed., *Adel und Bürgertum in Deutschland II*, 65–102.
11. Macdonogh, *Last Kaiser*, 406; Wolfgang Prinz von Hessen, *Aufzeichnungen*, 113–20.
12. Wolfgang Prinz von Hessen, *Aufzeichnungen*, 120. See more generally, Barry, *Great Influenza*.
13. For Prince Max assigning blame to Prince Friedrich Karl, see Maximilian Prinz von Baden, *Erinnerungen und Dokumente*, 527, 531.
14. Wolfgang Prinz von Hessen, *Aufzeichnungen*, 121.
15. Urbach and Buchner, "Prinz Max von Baden," 121–23. They note that access to his papers at Schloss Salem has been restricted.
16. Friedrich, *Before the Deluge*, 48; Ebert, *Friedrich Ebert*, 122–23.
17. Ebert, *Friedrich Ebert*, 122–23.
18. Wolfgang Prinz von Hessen, *Aufzeichnungen*, 129, 130, 131.
19. Malinowski, *Vom König zum Führer*, 203–10.
20. HStAM, 401/02, Nr. 18, Dr. von Helms in the Reich Interior Ministry to the Oberpräsident of Hessen-Nassau, 7 June 1944.
21. HHStAW, 520 D-Z, Nr. 519.563, Protocol of Karl Wolff, 18 September 1947. Wolff was also connected to Hessian royalty because his wife's father, Gustav von Römheld, was the director of Grand Duke Ernst Ludwig's chancellery. Lang, *Der Adjutant*.
22. Eyck, *Weimar Republic*, 62.

23. Ibid., 62.
24. The full title of the Adelsgesetz is "Gesetz über die Aufhebung der Standesvorrechte des Adels und die Auflösung der Hausvermögen" (Law for the suspension of class privileges of the aristocracy and the dissolution of house property).
25. Note that special rights for the nobility had gradually been eroded prior to World War I: e.g., by the late nineteenth century, there was no longer trial by peers. Even the divorce proceedings of the Grand Duke of Hessen-Darmstadt in 1884 and 1901 took place in ordinary courts. For more on special rights, including sumptuary laws (swords, hats with feathers, etc), see Ribeiro, *Dress in Eighteenth Century France*, 45, 167–206.
26. Weimar Constitution cited in Hoyningen-Huene, *Adel in der Weimarer Republik* 30.
27. In the Adelsgesetz, the nobles were given until 1 April 1921 to hand over the entailed property. This occurred in a number of instances, and the Prussian state received from these holders of entailments (Fideikommiss-Inhaber) "167 great art collections [and] 154 libraries." Hoyningen-Huene, *Adel in der Weimarer Republik*, 47.
28. Eyck, *Weimar Republic*, 62.
29. Wolfgang Prinz von Hessen, *Aufzeichnungen*, 149, 162. HHStAW, 520 D-Z, Nr. 519563, Kurhessische Hausstiftung to the Erster öffentlichen Kläger, 30 May 1947.
30. Rainer von Hessen, "Die Hessische Hausstiftung als Kulturstiftung: Festrede, gehalten anlässlich des siebzigjährigen Jubiläums der Hessischen Hausstiftung," (upublished lecture, Kronberg, 1998), 3.
31. See Stienicka, "Die Vermögensauseinandersetzung des Volksstaates Hessen," 255–308. Sheehan, *Museums*, 173. HStAD, 024 50/10, Gesetz über die Auseinandersetzung zwischen dem Volksstaate Hessen und dem vormals in Hessen regierenden Fürstenhaus, 29 January 1934.
32. Eyck, *Weimar Republic*, 62.
33. Wolfgang Prinz von Hessen, *Aufzeichnungen*, 149, 162.
34. Eyck, *Weimar Republic*, 63.
35. F. West, *Crisis of the Weimar Republic*, 268.
36. Ibid., 267.
37. Wolfgang Prinz von Hessen, *Aufzeichnungen*, 162.
38. F. West, *Crisis of the Weimar Republic*, 272.
39. Eyck, *Weimar Republic*, 65, 189.
40. Schmitz, "Adel in Deutschland," 212.
41. Schad, *Bayerns Königshaus*, 208. She notes that in 1923 Crown Prince Rupprecht created the Wittelsbacher Ausgleichsfonds and the Wittelsbacher Landesstiftung, which cared for family property, including art and certain castles.
42. Hoyningen-Huene, *Adel in der Weimarer Republik*, 21.
43. Schmitz, "Adel in Deutschland," 212.
44. Rainer von Hessen, " 'You didn't recommend a fool to me'—Elector Wilhelm I of Hesse and Meyer Amschel Rothschild," in Heuberger, ed., *Rothschilds*, 21–36. More generally, Ferguson, *House of Rothschild: Money's Prophets, 1798–1848* and *House of Rothschild: The World's Banker, 1848–1999*.

45. Hoyningen-Huene, *Adel in der Weimarer Republik*, 28.

46. Feuchtwanger, *From Weimar to Hitler*, 210.

47. Malinowski, *Vom König zum Führer*, 321–35; Hoyningen-Huene, *Adel in der Weimarer Republik*, 59, 321–475.

48. Hoyningen-Huene, *Adel in der Weimarer Republik*, 62–64.

49. Zentner and Bedürftig, eds., *Encyclopedia of the Third Reich*, 913. More generally, Berghahn, *Stahlhelm*.

50. Nelson, *Soldier Kings*, 442; Fromm, *Blood and Banquets*, 325; and Preradovich, "Regierende Fürsten," 28–30.

51. Zentner and Bedürftig, eds., *Encyclopedia of the Third Reich*, 385. See also Kaufmann, *Monarchism in the Weimar Republic*.

52. Fromm, *Blood and Banquets*, 308.

53. Tauber, *Beyond Eagle and Swastika*, 1400.

54. Mayer, *Persistence of the Old Regime*, 203.

55. Sheehan, *Museums*, 173. See also Franz, ed., *Erinnertes: Aufzeichnungen des letzten Grossherzhogs Ernst Ludwig von Hessen und bei Rhein*; Franz, ed., *Friede durch geistige Erneuerung*; and Knodt, *Ernst Ludwig*.

56. Sheehan, *Museums*, 173, 174.

57. Note that Constantine's wife, Queen Sophie, was the sister of Landgravine Margarthe and hence Philipp's aunt. Philipp mentions a two-month stay in spring 1921 and comments on a statue in Athens in his note to Sassoon. University Library, Cambridge (ULC), MS. Add. 9375/397, Prince Philipp to Sassoon, 18 June 1922.

58. Hart-Davis, ed., *Sassoon Diaries*, 257, entry for 29 September 1922.

59. HHStAW, 520 D-Z, Nr. 519.563, Klageschrift of Hessisches Staatsministerium, 22 October 1947.

60. Wolfgang Prinz von Hessen, *Aufzeichnungen*, 159.

61. ULC, MS. Add. 9375/404, Prince Philipp to Sassoon, 3 May 1923.

62. Hart-Davis, ed., *Sassoon Diaries*, 225: entry from 28 August 1922.

63. Ibid., 200–201 and 270–71: entries for 29 July 1922 and 20 October 1922.

64. Ellinghaus, "Der Prinz, der Hitlers Werkzeug war," *Hannoversche Presse*, 27 March 1948.

65. ULC, MS. Add. 9375/404, Prince Philipp to Sassoon, 3 May 1923.

66. ULC, MS. Add. 9375/407, Prince Philipp to Sassoon, 9 September 1923.

67. Hart-Davis, ed., *Sassoon Diaries*, 277, entry for 26 October 1922.

68. Ibid., 205, 257, and 269: entries for 3 August, 29 September, and 19 October 1922.

69. Institut für Zeitgeschichte, Munich (IfZG), ZS 918, Interrogation of the Prince of Hesse, 6 May 1947. See more generally, Feldman, *Great Disorder*.

70. Wolfgang Prinz von Hessen, *Aufzeichnungen*, 153.

71. Ibid., 155–56. See "No Bands nor Flags to Welcome Prince: Wolfgang von Hessen, Nephew of Ex-Kaiser, Arrives Here as 'Business Man,'" *New York Times*, 5 March 1924, 17; Cuneliffe-Owen, "Wolfgang of Hesse: A Rich, Royal Twin"; and "Kaiser's Nephew Departs," *New York Times*, 22 March 1924, 14.

72. ULC, MS. Add. 9375/411, Prince Philipp to Sassoon, 7 May 1924.

73. HHStAW, 520 D-Z, Nr. 519.563, statement of Landgravine Margarethe von Hessen, 15 July 1946.

74. ULC, MS. Add. 9375/411, Prince Philipp to Sassoon, 7 May 1924.
75. ULC, MS. Add. 9375/408, Prince Philipp to Sassoon, 10 March 1924.
76. Dahm, "Terrorapparat," in H. Müller, et al. eds., *Tödliche Utopie*, 148. For Bach-Zelewski and other nobles struggling economically in the 1920s, see Malinowski, *Vom König zum Führer*, 560–78.
77. FOIA request, Card of Hessen-Nassau, Prince Philipp of. Confidential Memo of Sixty-fifth CIC Detatchment, U.S. Army, Europe, n.d.
78. HHStAW, 520 D-Z, Nr. 519.563, Spruchkammer Protocol of Prince Philipp, 15–17 December 1947, 2.
79. IfZG, ZS 918, Interrogation of the Prince of Hesse, 4 March 1948.
80. HHStAW, 520 D-Z, Nr. 519.563, Response of Prince Philipp's attorney von Schlabrendorff to Spruchkammer Darmstadt, 21 November 1947.
81. Heinrich Prinz von Hessen, *Kristallene Lüster*, 66,
82. Ilsemann, *Kaiser in Holland*, 51, entry for 10 March 1927.
83. Heinrich Prinz von Hessen, *Kristallene Lüster*, 65.
84. Groueff, *Crown of Thorns*, 166.
85. Ibid., 166. See also Dino Campini, *La Principessa Martire*; and Renato Barneschi, *Frau von Weber*.
86. Courcy, *1939*, 42–43.
87. Groueff, *Crown of Thorns*, 166–67; and Katz, *Fall of the House of Savoy*, 280.
88. Lord Max Egremont, letter to author, 3 March 2004.
89. Wiskemann, *Rome-Berlin Axis*, 40–41.
90. Katz, *Battle for Rome*, 17; and Maclagan and Louda, *Lines of Succession*, 191.
91. PRO, FO 372/2162, Prince Friedrich Karl to King George V, 15 July 1925. Also ibid., Foreign Office to Lord D'Abernon, 1 October 1925, and ibid., British Embassy, Berlin to Foreign Office, 31 October 1925.
92. Heinrich Prinz von Hessen, *Kristallene Lüster*, 12–13.
93. Ellinghaus, "Der Prinz." Also HHStAW, 520 D-Z, Nr. 519.563, statement of Wilhelmine Heyer, 2 July 1946.
94. Heinrich Prinz von Hessen, *Kristallene Lüster*, 93. Rainer von Hessen to author, 20 October 2004.
95. For homosexual acts being made illegal in Italy in 1931, see Bosworth, *Mussolini*, 231. Note that Britain and Germany had legal prohibitions until the 1960s.
96. Hart-Davis, ed., *Sassoon Diaries*.
97. Hoare, *Serious Pleasures*, 89. See also J. Moorcroft-Wilson, *Siegfried Sassoon*; and J. S. Roberts, *Siegfried Sassoon*, 171–75.
98. For Sassoon fighting at the Somme and then, in 1917, issuing an antiwar statement that was read in the House of Commons, see Wohl, *Generation of 1914*, 95–100.
99. "Siegfried Sassoon" (by William J. Bean), www.geocities.com. Among Sassoon's semiautobiographical works is *Memoirs of a Fox-Hunting Man*.
100. See Stansky, *Sassoon: The World of Philip and Sybil*; and Kershaw, *Making Friends*, 88.
101. N. Rose, *Harold Nicolson*, 111.
102. Moorcroft-Wilson, *Siegfried Sassoon*, 145–46.

103. Jean Moorcroft-Wilson provides the insight that the passage quoted is about Prince Philipp. Moorcroft-Wilson, *Siegfried Sassoon*, 148. The poem was first published in *Nation* in December 1922.

104. ULC, MS. Add. 9375/390, Prince Philipp to Sassoon, 17 October 1921.

105. ULC, MS. Add. 9375/391, Prince Philipp to Sassoon, 28 October 1921.

106. Philipp wrote Sassoon, "I must say they [the poems] are beautiful. Wonderfully clever & brilliant—Limitations, Case for the Miners, Fragment of Autobiography & Falying [*sic*] Asleep—are my favourites. They are full of feeling & heart & you through & through. Some of the others—please forgive the comparison—are like beautiful ice crystals that look like diamonds in the sunlight but leave a cold & painful feeling when they melt in your hand—but all the same one must admire them!" ULC, MS. Add. 9375/406, Prince Philipp to Sassoon, 2 August 1923.

107. Hart-Davis, ed., *Sassoon Diaries*, 200–201, entry for 29 July 1922.

108. Ibid., 225, entry for 28 August 1922.

109. Ibid., 266, entry for 13 October 1922.

110. Ibid., 275–76, entry for 25 October 1922.

111. Ibid., 278–79, entry for 27 October 1922. Arthur Rackham (1867–1939), was best known for his illustration of children's books, such as *Peter Pan* and *Alice in Wonderland*.

112. Ibid., 216, entry for 15 August 1922. In this entry, he also writes, Philipp "is so sophisticated about 'affairs.'"

113. Ibid., 227, entry for 30 August 1922. Among evidence of Philipp's other relationships, see Prince Philipp's 31 October 1921 letter suggests a relationship with "L."—a "poor boy" who was coming from England to visit him; and his 22 December 1921 tells of a love affair with a woman from Berlin (Sassoon's biographer Lord Max Egremont suggests it is a Princess Galitzine). See ULC, MS. Add. 9375/392 and 394.

114. Hart-Davis, ed., *Sassoon Diaries*, 218, entry for 16 August 1922.

115. Ibid., 232, entry for 2 September 1922.

116. Ibid., 212, entry for 11 August 1922. Note that the milieu of "bright young things" of the interwar period is treated in Evelyn Waugh's satiric novel, first published in 1930, *Vile Bodies*.

117. ULC, MS. Add. 9375/404, Prince Philipp to Sassoon, 3 May 1923.

118. Ibid., MS. Add. 9375/410, Prince Philipp to Sassoon, 27 March 1924.

119. Hart-Davis, ed., *Sassoon Diaries*, 279, entry for 27 October 1922.

120. ULC, MS. Add. 9375/412, Prince Philipp to Sassoon, 29 September 1925.

121. According to recently declassified documents, a British intelligence offer described Dollmann as "a bon viveur, fond of women and luxury, but not a drunkard or a profligate. Is witty and an excellent raconteur. . . . It is thought that he has told the truth on all matters discussed with him." Katz, *Battle for Rome*, 24. Katz cites recently declassified OSS documents in NARA, RG 226, CIA, box 6, Doc/D 987: 6.

122. BAB, NS 19/3001, SS-Obersturmbannführer Dr. Eugen Dollmann to Generalmajor Schmundt, 14 and 15 September 1942.

123. HHStAW, 520 D-Z, Nr. 519.563, statement of Walter Rohrbach, 27 March 1947.

124. Diana Mosley quoted in Guppy, *Looking Back*, 190–91.
125. Bradford, *George VI*, 140.
126. Peter Millar, "The Other Prince," *The Sunday Times* (London), 26 January 2003.
127. Ibid.
128. Wiskemann, *Rome-Berlin Axis*, 40–41.
129. Heinrich Prinz von Hessen, *Kristallene Lüster*, 119.
130. H. Smith, ed., *Protestants, Catholics and Jews in Germany 1800–1914*.
131. Ritter, *Frederick the Great*, 13.
132. Cahill, *Philipp of Hesse and the Reformation*.
133. HHStAW, 520 D-Z, Nr. 519.563, Spruchkammer Protocol of Prince Philipp, 15–17 December 1947, 32: statement of Adelheid Fliege.
134. Ibid.
135. Heinrich Prinz von Hessen, *Kristallene Lüster*, 11.
136. Wolfgang Prinz von Hessen, *Aufzeichnungen*, 14. Note that the Hessens had not abided by the Kaiser's order and continued to see Princess Anna.
137. Schwarzmüller, *Zwischen Kaiser und "Führer,"* 214.
138. Preussen, *Haus Hohenzollern*, 17–26. Bruce Lincoln notes that the Romanovs created dynastic laws "modeled upon the 'House Statutes' of German ruling families," and that these related to hierarchy as well as rules concerning behavior. See Lincoln, *Romanovs*, 375.
139. Rijksarkiv Utrecht, Papers of Kaiser Wilhelm II, "Das Ex-Kaiser Wilhelm II, 1918–41, Korrespondenz mit mitgliedern der Kaiserlichen Familie, #8." See, in particular, Wilhelm II to Prince Philipp von Hessen, 31 October 1927. Ilsemann also reported in January 1929: "Downstairs in the Orangerie the Crown Princess lay on a chaise lounge, surrounded by several family members who joked and laughed. Upstairs, the younger generation convened in the room of Prince Paul of Greece: Prince Philipp with the daughter of the Italian king and both Darmstadt princes. Here princely ways were put aside and human inclinations given freer rein." Ilsemann, *Kaiser in Holland: Monarchie und Nationalsozialismus*, 121.
140. Heinrich Prinz von Hessen, *Kristallene Lüster*, 48.
141. Wolfgang Prinz von Hessen, *Aufzeichnungen*, 161. He notes that when Mafalda's sister Giovanna married King Boris III of Bulgaria in 1930, similar confessional difficulties induced them to move the ceremony to Assisi.
142. HHStAW, 520 D-Z, Nr. 519.563, Spruchkammer Protocol of Prince Philipp, 15–17 December 1947.
143. ULC, MS. Add. 9375/412, Prince Philipp to Sassoon, 29 September 1925.
144. More generally, see Cannadine and Price, eds., *Rituals of Royalty: Power*.
145. HHStAW, 520 D-Z, Nr. 519.563, statement of Landgravine Margarethe von Hessen, 15 July 1946.
146. ULC, MS. Add. 9375/412, Prince Philipp to Sassoon, 29 September 1925.
147. GStAPK, Rep 62 III, Nr. 49, Protocol of a discussion between Prince Auwi and Dr. Presber, 24 January 1928. See also Heinrich Prinz von Hessen, *Kristallene Lüster*, 32.
148. Heinrich Prinz von Hessen, *Kristallene Lüster*, 50.

149. Ross, *What Gardens Mean*.
150. After 1933, they needed Philipp's considerable but not enormous salary of RM 1,100 per month he earned as Oberpräsident in order to make ends meet. HHStAW, 520 D-Z, Nr. 519.563, statement of Adelheid Fliege, 8 July 1946.
151. BAB (formerly BDC), Partei Karte of Prince Philipp von Hessen.
152. Heinrich Prinz von Hessen, *Kristallene Lüster*, 57–58, 125.
153. HHStAW, 520 D-Z, Nr. 519.563, statement of Kriminalrat Kummel in the Darmstadt Kriminalpolizei, 28 June 1946. Among the schools they attended was one at Bieberstein in Hesse.
154. Heinrich Prinz von Hessen, *Kristallene Lüster*, 182.
155. GStAPK, Rep 62 III, Nr. 49, Protocol of discussion between Prince Auwi and Dr. Presber, 24 January 1928.
156. HHStAW, 520 D-Z, Nr. 519.563, statement of Landgravine Margarethe von Hessen, 15 July 1946.
157. Ferguson, "Das Haus Sachsen-Coburg und die europäische Politik des 19. Jahrhunderts," in Rainer von Hessen, ed., *Viktoria Kaiserin Friedrich*, 40.
158. Patricia Kollander, "Philanthropy as Agent for Social Change: The Charity Work of Empress Frederick of Germany and its Impact," (paper delivered at German Studies Association Conference, New Orleans, 20 September 2003). See also Albisetti, *Schooling German Girls and Women*, and Göttert, "Victoria und die deutsche Frauenbewegung," in Rainer von Hessen, ed., *Victoria Kaiserin Friedrich*, 94–112.
159. H. Smith, review of Jean Quataert, *Staging Philanthropy*, *American Historical Review* 107/5 (December 2002): 1651.
160. HHStAW, 520 D-Z, Nr. 519.563, Spruchkammer Protocol of Prince Philipp, 15–17 December 1947, 29: statement of Anne Aubel.
161. Ibid., 33: statement of Adelheid Fliege.
162. Ibid., Kreisbetreuungsstelle für ehemaligen politischen Häftlingen in Bad Homburg to the Sicherheitsnachprüfungsamt, 9 July 1946. Heinrich Prinz von Hessen, *Kristallene Lüster*, 125.
163. Heinrich Prinz von Hessen, *Kristallene Lüster*, 15.
164. HHStAW, 520 D-Z, Nr. 519.563, statement of Princess Margaret von Hessen-Darmstadt, 22 June 1946.
165. Vickers, *Alice*, 333.
166. Wolfgang Prinz von Hessen, *Aufzeichnungen*, 196.
167. See *Kasseler Post*, 19 October 1936, in *Volksgemeinschaft und Volksfeind*, eds. Jörg Kammler and others, 112. Note that Philipp would often take his sons out collecting for *Winterhilfswerk* (it was obligatory for members of Nazi organizations, including ten-year old "Pimpfe"). Heinrich Prinz von Hessen, *Kristallene Lüster*, 122.
168. HHStAW, 520 D-Z, Nr. 519.563, "Begründung," December 1947, 12.
169. Ibid.
170. Ibid., statement of von Schlabrendorff on behalf of Prince Philipp, 21 November 1947.
171. Ibid., "Begründung," December 1947, 12.
172. Ibid., Spruchkammer Protocol of Prince Philipp, 15–17 December 1947, 4.
173. Katz, *Battle for Rome*, 20.

174. HHStAW, 520 D-Z, Nr. 519.563, Spruchkammer Protocol of Prince Philipp, 15–17 December 1947.
175. Fenyvesi, *Royalty in Exile*, 92.
176. HHStAW, 520 D-Z, Nr. 519.563, statement of von Schlabrendorff on behalf of Prince Philipp, 9 March 1947.
177. Ibid.
178. Ibid., Klageschrift of Hessisches Staatsministerium, 22 October 1947.
179. BAB (formerly BDC), Prince Philipp von Hessen, "Lebenslauf," n.d. (1939?).
180. HHStAW, 520 D-Z, Nr. 519.563, statement of von Schlabrendorff on behalf of Prince Philipp, 21 November 1947.
181. HHStAW, 520 D-Z, Nr. 519.563, Spruchkammer Protocol of Prince Philipp, 15–17 December 1947.
182. Ibid. "Begründung," December 1947, 11.
183. BAB (formerly BDC), Prince Philipp, Lebenslauf, n.d. (1939?).
184. HHStAW, 520 D-Z, Nr. 519.563, Klageschrift of Hessisches Staatsministerium, 22 October 1947.
185. Ibid., statement of von Schlabrendorff on behalf of Prince Philipp, 21 November.
186. Wolfgang Prinz von Hessen, *Aufzeichnungen*, 137.
187. RvH: Prince Richard to Landgravine Margarethe, 1 September 1919. More generally, see McDougall, *France's Rhineland Diplomacy, 1914–1924*, and Fraenkel, *Military Occupation and the Rule of Law*.
188. See Oguntoye, Opitz, and Schultz, eds., *Showing Our Colors*.
189. Prince Friedrich Karl journal entry from 17 June 1919, in Wolfgang Prinz von Hessen, *Aufzeichnungen*, 141.
190. RvH: Prince Christoph to Landgravine Margarethe, 29 March 1920.
191. ULC, MS. Add. 9375/408, Prince Philipp to Sassoon, 10 March 1924.
192. Eckhart Franz, letter to author, 4 February 2004. See more generally, Schulze, *Freikorps und Republik, 1918–1920*.
193. RvH: Prince Christoph to Landgravine Margarethe, 27 March 1920
194. Ibid., Prince Christoph to Landgravine Margarethe, 4 October 1919.
195. See Hagen, *Germans, Poles and Jews: The Nationality Conflict in the Prussian East, 1772–1914*.
196. RvH: Prince Christoph to Landgravine Margarethe, 3 June 1921.
197. See Baranowski, *Sanctity of Rural Life*. See also Görlitz, *Die Junker*.
198. RvH, France: Prince Christoph to Landgravine Margarethe, 12 May 1921.
199. Birn, *Höheren SS- und Polizeiführer*, 330, 348. BAB, R 43/4063, Lammers to Göring, n.d. November 1938.
200. Wolfgang Prinz von Hessen, *Aufzeichnungen*, 149.
201. RvH, France: Prince Christoph to Landgravine Margarethe, undated (autumn 1923).
202. Ibid., Prince Christoph to Landgravine Margarethe, 20 November 1922.
203. Ibid., Prince Christoph to Landgravine Margarethe, 29 November 1921.
204. BAB (formerly BDC), SS Führerpersonalakten (SSF) 94A, file of Prince Christoph, Lebenslauf, 21 February 1933.
205. Rijksarkiv Utrecht, Papers of Wilhelm II ("Das Ex-Kaiser Wilhelm II, 1918–41, Korrespondenz mit mitgliedern der Kaiserlichen Familie, #8"), signature illegible to Oberstleutnant Lange, 13 September 1928.

206. BAB, SSF-94A, SS file of Prince Christoph, questionnaire, 25 February 1993.

207. RvH: Prince Christoph to Landgravine Margarethe, 31 August 1928.

208. Christoph notes that his flying lessons were terminated in June 1942 due to a shortage of fuel. Ibid., Prince Christoph to Princess Sophia, 19 June 1942.

209. Fritzsche, *Nation of Fliers*, 64, 82.

210. See Fritzsche's review of D. Siegfried, *Der Fliegerblick*, *American Historical Review* 107/3 (June 2002): 963.

211. Fritzsche, *Nation of Fliers*, 122.

212. Ibid., 125. See Fritzsche's fine analysis of "gliding and the revival of nationalism," 103–31.

213. Anonymous article on Prince Bernhard zur Lippe at www.rights.nl/ samenvattingen.drog.

214. Prince Paul Metternich-Winneburg married Tatiana Vassiltchikov (sister of Missie Vassiltchikov). See Metternich, *An der Rennstrecke*. Note that Prince Louis Ferdinand von Preussen also joined the Luftwaffe. See Fenyvesi, *Royalty in Exile*, 77.

215. Wohl, *Passion for Wings*.

216. Ibid., 1. More generally, see J. Wilson, *Lawrence of Arabia*.

217. Fritzsche, *Nation of Fliers*, 173–74.

218. Brooks, *Bobos in Paradise*, 24, 28.

219. Hanfstaengl, *Unheard Witness*, 46.

220. Pohl, Habeth, and Brüninghaus, *Daimler-Benz AG in den Jahren 1933 bis 1945*, 36.

221. Klemperer, *Language of the Third Reich*, 4.

222. National Socialism paradoxically combined pro- and antimodernist tendencies. See Herf, *Reactionary Modernism*.

223. Nelson, *Soldier Kings*, 446.

224. BAB (formerly BDC), SSF 94A, file of Prince Christoph, Lebenslauf, 21 February 1933.

225. HHStAW, 520 D-Z, Nr. 519.563, statement of Princess Sophia, 15 July 1946.

226. Ilsemann, *Kaiser in Holland: Amerongen und Doorn, 1918–1933*, 195. Also, John C. G. Röhl to author, 20 April 2005.

227. RvH: Prince Christoph to Princess Sophia, 4 November 1939.

228. Parker, *Prince Philip*, 75.

229. Cookridge, *From Battenberg to Mountbatten*, 255.

230. Parker, *Prince Philip*, 52.

231. Ibid., 53.

232. Ibid., 53. HRH Prince Philip, Duke of Edinburgh, shared similar recollections with the author, interview at Buckingham Palace, 3 March 2004.

233. HStAD, GF, D/24, 70/9. BAB, Sammlung Schumacher, R. 187/400, "Aufstellung derjenigen Parteigenossen, die Angehörige fürstlicher Häuser sind." For Prince Lu, who was given the membership number 5900 506, see HStAD, GF, D 24/76/2.

234. Duff, *Hessian Tapestry*, 352. Parker, *Prince Philip*, 66.

235. Parker, *Prince Philip*, 66. Michael Bloch maintains that Ribbentrop was one of the witnesses at the wedding. See Bloch, *Ribbentrop*, 144.

236. Cookridge, *From Battenberg to Mountbatten*, 265.

237. Vickers, *Alice*, 223.

238. Ibid., 225.

239. Hanfstaengl, *Unheard Witness*, 98.

240. Ibid., 165–66.

CHAPTER 3

1. Goebbels, *Tagebücher*, I/2, 15, entry for 31 January 1931.

2. Reichel, *Schöne Schein des Dritten Reiches*.

3. Moll, "Acts of Resistance," in Geyer and Boyer, eds., *Resistance Against the Third Reich*, 178.

4. Hanfstaengl, *Unheard Witness*, 154.

5. HHStAW, 520 D-Z, Nr. 519.563, statement of von Schlabrendorff on behalf of Prince Philipp, 21 November 1947, 43.

6. Malinowski, *Vom König zum Führer*, 477–79.

7. BAB, Sammlung Schumacher, R. 187/400, "Aufstellung derjenigen Parteigenossen, die Angehörige fürstlicher Häuser sind." See also Malinowski, *Vom König zum Führer*, 570.

8. Preradovich, "Regierende Fürsten," 28–30; Malinowski, *Vom König zum Führer*, 562.

9. BAB, NL 1470/37, Prince Friedrich Christian zu Schaumburg-Lippe, "Personalfragebogen," 18 January 1938.

10. Pool and Pool, *Who Financed Hitler?*, 421.

11. For the Prince von Hannover in the Reitersturm of the SS, see BAB, R43II/286a, Princess Frederike Luise von Braunschweig to Hitler, n.d. (1937?). She notes that two of her other brothers are in the Hitler Youth. Fromm, *Blood and Banquets*, 127. Preradovich, "Regierende Fürsten," 28–30.

12. PRO, FO 372/4831, memorandum by Sir Alan Lascelles, 10 April 1946. Also Fromm, *Blood and Banquets*, 304.

13. Fromm, *Blood and Banquets*, 318. See also Stockhorst, *5000 Köpfe*, 93.

14. Fromm, *Blood and Banquets*, 138.

15. Ibid., 299 (see also 48, 67, 216, 224). See also BAB, R 43/4073, Lammers, Vermerk, 25 February 1937; and Pool and Pool, *Who Financed Hitler?*, 420.

16. BAB (former BDC), SS file for Prince Friedrich Franz von Mecklenburg (b. 22 April 1910). He served in the Third SS-Panzer Korps. See also Malinowski, *Vom König zum Führer*, 566; and Herbert, *Best*.

17. Vassiltchikov. *Berlin Diaries*, 45. Note that Count Gottfried Bismarck-Schönhausen, who joined the NSDAP in 1931 and held various positions, including Landrat on the island of Rügen and Regierungspräsident in Stettin, became alienated from the regime and by 1941 was a "convinced anti-Nazi." He was later active in the July 20 plot, and appeared before Judge Freisler and the People's Court, where he was acquitted in October 1944 (but then re-arrested)."

18. Malinowski, *Vom König zum Führer*, 570. See also the list compiled by Preradovich, "Regierende Fürsten," 28–30.

19. Malinowski, *Vom König zum Führer*, 570.

20. Wied, *Vom Leben gelernt.*

21. Hanfstaengl, *Unheard Witness*, 161. Malinowski, *Vom König zum Führer*, 554.

22. Hanfstaengl, *Unheard Witness*, 44. For Winifred Wagner, see the book by her grandson, Gottfried Wagner, *Wer nicht mit dem Wolf heult* as well as Hamann, *Winifred Wagner.*

23. W. Schuster, "Hitler in München—privat?," in *München: "Hauptstadt der Bewegung,"* 127.

24. Dalley, *Diana Mosley*, 190.

25. Pryce-Jones, *Unity Mitford*, 281.

26. See Feldman, "A Collapse in Weimar Scholarship," *Central European History* 18 (June 1984), 159–77, 245–67. More generally, see Turner, *German Big Business and the Rise of Hitler.*

27. For the remarkable experiences of Princess Stephanie zu Hohenlohe, see Schad, *Hitlers Spionin.* For Nazi high society more generally, see Fromm, *Blood and Banquets.* Examples of seating charts and programs for dinners and parties can be found in the papers of Fritz Wiedemann and Heinrich Himmler, both in Bundesarchiv Koblenz (BAK), Kleine Erwerbungen 671 and NL 126/20. See also Wiedemann, *Mann der Feldherr werden wollte.*

28. HHStAW, 520 D-Z, Nr. 519.563, Spruchkammer Protocol of Prince Philipp, 15–17 December 1947, 7. Bullock notes that in January 1931, the NSDAP had 389,000 members; Philipp's number therefore appears appropriate. Bullock, *Hitler: A Study in Tyranny*, 171.

29. HHStAW, 520 D-Z, Nr. 519.563, Spruchkammer Protocol of Prince Philipp, 15–17 December 1947, 34: statement of Adelheid Fliege.

30. Ibid., statement of Adelheid Fliege, 8 July 1946.

31. Ibid., Spruchkammer Protocol of Prince Philipp, 15–17 December 1947, 34.

32. Ibid., "Begründung," December 1947, 21.

33. Ibid., statement of Landgravine Margarethe von Hessen, 15 July 1946.

34. Ibid., Spruchkammer Protocol of Prince Philipp, 15–17 December 1947, 10.

35. Ibid., "Begründung," December 1947, 21.

36. BAB, NS 10/516, Bl. 203, Landgravine Margarethe von Hessen to Hitler, 3 June 1940.

37. Jonas, *Life of Crown Prince William*, 97.

38. HHStAW, 520 D-Z, Nr. 519.563, statement of Kurt Jerschke, 22 July 1946.

39. Ibid., statement of Landgravine Margarethe von Hessen, 15 July 1946.

40. Manvell and Fraenkel, *Hermann Göring*, 41, 45. See also Overy, *Goering: The Iron Man*, 7–9; Paul, *Hermann Göring. Hitler Paladin or Puppet?*, 81; and Pool and Pool, *Who Financed Hitler?*, 301. The latter notes that Mussolini gave Göring no money.

41. Turner, *Hitler's Thirty Days to Power*, 114.

42. Guinness and Guinness, *House of Mitford*, 388.

43. Gellately, ed., *Nuremberg Interviews*, 131–32.

44. For the first visit, see Ilsemann, *Kaiser in Holland: Monarchie und National-sozialismus*, 152–54: entries for 8 January–19 January 1931. See also Thyssen, *I Paid Hitler*, 111.

45. Macdonogh, *Last Kaiser*, 447. See also Preussen, *Haus Hohenzollern*, 65.
46. Macdonogh, *Last Kaiser*, 447. Ilsemann, *Kaiser in Holland: Monarchie und Nationalsozialismus*, 190–95: entries for 3 May 1932 through 21 May 1932.
47. Ilsemann, *Kaiser in Holland: Monarchie und Nationalsozialismus*, 194, entry for 21 May 1932.
48. Macdonogh, *Last Kaiser*, 447.
49. Jonas, *Life of the Crown Prince*, 182.
50. Ibid.
51. Macdonogh, *Last Kaiser*, 447, 451, 446.
52. Hanfstaengl, *Unheard Witness*, 165–66.
53. For the phrase "totalitarian temptation," see Stern, *Dreams and Delusions*. See also Machtan, *Kaisersohn*.
54. Ellinghaus, "Der Prinz."
55. HHStAW, 520 D-Z, Nr. 519.563, statement of von Schlabrendorff on behalf of Prince Philipp, 9 March 1947.
56. Ibid., Spruchkammer Protocol of Prince Philipp, 15–17 December 1947, 5.
57. Ibid., statement of von Schlabrendorff on behalf of Prince Philipp, 21 November 1947.
58. Spruchkammer Protocol of Prince Philipp, 15–17 December 1947, 5.
59. See Hanfstaengl, *Unheard Witness*, 25.
60. Pryce-Jones, *Unity Mitford*, 102.
61. HHStAW, 520 D-Z, Nr. 519.563, Klageschrift of Hessisches Staatsministerium, 22 October 1947.
62. Ibid., Freilassungsantrag Philipp Prinz von Hessen, n.d. (1946).
63. Eric Strasser, letter to author, 6 March 2002.
64. Thyssen, *I Paid Hitler*, 110.
65. PRO, FO 371/16719, minutes of 7 March 1933 meeting between Franz von Papen and British Ambassador to Germany Eric Phipps.
66. Macdonogh, *Last Kaiser*, 451.
67. Preussen, *Haus Hohenzollern*, 90–92, 193. Ilsemann, *Kaiser in Holland: Monarchie und Nationalsozialismus*, 191.
68. Preussen, *Haus Hohenzollern*, 207.
69. W. Dodd and M. Dodd, eds., *Ambassador Dodd's Diary, 1933–1938*, 48–49, entry for 11 September 1933.
70. The "Duke of Hesse" would presumably have been Ernst Ludwig von Hessen-Darmstadt. Note that Goebbels did not exclude the possibility of a restoration in 1933 but thought that it would intensify class conflict and was something for the future after the *Volksgemeinschaft* had been realized. Schaumburg-Lippe, *Dr. G. Ein Porträt des Propagandaministers*, 67.
71. Macdonogh, *Last Kaiser*, 452. Von Dommes was Hausminister of the Kaiser and his meeting with Hitler took place on 27 April 1934.
72. HHStAW, 520 D-Z, Nr. 519.563, Spruchkammer Protocol of Prince Philipp, 15–17 December 1947, 7.
73. For pro-restoration sympathies of the Hessens, see Ilsemann, *Kaiser in Holland: Amerongen und Doorn*, 195, entry for 28 December 1921.

74. Rijksarkiv Utrecht, Papers of Wilhelm II ("Das Ex-Kaiser Wilhelm II, 1918–41, Korrespondenz mit mitgliedern der Kaiserlichen Familie, #8"). Prince Philipp von Hessen to Wilhelm II, 25 April 1928, is among the many items of correspondence between the Hessens and the Kaiser.

75. Macdonogh, *Last Kaiser*, 451. The speech occurred on 24 March 1933.

76. For Hitler's remarks concerning the "Gesetz üben den Neuaufbau des Reiches," see Preussen, *Haus Hohenzollern*, 214.

77. PRO, FO 371/17758, Ambassador Eric Phipps to Sir John Simon, 8 February 1934.

78. PRO, FO 371/17758, Ambassador Eric Phipps to Sir John Simon, 25 January 1934. This speech was covered in the international press: see "Anniversary of the Reich: Nazi Warnings to Monarchists," *The Times* (London), 19 January 1934.

79. PRO, FO 371/17758, Sir Eric Phipps to Sir Orme Sargent, 13 January 1934.

80. BAB, R 43 II/216, Duke Carl Eduard von Sachsen-Coburg und Gotha to Hitler, 6 November 1933, and the responses from Lammers, 16 November 1933, and Darré, 23 November 1933.

81. BAB, R 43 II/287, Reich Interior Minister Frick to Hitler, 8 March 1938. See ibid., for the above mentioned *Denkschrift*.

82. Reichsgesetzblatt (RGBL) 1 February 1939, 139.

83. BAB, R 43/4063, Darré to Lammers, 23 September 1938.

84. BAB, R 43 II/287, Lammers to Sauckel, 15 April 1939.

85. Preussen, *Haus Hohenzollern*, 230.

86. BAB, SSF 112A, SS-Obersturmbannführer Franke-Gricksch memorandum, n.d., 1939. See also Preradovich, "Regierende Fürsten," 28–30. More generally, see Campbell, *SA Generals and the Rise of Nazism*; and Longerich, *Die braunen Battaillone*.

87. It also helped that Röhm was well disposed toward princes. He was quoted as saying in the mid-1920s, "I remain what I have always been, a Bavarian monarchist." Hanfstaengl, *Unheard Witness*, 133. See more generally, Kater, "Zum gegenseitigen Verhältnis," *Vierteljahrshefte für Sozial- und Wirtschaftsgeschichte* 2 (1975): 330–50.

88. BAB, PK 1597, file of Prince Philipp von Hessen, "Personalfragebogen für die Anlegung der SA-Personalakte," 20 November 1937.

89. HHStAW, 520 D-Z, Nr. 519.563, statement of von Schlabrendorff on behalf of Prince Philipp, 9 March 1947.

90. Private papers of Rainer von Hessen: Princess Sophia to Landgravine Margarethe, 22 January 1934.

91. HHStAW, 520 D-Z, Nr. 519.563, Spruchkammer Protocol of Prince Philipp, "Begründung," December 1947, 5.

92. www.skalman.nu/third-reich/sa-fuhrung-1932.htm.

93. BAB, PK 1597, file of Prince Philipp von Hessen, "Personalfragebogen für die Anlegung der SA-Personalakte," n.d. The party files say on 9 November 1938—the anniversary of the failed Beer Hall putsch but also Kristallnacht. The denazification board believed the party files were in error and the

promotion came in October 1937, before the SA-led pogrom against German Jews. HHStAW, 520 D-Z, Nr. 519.563, Spruchkammer of Prince Philipp, "Begründung," December 1947, 5.

94. BAB, PK, file of Wolfgang Prinz von Hessen, Sprenger to Schwarz, 19 July 1933.

95. Wolfgang Prinz von Hessen, *Aufzeichnungen*, 172.

96. Speer, *Inside the Third Reich*, 88.

97. Wolfgang Prinz von Hessen, *Aufzeichnungen*, 173.

98. HHStAW, 520 D-Z, Nr. 519.563, Spruchkammer Protocol of Prince Philipp, 15–17 December 1947, 7.

99. Ibid., statement of von Schlabrendorff on behalf of Prince Philipp, 9 March 1947.

100. BAB, PK 1597, file of Prince Philipp von Hessen, Prince Philipp to Röhm, 18 May 1933.

101. Malinowski, *Vom König zum Führer*, 482.

102. Wolfgang Prinz von Hessen, *Aufzeichnungen*, 21. For more on resentment of Jewish social climbers of bourgeois descent, see Stern, *Gold and Iron: Bismarck and His Banker Bleichröder*.

103. Claudia Koonz, summary of paper "The Dissemination of Racial Phobia as Knowledge" at German Studies Association Conference, 2003 at h-german @h-net.msu.edu. More generally, see Koonz, *Nazi Conscience*.

104. HRH Prince Philip, Duke of Edinburgh, interview with author, Buckingham Palace, 3 March 2004.

105. Klein, *Lageberichte der Geheimen Staatspolizei über die Provinz Hessen-Nassau, 1933–1936*, 904–11 and 922–27: reports from Prince Philipp to the Reich Minister of the Interior, 9 August 1934 and 9 May 1935.

106. Parker, *Prince Philip*, 74. He cites a taped telephone conversation introduced as evidence at the IMT in Nuremberg on 29 November 1945.

107. Washington State University, Hans Rosbaud Papers, folder 74, Landgrave Alexander Friedrich von Hessen to Hans Rosbaud, 8 March 1941.

108. Irving, *Göring*, 135.

109. BAB, PK 4793, file of Prince Christoph, Prince Christoph to Ortsgruppe Dahlem der NSDAP, 8 March 1937.

110. Ibid., Julius Stilke to Prince Christoph, 1 February 1937.

111. Ibid., Marquart to Gauschatzmeister des Gaues Berlin der NSDAP, 6 October 1937.

112. BAB, NL 1470/37, Prince Friedrich Christian zu Schaumburg-Lippe, Personalfragebogen, 18 January 1938.

113. Prince zu Waldeck quoted from his 1949 denazification trial in Schmeling, *Waldeck*, 36.

114. BAB, PK 4793, file of Prince Christoph, Karl Hanke, "Bescheinigung," 21 January 1935.

115. Ibid., Prince Christoph to Ortsgruppe Dahlem, 8 March 1937.

116. Ibid., Hauptamtsleiter Stenger to Bormann, 28 October 1936, and BAB (formerly BDC), SSF 94A, file of Prince Christoph, statement signed by Hermann Göring, 24 January 1936.

117. BAB, PK 4793, file of Prince Christoph, Hauptamtsleiter Stenger to Bormann, 28 October 1936, and BAB (formerly BDC), SSF 94A, file of Prince Christoph, statement signed by Hermann Göring, 24 January 1936.
118. BAB, PK 4793, file of Prince Christoph, Marquart to Gauschatzmeister des Gaues Berlin der NSDAP, 13 December 1937.
119. HHStAW, 520 D-Z, Nr. 519.563, statement of Princess Sophia, 15 July 1946. Irving, *Reich hört mit*, 35.
120. RvH: Prince Christoph to Landgravine Margarethe, 24 April 1932.
121. Ibid., Princess Sophia to Landgravine Margarethe, 30 May 1932.
122. Ibid., Princess Sophia to Landgravine Margarethe, 30 June 1932.
123. Ibid., Princess Sophia to Landgravine Margarethe, 27 February 1933.
124. Ibid.
125. Ibid., Princess Sophia to Landgravine Margarethe, 22 January 1934.
126. Rainer von Hessen to author, 17 October 2004.
127. Wegner, *Waffen-SS*, 252–62.
128. BAB, RS, file of Prince Wilhelm von Hessen (b. 1 March 1905): Lebenslauf of Prinz Wilhelm, 1937.
129. See the description of the wedding, which included dueling Nazi and Stahlhelm choirs, a toast to the Kaiser, the announcement of Hitler's appointment, and the raucous celebration of some wedding guests in Louis Ferdinand Prince von Preussen, *Im Strom der Geschichte*, 194.
130. Hermann Prinz von Hessen (son of Prince Wilhelm von Hessen) to author, 6 March 2005.
131. Ibid.
132. HHStAW, 520 D-Z, Nr. 519.563, statement of Princess Sophia, 15 July 1946.
133. BAB, PK 4793, file of Prince Christoph, Reichsschatzmeister to Gauleitung Gross Berlin der NSDAP, 21 November 1933.
134. Hamilton, *Who Voted for Hitler?*, 413. See also Bracher, *Auflösung der Weimarer Republik*, 120, 546.
135. Macdonogh, *Last Kaiser*, 449.
136. HHStAW, 520 D-Z, Nr. 519.563, Klageschrift of Hessisches Staatsministerium, 22 October 1947.
137. RvH: Princess Sophia to Landgravine Margarethe, 27 February 1933.
138. Wolfgang Prinz von Hessen, *Aufzeichnungen*, 168.
139. IfZG, MA-1300/2 (0281–83), Anonymous report, "Hesse, Prince Philipp," 21 July 1945. Other princes also helped the Nazi leaders with introductions. The Prince and Princess zu Wied, for example, had been among Carin Göring's best friends and continued to help the future Reichsmarschall. See Frischauer, *Goering*, 122. Note also that a Prince Eulenburg-Hertefeldt "sent [a circular] to his peers in February 1931 . . . if they did not want Bolshevism there was no choice but to join 'the Party.'" Padfield, *Himmler*, 98, 102.
140. Pool and Pool, *Who Financed Hitler?*, 301.
141. Goebbels, *Tagebücher* I/2, 18—19, entry for 9 February 1931.
142. Ibid., I/2, 425–28, entry for 4 June 1933.
143. Ibid., I/2, 434, entry for 16 June 1933.
144. Fromm, *Blood and Banquets*, 99.

145. Ibid., 113.
146. Ibid., 118, 326. Schellenberg uses the phrase, "society espionage" and has a chapter on the subject in Walter Schellenberg, *Schellenberg Memoirs*, 190–99.
147. M. Dodd, *Through Embassy Eyes*. See also Brysac, *Resisting Hitler*.
148. BAB (former BDC), SS file for Prince Friedrich Franz von Mecklenburg (b. 22 April 1910): Reinhard Heydrich to Heinrich Himmler, 31 January 1941.
149. Courcy, *Diana Mosley*, 174–75 and 376–403. The 2 October 1940 interview with Diana Mosley reproduced here is particularly revealing.
150. For an account of the April 1935 luncheon and Mosley's remark, see Dalley, *Diana Mosley*, 191; and D. Mosley, *A Life of Contrasts*, 125.
151. Turner, *Hitler's Thirty Days*, 115.
152. Ibid. Fritz Thyssen later maintained that "old President von Hindenburg did not disdain to accept a castle and several thousand hectares and forests from the hands of Göring, whom he had just made a general." Thyssen, *I Paid Hitler*, 169. Reich Chancellery chief Hans Lammers confirmed this after the war. See Overy, *Interrogations*, 272–76.
153. Turner, *Hitler's Thirty Days*, 116.
154. Gerhard Weinberg, review of "Hitler: The Rise of Evil," on H-German, April 2003.
155. Goebbels, *Tagebücher* I/2, 366, entry for 5 February 1933.
156. Hanfstaengl, *Unheard Witness*, 213.
157. Diels, *Lucifer ante portas*, 193–94.
158. For Göring's visit to Italy between 10 and 20 April 1933, see Maser, *Hermann Göring*, 187–88.
159. Wolfgang Prinz von Hessen, *Aufzeichnungen*, 170–73. See also Prince Wolfgang's denazification trial records in HHStAW, 520 F.
160. BAB, SA file of Richard Prinz von Hessen (b. 14 May 1901), undated file cards; also Prince Richard's denazification trial records in HHStAW, 520 F.
161. Zentner and Bedürftig, eds., *Encyclopedia of the Third Reich*, 634. For more on the NSKK, see Pohl, Habeth, and Brüninghaus, *Daimler-Benz*, 54–56.
162. Prince Auwi testimony of 14 May 1947 in Kempner, *Dritte Reich im Kreuzverhör*, 134.
163. HHStAW, 520 D-Z, Nr. 519563, statement of Prince Philipp, 21 February 1947.
164. Ibid.
165. Ibid., Spruchkammer Protocol of Prince Philipp, 15–17 December 1947, 8. Note that Gauleiter Karl Weinrich's Spruchkammer files are in HHStAW, 520/4960.
166. HHStAW, 520 D-Z, Nr. 519.563, Spruchkammer Protocol of Prince Philipp, 15–17 December 1947, 8. For Mafalda's opposition, see ibid., Beiakten II, statement of Princess Sophia von Hannover, 15 July 1946.
167. Ibid., Spruchkammer Protocol of Prince Philipp, 15–17 December 1947, 8.
168. Ibid., statement of Prince Philipp, 21 February 1947.
169. Ibid.
170. Ibid.
171. Ibid.

172. Kube, *Pour le Mérite und Hakenkreuz*, 33.

173. On 7 June he was appointed Kommissarische Oberpräsident (there were press reports that this would occur in May). Bayerisches Hauptstaatsarchiv (BHSA), Slg. Personen 5458, "Oberpräsident Prinz Philipp von Hessen," *Hamburger Nachrichten*, 236, 22 May 1933.

174. HHStAW, 520 D-Z, Nr. 519.563, statement of Kurt Jerschke, 22 July 1946. See also Kempner, *Dritte Reich im Kreuzverhör*, 142. More generally, see Rebentisch, "Nationalsozialistische Revolution," in U. Schultz, ed., *Die Geschichte Hessens*, 232–48; and Hennig, ed., *Hessen unterm Hakenkreuz*.

175. For more on the position of Oberpräsident, see Caplan, *Government Without Administration*, 43, 154.

176. Speer, *Inside the Third Reich*, 417. Speer notes that he earned a salary of RM 6,000 annually.

177. HHStAW, 520 D-Z, Nr. 519.563, statement of von Schlabrendorff on behalf of Prince Philipp, 21 November 1947: Wilhelmine Heyer quoted in extracts of testimony, 5.

178. Thyssen, *I Paid Hitler*, 127. He notes how meetings sometimes felt like a "course on National Socialism" and that speakers included Julius Streicher, the radical Gauleiter from Nuremberg.

179. HHStAW, 520 D-Z, Nr. 519.563, Haftprüfungsamt Kassel, "Beschluss," 26 July 1946.

180. Ibid., statement of von Schlabrendorff on behalf of Prince Philipp, 21 November 1947, 40.

181. Anfuso, *Beiden Gefreiten*, 24.

182. IfZG, ZS 918, Interrogation of the Prince of Hesse, 4 March 1948.

183. Streets throughout Germany had their names changed to reflect the new political order: in Kassel, the Rasen-Allee became the Horst Wessel Allee, and so forth. HHStAW, 520 D-Z, Nr. 519.563, Spruchkammer of Prince Philipp, 15–17 December 1947, 15: testimony of Karl Vötterle.

184. BHSA, Slg. Personen 5458, "Prinz Philipp von Hessen. Mittler zwischen Deutschland und Italien," *Berliner Illustrierte Zeitung*, 8 June 1933.

185. HHStAW, 520 D-Z, Nr. 519.563, Spruchkammer Protocol of Prince Philipp, 15–17 December 1947, 9. The quote comes from the chair, Hans Quambusch.

186. Ibid., statement of Dr. Ernst Gall, 30 July 1946.

187. Wistrich, *Who's Who in Nazi Germany*, 102. See also the account in Diels, *Lucifer ante portas*, 227–42.

188. BAB, NS 19/1647, Heinrich Himmler, "Akten-Notiz," 8 May 1933.

189. Gellermann, *. . . und lauschten für Hitler. Geheime Reichssache: Die Abhörzentralen des Dritten Reiches*, 20.

190. Wolfgang Prinz von Hessen, *Aufzeichnungen*, 173.

191. L. Mosley, *Reich Marshal*, 132; Overy, *Goering*, 35.

192. Kempner quoted by Maser, *Göring*, 91.

193. Kahn, *Hitler's Spies*, 179.

194. BAB, Kleine Erwerbungen, 272–10, CIC Detachment 970/41, James Olsen and Harvey Gutman, Memorandum for the Officer in Charge, 3 September 1945. See also Flicke, *War Secrets in the Ether*, vol. 1, 107.

195. Note that in the summer of 1944, Schellenberg took control of German Military Intelligence (the Abwehr). See Bullock, "Introduction," in Schellenberg, *Memoirs*, 11–12. See also Watt, "Introduction," in Irving, ed., *Breach of Security*, 20.

196. Gellermann, *und lauschten für Hitler*, 20. See also Kahn, *Codebreakers*.

197. Gellermann, *und lauschten für Hitler*, 20.

198. RvH: Princess Sophia to Landgravine Margarethe, 12 April 1935.

199. Kahn, *Hitler's Spies*, 179. See also Wolfgang Prinz von Hessen, *Aufzeichnungen*, 174.

200. Rainer von Hessen to author, 17 October 2004.

201. HHStAW, 520 D-Z, Nr. 519.563, statement of Princess Sophia, 15 July 1946.

202. Ibid., statement of von Schlabrendorff on behalf of Prince Philipp, 21 November 1947.

203. Ibid., statement of Constantin von Neurath, 15 October 1947.

204. Maser, *Göring*, 247. Schwarzmüller, *Zwischen Kaiser und "Führer,"* 310. Singer, *Göring*, 253.

205. Heinrich Prinz von Hessen, *Kristallene Lüster*, 170.

206. E. Göring, *An der Seite meines Mannes*, 32–33.

207. Courcy, *1939*, 62. Kershaw, *Making Friends*, 194–96.

208. PRO, FO 371/20734, Ambassador Eric Phipps to Foreign Office, 28 February 1937.

209. Broadlands Archives, MB1/A110, for Mountbatten documents concerning the funeral of King George V. An early biographer of Göring, Willi Frischauer, claimed that Göring actually traveled to London the day before the coronation and stayed at the German Embassy at Carlton House Terrace, but that he succumbed to pressure from "a well-known British peer" and returned to Germany on his private plane; this report remains unconfirmed and must be regarded as highly dubious. Frischauer, *Goering*, 145.

210. Frischauer, *Goering*, 124.

212. Kube, *Pour le Mérite und Hakenkreuz*, 84. Frischauer, *Goering*, 131–35.

213. E. Göring, *An der Seite*, 139. Balfour and Mackay, *Paul of Yugoslavia*, 114–15.

214. Martens, *Hermann Göring*, 61.

215. HHStAW, 520 D-Z, Nr. 519.563, statement of Wilhelmine Heyer, 2 July 1946.

216. Ueberschär and Vogel, *Dienen und Verdienen. Hitlers Geschenke an seine Eliten.*

217. NARA, RG 259, Entry 1082, box 2, "Von Hessen, Prince Philip: Background Information. Interrogation," 21 July 1942.

CHAPTER 4

1. Wegner, *Waffen-SS: Organization*, 245. Wegner notes that in 1935, 21.9 percent of the army officer corps had titles (this figure dropped to 6.5 percent over the next ten years). See also Funck, "Shock und Chance. Der Preussische Militäradel in der Weimarer Republik zwischen Stand und Profession," in Reif, ed., *Adel und Bürgertum in Deutschland II*, 163; and Craig, *Politics of the Prussian Army, 1640–1945*, 471, 483.

2. The other barons present were Werner von Fritsch, Curt von Gienanth, and Erich von dem Bussche-Ippenburg. See Wirsching, " 'Man kann nur Boden Germanisieren,' " *Vierteljahrshefte für Zeitgeschichte* 49 (3/2001): 517–50.

3. Ribbentrop, *Ribbentrop Memoirs*, 63–65.

4. BAB, NL 1470/37, Prince Friedrich Christian zu Schaumburg-Lippe, Personalfragebogen, 18 January 1938. See also Schaumburg-Lippe, *Dr. G.*, 5. He held the latter post for three years but remained an employee of the Ministry until 1945.

5. See the 9 May 1933 letter from Schaumburg Lippe to the Deutsche Studentenschaft where he secures Goebbels's involvement, reproduced at www.bayern.de/HDBG/buecher.

6. Schaumburg-Lippe rose through the ranks from *Gauredner* (regional speaker) to *Reichsredner* (national speaker) in 1932. He had also worked with Dr. Robert Ley to build up the Nazi press in the Rhineland, helping found six papers and publishing houses. BAB, NL 1470/37, Prince Friedrich Christian zu Schaumburg-Lippe, Personalfragebogen, 18 January 1938.

7. Kempner, *Dritte Reich im Kreuzverhör*, 157. See Schaumburg-Lippe, ed., *Deutsche Sozialisten am Werk*, as well as his three volumes of memoirs: *Verdammte Pflicht und Schuldigkeit*; *Als die goldne Abendsonne*; and *Damals fing das neue an*. See also Malinowski, *Vom König zum Führer*, 565.

8. For Duke Carl Eduard, including his role as leader of the influential Nationalklub, see Malinowski, *Vom König zum Führer*, 449–52, 568. See also Eilers, *Queen Victoria's Descendants*; and www.geocities.com/evestrehl/KarlEduard.html.

9. For the report of the Duke von Sachsen-Coburg from 1936, which includes discussions of his meetings with King George V, King Edward VIII, and the Dukes of Kent and York, among others, see *Documents on German Foreign Policy, 1918–1945*, Series C, Vol. 4, 1061–72: document 531. Copies of this report went to both Hitler and Göring.

10. "German Red Cross Chief Faces Pickets," *Chicago Daily Times*, 28 March 1940.

11. The literature mentioning Duke Carl Eduard has been mostly of a popular variety: see P. Allen, *Crown and the Swastika*, 49–53; Shaw, *Royal Babylon*, 314. See also D. Mosley, *Life of Contrasts*, 133.

12. Bamford, *Puzzle Palace*, 2, 98.

13. Frei, *Adenauer's Germany and the Nazi Past*, 50.

14. Irving, *Reich hört mit*, 5, 176. See also Kahn, *Hitler's Spies*, 179.

15. "Diese Haderlumpen," *Der Spiegel* 31 (30 July 1979): 60–66.

16. Gellermann, *und lauschten für Hitler*, 61.

17. Kahn, *Hitler's Spies*, 179.

18. Watt, "Introduction," 15.

19. BAB, Kleine Erwerbungen, 272–10, CIC Detachment 970/41, Memorandum for the Officer in Charge, 3 September 1945. Note that the intelligence in this document is very sketchy: the author(s) confuse Princes Christoph and Philipp and think the latter headed the agency. They also fail to note that the agency was initially founded in the attic of Göring's air building in April 1933. See Kahn, *Hitler's Spies*, 179; and Schellenberg, *Memoirs*, 300.

20. In principle, Himmler and Reich Minister of the Interior Wilhelm Frick shared authority over the police, but Himmler had the upper hand (and took Frick's position outright in 1943). See Overy, *Goering*, 27.
21. Irving, *Göring*, 176.
22. Kahn, *Hitler's Spies*, 178.
23. BAB, Kleine Erwerbungen, 272–10, CIC Detachment 970/41, James Olsen and Harvey Gutman, Memorandum for the Officer in Charge, 3 September 1945.
24. Ibid.
25. Gellermann, *und lauschten für Hitler*, 31.
26. BAB, Kleine Erwerbungen, 272–10, CIC Detachment 970/41, James Olsen and Harvey Gutman, Memorandum for the Officer in Charge, 3 September 1945.
27. BAB, Kleine Erwerbung, 671/7: Fritz Wiedemann to Bodenschatz, 25 August 1938. The same file includes Wiedemann to Heydrich, 29 June 1938. Both letters are marked "persönlich und vertraulich!"
28. Watt, "Introduction," 16.
29. Irving, *Reich hört mit*, 177. See Prince Christoph's memoranda on security measures for FA materials reproduced in Irving, ed., *Breach of Security*, 184–90.
30. BAB, Kleine Erwerbungen, 272–10, CIC Detachment 970/41, James Olsen and Harvey Gutman, Memorandum for the Officer in Charge, 3 September 1945.
31. Ibid. Flicke, *War Secrets in the Ether*, 103.
32. RvH, Prince Christoph to Adjudantur des Führers, 4 June 1938. For the FA's "Richtlinien für Geheimhaltung," see Gellermann, . . . *und lauschten für Hitler*, 198.
33. Irving, *Göring*, 124.
34. Wolfgang Prinz von Hessen, *Aufzeichnungen*, 173.
35. Kahn, *Hitler's Spies*, 180.
36. BAB, Kleine Erwerbungen, 272–10, CIC Detachment 970/41, James Olsen and Harvey Gutman, Memorandum for the Officer in Charge, 3 September 1945. For intercepts of conversations of Czechoslovak leaders during the Munich crisis in 1938, see "Diese Haderlumpen," *Der Spiegel* 31, 30 July 1979, 66.
37. BAB, Kleine Erwerbungen, 272–10, CIC Detachment 970/41, James Olsen and Harvey Gutman, Memorandum for the Officer in Charge, 3 September 1945.
38. "Diese Haderlumpen," *Der Spiegel* 31, 30 July 1979, 66. See also Irving, ed., *Breach of Security*. Note that during the war, the FA did not retain a monopoly on intercepting communications, as the SS and Wehrmacht also had important operations.
39. BAB, Kleine Erwerbungen 272–2, Ulrich Kittel, "Reichsluftfahrtministerium Forschungsamt. Geschichte und Arbeitsweise eines Nachrichtenamtes. Ergänzung," March 1958.
40. Kahn, *Hitler's Spies*, 181. See also Black, *IBM and the Holocaust*, 134, 223–26. Black does not identify all of the agencies that utilized Hollerith machines, but the operations he describes and the linkages between IBM chief Thomas Watson and Göring make it almost certain that the Forschungsamt employed the new technology.

41. "Hinter den Kulissen des Nazi-Geheimdienstes," *Hessische Nachrichten* 77, 27 July 1946.
42. RvH: Princess Sophia, "Memories," unpublished handwritten manuscript.
43. See Gellately, *Gestapo and German Society*, 44, 253.
44. BAB, Kleine Erwerbungen, 272-10, CIC Detachment 970/41, James Olsen and Harvey Gutman, Memorandum for the Officer in Charge, 3 September 1945. "Diese Haderlumpen," *Der Spiegel* 31, 30 July 1979, 60–66.
45. Irving, *Reich hört mit*, 5–6.
46. BAB, Kleine Erwerbungen, 272-10, CIC Detachment 970/41, James Olsen and Harvey Gutman, Memorandum for the Officer in Charge, 3 September 1945.
47. The U.S. government is still in the process of declassifying its findings from the immediate postwar period. The Germans also long protected their research—for example, one general study that was begun in 1951 and expanded upon the request of the German Federal Archives—was for the relevant archivists' use only until the 1970s. BAB, Kleine Erwerbungen 272-2, Kittel, "Reichsluftfahrtministerium Forschungsamt."
48. BAB, Kleine Erwerbungen, 272-10, CIC Detachment 970/41, James Olsen and Harvey Gutman, Memorandum for the Officer in Charge, 3 September 1945.
49. Jacobson, "Zur Rolle der Diplomatie im Dritten Reich," in Schwabe, ed., *Diplomatische Korps, 1871–1945*, 182.
50. The Duke of Hamilton evidently worked for the airforce intelligence service. See Padfield, *Hess: Flight for the Führer*, 89; and Picknett, Prince, and Prior, *Double Standards*, 159.
51. Persico, *Roosevelt's Secret War*, 16, 50–51.
52. L. Mosley, *Reich Marshal*, 188. For more on the daily FA reports and the Röhm Purge, see Gellermann, *. . . und lauschten für Hitler*, 85.
53. L. Mosley, *Reich Marshal*, 190. For the number of victims, see Koehl, *Black Corps*, 100.
54. Padfield, *Hess: The Führer's Disciple*, 70.
55. For a list of victims, see www.axishistory.com.
56. RvH: Landgravine Margarethe to Landgrave Friedrich Karl, 2 July 1934.
57. L. Mosley, *Reich Marshal*, 193.
58. Ibid., 194. See also the testimony of SS officers involved in the purge in Kempner, *SS im Kreuzverhör*, 253–70.
59. Koehl, *Black Corps*, 100. See also Padfield, *Hess: Flight*, 68. Note that Koehl places Prince zu Waldeck at Lichterfelde among the executioners. Anke Schmeling is apparently correct when she writes of him fulfilling a similar function in Munich. Schmeling, *Waldeck*, 48.
60. Rainer von Hessen, interview with author, 20 July 2002.
61. RvH: Landgravine Margarethe to Landgrave Friedrich Karl, 2 July 1934.
62. BAB, SSF-217B, Heinrich Himmler circular, 11 August 1936.
63. Höhne, *Order of the Death's Head*, 137. P. J. Wilson, *Himmler's Cavalry*.
64. In the case of Buchenwald, this included stables and both indoor and outdoor rings, lavish facilities that the camp commandant Karl Koch paid for by

stealing from prisoners. Zentner and Bedürftig, eds., *Encyclopedia of the Third Reich*, 118.

65. Guenther, *Nazi "Chic"?*, 12.

66. BAB (formerly BDC), SSF-94A, Prince Christoph to Chef des SS-Hauptamtes, 1 July 1937.

67. HHStAW, 520 D-Z, Nr. 519.563, statement of von Schlabrendorff on behalf of Prince Philipp, 21 November 1947, 30.

68. Ibid.

69. Hüttenberger, *Die Gauleiter*. See also "Weinrich wusste, was in den KZs vor sich ging," in *Hessische Nachrichten*, 5 July 1949.

70. Heinrich Prinz von Hessen, *Kristallene Lüster*, 129.

71. HHStAW, 520 D-Z, Nr. 519.563, statement of Dr. Franz Ulbrich, 16 December 1947.

72. Ibid., Spruchkammer Protocol of Prince Philipp, 15–17 December 1947, 29: statement of Anne Aubel.

73. Ibid., statement of Erste öffentliche Kläger, 19 March 1947.

74. Paret, *An Artist Against the Third Reich*, 37, 48, 77.

75. HHStAW, 520 D-Z, Nr. 519.563, statement of Dr. Bleibaum, 23 April 1947.

76. Ibid., Spruchkammer Protocol of Prince Philipp, 15–17 December 1947, 14.

77. Ibid., Spruchkammer Protocol of Prince Philipp, 15–17 December 1947, 24: statement of Dr. Bleibaum, Landeskonservator of Hesse.

78. See www.elisabethkirche-mr.de

79. Ibid., Spruchkammer Protocol of Prince Philipp, 15–17 December 1947, 24: statement of Kurt Jerschke.

80. Ibid., statement of Josef Leis (a conservation expert), 17 June 1946, and statement of Professor Dr. Philipp Losch, 12 March 1947.

81. Rainer von Hessen, "Hessische Hausstiftung," 4.

82. Dr. Bernhard Schackenburg to author, 17 July 2002. See also Gercke, "Die Antikensammlung," *Kunst in Hessen und am Mittelrhein* 28 (1988): 95–106.

83. Sheehan, *Museums*, 17–18.

84. "Die Weihe des Landgrafen-Museums: Reichsminister Dr. Rust über den Weg der Kunst," *Kasseler Post*, 20 May 1935. Among other examples of the press coverage of the opening and subsequent developments, see "Das grosse Vermächtnis der hessischen Landgrafen," *Kurhessische Landeszeitung*, 18/19 May 1935; "Das Landgrafen-Museum. Zu seiner Entstehung und Geschichte," *Kasseler Neue Nachrichten*, 19 May 1935; and "Denkmäler antiker Malerei in Kassel: Eine Schenkung des Prinzen Philipp von Hessen," *Kasseler Post*, 28 March 1936. More generally, see Schnackenburg, "Der Kasseler Gemäldegalerie," *Münchner Jahrbuch der bildenden Kunst* 49 (1998): 163–84.

85. FOIA request, Card of Hessen-Nassau, Prince Philipp of.

86. HHStAW, 520 D-Z, Nr. 519.563, Spruchkammer Protocol of Prince Philipp, 15–17 December 1947, 21: statement of Heinrich Lange.

87. IfZG, ZS 918, Interrogation of the Prince of Hesse, 20 July 1945.

88. IfZG, MA-1300/2 (0281-83), anonymous report, "Hesse, Prince Philipp," 21 July 1945.

89. Rainer von Hessen to author, 24 October 2004.

90. Note that self-control is valued in many non-European aristocratic cultures, such as the Japanese Samurai and their code of conduct known as Bushido. See also the pretender to the Bulgarian throne, King Simeon, quoting Louis XIV, "Control your rage and don't give offense." Fenyvesi, *Royalty in Exile*, 161.

91. IfZG, ZS 918, Interrogation of the Prince of Hesse, 6 May 1947.

92. BHSA, Slg. Personnen, 5458, "Oberpräsident Prinz von Hessen besucht den Stahlberg," in *Kreis Beobachter* 159, 11 July 1933.

93. Enigl, "Der Adel und die Nazis," 34.

94. HHStAW, 520 D-Z, Nr. 519563, statement of Prince Philipp, 21 February 1947.

95. BHSA, Slg. Personnen, 5458, K. B, "Ein Prinz?—Nein, unser Prinz kommt!" *Kreis Beobachter* 155 (6 July 1933).

96. HHStAW, 520 D-Z, Nr. 519.563, statement of von Schlabrendorff on behalf of Prince Philipp, 21 November 1947.

97. Ibid.

98. Ibid., Spruchkammer Protocol of Prince Philipp, 15–17 December 1947, 24: statement of Kurt Jerschke.

99. BHSA, Slg. Personnen, 5458, "Unverbrüchliche Treue," *Berliner Börsen Zeitung* 266, 19 June 1933.

100. HHStAW, 520 D-Z, Nr. 519.563, Spruchkammer of Prince Philipp, "Begründung," December 1947, 10.

101. IfZG, MA-1300/2 (0281–83), anonymous report, "Hesse, Prince Philipp," 21 July 1945.

102. Kershaw, *Hitler: 1936–1945*, 728.

103. HHStAW, 520 D-Z, Nr. 519.563, Spruchkammer Protocol of Prince Philipp, 15–17 December 1947, 39.

104. Ibid., "Begründung," December 1947, 9–10.

105. This line is repeated in Speer, *Inside the Third Reich*, 25.

106. Lothar Machtan, statement to author, Bremen, Germany, 24 July 2002.

107. "Der Führer besuchte den Gauleiter und den Oberpräsident," *Kasseler Post*, 5 June 1939.

108. Machtan, *Hidden Hitler*. Also Lothar Machtan to author, 28 February 2005.

109. Geoffrey Giles noted, "Many homosexuals only emerged into the public eye if they were unfortunate enough to fall afoul of the police; otherwise they led very private lives." See Giles, "A Gray Zone Among the Field Gray Men," in Petropoulos and Roth, eds., *Gray Zones*.

110. Heineman, "Sexuality and Nazism" *Journal of the History of Sexuality* 11:1/2 (January/April 2002). Heineman references the work of Wilhelm Reich and Erich Fromm, among others. See also Hancock, " 'Only the Real, the True, the Masculine Held Its Value' " *Journal of the History of Sexuality* 8/4 (April 1998).

111. Theweleit, *Male Fantasies*.

112. "Karl Weinrich gestorben," *Hessische Allgemeine Zeitung*, 27 July 1973; "Weinrich wusste, was in den KZs vor sich ging," *Hessische Nachrichten*, 5 July 1949; and HHStAW, 520/4960. More generally, see Rebentisch, "Persönlichkeitsprofil," 293–332.

113. For more on Sprenger and the local Gauleiter, see Zibell, *Jakob Sprenger*.

114. See Heberer, "'Exitus Heute in Hadamar,'" 158. For the Gesetz über die Erweiterung der Befugnisse des Oberpräsident of 15 December 1935, see Winter, "Die Geschichte der NS-'Euthanasie'-Anstalt Hadamar," in Baader, Cramer, and Winter, eds., *"Verlegt nach Hadamar,"* 42.

115. IfZG, ZS 918, Interrogation of the Prince of Hesse, 20 July 1945.

116. Heinrich Prinz von Hessen, *Kristallene Lüster*, 74, 121.

117. HHStAW, 520 D-Z, Nr. 519.563, statement of Dr. Franz Ulbrich, 16 December 1947.

118. Burleigh, *Death and Deliverance*, 47, 278.

119. HHStAW, 520 D-Z, Nr. 519.563, statement of Dr. Ernst Beckmann, 29 May 1947.

120. Ibid., statement of Prince Philipp, 21 February 1947.

121. Ibid., statement of Dr. Ernst Gall, 30 July 1946.

122. Ibid., statement of Hans Steegmann, 28 March 1947.

123. IfZG, ZS 918, Interrogation of the Prince of Hesse, 6 May 1947.

124. HHStAW, 520 D-Z, Nr. 519.563, Prince Philipp to Hessische Minister für politische Befreiung, 7 October 1947.

125. Ibid., "Protocol" of Karl Wolff, 18 September 1947.

126. Goebbels, *Tagebücher* I/2, 543, entry for 23 November 1935.

127. HHStAW, 520 D-Z, Nr. 519.563, statement of Dr. Nollau, 5 July 1946.

128. Ibid., statement of Dr. Ernst Beckmann, 29 May 1947.

129. IfZG, ZS 918, Interrogation of the Prince of Hesse, 6 May 1947.

130. HHStAW, 520 D-Z, Nr. 519.563, statement of Prince Philipp, 21 February 1947.

131. Ibid.

132. Ibid.

133. Ibid.

134. Ibid., statement of von Schlabrendorff on behalf of Prince Philipp, 21 November 1947, 29.

135. "Mittler zwischen Deutschland und Italien," *Berliner Illustrierte Zeifung*, 8 June 1933.

136. FOIA request, William Philip, memorandum on Prince Philipp, n.d.

137. For more on the Adolf Hitler Spende der Deutschen Wirtschaft, see, among others, Hayes, *Industry and Ideology*; and Bajohr, *Parvenüs und Profiteure*, 34–36.

138. Schad, *Hitlers Spionin*, 72.

139. IfZG, MA-255, Bl. 21, Alfred Rosenberg "Aktennotiz," 20 February 1934.

140. "Hitler hatte eine jüdische Beraterin," *Frankenpost*, 5 September 1950. See also "Missions" in *Time*, 30 January 1939, 19–20, and the press clippings collected in BAB, Kleine Erwerbungen 671/2. More generally, see Schad, *Hitlers Spionin*.

141. John Weitz writes, "The German Embassy expert in matters concerning royalty and its affairs of the heart was 'Lu' Hessen, a great-grandson of Queen Victoria and a young official of the Ribbentrop Büro. The prince was told by the ambassador to stay as close as possible to Buckingham Palace and to report any rumors about the durability and future of the King." Weitz, *Hitler's Diplomat*, 120. See also the "Registry of Cards" at the British Embassy

in Berlin, 1935, where Prince Ludwig identifies himself as a member of the Büro Ribbentrop, in Churchill Archives, Cambridge University, Papers of Ambassador Eric Phipps, PHPP III/6/5.

142. See Hauser, *England und das Dritte Reich. Erster Band*; and *England und das Dritte Reich. Zweiter Band*, 23–38. After leaving London, Prince Otto von Bismarck moved to Rome, where he became the deputy of Ambassador Mackensen. See Hoettl, *Secret Front*, 228–31.

143. Parker, *Prince Philip*, 64.

144. PRO, FO 372/3247, German Embassy to State Secretary, British Foreign Office, 23 May 1938.

145. See also Broadlands Archives, Victoria Milford Haven declaration, 9 July 1946, and ibid., King George VI to Victoria Milford Haven, 4 July 1946. Vickers, *Cecil Beaton*, 196. Among other members of the German high nobility who worked to forge better Anglo-German relations was Princess Marie Elisabeth zu Wied, who visited the Londonderrys with Ribbentrop, and Prince Adolf zu Mecklenburg was a member of a German delegation that met with Foreign Minister Halifax in London in June 1939. See Kershaw, *Making Friends*, 160.

146. Auswärtiges Amt Politisches Archiv (AAPA), R 102 823, Woermann, Vermerk, 20 December 1937. The Second Duke of Westminster was Hugh Richard Arthur Bendor Grosvenor (1879–1953).

147. Kershaw, *Making Friends*, 62–64, 174, 208.

148. Ibid., 209.

149. AAPA, 102823, British Foreign Office (anonymous) to German Ambassador Dr. Herbert von Dirksen, 5 July 1938.

150. HRH Viktoria Luise, *Kaiser's Daughter: Memoirs of H.R.H. Viktoria Luise, Duchess of Brunswick and Lüneburg, Princess of Prussia*, 180.

151. Paget, *Lineage and Ancestry of H.R.H. Prince Charles, Prince of Wales*, 40.

152. Viktoria Luise, *Kaiser's Daughter*, 188. See the more expansive treatment in the original German volumes: *Im Glanz der Krone* and *Im Strom der Zeit*.

153. Channon, *Chips*, 238. A more complete description of the state visit is in Balfour and Mackay, *Paul of Yugoslavia*, 174–78. See also Columbia University Libraries, Bakhmeteff Archive (CULBA), Prince Paul Karageorgevich, notes on meetings with Hitler and Göring, June 1939. BAB, NS 10/10, "Aufzeichnungen über Prinzregent Paul von Jugoslawien," 1 June 1939. This file also contains guest lists for dinners, which include members of Bismarck, Toerring-Jettenbach, and Hessen families.

154. Balfour and Mackay, *Paul of Yugoslavia*, 177–78.

155. Ibid., 178.

156. Ibid., 272. They cite PRO, FO 371/30265, a Foreign Office memorandum, 27 June 1941.

157. Emblematic of King Carol II's quandary is that his father was Ferdinand von Hohenzollern-Sigmaringen (1865–1927) and his mother, born Princess Marie of Edinburgh (1879–1938), was a granddaughter of Queen Victoria.

158. Preussen, *Haus Hohenzollern*, 185.

159. Reuter, "This War Has Been Madness: Crown Prince's Views," *The Times* (London), 12 May 1945.

160. Preussen, *Haus Hohenzollern*, 159, 176, 182. See also Machtan, *Kaisersohn*.
161. HHStAW, 520 D-Z, Nr. 519.563, Protocol of Karl Wolff, 18 September 1947.
162. Prince Franz von Hohenzollern-Emden was a son of Prince Wilhelm von Hohenzollern and Princess Maria Theresia von Bourbon-Sicily. He took the latter part of his name after World War I in honor of the heroic deeds of the light cruiser *Emden* during the Great War. Throughout the 1930s, the prince was responsible for cooperation between the NSDAP colonial political office and the Reich colonial association. An SS-Major (Sturmbannführer) he was also attached to the Staff of the SS Head Office. In 1939, he volunteered for military service, where he commanded a marine flak battery at the Cuxhaven naval base until 1944. However, the prince also eventually became suspect in the eyes of Himmler and party radicals. He was released from active service in the Armed Forces in June 1944 and then expelled from the SS on Himmler's personal order in November 1944, despite pleading for reinstatement. BAB, SSF 112A, Prince von Hohenzollern-Emden to Himmler, 3 January 1945.
163. Nelson, *Soldier Kings*, 444; Heinrich Prinz von Hessen, *Kristallene Lüster*, 189–90.
164. Hanfstaengl, *Unheard Witness*, 165–66. Hanfstaengl adds that Hitler "had a certain affection for" Auwi, but "had no illusions about his capacity."
165. Preussen, *Haus Hohenzollern*, 158.
166. Vassiltchikov, *Berlin Diaries*, 9.
167. Ilsemann, *Kaiser in Holland: Monarchie und Nationalsozialismus*, 17: entry for 10 October 1924.
168. Preussen, *Haus Hohenzollern*, 176, 179.
169. Ibid., 274. Note that Crown Prince Wilhelm's adjutant, von Müldner, was briefly imprisoned in the wake of the Röhm Purge.
170. Ibid., 185. Prince Auwi was apparently not mentioned in the *Völkischer Beobachter* after 1935.
171. For Prince August Wilhelm visiting the head of the RSHA (Heydrich) and the head of the Gestapo (Müller), see BAB, R 43/4064, General Wilhelm von Dommes to Dr. Meerwald, 20 August 1940.
172. See the documents reproduced in Preussen, *Haus Hohenzollern*, 186, 321–57.
173. Ibid., 192. Viktoria Luise, *Ein Leben als Tochter des Kaisers*, 272.
174. Nelson, *Soldier Kings*, 444. See also Herre, *Kronprinz Wilhelm*; and Preussen, *Haus Hohenzollern*, 193–225.
175. BAB, Kleine Erwerbungen 671/2, Hofrat A. Berg to Frau von Dirksen, 18 January 1936.
176. Preussen, *Haus Hohenzollern*, 209–12.
177. The crown prince was so close to Röhm that he and his adjutant were threatened with arrest (and worse) during the June 1934 purge. Preussen, *Haus Hohenzollern*, 199–201, 218.
178. BAB, R 43/4063, Crown Prince Wilhelm von Preussen to Hitler, 17 May 1936. Note that Hitler and the crown prince met at Cecilienhof in 1926 but initially did not get along well.

179. BAB, R 43/4063, Crown Prince Wilhelm von Preussen to Hitler, 25 June 1940. The crown prince had sent another openly supportive telegram to Hitler on 7 May 1940.

180. Nelson, *Soldier Kings*, 450.

181. Preussen, *Haus Hohenzollern*, 223.

182. BAB, Kleine Erwerbungen 671/2, Hofrat A. Berg to Frau von Dirkson, 18 January 1936.

183. Preussen, *Haus Hohenzollern*, 219.

184. Ibid., 221.

185. Ilsemann, *Kaiser in Holland: Monarchie und Nationalsozialismus*, 280: entry for 17 May 1935.

186. Röhl, "Kaiser and the Jews."

187. Kaiser Wilhelm II to Landgravine Margarethe, 3 November 1940, in Röhl, *Kaiser and his Court*, 212.

188. BAB, R43/4064, General von Dommes to Hitler, 25 September 1939.

189. BAB, R43/4064, Lammers, Vermerk, 6 November 1939. Note that the British also expressed preparedness to take steps to insure the safety of Wilhelm II. Ilsemann, *Kaiser in Holland: Monarchie und Nationalsozialismus*, 341.

190. Preussen, *Haus Hohenzollern*, 223.

191. Ilsemann, *Kaiser in Holland: Monarchie und Nationalsozialismus*, 345.

192. BAB, R43/4064, General von Dommes to Reichskabinettsrat von Stutterheim, 7 May 1939. Ibid., Graf von Moltke to *Daily Telegraph and Morning Post*, 9 May 1939. The letter from von Dommes includes the assurance, "Der Kaiser nimmt an allem, was in Deutschland geschieht, wärmsten Anteil." For more on the interview with journalist W. Burkhardt, see Preussen, *Haus Hohenzollern*, 147–49. It remains unclear whether the interview was a fabrication.

193. BAB, R 43/4063, Lammers to Crown Prince Wilhelm and Crown Princess Cecilie, 28 May 1940.

194. PRO, FO 371/29467, report of R. A. Butler, 16 July 1941.

195. Fenyvesi, *Royalty in Exile*, 80. He writes, "Louis Ferdinand concedes that in the summer of 1944 he was closer to the throne than at any other time in his life." See also Louis Ferdinand, Prince von Preussen, *Im Strom der Geschichte*, 288–308.

196. Preussen, *Haus Hohenzollern*, 229–30.

197. PRO, FO 371/26467, Foreign Office report, "Monarchy in Europe," 18 March 1941.

198. Preussen, *Haus Hohenzollern*, 269.

199. Mann, *Deutsche Geschichte*, 578.

200. Weyerer, "Bestattet wie ein König."

201. *Biographisch-Bibliographisches Kirchenlexikon*, 22, at www.bautz.de. Note that even though Rupprecht was the presumptive Bavarian monarch after 1921, he was customarily referred to as the crown prince.

202. Preussen, *Haus Hohenzollern*, 176.

203. Weyerer, "Bestattet wie ein König."

204. Aretin, *Krone und Ketten*.

205. PRO, FO 371/18859, Ambassador Eric Phipps to Foreign Office, 27 December 1935.

206. *Biographisch-Bibliographisches Kirchenlexikon*, 22, at www.bautz.de.

207. PRO, FO 371/33219, British Legation Berne to Central Department, Foreign Office, 9 June 1942; and PRO, FO 371/34438, Madrid Chancellery to General Department, 5 October 1943.

208. PRO, FO 371/3458, Hugh Montgomery to Sir Orme Sargent, Foreign Office, 3 May 1943.

209. Schad, *Bayerns Königshaus*, 208–9, 226.

210. Ibid., 209.

211. Weyerer, "Bestattet wie ein König."

212. Wilhelm Liebhart, *Königtum und Politik in Bayern*, 236.

213. Cannadine, *Aspects of Aristocracy*, 2.

214. Churchill, *My Early Life*.

215. Ishiguro, *Remains of the Day*, 197–99.

CHAPTER 5

1. See, among other sources, Kropat, "Die Verfolgung der Juden in Hessen und Nassau," in Knigge-Tesche and Ulrich, *Verfolgung und Widerstand in Hessen*, 86, 96.

2. More generally, see Weinberg, *Foreign Policy of Hitler's Germany: Starting World War II, 1937–1939*.

3. HHStAW, 520 D-Z, Nr. 519.563, Oberregierungsrat Hill to Regierungs-direktor Schleich, 22 July 1947.

4. Ibid., statement of Ernst von Weiszäcker, 17 September 1947.

5. Ribbentrop, *Ribbentrop Memoirs*, 79.

6. HHStAW, 520 D-Z, Nr. 519.563, statement of Constantin von Neurath, 15 October 1947.

7. Wiskemann, *Rome-Berlin Axis*, 114; Weinberg, *Foreign Policy of Hitler's Germany Starting World War II*, 286.

8. HHStAW, 520 D-Z, Nr. 519.563, statement of von Schlabrendorff on behalf of Prince Philipp, 21 November 1947. He cites a statement of Schellenberg. The RSHA was created in September 1939 and oversaw a network of agencies, including the Gestapo and the Criminal Police, and also instruments of genocide, including the concentration camp guard staff and the Order Police.

9. CULBA, Prince Paul Karageorgevich, notes on meeting with Göring, June 1939.

10. HHStAW, 520 D-Z, Nr. 519.563, statement of Adelheid Fliege, 8 July 1946.

11. CULBA, Prince Philipp von Hessen to Prince Paul Karageorgevich, 13 January 1935.

12. BAB, R43 II/1292, Prince Philipp von Hessen to Lammers, 11 December 1933 (marked *Geheim*); and ibid., Blomberg to all offices of the Reichswehrministerium, with a copy to Lammers, 21 February 1934.

13. Hanfstaengl, *Unheard Witness*, 244.

14. Redlich, *Hitler*, 138–39.
15. D. Mack Smith, *Mussolini*, 8. IfZG, ZS 918, Interrogation of the Prince of Hesse, 6 May 1947.
16. PRO, FO 371/18357, Sir Eric Drummond to Foreign Office, 7 October 1934.
17. It might be added that these four events were *the* most critical of the crises leading to World War II, and it is no coincidence that they served as the subject of Oxford historian A. J. P. Taylor in his controversial 1961 study, *Origins of the Second World War*; and Martel, ed., *Origins of the Second World War Reconsidered*.
18. Bullock, *Hitler*, 406.
19. Schellenberg, *Memoirs*, 53.
20. Philipp is featured in a picture with Hitler at the Colosseum in Rome, in Lang, ed., *Hitler Close-Up*, 76.
21. HHStAW, 520 D-Z, Nr. 519.563, statement of von Schlabrendorff, 10 July 1946. See also Weizsäcker, *Memoirs*, 129. For more on Hitler's visits to the Italian royal family, see Heinrich Prinz von Hessen, *Kristallene Lüster*, 78–80.
22. Picker, ed., *Hitlers Tischgespräche*, 133–35, entry from 21 July 1941.
23. HHStAW, 520 D-Z, Nr. 519.563, Spruchkammer Protocol of Prince Philipp, 15–17 December 1947, 40.
24. Ibid., "Begründung," December 1947, 12.
25. Ibid.
26. Ellinghaus, "Der Prinz."
27. "Mussolini Sought Excommunication of Hitler," *Los Angeles Times*, 28 September 2003, A12.
28. Weizsäcker, *Memoirs*, 131.
29. Wiskemann, *Rome-Berlin Axis*, 122.
30. IfZG, ZS 918, Interrogation of the Prince of Hesse, 6 May 1947.
31. HHStAW, 520 D-Z, Nr. 519.563, anonymous, "Bericht über die Vernehmung verschiedener Mitglieder des Auswärtigen Amtes über Prinz von Hessen," 1 September 1947.
32. Ibid., statement of von Schlabrendorff on behalf of Prince Philipp, 11 November 1947.
33. IfZG, ZS 918, Interrogation of the Prince of Hesse, 6 May 1947.
34. HHStAW, 520 D-Z, Nr. 519.563, Spruchkammer Protocol of Prince Philipp, "Begründung," December 1947, 13. See also Shirer, *Rise and Fall*, 421–22.
35. HHStAW, 520 D-Z, Nr. 519.563, Spruchkammer Protocol of Prince Philipp, "Begründung," December 1947, 13.
36. Ellinghaus, "Der Prinz."
37. IMT, *Trial of the Major War Criminals*, vol. 2, 422–23 and vol. 31, 368–70: doc. 2949-PS.
38. HHStAW, 520 D-Z, Nr. 519.563, Spruchkammer Protocol of Prince Philipp, "Begründung," December 1947, 14.
39. Ibid., statement of Prince Philipp, 24 June 1947.
40. Ibid., statement of von Schlabrendorff on behalf of Prince Philipp, 21 November 1947, 32.
41. Ibid., "Begründung," December 1947, 13.
42. Wheeler-Bennett, *King George VI*, 333.

43. Kershaw, *Hitler: 1936–1945*, 83.
44. Weinberg, *Foreign Policy of Hitler's Germany: Starting World War II*, 413.
45. For Prince Philipp's efforts to secure a military alliance between Germany and Italy, which include discussions with Ciano in July 1938, September 1938 and October 1938, see Toscano, *Origins of the Pact of Steel*, 36–37, 41, 48. Ciano, *Hidden Diary*, 135, 153–54, 176–77.
46. Weinberg, *Foreign Policy of Hitler's Germany: Starting World War II*, 454.
47. Watt, *How War Came*, 49–50. With regard to Prince Philipp's 11 October 1938 meeting with Ciano, Watt writes, "Nothing more was heard of this proposal, the first of Göring's attempts to conduct an alternative foreign policy to that of Ribbentrop." Ernst von Weizsäcker to Hans Georg von Mackensen, 11 October 1938, in *Documents on German Foreign Policy, 1918–1945, Series D, Vol. 4*, 436: document 337.
48. HHStAW, 520 D-Z, Nr. 519.563, Spruchkammer Protocol of Prince Philipp, 15–17 December 1947, 41.
49. Bullock, *Hitler*, 428.
50. For the "Memorandum on the First Meeting Between the British and French Prime Ministers, the Duce and the Führer at Munich, 29 September 1938," see *Documents on German Foreign Policy Series D, Vol. 2*, 1003–16; document 670. More generally, see Robbins, *Munich 1938*.
51. HHStAW, 520 D-Z, Nr. 519.563, statement of Baurat Erwin Schwarzer, 1 July 1946. For more on the Hitler-Chamberlain negotiations, see Kershaw, *Hitler 1936–1945*, 110–14.
52. Shirer, *Rise and Fall*, 516.
53. HHStAW, 520 D-Z, Nr. 519.563, Spruchkammer Protocol of Prince Philipp, "Begründung," December 1947, 15.
54. Ellinghaus, "Der Prinz." See Ciano's entry for 15 March 1939 in Muggeridge, ed., *Ciano's Diary*, 45. See also Kley, *Hitler, Ribbentrop und die Entfesselung des Zweiten Weltkrieges*, 238.
55. Von Weizsäcker to von Mackensen, 11 March 1939, cited in Toscano, *Origins of the Pact of Steel*, 166.
56. HHStAW, 520 D-Z, Nr. 519.563, Spruchkammer Protocol of Prince Philipp, 15–17 December 1947, 41.
57. Ibid.
58. Ibid.
59. Ibid. See more generally, Bosworth, *Mussolini*.
60. Toscano, *Origins of the Pact of Steel*, 168. He cites a telegram from von Mackensen to Ribbentrop, 16 March 1939.
61. HHStAW, 520 D-Z, Nr. 519.563, translation of diaries of Count Ciano from 15 March 1939 to 8 February 1940. See also Bullock, *Hitler*, 447.
62. HHStAW, 520 D-Z, Nr. 519.563, translation of diaries of Count Ciano, 15 March 1939.
63. Ibid.
64. Below, *At Hitler's Side*, 28.
65. See Ambassador von Mackensen to Ribbentrop, 17 March 1938, in *Documents on German Foreign Policy, 1918–1945, Series D, Vol. 6*, 15–16: document 15.
66. HHStAW, 520 D-Z, Nr. 519.563, translation of diaries of Count Ciano.

67. Ibid.
68. IfZG, ZS 918, Interrogation of the Prince of Hessen, 6 May 1947.
69. CULBA, Prince Philipp von Hessen to Prince Paul Karageorgevich, 13 January 1935.
70. Prince Auwi testimony of 14 May 1947 in Kempner, *Dritte Reich im Kreuzverhör*, 133.
71. PRO, FO 371/24407, memorandum by J. K. Roberts, 16 July 1940.
72. Hoare evidently entertained notions of replacing Churchill as head of the British government. Picknett, Prince, and Prior, *Double Standards*, 109. See also Padfield, *Hess: Flight*, 165–68; and CUL, Templewood Papers, Part 13, file 18, Sir Samuel Hoare to Sir Alexander Cadogan, 6 March 1941.
73. Albrecht Haushofer was the son of Karl Haushofer (1869–1946), architect of a theory of geopolitics and teacher of Rudolf Hess. The Haushofers and others evidently believed that Churchill's government could be bypassed or the prime minister forced out and that this would be an avenue to peace. Picknett, Prince, and Prior, *Double Standards*, 152–53.
74. Nolte, *Three Faces of Fascism*, 276.
75. MacDonnell, *Daylight Upon Magic*, 43. King, *Princess Marina*, 115, 144.
76. Heinrich Prinz von Hessen, *Kristallene Lüster*, 252.
77. Balfour and Mackay, *Paul of Yugoslavia*, 205, 272.
78. PRO, FO 371/28765, "Der Bund," 11 August 1937.
79. Balfour and Mackay, *Paul of Yugoslavia*, 181.
80. Whiting, *The Kents*, 97–98.
81. MacDonnell, *Daylight Upon Magic*, 227. He cites the Mackenzie King papers, in the National Archives of Canada, King entry for 10 June 1939. See http://king.archives.ca.
82. Bradford, *King George VI*, 302; Whiting, *The Kents*, 97.
83. HRH Prince Philip, Duke of Edinburgh, interview with author, Buckingham Palace, 3 March 2004.
84. Philipp and the Duke of Kent evidently had a close personal relationship, although the documentation is missing. Officials at the Royal Archives at Windsor claim to have no correspondence between the two men, and among the letters provided to the author by the Hessen family, none comes from British royals. There are only indirect clues: Philipp, for example, was very close to Prince Paul of Yugoslavia and his wife, Olga (as noted earlier, both played a role in the courtship of Philipp and Mafalda in Rome); Olga was the sister of Marina, the Duchess of Kent. Philipp wrote, in 1935, "Please give lots of love to dear Olga + tell her how pleased I am about Marina's marriage [to the Duke of Kent]." CULBA, Prince Philipp von Hessen to Prince Paul Karageorgevich, 13 January 1935.
85. Higham, *Mrs. Simpson*, 109.
86. For the Duke of Kent's attendance at the funeral, see PRO, FO 371/21663, memorandum by Will Stang, 21 July 1938. The memorandum also discusses the feasibility of the Duke of Kent visiting Germany. See also the French newspaper, *Le Moment*, 22 July 1938, 3. This article notes that the Duke of Kent was the second cousin of King Carol II of Romania. For more on

Queen Marie's funeral, see Kent State University, Department of Special Collections, Queen Marie of Romania Papers, document 86.

87. Wheeler-Bennett, *King George VI*, 396. He cites RA, King George VI to Chamberlain, 3 July 1939.

88. Parker, *Prince Philip*, 81. Balfour and Mackay, *Paul of Yugoslavia*, 54.

89. Bradford, *King George VI*, 302.

90. Wheeler-Bennett, *King George VI*, 333.

91. PRO, FO 371/23827: the actual file is missing; only the description in the Foreign Office finding aid remains under the heading, "Duke of Kent having to propose a toast to the King of Italy and Albania."

92. PRO, FO 371/23827, Pierson Dixon to Viscount Halifax, 7 July 1939.

93. Ibid.

94. HHStAW, 520 D-Z, Nr. 519.563, statement of von Schlabrendorff on behalf of Prince Philipp, 11 November 1947.

95. Ibid., Spruchkammer Protocol of Prince Philipp, 15–17 December 1947, 44.

96. Ibid., 43.

97. Hanfstaengl, *Unheard Witness*, 240.

98. Picknett, Prince, and Prior, *Double Standards*, 286, 296.

99. Ibid., 296.

100. HHStAW, 520 D-Z, Nr. 519.563, Spruchkammer Protocol of Prince Philipp, 15–17 December 1947, 44.

101. Ibid., statement of von Schlabrendorff on behalf of Prince Philipp, 11 November 1947.

102. Ibid., Spruchkammer Protocol of Prince Philipp, 15–17 December 1947, 44.

103. Ibid.

104. Ibid., statement of von Schlabrendorff on behalf of Prince Philipp, 9 March 1947.

105. Ibid., statement of Prince Philipp, 21 February 1947.

106. Dönhoff, *Um der Ehre Willen*, 26. HHStAW, 520 D-Z, Nr. 519.563, Spruchkammer Protocol of Prince Philipp, "Begründung," December 1947, 19.

107. HHStAW, 520 D-Z, Nr. 519.563, Spruchkammer Protocol of Prince Philipp, 15–17 December 1947, 44.

108. IfZG, ZS 918, Interrogation of the Prince of Hesse, 6 May 1947.

109. Ibid.

110. PRO, FO 371/24937, Report of Axel Munthe, 10 May 1940. Axel Munthe was known for his accounts of World War I and *The Story of San Michele*. See also Heinrich Prinz von Hessen, *Kristallene Lüster*, 95; and Jangfeldt, *En Osalig Ande*, 585–92.

111. PRO, FO 371, 24948, unsigned report to Viscount Halifax, 30 May 1940. Crown Prince Umberto is envisioned as the successor to Vittorio Emmanuele.

112. Muggeridge, ed., *Ciano's Diary*, 175.

113. HHStAW, 520 D-Z, Nr. 519.563, translation of diaries of Count Galeazzo Ciano.

114. Ibid., Spruchkammer Protocol of Prince Philipp, 15–17 December 1947, 43.

115. Goebbels, *Tagebücher*, I/4, 118, entry for 19 April 1940.

116. See Corvaja, *Hitler and Mussolini*, 117. More generally, see Overy and Wheatcroft, *Road to War*, 179; and Wiskemann, *Rome-Berlin Axis*, 241–43.

117. HHStAW, 520 D-Z, Nr. 519.563, Spruchkammer Protocol of Prince Philipp, 15–17 December 1947, 19: statement of Carl Radl.

118. Ibid.

119. Ibid., "Protocol" of Karl Wolff, 18 September 1947.

120. Ibid.

121. Ibid., statement of Willy Heine, 29 November 1947.

122. Speer, *Inside the Third Reich*, 148.

123. HHStAW, 520 D-Z, Nr. 519.563, "Protocol" of Karl Wolff, 18 September 1947.

124. Ibid., "Begründung," December 1947, 9.

125. Kenneth Rose, *George V*, 229.

126. A. Roberts, *Eminent Churchillians*, 12.

127. Radzinsky, *Last Tsar*, 205. Rose, *George V*, 208–18.

128. For the two views of George V, see K. Rose, *George V*, 229; and A. Roberts, *Eminent Churchillians*, 6.

129. See "Power Behind the Throne," at http:www.pharo.com/20th_century_ mysteries/duke_of_kent. Last accessed 10 June 2003.

130. For the Kents' visits to Munich in July 1936, and January 1939, see APA, R 102823, "Staatsoberhaupten und deren Familie, 1936–1939."

131. HStAD, GF, D 26, 83/5, notes of Prince Ludwig von Hessen-Darmstadt, n.d.

132. Kershaw, *Making Friends*, 340.

133. CULBA, Duke of Kent to Prince Paul Karageorgevich, 5 December 1939.

134. Ibid., Duke of Kent to Prince Paul Karageorgevich, 17 July 1940.

135. Picknett, Prince, and Prior, *Double Standards*, 279. For more on de Ropp and the Duke of Kent, but with certain errors, see P. Allen, *Crown and the Swastika*, 44–46; and Whiting, *The Kents*, 97.

136. Picknett, Prince, and Prior, *Double Standards*, 278. Winterbotham, *Secret and Personal*, 81; and Winterbotham, *Nazi Connection*. See also Newton, *Profits of Peace*, 83. Newton cites a 1937 Foreign Office Report that notes the Duke of Kent's ties to German Ambassador Ribbentrop.

137. Lukacs, *Five Days in London*, 56.

138. Masters, *Nancy Astor*, 187. Andrew Roberts argues that the Cliveden Set's pro-Nazi views have been exaggerated. A. Roberts, *Eminent Churchillians*, 18.

139. Lukacs, *Five Days*, 128. See also A. Roberts, *Holy Fox*, 140. The king remarked in 1939 in one unguarded discussion, "He would never wish to appoint Churchill to any office unless it was absolutely necessary in time of war." MacDonnell, *Daylight Upon Magic*, 227. He cites the Mackenzie King papers, National Archives of Canada, MK 10/6/39.

140. Kershaw, *Making Friends*, 64, 210.

141. AAPA, R 102776, "Politische Beziehungen England und Deutschland," program for "Anglo-German Fellowship Second Annual Dinner," 2 December 1937. See also Henderson, *Failure of a Mission*, 19; and Kershaw, *Making Friends*, 141–44, 174.

142. Lukacs, *Five Days*, 57, 109.

143. Picknett, Prince, and Prior, *Double Standards*, 111.

144. Lukacs, *Five Days*, 57. He notes as examples the removal of documents from the Halifax papers at the University of York, the papers of Maurice Hankey and David Margesson in the Churchill Archives at Cambridge, and the R. A. Butler Papers at Trinity College, Cambridge.

145. Rowse quoted by Padfield, *Hess: Flight*, 109.

146. A vivid, if unreliable, indicator or pro-appeasement sentiment was provided by the German academic Albrecht Haushofer, who, after Hess's May 1941 flight to Scotland, was ordered to dictate a report on the people Hess might try to visit in the UK: "Among those named by Albrecht Haushofer as being in favour of an Anglo-German agreement were Lord Halifax, Foreign Secretary from 1938 to 1940, and his deputy, R. A. Butler, Lord Dunglass [the Prime Minister's Parliamentary private secretary], the Duke of Hamilton, Owen O'Malley [British Minister to Hungary], William Strang [Assistant under-secretary of state at the Foreign Office], Lord Lothian [British ambassador to Washington], Oliver Stanley [secretary of state for war] and Sir Samuel Hoare [ambassador to Madrid]." Thomas, *Hess*, 96, 161. Among the elite in the pro-appeasement camp, one might also count the following: the Duke of Westminister; the Duke of Buccleugh; the Duke of Bedford; Lord Londonderry; Lord Walter Runciman; Viscount Rothermere; the Marquess Lothian; Baron Brocket; Baron McGowan, Baron Mottistone, Baron Redesdale; Baron Semphill; the Earl of Glasgow; and Edwina Mountbatten's father, Lord Mount Temple, who met with Hitler in Berlin in 1936 and received an inscribed picture from the dictator. See Broadlands Archives, MB1/A110, Doc. 15: a note from Lord Louis Mountbatten, 27 June 1966, and the signed photograph. Kershaw, *Making Friends*, xvi, 144; and more generally Pugh, *"Hurrah for the Blackshirts!"*

147. Lukacs, *Five Days*, 56.

148. Speer, *Inside the Third Reich*, 74.

149. PRO, KV2/837 and KV2/838, for the British intelligence services files on Sir Barry Domville. Domville also wrote for the *Anglo-German Review*, which was staunchly pro-Nazi and elicited positive comments from Himmler, among others. See BAB, NS 19/1139, for correspondence between Domville and Himmler concerning the magazine.

150. G. King, *Duchess of Windsor*, 149; and more generally, Kershaw, *Making Friends*, 247.

151. Stephen Dorril communication to author, 8 December 2004. See Dorril, *Blackshirt*.

152. For the vicissitudes in Anglo-German relations, see Kershaw, *Making Friends*, 194.

153. Lukacs, *Five Days*, 177.

154. Costello, *Ten Days to Destiny*, xv.

155. Costello, *Ten Days*, caption to photo, no page.

156. Lukacs, *Five Days*, 96.

157. In 1944, King Leopold and his family were transferred to a "mansion on the Elbe near Dresden" and then to the Austrian Alps in early 1945 on Himmler's orders. PRO, KV2/272, "Summary of Information from Kaltenbrunner and Schellenberg on Visits to the King of the Belgians," 18 July 1945. See also

Staercke, "*Tout cela a passé comme une ombre*," and Aronson, *Coburgs of Belgium*, 268–71.

158. Höhne, *Canaris*, 485–86.

159. Padfield, *Hess: Flight*, 110.

160. Höhne, *Order of the Death's Head*, 519.

161. Ibid.

162. Padfield, *Hess: Flight*, 180.

163. A. Roberts, *Holy Fox*, 182.

164. See Gellermann, *Geheime Wege*; as well as Martin, *Friedensinitiativen und Machtpolitik*.

165. Note that there is no mention of the Princes von Hessen in Dahlerus, *Letzte Versuch*.

166. Gellermann, *Geheime Wege*, 117–37. See also Höhne, *Canaris*, 485–86; and Gerhard Ritter, *Carl Goerdeler*, 569; and Bassett, *Hitler's Spy Chief: The Wilhelm Canaris Mystery*, 240–60.

167. Parker, *Prince Philip*, 76.

168. Ibid., 55.

169. Weinberg, *Foreign Policy of Hitler's Germany: Starting World War II*, 63.

170. Schad, *Hitlers Spionin*, 72. See also Philip Ziegler, *King Edward VIII: The Official Biography* (London: Collins, 1990), 267–72.

171. Schad, *Hitlers Spionin*, 73.

172. Weinberg, *Foreign Policy of Hitler's Germany: Starting World War II*, 63.

173. *New York Times*, 23 October 1937, quoted in Costello, *Ten Days*, 353.

174. FOIA file of the Duke and Duchess of Windsor, anonymous letter to Major General Edwin Watson, secretary to the president, 22 April 1942.

175. Brendon and Whitehead, *Windsors*, 34. Note that all of the Duke of Windsor's trips abroad are summarized in the appendix of his memoirs, Duke of Windsor, *A King's Story*. From 2 to 30 July 1913, he visited Berlin, Hamburg, Nuremberg, and Dresden, among various cities, and from 9 to 19 January 1919, he was in Bonn, Koblenz, and Cologne.

176. The Duke of Windsor is quoted by Fox, "Oddest Couple," *Vanity Fair*, August 2003, 288. Mosley, *Life of Contrasts*, 246.

177. PRO, FO 371/16736, Hugh Lloyd Thomas to E. D. Sandys in the Foreign Office, 8 March 1933.

178. RA, DW/3434, Duke von Sachsen-Coburg und Gotha to Duke of Windsor, 30 September 1937.

179. Ibid. See also RA, DW/3450, Duke von Sachsen-Coburg to the Duke of Windsor, 10 October 1937, where he confirms their plans for dinner on 19 October in Nuremberg.

180. Higham, *Mrs. Simpson*, 255.

181. RA, DW 3475, Winston Churchill to Duke of Windsor, 28 October 1937.

182. Schad, *Hitlers Spionin*, 76. For the Windsors's itinerary during their visit to Germany in 1937, see RA, GVI/C 042/60, 25 October 1937 memorandum from Ambassador Arthur Henderson. Goebbels, *Tagebücher*, I /4, 357, entry for 12 October 1937. See also Ziegler, *King Edward VIII*, 386–401.

183. M. Allen, *Hidden Agenda*, 87–96.

184. Ibid., 96. For the Duke of Windsor and the Nazi salute, see King, *Duchess of Windsor*, 280.
185. M. Allen, *Hidden Agenda*, 96.
186. Costello, *Ten Days*, 353.
187. RA, GVI/C 042/60, Ambassador Arthur Henderson memorandum, 25 October 1937.
188. Parker, *Prince Philip*, 75.
189. RA, PS/GVI/C 042/060A, Donald Gainer, British Consul General in Munich to Ambassador Nevile Henderson, 1 October 1937.
190. Ibid. Note that a "Herr von Yorry" does not appear in any lexica or handbooks of aristocracy and may be an assumed name.
191. RA, GVI/C 042/63, extract of report of British Consul in Dresden, 18 November 1937.
192. FOIA, FBI file of Duke and Duchess of Windsor, Edward Tamm to J. Edgar Hoover, 13 September 1940. For more on Wallis Simpson's views about Germany, see Donaldson, *Edward VIII*, chap. 15.
193. FOIA, FBI file of Duke and Duchess of Windsor, report of P. E. Foxworth to the director of the FBI (J. Edgar Hoover), 2 May 1941.
194. Schad, *Hitlers Spionin*, 74.
195. Ibid., 75. Similar formulations appeared in the press—such as an article in the *Statesman* by Helena Normanton on 31 May 1937—although most authors spoke about "social" connections and fell short of alleging a sexual relationship. Normanton, "Truth About Mrs. Simpson," *Statesman*, 31 May 1937. Note that a copy of the article is in the German Foreign Office Archives, AAPA, R 102775, "Politische Beziehungen England zu Deutschand."
196. Higham, *Duchess of Windsor*. Hugo Vickers to the author, 3 June 2003. Among the recent articles in the press about the Duchess of Windsor and Ribbentrop, see Rob Evans and Hencke, "Wallis Simpson, the Nazi Minister, the Telltale Monk, and an FBI Plot." *Manchester Guardian*, 29 June 2002, 1; and "Mrs. Simpson Cheated on Edward, Papers Show," *Los Angeles Times*, 30 January 2003, A4.
197. Middlemas and Barnes, *Baldwin*, 980. Rob Evans and Hencke, "Hitler Saw Duke of Windsor as 'no enemy' US File Reveals." *Manchester Guardian*, 25 June 2003.
198. FOIA, FBI file of Duke and Duchess of Windsor, Edward Tamm to J. Edgar Hoover, 13 September 1940. The above-noted FBI report to Hoover report portrays the Windsors consciously spying for the Germans.
199. M. Allen, *Hidden Agenda*. Note that allegations have been made that Martin Allen forged a critical document for this argument: a November 1939 letter purportedly from the Duke of Windsor to Hitler. See D. Leppard, "Historian in Himmler dispute was in an earlier forgery furore," *The Sunday Times* (London), 3 July 2005, 15.
200. Costello, *Ten Days*, 356.
201. Martin Allen has even been charged with forging a key document that implicated the Duke of Windsor as a Nazi informant. The allegation of forgery remains unproven. See note 199.
202. P. Allen, *Crown and the Swastika*, 245.

203. Bloch, *Secret File of the Duke of Windsor*, 108.

204. Ibid., 108.

205. RA, DW 3200, Oscar Solbert to the Duke of Windsor, 27 April 1937. See also Bloch, *Secret File of the Duke of Windsor*, 109–10.

206. RA, DW 3409, Charles Bedaux to Oscar Solbert, 23 August 1937

207. Bloch, *Secret File of the Duke of Windsor*, 111.

208. PRO, WO 106/1678, for the Duke of Windsor's five reports on his tours of French headquarters and troops between 4 October 1939 and 10 October 1940. The reports, signed "Edward, Major-General," are quite sophisticated, displaying an impressive knowledge of military affairs and geography. See also Ziegler, *King Edward VIII*, 408–16.

209. Higham, *Duchess of Windsor*, 270. Note that Higham also sees the Duchess of Windsor as the main source of the information leaked to Bedaux.

210. Gerhard Weinberg to author, 22 February 2004.

211. "King's Safety," *Edinburgh Scotsman*, 17 July 1936.

212. "Mountbatten Tribute to Spell-Binder," *Daily Telegraph*, 5 June 1972.

213. Ziegler, *King Edward VIII*, 374, 522; Ziegler cites RA, KEVIII, Ab. Box 3, Alexander Hardinge memorandum, 7 July 1940.

214. Broadlands Archives, MB1/A116, notes from Lord Louis Mountbatten, as well as a copy of the leaflet.

215. Among the books treating the Windsors's experiences in 1940 are the aforementioned Costello, *Ten Days*; Higham, *Mrs. Simpson*; P. Allen, *Crown and the Swastika*; Bloch, *Duke of Windsor's War*; Bloch, *Operation Willi*; Bloch, ed., *Wallis and Edward*; and Bloch, *Secret File of the Duke of Windsor*. Note also that Himmler, according to Schellenberg, still hoped for a negotiated peace in August 1942. PRO, KV2/294, Report on the Interrogation of Walter Schellenberg, 10 April 1945. The peace feelers sent out by Himmler and others later in the war—in 1944 and 1945—where he had contact with individuals in Sweden and Switzerland—also reflected hopes for a compromise with the Western Allies.

216. RA, DW Trunk 2, Duke of Windsor to Adolf Hitler, 27 August 1939; and ibid., Hitler to the Duke of Windsor, 29 August 1939.

217. Shaw, *Royal Babylon*, 315.

218. Bloch, *Operation Willi*, 192: Don Angel's report as conveyed by Stohrer to Ribbentrop, 31 July 1940.

219. Ibid., 61, 195: Ribbentrop to Baron von Hoyningen-Huene, 31 July 1940. See more generally, Strobl, *Germanic Isle*.

220. Blandford, *SS Intelligence*, 194.

221. Parker, *Prince Philip*, 81. See also Ilija Jukie, *Fall of Yugoslavia*.

222. Parker, *Prince Philip*, 81. For a critical treatment of Prince Paul, see R. West, *Black Lamb and Grey Falcon*, 1137–42.

223. Parker, *Prince Philip*, 81. See also Gilbert, *Finest Hour*, 1043.

224. Besides King Peter II of Yugoslavia, other monarchs in exile in Great Britain during the war included those of Norway, Denmark, Luxembourg, the Netherlands, and Albania. Fenyvesi, *Royalty in Exile*, 211–17.

225. Schellenberg, *Memoirs*, 130.

226. Blandford, *SS Intelligence*, 194.

227. Costello, *Ten Days*, 360–61.

228. Ibid., 369.

229. Ibid., 361. Note that many of Churchill's telegrams to the Duke of Windsor remain officially closed until 2016, but "the index to the empty Foreign Office file that contained them outlines the progress of the row." See also Schellenberg, *Memoirs*, 127–43.

230. FOIA, file of Duke and Duchess of Windsor, unspecified newspaper clipping, "Windsor Denies Story of 1940 Nazi Bribe," 27 July 1956; and Schellenberg, *Memoirs*, 129. See also Ziegler, *King Edward VIII*, 431.

231. CULBA, Duke of Kent to Prince Paul Karageorgevich, 17 July 1940.

232. Costello, *Ten Days*, 370.

233. Padfield *Hess: Flight*, 128 and 335: he cites APA, F & C B 15 B002609 and B002633, Hoyningen-Huene to Auswärtiges Amt, 30 July 1940 and 2 August 1940.

234. Carter, *Anthony Blunt*, 312. Letter from Miranda Carter to the author, 10 January 2005. Higham, *Mrs. Simpson*, 320, 324. Higham statement via telephone to the author, 24 October 2004.

235. Higham, *Mrs. Simpson*, 279–88.

236. For the FA tapping Henderson's phone, see Watt, "Introduction," 25.

237. A. Roberts, *Holy Fox*, 184. Sir Alexander Cadogan was the permanent under secretary of the Foreign Office.

238. C. Simpson, Leitch, and Knightly, "Blunt was Emissary for King George VI," *The Sunday Times* (London), 25 November 1979, 1.

239. PRO, KV2/294, Report on the Interrogation of Walter Schellenberg, 10 April 1945. He blamed Admiral Canaris, the head of the Abwehr, for the shortcomings in the recruitment of agents.

240. Wheeler-Bennett, *King George VI*, 469.

241. Posner, "Secrets of the Files," *New Yorker*, 14 March 1994; and Giles, "Who Owns the Past?" in *User's Guide to German Cultural Studies*, ed. Denham, Kacandes, and Petropoulos, 377–88.

242. Thompson, "Lebensborn and the Eugenics Policy of the Reichsführer-SS," *Central European History*, 4 (1971): 54–77.

243. Ibid., 54.

244. Ibid., 54–77. More generally see Lillienthal, *Lebensborn*.

245. Thompson, "Lebensborn," 55.

246. Ibid., 61.

247. Ibid., 62.

248. Ibid., 67.

249. BAB, SSO, Personal file of Prince Christoph, SS-Personal-Akte, Prince Christoph, "Erklärung," 26 August 1936.

250. Ibid., card file.

251. Ibid., Adjutant, Chef der Sicherheitspolizei to SS-Gruppenführer Schmitt, 27 January 1939.

252. Ibid., card file. On another form, it states that his "Truppenteil" was "Reichsführer-SS." Ibid., "Dienstlaufbahn." See also the *Dienstaltersliste der Schutzstaffel*, 28.

253. Ibid., Prince Christoph to Personalkanzlei des Reichsführer-SS, 5 October 1937; ibid., and Chef der Personalkanzlei to Prince Christoph, 6 October 1937.

254. Ibid., Chef der SS-Personalkanzlei to Prince Christoph von Hessen, 2 March 1938; and ibid., Hildebrandt to Himmler, 5 November 1943.

255. RvH: Princess Sophia to Landgravine Margarethe, 18 January 1941.

256. Ibid., Princess Sophia to Landgravine Margarethe, 14 March 1936.

257. AHH, Landgravine Margarethe to Prince Richard, 8 June 1942.

258. Watt, "Introduction," 40.

259. Irving, *Reich hört mit*, 293. Irving cites a letter from Graf Soltikow of 28 March 1981.

260. Picknett, Prince, and Prior, *Double Standards*, 167, 182; and Padfield, *Hess: Flight*, 196.

261. www.histoiredumonde.net.

262. Vassiltchikov, *Berlin Diaries*, 88, 141, 144. See H. Müller, "Heinrich Prinz zu Sayn-Wittgenstein," at www.bendorf-geschichte.de.

263. Vassiltchikov, *Berlin Diaries*, 144.

264. This is the interpretation that Günther Gellermann seems most inclined to support. See Gellermann, *und lauschten für Hitler*, 23–24.

265. Bradford, *George VI*, 425. Note that Christoph's family members have pressed Bradford to reveal the source of this comment, but she has refused to do so.

266. W. Smith, *Ideological Origins of Nazi Imperialism*.

267. Thomas, *Hess*, 65. Thomas believes that the real Rudolf Hess was shot down on Göring's orders by the Luftwaffe as he tried to reach a neutral Scandinavian country and that a double was sent to Scotland—also with the intent of making peace (but with less risk because he would not have known precious secrets).

268. Pryce-Jones, *Unity Mitford*, 240. He cites as his source a correspondence with author Leonard Mosley.

269. Costello, *Ten Days*, 373–74.

270. Penny Russell-Smith, Press Secretary to the Queen, to author, 8 June 2001.

271. Rainer von Hessen to author, 24 October 2004.

272. Gellermann, *und lauschten für Hitler*, 25. Gellermann notes that retaining an assistant for wartime leave was unusual.

273. BAB, R 2/11831, Pilli Körner to Count Schwerin von Krosigk, 18 November 1940. See also Gellermann, *und lauschten für Hitler*, 22.

274. Wolfgang Prinz von Hessen, *Aufzeichnungen*, 173.

275. Ibid., 178. Wolfgang joined the Wehrmacht in early 1940 and was initially part of the German occupation administration in Norway before being deployed to Finland, where he helped build roads. Prince Richard joined in August 1939 and primarily helped build roads and bridges.

276. BAB, SSO, Personal file of Prince Christoph, SS-Personal-Akte, card file. For the promotion to major, see BAB, SS-Führerakten, 94A, Hildebrandt (secretary of Prince Christoph) to Himmler, 7 August 1943.

277. Loerzer was not only part of Göring's entourage but also corrupt: Albert Speer reported on how Loerzer and Pilli Körner engaged in "wholesale black

market activities" during the war, including smuggling ladies undergarments from Italy. See Speer, *Spandau*, 115.

278. RvH: Prince Christoph to Princess Sophia, 13 May 1940.
279. Ibid., Prince Christoph to Princess Sophia, 24 June 1940.
280. Ibid., Prince Christoph to Princess Sophia, 10 July 1940.
281. Zentner and Bedürftig, eds., *Encyclopedia of the Third Reich*, 815. Maas, *Netherlands at War*, 40.
282. Maas, *Netherlands at War*, 40.
283. RvH: Prince Christoph to Princess Sophia, 10 July 1940.
284. For more on the Feindnachrichtendienst, see Boog, *Deutsche Luftwaffeführung*, 76–83.
285. RvH: Prince Christoph to Princess Sophia, 21 May 1940.
286. Ibid., Prince Christoph to Princess Sophia, 2 September 1940.
287. Ibid., Prince Christoph to Princess Sophia, 9 September 1940.
288. Bradford, *George VI*, 323.
289. Ibid., Rainer von Hessen, "Christoph von Hessen: Standorte/Aufenthalte im Krieg reconstruiert anhand von Briefen und Fotoalben."
290. Ibid., Prince Christoph to Princess Sophia, 11 September 1940.
291. *Jane's All the World's Aircraft*, 108c.
292. PRO, H0202/1, R. Garnons Williams, "Appreciation for the Period 0600 Hours 13th to 0600 14th September 1940"; "Appreciation for the Period 0600 Hours 15th to 0600 16th September 1940: Part III, Special Damage Report," 6. See also, PRO, H0203/4, "Home Security Intelligence Summary No. 757 for the Period 0600 to 1800 Hours, 15th September 1940," 3, 6.
293. Bradford, *George VI*, 324. See also Wheeler-Bennett, *King George VI*, 467–68. Both authors quote the king's diary from 13 September 1940.
294. Wheeler-Bennett, *King George VI*, 468.
295. PRO, H0202/1, R. Garnons Williams, report on bombing activity, 16 September 1940.
296. Bradford, *George VI*, 324.
297. Ibid.
298. Ibid.
299. Parker, *Prince Philip*, 75.
300. Hilberg, *Sources of Holocaust Research*, 162.
301. HHStAW, 520 D-Z, Nr. 519.563, Spruchkammer Protocol of Prince Philipp, 15–17 December 1947, 41. See also Petropoulos, *Faustian Bargain*, 106–10.
302. Spotts, *Hitler and the Power of Aesthetics*, 208.
303. Ibid., 209. Heinrich Prinz von Hessen claims that a fund-raising drive at German universities helped pay for the Lancellotti statue. See Heinrich Prinz von Hessen, *Kristallene Lüster*, 68.
304. Spotts, *Hitler and the Power of Aesthetics*, 209. Nicholas, *Rape of Europa*, 29.
305. Nicholas, *Rape of Europa*, 436–40.
306. PRO, GFM 33/318, Mackensen telegram, 8 November 1941. Marked "*Geheime Reichssache*."
307. See the summary of Siviero's *L'Arte e il Nazismo* at www.lootedart.com.

308. FOIA, Prince Philipp of Hesse, High Commissioner of Germany-Frankfurt to Department of State, "Foreign Service Despatch," 8 May 1951. This list of "Individuals Involved in Art Looting" was based upon the Art Looting Investigation Unit Final Report of 1946.

309. Feliciano, *Lost Museum*, 4.

310. HHStAW, 520 D-Z, Nr. 519.563, statement of Princess Sophia, 15 July 1946.

311. Rainer von Hessen, ed. and trans., *Wir Wilhelm von Gottes Gnaden*, 544–45.

312. Rainer von Hessen to author, 11 July 2001.

313. NARA, RG 260, OMGUS, Munich Central Collecting Point, box 486, "Items Purchased for Hitler by Prince Philip in Italy, 1941" (n.d.). They note a price difference of 24,500 lire on a purchase of 76,000 lire.

314. NARA, M 1944/46, Card for "Hesse-Nassau, Prince Philip [*sic*] of," n.d.

315. Ibid.

316. NARA, RG 260, OMGUS, Munich Central Collecting Point, box 486, "Items Purchased for Hitler by Prince Philip [*sic*] in Italy, 1941" (n.d.). NARA, RG 260, OMGUS Education and Cultural Relations Branch, box 229, "Personal Statement of Phillip [*sic*] Prince von Hessen on His Activities as Art Negotiator For Hitler [and Goering]," 15 July 1945.

317. HHStAW, 520 D-Z, Nr. 519.563, Spruchkammer Protocol of Prince Philipp, 15–17 December 1947, 20: statement of Karl Anton Schulte.

318. The most thorough study of the bank Lippmann, Rosenthal & Co. is Aalders, *Geraubt!*, 221–56. See also Aalders, *Nazi Looting*, 127–45.

319. HHStAW, 520 D-Z, Nr. 519.563, Grosshessisches Staatsministerium, Öffentlicher Kläger, memorandum, 27 March 1947.

320. Ibid., statement of Hermann Schultze, 30 December 1946.

321. NARA, RG 260, OMGUS Education and Cultural Relations Branch, box 229, "Personal Statement of Phillip [*sic*] Prince von Hessen on His Activities as Art Negotiator For Hitler [and Goering]," 15 July 1945; see the list attached to the report as appendix 2. Faison, *Supplement to CIR No. 4*: Attachment 65: "List of Works of Art Received in Munich from Prince Philipp von Hessen." Documents concerning Prince Philipp's art purchases in Italy are in BAK, B 323/147, 305–47 and B 323/121, 348–62.

322. NARA, M 1944/46, Card for "Hesse-Nassau, Prince Philip [*sic*] of," n.d. By May 1942, Hitler had spent over 40 million lire (RM 5 million) on artworks in Italy, with Philipp involved in the vast majority of these purchases.

323. Note that recent scholarship has determined that only some 1,200 works were actually earmarked for the Führermuseum; however, the total number that formed the selection pool in 1945 was more than 8,000. See B. Schwarz, *Hitlers Museum*.

324. NARA, RG 260, OMGUS, Munich Central Collecting Point, box 486, Posse to Prince Philipp, 23 February 1943.

325. According to extant inventories, Prince Philipp acquired several works for Göring, including a sixteenth-century painting of a Madonna with Child of Franconian origin and a Renaissance wooden sculpture from Sienna that the Nazi leader kept in his office. The latter was acquired in November 1938.

See NARA, RG 260, OMGUS, Munich Central Collecting Point, box 442, document 167.

326. See the report in OMGUS 5/346-1/40: Procurement of Art Objects for Hitler by Prinz Philipp von Hessen in 1941–1942 (based on interviews conducted on 12–14 July 1945). See also Nicholas, *Rape of Europa*, 156.

327. NARA, RG 260, OMGUS, Munich Central Collecting Point, box 486, Walter Hanssen to Prince Philipp, 13 June 1941 (also BAB, R43 II/1649c).

328. Art Looting Investigation Unit, *Final Report*, 20, 50, 69.

329. Rousseau, *CIR No. 2*, 106–9. See also Haase, *Kunstraub und Kunstschutz*, 135.

330. Alford, *Spoils of World War II*, 113.

331. Art Looting Investigation Unit, *Final Report*, 21.

332. Spotts, *Hitler and the Power of Aesthetics*, 210. Faison, *CIR No. 4*, 10. Note that Prince Philipp had a special account created for his use at the German Embassy in Rome and that at one point in June 1941, it contained over 13 million lire. The funds were earmarked for the purchase of artworks. See Faison, *Supplement to CIR No. 4*, Attachment 13: Bormann to Posse, 28 June 1941. Note that Yeide, Akinsha, and Walsh claim that the Memling was sold by Alessandro Contini-Bonacossi, a prominent Fascist and close financial advisor to Mussolini. See Yeide, Akinsha, and Walsh, *AAM Guide to Provenance Research*, 294.

333. Faison, *Supplement to CIR No. 4*, Attachment 46: W. Wirth to K. Haberstock, 11 October 1941.

334. NARA, RG 260, Education and Cultural Relations Branch, box 229, "Procurement of Art Objects for Hitler by Prinz Philipp von Hessen in 1941–1942 (based on interviews conducted on 12–14 July 1945)."

335. Ibid., Colonel L. E. Dostert, "Interrogation of Philipp, Prince of Hessen," 21 July 1945. The Cranach painting of the Prince of Saxony was recovered with the bulk of Göring's collection at Berchtesgaden in 1945; it later had the inventory number 6165 at the Munich Central Collecting Point.

336. BAK, B 323/103/47, doc. 217, Posse Vermerk, 11 April 1940.

337. Petropoulos, *Faustian Bargain*, 90. Flanner, *Men and Monuments*, 228. See also Faison, *CIR No. 4*, 8. After the war, Haberstock disputed that the payment was made by a land grant. See National Gallery of Art, Papers of S. Lane Faison, Jr., box 2, Karl Haberstock statement of August 1947.

338. Siviero, *L'Arte e il Nazismo*. See also Petropoulos, *Art as Politcs*, 301.

339. NARA, M 1944/46, Card for "Hesse-Nassau, Prince Philip [*sic*] of," n.d.

340. NARA, RG 260, Education and Cultural Relations Branch, box 229, "Procurement of Art Objects for Hitler by Prinz Philipp von Hessen in 1941–1942 (based on interviews conducted on 12–14 July 1945)."

341. *The Plague of Florence* belonged to the Landau-Finaly family, which was a branch of the Rothschilds. They had refused to sell the works for a variety of reasons stemming from their anti-Nazi views. Mussolini not only arranged for the confiscation of the work from the Florentine Jewish family (seizing their entire villa and its contents in the process), but also bestowed it to the German dictator as a present in the autumn of 1940. Petropoulos, *Art as Politics*, 271–72. See also Faison, *CIR No. 4*, 28; and Faison, *Supplement to CIR No. 4*: Attachments 24 and 24a.

342. Spotts, *Hitler and the Power of Aesthetics*, 211.

343. Petropoulos, *Art as Politics*, 271–73, 285–86.

344. Goebbels, *Tagebücher* II/4, 195, entry for 28 April 1942.

345. RvH: Landgravine Margarethe to Prince Richard, 18 October 1940.

346. Note that Christoph moved around a great deal in the fall of 1940 and spring of 1941. This included trips back to Mariakerk near Ghent, Christmas in Kronberg, and several trips to Berlin.

347. RvH: Prince Christoph to Princess Sophia, 20 June 1941.

348. Ibid., Prince Christoph to Princess Sophia, 4 June 1941.

349. Ibid., Princess Sophia to Landgravine Margarethe, 3 August 1941.

350. Ibid., Princess Sophia to Landgravine Margarethe, 6 August 1941.

351. Ibid., Prince Christoph to Princess Sophia, 23 July 1941.

352. See Hamburger Institut für Sozialforschung, *Verbrechung der Wehrmacht*.

353. Vinen, *History in Fragments*, 185.

354. RvH: Prince Christoph to Princess Sophia, 19 September 1941.

355. Zentner and Bedürftig, eds., *Encyclopedia of the Third Reich*, 94, 602. See also RvH: Prince Christoph to Princess Sophia, 8 October 1941.

356. RvH: Prince Christoph to Princess Sophia, 25 November 1941. See also Gellermann, *und lauschten für Hitler*, 23.

357. Werner Röhr, "Stalingrad: von der Hybris zur Nemesis: Wissenschaftliches Colloquium zum 60. Jahrestag der Schlacht von Stalingrad" (2003) at www.hco.hagen.de/forum/roehro3-1.html.

358. RvH: Prince Christoph to Princess Sophia, 25 November 1941.

359. Viktoria Luise, *Kaiser's Daughter*, 215–16.

360. Ibid., 209.

361. Ibid., 212. See Preussen, *Haus Hohenzollern*, 260. Parker, *Prince Philip*, 75. See HStAD, 024 50/15, Princess Margaret von Hessen-Darmstadt, "Memorandum," 7 July 1946.

362. HStAD, GF, D 24/76/2, Order from General Field Marshal Keitel, 30 December 1943.

363. BAB, Sammlung Schumacher, R. 187/400, Liste der aus der Wehrmacht entlassenen Angehörigen ehemalsregierender Fürstenhäuser, n.d. (1944). The list has thirty members in the army, three in the navy, and six in the air force.

364. RvH: Prince Christoph to Princess Sophia, 23 February 1942.

365. Ibid., Prince Christoph to Princess Sophia, 6 March 1942.

366. Ibid., Landgravine Margarethe to Prince Richard, 21 March 1943.

367. Ibid., Landgravine Margarethe to Prince Richard, 29 June 1942.

368. Ibid., Prince Christoph to Princess Sophia, 25 June 1942.

369. Ibid., Prince Christoph to Princess Sophia, 1 September 1942.

370. Ibid., Prince Christoph to Princess Sophia, 6 September, 23 September 1942, and 18 December 1942.

371. Ibid., Prince Christoph to Princess Sophia, 28 December 1942.

372. Ibid., Prince Christoph to Princess Sophia, 5 February 1943 and 24 February 1943.

373. Ibid., Prince Christoph to Princess Sophia, 17 April 1943.

374. Ibid., Prince Christoph to Princess Sophia, 8 May 1943.

375. Ibid., Prince Christoph to Princess Sophia, 8 May 1943.

376. Ibid., Prince Christoph to Princess Sophia, 8 May 1943.

377. Ibid., Prince Christoph to Princess Sophia, 8 May 1943.

378. The testament is located in the archives of the Hessische Hausstiftung, Schloss Fasanerie.

379. RvH: Prince Christoph to Princess Sophia, 3 July 1943.

380. Ibid., Prince Christoph to Princess Sophia, 9 July 1943.

381. Ibid., Prince Christoph to Princess Sophia, 17 July 1943.

382. Ibid., Prince Christoph to Princess Sophia, 9 August 1943.

383. Vickers, *Alice*, 314. Prince Philip was in the Royal Navy, and fought from 1940 to 1945 in theaters ranging from the Indian Ocean to North Africa to the North Sea and the Mediterranean. Philip had a distinguished naval career and was even aboard the HMS *Whelp*, a destroyer that was present in Tokyo Bay when the Japanese signed the surrender in August 1945.

384. HRH Prince Philip, Duke of Edinburgh, interview with author, Buckingham Palace, 3 March 2004.

385. For an example of Christoph learning news of his brother-in-law Prince Philip, see RvH: Prince Christoph to Princess Sophia, 26 July 1941.

386. CULBA, Duke of Kent to Prince Paul Karageorgevich, 25 March 1942. He wrote in the margin that his note was to accompany the letter that his wife, Marina, was sending to her sister, Paul's wife, Olga.

387. Friedlander, *Origins of Nazi Genocide*. See also Burleigh, *Death and Deliverance*.

388. Lagerwey, "Nurses's Trial at Hadamar," in Baer and Goldenberg, eds., *Experience and Expression*, 116.

389. The responsible agency within the Reich Interior Ministry was the Gemeinnützige Stiftung für Anstaltspflege. Note that a copy of the signed transfer agreement of 15 February 1941 is in HHStAW, 520 D-Z, Nr. 519.563. The German name of the facility was Landesheil und Pflegeanstalt Hadamar.

390. FOIA, Card of Hessen-Nassau, Prince Philipp of. Dachau Detachment, War Crimes Group, memo of 8 October 1945.

391. Sax and Kuntz, *Inside Hitler's Germany*, 210.

392. Klein, *Lageberichte der Geheimen Staatspolizei*, 943–44.

393. Sax and Kuntz, *Inside Hitler's Germany*, 214. Note also that the publisher of the Bärenreiter Verlag, Karl Vötterle in Kassel, said that Philipp helped protect him when his establishment published a "Schrift gegen das Sterilisationsgesetz." HHStAW, 520 D-Z, Nr. 519.563, statement of von Schlabrendorff on behalf of Prince Philipp, 21 November 1947 and ibid., 15: testimony of Karl Vötterle.

394. BAB, RS, file of Prince Wilhelm von Hessen (b. 1 March 1905).

395. Ibid., Chief of the Sippenamt in the RuSHA to the Staatliche Gesundheitsamt, 5 July 1938; and ibid., report of Dr. Heinrich Hardt, 2 December 1937.

396. Hermann Prinz von Hessen to author, 6 March 2005. He also notes that there are no other known cases of epilepsy in the family.

397. BAB, RS, file of Prince Wilhelm von Hessen (b. 1 March 1905), Medizinalrat to the Reichsführer-SS, RuSHA, 27 July 1938.

398. See http://gsteinbe.intrasun.tcnj.edu.

399. Friedemann and Bedürftig, eds., *Encyclopedia of the Third Reich*, 357.
400. Friedlander, *Origins of Nazi Genocide*, 92–93.
401. Ibid.
402. HHStAW, 520 D-Z, Nr. 519.563, Spruchkammer Protocol of Prince Philipp, 15–17 December 1947, 12.
403. Ibid.
404. Ibid., Aufzeichnung über die Verpachtung der Landesheilanstalt Hadamar, 2 January 1947.
405. Ibid., Spruchkammer Protocol of Prince Philipp, 15–17 December 1947, 12.
406. Ibid.
407. Friedlander, *Origins of Nazi Genocide*, 197.
408. Burleigh, *Death and Deliverance*, 278.
409. HHStAW, 520 D-Z, Nr. 519.563, statement of von Schlabrendorff on behalf of Prince Philipp, 21 November 1947, 45.
410. IfZG, ZS 918, Interrogation of the Prince of Hesse, 6 May 1947. See also Kempner, *Dritte Reich im Kreuzverhör*, 144. One scholar of the T-4 program also described how in mid-1941 "Hadamar celebrated the cremation of its ten-thousandth patient in a special ceremony, where everyone in attendance [including] secretaries, nurses, and psychiatrists, received a bottle of beer for the occasion." While Philipp was not an employee of the facility, the episode nonetheless speaks to the lack of secrecy surrounding the measures to end those "lives unworthy of life." Benedict, "Caring While Killing," in Baer and Goldenberg, eds., *Experience and Expression*, 97. Proctor, "Nazi Doctors, Racial Medicine, and Human Experimentation," 25.
411. Griech-Polelle, *Bishop von Galen*, 75–76.
412. HHStAW, 520 D-Z, Nr. 519.563, statement of von Schlabrendorff on behalf of Prince Philipp, 21 November 1947, 45. See also HHStAW, 520 D-Z, Nr. 519.563, Spruchkammer Protocol of Prince Philipp, 15–17 December 1947, 39.
413. IfZG, ZS 918, Interrogation of the Prince of Hesse, 6 May 1947.
414. HHStAW, 520 D-Z, Nr. 519.563, Spruchkammer Protocol of Prince Philipp, 15–17 December 1947, 12.
415. Heberer, "'*Exitus Heute* in Hadamar,'" 293.
416. IfZG, No. 2854, "Beglaubigte Abschrift" of Prince Philipp von Hessen, 6 March 1947.
417. HHStAW, 461/32061/6, summary of interrogation of Prince Philipp, 14 January 1947. See also Griech-Polelle, *Bishop von Galen*, 92. For "wild euthanasia," see Friedlander, *Origins of Nazi Genocide*, 152.
418. HHStAW, 520 D-Z, Nr. 519.563, Spruchkammer Protocol of Prince Philipp, 15–17 December 1947, 12.
419. Ibid., statement of von Schlabrendorff on behalf of Prince Philipp, 21 November 1947, 46.
420. IfZG, ZS 918, Interrogation of the Prince of Hesse, 4 March 1948.
421. HHStAW, 520 D-Z, Nr. 519.563, statement of von Schlabrendorff on behalf of Prince Philipp, 21 November 1947, 46.
422. HHStAW, Abt. 461, Nr. 32061/7, Verfahren gegen Adolf Walhlmann, et al. (Frankfurt Hadamar Trial), interrogation of Prince Philipp, 6 March 1947.

423. HHStAW, 520 D-Z, Nr. 519.563, Spruchkammer Protocol of Prince Philipp, 15–17 December 1947, 12.

424. HHStAW, Abt. 461, Nr. 32061/6, summary of interrogation of Prince Philipp, 14 January 1947.

425. HHStAW, Abt. 461, Nr. 32061/7, Verfahren gegen Adolf Wahlmann, et al. (1947 Frankfurt Hadamar Trial), interrogation of Prince Philipp, 6 March 1947.

426. Prince Philipp's testimony compiled from three interviews in May 1947 and March 1948 in Kempner, *Dritte Reich im Kreuzverhör*, 145.

427. NARA, RG 260, OMGUS, Munich Central Collecting Point, box 482, report on Bruno Lohse, 20 December 1947.

428. HHStAW, 520 D-Z, Nr. 519.563, statement of von Schlabrendorff on behalf of Prince Philipp, 21 November 1947, 46.

429. Ibid., Spruchkammer Protocol of Prince Philipp, 15–17 December 1947, 12.

430. Ibid., Spruchkammer Protocol of Prince Philipp, 15–17 December 1947, 13.

431. Ellinghaus, "Der Prinz."

432. HHStAW, 520 D-Z, Nr. 519.563, Grosshessisches Staatsministerium, Minister der Justiz, 1 August 1946. The case number is 4a Js 24/46.

433. Barnett, *Bystanders*, 7.

434. Elon, *Pity of It All*, 362–63; Wippermann, *Leben in Frankfurt*; Heinemann, ed., *Neunhundert Jahre Geschichte*; and Friedman, *Lion and the Star*.

435. Prinz, "Die Judenverfolgung in Kassel," in Frenz, Kammler, and Krause-Vilmar, eds., *Volksgemeinschaft*, 149.

436. Rebentisch, "Nationalsozialistische Revolution," 243.

437. See, among other works, Kropat, *Kristallnacht in Hessen:*; Monica Kingreen, ed., *"Nach Kristallnacht."*

438. Prinz, "Judenverfolgung in Kassel," 196. See also the 9 November 1938 report of Heydrich to Lammers in Kropat, *"Reichskristallnacht,"* 206.

439. HHStAW, 520 D-Z, Nr. 519.563, Spruchkammer Protocol of Prince Philipp, 15–17 December 1947, 10.

440. Ibid.

441. Ibid.

442. Ibid., 11.

443. Ibid., statement of von Schlabrendorff on behalf of Prince Philipp, 21 November 1947, 44.

444. Ibid., statement of Dr. Rohrbach, 27 March 1947. In Rome, the Hessens were friends with the head of the archeological institute, Professor Caro, who was Jewish. HHStAW, 520 D-Z, Nr. 519.563, statement of Dr. Schrenk, Deutsches Rotes Kreuz, 13 July 1946.

445. See the summary of these post-Kristallnacht discriminatory measures in Prinz, "Judenverfolgung in Kassel," 201–2.

446. Prinz, "Die Judenverfolgung in Kassel," 192.

447. Kammler, et. al., *Volksgemeinschaft und Volksfeinde*, 266.

448. Monica Kingreen to author 14 April 2004.

449. For an example of the Oberfinanzdirektion Kassel lists of seized assets, see Kammler, et. al., *Volksgemeinschaft und Volksfeinde*, 270.

450. Prinz, "Judenverfolgung in Kassel," 209.

451. IfZG, ZS 918, Interrogation of the Prince Philipp, 4 March 1948. See also Kempner, *Dritte Reich im Kreuzverhör*, 135.
452. HHStAW, 520 D-Z, Nr. 519.563, Spruchkammer Protocol of Prince Philipp, 15–17 December 1947, 11.
453. Ibid., statement of Herbert von Marx, 25 March 1946.
454. Ibid., Spruchkammer Protocol of Prince Philipp, 15–17 December 1947, 10. For more on Rothschild-Goldschmidt family, see Kopper, "Rothschild Family During the Third Reich," in Heuberger, ed., *Rothschilds*, 322–23 and 326.
455. HHStAW, 520 D-Z, Nr. 519.563, Spruchkammer Protocol of Prince Philipp, 15–17 December 1947, 31: statement of de la Fontaine.
456. Ibid.
457. Ibid.; and ibid., statement of von Schlabrendorff on behalf of Prince Philipp, 21 November 1947, 43.
458. Kopper, "Rothschild Family During the Third Reich," 326.
459. Moseley, *Mussolini's Shadow*, 49.
460. Kopper, "Rothschild Family During the Third Reich," 325–26. On plundering from Frankfurt's Jewish community more generally, see Kingreen, "Wie sich Museen Kunst aus jüdischem Besitz aneigneten."
461. HHStAW, 520 D-Z, Nr. 519.563, Spruchkammer Protocol of Prince Philipp, 15–17 December 1947, 24: statement of Kurt Jerschke.
462. Krause-Schmitt, "Das NS-Lagersystem in Hessen," in Knigge-Tesche and Ulrich, *Verfolgung und Widerstand in Hessen*, 44–63.
463. IfZG, MA-1300/2 (0281-83), anonymous report, "Hesse, Prince Philipp," 21 July 1945.
464. IfZG, ZS 918, Interrogation of the Prince of Hesse, 4 March 1948.
465. Ibid.
466. HHStAW, 520 D-Z, Nr. 519.563, Spruchkammer Protocol of Prince Philipp, 15–17 December 1947, 11.
467. H. Ziegler, *Nazi Germany's New Aristocracy*, xiv. Höhne, *Order of the Death's Head*, 135. The Fritz Bauer Institute has also organized exhibitions exploring the theft of Jewish property in Hessen.
468. The data bank of the former Berlin Document Center as well as BAB, Berlin Document Center Series 6400 (SS Officers' Service Records), provide the basis for the above-noted list of *Freiherrn* in the SS. See also www.stengerhistorica.com. For more on the father of Princess Michael of Kent, see Palmer, *Crowned Cousins*, 227.
469. For Prince Alfred Auersperg in the SS, see Enigl, "Der Adel und die Nazis," *Profil* 22 (24 May 2004): 37. For more on aristocrats in the SS, see Jakobs, *Himmlers Mann in Hamburg*; and Vassiltchikov, *Berlin Diaries*, 308.
470. Ziegler, *Nazi Germany's New Aristocracy*, xv.
471. Graber, *History of the SS*, 66.
472. Wegner, *Waffen-SS*, 77.
473. See Otto Freiherr von Waldenfels, "Legendenbildung um Himmler," *Zeitschrift für bayerische Landesgeschichte* 26 (1963): 400–407.
474. Hanfstaengl, *Unheard Witness*, 22.
475. Ibid., 21, 26.
476. Padfield, *Himmler*, 21.

477. Ibid., 29.

478. Hüser, ed., *Wewelsburg 1933 bis 1945*; and BAB, NS 19/3356, Himmler to Oswald Pohl, 26 February 1944.

479. Höhne, *Order of the Death's Head*, 154. See also Kater, *Das "Ahnenerbe,"* 44.

480. Padfield, *Himmler*, 96.

481. Birn, *Höheren SS- und Polizeiführer*, 10, 332.

482. Count Folke Bernadotte was born Prince Oscar of Sweden and later took the title Count of Wisborg. On his activities at war's end, see Bauer, *Jews for Sale?*

483. Reitlinger, *SS: Alibi of a Nation*, 239.

484. Ibid., 239.

485. "Fürst Josias zu Waldeck gestorben," *Kasseler Allgemeine Zeitung*, 2 December 1967, in Kassel Stadtarchiv, SL 2392. Waldeck had been an Oberleutnant in the 3. Kurhessische Infantry Regiment, Number 83, seeing action in France and the Balkans. See Schmeling, *Waldeck*, 19.

486. Preradovich, "Regierende Fürsten," 28–30.

487. Padfield, *Himmler*, 102. Schmeling, *Waldeck*, 60–69, 82. Note that the position as Himmler's adjutant was later held by another aristocrat, Ludolf von Alvensleben.

488. In German, Büro zur Eindeutschung der Ostvölker. Preradovich, "Regierende Fürsten," 28–30.

489. BAB SSF-217B, appointment of Waldeck as General der Polizei, signed by Hitler, 8 April 1941. Browning, *Ordinary Men*.

490. Schmeling, *Waldeck*, 48. BAB SSF-217B, Waldeck to Himmler, 12 March 1938.

491. Kropat, *"Reichskristallnacht,"* 78, 174.

492. BAB, SSF-217B, SS-Standartenführer Moreth to the judge (Scheidmann des Schiedhofes beim Reichsführer-SS), 24 September 1941.

493. Schmeling, *Waldeck*, 93–104.

494. Eugen Kogon holds Waldeck responsible for Koch's execution. Kogon, *Theory and Practice of Hell*, 265. Anke Schmeling argues that the matter was decided by an SS court in Munich and acquits him of direct involvement in the execution; however, she details his involvement in the deaths that resulted from the evacuation of Buchenwald. Schmeling, *Waldeck*, 111–15, 118.

495. Schmeling, *Waldeck*, 116–20. Kogon, *Theory and Practice of Hell*, 89.

496. Schmeling, *Waldeck*, 71–72.

497. Reichsgesetzblatt Jahrgang 1938, Teil I, 825, "Gesetz über das Erlöschen der Fideikommisse und sonstiger gebundener Vermögen," 6 July 1938.

498. Schmeling, *Waldeck*, 71–72.

499. BAB, SSF-217B, Darré to Himmler, 11 February 1939.

500. BAB, R 43/4063, Lammers to Göring, n.d. November 1938.

501. Malinowski, *Vom König zum Führer*, 566.

502. Zentner and Bedürftig, eds., *Encyclopedia of the Third Reich*, 397.

503. BAB, SSF-217B, Adjutant of Waldeck to Himmler, 7 April 1938.

504. Ibid., Himmler "Aktennotiz," 13 April 1938.

505. Ibid., Himmler to Waldeck, 22 December 1944 and 13 January 1945.

506. Ibid., Dr. Fitsner to Dr. Rudolf Brandt, Personal Staff of the Reichsführer-SS, 5 March 1943.

507. Ibid., SS-Obergruppenführer Udo von Woyrsch to Himmler, 25 January 1944.

448 ❧ *Notes to Pages 265–269*

508. Ibid.
509. Schmeling, *Waldeck*, 115.
510. For the 17 September 1949 judgment of the Spruchkammer concerning Prince zu Waldeck, see Schmeling, *Waldeck*, 129.
511. Schmeling, *Waldeck*, 132, 137.
512. Birn, *Höheren SS- und Polizeiführer*, 347.
513. SAK, SL 2392, "Eine Prinzenhochzeit," in *Kassel Allgemeine Zeitung*, 4 March 1968.
514. Bramwell, *Blood and Soil*, 46–48.
515. Wegner, *Waffen-SS*, 237.
516. Ibid. See also Richard Evans, *Coming of the Third Reich*, 274.
517. Preradovich, "Regierende Fürsten," 28–30.
518. Zentner and Bedürftig, eds., *Encyclopedia of the Third Reich*, 747.
519. Ibid., 747.
520. Lippe, *Nordische Frau*.
521. Zentner and Bedürftig, eds., *Encyclopedia of the Third Reich*, 183.
522. Hatch, *H.R.H. Prince Bernhard of the Netherlands*. He claims that he and some friends "put on their uniforms and met once a week for what almost amounted to a sportscar rally." Nikolaus von Preradovich states that Prince Bernhard was a candidate (*Anwärter*) for the SS. See Preradovich, "Regierende Fürsten," 28–30. For another source claiming membership in the Reiter-SS," see http://en.wikipedia.org.
523. Ruby, "A Slap for the Prince," *Newsweek*, 5 April 1976, 24.
524. "Prince Bernhard (1911–2004): Royal Consort Who Admitted Taking Bribes Worth $1 million," *The Week*, 11 December 2004, 38.
525. Prince Bernhard had an extraordinary life, characterized by both accomplishment and scandal. In terms of the latter, besides his early support for National Socialism, he made remarks many considered insensitive after the war (e.g., he felt sorry for General Blaskowitz, the German military commander in the Netherlands) and was involved in corporate scandals (e.g., bribes from the Lockheed Corporation). On the positive side, he played a key role in founding the World Wildlife Fund, has aided many charities, and organized the Bilderberg discussion forum: an important event held annually from 1954 to 1976. See www.nationmaster.com/encyclopedia/prince-bernhard; www.koninklijhuis.nl; and www.bilderberg.org.
526. Preradovich, "Regierende Fürsten," 28–30.
527. Ibid.
528. Gerlach, "German Economic Interest," in Herbert, ed., *National Socialist Extermination Policies*, 220. See also Angrick, "Erich von dem Bach-Zelewski," in Smelser and Syring, *Die SS: Elite Unter dem Totenkopf*, 28–44.
529. Gerlach, "German Economic Interest," 220.
530. Ibid., 216.
531. See Bach-Zelewski's obituary, *New York Times*, 21 March 1972, 44.
532. NARA, T-175/90/2612447, Himmler to SS-Gruppenführer, 11 August 1937. Also Ziegler, *Nazi Germany's New Aristocracy*, 52.
533. Höhne, *Order of the Death's Head*, 134.
534. Ibid., 135. Wegner, *Waffen-SS*, 245.

535. Birn, *Höheren SS- und Polizeiführer*, 353. Note that the category *Oberschicht* is comprised of *Rittergutsbesitzer* (estate owners) and *Hochadel* (high aristocracy).
536. Wegner, *Waffen-SS*, 245.

CHAPTER 6

1. Muggeridge, ed., *Ciano's Diary*, 205: entry for 6 February 1940. See also Moseley, *Mussolini's Shadow*, 91; Wiskemann, *Rome-Berlin Axis*, 249; and Overy, *Goering*, 233.
2. Moseley, *Mussolini's Shadow*, 67. See also AAPA, "Botschaft Rom (Quirinal)," Bd. 77, for correspondence from 1940 concerning these awards. Note also Putzi Hanfstaengl's observation about Göring: "He collected decorations the way other people collect stamps and used to blackmail his acquaintances among the old princely families to disgorge the grand cross of their ancestral order." Hanfstaengl, *Unheard Witness*, 240.
3. HHStAW, 520 D-Z, Nr. 519.563, statement of Prince Philipp, 21 February 1947.
4. Interview with Heinrich von Schuschnigg in *Profil* 22 (24 May 2004): 37.
5. Gellately, *Backing Hitler*, 236–41, for the section, "Final Effort to Deal with Nazism's 'Enemies.'"
6. Giles, "Why Bother About Homosexuals?" 17. See also BAB (former BDC), Personal file of Prince Friedrich von Mecklenburg (b. 22 April 1910).
7. Herzstein, *War That Hitler Won*, 27.
8. Amtsgericht Munich, Arno Breker Spruchkammer files, Breker "Lebenslauf," 9 June 1947, 4.
9. Hart-Davis, ed., *Sassoon Diaries*, 278–, entry for 27 October 1922.
10. HHStAW, 520 D-Z, Nr. 519.563, statement of von Schlabrendorff on behalf of Prince Philipp, 21 November 1947, 44.
11. HHStAW, 520 D-Z, Nr. 519.563, Spruchkammer Protocol of Prince Philipp, 15–17 December 1947, 14.
12. See, among many other works, Bergen, *Twisted Cross*; and Spotts, *Churches and Politics in Germany*, 3–21.
13. HHStAW, 520 D-Z, Nr. 519.563, Spruchkammer Protocol of Prince Philipp, 15–17 December 1947, 14.
14. Ibid., statement of von Schlabrendorff on behalf of Prince Philipp, 21 November 1947, 44.
15. Klein, *Lageberichte*, 943–44: "Erlass des Oberpräsident der Provinz Hessen-Nassau an den Regierungspräsidenten in Kassel wegen Intensivierung des Kirchenkampfes," 26 July 1935.
16. HHStAW, 520 D-Z, Nr. 519.563, Spruchkammer Protocol of Prince Philipp, 15–17 December 1947, 14. Note that the denazification board counted this as his only success in terms of protecting Catholic cloisters.
17. Ibid.
18. Ibid.
19. The Gauleiter and the Gauamtsleiter der NSV had wanted to transform the local Kassel orphanage into a "National Socialist facility" [Anstalt] and

Philipp defended its traditional status. Ibid., statement of von Schlabrendorff on behalf of Prince Philipp, 21 November 1947.

20. Ibid., statement of Dr. Bleibaum, 23 April 1947.

21. Muggeridge, ed., *Ciano's Diary*, 194: entry for 8 January 1940.

22. Ibid., statement of Prince Philipp, 21 February 1947.

23. Marrus, "Pius XII and the Holocaust," in Rittner and Roth, *Pope Pius XII and the Holocaust*, 47. Note also that Prince Philipp does not appear in any of the studies on the Vatican during the Third Reich, including books by Anthony Rhodes, John Morley, John Cornwall, Pierre Blet, Susan Zuccotti, Daniel Goldhagen, and Michael Phayer, among others.

24. Adelheid Fliege testified that she believed Princess Mafalda was imprisoned because "The princess had undertaken steps with the pope that would bring about an end to the war." HHStAW, 520 D-Z, Nr. 519.563, statement of Adelheid Fliege, 8 July 1946.

25. HHStAW, 520 D-Z, Nr. 519.563, statement of Prince Philipp, 21 February 1947.

26. Ibid., Spruchkammer Protocol of Prince Philipp, 15–17 December 1947, 42.

27. Ibid.

28. Ibid., Spruchkammer Protocol of Prince Philipp, 15–17 December 1947, 11–12.

29. Ibid., statement of Princess Sophia, 15 July 1946.

30. AHH, Landgravine Margarethe to Prince Richard, 8 June 1942. See also Vickers, *Alice*, 301.

31. HHStAW, 520 D-Z, Nr. 519.563, Spruchkammer Protocol of Prince Philipp, 15–17 December 1947, 45.

32. Conze, "Adel und Adeligkeit im Widerstand," 269–95.

33. Preussen, *Haus Hohenzollern*, 275.

34. Mommsen, "Widerstand gegen Hitler," in Schmädeke and Steinbach, *Widerstand gegen den Nationalsozialismus*, 8.

35. Mommsen, "Widerstand gegen Hitler," 10.

36. Schlabrendorff, *Secret War Against Hitler*, 211.

37. Nelson, *Soldier Kings*, 445.

38. Dönhoff, *Um der Ehre Willen*, 144–45.

39. A statement by his in-law, Ferdinand Karl Prince von Isenberg (House of Savoy), confirmed Philipp's ties to von Hassell, who was killed in the wake of 20 July. HHStAW, 520 D-Z, Nr. 519.563, statement of Ferdinand Karl Prinz von Isenburg, 8 September 1947.

40. *Biographisch-Bibliographisches Kirchenlexikon*, 22 at www.bautz.de.

41. Peter Hoffmann, statement to author, New Orleans, 19 September 2003.

42. Broadlands Archives Princess Sophia to Princess Alice, 14 May 1945.

43. HHStAW, 520 D-Z, Nr. 519.563, Spruchkammer Protocol of Prince Philipp, 15–17 December 1947, 45.

44. Ibid., Dr. Ortweiler, Berufungskammer "Begründung," 10 February 1949.

45. Ibid, Spruchkammer of Prince Philipp, "Begründung," December 1947, 25.

46. Remy, *Heidelberg Myth*, 154–55.

47. BAB, PK 4793, file of Prince Philipp von Hessen, Mauss to Schwarz, 22 January 1941.

48. HHStAW, 520 D-Z, Nr. 519.563, statement of Landgravine Margarethe von Hessen, 15 July 1946.

49. Rainer von Hessen to author, 14 September 2003.

50. See Weinberg, *World at Arms*. See also Winton, *ULTRA at Sea*.

51. Overy, *Goering*, 220. See also Perrault, *Red Orchestra*; and Paul Brown, "Report on the IRR File on the Red Orchestra," at http://archives.gov/iwg/research; and Brysac, *Resisting Hitler*.

52. HHStAW, 520 D-Z, Nr. 519.563, statement of Princess Margaret von Hessen-Darmstadt, 22 June 1946.

53. Ibid, statement of von Schlabrendorff on behalf of Prince Philipp, 21 November 1947, 30.

54. Ibid.

55. See, for example, the complaint made to Gauleiter Sprenger about Prince Philipp's ties to the Rothschilds in HStAD, G 5, Nr. 21: A. Luthmann to Gauleiter Sprenger, 12 February 1934.

56. Macdonogh, *Last Kaiser*, 458. See also Vassiltchikov, *Berlin Diaries*, 16; and Kronprinzessin Cécile, *Erinnerungen*, 147.

57. Louis Ferdinand Prince von Preussen, *Im Strom der Geschichte*, 282. See also Macdonogh, *Last Kaiser*, 458.

58. IfZG, ZS-145, statement of Lutz Graf Schwerin von Krosigk, 23 February 1949, who told about a report he received from a cousin of his wife, Baron Kurt von Plettenberg (1891–1945), who administered the Hohenzollern crown prince's property.

59. Vassiltchikov, *Berlin Diaries*, 18.

60. PRO, FO 371/30900, "Report on Interrogation of American Newspaper Correspondents Repatriated from Germany Aboard the Liner *Drottningholm*."

61. IfZG, ZS-145, statement of Reich Finance Minister Count Schwerin von Krosigk, 23 February 1949.

62. BAB, NS 19/2481, Himmler to Heydrich, 24 February 1942. BAB, NS 19/2209, Rudolph Brandt (on behalf of Himmler) to Gruppenführer Berger, 20 August 1942.

63. Steinberg, *All or Nothing*, 136.

64. RvH: Landgravine Margarethe to Prince Richard, 2 June 1942.

65. BAB (former BDC), Sonderakte 4 , "Erlass des Führers über die Fernhaltung international gebundener Männer in Staat, Partei, und Wehrmacht," 19 May 1943. This file also includes the 30 April 1944 list of aristocrats released from positions in Nazi Germany.

66. Cave Brown, introduction to F. Hassell, *Hostage of the Third Reich*, xi.

67. BAB, Sammlung Schumacher, R. 187/400, "Aufstellung derjenigen Parteigenossen, die Angehörige fürstlicher Häuser sind" (see translation of document in appendix 1).

68. BAB, NL 1470/37, anonymous "*Vermerk*," marked "*Geheim*," 23 December 1943.

69. Ibid., 18 January 1944.

70. Friedrich Christian Prince zu Schaumburg-Lippe, *Damals fing das neue an*, 9, 12.

71. BAB,O/915, Bl. 136/429, Hitler and Göring, Removal from Office of Prince Philipp von Hessen, 25 January 1944.

72. PRO, FO 371/3443, anonymous report on the German Propaganda Ministry, 27 September to 3 October 1943.
73. PRO, KV2/272, Progress Report on the Case of Ernst Kaltenbrunner, 13 July 1945, Appendix 3. More generally, see Hoffmann, *History of the German Resistance*; and Hett and Tuchel, "Reaktionen des NS-Staates," in Steinbach and Tuchel, *Widerstand gegen Nationalsozialismus*, 377–89.
74. PRO, KV2/272, Progress Report on the Case of Ernst Kaltenbrunner, 13 July 1945, Appendix 3.
75. Ibid.
76. Dönhoff, *Um der Ehre Willen*, 175.
77. Wheeler-Bennett, *Nemesis of Power*, 685.
78. Aretin, *Wittelsbacher ins KZ*, 8. See also the *Biographisch-Bibliographisches Kirchenlexikon*, 22 at www.bautz.de.
79. Wheeler-Bennett, *Nemesis of Power*, 685. Cave Brown, introduction, ix.
80. Vassiltchikov, *Berlin Diaries*, 240.
81. Ley, "Gott schütze den Führer," *Der Angriff* (23 July 1944). See also Smelser, *Robert Ley*, 290–91; and Semmler, *Goebbels*, 140.
82. RvH, Abschrift: "Was Himmler seinem Arzt sagte. Aus dem Artikel der *Sunday Express*, London, 30 March 1947."
83. Preussen, *Haus Hohenzollern*, 275.
84. Ellinghaus, "Der Prinz." Philipp signed the papers for Landesrat Franz Antoni to continue to administer the social institutions in the province of Hesse Nassau.
85. HHStAW, 520 D-Z, Nr. 519.563, brief to Spruchkammer by de la Fontaine, 20 February 1948.
86. Ibid., statement of Prince Philipp, 21 February 1947.
87. Ibid.
88. Hoettl, *Secret Front*, 230–31. Höttl notes that he also penned a report that was submitted to Hitler in April 1943 that "exposed the weakness of the Fascist regime."
89. HHStAW, 520 D-Z, Nr. 519.563, statement of von Schlabrendorff on behalf of Prince Philipp, 21 November 1947, 46.
90. Redlich, *Hitler*, 201.
91. Ibid.
92. Speer, *Inside the Third Reich*, 399.
93. CULBA, Prince Paul Karageorgevich, notes on meeting with Göring, June 1939.
94. HHStAW, 520 D-Z, Nr. 519.563, statement of von Schlabrendorff on behalf of Prince Philipp, 21 November 1947.
95. Ibid., statement of Landgravine Margarethe von Hessen, 15 July 1946.
96. U. Hassell, *Hassell-Tagebücher*, 154.
97. HHStAW, 520 D-Z, Nr. 519.563, statement of Prince Philipp, 21 February 1947.
98. RvH: Landgravine Margarethe to Prince Richard, 21 March 1942.
99. Ibid.: Landgravine Margarethe to Prince Richard, 15 February 1942.
100. HHStAW, 520 D-Z, Nr. 519.563, "Protocol" of Karl Wolff, 18 September 1947.

101. Ibid., brief to Spruchkammer by de la Fontaine, 20 February 1948.

102. Ibid., statement of Adelheid Fliege, 8 July 1946.

103. Ibid., statement of Prince Philipp, 21 February 1947. See also AAPA, Büro des Staatssekretär Italiens, Bd. 14, Doc. 72340, Sonnleithner to Mackensen, 22 July 1943.

104. Heinrich Prinz von Hessen, *Kristallene Lüster*, 143; and Katz, *Fall of the House of Savoy*, 353–79. See also what are purported to be Mussolini's notes on his arrest and imprisonment in Hoettl, *Secret Front*, 240–70.

105. For an account of Himmler, Bormann, and Ribbentrop discussing the situation in Italy, see AAPA, Büro des Staatssekretär Italiens, Bd. 14, Doc. 72411, Brandt to Wagner, 19 July 1943.

106. HHStAW, 520 D-Z, Nr. 519.563, "Protocol" of Karl Wolff, 18 September 1947. See also IfZG, ZS 918, Interrogation of the Prince of Hesse, 6 May 1947.

107. HHStAW, 520 D-Z, Nr. 519.563, statement of the priest Dr. W. Borngässer, 28 November 1947.

108. Heinrich Prinz von Hessen, *Kristallene Lüster*, 144.

109. HHStAW, 520 D-Z, Nr. 519.563, Bericht über die Vernehmung verschiedener Mitglieder des auswärtigen Amtes über Prinz von Hessen, 1 September 1947.

110. Ibid., statement of Princess Margaret von Hessen-Darmstadt, 22 June 1946.

111. Steinberg, *All or Nothing*, 136.

112. Katz, *Battle for Rome*, 18.

113. Hoettl, *Secret Front*, 279. Note that Marie-José, later queen of Italy, had been born Princess of Belgium from the Sachsen-Coburg und Gotha family (1906–2001) and had met with Hitler at the Berghof on 17 October 1940.

114. RvH: Prince Christoph to Princess Sophia, 19 September 1943.

115. HHStAW, 520 D-Z, Nr. 519.563, statement of von Schlabrendorff, 10 July 1946.

116. Heinrich Prinz von Hessen, *Kristallene Lüster*, 146–47.

117. Smyth, *Secrets of the Fascist Era*, 27.

118. Heinrich Prinz von Hessen, *Kristallene Lüster*, 148.

119. Swiss Federal Archives, Bern, E 4320 (B) 1991/243, Bd. 98, declaration of Eddie von Bismarck, 3 February 1944. Special thanks to Professor Lothar Machtan for providing the author with this document.

120. HHStAW, 520 D-Z, Nr. 519.563, statement of von Schlabrendorff on behalf of Prince Philipp, 21 November 1947, 47.

121. "So verriet der Lügen-König den Duce," in *Völkischer Beobachter* 253, 10 September 1943 (Berlin edition), 2. Note that Prince Philipp was not mentioned in this article (or subsequent ones), although the "court camarilla" is accused of plotting with Free Masons and Jewish leaders, and there were subsequent calls to "overthrow the plutocrats" (*Beseitigung der Plutokratie*). For the latter, see "Niemand in Italien glaubt mehr der Monarchie," in *Völkischer Beobachter* 263, 26 September 1943 (Berlin edition), 2.

122. HHStAW, 520 D-Z, Nr. 519.563, statement of Franz Ulbrich, 15 July 1946.

123. IfZG, ZS 576, statement of General Enno von Rintelen, 11 April 1957.

124. HHStAW, 520 D-Z, Nr. 519.563, Spruchkammer Protocol of Prince Philipp, 15–17 December 1947, 46.

125. Ibid., "Begründung," December 1947, 10.
126. Kershaw, *Hitler, 1936–1945*, 600.
127. HHStAW, 520 D-Z, Nr. 519.563, statement of Prince Philipp, 21 February 1947.
128. NARA, M 1204/5, Record of Testimony in the Trial of the United States versus Friedrich Becker, et al., 12 June 1946, 3434. Kershaw, *Hitler, 1936–1945*, 600.
129. NARA, M 1204/5, Record of Testimony in the Trial of the United States versus Friedrich Becker, et al., 12 June 1946, 3434.
130. Bundesarchiv Zentralnachweisstelle, Aachen, Sign. F573/c–S. 1: Personalveränderungen in der Dienstaltersliste C, 16 October 1943.
131. BAB, O/915, Bl. 136/429, Hitler and Göring, Removal from Office of Prince Philipp von Hessen, 25 January 1944.
132. "Ab 1. Juli Provinz Kurhessen. Aufteilung der Provinz Hessen-Nassau— Einheitliche Verwaltungsräume—Stellv. Gauleiter Karl Gerland der neue Oberpräsident," *Kurhessische Landeszeitung*, 2 July 1944; "Gefallener wurde 'Hauptschuldiger,'" *Kasseler Post*, 2 March 1950. See SAK, Nr. 237, for the efforts of the German Red Cross to determine Gerland's fate. Note that Gauleiter Sprenger assumed the responsibilities of the Oberpräsident for the Wiesbaden region.
133. HHStAW, 520 D-Z, Nr. 519.563, statement of Prince Philipp, 21 February 1947.
134. IfZG, ZS 918, Interrogation of the Prince of Hesse, 20 July 1945. See more generally, Orth, *System der nationalsozialistischen Konzentrationslager*.
135. HHStAW, 520 D-Z, Nr. 519.563, "Protocol" of Karl Wolff, 18 September 1947.
136. IfZG, ZS 918, Interrogation of the Prince of Hesse, 20 July 1945.
137. Ibid.
138. HHStAW, 520 D-Z, Nr. 519.563, statement of Prince Philipp, 21 February 1947.
139. Goebbels, *Tagebücher* II/9, 255 entry of 10 August 1943.
140. HHStAW, 520 D-Z, Nr. 519.563, statement of von Schlabrendorff on behalf of Prince Philipp, 21 November 1947. He cites a statement of Johann Harnyss.
141. Ibid., Spruchkammer Protocol of Prince Philipp, 15–17 December 1947, 26: statement of Johannes Harnyss.
142. Ibid., Spruchkammer Protocol of Prince Philipp, 15–17 December 1947, 33: statement of Adelheid Fliege.
143. Ibid.
144. Ibid.
145. Ibid., statement of von Schlabrendorff on behalf of Prince Philipp, 21 November 1947.
146. Ibid., statement of von Schlabrendorff on behalf of Prince Philipp, 21 November 1947.
147. Ibid., statement of Adelheid Fliege, 8 July 1946.
148. Ibid., statement of Adelheid Fliege, 2 July 1946.

149. Ibid., statement of Prince Philipp, 21 February 1947.
150. Ibid., statement of von Schlabrendorff on behalf of Prince Philipp, 21 November 1947, 47.
151. Ibid., statement of von Schlabrendorff, 10 July 1946.
152. NARA, RG 259, Entry 1082, box 2, "Von Hessen, Prince Philip [*sic*]: Background Information. Interrogation," 21 July 1945.
153. Goebbels, *Tagebücher* II/9, 458, entry for 10 September 1943.
154. NARA, M 1204/5, Record of Testimony in the Trial of the United States versus Friedrich Becker, et al., 12 June 1946, 3435–36, 3440, 3449–50, 3455.
155. HHStAW, 520 D-Z, Nr. 519.563, statement of Prince Philipp, 21 February 1947.
156. NARA, M 1204/5, Record of Testimony in the Trial of the United States versus Friedrich Becker, et al., 12 June 1946, 3441.
157. See the website for the Flossenbürg memorial at www.gedenkstaette-flossenbuerg.de.
158. IfZG, ZS 918, Interrogation of the Prince of Hesse, 4 March 1948.
159. HHStAW, 520 D-Z, Nr. 519.563, statement of von Schlabrendorff, 10 July 1946.
160. Schlabrendorff, *Revolt Against Hitler*, 164.
161. HHStAW, 520 D-Z, Nr. 519.563, statement of Robert Hellwig, 1 July 1946.
162. Note that Philipp testified that he had never before heard of Flossenbürg, although he had heard of Dachau and Oranienburg. NARA, M 1204/5, Record of Testimony in the Trial of the United States versus Friedrich Becker, et al., 12 June 1946, 3466.
163. Heinrich Prinz von Hessen, *Kristallene Lüster*, 149–50.
164. Obituary, "Queen Giovanna of the Bulgarians," *The Times* (London), 28 February 2000. See also Dimitroff, *Boris III*, 3–15, 102–11.
165. Groueff, *Crown of Thorns*, 381. See also Devere-Summers, *War and the Royal Houses*, 127–30.
166. Groueff, *Crown of Thorns*, 380–81. Goebbels, *Tagebücher* 2/9, 481–84, entry for 11 September 1943.
167. BAB, NS 19/2348, "Rudi" to SS-Obersturmbannführer Paul Baumert, Persönlicher Stab RF-SS, 14 September 1943. Himmler is copied on the letter, which is marked "Geheim!"
168. HHStAW, 520 D-Z, Nr. 519.563, statement of von Schlabrendorff on behalf of Prince Philipp, 21 November 1947. Also Ellinghaus, "Der Prinz."
169. Heinrich Prinz von Hessen, *Kristallene Lüster*, 153–66. Katz, *Fall of the House of Savoy*, 353–75.
170. Hoettl, *Secret Front*, 230–31.
171. HHStAW, 520 D-Z, Nr. 519.563, statement of von Schlabrendorff on behalf of Prince Philipp, 21 November 1947.
172. Ibid.
173. Ibid.
174. Ibid.
175. Ibid., Spruchkammer Protocol of Prince Philipp, 15–17 December 1947, 32: statement of Adelheid Fliege.

176. See the account by Mrs. Tony Breitscheid in a 14 July 1945 letter to King Vittorio Emmanuele III in Heinrich Prinz von Hessen, *Kristallene Lüster*, 272–77.

177. Ellinghaus, "Der Prinz." More generally, Hackett, *Buchenwald Report*.

178. HHStAW, 520 D-Z, Nr. 519.563, statement of von Schlabrendorff on behalf of Prince Philipp, 21 November 1947. He cites a statement of Johannes Harnyss.

179. HHStAW, 520 D-Z, Nr. 519.563, Spruchkammer Protocol of Prince Philipp, 15–17 December 1947, 26: statement of Johannes Harnyss.

180. Ibid.

181. Hoettl, *Secret Front*, 229.

182. Katz, *Battle for Rome*, 47, 51, 75, 233–65. Kappler was charged with complicity in the deportation of 8,000 Jews from Rome. See his testimony at the Eichmann trial on 30 May 1961 at www.nizkor.org.

183. Heinrich Prinz von Hessen, *Kristallene Lüster*, 163.

184. HHStAW, 520 D-Z, Nr. 519.563, Spruchkammer Protocol of Prince Philipp, 15–17 December 1947, 27: statement of Johannes Harnyss.

185. Ibid., statement of von Schlabrendorff on behalf of Prince Philipp, 21 November 1947.

186. Recollection of Armin Walther, in Hackett, *Buchenwald Report*, 232–33.

187. Ellinghaus, "Der Prinz." See also Armin Walther, in Hackett, *Buchenwald Report*, 232–33.

188. HHStAW, 520 D-Z, Nr. 519.563, Spruchkammer Protocol of Prince Philipp, 15–17 December 1947, 26: statement of Johannes Harnyss.

189. Recollection of Armin Walther, in Hackett, *Buchenwald Report*, 232–33.

190. HHStAW, 520 D-Z, Nr. 519.563, Spruchkammer Protocol of Prince Philipp, 15–17 December 1947, 27: statement of Johannes Harnyss.

191. Marshall, *White Rabbit*, 193. In this inaccurate account, Mafalda is said to have died in the arms of a prostitute.

192. HHStAW, 520 D-Z, Nr. 519.563, Spruchkammer Protocol of Prince Philipp, 15–17 December 1947, 27: statement of Johannes Harnyss.

193. Tony Breitscheid to King Vittorio Emmanuele III, 14 July 1945, in Heinrich Prinz von Hessen, *Kristallene Lüster*, 272–77; Frey, ed., *Prominente ohne Maske. 2. Bd.*, 276; Ellinghaus, "Der Prinz."

194. Different versions have emerged concerning the disposition of her body. Kogon, *Theory and Practice of Hell*, 128–29. See also Marshall, *White Rabbit*, 193.

195. HHStAW, 520 D-Z, Nr. 519.563, statement of Niemöller, 27 June 1946. See also HHStAW, 520 D-Z, Nr. 519.563, statement of von Schlabrendorff, 10 July 1946.

196. Ibid., statement of Adelheid Fliege, 8 July 1946. Heinrich Prinz von Hessen, *Kristallene Lüster*, 210.

197. Ellinghaus, "Der Prinz."

198. HHStAW, 520 D-Z, Nr. 519.563, statement of von Schlabrendorff on behalf of Prince Philipp, 21 November 1947.

199. Shirer, *Rise and Fall*, 1191.

200. Ibid. Also Gilbert, *Hitler Directs His War*, 37; and Warlimont, *Im Hauptquartier der Deutschen Wehrmacht*, 342–43.

201. HHStAW, 520 D-Z, Nr. 519.563, statement of von Schlabrendorff on behalf of Prince Philipp, 10 February 1946.

202. Ibid., Spruchkammer Protocol of Prince Philipp, "Begründung," December 1947, 11. See also PRO, HW 19/238, item 6503, an ULTRA decryption which was that "on the representation of the Reichsmarschall, the Führer has decided to have the Duke of Calvi brought to Germany immediately." The Germans decided that the duke could be trusted and appointed him commander of Rome.

203. Heinrich Prinz von Hessen, *Kristallene Lüster*, 158, 173.

204. HHStAW, 520 D-Z, Nr. 519.563, statement of von Schlabrendorff on behalf of Prince Philipp, 21 November 1947, 48. Heinrich Prinz von Hessen, *Kristallene Lüster*, 246.

205. Zuccotti, *Italians and the Holocaust*, 7. See also Kershaw, *Hitler, 1936–1945*, 600.

206. Zuccotti, *Italians and the Holocaust*, 272.

207. Wolfgang Prinz von Hessen, *Aufzeichnungen*, 183–94.

208. Ibid., 193.

209. RvH: Prince Christoph to Princess Sophia, 17 July 1943.

210. Ibid., Prince Christoph to Princess Sophia, 11 August 1943.

211. Ibid., Prince Christoph to Princess Sophia, 19 September 1943.

212. Ibid., Prince Christoph to Princess Sophia, 7 September 1943.

213. Ibid., Prince Christoph to Princess Sophia, 28 September 1943.

214. RvH: Princess Sophia to Prince Christoph, 17 September 1943.

215. Ibid., Prince Christoph to Princess Sophia, 19 September 1943.

216. Ibid., Prince Christoph to Princess Sophia, postage stamp of 8 October 1943. Note that this was the last letter Christoph wrote to his wife Sophia; it concludes, "I hope to come soon! Tender love and 1,000 kisses from Peech."

217. Ibid., Major Bennemann to Prince Wolfgang, 3 December 1943. According to some reports, Christoph was flying directly to Berlin. This is what his brother Richard claimed in his denazification trial in 1948 in Wolfgang Prinz von Hessen, *Aufzeichnungen*, 195. Popular author Karl Shaw claims that he "was on a top-secret Nazi assignment" (without suggesting the nature of such a mission). Shaw, *Royal Babylon*, 287.

218. Report of Dreifke in Gellermann, *und lauschten für Hitler*, 28.

219. Vickers, *Alice*, 301.

220. RvH, Major Bennemann to Prince Wolfgang, 3 December 1943.

221. Ibid.

222. HRH Prince Philip, Duke of Edinburgh, interview with author, Buckingham Palace, 3 March 2004.

223. Richard Evans, *Telling Lies About Hitler*, 97–99.

224. See Richard Breitman and Timothy Naftali, "Report to the Interagency Working Group on Previously Classified OSS Records," (June 200) at http://www.archives.gov/iwg/reports.

225. Lambton, *Mountbattens*, 36.

226. For more on the Duke of Kent's death, see Bradford, *King George VI*, 344–46; Whiting, *The Kents*, 102–04; King, *Princess Marina*, 167–69.

227. See Picknett, Prince, and Prior, *Double Standards*. With regard to the death of the Duke of Kent, they point out that "it was a strange accident indeed in which a flying boat should crash into a hillside inland (their standing orders were to fly over water whenever possible), and if it were an accident, why has the Establishment ensured that it is next to impossible to find out what really happened from the official records, for the simple reason that most of them have 'disappeared.'"

228. Wolfgang Prinz von Hessen, *Aufzeichnungen*, 189.

229. Note that Hugo von Windisch-Graetz died test-flying a plane in Italy in 1942. The son of Hungary Regent Admiral Horthy also died in a plane accident. Vassiltchikov, *Berlin Diaries*, 67, 74.

230. Gellermann, *und lauschten für Hitler*, 29.

231. *Völkischer Beobachter* 291, 18 October 1943.

232. Vickers, *Alice*, 301.

233. Ibid. Note that the letter from Victoria, Marchioness of Milford Haven to Earl Mountbatten of Burma is dated somewhat later, 4 February 1944.

234. Vickers, *Alice*, 302.

235. Gellermann, *und lauschten für Hitler*, 29. See Hüser, ed., *Wewelsburg*, 62.

236. BAB (formerly BDC), SSF 94A, file of Prince Christoph, SS-Obergruppenführer und General der Waffen-SS Taubert to Himmler, 30 November 1943.

237. Ibid.

238. Heinrich Prinz von Hessen, *Kristallene Lüster*, 115. See also Alford, *Spoils of World War II*, 169.

239. BAB (formerly BDC), SSF 94A, file of Prince Christoph Taubert to Himmler, 30 November 1943.

240. Rainer von Hessen reports the analysis of Taubert's report of the conversation and noted the formulation, "auf der Wewelsburg hörte und erführe ich von solchen und ähnlichen Dingen rein garnichts." Rainer von Hessen to the author, telephone conversation, 22 September 2003.

241. Wolfgang Prinz von Hessen, *Aufzeichnungen*, 195.

242. Ibid.

243. Ibid., 190.

244. Wolfgang Prinz von Hessen, *Aufzeichnungen*, 195.

245. BAB (formerly BDC), SSF 94A, file of Prince Christoph, Taubert to Himmler, 30 November 1943.

246. Letter from Princess Alice to her son, Prince Philip, from 23 April 1944 is cited in Vickers, *Alice*, 302.

247. HHStAW, 520 D-Z, Nr. 519.563, "Begründung," December 1947, 20.

248. Ibid., statement of Generaldirektor of the diocese in Vallendar-Schönstatt, 31 July 1946.

249. Ibid., statement of Dr. Michael Höck, 5 July 1946.

250. Ibid., statement of von Schlabrendorff, 10 July 1946.

251. Marcuse, *Legacies of Dachau*, 49.

252. Padfield, *Himmler*, 588.

253. Höhne, *Canaris*, 579.

254. F. Hassell, *Hostage of the Third Reich*, 200–202.

255. PRO, FO 371/46888, Mr. Macmillan, Caserta, report of 10 May 1945.

256. HHStAW, 520 D-Z, Nr. 519.563, statement of von Schlabrendorff, 10 July 1946.

257. F. Hassell, *Hostage of the Third Reich*, 198.

258. Ibid.

259. Naftali, "Creating the Myth of the *Alpenfestung*," 203–46.

260. Cave Brown, introduction, xiv.

261. IfZG, ZS 918, Interrogation of the Prince of Hesse, 6 May 1947. Ellinghaus, "Der Prinz." See also F. Hassell, *Hostage of the Third Reich*, 203.

262. See, for example, "Schacht Saved by Fifth," *Daily Mail*, 8 May 1945, 1.

263. PRO, FO 371/46888, G. W. Harrison memorandum, 12 May 1945.

264. Ibid., John Wheeler-Bennett to G. W. Harrison, 15 May 1945.

265. Ibid., Mr. Macmillan, Caserta, report of 10 May 1945.

266. F. Hassell, *Hostage of the Third Reich*, 209.

267. Ibid., 211.

268. HHStAW, 520 D-Z, Nr. 519.563, statement of von Schlabrendorff on behalf of Prince Philipp, 21 November 1947, 47.

269. Ibid., statement of Priest J. Neuhäusler, 5 July 1946.

270. Read, *Devil's Disciples*, 1–10. See also Overy, *Interrogations*, 60–61.

271. NARA, RG 59, Entry 1082, box 3, Donald Heath to Ambassador Murphy, 18 June 1945.

272. HHStAW, 520 D-Z, Nr. 519.563, statement of Robert Hellwig, 1 July 1946.

273. Ibid., statement of Hans Schneider, 17 July 1946.

274. Heinrich Prinz von Hessen, *Kristallene Lüster*, 225.

275. Wolfgang Prinz von Hessen, *Aufzeichnungen*, 203.

276. Alford, *Spoils of World War II*, 114.

277. Heinrich Prinz von Hessen, *Kristallene Lüster*, 208, 210. See also Broadlands Archives Princess Sophia to Princess Alice, 14 May 1945.

278. Wolfgang Prinz von Hessen, *Aufzeichnungen*, 205.

279. Ibid., 203. Heinrich Prinz von Hessen, *Kristallene Lüster*, 189.

280. Landgrave Moritz von Hessen, interview with author, Kronberg, 22 July 2002.

281. Alford, *Spoils of World War II*, 115.

282. Heinrich Prinz von Hessen, *Kristallene Lüster*, 193.

283. Wolfgang Prinz von Hessen, *Aufzeichnungen*, 198. Heinrich Prinz von Hessen, *Kristallene Lüster*, 115. See also Alford, *Spoils of World War II*, 111.

284. IfZG, ZS 918, Interrogation of the Prince of Hesse, 4 March 1948.

285. Heinrich Prinz von Hessen, *Kristallene Lüster*, 233.

286. Wolfgang Prinz von Hessen, *Aufzeichnungen*, 198–99.

287. Heinrich Prinz von Hessen, *Kristallene Lüster*, 177–79. More generally, Dettmar, *Zerstörung Kassels*, 153. Note that Kassel was bombed at least forty times between 22 June 1940 and 21 March 1945.

288. Berg and Röbel, "Beutekunst: Von Sanssouci nach Moskau," *Der Spiegel* 38, 15 September 2003. See also Harding, "A Rubens in Recovered," *ARTnews*, November 2003, 70.

289. Metternich, *Bericht eines ungewöhnlichen Lebens*, 312.

290. Duff, *Hessian Tapestry*, 363. See also Neumann, *1945 Nachgetragen*.

291. BAB, SSO/BDC, file of Prince Wilhelm von Hessen (b. 1 March 1905). See also BA Zentralnachweisstelle, Wehrmacht-Personalkartei for Prince Wilhelm von Hessen.

292. Bundesarchiv Zentralnachweisstelle, Abgangskartei, card for Prince Wilhelm von Hessen. Also Hermann Prinz von Hessen (son of Prince Wilhelm von Hessen) to author, 6 March 2005.

293. See the war diary of Magnus Erd at http://haiku-plus.de/kriegstagebuch/tagebucheng.html.

294. Hermann Prinz von Hessen to author, 6 March 2005.

295. Preussen, *Haus Hohenzollern*, 231.

296. Macdonogh, *Last Kaiser*, 459.

297. Ibid.

298. Preussen, *Haus Hohenzollern*, 192–93.

299. Nelson, *Soldier Kings*, 455.

300. Preussen, *Haus Hohenzollern*, 226. Jonas, *Life of Crown Prince Wilhelm*, 225–26.

301. Jonas, *Life of Crown Prince Wilhelm*, 225–26. Prior to his death, the crown prince had carried out a legal fight to recover his father's house in Doorn, Holland, which he had inherited after the ex-Kaiser's death in 1941. The Dutch government decided in June 1949, however, that the house was enemy property and confiscated it (it was turned into a museum open to the public).

302. Prusczynski, "Poland: The War Losses," in E. Simpson, *Spoils of War*, 51.

303. Aalders, *Nazi Looting*, 43.

CHAPTER 7

1. Picknett, Prince, and Prior, *War of the Windsors*, 195.

2. Wolfgang Prinz von Hessen, *Aufzeichnungen*, 221. See Weinrich's Spruchkammer file in HHStAW, 520/4960.

3. In late 1947, as the trial reached its peak, Schaub, von Weizsäcker and Schellenberg were still imprisoned in the Palace of Justice in Nuremberg, where they testified before the IMT. HHStAW, 520 D-Z, Nr. 519.563, statement of Dr. Quambusch, 24 November 1947.

4. Heinrich Prinz von Hessen, *Kristallene Lüster*, 226. Metternich, *Bericht*, 312–18.

5. Kronprinzessin Cecilie, *Erinnerungen*, 179–80.

6. Heinrich Prinz von Hessen, *Kristallene Lüster*, 197.

7. HStAD, Q4 8/78-1/13, Captain Orson Jones to Mr. Yakoubian, 17 September 1946.

8. Wolfgang Prinz von Hessen, *Aufzeichnungen*, 220.

9. See Prince Auwi's testimony of 14 May 1947 in Kempner, *Dritte Reich im Kreuzverhör*, 129.

10. HHStAW, 520 D-Z, Nr. 519.563, statement of Hans Schneider, 17 July 1946.

11. Wolfgang Prinz von Hessen, *Aufzeichnungen*, 221.

12. FOIA request, Cryptocenter HQ 66th CIC DE, U.S. Army, Europe, n.d.

13. HHStAW, 520 D-Z, Nr. 519.563, statement of Hans Schneider, 17 July 1946.
14. Heinrich Prinz von Hessen, *Kristallene Lüster*, 249.
15. HHStAW, 520 D-Z, Nr. 519.563, statement of the Bishop of Limburg Kilfrisch, 1 July 1946.
16. Ibid., statement of Pastor Martin Niemöller, 27 June 1946.
17. Ibid., statement of Princess Margaret von Hessen-Darmstadt, 22 June 1946.
18. FOIA request, memorandum, 29 January 1947.
19. IfZG, ZS 918, Interrogation of the Prince of Hesse, 6 May 1947.
20. HHStAW, 520 D-Z, Nr. 519.563, Sitzung des Deutschen Sicherheitsnach-prüfungsamt, 1 August 1946.
21. Wolfgang Prinz von Hessen, *Aufzeichnungen*, 237.
22. HStAD, Q4 8/214-3/12, James Newman to von Schlabrendorff, 23 December 1947, and previously, Schlabrendorff to Newman, 20 December 1947.
23. FOIA request, Cryptocenter HQ 66th CIC DE, U.S. Army, Europe, n.d.
24. NARA, M 1204/5, Record of Testimony in the Trial of the United States versus Friedrich Becker, et al., 12 June 1946, 3437.
25. Ibid., 3458.
26. See the article in the newspaper, *Telegraf*, 10 December 1946.
27. Heberer, "*'Exitus Heute* in Hadamar,'" 159.
28. Kintner, ed., *Hadamar Trial*, 247.
29. HHStAW, Abt. 461, Nr. 32061/7, Verfahren gegen Adolf Wahlmann, et al. (1947 Frankfurt Hadamar Trial), interrogation of Prince Philipp, 6 March 1947.
30. For Weinrich's denazification trial, including the judgment of the Zentral-berufungskammer Hessen-Nord, see HHStAW, 520/4960. See also the documents from the Landespersonalamt in HHStAW, 527/5004 and 14888.
31. "Weinrich wusste, was in den KZs vor sich ging," *Hessische Nachrichten*, 5 July 1949.
32. IfZG, ZS 918, Interrogation of the Prince of Hesse, 4 March 1948. Note that these interviews were still going on in March 1948. See also Kempner, *SS im Kreuzverhör*, 207; and Kempner, *Dritte Reich im Kreuzverhör*, 135–42.
33. IfZG, ZS 918, Interrogation of the Prince of Hesse, 6 May 1947.
34. Ibid.
35. HHStAW, 520 D-Z, Nr. 519.563, Bericht über die Vernehmung ver-schiedener Mitglieder des Auswärtigen Amtes über Prinz von Hessen, 1 September 1947.
36. HHStAW, 520 D-Z, Nr. 519.563, statement of Hans Schneider, 17 July 1946.
37. Ibid., statement of Princess Margaret von Hessen-Darmstadt, 22 June 1946.
38. Ibid., Deutsche Sicherheitsnachprüfungsamt, Sitzung of 1 August 1946.
39. Heinrich Prinz von Hessen, *Kristallene Lüster*, 283.
40. HHStAW, 520 D-Z, Nr. 519.563, Declaration of Karl Anton Schulte, 13 September 1946.
41. HStAD, Q4 8/214-3/12, Chief of Denazification Division, Herbert Teitelbaum to the Minister for Political Liberation, Hesse, 6 January 1947. See also HHStAW, 520 D-Z, Nr. 519.563, Prince Philipp to Minister für politische Befreiung, 7 October 1947.

42. HHStAW, 520 D-Z, Nr. 519563, Raymond Didlo of the Miltitary Government Liaison Office Darmstadt German Labor Camp to Mr. Bojunga, chief prosecutor before the Tribunal at the Darmstadt Labor Camp, 21 February 1947.

43. Ibid., "Begründung," December 1947, 21.

44. Ibid., 22.

45. Ibid.

46. Ibid., statement of Hermann Gorhn, 20 March 1947.

47. HHStAW, Denazification file of Prince Richard, # 4610, Protocol, 25 May 1949.

48. Wolfgang Prinz von Hessen, *Aufzeichnungen*, 222, 232.

49. "Gesetz zur Befreiung von Nationalsozialismus und Militarismus," 5 March 1946.

50. The 24 July 1950 ruling by the Zentral-Berufungskammer Hessen and the information about the 30 November 1949 Gesetz über den Abschluss der politischen Befreiung in Hessen was communicated to the author by Dr. Diether Degreif of the Hessisches Hauptstaatsarchiv Wiesbaden, 10 February 2005. See more generally, A. Schuster, *Entnazifizierung in Hessen, 1945–1954.*

51. HHStAW, 520 D-Z, Nr. 519.563, statement of von Schlabrendorff, 10 July 1946.

52. Ibid., "Begründung," December 1947, 10.

53. Ibid., statement of von Schlabrendorff, 10 July 1946.

54. Ibid. For more on Schlabrendorff, see his memoirs, Schlabrendorff, *Begegnungen* and *Secret War Against Hitler.*

55. HHStAW, 520 D-Z, Nr. 519.563, Prince Philipp to Hessische Minister für politische Befreiung, 7 October 1947.

56. Ibid., statement of von Schlabrendorff on behalf of Prince Philipp, 21 November 1947, 31.

57. Ibid., 49.

58. Ibid., Spruchkammer Protocol of Prince Philipp, 15–17 December 1947, 29: statement of Anne Aubel.

59. Ibid., Spruch for Prince Philipp, 17 December 1947, 1. See also IfZG, clipping file of Prince Philipp, article of unspecified newspaper, 19 December 1947.

60. HHStAW, 520 D-Z, Nr. 519.563, Spruch for Prince Philipp, 17 December 1947, 1.

61. Ibid., "Begründung," December 1947, 27.

62. Ibid.

63. Ibid., 28.

64. Niethammer, *Mitläufer-fabrik*, 645–52. See also I. Müller, *Hitler's Justice: The Courts of the Third Reich*, 201–300.

65. HHStAW, 520 D-Z, Nr. 519.563, brief to Spruchkammer by de la Fontaine, 20 February 1948. Note that von Schlabrendorff was still listed as one of Philipp's attorneys at the appeal trial but also as a witness. Ibid., Berufung-skammer Darmstadt, Protokol der öffentlichen Sitzung, 10 February 1949.

66. Ibid., brief to Spruchkammer by de la Fontaine, 20 February 1948.
67. Ibid., Minister für politische Befreiung to the Erster öffentliche Kläger der Berufungskammer, 23 February 1948.
68. Ibid.
69. Ibid., Minister für politische Befreiung to the Erster öffentliche Kläger der Berufungskammer, 2 February 1948.
70. Ibid., Dr. Ortweiler, Berufungskammer "Begründung," 10 February 1949.
71. Ibid.
72. Ibid., de la Fontaine to the Staatskasse Frankfurt, 8 January 1950.
73. Ibid., Treuhander der kurhessische Hausstiftung to the Ersten Öffentlichen Kläger der Spruchkammer, 2 May 1947.
74. Ibid.
75. HStAD, 024 53/9, [author's signature illegible], "Denkschrift über die Behandlung des Vermögens der Kurhessischen Hausstiftung," 24 August 1947.
76. Heinrich Prinz von Hessen, *Kristallene Lüster*, 297.
77. See www.geocities.com/evestrehl/KarlEduard.html. Note that Duke Carl Eduard astonished his Allied captors in April 1945 by his "ignorance, lack of contrition, and by American standards, unbridled arrogance": for example, he maintained that the Poles had attacked Germany, believed up until the last days that the Germans would prevail in the war, and described National Socialism as a "wonderful" idea. Bernd Junior, "Wer im November 1994 den 13. Bundestag in Berlin eröffnete," at www.pdsgotha.de. He comments on Stefan Heym's "Report to Luxemburg" of 17 April 1945.
78. BAB, NL 1470/37, Prince Friedrich Christian zu Schaumburg-Lippe to Robert Kempner, 3 April 1980. More generally, Friedrich Christian zu Schaumburg-Lippe, *Damals fing das neue an*, 95, 163, 293–307.
79. HHStAW, 520 D-Z, Nr. 519.563, Löber of the Amtsgericht to de la Fontaine, 31 October 1950.
80. RvH, declaration of the Zentralberufungskammer in Frankfurt, 17 April 1950.
81. Frei, *Adenauer's Germany*; Moeller, *War Stories*; and Reichel, *Erfundene Erinnerung*.
82. HHStAW, 520 D-Z, Nr. 519.563, de la Fontaine to the Staatskasse Frankfurt, 8 January 1950.
83. Ibid., Magistrat der Stadt Kassel to das Finanzamt Frankfurt, 27 June 1955.
84. Picknett, Prince, and Prior, *Double Standards*; K. Alford, *Spoils of World War II*; M. Allen, *Hidden Agenda*, 2; and Picknett, Prince, and Prior, *War of the Windsors*, 195–200.
85. M. Allen, *Hidden Agenda*, 2.
86. Ibid., 1.
87. Carter, *Anthony Blunt*, 311.
88. Ibid., 312. For the letters being returned, see RA, VIC/Add A 1/10, Sir Owen Morshead's Mission to Germany, 3–5 August 1945, documents 21 (Queen Mary to Morshead, 18 October 1951) to 35, Michael Wilforn, Foreign Office, to Morshead, 31 December 1951.
89. RA, VIC/Add A 1/22 ADD Mss., No. 22: Landgravine Margarethe to Queen Mary, 15 October 1951.
90. Carter, *Anthony Blunt*, 312.

91. Ibid.
92. NARA, RG 260/OMGUS Education and Cultural Relations, box 226, Colonel John Allen to G-5 USFET, 6 August 1946.
93. RA, VIC/Add, report of Owen Morshead, 9 August 1945. See also RA, MSS, Sir Owen Morshead's Mission to Germany, 3–5 August 1945: Morshead offers a detailed account of the trip, including lists with inventories of the letters and books that he removed (see document 6).
94. RA, VIC/Add 1/10, report of Owen Morshead, 9 August 1945.
95. Nicholas, *Rape of Europa*, 374.
96. Carter, *Anthony Blunt*, 315.
97. Ibid., 316.
98. Ibid., 315.
99. C. Simpson, Leitch, and Knightly, "Blunt was Emissary," 1.
100. Wright, *Spycatcher*, 223.
101. Martin Allen to author, 2 April 2002.
102. Wright, *Spycatcher*, 223.
103. Carter, *Anthony Blunt*, 313.
104. RA, GVI/C042/ ADD Mss., No. 7: Anthony Blunt, "English Paintings from the Collection of Empress Frederick Preserved at Schloss Friedrichshof," August 1945.
105. C. Simpson, Leitch, and Knightly, "Blunt was Emissary," 1.
106. "Phoenix" is reportedly an ex-MI5 agent whom they interviewed. They also suggest that Prince Philipp von Hessen may have secured sensitive papers for the Duke and Duchess of Windsor in Paris during the war. See Picknett, Prince, and Prior, *War of the Windsors*, 196–98.
107. Royal Archivist Pamela Clark, statement to author, Windsor Castle, 9 June 2003.
108. Box 24 of Monckton's papers, which concerns correspondence from 1936–51, remains closed to researchers. Colin Harris, Supervisor, Department of Special Collections and Western Manuscripts, New Bodleian Library, Oxford University, to author, 4 January 2005.
109. Carter, *Anthony Blunt*, 313. See also P. Ziegler, *King Edward VIII*, 551.
110. Costello, *Ten Days*, 367.
111. Ibid.
112. Note that certain British historians evaluating the German archives also pushed for the inclusion of the Windsor documents in the published volumes. See Wheeler-Bennett, *Friends, Enemies and Sovereigns*, 80–82. Most of the Windsor papers were published in *Documents on German Foreign Policy, 1918–1945, Series D, Vol. 10*.
113. Costello, *Ten Days*, 368. See more generally, A. Eckert, *Kampf um die Akten*.
114. Alford, *Spoils of World War II*, 122. Parker, *Prince Philip*, 104.
115. Alford, *Spoils of World War II*, 112.
116. "Tafelsilber der Bismarcks ausgegraben," in *Süddeutsche Zeitung* 165, 20 July 2000, 12.
117. Wolfgang Prinz von Hessen, *Aufzeichnungen*, 223. NARA, RG 260/OMGUS Education and Cultural Relations, box 226, Captain Ralph Brant to Commanding General, U.S. Forces European Theater, 6 May 1946.

118. American General Saunders, for example, requisitioned furniture and rugs from Kronberg for his official residence at Königstein, and by providing a receipt, this would appear to be consistent with U.S. policy. Heinrich Prinz von Hessen, *Kristallene Lüster*, 203. See also Petropoulos, "Postwar Justice and the Treatment of Nazis' Assets," in Petropoulos and Roth, eds., *Gray Zones.*

119. NARA, RG 260, OMGUS, Education and Cultural Relations Division, box 226, Lloyd Norman, "Royal German Silver Taken by War Department," *Chicago Tribune* (n.d., February 1946). Note that after World War I, the silver had been on display at a Berlin museum.

120. NARA, RG 260, OMGUS, Education and Cultural Relations Division, box 226, "Army Studies Status of Seized Silver," *Stars and Stripes*, 29 December 1946.

121. Günter Bischof quoted in Tim Golden, "G.I.'s Are Called Looters of Jewish Riches," *New York Times*, 15 October 1999, A1. See more generally, Akinsha, Kozlov, and Hochfield, *Beautiful Loot.*

122. NARA, RG 260, Ardelia Hall Collection, box 16: Maurice de Vienna to Captain Patrick Kelleher, 8 March 1946. See also Presidential Advisory Commission on Holocaust Assets in the United States, *Plunder and Restitution*, SR-119.

123. Alford, *Spoils of World War II*, 115.

124. Heinrich Prinz von Hessen, *Kristallene Lüster*, 101.

125. NARA, RG 260/OMGUS, Education and Cultural Relations, box 226, Edward Peck report to MFA&A Section, 25 September 1946.

126. Parker, *Prince Philip*, 104–5.

127. NARA, RG 260/OMGUS, Education and Cultural Relations, box 226, Captain Ralph Brant to Commanding General, U.S. Forces European Theater, 6 May 1946.

128. Wolfgang Prinz von Hessen, *Aufzeichnungen*, 225.

129. Heinrich Prinz von Hessen, *Kristallene Lüster*, 288.

130. NARA, RG 260/OMGUS, Education and Cultural Relations, box 226, Captain Ralph Brant to Commanding General, U.S. Forces European Theater, 6 May 1946.

131. Parker, *Prince Philip*, 105.

132. Wolfgang Prinz von Hessen, *Aufzeichnungen*, 225.

133. "Der Kronbergprozess," *Frankfurter Neuen Presse*, 1/41, 2 September 1946. See also Heinrich Prinz von Hessen, *Kristallene Lüster*, 291.

134. "Der Kronbergprozess."

135. Parker, *Prince Philip*, 105.

136. HStAD, 024 53/8, Ministerialrat Hesse to Oberfinanzrat Lucius, 5 August 1946. HStAD, 024 53/8, Oberfinanzrat Lucius to Ministerialrat Hesse, 8 August 1946. Wolfgang Prinz von Hessen, *Aufzeichnungen*, 226.

137. HStAD, 024 53/8, Ministerialrat Hesse to Oberregierungsrat Dr. Oppler, 5 August 1946.

138. Alford, *Spoils of World War II*, 124.

139. Wolfgang Prinz von Hessen, *Aufzeichnungen*, 227.

140. Ibid., 227–28. Parker, *Prince Philip*, 106.

141. David Hartley to National Personnel Records Center, n.d. (copy of letter in author's possession).
142. David Hartley to Professor Dr. Detlef Junker, n.d. (copy of letter in author's possession).
143. See Honan, *Treasure Hunt*.
144. Landgrave Moritz von Hessen to Dr. David Hartley, 7 July 1999 (copy of letter in author's possession).
145. Ibid.
146. Lesley, "Tante Mossy," *Times Literary Supplement* 2846, 14 September 1956, 539. See also the review of Richard Barkeley, *The Empress Friedrich* in *Times Literary Supplement* 2842, 17 August 1956, 481–82. Note that a number of German aristocratic women ended up marrying American soldiers: e.g., Marie Vassiltchikov married Peter Harnden from U.S. Intelligence; and her friend, Loremarie Schönburg, who also found work with the U.S. Army, married an American officer. Vassiltchikov. *Berlin Diaries*, 305–9.
147. Lesley, "Tante Mossy."
148. Heinrich Prinz von Hessen, *Kristallene Lüster*, 212.
149. Macdonogh, *Last Kaiser*, 459.
150. Browning, *Ordinary Men*; Goldhagen, *Hitler's Willing Executioners*.
151. Conze, "Adel und Adeligkeit im Widerstand," 291.
152. Hammerow, *On the Road to the Wolf's Lair*, 388–405. See also Ueberschär, ed., *Der 20. Juli 1944*.

CHAPTER 8

1. There have been many studies comparing the Weimar and Bonn republics, such as Allemann, *Bonn ist nicht Weimar*.
2. Mayer, *Persistence of the Old Regime*, 94. See also the specific case of Prince Louis Ferdinand von Preussen in Fenyvesi, *Royalty in Exile*, 83.
3. Marie Waldburg, "Society," *Bunte* 24 (2004): 116.
4. Vinen, *History in Fragments*, 185.
5. Naimark, *Russians in Germany*, 142–43. See also C. Goeschel, "Suicide at the End of the Third Reich," *Journal of Contemporary History* (forthcoming, 2006).
6. Fenyvesi, *Royalty in Exile*, 83.
7. N. Clarion, "Does Democracy Need Nazi Partners?" *Commentary* 7/4 (April 1949). Also, Bauerkämper, ed., *"Junkerland in Bauernhand"*?
8. Based in Owschlag, the Institut für Adelsforschung publishes an almanac, as well as the Deutsches Biographisches Adels-Repertorium. It also has an Internet site at http://tsx.de/adel.
9. McGee, *Berlin*, 12, 14. Ledanff, "The Palace of the Republic versus the Stadtschloss," *German Politics and Society* 21/4 (May 2004): 30–73.
10. McGee, *Berlin*, 18.
11. Ibid.

12. Ibid. The East German Communist Party was the Socialist Unity Party of Germany: Sozialistischer Einheitspartei Deutschlands or SED.

13. Ibid., 20.

14. Ibid., 22.

15. Ibid., 14.

16. Among the many websites that cover royalty, one finds the following: http://pages.prodigy.net/ptheroff/gotha.html; http://www.royalty.nu; http://www.worldroots.com; http://gsteinb.intrasun.tcnj.edu; http://www.royal.gov.uk; http://www.thePeerage.com; http://www.imperialcollegeofprincesandcourts.org.

17. Heinrich Prinz von Hessen, *Kristallene Lüster*, 214.

18. Ibid., 131.

19. Horowitz, "Italy Moves to End Exile of Its Princes," *Boston Sunday Globe* 262, 28 July 2002, A4; and Holley, "Exiled Italian Royal Family," *Los Angeles Times*, 24 December 2002.

20. Rainer von Hessen, "Hessische Hausstiftung," 4.

21. http://www.schloss-fasanerie.de. See also www.bornpower.de.

22. HHStAW, 520 D-Z, Nr. 519.563, statement of Princess Sophia, 15 July 1946.

23. Rainer von Hessen, "Hessische Hausstiftung," 5.

24. Author's visit to Schloss Fasanerie, 19 April 2001.

25. See, for example, "Landgraf Philipp von Hessen 60 Jahre," *Kasseler Post*, 6 November 1956; and "Landgraf Philipp von Hessen 70 Jahre," *Hessische Allgemeine Zeitung*, 5 November 1966.

26. Kronprinzessin Cecilie, *Erinnerungen*, 179–80.

27. Vassiltchikov, *Berlin Diaries*, 63.

28. HStAD, 024 53/9, [author's signature illegible], "Denkschrift über die Behandlung des Vermögens der Kurhessischen Hausstiftung," 24 August 1947.

29. Renkhoff, *Nassauische Biographie*, 317.

30. Landgrave Moritz von Hessen, interview with author, Kronberg, 23 July 2002.

31. Heinrich Prinz von Hessen, *Kristallene Lüster*, 66. See also Hania Heinzinger, "Prinz Heinrich von Hessen: Ich male mir den Schmerz von der Seele," *Frau im Spiegel* 13, 25 March 1993, 22–28.

32. The four children of Philipp and Mafalda are as follows: Prince Moritz (b. 1926), who became the head of the House of Hessen upon his father's death in October 1980; Heinrich von Hessen (1927–99), an artist and set-designer who never married; Otto (1937–98), who was born at the Villa Savoia in Rome and became an archeologist; Elisabeth (b. 1940), who was also born in Rome and later married Count Friedrich Karl von Oppersdorff (1925–85).

33. Courcy, *Diana Mosley*, 306.

34. RA, EDW/10,837: Oswald Mosley to Duke of Windsor, 3 January 1963.

35. D. Mosley, *Life of Contrasts*, 264–67. D. Mosley, *Duchess of Windsor*.

36. Mona Bismarck's brother-in-law, Prince Otto von Bismarck, was also in this circle: e.g., the duke and duchess visited on occasion at Friedrichsruh—including a Peasants's Ball (*Bauernball*) in the summer of 1966. RA, EDW/11,324, Otto von Bismarck to Duke of Windsor, 9 August 1966. Mona Bismarck

(née Williams), was a wealthy American who had lived in Capri with her husband Eddie. She was also a close friend of Peg von Hessen-Darmstadt.

37. Frey, ed., *Prominente ohne Maske*, 276.
38. "Landgraf Philipp. Morgen Beisetzung auf der Burg Kronberg," *Hessische Allgemeine Zeitung*, 31 October 1980.
39. Heinrich Prinz von Hessen, *Kristallene Lüster*; it appeared first in Italian in 1992 as *Il Lampe adario di Cristello*.
40. Heinrich Prinz von Hessen, *Kristallene Lüster*, 297.
41. Niethammer, *Mitläufer-fabrik*. See also Zentner and Bedürftig, eds., *Encyclopedia of the Third Reich*, 190.
42. Parker, *Prince Philip*, 91.
43. Kempner, *SS im Kreuzverhör*, 207–8.
44. Weiss, *Biographisches Lexicon*, 272–73.
45. RvH: Dr. jur. Hans-Georg Tovote to Spruchkammer Berlin, 6 March 1953.
46. PRO, FO 372/4831, Ernest August Duke of Brunswick to King George VI, 22 March 1946.
47. Ibid., Foreign Office to Political Adviser to Commander-in-Chief, Germany, 18 April 1946.
48. Ibid., P. J. Dixon to Sir Alan Lascelles, 17 April 1946.
49. Ibid., W. E. Beckett to G. G. Fitzmaurice, 15 April 1946. In early 1946, a British journalist who learned of the difficulties of Princess Hermine, the Kaiser's second wife, who had been captured by the Soviets in Frankfurt an der Oder, had written to Foreign Minister Bevin and King George VI. The response was basically the same, "It is not thought desirable for His Majesty's Government to take any action in this matter" and "any suggestion that we were hobnobbing with the German royal family would be eagerly seized on by the Russians or anyone else who likes to call us reactionary." PRO, FO 1049/475, Patrick Dean to Graham Scott, 1 August 1946 and Hillary Young to Cecil King, 14 January 1946. The Grand Duchess von Sachsen-Weimar (Feodora von Sachsen-Meiningen) and her daughter Sophie were also imprisoned in the Soviet zone in 1945 and in danger of being deported. Family members wrote to Queen Mary asking for her help, and she was also advised by the Foreign Office to do nothing.
50. Vickers, *Alice*, 321.
51. RA GeoV-CC, No 1452, Queen Mary to Princess Alice, 26 January 1946.
52. Vickers, *Alice*, 315, 321, 340.
53. Ibid., 327.
54. Ibid., 328.
55. Ibid., 345.
56. Ibid.
57. Shaw, *Royal Babylon*, 287.
58. Parker, *Prince Philip*, 134.
59. Vickers, *Alice*, 343.
60. Balfour and Mackay, *Paul of Yugoslavia*, 290, 297.
61. Parker, *Prince Philip*, 147. H.R.H. Prince Philip, Duke of Edinburgh, interview with author, Buckingham Palace, 3 March 2004.

62. Vickers, *Alice*, 348.

63. Ibid., 381.

64. H.R.H. Prince Philip, Duke of Edinburgh, interview with author, Buckingham Palace, 3 March 2004.

65. For more on "Moral Rearmament," see www.caux.ch/de/urspruenge.php.

66. Rainer von Hessen, telephone conversation with author, 9 September 2003.

67. Funck and Malinowski, "Masters of Memory: the Strategic Use of Autobiographical Memory by the German Nobility," in Fritzsche and Confino, eds., *Work of Memory*.

68. Wolfgang Prinz von Hessen, *Aufzeichnungen*, 232. Wolfgang was based at Schloss Kronberg, where he worked on his memoirs, until his death in 1989.

69. HHStAW, 520 F, Spruchkammer trial of Prince Wolfgang, ruling by the Zentral-Berufungskammer Hessen, 24 July 1950.

70. Rainer von Hessen to author, 20 April 2005.

71. See, for example, Rainer von Hessen, "Landgraf Carl von Hessen (1774–1836)," in Heinemeyer, *Hundert Jahre Historische Kommission*, 680–712. See also his translation and editing of the memoirs of Kurfürst Wilhelm, *Wir Wilhelm von Gottes Gnaden*, and his article in the volume he edited, *Victoria Kaiserin Friedrich*. Note that Rainer von Hessen also edited the memoirs of his uncle, Prince Wolfgang.

72. Rainer von Hessen to author, 2 December 2003.

73. Marie Waldburg, "In Bayern sind selbst Dackel königlich," *Bunte* 31, 24 July 2003, 28.

74. This theory is articulated in BAB, Kleine Erwerbungen 242/1: a "confidential report" (vertraulicher Bericht), by Henning Borcke, 30 April 1947. He notes that Junkers have become a kind of "whipping boy" (*Prügelknabe*).

75. Malinowski, *Vom König zum Führer*, 562.

76. "Kaiser and the Jews." See also Fenyvesi, *Royalty in Exile*, 80–84.

77. P. Ziegler, *Mountbatten*, 656.

78. Wheeler-Bennett, *King George VI*, 11.

79. "Voters Hand Prince Wide-Ranging Powers," *Los Angeles Times*, 17 March 2003, A5.

80. Otto von Habsburg (b. 1912) was a Christian Socialist Union member of the European Parliament from 1979 to 1999. His son, Karl von Habsburg, was a member from 1996 to 1999. Both have also served as president of the Pan-European Union of Austria. Among the websites devoted to them see http://www.tschwarzer.de/karl.htm and http://www.otto.tschwarzer.de.

81. Michael Nikbakhsh, "Ich bin Promi-Kandidat. Basta!" *Profil* 25, 15 June 2004, 34.

82. See Blacksell, Born, and Bohlander, "Settlement of Property Claims in Former East Germany," *Geographical Review* 86/2 (April 1996): 198–215.

83. Clem Cecil and Adam LeBor, "Aristocrats Fight for Return of Prague Castles," *The Times* (London), 17 May 2003.

84. CTK News Agency, "Disputes on Former Aristocratic Estates Still Unsettled," 2 July 2003.

85. Younge, "British Racism Can Be a Royal Pain," *Los Angeles Times*, 27 May 2004, B 13.

CONCLUSION

1. HRH Prince Philip, Duke of Edinburgh, interview with author, Buckingham Palace, 3 March 2004.
2. BAB, Sammlung Schumacher, R. 187/400, "Aufstellung derjenigen Parteigenossen, die Angehörige fürstlicher Häuser sind." See also Malinowski, *Vom König zum Führer*, 570.
3. Viktoria Luise, *Kaiser's Daughter*, 252.
4. Eckhart Franz to author, 4 February 2004.
5. Ibid.
6. Goethe quoted in Lincoln, *Romanovs*, 383–84.
7. HHStAW, 520 D-Z, Nr. 519.563, statement of Princess Margaret von Hessen-Darmstadt, 22 June 1946.
8. Dahrendorf, *Gesellschaft und Demokratie*, 464–80. See also Conze, "Adel und Adeligheit im Widerstand," 293.
9. See Martin Broszat's argument about the "historicization" of the Third Reich and Saul Friedländer's trenchant critique—that focusing on modernizing tendencies masks the epoch's murderous features—as well as Peter Baldwin's excellent analysis, in Baldwin, ed., *Reworking the Past*, 13–17, 77–134.
10. Heinrich Prinz von Hessen, *Kristallene Lüster*, 163.
11. Rogasch, *Schatzhäuser Deutschlands*, 41.
12. Cannadine, *Aspects of Aristocracy*, 157.
13. Ibid.
14. Steiner, *In Bluebeard's Castle*, 5–6.

Bibliography

Aalders, Gerard. *Geraubt! Die Enteignung jüdischen Besitzes im Zweiten Weltkrieg.* Cologne: Dittrich Verlag, 2000.

———. *Nazi Looting: the Plunder of Dutch Jewry During the Second World War.* Oxford: Berg, 2004.

"Adels-Hochzeit des Jahres: Fürsten und Prinzessinnen feierten drei Tage." *Bunte* 22 (22 May 2003).

Akinsha, Konstantin, Grigorii Kozlov, and Sylvia Hochfield. *Beautiful Loot: The Soviet Plunder of Europe's Art Treasures.* New York: Random House, 1995.

Albisetti, James. *Schooling German Girls and Women.* Princeton: Princeton University Press, 1988.

Alford, Kenneth D. *The Spoils of World War II: The American Military's Role in the Stealing of Europe's Treasures.* New York: Birch Lane Press, 1994.

Allemann, Fritz René. *Bonn ist nicht Weimar.* Cologne: Kiepenheuer & Witsch, 1956.

Allen, Martin. *Hidden Agenda: How the Duke of Windsor Betrayed the Allies.* London: Macmillan, 2000.

Allen, Peter. *The Crown and the Swastika: Hitler, Hess and the Duke of Windsor.* London: Robert Hale, 1983.

Almanach de Gotha: Annuaire Généalogique, Diplomatique et Statistique. Gotha: Justus Perthes, 1941.

Anfuso, Filippo. *Die beiden Gefreiten. Ihr Spiel um Deutschland und Italien.* Munich: Pohl, 1952.

Angrick, Andrej. "Erich von dem Bach-Zelewski: Himmlers Mann für all Fälle." In *Die SS: Elite Unter dem Totenkopf. 30 Lebensläufe*, edited by Ronald Smelser and Enrico Syring, 28–44. Paderborn: Schöningh, 2000.

Aretin, Erwein von. *Krone und Ketten: Erinnerungen eines bayerischen Edelmannes.* Munich: Süddeutscher Verlag, 1955.

———. *Wittelsbacher ins KZ.* Munich: Münchener Dom-Verlag, n.d.

Aronson, Theo. *The Coburgs of Belgium.* London: Cassell, 1968.

———. *The Kaisers.* London: Cassell, 1971.

Art Looting Investigation Unit. *Art Looting Investigation Unit Final Report.* Washington, DC: War Department, 1 May 1946.

Baader, Gerhard, Johannes Cramer, and Bettina Winter, eds. *"Verlegt nach Hadamar": Die Geschichte einer NS-"Euthanasie"-Anstalt.* Kassel: Eigenverlag des LWV Hessen, 1991.

Baden, Maximilian Prinz von. *Erinnerungen und Dokumente.* Edited by Golo Man and Andreas Burckhardt. Stuttgart: Ernst Klett, 1968.

Baer, Elizabeth, and Myrna Goldenberg, eds. *Experience and Expression: Women, the Nazis and the Holocaust.* Detroit: Wayne State University Press, 2003.

Bajohr, Frank. *Parvenüs und Profiteure. Korruption in der NS-Zeit.* Frankfurt: S. Fischer, 2001.

Baldwin, Peter. "The *Historikerstreit* in Context." In *Reworking the Past: Hitler, the Holocaust, and the Historians' Debate,* edited by Peter Baldwin, 3–37. Boston: Beacon Press, 1990.

Balfour, Neil, and Sally Mackay. *Paul of Yugoslavia: Britain's Maligned Friend.* London: Hamish Hamilton, 1980.

Bamford, James. *The Puzzle Palace: A Report on America's Most Secret Agency.* Boston: Houghton Mifflin, 1982.

Baranowski, Shelley. *The Sanctity of Rural Life: Nobility, Protestantism, and Nazism in Weimar Prussia.* New York: Oxford University Press, 1995.

Barneschi, Renato. *Frau von Weber: Vita e Morte di Mafalda di Savoia a Buchenwald.* Milan: Rusconi, 1982.

Barnett, Victoria. *Bystanders: Conscience and Complicity During the Holocaust.* Westport: Greenwood, 1999.

Barry, John. *The Great Influenza: The Epic Story of the Deadliest Plague in History.* New York: Viking, 2004.

Bassett, Richard. *Hitler's Spy Chief: The Wilhelm Canaris Mystery.* London: Weidenfeld & Nicolson, 2005.

Bauer, Yehuda. *Jews for Sale? Nazi-Jewish Negotiations, 1933–1945.* New Haven: Yale University Press, 1994.

Bauerkämper, Arnd, ed. *"Junkerland in Bauernhand"?: Durchführung, Auswirkungen, und Stellenwert der Bodenreform in der Sowjetischen Besatzungszone.* Stuttgart: F. Steiner, 1996.

Beaucamp, Eduard. "Vorsicht Getty! Was Raffael mit Holbein verbindet." *Frankfurter Allgemeine Zeitung,* 7 November 2002.

Below, Nicolaus von. *Als Hitlers Adjutant, 1937–1945.* Mainz: v. Hase & Koehler Verlag, 1980.

———. *At Hitler's Side: The Memoirs of Hitler's Luftwaffe Adjutant 1937–1945.* London: Greenhill, 2001.

Benedict, Susan. "Caring While Killing." In *Experience and Expression: Women, the Nazis and the Holocaust,* edited by Elizabeth Baer and Myrna Goldenberg. Detroit: Wayne State University Press, 2003, pages 95–110.

Berg, Stefan, and Sven Röbel. "Beutekunst: Von Sanssouci nach Moskau." *Der Spiegel* 38, 15 September 2003.

Bergen, Doris. *The Twisted Cross: The German Christian Movement in the Third Reich*. Chapel Hill: University of North Carolina Press, 1996.

Berghahn, Volker. *Der Stahlhelm—Bund der Frontsoldaten 1918–1935*. Düsseldorf: Droste, 1966.

"Bernhard (Prince): Royal Consort Who Admitted Taking Bribes Worth $1 million." *The Week*, 11 December 2004, 38.

Biographisch-Bibliographisches Kirchenlexikon. Munich: Verlag Traugott Bautz, 2004.

Birn, Ruth Bettina. *Die höheren SS- und Polizeiführer: Himmlers Vertreter im Reich und in den besetzten Gebieten*. Düsseldorf: Droste, 1986.

Black, Edwin. *IBM and the Holocaust*. New York: Random House, 2001.

Blacksell, M., K. M. Born, and M. Bohlander. "Settlement of Property Claims in Former East Germany." *Geographical Review* 86/2 (April 1996): 198–215.

Blandford, Edmund L. *SS Intelligence: The Nazi Secret Service*. Edison, NJ: Castle Books, 2000.

Bloch, Michael. *The Duke of Windsor's War*. London: Weidenfeld & Nicolson, 1982.

———. *Operation Willi: The Nazi Plot to Kidnap the Duke of Windsor*. New York: Weidenfeld & Nicolson, 1984.

———. *Ribbentrop*. London: Bantam Press, 1992.

———. *Secret File of the Duke of Windsor*. New York: Harper & Row, 1988.

———, ed. *Wallis and Edward: Letters, 1931–1937*. New York: Summit Books, 1986.

Boog, Horst. *Die Deutsche Luftwaffeführung 1935–1945*. Stuttgart, Deutsche Verlags-Anstalt, 1982.

Bosworth, R. J. B. *Mussolini*. London: Arnold, 2002.

Bracher, Karl Dietrich. *Die Auflösung der Weimarer Republik*. Villingen: Ring Verlag, 1964.

Bradford, Sarah. *George VI*. London: Weidenfeld & Nicolson, 1989.

Bramwell, Anna. *Blood and Soil: Walter Darré and Hitler's Green Party*. Abbotsbrook: Kensal House, 1985.

Brendon, Piers, and Philip Whitehead. *The Windsors: A Dynasty Revealed, 1917–2000*. London: Pimlico, 2000.

Brooks, David. *Bobos in Paradise: The New Upper Class and How They Got There*. New York: Simon & Schuster, 2000.

Brose, Eric Dorn. *The Kaiser's Army: The Politics of Military Technology in Germany During the Machine Age*. Oxford: Oxford University Press, 2001.

Brown, Anthony Cave. "Introduction." In *Hostage of the Third Reich: The Story of My Imprisonment and Rescue from the SS*, by Fey von Hassell. New York: Charles Scribner's Sons, 1989.

Browning, Christopher. *Nazi Policy, Jewish Workers, German Killers*. Cambridge: Cambridge University Press, 2000.

———. *Ordinary Men: Reserve Police Battalion 101 and the Final Solution in Poland*. New York: HarperPerennial, 1998 (1992).

Brysac, Shareen Blair. *Resisting Hitler: Mildred Harnack and the Red Orchestra*. Oxford: Oxford University Press, 2000.

Bullock, Alan. *Hitler: A Study in Tyranny*. London: Odhams Press, 1959. 1st edition 1952.

———. "Introduction." In *The Schellenberg Memoirs*, by Walter Schellenberg. London: Andre Deutsche, 1956.

Burleigh, Michael. *Death and Deliverance: "Euthanasia" in Germany, 1900–1945*. London: Pan, 2002.

Cahill, Richard Andrew. *Philipp of Hesse and the Reformation*. Mainz: Philipp von Zabern, 2001.

Campbell, Bruce. *The SA Generals and the Rise of Nazism*. Lexington: University Press of Kentucky, 1998.

Campini, Dino. *La Principessa Martire: Mafalda di Savoia*. Milan: E.L.I., 1955.

Cannadine, David. *Aspects of Aristocracy: Grandeur and Decline in Modern Britain*. New Haven: Yale University Press, 1994.

Cannadine, David, and Simon Price, eds. *Rituals of Royalty: Power and Ceremonial in Traditional Societies*. Cambridge: Cambridge University Press, 1987.

Caplan, Jane. *Government Without Administration: State and Civil Service in Weimar and Nazi Germany*. New York: Oxford University Press, 1988.

Carter, Miranda. *Anthony Blunt: His Lives*. New York: Farrar, Straus & Giroux, 2001.

Cecil, Clem, and Adam LeBor. "Aristocrats Fight for Return of Prague Castles." *The Times* (London), 17 May 2003.

Churchill, Winston. *My Early Life: A Roving Commission*. London: T. Butterworth, 1930.

Ciano, Galeazzo. *Hidden Diary, 1937–1938*. New York: Dutton, 1953.

Clarion, Nicolas. "Does Democracy Need Nazi Partners?" *Commentary* 7/4 (April 1949).

Conway, John. Review of Beth Griech-Polelle, *Bishop von Galen: German Catholicism and National Socialism*. New Haven: Yale University Press, 2002; H-German, April 2003.

Conze, Eckart. "Adel und Adeligkeit im Widerstand des 20. Juli 1944." In *Adel und Bürgertum in Deutschland III*, edited by Heinz Reif, 269–95. Berlin: Akademie Verlag, 2001.

———. *Von Deutschem Adel. Die Grafen von Bernstorff im zwanzigsten Jahrhundert*. Stuttgart: Deutsche Verlags-Anstalt, 2000.

Conze, Eckart, and Monika Wienfort, eds. *Adel und Moderne. Deutschland im europäischen Vergleich im 19. und 20. Jahrhundert*. Cologne: Böhlau, 2004.

Cookridge, E. H. *From Battenberg to Mountbatten*. New York: John Day, 1968.

Corvaja, Santi. *Hitler and Mussolini: The Secret Meetings*. New York: Enigma Books, 2001.

Cooper, Duff (Viscount Norwich). *Old Men Forget: An Autobiography of Duff Cooper*. London: Rupert Hart-Davis, 1953.

Costello, John. *Ten Days to Destiny: The Secret Story of the Hess Peace Initiative and British Efforts to Strike a Deal With Hitler*. New York: William Morrow, 1991.

Courcy, Anne de. *Diana Mosley: Mitford Beauty, British Fascist, Hitler's Angel*. New York: William Morrow, 2003.

———. *1939: The Last Season*. London: Thames & Hudson, 1989.

Craig, Gordon. *The Politics of the Prussian Army, 1640–1945*. Oxford: Oxford University Press, 1955.

Crankshaw, Edward. *The Fall of the House of Habsburg*. London: Penguin, 1963.

Cuneliffe-Owen, Frederick. "Kaiser's Nephew Departs." *New York Times*, 22 March 1924, 14.

———. "Wolfgang of Hesse: A Rich, Royal Twin." *New York Times*, 9 March 1924, 5.

Dahlerus, Johann Birger. *Der letzte Versuch: London-Berlin, Sommer 1939*. Munich: Nymphenburg Verlagshandlung, 1948.

Dahm, Volker. "Der Terrorapparat." In *Die Tödliche Utopie. Bilder, Texte, Dokumente, Daten zum Dritten Reich*, edited by Horst Müller et al. Munich: Institut für Zeitgeschichte, 2001, pages 91–172.

Dahrendorf, Ralf. *Gesellschaft und Demokratie in Deutschland*. Munich: Piper, 1965.

Dalley, Jan. *Diana Mosley*. New York: Alfred Knopf, 2000.

Denham, Scott, Irene Kacandes, and Jonathan Petropoulos, eds. *A User's Guide to German Cultural Studies*. Ann Arbor: University of Michigan Press, 1997.

Dettmar, Werner. *Die Zerstörung Kassels im Oktober 1943: eine Dokumentation*. Fuldabrück: Hesse, 1983.

Devere-Summers, Anthony. *War and the Royal Houses of Europe in the Twentieth Century*. New York: Arms & Armour Press, 1996.

Diels, Rudolf. *Lucifer ante portas: von Severing bis Heydrich*. Zurich: Interverlag, 1950.

Dienstaltersliste der Schutzstaffel der NSDAP. Berlin: Reichsdruckerei, 1938.

Dimitroff, Pashanko. *Boris III of Bulgaria: Toiler, Citizen, King*. Lewes: Book Guild, 1986.

Documents on German Foreign Policy, 1918–1945, Series C, Vol. 4. London: His Majesty's Stationery Office, 1950.

Documents on German Foreign Policy, 1918–1945, Series D, Vol. 10. London: His Majesty's Stationery Office, 1950.

Dodd, Martha. *Through Embassy Eyes*. New York: Harcourt, Brace, 1939.

Dodd, William, and Martha Dodd. *Ambassador Dodd's Diary, 1933–1938*. London: Victor Gallancz, 1941.

Donaldson, Frances. *Edward VIII*. London: Weidenfeld & Nicolson, 1974.

Dönhoff, Marion Gräfin von. *Um der Ehre Willen: Erinnerungen an die Freunde vom 20. Juli*. Berlin: Siedler Verlag, 1994.

Dönhoff, Marion Gräfin von, and Richard von Weizsäcker. "Wider die Selbstgerechtigkeit der Nachgeborenen: Wehrmachtsverbrechen und die Männer des 20. Juli." *Die Zeit* 11, 8 March 1996, 63.

Dorril, Stephen. *Blackshirt: Sir Oswald Mosley and British Fascism*. London: Penguin, 2005.

Duff, David. *Hessian Tapestry*. London: Frederick Muller, 1967.

Easton, Laird Mcleod. *The Red Count: The Life and Times of Count Harry Kessler*. Berkeley: University of California Press, 2003.

Eatwell, Roger. *Fascism: A History*. New York: Penguin Books, 1995.

Ebert, Friedrich. *Friedrich Ebert, 1871–1927*. Bonn: Inter Nationes, 1971.

Eckert, Astrid. *Kampf um die Akten: Die Westalliierten und die Rückgabe von deutschem Archivgut nach dem Zweiten Weltkrieg*. Stuttgart: F. Steiner, 2004.

Eckert, Jörn. *Der Kampf um die Fideikommisse in Deutschland.* Frankfurt: Peter Lang, 1992.

Eghigian, Greg, and Matthew Paul Berg, eds., *Sacrifice and National Belonging in Twentieth-Century Germany.* Arlington: Texas A & M University Press, 2002.

Eilers, Marlene. *Queen Victoria's Descendants.* New York: Altantic International, 1987.

Ellinghaus, Wilhelm. "Der Prinz, der Hitlers Werkzeug war," *Hannoversche Presse,* 27 March 1948.

Elon, Amos. *The Pity of It All: A History of Jews in Germany, 1743–1933.* New York: Metropolitan Books, 2002.

Enigl, Marianne. "Der Adel und die Nazis." *Profil* 22, 24 May 2004, 34–42.

Evans, Richard. *The Coming of the Third Reich.* London: Allen Lane, 2003.

———. *Telling Lies About Hitler: The Holocaust, History, and the David Irving Trial.* London: Verso, 2002.

Evans, Rob, and David Hencke. "Hitler Saw Duke of Windsor as 'no enemy' US File Reveals." *Manchester Guardian,* 25 June 2003, 1.

———. "Wallis Simpson, the Nazi Minister, the Telltale Monk, and an FBI Plot." *Manchester Guardian,* 29 June 2002, 1.

Eyck, Erich. *A History of the Weimar Republic.* Cambridge: Harvard University Press, 1964.

Faison, S. Lane Jr. *Consolidated Interrogation Report No. 4: Linz: Hitler's Museum and Library.* Washington, DC: Strategic Service Unit, 1945.

———. *Supplement to Consolidated Interrogation Report No. 4: Linz: Hitler's Museum and Library.* Washington, DC: Strategic Service Unit, 1946.

Farago, Ladislas, and Andrew Sinclair. *Royal Web: The Story of Princess Victoria and Frederick of Prussia.* New York: McGraw Hill, 1982.

Feldman, Gerald. "A Collapse in Weimar Scholarship." *Central European History* 18 (June 1984): 159–77, 245–67.

———. *The Great Disorder: Politics, Economics, and Society in the German Inflation, 1914–1924.* New York: Oxford University Press, 1993.

Feliciano, Hector. *The Lost Museum: The Nazi Conspiracy to Steal the World's Greatest Works of Art.* New York: Basic Books, 1997.

Fenyvesi, Charles. *Royalty in Exile.* London: Robson Books, 1981.

Ferguson, Niall. "Das Haus Sachsen-Coburg und die europäische Politik des 19. Jahrhunderts." In *Victoria Kaiserin Friedrich (1840–1901). Mission und Schicksal einer englischen Prinzessin in Deutschland,* edited by Rainer von Hessen, 27–48. Frankfurt: Campus Verlag, 2002.

———. *The House of Rothschild: Money's Prophets, 1798–1848.* New York: Penguin Books, 1998.

———. *The House of Rothschild: The World's Banker, 1848–1999.* New York: Penguin Books, 1998.

———. *The Pity of War.* New York: Basic Books, 1999.

Fest, Joachim. *Hitler.* New York: Vintage, 1975.

Feuchtwanger, E. J. *From Weimar to Hitler: Germany, 1918–1933.* New York: St. Martin's Press, 1993.

Flanner, Janet. *Men and Monuments.* New York: Harper & Row, 1957.

Flicke, Wilhelm. *War Secrets in the Ether.* 2 vols. Laguna Hills: Aegean Park Press, 1977.

Fox, James. "The Oddest Couple." *Vanity Fair*, August 2003, 200–290.

Fraenkel, Ernst. *Military Occupation and the Rule of Law: the Occupation Government of the Rhineland, 1918–1923*. London: Oxford University Press, 1944.

Francini, Esther Tisa, Anja Heuss, and Georg Kreis. *Fluchtgut—Raubgut: Der Transfer von Kulturgütern in und über die Schweiz 1933–1945 und die Frage der Restitution*. Zürich: Chronos Verlag, 2001.

Franz, Eckhart, ed. *Erinnertes: Aufzeichnungen des letzten Grossherzhogs Ernst Ludwig von Hessen und bei Rhein*. Darmstadt: Eduard Roether Verlag, 1983.

———, ed. *Friede durch geistige Erneuerung: Fritz von Unruh und Grossherzog Ernst Ludwig von Hessen*. Darmstadt: Justus von Liebig Verlag, 1987.

Franz, Eckhart, and Hans-Peter Lachmann, eds. *Das kulturelle Erbe des Hauses Hessen*. Marburg: Historische Kommission für Hessen, 2002.

Frei, Norbert. *Adenauer's Germany and the Nazi Past: The Politics of Amnesty and Integration*. New York: Columbia University Press, 2002.

———. *Karrieren im Zwielicht. Hitlers Eliten nach 1945*. Frankfurt: Campus, 2001.

———. *1945 und Wir. Das Dritte Reich im Bewusstsein der Deutschen*. Munich: C. H. Beck, 2005.

Frey, Gerhard, ed. *Prominente ohne Maske*. Munich: FZ-Verlag, 1985.

Friedlander, Henry. "Der deutsche Strafprozess als historische Quelle." In *Keine "Abrechnung": NS-Verbrechen, Justiz und Gesellschaft in Europa nach 1945*, edited by Claudia Kuretsidis-Haider and Winfried Garscha. Vienna: Akademische Verlagsanstalt, 1998.

———. *The Origins of Nazi Genocide: From Euthanasia to the Final Solution*. Chapel Hill: University of North Carolina Press, 1995.

Friedman, Jonathan. *The Lion and the Star: Gentile-Jewish Relations in Three Hessian Communities, 1919–1945*. Lexington: University of Kentucky Press, 1998.

Friedrich, Jörg. *Der Brand. Deutschland im Bombenkrieg 1940–1945*. Berlin: Propyläen, 2002.

Friedrich, Otto. *Before the Deluge: A Portrait of Berlin in the 1920s*. New York: HarperPerennial, 1995.

Friderici, Robert. *1866: Bismarcks Okkupation und Annexion Kurhessens*. Kassel: Georg Wenderoth Verlag, 1989.

Frischauer, Willi. *Goering*. London: Odhams Press, 1951.

Fritzsche, Peter. *A Nation of Fliers: German Aviation and Popular Imagination*. Cambridge: Harvard University Press, 1992.

Fritzsche, Peter, and Alon Confino, eds. *The Work of Memory: New Directions in the Study of German Society and Culture*. Urbana: University of Illinois Press, 2002.

Fromm, Bella. *Blood and Banquets: A Berlin Social Diary*. 1943. Reprint, New York: Kensington, 2002.

Fulford, Roger. *Friedrichshof: The Home of Empress Frederick*. Regensburg: Verlag Schnell & Steiner, 1997.

Funck, Marcus. "The Meaning of Dying: East Elbian Noble Families as 'Warrior-Tribes.'" In *Sacrifice and National Belonging in Twentieth-Century Germany*, edited by Greg Eghigian and Matthew Paul Berg. Arlington: Texas A & M University Press, 2002.

———. "Shock und Chance. Der Preussische Militäradel in der Weimarer Republik zwischen Stand und Profession." In *Adel und Bürgertum in Deutschland II*, edited by Hans Reif. Berlin: Akademie Verlag, 2001.

Funck, Marcus, and Stephan Malinowski. "Masters of Memory: the Strategic Use of Autobiographical Memory by the German Nobility." In *The Work of Memory: New Directions in the Study of German Society and Culture*, edited by Peter Fritzsche and Alon Confino. Urbana: University of Illinois Press, 2002, pages 86–103.

Gallus, Alexander. "Biographik und Zeitgeschichte." *Aus Politik und Zeitgeschichte* 1–2 (January 2005): 40–46.

Gellately, Robert. *Backing Hitler: Consent and Coercion in Nazi Germany*. Oxford: Oxford University Press, 2001.

———. *The Gestapo and German Society: Enforcing Racial Policy, 1933–1945*. New York: Oxford University Press, 1990.

———, ed. *The Nuremberg Interviews. Conducted by Leon Goldensohn*. New York: Alfred Knopf, 2004.

Gellermann, Günther. *Geheime Wege zum Frieden mit England: Ausgewählte Initiativen zur Beendung des Krieges, 1940–1942*. Bonn: Bernard & Graefe, 1995.

———. *. . . und lauschten für Hitler. Geheime Reichssache: Die Abhörzentralen des Dritten Reiches*. Bonn: Bernard & Graefe, 1991.

Gercke, Peter. "Die Antikensammlung." *Kunst in Hessen und am Mittelrhein* 28 (1998): 95–106.

Gerlach, Christian. "German Economic Interest, Occupation Policy, and the Murder of the Jews in Belorussia, 1941–1943." In *National Socialist Extermination Policies*, edited by Ulrich Herbert. New York: Berghahn Books, 2000.

———. "Men of 20 July and the War in the Soviet Union." In *War of Extermination: The German Military in World War II, 1941–1944*, edited by Hannes Heer and Klaus Naumann, 127–45. New York: Berghahn Books, 2000.

Gilbert, Felix. *Finest Hour*. London: Heinemann, 1983.

———. *Hitler Directs His War: The Secret Records of his Daily Military Conferences*. New York: Oxford University Press, 1950.

Giles, Geoffrey. "A Gray Zone Among the Field Gray Men: Confusion in the Discrimination against Homosexuals in the *Wehrmacht*." In *Gray Zones: Ambiguity and Compromise in the Holocaust and Its Aftermath*, edited by Jonathan Petropoulos and John Roth. New York: Berghahn Books, 2005, pages 127–46.

———. "Who Owns the Past? The Surrender of the Berlin Document Center." In *A User's Guide to German Cultural Studies*, edited by Scott Denham, Irene Kacandes, and Jonathan Petropoulos, 377–88. Ann Arbor: University of Michigan Press, 1997.

———. "Why Bother About Homosexuals? Homophobia and Sexual Politics in Nazi Germany." Washington, DC: United States Holocaust Memorial Museum, 2002.

Goebbels, Joseph. *Die Tagebücher von Joseph Goebbels. Sämtliche Fragmente*. Edited by Elke Fröhlich. Munich: K. G. Sauer, 1987.

Golden, Tim. "G.I.'s Are Called Looters of Jewish Riches." *New York Times*, 15 October 1999, A1.

Goldhagen, Daniel Jonah. *Hitler's Willing Executioners: Ordinary Germans and the Holocaust*. New York: Alfred Knopf, 1996.

Göring, Emmy. *An der Seite meines Mannes*. Göttingen: Schültz, 1967.

Görlitz, Walter. *Die Junker. Adel und Bauer im deutschen Osten*. Limburg: Starke Verlag, 1964.

Göttert, Margit. "Victoria und die deutsche Frauenbewegung." In *Victoria Kaiserin Friedrich (1840–1901). Mission und Schicksal einer englischen Prinzessin in Deutschland*, edited by Rainer von Hessen, 94–112. Frankfurt: Campus Verlag, 2002.

Graber, G. S. *History of the SS*. New York: David McKay, 1978.

"Greatest Holbein for Sale." *Art Newspaper* 124, April 2002.

Green, Peter. "Habsburgs Ask Austria to Return Estates Seized by Nazis." *New York Times*, 10 May 2003.

Griech-Polelle, Beth. *Bishop von Galen: German Catholicism and National Socialism*. New Haven: Yale University Press, 2002.

Groueff, Stéphane. *Crown of Thorns: The Reign of King Boris III of Bulgaria, 1918–1943*. Lanham, DM: Madison Books, 1987.

Guenther, Irene. *Nazi 'Chic'? Fashioning Women in the Third Reich*. Oxford: Berg, 2004.

Guinness, Jonathan, and Catherine Guinness. *The House of Mitford*. New York: Penguin, 1984.

Guppy, Shusha. *Looking Back: A Panoramic View of a Literary Age by the Grandes Dames of European Letters*. Latham: Paris Review Editions, 1991.

Haase, Günther. *Kunstraub und Kunstschutz: Eine Dokumentation*. Hildesheim: Georg Olms, 1991.

Hackett, David, ed. *The Buchenwald Report*. Boulder: Westview Press, 1995.

"Haderlumpen, Diese." *Der Spiegel* 31, 30 July 1979, 60–66.

Hagen, William. *Germans, Poles and Jews: The Nationality Conflict in the Prussian East, 1772–1914*. Chicago: University of Chicago Press, 1980.

Hamburger Institut für Sozialforschung. *Verbrechen der Wehrmacht: Dimensionen des Vernichtungskrieges 1941–1944*. Hamburg: Hamburger Edition, 2002.

Hamilton, Richard. *Who Voted for Hitler?* Princeton: Princeton University Press, 1982.

Hamann, Brigitte. *Winifred Wagner: A Life at the Heart of Hitler's Bayreuth*. London: Granta, 2005.

Hammerow, Theodore. *On the Road to the Wolf's Lair: German Resistance to Hitler*. Cambridge: Harvard University Press, 1997.

Hancock, Eleanor. " 'Only the Real, the True, the Masculine Held Its Value': Ernst Röhm, Masculinity, and Male Homosexuality." *Journal of the History of Sexuality* 8/4 (April 1998).

Hanfstaengl, Ernst. *Unheard Witness*. Philadelphia: J. B. Lippincott, 1957.

Harding, Luke. "A Rubens is Recovered." *ARTnews* (November 2003): 70.

Hart-Davis, Rupert, ed. *Siegfried Sassoon Diaries, 1920–1922*. London: Faber & Faber, 1981.

Hassell, Fey von. *Hostage of the Third Reich: The Story of My Imprisonment and Rescue from the SS*. New York: Charles Scribner's Sons, 1989.

Hassell, Ulrich von. *Die Hassell-Tagebücher. Aufzeichnungen von andern Deutschland, 1938–1944*. Berlin: Siedler, 1988.

Hatch, Alden. *H.R.H. Prince Bernhard of the Netherlands: An Authorized Biography*. New York: Harrap, 1962.

Hauser, Oswald. *England und das Dritte Reich. Erster Band, 1933 bis 1936.* Stuttgart: Seewald Verlag, 1972.

———. *England und das Dritte Reich. Zweiter Band, 1936 bis 1938.* Göttingen: Muster-Schmidt Verlag, 1982.

Hayes, Peter. *Industry and Ideology: IG Farben in the Nazi Era.* Cambridge: Cambridge University Press, 1987.

Heberer, Patricia. "'*Exitus Heute* in Hadamar': The Hadamar Facility and 'Euthanasia' in Nazi Germany." PhD diss., University of Maryland, 2001.

Heer, Hannes, and Klaus Naumann, eds. *War of Extermination: The German Military in World War II, 1941–1944.* New York: Berghahn Books, 2000.

Heineman, Elizabeth. "Sexuality and Nazism: The Doubly Unspeakable?" *Journal of the History of Sexuality* 11:1/2 (January/April 2002).

Heinemann, Christine, ed. *Neunhundert Jahre Geschichte der Juden in Hessen.* Wiesbaden: Kommission für die Geschichte der Juden in Hessen, 1983.

Henderson, Nevile. *Failure of a Mission. Berlin, 1937–1939.* London: Hodder & Stoughton, 1940.

Hennig, Eike, ed. *Hessen unterm Hakenkreuz. Studien zur Durchsetzung der NSDAP in Hessen.* Frankfurt: Insel Verlag, 1983.

Herbert, Ulrich. *Best. Biographische Studien über Radikalismus, Weltanschauung und Vernunft, 1903–1989.* Bonn: J. H. W. Dietz, 1996.

———. "Extermination Policy: New Answers and Questions about the History of the 'Holocaust' in German Historiography." In Herbert. *National Socialist Extermination Policies*, pages 1–52.

———, ed. *National Socialist Extermination Policies. Contemporary German Perspectives and Controversies.* New York: Berghahn Books, 2000.

Herf, Jeffrey. *Reactionary Modernism: Technology, Culture and Politics in Weimar and the Third Reich.* Cambridge, MA: Harvard University Press, 1984.

Herre, Paul. *Kronprinz Wilhelm. Seine Rolle in der deutschen Politik.* Munich: C. H. Beck, 1954.

Herzstein, Robert Edwin. *The War That Hitler Won: The Most Infamous Propaganda Campaign in History.* London: Hamish Hamilton, 1979.

Hessen, Heinrich Prinz von. *Der kristallene Lüster. Meine deutsch-Italienische Jugend.* Munich: Piper, 1994.

Hessen, Rainer von. "Einführung." In *Victoria Kaiserin Friedrich: Mission und Schicksal einer englischen Prinzessin in Deutschland,* edited by Rainer von Hessen. Frankfurt: Campus Verlag, 2002, pages 11–26.

———. "Friedrichshof: 'A Country Home.' Der Witwensitz der Kaiserin Friedrich in Kronberg (Taunus)." In *Das kulturelle Erbe des Hauses Hessen,* edited by Eckhart Franz and Hans-Peter Lachmann, 123–30. Marburg: Historische Kommission für Hessen, 2002).

———. "Die Hessische Hausstiftung als Kulturstiftung: Festrede, gehalten anlässlich des siebzigjährigen Jubiläums der Hessischen Hausstiftung" (unpublished lecture, Kronberg, 1998).

———. "Landgraf Carl von Hessen (1774–1836): Eine Reise durch Freimauerei und Geheimwissenschaften." In *Hundert Jahre Historische Kommission für Hessen, 1897–1997,* edited by Walter Heinemeyer. Marburg: N.C. Elwert, 1997.

———, ed. and trans. *Wir Wilhelm von Gottes Gnaden: Die Lebenserinnerungen Kurfürst Wilhelms I. von Hessen, 1743–1821*. Frankfurt: Campus Verlag, 1996.

Hessen, Wolfgang Prinz von. *Aufzeichnungen*. Edited by Rainer von Hessen. Kronberg: Privatdruck, 1986.

Hett, Ulrike, and Johannes Tuchel. "Die Reaktionen des NS-Staates auf den Umsturzversuch vom 20. Juli 1944." In *Widerstand gegen Nationalsozialismus*, edited by Peter Steinbach and Johannes Tuchel, 377–89. Berlin: Akademie Verlag, 1994.

Heuberger, Georg, ed. *The Rothschilds: Essays on the History of a European Family*. Woodbridge: Boydell & Brewer, 1995.

Higham, Charles. *The Duchess of Windsor: The Secret Life*. New York: McGraw Hill, 1988.

———. *Mrs. Simpson: Secret Lives of the Duchess of Windsor*. London: Sidgwick & Jackson, 2004.

Hilberg, Raul. *Sources of Holocaust Research: An Analysis*. Chicago: Ivan Dee, 2001.

Hoare, Philip. *Serious Pleasures: The Life of Stephen Tennant*. London: Hamish Hamilton, 1990.

Hoettl, Wilhelm. *The Secret Front: The Story of Nazi Political Espionage*. London: Weidenfeld & Nicolson, 1953.

Hoffmann, Peter. *The History of the German Resistance, 1933–1945*. Cambridge, MA: MIT Press, 1977.

Höhne, Heinz. *Canaris*. London: Secker & Warburg, 1979.

———. *The Order of the Death's Head: The Story of Hitler's SS*. New York: Penguin, 2000 (1967).

Holley, David. "Exiled Italian Royal Family Makes Lightning Visit to Homeland." *Los Angeles Times*, 24 December 2002.

Honan, William. *Treasure Hunt: A New York Times Reporter Tracks the Quedlinburg Hoard*. New York: Delta, 1997.

Horowitz, Jason. "Italy Moves to End Exile of Its Princes," *Boston Sunday Globe* 262, 28 July 2002.

Hoyningen-Huene, Iris Freifrau von. *Adel in der Weimarer Republik*. Limburg: C. A. Starke Verlag, 1992.

Huberty, Michel. *L'Allemagne dynastique*. Le Perreux: A. Giraud, 1976.

Huldén, Anders. *Finnlands Deutsches Königsabenteuer 1918*. Reinbek: Traute Warnke Verlag, 1997.

Hüser, Karl, ed. *Wewelsburg 1933 bis 1945: Kult- und Terrorstätte der SS. Eine Dokumentation*. Paderborn: Verlag Bonifatius, 1982.

Hüttenberger, Peter. *Die Gauleiter: Studie zur Wandel der Machtgefüges in der NSDAP*. Stuttgart: Deutsche Verlags-Anstalt, 1969.

Ilsemann, Sigurd von. *Der Kaiser in Holland: Amerongen und Doorn, 1918–1933*. Munich: Biederstein Verlag, 1967.

———. *Der Kaiser in Holland: Monarchie und Nationalsozialismus, 1924–1941*. Munich: Biderstein Verlag, 1968.

International Military Tribunal. *Trial of the Major War Criminals*. Nuremberg: International Military Tribunal, 1948.

Irving, David. *Das Reich hört mit. Görings "Forschungsamt": Der geheimste Nachrichtendienst des Dritten Reiches*. Kiel: Arndt, 1989.

————. *Breach of Security: The German Secret Intelligence File on Events Leading to the Second World War*. London: William Kimber, 1968.

————. *Göring*. Munich: Albrecht Knaus, 1986.

Ishiguro, Kazuo. *The Remains of the Day*. New York: Vintage International, 1989.

Jacobson, Hans-Adolf. "Zur Rolle der Diplomatie im Dritten Reich." In *Das Diplomatische Korps, 1871–1945*, edited by Klaus Schwabe. Boppard: Harald Boldt Verlag, 1985.

Jakobs, Tino. *Himmlers Mann in Hamburg: Georg Henning Graf von Bassewitz-Behr als höher SS- und Polizeiführer im Wehrkreis X, 1933–1945*. Hamburg: Ergebnisse-Verlag, 2001.

James, Robert Rhodes, ed. *"Chips": The Diaries of Sir Henry Channon*. London: Phoenix, 1993.

Jane's All the World's Aircraft. London: Sampson, Low, Marstron & Co., 1943.

Jangfeldt, Bengt. *En Osalig Ande. Berättelsen om Axel Munthe*. Stockholm: Wahlstrom & Widstrand, 2003.

Jonas, Klaus. *The Life of Crown Prince William*. London: Routledge & Kegan Paul, 1961.

Jukie, Ilija. *The Fall of Yugoslavia*. New York: Harcourt Brace, Jovanovich, 1971.

Kahn, David. *The Codebreakers: The Story of Secret Writing*. New York: Scribner, 1996.

Kammler, Jörg, and others, ed. *Volksgemeinschaft und Volksfeinde: Kassel, 1933–1945. Eine Dokumentation*. Fuldabrück: Druckerei Hesse, 1984.

————. *Hitler's Spies: German Military Intelligence During World War II*. New York: Macmillan, 1978.

Kater, Michael. *Das "Ahnenerbe" der SS 1935–45: Ein Beitrag zur Kulturpolitik des Dritten Reiches*. 2nd ed. Munich: R. Oldenbourg, 1997.

————. *Doctors under Hitler*. Chapel Hill: University of North Carolina Press, 1989.

————. *The Nazi Party: A Social Profile of Members and Leaders, 1919–1945*. Oxford: Blackwell, 1983.

————. "Zum gegenseitigen Verhältnis von SA und SS in der Sozialgeschichte des Nationalsozialismus von 1925 bis 1939." *Vierteljahrshefte für Sozial- und Wirtschaftsgeschichte* 2 (1975): 330–50.

Katz, Robert. *The Battle for Rome*. New York: Simon & Schuster, 2003.

————. *The Fall of the House of Savoy*. London: Allen & Unwin, 1971.

Kaufmann, Walter. *Monarchism in the Weimar Republic*. New York: Bookman, 1953.

Keil, Lars-Broder, and Sven Felix Kellerhoff. *Deutsche Legenden: Vom "Dolchstoss" und anderen Mythen der Geschichte*. Berlin: Ch. Links, 2002.

Kempner, Robert. *Das Dritte Reich im Kreuzverhör. Aus dem unveröffentlichen Vernehmungsprotokollen des Anklägers*. Munich: Bechtle, 1969.

————. *SS im Kreuzverhör*. Munich: Rütten & Loening, Verlag, 1964.

Kershaw, Ian. *Hitler, 1889–1936: Hubris*. London: Allen Lane, 1998.

————. *Hitler, 1936–1945: Nemesis*. New York: W. W. Norton, 2000.

————. *Making Friends with Hitler: Lord Londonderry and Britain's Road to War*. London: Allen Lane, 2004.

Kessler, Count Harry. *Diaries of a Cosmopolitan*. London: Weidenfeld & Nicholson, 1971.

King, Greg. *The Duchess of Windsor: The Uncommon Life of Wallis Simpson*. London: Aurum, 1999.

King, Stella. *Princess Marina: Her Life and Times*. London: Cassell, 1969.

Kingreen, Monica, ed. *"Nach kristallnacht": Jüdisches Leben und antijüdische Politik in Frankfurt am Main, 1938–1945*. Frankfurt: Fritz Bauer Institut, 1999.

———. "Wie sich Museen Kunst aus jüdischem Besitz aneigneten. Städte als skrupellose Profiteure der Vertreibungs- und Vernichtungspolitik der NS-Staates: das Beispiel Frankfurt am Main." *Frankfurter Rundschau*, 8 May 2000.

Kintner, Earl, ed. *Trial of Alfons Klein, Adolf Washlmann, Heinrich Ruoff, Karl Willig, Adolf Merkle, Irmgard Huber, and Philip Blum (The Hadamar Trial)*. London: William Hodge, 1948.

Klein, Thomas. *Die Lageberichte der Geheimen Staatspolizei über die Provinz Hessen-Nassau, 1933–1936*. Vienna: Böhlau, 1986.

Klemperer, Victor. *The Language of the Third Reich*. London: Continuum, 2000 (1947).

Kley, Stefan. *Hitler, Ribbentrop und die Entfesselung des Zweiten Weltkrieges*. Paderborn: Schöningh, 1996.

Knigge-Tesche, Renate, and Axel Ulrich, eds. *Verfolgung und Widerstand in Hessen, 1933–1945*. Frankfurt: Eichborn, 1996.

Knodt, Manfred. *Ernst Ludwig: Grossherzog von Hessen und bei Rhein. Sein Leben und seine Zeit*. Darmstadt: Schlapp, 1978.

Koehl, Robert. *The Black Corps: The Structure and Power Struggles of the Nazi SS*. Madison: University of Wisconsin Press, 1983.

Kogon, Eugen. *The Theory and Practice of Hell: The German Concentration Camps and the System Behind Them*. London: Secker & Warburg, 1950 (1947).

Kohlrausch, Martin. "Die Flucht des Kaisers: Doppeltes Scheitern adlig-bürgerlicher Monarchiekonzepte." In *Adel und Bürgertum in Deutschland II*, edited by Heinz Reif, 65–102. Berlin: Akademie Verlag, 2001.

Koonz, Claudia. *The Nazi Conscience*. Cambridge: Harvard University Press, 2004.

Kopper, Christopher. "The Rothschild Family During the Third Reich." In Heuberger, *The Rothschilds*, 320–45.

Krause-Schmitt, Ursula. "Das NS-Lagersystem in Hessen." In Knigge-Tesche and Ulrich, *Verfolgung und Widerstand in Hessen*, 44–63.

"Kronbergprozess." *Frankfurter Neuen Presse*, 1/41, 2 September 1946.

Kropat, Wolf-Arno. *Kristallnacht in Hessen: Der Judenpogrom vom November 1938. Eine Dokumentation*. Wiesbaden: Kommission für die Geschichte der Juden in Hessen, 1988.

———. *"Reichskristallnacht": Der Judenpogrom vom 7. bis 10. November 1938—Urheber, Täter, Hintergründe*. Wiesbaden: Kommission für die Geschichte der Juden in Hessen, 1997.

———. "Die Verfolgung der Juden in Hessen und Nassau." In Knigge-Tesche and Ulrich, *Verfolgung und Widerstand in Hessen*, 86–101.

Kube, Alfred. *Pour le Mérite und Hakenkreuz: Hermann Göring im Dritten Reich*. Munich: Oldenbourg, 1986.

Kuretsidis-Haider, Claudia, and Winfried Garscha, eds. *Keine "Abrechnung": NS-Verbrechen, Justiz und Gesellschaft in Europa nach 1945*. Vienna: Akademische Verlagsanstalt, 1998.

Lagerwey, Mary. "The Nurses's Trial at Hadamar." In Elizabeth Baer and Myrna Goldenberg, eds. *Experience and Expression: Women, the Nazis and the Holocaust.* Detroit: Wayne State University Press, 2003, 111–26.

Lambton, Antony. *The Mountbattens: The Battenbergs and Young Mountbatten.* London: Constable, 1989.

Lang, Jochen von. *Der Adjutant: Karl Wolff. Der Mann zwischen Himmler und Hitler.* Munich: Herbig, 1985.

———, ed. *Hitler Close-Up.* New York: Macmillan, 1973.

Ledanff, Susanne. "The Palace of the Republic versus the Stadtschloss: The Dilemmas of Planning in the Heart of Berlin." *German Politics and Society* 21/4 (May 2004): 30–73.

Leppard, David. "Historian in Himmler dispute was in earlier fogery furore." *The Sunday Times* (London), 3 July 2005, 15.

Lesley, Parker. "Tante Mossy." *Times Literary Supplement* 2846, 14 September 1956, 539.

Ley, Robert. "Gott schutz den Führer." *Der Angriff*, 23 July 1944, 1.

Liebhart, Wilhelm. *Königtum und Politik in Bayern.* Frankfurt: Peter Lang, 1994.

Lieven, Dominic. *The Aristocracy in Europe, 1815–1914.* New York: Columbia University Press, 1992.

Lillienthal, Georg. *Der Lebensborn e.V.: eine Instrument Nationalsozialistischer Rassenpolitik.* Frankfurt: S. Fischer Taschenbuch, 2003.

Lincoln, W. Bruce. *The Romanovs: Autocrats of All the Russians.* New York: Anchor Books, 1981.

Lippe, Princess Marie Adelheid zur. *Nordische Frau und nordischer Glaube.* Berlin: Flugschriften der Nordischen Glaubensbewegung, 1934.

Longerich, Peter. *Die braune Battaillone: Geschichte der SA.* Munich: C. H. Beck, 1989.

Lukacs, John. *Five Days in London: May 1940.* New Haven: Yale University Press, 1999.

Maas, Walter. *The Netherlands at War: 1940–1945.* London: Abelard-Schuman, 1970.

MacDonnell, Tom. *Daylight Upon Magic: The Royal Tour of Canada—1939.* Toronto: Macmillan of Canada, 1989.

Macdonogh, Giles. *The Last Kaiser: The Life of Wilhelm II.* New York: St. Martin's Press, 2000.

Machtan, Lothar. *The Hidden Hitler.* New York: Basic Books, 2001.

———. *Der Kaisersohn bei Hitler. August Wilhelm im Hexenkessel der deutschen Geschichte.* Hamburg: Hoffmann & Campe, 2006.

Mack Smith, Denis. *Mussolini: A Biography.* New York: Vintage Books, 1983.

Maclagan, Michael, and Jiri Louda. *Lines of Succession: Heraldry of the Royal Families of Europe.* New York: Barnes & Noble, 2002.

Manvell, Roger, and Heinrich Fraenkel. *Hermann Göring.* London: Heinemann, 1962.

Maier, Charles. *The Unmasterable Past: History, Holocaust, and German National Identity.* Cambridge, MA: Harvard University Press, 1990.

Malinowski, Stephan. " 'Führertum' und 'Neuer Adel': Die Deutsche Adelsgenossenschaft und der Deutsche Herrenklub in der Weimarer Republik." In Reif, *Adel und Bürgertum in Deutschland II*, 173–212.

———. *Vom König zum Führer: Sozialer Niedergang und politische Radikalisierung im deutschen Adel zwischen Kaiserreich und NS-Staat.* Berlin: Akademie Verlag, 2003.

Mann, Golo. *Deutsche Geschichte des neunzehnten und zwanzigsten Jahrhunderts.* Frankfurt: S. Fischer, 1960.

Marcuse, Harold. *Legacies of Dachau: The Uses and Abuses of a Concentration Camp, 1933–2001.* Cambridge: Cambridge University Press, 2001.

Marrus, Michael. "Pius XII and the Holocaust: Ten Essential Themes." In *Pope Pius XII and the Holocaust,* edited by Carol Rittner and John Roth. London: Leicester University Press, 2002, 43–55.

Marshall, Bruce. *The White Rabbit.* New York: Houghton Mifflin, 1952.

Martel, Gordon, ed. *The Origins of the Second World War Reconsidered. A. J. P. Taylor and the Historians.* New York: Routledge, 1999.

Martens, Stefan. *Hermann Göring: "erster Paladin des Führers" und "zweiter Mann im Reich."* Paderborn: Schöningh, 1985.

Martin, Berndt. *Friedensinitiativen und Machtpolitik im Zweiten Weltkrieg, 1939–1942.* Düsseldorf: Droste, 1974.

Maser, Werner. *Hermann Göring. Hitlers janusköpfiger Paladin. Die politische Biographie.* Berlin: edition q, 2000.

Massie, Robert. *Nicholas and Alexandra.* New York: Atheneum, 1967.

Masters, Anthony. *Nancy Astor: A Biography.* New York: McGraw Hill, 1981.

Mayer, Arno. *The Persistence of the Old Regime: Europe to the Great War.* New York: Pantheon, 1981.

McDougall, Walter. *France's Rhineland Diplomacy, 1914–1924: The Last Bid for a Balance of Power in Europe.* Princeton: Princeton University Press, 1978.

McGee, Mark. *Berlin: A Visual and Historical Documentation from 1925 to the Present.* New York: Overlook Press, 2002.

Messenger, Charles. *Hitler's Gladiator: The Life and Times of Oberstgruppenführer and Panzergeneral-Oberst der Waffen-SS Sepp Dietrich.* London: Brassey's, 1988.

Metternich, Tatiana. *An der Rennstrecke. Erinnerungen an Paul Fürst Metternich.* Munich: Langen Müller, 1995.

———. *Bericht eines ungewöhnlichen Lebens.* Vienna: Verlag Fritz Molden, 1976.

Michael, Prince of Greece. "The Case for Kings." *Vanity Fair,* September 2003, 400–58.

Middlemas, Keith, and John Barnes. *Baldwin: A Biography.* London: Weidenfeld & Nicolson, 1969.

Miller, Markus. "Schloss Fasanerie. 50 Jahre Museum der Hessischen Hausstiftung." In *Das kulturelle Erbe des Hauses Hessen,* edited by Eckhart Franz and Hans-Peter Lachmann, 161–70. Marburg: Historische Kommission für Hessen, 2002.

Moeller, Robert. *War Stories: The Search for a Usable Past in the Federal Republic of Germany.* Berkeley: University of California Press, 2001.

Moll, Christiane. "Acts of Resistance: The White Rose in Light of New Archival Evidence." In *Resistance Against the Third Reich,* edited by Michael Geyer and John Boyer. Chicago: University of Chicago Press, 1992, 173–200.

Mommsen, Hans. "Der Widerstand gegen Hitler und die deutsche Gesellschaft." In *Der Widerstand gegen den Nationalsozialismus. Die deutsche Gesellschaft und der Widerstand gegen Hitler,* edited by Jürgen Schmädeke and Peter Steinbach. Munich: Piper, 1986.

"Montesi-Skandal: Das Ablenkungsmanöver." *Der Spiegel* 39, 22 September 1954, 29–30.

Montgomery-Massinberd, Hugh, ed. *Burke's Royal Families of the World, Vol. I: Europe and Latin America*. London: Burke's Peerage, 1977.

Moorcroft-Wilson, Jean. *Siegfried Sassoon: The Journey from the Trenches. A Biography*. London: Duckworth, 2003.

Moseley, Ray. *Mussolini's Shadow: The Double Life of Count Galeazzo Ciano*. New Haven: Yale University Press, 1999.

Mosley, Diana. *The Duchess of Windsor*. London: Sidgwick & Jackson, 1980.

———. *A Life of Contrasts: An Autobiography*. New York: Times Books, 1977.

Mosley, Leonard. *The Reich Marshal: A Biography of Hermann Göring*. Garden City: Doubleday, 1974.

Muggeridge, Malcolm, ed. *Ciano's Diary, 1939–1943*. London: William Heinemann, 1947.

Müller, Horst, et al., eds., *Die Tödliche Utopie. Bilder, Texte, Dokumente, Daten zum Dritten Reich*. Munich: Institut für Zeitgeschichte, 2001.

Müller, Ingo. *Hitler's Justice: The Courts of the Third Reich*. Cambridge: Harvard University Press, 1991.

Munthe, Axel. *The Story of San Michele*. New York: Dutton, 1929.

Naftali, Timothy. "Creating the Myth of the *Alpenfestung*: Allied Intelligence and the Collapse of the Nazi Police State." *Contemporary Austrian Studies* 5 (1996): 203–46.

Naimark, Norman. *The Russians in Germany: A History of the Soviet Zone of Occupation, 1945–1949*. Cambridge: Harvard University Press, 1995.

Nelson, Walter Henry. *The Soldier Kings: The House of Hohenzollern*. New York: G. P. Putnam, 1970.

Neumann, Moritz. *1945 Nachgetragen: In den Trummern von Darmstadt. Das Ende der Diktatur und die Monate nach dem Krieg*. Darmstadt: Roether Verlag, 1995.

Newton, Scott. *Profits of Peace: The Political Economy of Anglo-German Appeasement*. Oxford: Clarendon Press, 1996.

Niethammer, Lutz. *Die Mitläufer-fabrik. Die Entnazifizierung am Beispiel Bayerns*. Berlin: J. H. W. Dietz, 1982.

Nicholas, Lynn H. *The Rape of Europa: The Fate of Europe's Treasures in the Third Reich and the Second World War*. New York: Alfred Knopf, 1994.

Nikbakhsh, Michael. "Ich bin Promi-Kandidat. Basta!" *Profil* 25, 15 June 2004, 34.

Nolte, Ernst. *The Three Faces of Fascism: Action Francaise, Italian Fascism, National Socialism*. New York: Signet, 1969 (1963).

Normanton, Helena. "The Truth About Mrs. Simpson." *Statesman*, 31 May 1937.

Offiziervereinigung "Alt 81," eds. *Das Königlich Preussische Infanterie-Regiment Landgraf Friedrich I. von Hessen-Kassel (I. Kurhessisches) Nr. 81*. Bad Warmbrunn: Privatdruck, 1932.

Oguntoye, Katharina, May Opitz, and Dagmar Schultz, eds. *Showing Our Colors: Afro-German Women Speak Out*. Amherst: University of Massachusetts Press, 1992.

Ondaatje, Michael. *The English Patient*. New York: Alfred Knopf, 1992.

Orth, Karin. *Das System der nationalsozialistischen Konzentrationslager: eine politische Organisationsgeschichte*. Zurich: Pendo, 2002.

Osterkorn, Thomas. "Danke, Alice Schwarzer." *Stern* 24, 2001, 3.

Overy, Richard. *Goering: The Iron Man.* London: Routledge & Kegan Paul, 1984.

————. *Interrogations: The Nazi Elite in Allied Hands, 1945.* New York: Viking, 2001.

Overy, Richard, and Andrew Wheatcroft. *The Road to War.* London: Macmillan, 1989.

Padfield, Peter. *Hess: Flight for the Führer.* London: Weidenfeld & Nicolson, 1991.

————. *Hess: The Führer's Disciple,* Weidenfeld & Nicolson, 1995.

————. *Himmler: Reichsführer-SS.* New York: Holt, 1991.

Paget, Gerald. *The Lineage and Ancestry of H.R.H. Prince Charles, Prince of Wales.* 2 vols. Edinburgh: Charles Skilton, 1977.

Palmer, Alan. *Crowned Cousins: The Anglo-German Royal Connection.* London: Weidenfeld & Nicolson, 1985.

Paret, Peter. *An Artist Against the Third Reich: Ernst Barlach, 1933–1938.* Cambridge: Cambridge University Press, 2003.

Parker, John. *Prince Philip: A Critical Biography.* London: Sidgwick & Jackson, 1990.

"Passings: Queen Susan, 63; Her Husband Claimed Albanian Throne." *Los Angeles Times,* 19 July 2004, B9.

Paul, Wolfgang. *Hermann Göring. Hitler Paladin or Puppet?* London: Arms & Armour, 1998.

Perrault, Gilles. *The Red Orchestra.* New York: Schocken, 1989.

Persico, Joseph. *Roosevelt's Secret War.* New York: Random House, 2001.

Petropoulos, Jonathan. *Art as Politics in the Third Reich.* Chapel Hill: University of North Carolina Press, 1996.

————. *The Faustian Bargain: The Art World in Nazi Germany.* New York: Oxford University Press 2000.

————. "The History of the Second Rank: The Art Plunderer Kajetan Mühlmann." *Contemporary Austrian Studies* 4 (1995): 177–221.

————. "Postwar Justice and the Treatment of Nazis' Assets." In *Gray Zones: Ambiguity and Compromise in the Holocaust and Its Aftermath,* edited by Jonathan Petropoulos and John Roth, 319–32. New York: Berghahn Books, 2005.

Petropoulos, Jonathan, and John Roth, eds. *Gray Zones: Ambiguity and Compromise in the Holocaust and Its Aftermath.* New York: Berghahn Books, 2005.

Pflanze, Otto. *Bismarck and the Development of Germany: The Period of Unification, 1815–1871.* Princeton: Princeton University Press, 1963.

Philippi, Hans. *Das Haus Hessen: ein europäisches Fürstengeschlecht.* Kassel: Thiele & Schwarz, 1983.

Picker, Henry, ed. *Hitlers Tischgespräche im Führerhauptquartier, 1941–1942.* Stuttgart: Seewald Verlag, 1965.

Picknett, Lynn, Clive Prince, and Stephen Prior. *Double Standards: The Rudolf Hess Cover-Up.* London: Time Warner Books, 2001.

————. *War of the Windsors: A Century of Unconstitutional Monarchy.* Edinburgh: Mainstream Publishing, 2002.

Plaut, James. "Attachment 65: List of Works of Art Received in Munich from Prince Philipp von Hessen." *Supplement to Consolidated Interrogation Report No. 1.* Washington, DC: Strategic Services Unit, 1945.

Pohl, Hans, Stephanie Habeth, and Beate Brüninghaus. *Die Daimler-Benz AG in den Jahren 1933 bis 1945.* Wiesbaden: F. Steiner, 1986.

Pool, James, and Suzanne Pool. *Who Financed Hitler? The Secret Funding of Hitler's Rise to Power, 1919–1933.* London: Macdonald & Jane's, 1978.

Posner, Gerald. "Secret of the Files." *New Yorker,* 14 March 1994.

Preradovich, Nikolaus von. "Regierende Fürsten im Dritten Reich: Die Herrschaftsgeschlechter des Deutschen Reiches und die NSDAP." *Deutschland in Geschichte und Gegenwart* 2 (1981): 28–30.

Presidential Advisory Commission on Holocaust Assets in the United States. *Plunder and Restitution: The U.S. and Holocaust Victims's Assets.* Washington, DC: Government Printing Office, 2000.

(Preussen) Kronprinzessin Cécile. *Erinnerungen an den Deutschen Kronprinzen.* Biebrach: Koehlers, 1952.

Preussen, Friedrich Wilhelm Prinz von. *Das Haus Hohenzollern, 1918–1945.* Munich: Langen Müller, 1985.

(Preussen) Louis Ferdinand, Prince of Prussia. *Im Strom der Geschichte.* Munich: Langen Müller, 1983.

———. *The Rebel Prince.* Chicago: Henry Regnery, 1952.

Prinz, Wolfgang. "Die Judenverfolgung in Kassel," in *Volksgemeinschaft und Volksfeinde Kassel 1933–1945,* edited by Wilhelm Frenz, Jörg Kammler, and Dietfried Krause-Vilmar. Kassel: Druckerei Hesse, 1987.

Proctor, Robert. "Nazi Doctors, Racial Medicine, and Human Experimentation." In *The Nazi Doctors and the Nuremberg Code.* New York: Oxford University Press, 1992, 17–32.

Prusczynski, Jan. "Poland: The War Losses." In *The Spoils of War: World War II and Its Aftermath. The Loss, Disappearance and Recovery of Cultural Property,* edited by Elizabeth Simpson, 49–52. New York: Harry Abrams, 1997.

Pryce-Jones, David. *Unity Mitford: An Enquiry into Her Life and the Frivolity of Evil.* New York: Dial Press, 1977.

Pugh, Martin. *"Hurrah for the Blackshirts!" Fascists and Fascism in Britain Between the Wars.* London: Jonathan Cape, 2005.

Quataert, Jean. *Staging Philanthropy: Patriotic Women and the National Imagination in Dynastic Germany, 1813–1916.* Ann Arbor: University of Michigan Press, 2001.

Radzinsky, Edvard. *The Last Tsar: The Life and Death of Nicholas I.* New York: Doubleday, 1992.

Read, Anthony. *The Devil's Disciples: The Lives and Times of Hitler's Inner Circle.* London: Pimlico, 2003.

Rebentisch, Dieter. "Nationalsozialistische Revolution, Partei herrschaft und totaler Krieg in Hessen, 1933–1945." In *Die Geschichte Hessens,* edited by Uwe Schultz, 232–48. Stuttgart: Konrad Theiss Verlag, 1983.

———. "Persönlichkeitsprofil und Karriereverlauf der nationalsozialistischen Führungskader in Hessen, 1928–1945." *Hessisches Jahrbuch für Landesgeschichte* 33 (1983): 293–332.

Redlich, Fritz. *Hitler: Diagnosis of a Destructive Prophet.* New York: Oxford University Press, 1999.

Reeves, Richard. "A Nation of Servants." *Hartford Courant,* 28 December 2002, A9.

Reichel, Peter. *Erfundene Erinnerung: Weltkrieg und Judenmord in Film und Theater.* Munich: Hanser, 2004.

———. *Der schöne Schein des Dritten Reiches. Faszination und Gewalt des Faschismus.* Munich: Hanser, 1991.

Reif, Heinz. *Adel im 19. und 20. Jahrhundert.* Munich: R. Oldenbourg Verlag, 1999.

———, ed. *Adel und Bürgertum in Deutschland II.* Berlin: Akademie Verlag, 2001.

Reitlinger, Gerald. *The SS: Alibi of a Nation, 1922–1945.* London: Heinemann, 1956.

Remy, Steven. *The Heidelberg Myth: The Nazification and Denazification of a German University, 1933–1957.* Cambridge: Harvard University Press, 2002.

Renkhoff, Otto. *Nassauische Biographie.* Wiesbaden: Historische Kommission für Nassau, 1992.

"Return of Exiled Royals Marred by Scuffles." *Los Angeles Times,* 16 March 2003, A4.

Rezzori, Gregor von. *Memoirs of an Anti-Semite: A Novel in Five Stories.* New York: Vintage Books, 1991.

Ribbentrop, Joachim von. *The Ribbentrop Memoirs.* London: Weidenfeld & Nicolson, 1953.

Ribeiro, Aileen. *Dress in Eighteenth Century France.* New Haven: Yale University Press, 2002.

Ritter, Gerhard. *Carl Goerdeler und die deutsche Widerstandsbewegung.* Stuttgart: Deutsche Verlags-Anstalt, 1956.

Rittner, Carol, and John Roth, eds. *Pope Pius XII and the Holocaust.* London: Leicester University Press, 2002.

Rittner, Gerhard. *Frederick the Great.* Berkeley: University of California Press, 1974.

Robbins, Keith. *Munich 1938.* London: Cassell, 1968.

Roberts, Andrew. *Eminent Churchillians.* New York: Simon & Schuster, 1994.

———. *The Holy Fox.* London: Weidenfeld & Nicolson, 1991.

Roberts, John Stuart. *Siegfried Sassoon (1886–1967).* London: Richard Cohen Books, 1999.

Rogasch, Wilfried. *Schatzhäuser Deutschlands: Kunst in adligen Privatbesitz.* Munich: Prestel, 2004.

Röhl, John C. G. *The Kaiser and His Court: Wilhelm II and the Government of Germany.* Cambridge: Cambridge University Press, 1994.

———. "The Kaiser and the Jews," unpublished lecture delivered at the German Historical Institute, London, 23 February 2005.

———. "Die Kaiserwitwe als Kritikerin der Persönlichen Monarchie Wilhelms II." In *Victoria Kaiserin Friedrich: Mission und Schicksal einer englischen Prinzessin in Deutschland,* edited by Rainer von Hessen. Frankfurt: Campus Verlag, 2002, 208–21.

———. *Wilhelm II: The Kaiser's Personal Monarchy, 1888–1900.* Cambridge: Cambridge University Press, 2004.

Röhl, John C. G., Martin Warren, and David Hunt, *Purple Secret: Genes, "Madness," and the Royal Houses of Europe.* London: Bantam, 1998.

Rousseau, Theodore. *Consolidated Interrogation Report No. 2: The Goering Collection.* Washington, DC: War Department, 1945.

Rose, Kenneth. *Intimate Portraits of Kings, Queens and Courtiers.* London: Spring Books, 1985.

———. *George V.* London: Weidenfeld & Nicolson, 1983.

Rose, Norman. *Harold Nicolson.* London: Jonathan Cape, 2004.

Ross, Stephanie. *What Gardens Mean.* Chicago: University of Chicago Press, 1988.

Ruby, Michael. "A Slap for the Prince." *Newsweek,* 5 April 1976, 24.

Ruck, Michael. *Bibliographie zum Nationalsozialismus,* 2 vols. Darmstadt: Wissenschaftliche Buchgesellschaft, 2000 (1995).

Sassoon, Siegfried. *Memoirs of a Fox-Hunting Man.* London: Faber & Faber, 1999 (1928).

Sax, Benjamin, and Dieter Kuntz, eds. *Inside Hitler's Germany: A Documentary History of Life in the Third Reich.* Lexington: DC Heath, 1992.

Schad, Martha. *Bayerns Königshaus.* Regensburg: Verlag Friedrich Pustet, 1994.

———. *Hitlers Spionin. Das Leben der Stephanie von Hohenlohe.* Munich: Wilhelm Heyne, 2002.

Schaumburg-Lippe, Friedrich Christian Prinz zu. *Als die goldne Abendsonne: Aus meinen Tagebüchern der Jahre 1933–1937.* Wiesbaden: Limes, 1971.

———. *Damals fing das neue an: Erlebnisse und Gedanken eines Gefangenen, 1945–1948.* Hanover: H. Pfeiffer, 1969.

———. *Dr. G. Ein Porträt des Propagandaministers.* Wiesbaden: Limes Verlag, 1964.

———. *Verdammte Pflicht und Schuldigkeit: Weg und Erlebnis, 1914–1933.* Leoni am Starnberger See: Druffel Verlag, 1966.

———, ed. *Deutsche Sozialisten am Werk.* Berlin: Deutscher Verlag für Politik und Wirtschaft, 1936.

Schlabrendorff, Fabian von. *Begegnungen in Fünf Jahrzehnten.* Tübingen: Wunderlich, 1979.

———. *Revolt Against Hitler: The Personal Account of Fabian von Schlabrendorff.* London: Eyre & Spottiswoode, 1948.

———. *The Secret War Against Hitler.* London: Hodder & Stoughton, 1965.

Schellenberg, Walter. *The Schellenberg Memoirs.* London: Andre Deutsche, 1956.

Schmeling, Anke. *Josias Erbprinz zu Waldeck und Pyrmont. Der politische Weg eines hohen SS-Führers.* Kassel: Verlag Gesamthochschul-Bibliothek Kassel, 1993.

Schmitz, Werner. "Adel in Deutschland: Die Neue Generation." *Stern* 24 (2001).

Schnackenburg, Bernhard. "Der Kasseler Gemäldegalerie des 18. Jahrhunderts und neuentdeckte Pläne von François de Cuvilliés D.Ä." *Münchner Jahrbuch der bildenden Kunst* 49 (1998): 163–84.

Schönburg, Alexander von. "Konferenz für Königskinder." *Frankfurter Allegemeine Zeitung,* 10 September 2001.

Schultz, Uwe, ed. *Die Geschichte Hessens.* Stuttgart: Konrad Theiss Verlag, 1983.

Schulz, Günther, and Markus Denzel, eds. *Deutscher Adel im 19. und 20. Jahrhundert.* St. Katharinen: Scripta Mercaturae, 2004.

Schulze, Hagen. *Freikorps und Republik, 1918–1920.* Boppard: H. Boldt, 1969.

Schuster, Armin. *Die Entnazifizierung in Hessen, 1945–1954: Vergangenheitspolitik in der Nachkriegszeit.* Wiesbaden: Historische Kommission für Nassau, 1999.

Schuster, Wolfgang. "Hitler in München—privat?" In *München: "Hauptstadt der Bewegung,"* edited by Münchener Stadtmuseum. Munich: Münchener Stadtmuseum, 1993, 125–30.

Schwabe, Klaus, ed. *Das Diplomatische Korps, 1871–1945*. Boppard: Harald Boldt Verlag, 1985.

Schwarz, Birgit. *Hitlers Museum. Die Fotoalben Gemäldegalerie Linz: Dokumente zum "Führermuseum."* Vienna: Böhlau, 2004.

Schwarz, Paul. *This Man Ribbentrop*. New York: Messner, 1943.

Schwarzmüller, Theo. *Zwischen Kaiser und "Führer": Generalfeldmarschall August von Mackensen. Eine politische Biographie*. Paderborn: Schöningh, 1996.

Sebald, Winfried. *On the Natural History of Destruction*. New York: Random House, 2002.

Shaw, Karl. *Royal Babylon: The Alarming History of European Royalty*. New York: Broadway Books, 2001.

Sheehan, James. *Museums in the German Art World: From the End of the Old Regime to the Rise of Modernism*. New York: Oxford University Press, 2000.

Shirer, William. *The Rise and Fall of the Third Reich*. London: Pan Books, 1960.

Shnayerson, Michael. "Treacherous Inheritance." *Vanity Fair*, August 2002, 127–72.

Showalter, Dennis. *The Wars of German Unification*. London: Arnold, 2004.

Siegfried, Detlef. *Der Fliegerblick: Intellektuelle, Radikalismus und Flugzeugproduktion bei Junkers 1914 bis 1934*. Bonn: J. H. W. Dietz, 2001.

Simpson, Colin, David Leitch, and Phillip Knightly. "Blunt was Emissary for King George VI." *The Sunday Times* (London), 25 November 1979, 1.

Simpson, Elizabeth, ed. *The Spoils of War: World War II and Its Aftermath. The Loss, Disappearance and Recovery of Cultural Property*. New York: Harry Abrams, 1997.

Sinclair, Andrew. *Death by Fame: A Life of Elisabeth, Empress of Austria*. New York: St. Martin's Press, 1998.

Singer, Kurt. *Göring*. London: Hutchinson, 1940.

Siviero, Rodolfo. *L'Arte e il Nazismo*. Florence: Edizioni d'Arte, 1984.

Smelser, Ronald. *Robert Ley: Hitler's Labor Front Leader*. Oxford: Berg, 1988.

Smelser. Ronald, and Enrico Syring, eds. *Die SS: Elite unter dem Totenkopf. 30 Lebensläufe*. Paderborn: Schöningh, 2000.

Smith, Helmut Walser, ed. *Protestants, Catholics, and Jews in Germany 1800–1914*. Oxford: Berg, 2002.

Smith, Woodruff. *The Ideological Origins of Nazi Imperialism*. New York: Oxford University Press, 1993.

Smyth, Howard McGraw. *Secrets of the Fascist Era: How Uncle Sam Obtained Some of the Top-Level Documents of Mussolini's Period*. Carbondale: Southern Illinois University Press, 1975.

Speer, Albert. *Inside the Third Reich*. New York: Macmillan, 1970.

———. *Spandau: The Secret Diaries*. London: Phoenix, 1976.

Spielvogel, Jackson. *Hitler and Nazi Germany: A History*. Upper Saddle River: Prentice Hall, 2001.

Spotts, Frederic. *The Churches and Politics in Germany*. Middletown: Wesleyan University Press, 1973.

———. *Hitler and the Power of Aesthetics*. New York: Overlook Press, 2002.

Staercke, André de. *"Tout cela a passé comme une ombre": Mémoires sur la Régence et la Question royale*. Brussels: Editions Racine, 2003.

Stansky, Peter. *Sassoon: The World of Philip and Sybil*. New Haven: Yale University Press, 2003.

Steinbach, Peter. *Der Widerstand gegen den Nationalsozialismus. Die deutsche Gesellschaft und der Widerstand gegen Hitler*. Munich: Piper, 1986.

Steinberg, Jonathan. *All or Nothing: The Axis and the Holocaust, 1941–1943*. London: Routledge, 1990.

Steiner, George. *In Bluebeard's Castle: Some Notes Towards the Redefinition of Culture*. New Haven: Yale University Press, 1971.

Stern, Fritz. *Dreams and Delusions: The Drama of German History*. New York: Alfred Knopf, 1984.

———. *Gold and Iron: Bismarck and His Banker Bleichröder*. New York: Alfred Knopf, 1977.

Stienicka, Norbert. "Die Vermögensauseinandersetzung des Volksstaates Hessen und seiner Rechtsnachfolger mit der ehemals grossherzoglichen Familie 1918–1953." *Archiv für Hessische Geschichte* 56 (1998): 255–308.

Stockhorst, Erich. *5000 Köpfe: Wer war Was im Dritten Reich*. Kiel: Arndt Verlag, 1985.

Strandmann, Hartmut Pogge von. "Nationalisierungsdruck und königliche Namensänderung in England. Das Ende der Grossfamilie europäischer Dynastien." In *Veröffentlichungen des Deutschen Historischen Instituts London*, edited by Peter Wende. Paderborn: Schöningh, 1999.

Strobl, Gerwin. *The Germanic Isle: Nazi Perceptions of Britain*. Cambridge: Cambridge University Press, 2000.

Tauber, Kurt. *Beyond Eagle and Swastika: German Nationalism Since 1945*. Middletown, CT: Wesleyan University Press, 1967.

Taylor, A. J. P. *Bismarck: The Man and the Statesman*. New York: Vintage, 1967 (1955).

———. *The Origins of the Second World War*. New York: Touchstone Books, 1996 (1961).

Theweleit, Klaus. *Male Fantasies*. Minneapolis: University of Minnesota Press, 1987.

Thomas, Hugh. *Hess: A Tale of Two Murders*. London: Hodder & Stoughton, 1988.

Thompson, Larry V. "Lebensborn and the Eugenics Policy of the Reichsführer-SS." *Central European History* 4 (1971): 54–77.

Thyssen, Fritz. *I Paid Hitler*. New York: Farrar & Rinehart, 1941.

Toscano, Mario. *The Origins of the Pact of Steel*. Baltimore: The Johns Hopkins University Press, 1967.

Tuchman, Barbara. *The Guns of August*. New York: Bantam Books, 1979 (1962).

Turner, Henry Ashby. *German Big Business and the Rise of Hitler*. New York: Oxford University Press, 1985.

———. *Hitler's Thirty Days to Power: January 1933*. Reading: Addison-Wesley, 1996.

Ueberschär, Gerd, ed. *Der 20. Juli 1944. Bewertung und Rezeption des deutschen Widerstandes gegen das NS-Regime*. Cologne: Bund-Verlag, 1994.

Ueberschär, Gerd, and Winfried Vogel. *Dienen und Verdienen. Hitlers Geschenke an seine Eliten*. Frankfurt: S. Fischer, 1999.

Urbach, Karina, and Bernd Buchner. "Prinz Max von Baden und Houston Stewart Chamberlain. Aus dem Briefwechsel 1909–1919." *Vierteljahrshefte für Zeitgeschichte* 1 (2004): 121–77.

Vassiltchikov, Marie. *Berlin Diaries: 1940–1945*. New York: Vintage Books, 1988.

Verhey, Jeffrey. *The Spirit of 1914: Militarism, Myth, and Mobilization in Germany*. Cambridge: Cambridge University Press, 2000.

Vickers, Hugo. *Alice: Princess Andrew of Greece*. London: Hamish Hamilton, 2000.

———. *Cecil Beaton: An Authorized Biography*. London: Weidenfeld & Nicolson, 1985.

Viktoria Luise, Princess. *Ein Leben als Tochter des Kaisers*. Hanover: Göttinger Verlagsanstalt, 1965.

———. *Im Glanz der Krone*. Hanover: Göttinger Verlagsanstalt, 1967.

———. *Im Strom der Zeit*. Hanover: Göttinger Verlagsanstalt, 1974.

———. *The Kaiser's Daughter: Memoirs of H.R.H. Viktoria Luise, Duchess of Brunswick and Lüneburg, Princess of Prussia*. Englewood Cliffs: Prentice Hall, 1977.

Vinen, Richard. *A History in Fragments: Europe in the Twentieth Century*. New York: Da Capo Press, 2000.

"Voters Hand Prince Wide-Ranging Powers." *Los Angeles Times*, 17 March 2003, A5.

Wagner, Gottfried. *Wer nicht mit dem Wolf heult: Autobiographische Aufzeichnungen eines Wagner-Urenkels*. Cologne: Kiepenheuer & Witsch, 1997.

Waldburg, Marie. "In Bayern sind selbst Dackel königlich." *Bunte* 31, 24 July 2003, 28.

Waldenfels, Otto Freiherr von. "Legendenbildung um Himmler: Die königlich-bayerischen Edelknaben und die SS." *Zeitschrift für bayerische Landesgeschichte* 26 (1963): 400–407.

Warlimont, Walter. *Im Hauptquartier der Deutschen Wehrmacht, 1939–1945*, Bd. 2. Augsburg: Novato, 1990.

Watt, D. C. *How War Came: The Immediate Origins of the Second World War, 1938–1939*. London: Heineman, 1989.

———. "Introduction." In *Breach of Security: The German Secret Intelligence File on Events Leading to the Second World War*, edited by David Irving. London: William Kimber, 1968.

Waugh, Evelyn. *Vile Bodies*. London: Folio Society, 1999 (1930).

Weale, Adrian. *Renegades: Hitler's Englishmen*. London: Weidenfeld & Nicholson, 1994.

Wegner, Bernd. *The Waffen-SS: Organization, Ideology and Function*. Cambridge: Basil Blackwell, 1990.

Weinberg, Gerhard. *The Foreign Policy of Hitler's Germany: Starting World War II, 1937–1939*. Chicago: University of Chicago Press, 1980.

———. *A World at Arms: A Global History of World War II*. Cambridge: Cambridge University Press, 1994.

Weiss, Hermann, ed. *Biographisches Lexikon zum Dritten Reich*. Frankfurt: S. Fischer, 1998.

Weizsäcker, Ernst von. *Memoirs of Ernst von Weizsäcker*. London: Victor Gollancz, 1951.

Weitz, John. *Hitler's Diplomat: The Life and Times of Joachim von Ribbentrop*. New York: Ticknor & Fields, 1992.

West, Franklin. *A Crisis of the Weimar Republic: A Study of the German Referendum of 20 June 1926*. Philadelphia: Memoirs of the American Philosophical Society, 1985.

West, Nigel. *MI 6: British Secret Intelligence Service Operations, 1909–1945*. London: Weidenfeld & Nicolson, 1983.

West, Rebecca. *Black Lamb and Grey Falcon: A Journey through Yugoslavia*. London: Macmillan, 1977 (1943).

Weyerer, Benedikt. "Bestattet wie ein König." *Süddeutsche Zeitung* 178, 4 August 2000.

Whalen, Robert Weldon. *Bitter Wounds: German Victims of the Great War, 1914–1939*. Ithaca: Cornell University Press, 1984.

Wheeler-Bennett, John. *Friends, Enemies and Sovereigns*. London: Macmillan, 1976.

———. *King George VI: His Life and Reign*. London: Macmillan, 1958.

———. *The Nemesis of Power: The German Army in Politics, 1918–1945*. London: Macmillan, 1953.

Whiting, Audrey. *The Kents*. London: Hutchinson, 1985.

Wied, Fürstin zu. *Vom Leben gelernt*. Ludwigsberg: Ungeheuer & Ulmer, 1953.

Wiedemann, Fritz. *Der Mann der Feldherr werden wollte*. Velbert: Blick und Bild Verlag, 1964.

Wilson, Jeremy. *Lawrence of Arabia: The Authorized Biography of T. E. Lawrence*. London: Heineman, 1989.

Wilson, Paul J. *Himmler's Cavalry: The Equestrian SS, 1930–1945*. Atglen: Schiffer Publishing, 2000.

Windsor, Duke of. *A King's Story: The Memoirs of H.R.H. The Duke of Windsor*. London: Cassel, 1951.

Winter, Bettina. "Die Geschichte der NS-'Euthanasie'-Anstalt Hadamar." In *"Verlegt nach Hadamar": Die Geschichte einer NS-"Euthanasie"-Anstalt*, edited by Gerhard Baader, Johannes Cramer, and Bettina Winter. Kassel: Eigenverlag des LWV Hessen, 1991.

Winterbotham, Frederick. *The Nazi Connection*. London: Weidenfeld & Nicolson, 1978.

———. *Secret and Personal*. London: William Kimber, 1969.

Winton, John. *ULTRA at Sea: How Breaking the Nazi Code Affected Allied Naval Strategy during World War II*. New York: W. Morrow, 1988.

Wippermann, Wolfgang. *Das Leben in Frankfurt zur NS-Zeit. Die nationalsozialistische Judenverfolgung*. Frankfurt: Kramer Verlag, 1986.

Wirsching, Andreas. "'Man kann nur Boden Germanisieren': Eine neue Quelle zu Hitlers Rede vor den Spitzen der Reichswehr am 3. Februar 1933." *Vierteljahrshefte für Zeitgeschichte* 49 (3/2001): 517–50.

Wiskemann, Elizabeth. *The Rome-Berlin Axis: A Study of Relations Between Hitler and Mussolini*. London: Collins, 1966.

Wistrich, Robert. *Who's Who in Nazi Germany*. New York: Bonanza Books, 1982.

Wohl, Robert. *The Generation of 1914*. Cambridge: Harvard University Press, 1979.

————. *A Passion for Wings: Aviation and the Western Imagination, 1908–1918.* New Haven: Yale University Press, 1994.

Wright, Peter. *Spycatcher: The Candid Autobiography of a Senior Intelligence Officer.* New York: Viking, 1987.

Yeide, Nancy, Konstantin Akinsha, and Amy Walsh. *The AAM Guide to Provenance Research.* Washington, DC: AAM, 2001.

Younge, Gary. "British Racism Can Be a Royal Pain." *Los Angeles Times,* 27 May 2004, B13.

Zentner, Christian, and Friedemann Bedürftig, eds. *The Encyclopedia of the Third Reich.* New York: Macmillan, 1991.

Zibell, Stephanie. *Jakob Sprenger (1884–1945). NS-Gauleiter und Reichsstatthalter in Hessen.* Darmstadt: Hessische Historische Kommission, 1999.

Ziegler, Herbert. *Nazi Germany's New Aristocracy: The SS Leadership, 1925–1939.* Princeton: Princeton University Press, 1989.

Ziegler, Philip. *King Edward VIII. The Official Biography.* London: Collins, 1990.

————. *Mountbatten: The Official Biography.* London: Collins, 1985.

————, ed. *From Shore to Shore: The Tour Diaries of Earl Mountbatten of Burma, 1953–1979.* London: Collins, 1989.

Zuccotti, Susan. *The Italians and the Holocaust: Persecution, Rescue, and Survival.* London: Peter Halban, 1987.

Index

Note: Page numbers in *italics* indicate photographs and illustrations.